QUESTIONS OF LIABILITY

In this collection, one of the key commentators on the modern law of tort presents 12 of his most important articles and book chapters. These are accompanied by an introductory chapter in which the author comments on the impact and reception of the pieces that make up the collection, and by a provocative new essay in which he argues against strict product liability in the law of tort. A coherent and compelling exploration of topical issues in core areas of tort law, the collection is divided into three parts, dealing with negligence; nuisance and *Rylands v Fletcher*; and tort in general. The essays in this collection are a significant contribution to debates about the limits and scope of tortious liability in common law systems. Students, scholars and practitioners alike will find it an invaluable resource for understanding tort law in the early 21st century.

Questions of Liability

Essays on the Law of Tort

Donal Nolan

·HART·

OXFORD · LONDON · NEW YORK · NEW DELHI · SYDNEY

HART PUBLISHING

Bloomsbury Publishing Plc

Kemp House, Chawley Park, Cumnor Hill, Oxford, OX2 9PH, UK

1385 Broadway, New York, NY 10018, USA

29 Earlsfort Terrace, Dublin 2, Ireland

HART PUBLISHING, the Hart/Stag logo, BLOOMSBURY and the Diana logo are
trademarks of Bloomsbury Publishing Plc

First published in Great Britain 2023

First published in hardback, 2023

Paperback edition, 2025

A catalogue record for this book is available from the British Library.

A catalogue record for this book is available from the Library of Congress.

Library of Congress Control Number: 2023941118

ISBN: PB: 978-1-50996-196-2
       ePDF: 978-1-50996-194-8
       ePub: 978-1-50996-193-1

Typeset by Compuscript Ltd, Shannon

In Memoriam
John Windsor Davies (1934–2020)

Preface

THIS BOOK IS a collection of previously published work on tort law, accompanied by an introductory overview (chapter 1) and a new essay on product liability (chapter 14). I am grateful to the publishers of the original versions of the essays in chapters 2–13 for giving their permission for their reproduction. In writing those essays I incurred debts of gratitude to many anonymous referees and to the editors of the journals and collections in which they first appeared. I also benefited from the advice and observations of Bjarte Askeland, Stephen Bailey, Elise Bant, Katy Barnett, Peter Cane, Andrew Dickinson, Matthew Dyson, Chris Essert, Joshua Getzler, James Goudkamp, Harold Luntz, John Mee, Jonathan Morgan, Jason Neyers, Ken Oliphant, James Penner, Joshua Pike, James Plunkett, Andrew Robertson, Marc Stauch, Sandy Steel, Robert Stevens, Frederick Wilmot-Smith and Christian Witting. I am also grateful to the many colleagues who commented on drafts of these essays which were presented at conferences and workshops, and especially to James Goudkamp for presenting a draft of chapter 10 at a workshop in Hong Kong which I was unable to attend for family reasons. Marco Cappelletti, James Goudkamp and Chris Hodges were kind enough to provide comments on a draft of chapter 14, as were the participants in a seminar at the Institute of European and Comparative Law at Oxford. Finally, I am grateful to James Plunkett for looking over a draft of chapter 1. The usual disclaimer applies.

In the preparation of this volume I was ably assisted by Daniel Leyva, who converted the existing material into Hart's style, and I am grateful to the University of Oxford Law Faculty's Research Support Fund for its financial assistance with that process. I am also indebted to Sinead Moloney for agreeing to publish the collection, to the referees for their thoughtful comments on the book proposal, and to all at Hart Publishing (particularly Tom Adams and Sasha Jawed) for their customary efficiency and patience. Thanks are also due to Helen Kitto for her excellent copy-editing. Finally, I owe a debt of gratitude to my wife Maria for tolerating yet another project that took longer to bring to completion than originally hoped.

The publication of this collection provides me with an opportunity to pay tribute to the many superb tort scholars with whom I have had the privilege of working over the last thirty years, first at King's College London and then at the University of Oxford. They have shaped my thinking about the subject in countless ways, as have numerous other scholars from across the common law and civil law worlds. I have also learned a huge amount over the course of three decades of teaching tort law from my interactions with many generations of excellent students.

The collection is dedicated to the memory of John Davies, the tutor who first introduced me to this endlessly fascinating subject during my undergraduate studies at Brasenose College, Oxford.

Donal Nolan
Oxford
16 March 2023

Acknowledgements

CHAPTER 2 WAS first published by Sweet & Maxwell Ltd as Donal Nolan, 'Deconstructing the Duty of Care' (2013) 129 *Law Quarterly Review* 559 and is reproduced by agreement with the publishers.

Chapter 3 was first published by Appellate Press as Donal Nolan, 'The Duty of Care After *Robinson v Chief Constable of West Yorkshire Police*' in Daniel Clarry (ed), *The UK Supreme Court Yearbook, Volume 9: 2017–2018 Legal Year* (London, Appellate Press, 2019) and is reproduced by agreement with the publishers.

Chapter 4 was first published by Sweet & Maxwell Ltd as Donal Nolan, 'The Liability of Public Authorities for Failing to Confer Benefits' (2011) 127 *Law Quarterly Review* 260 and is reproduced by agreement with the publishers.

Chapter 5 was first published by Oxford University Press as Donal Nolan, 'Assumption of Responsibility: Four Questions' (2019) 72 *Current Legal Problems* 123 and is reproduced by agreement with the publishers.

Chapter 6 was first published by The Modern Law Review Ltd and Blackwell Publishing as Donal Nolan, 'New Forms of Damage in Negligence' (2007) 70 *Modern Law Review* 59 and is reproduced by agreement with the publishers.

Chapter 7 was first published by Cambridge University Press as Donal Nolan, 'Varying the Standard of Care in Negligence' [2013] *Cambridge Law Journal* 651 and is reproduced by agreement with the publishers.

Chapter 11 was first published by Sweet & Maxwell Ltd as Donal Nolan, 'The Distinctiveness of *Rylands v Fletcher*' (2005) 121 *Law Quarterly Review* 421 and is reproduced by agreement with the publishers.

Chapter 12 was first published by Sweet & Maxwell Ltd as Donal Nolan, 'Preventive Damages' (2016) 132 *Law Quarterly Review* 68 and is reproduced by agreement with the publishers.

Chapter 13 was first published by Oxford University Press as Donal Nolan, 'Rights, Damage and Loss' (2017) 37 *Oxford Journal of Legal Studies* 255 and is reproduced by agreement with the publishers.

Contents

Preface..*vii*

Acknowledgements..*ix*

Table of Cases...*xiii*

Table of Legislation...*xxxvii*

1. Introduction...*1*

PART I
NEGLIGENCE

2. *Deconstructing the Duty of Care* 27

3. *The Duty of Care After* Robinson v Chief Constable of
   West Yorkshire Police...63

4. *The Liability of Public Authorities for Failing to Confer Benefits* 92

5. *Assumption of Responsibility: Four Questions*....................................125

6. *Varying the Standard of Care in Negligence* 157

7. *New Forms of Damage in Negligence* 193

8. *Causation and the Goals of Tort Law* 226

PART II
NUISANCE AND *RYLANDS v FLETCHER*

9. *'A Tort Against Land': Private Nuisance as a Property Tort* 255

10. *The Essence of Private Nuisance* 284

11. *The Distinctiveness of* Rylands v Fletcher...305

PART III
TORT IN GENERAL

12. *Preventive Damages* *339*

13. *Rights, Damage and Loss* *371*

14. *Against Strict Product Liability* *392*

Index *427*

Table of Cases

1688782 Ontario Inc v Maple Leaf Foods Inc 2020 SCC 35,
450 DLR (4th) 181 21
A v Essex CC [2003] EWCA Civ 1848, [2004] 1 FLR 749 54
A v National Blood Authority [2001] 3 All ER 289 (QBD) 395, 396, 404
A v Secretary of State for the Home Department [2004] EWHC 1585
(Admin) 112
Abbahall Ltd v Smee [2002] EWCA Civ 1831, [2003] 1 WLR 1472 .... 175–6, 281
Abouzaid v Mothercare (UK) Ltd, The Times (CA, 20
February 2001) 394, 396, 397
ACB v Thomson Medical Pte Ltd [2017] SGCA 20, [2017] 1 SLR 918 13
Accident Compensation Corporation v Ambros [2007] NZCA 304 234
Adams v Bracknell Forest DC [2004] UKHL 29, [2005] 1 AC 76........ 218–9, 220
Adams v Star Enterprise 51 F 3d 417 (4th Cir 1995) 289
Adkins v Thomas Solvent Co 487 NW 2d 715 (Mich 1992) 289
A-G v Birmingham Borough Council (1858) 4 K & J 528,
70 ER 220 .... 277, 282–3
A-G v Prince [1998] 1 NZLR 262 (NZCA) 103
Alcan Gove Pty Ltd v Zabic [2015] HCA 33, 257 CLR 1 13
Alcock v Chief Constable of South Yorkshire Police [1992]
1 AC 310 (HL) 36, 41, 42,
59, 75, 81, 86
Alcock v Wraith (1991) 59 BLR 20 (CA) 320
Aldred's Case (1610) 9 Co Rep 57b, 77 ER 816 ....261, 263, 293
Aldridge v Van Patter [1952] 4 DLR 93 (Ont HC) 318
Alexandrou v Oxford [1993] 4 All ER 328 (CA) 103, 115
Aliakmon, The. See Leigh & Sillivan Ltd v Aliakmon Shipping Co Ltd
(The Aliakmon)
Allied Maples Group Ltd v Simmons & Simmons (a firm) [1995]
1 WLR 1602 (CA) 245
Amphitheaters Inc v Portland Meadows 198 P 2d 847 (Or 1948) 266
Anderson v Forth Valley Health Board (1997) 44 BMLR 108 (CSOH) 208
Andreae v Selfridge & Co Ltd [1938] Ch 1 (CA) 274
Anglian Water Services Ltd v Crawshaw Robbins & Co Ltd
[2001] BLR 173 (QBD) 262, 291, 293, 382
Anns v Merton London Borough [1978] AC 728 (HL) 45, 53, 56, 73,
82, 83, 84, 85,
95, 352, 360

Appleby v Erie Tobacco (1910) 22 OLR 533 (Ont DC) 287
Armitage v Nurse [1998] Ch 241 (CA) 177, 181
Arscott v Coal Authority [2004] EWCA Civ 892, [2005] EnvLR 6 321
Arthur JS Hall & Co (a firm) v Simons [2000] UKHL 38, [2002]
    1 AC 615 (HL) 40, 135
Ashby v White (1703) 2 Ld Raym 938, 92 ER 126 376
Ashley v Chief Constable of Sussex Police [2008] UKHL 25,
    [2008] AC 962 359–60
Ashton v Turner [1981] QB 137 (QBD) 42
Associated Provincial Picture Houses v Wednesbury Corp
    [1948] 1 KB 223 (CA) 157, 158, 165, 166,
                                                                        171, 172, 173, 174
Ata Textile Co v Schwartz (1976) 30(3) PD 785 (Sup Ct Isr) 277
Attorney General v Blake [2000] UKHL 45, [2001] 1 AC 268 276
Attorney-General v PYA Quarries Ltd [1957] 2 QB 169 (CA) 280, 323
Attorney General of the British Virgin Islands v Hartwell
    [2004] UKPC 12, [2004] 1 WLR 1273 .... 51, 52, 74
Ayers v Jackson Township 525 A 2d 287 (NJ 1987) 355, 356, 365
B v AG of New Zealand [2003] UKPC 61, [2003] 4 All ER 833 103
Backhouse v Bonomi (1861) 9 HL Cas 503, 11 ER 825 296
Bacon v Howard Kennedy (a firm) [1999] PNLR 1 (Ch D) 383
Balfour v Balfour [1919] 2 KB 571 (CA) 136
Balfour v Barty-King [1956] 1 WLR 779 (QBD); affirmed [1957]
    1 QB 496 (CA) 327
Bamford v Turnley (1862) 3 B & S 66, 122 ER 27 .... 265, 299
Banbury v Bank of Montreal [1918] AC 626 (HL) 153
Banca Nazionale del Lavoro SPA v Playboy Club London Ltd
    [2018] UKSC 43, [2018] 1 WLR 4041 .... 132, 136, 137,
                                                                          138, 142, 148
Bank of East Asia Ltd v Tsien Wui Marble Factory Ltd (1999)
    2 HKCFAR 349, [2000] 1 HKLRD 268 389
Barbagallo v J & F Catelan Pty Ltd [1986] 1 Qd R 245 (QSC) 344, 360
Barber v Somerset CC [2004] UKHL 13, [2004] 1 WLR 1089 75
Barclays Bank plc v Grant Thornton UK LLP [2015] EWHC 320 (Comm),
    [2015] 2 BCLC 537 136
Barker v Corus (UK) Ltd [2006] UKHL 20, [2006] 2 AC 572 .... 14, 228, 233,
                                                                       234, 236, 238,
                                                                        239, 249, 251
Barnes v Mac Brown & Co Inc 342 NE 2d 611 (Ind 1976) 361
Barnett v Chelsea and Kensington Hospital Management
    Committee [1969] 1 QB 428 (QBD) 116, 153
Barr v Biffa Waste Services Ltd [2012] EWCA Civ 312, [2013] QB 455 284
Barratt Homes Ltd v DWR Cymru Cyfyngedig (Welsh Water)
    (No 2) [2013] EWCA Civ 233, [2013] 1 WLR 3486 .... 291, 296, 297

Barrett v Enfield London Borough Council [2001] 2 AC 550 (HL) 100, 114,
120, 131, 147,
151, 153, 166,
167, 168, 186, 188

Barrett v Ministry of Defence [1995] 1 WLR 1217 (CA) 46, 114, 141

Bartlett v Tottenham [1932] 1 Ch 114 (Ch D) 319

Bass v Gregory (1890) 25 QBD 481 (QBD) 297

Bellew v Cement Ltd [1948] IR 61 (Sup Ct Ire) 277

Benning v Wong (1969) 122 CLR 249 (HCA) 307, 314, 318, 329

Ben Nevis Distillery (Fort William) Ltd v North British
Aluminium Co Ltd 1948 SC 592 (CSIH) 277

BGH 21 December 1970, BGHZ 55, 153 (Fleet Case) 303

BGH 26 November 1968, BGHZ 51, 91 (Chicken Pest Case) 422

Bhamra v Dubb (t/a Lucky Caterers) [2010] EWCA Civ 13 51

Biddick (decd) v Morcom [2014] EWCA Civ 182 .... 125, 131, 135,
137–8, 141, 153

Bird v Pearce (Somerset CC, third party) (1979) 77 LGR 753 (CA) 110–11

Birmingham Development Co Ltd v Tyler [2008] EWCA Civ 859,
[2008] BLR 445 .... 289, 297

Blake v Galloway [2004] EWCA Civ 814, [2004] 1 WLR 2844 161–2

Blyth v Birmingham Waterworks Co (1856) 11 Exch 781,
156 ER 1047 .... 157, 179

Body Corporate No 207624 v North Shore CC [2012] NZSC 83,
[2013] 2 NZLR 297 351

Bolam v Friern Hospital Management Committee [1957]
1 WLR 582 (QBD) 160, 166, 167

Bolton v Stone [1951] AC 850 (HL), ... 279

Bond v Norman [1940] 2 All ER 12 (CA) 281

Bone v Seale [1975] 1 WLR 797 (CA) 256, 284

Bonnington Castings Ltd v Wardlaw [1956] AC 613 (HL) 229

Boomer v Atlantic Cement Co 257 NE 2d 870 (NY 1970) 264, 277

Bourhill v Young [1943] AC 92 (HL) 240

Bower v Peate (1876) 1 QBD 321 (QBD) 316

Bowry and Pope's Case (1589) 1 Leon 168, 74 ER 155 297

Box v Jubb (1879) 4 Ex D 76 (Exch D) 329

Bradburn v Lindsay [1983] 2 All ER 408 (Ch D) 281

Bradford Corp v Pickles [1895] AC 587 (HL) 17, 261, 293

Brady's Ltd v CNR [1929] 2 DLR 549 (Alta SC) 327

Bridlington Relay Ltd v Yorkshire Electricity Board [1965] Ch 436 (Ch D) 263

British Celanese Ltd v AH Hunt (Capacitors) Ltd [1969] 1 WLR 959
(QBD) 317, 322

British Railways Board v Herrington [1972] AC 877 (HL) 162, 163, 188

British Westinghouse Electric and Manufacturing Co v Underground
Electric Railways Co of London [1912] AC 673 (HL) 342

Brodie v Singleton Shire Council [2001] HCA 29, 206 CLR 512 .....112, 113, 279
Brookfield Multiplex Ltd v Owners Corporation Strata Plan 61288
    [2014] HCA 36, 254 CLR 185 351
Brooks v Canadian Pacific Railway Ltd (2007) 283 DLR (4th) 540
    (Sask Ct of QB) 347
Brooks v Commissioner of Police of the Metropolis [2005]
    UKHL 24, [2005] 1 WLR 1495.. 75, 81, 186
Brownie Wills v Shrimpton [1998] 2 NZLR 320 (NZCA)............................ 126
Browning v War Office [1963] 1 QB 750 (CA) 5
Brunsden v Humphrey (1884) 14 QBD 141 (CA) 6, 31
Bryan v Moloney (1995) 182 CLR 609 (HCA) 351
Burnett v Grampian Fire and Rescue Services [2007] CSOH 3,
    2007 SLT 61..116, 118, 119
Burnie Port Authority v General Jones Pty Ltd [1991] Tas R 203
    (Tas SC) 327
Burnie Port Authority v General Jones Pty Ltd (1994) 179 CLR 520
    (HCA)... 19, 306, 325,
                                                                        326, 327, 328,
                                                                        329, 330, 333
Caltex Refineries (Qld) Pty Ltd v Stavar [2009] NSWCA 258, 75
    NSWLR 649 .... 7, 55
Calvert v William Hill Credit Ltd [2008] EWCA Civ 1427,
    [2009] Ch 330 .... 52, 120, 137
Camarata Property Inc v Credit Suisse Securities (Europe) Ltd
    [2011] EWHC 479 (Comm), [2011] 2 BCLC 54 181
Cambridge Water Co Ltd v Eastern Counties Leather plc [1994]
    2 AC 264 (HL) 305, 306, 308, 309,
                                                                        310, 316, 317, 318,
                                                                        322, 325, 326, 327,
                                                                        328, 330, 331, 333
Caparo Industries plc v Dickman [1990] 2 AC 605 (HL) 6, 7, 40, 45, 53,
                                                                        55, 56, 57, 64, 65,
                                                                        66, 67, 68, 69, 70,
                                                                        71, 81, 83, 84, 86,
                                                                        87, 88, 90, 126,
                                                                        138, 144, 146
Capital and Counties plc v Hampshire County Council [1997]
    QB 1004 (CA)... 54, 103, 106, 107,
                                                                        112, 115, 116,
                                                                        118, 132, 134
Carr-Saunders v Dick McNeil Associates Ltd [1986] 1 WLR 922
    (Ch D).. 266
Carstairs v Taylor (1871) LR 6 Exch 217 (Exch) 329
Cartledge v E Jopling & Sons Ltd [1963] AC 758 (HL) 389

Carty v Croydon London Borough Council [2005] EWCA Civ 19,
 [2005] 1 WLR 2312 ....99, 167
Cashill v Wright (1856) 6 El & Bl 891, 119 ER 1096............................... 179
Cassidy v Ministry of Health [1951] 2 KB 343 (CA) 135
Cattanach v Melchior [2003] HCA 38, 215 CLR 1.......................... 35, 43, 207,
 214, 215
Cattle v Stockton Waterworks (1875) LR 10 QB 453 (QBD) 318
Cattley v St John's Ambulance Brigade (QBD, 25 November 1988) 159
Chandler v Cape plc [2012] EWCA Civ 525, [2012] 1 WLR 3111 125,
 141, 153
Chaplin v Hicks [1911] 2 KB 786 (CA).. 245
Charing Cross Electricity Supply Co v Hydraulic Power Co
 [1914] 3 KB 772 (CA) 317, 320, 322
Charitable Corporation v Sutton (1742) 2 Atk 400, 26 ER 642 179
Charlotte, The [1908] P 206 (CA) 387
Chasemore v Richards (1859) 7 HL Cas 349, 11 ER 140 .... 261, 293
Chaudhry v Prabhakar [1989] 1 WLR 29 (CA) 136
Chester v Afshar [2004] UKHL 41, [2005] 1 AC 134 216
Christie v Davey [1893] 1 Ch 316 (Ch D).. 265
City of Kamloops v Nielsen (1984) 10 DLR (4th) 641 (SCC)........................ 98
Clarke v Crew (1999) 149 NLJ 899 (CA) 196, 199
Clemente v United States 567 F 2d 1140 (1st Cir 1977)............................. 122
Clements v Clements 2012 SCC 32, [2012] 2 SCR 181 14
Clunis v Camden and Islington HA [1998] QB 978 (CA) 49
Coggs v Barnard (1703) 2 Ld Raym 909, 92 ER 107 178
Coles v Hetherton [2013] EWCA Civ 1704, [2015] 1 WLR 160 378
Colls v Home and Colonial Stores Ltd [1904] AC 179 (HL) 267, 297
Colour Quest Ltd v Total Downstream UK plc [2010] EWCA Civ 180,
 [2011] QB 86; [2009] EWHC 540 (Comm), [2009] 2 Lloyd's Rep 1 19
Commission v United Kingdom (Case C-300/95) [1997] ECR I-2649.....396, 416
Condon v Basi [1985] 1 WLR 866 (CA).. 162
Conques v Hardy 337 So 2d 627 (La Ct App 1976) 45
Connor v Surrey CC [2010] EWCA Civ 286, [2011] QB 429........................ 160
Constantine v Imperial Hotels Ltd [1944] KB 693 (KBD)...................... 155, 194
Cook v Lewis [1951] SCR 830 (SCC) 227, 230, 236, 237
Cooper v Hobart [2001] 3 SCR 537 (SCC) 35, 45, 102
Cope v Sharpe (No 2) [1912] 1 KB 496 (CA) 360
Corby Group Litigation Claimants v Corby Borough Council
 [2008] EWCA Civ 463, [2009] QB 335 ....256, 275, 279
Corpus Christi Oil & Gas Co v Zapata Gulf Marine Corp
 71 F 3d 198 (5th Cir 1995) 348
Costello v Chief Constable of the Northumbria Police [1999]
 1 All ER 550 (CA)...115, 141

Couch v A-G [2008] NZSC 45, [2008] 3 NZLR 725 .... 59, 98, 112
Cowan v Chief Constable of Avon and Somerset Constabulary
    [2001] EWCA Civ 1699, [2002] HLR 44 ....50, 193
Creative Foundation v Dreamland Leisure Ltd [2015] EWHC 2556 (Ch),
    [2016] Ch 253 389
Cremidas v Fenton 111 NE 855 (Mass 1916) 266
Crimmins v Stevedoring Industry Finance Committee (1999)
    200 CLR 1 (HCA) 89, 90, 102,
                                                                                       103, 188
Critelli Ltd v Lincoln Trust & Savings Co (1978) 86 DLR (3d) 724
    (Ont HC) 345
Crosby v Regency Security Services Ltd (Colchester CC, 18 May 2006) 170
Crown River Cruises Ltd v Kimbolton Fireworks Ltd [1996] 2 Lloyd's
    Rep 533 (QBD) 320, 321
Cunard v Antifyre Ltd [1933] 1 KB 551 (KBD) 256
Customs and Excise Commissioners v Barclays Bank plc [2004]
    EWCA Civ 1555, [2005] 1 WLR 2082 ....56, 146
Customs and Excise Commissioners v Barclays Bank plc [2006]
    UKHL 28, [2007] 1 AC 181 ....86, 90, 119–20,
                                                                                      126, 131, 138,
                                                                                      139, 142, 146
D & F Estates Ltd v Church Commissioners for England [1989]
    AC 177 (HL) 349, 351, 352
D Pride & Partners (a firm) v Institute for Animal Health [2009]
    EWHC 685 (QB), [2009] NPC 56 290
Daborn v Bath Tramways Motor Co Ltd [1946] 2 All ER 333 (CA) 161
Dalton v Henry Angus & Co (1881) LR 6 App Cas 740 (HL) 263
Daniels and Daniels v R White & Sons Ltd [1938] 4 All ER 258 (KBD) 418
Darnley v Croydon Health Services NHS Trust [2018] UKSC 50,
    [2019] AC 831 84
Das v Ganju [1999] PIQR P260 (CA) 208
Davey v Harrow Corpn [1958] 1 QB 60 (CA) 300
Davidson v Chief Constable of North Wales [1994] 2 All ER 597 (CA) 203
Davies v Taylor (No 1) [1974] AC 207 (HL) 245
Davis v Foots [1940] 1 KB 116 (CA) 130
De Freville v Dill (1927) 96 LJKB 1056 (KBD) 198, 203
Deepcliffe Pty Ltd v Council of the City of Gold Coast [2001]
    QCA 342, 118 LGERA 117 289
Delaware Mansions Ltd v Westminster CC [2001] UKHL 55,
    [2002] 1 AC 321 ....162, 343, 358
Deloitte & Touche v Livent Inc (Receiver of) [2017] SCC 63,
    [2017] 2 SCR 855 126
Dennis v Ministry of Defence [2003] EWHC 793 (QB), [2003]
    Env LR 34 ....265, 277, 320–1

Denny v Supplies and Transport Co [1950] 2 KB 374 (CA) 342
DeShaney v Winnebago County Department of Social Services 489
    US 189 (1989) 108–9
Devon Lumber Co Ltd v MacNeill (1987) 45 DLR (4th) 300
    (New Brunswick CA) 269
Dickinson v Cornwall CC (QBD, 10 December 1999) 170
D' Jan of London Ltd, Re [1994] 1 BCLC 561 (Ch D) 181
Dobson v Thames Water Utilities Ltd [2011] EWHC 3523 (TCC),
    140 Con LR 135 284
Dobson v Thames Water Utilities Ltd [2009] EWCA Civ 28,
    [2009] 3 All ER 319 .... 272, 273
Donoghue v Folkestone Properties Ltd [2003] EWCA Civ 231,
    [2003] QB 1008 164
Donoghue v Stevenson [1932] AC 562 (HL) 37, 54, 56, 82, 85, 88,
                                                                    89, 132, 139, 142, 146,
                                                                    154, 163, 185, 353, 404
Donohue v Copiague Union Free School District 407 NYS 2d 874
    (NY App Div 1978) 221
Doughty v Turner [1964] 1 QB 518 (CA) 52
Dovuro Pty Ltd v Wilkins [2000] FCA 1902, 105 FCR 476 .... 357, 359,
                                                                    360, 361, 362
Dovuro Pty Ltd v Wilkins [2003] HCA 51, 215 CLR 317 360
Dryden v Johnson Matthey plc [2018] UKSC 18, [2019] AC 403 .... 13, 21
Duff v Highland and Islands Fire Board 1995 SLT 1362 (CSOH) 116
Dunn v Birmingham Canal Co (1872) LR 7 QB 244 (QBD) 329
Dutton v Bognor Regis UDC [1972] 1 QB 373 (CA) 351–2
DW Moore & Co Ltd v Ferrier [1988] 1 WLR 267 (CA) 379
E (a minor) v Dorset County Council [1994] 3 WLR 853 (CA) 194, 195,
                                                                    218, 220
East Suffolk Rivers Catchment Board v Kent County Council
    [1941] AC 74 (HL) 94–5, 96,
                                                                    98, 106, 115
Elguzouli-Daf v Commissioner of Police of the Metropolis
    [1995] QB 335 (CA) 198–9, 205
Ellison v Ministry of Defence (1996) 81 BLR 101 (QBD) 309, 319
England v Cowley (1873) LR 8 Ex 126 (Exch) 303
Equitas Insurance Ltd v Municipal Mutual Insurance Ltd [2019]
    EWCA Civ 718, [2020] QB 418 15
Escola v Coca-Cola Bottling Co of Fresno 150 P 2d 436 (Cal 1944) 407, 408,
                                                                    409, 410, 417,
                                                                    419, 420, 426
Evans v Triplex Safety Glass Co Ltd [1936] 1 All ER 283 (KBD) 419, 422
Everett v Comojo (UK) Ltd (t/a The Metropolitan) [2011]
    EWCA Civ 13, [2012] 1 WLR 150 .... 57, 58, 87

Everett v Griffiths [1920] 3 KB 163 (CA) 196, 198, 203

Everett v Griffiths [1921] 1 AC 631 (HL) 198

Exxon Corp v Yarema 516 A 2d 990 (Md App 1986) 290

Fairchild v Glenhaven Funeral Services Ltd [2002] UKHL 22,
    [2003] 1 AC 32 .... 14, 15, 228, 229,
                                            230–2, 233, 234, 235,
                                            236, 237, 238, 239–40,
                                            243, 244, 250, 251

Farr v Butters Bros & Co [1932] 2 KB 606 (CA) 342

Fear v Vickers (1911) 27 TLR 558 (CA) 297

Fearn v Board of Trustees of the Tate Gallery [2023] UKSC 4,
    [2023] 2 WLR 339 .... 16, 17, 18

Fennell v Robson Excavations Pty Ltd [1977] 2 NSWLR 486 (NSWCA) 270

Fisher v Ruislip-Northwood UDC [1945] KB 584 (CA) 106

Fletcher v Bealey (1885) 28 Ch D 688 (Ch D) 360

Fletcher v Rylands (1865) 3 H & C 774, 159 ER 737 (Exch) 311–2, 313,
                                            314, 329

Fletcher v Rylands (1866) LR 1 Exch 265 (Exch Ch) 308, 313

Florence v Goldberg 375 NE 2d 763 (NY 1978) 110

Foley v Harris 286 SE 2d 186 (Va 1982) 291

Fontainebleau Hotel Corp v Forty-Five Twenty-Five Inc 114 So 2d 357
    (Fla Dist Ct App 1959) 263, 297

Fowler v Lanning [1959] 1 QB 426 (QBD) 204

Fowler v Sanders (1617) Cro Jac 446, 79 ER 382 279

Froom v Butcher [1976] QB 286 (CA) 341

Furnell v Flaherty [2013] EWHC 377 (QB) 132

Gala v Preston (1991) 172 CLR 243 (HCA) 42, 56

Geary v JD Wetherspoon plc [2011] EWHC 1506 (QB) 42

Gee v DePuy International Ltd [2018] EWHC 1208 (QB), [2018]
    Med LR 347 396

George Fischer Holding Ltd v Multi Design Consultants Ltd
    (1998) 61 Con LR 85 (QBD) 353

Giblin v McMullen (1868) LR 2 PC 317 (PC) 177

Gibson v Orr 1999 SC 420 (CSOH) 116, 118

Gilchrist Watt & Sanderson Pty Ltd v York Products Pty Ltd
    [1970] 1 WLR 1262 (PC) 135

Gladwell v Steggall (1839) 5 Bing NC 733, 132 ER 1283 141

Glanzer v Shepard 135 NE 275 (NY 1922) 125, 135

Glasgow Corporation v Muir [1943] AC 448 (HL) 170

Godden v Kent & Medway SHA [2004] EWHC 1629 (QB),
    [2004] Lloyd's Rep Med 521 186

Godfrey v Gloucestershire Royal Infirmary NHS Trust [2003]
    EWHC 549 (QB), [2003] Lloyd's Rep Med 398 208

Gold v Essex County Council [1942] 2 KB 293 (CA)...................................138
Goldman v Hargrave [1967] 1 AC 645 (PC)...............................142, 162, 163,
169, 188, 322
Goodbody v Poplar Borough Council (1914) 84 LJKB 122 (KBD)...............317
Goodes v East Sussex County Council [2000] 1 WLR 1356 (HL)...................97
Goodwill v British Pregnancy Advisory Service [1996] 1 WLR 1397 (CA)....207
Gore v Stannard (t/a Wyvern Tyres) [2012] EWCA Civ 1248,
[2014] 1 QB 1... 19, 342, 344
Gorham v British Telecommunications plc [2000] 1 WLR 2129 (CA)..............54
Gorringe v Calderdale Metropolitan Borough Council [2002]
EWCA Civ 595, [2002] RTR 446..97
Gorringe v Calderdale Metropolitan Borough Council [2004]
UKHL 15, [2004] 1 WLR 1057... 8, 9, 71, 73, 77, 93,
96, 97, 98, 99, 100,
101, 102, 103, 104,
105, 106, 110, 111,
112, 113, 114, 115,
120, 121, 123, 141
Gower v London Brorough of Bromley [1999] ELR 356 (CA).......................222
Graham Barclay Oysters Pty Ltd v Ryan [2002] HCA 54, 211 CLR 540........102
Graham and Graham v ReChem International Ltd [1996]
Env LR 158 (QBD)...321
Grant v Australian Knitting Mills Ltd [1936] AC 85 (PC).......................56, 395
Gray v Thames Trains Ltd [2009] UKHL 33, [2009] 1 AC 1339......................49
Greenock Corporation v Caledonian Rly Co [1917] AC 556 (HL)................329
Greenway v Johnson Mathey plc [2014] EWHC 3957 (QB), [2015]
PIQR P10 350
Gregg v Scott [2002] EWCA Civ 1471, (2003) 71 BMLR 16..........................248
Gregg v Scott [2005] UKHL 2, [2005] 2 AC 176............................... 241, 242–4,
245, 247, 251
Greystoke Castle, The. See Morrison Steamship Co v Greystoke
Castle (Cargo Owners) (The Greystoke Castle)
Grinham v Willey (1859) 4 H & N 496, 157 ER 934 202
Gunnersen v Henwood [2011] VSC 440 ....346, 357, 359
Guppys (Bridport) Ltd v Brookling (1984) 14 HLR 1 (CA) 291–2
Hale v Jenning Bros [1938] 1 All ER 579 (CA)..317
Hall v Beckenham Corp [1949] 1 KB 716 (KBD).......................................270
Hall v Hebert [1993] 2 SCR 159 (SCC) 42, 45, 47, 60
Halsey v Esso Petroleum Co Ltd [1961] 1 WLR 683 (QBD) 270, 274,
284, 317
Harris v Evans [1998] 1 WLR 1285 (CA)..54
Harrison v Good (1871) LR 11 Eq 338 (Ch) 260, 288
Harrison v Southwark and Vauxhall Water Co [1891] 2 Ch 409 (Ch D) 265
Harriton v Stephens [2006] HCA 15, 226 CLR 52 ....30, 54, 195, 210, 224

Hawkins v Clayton (1988) 164 CLR 539 (HCA) 56

Hedley Byrne & Co Ltd v Heller & Partners Ltd [1964]
   AC 465 (HL) 46, 88, 90, 125, 126,
                                                           127, 129, 130, 132, 133,
                                                           134, 135, 136, 138, 141,
                                                           142, 142, 143, 144, 145,
                                                           146, 147, 148, 149, 152,
                                                           153, 156, 222, 383

Hellespont Ardent, The [1997] 2 Lloyd's Rep 547 (QBD) 181

Henderson v Merrett Syndicates Ltd [1995] 2 AC 145 (HL) 46, 90, 120,
                                                           130, 131, 134, 135,
                                                           141, 148, 150, 153

Hepburn v A Tomlinson (Hauliers) Ltd [1966] AC 451 (HL) 388

Hercules Managements Ltd v Ernst & Young [1997] 2 SCR 165 (SCC) 138

Herrington v British Railways Board [1971] 2 QB 107 (CA)..........................177

Hill v Chief Constable of West Yorkshire [1989] AC 53 (HL)............. 41, 64, 65,
                                                           67, 73, 74, 75,
                                                           76, 77, 79, 80

Hinton v Dibbin (1842) 2 QB 646, 114 ER 253 ....179, 180

Hirose Electrical UK Ltd v Peak Ingredients Ltd [2011] EWCA Civ 987,
   [2011] Env LR 34 266

Hobbs (Farms) Ltd v Baxenden Chemical Co Ltd [1992] 1 Lloyd's
   Rep 54 (QBD)..368

Holbeck Hall Hotel Ltd v Scarborough BC [2000] QB 836 (CA).................163

Homburg Houtimport BV v Agrosin Private Ltd (The Starsin) [2003]
   UKHL 12, [2004] 1 AC 715...388

Hollywood Silver Fox Farm Ltd v Emmett [1936] 2 KB 468 (KBD)..............265

Home Office v Dorset Yacht Co Ltd [1970] AC 1004 (HL)............. 41, 82, 86–7,
                                                           89, 90, 100, 106,
                                                           142, 165, 168, 170

Hooper v Rogers [1975] Ch 43 (CA) 343–4, 346, 360

Hotson v East Berkshire Area Health Authority [1987]
   2 WLR 287 (CA)..195, 241

Hotson v East Berkshire Health Authority [1987]
   AC 750 (HL).. 236, 241–2, 243,
                                                           244, 246–7, 248

Howard Electric Ltd v AJ Mooney Ltd [1974] 2 NZLR 762 (NZSC)............274

Howell v Young (1826) 5 B & C 259, 108 ER 97 155

HR Moch Co Inc v Rensselaer Water Co 159 NE 896 (NY 1928) 130

Hubbard v Pitt [1976] QB 142 (CA) 262, 270

Hunt v Peake (1860) John 705, 70 ER 603 296

Hunter v British Coal Corp [1999] QB 140 (CA) 36

Hunter v Canary Wharf Ltd [1996] 2 WLR 348 (CA)............................195, 269

Hunter v Canary Wharf Ltd [1997] AC 655 (HL) 256, 257, 258, 261,
262, 263, 268, 269,
271, 272, 273–4,
275, 279, 280, 286,
287, 288, 293, 298,
299, 316, 318, 389
Hussain v Lancaster City Council [2000] QB 1 (CA) 271
HXA v Surrey County Council [2022] EWCA Civ 1196, [2023]
1 WLR 116 9
Informer v Chief Constable [2012] EWCA Civ 197, [2013] QB 579 40
International Energy Group Ltd v Zurich Insurance plc [2015] UKSC 33,
[2016] AC 509 15
Invercargill City Council v Hamlin [1994] 3 NZLR 513 (NZCA);
affirmed [1996] AC 624 (PC) 98
J Lyons & Sons v Wilkins [1899] 1 Ch 255 (CA) 262
Jackson v Harrison (1978) 138 CLR 438 (HCA) 45
Jacque v Steenberg Homes 563 NW 2d 154 (Wis 1997) 5
Jain v Trent Strategic Health Authority [2009] UKHL 4, [2009]
1 AC 853 ....45, 50, 105, 123
James-Bowen v Commissioner of Police of the Metropolis [2018]
UKSC 40, [2018] 1 WLR 4021 84
Jan de Nul (UK) Ltd v Axa Royale Belge SA [2002] EWCA Civ 209,
[2002] 1 Lloyd's Rep 583 274
JD v East Berkshire Community NHS Trust [2003] EWCA
Civ 1151, [2004] QB 558 ....100, 101, 102,
103, 104, 122
JD v East Berkshire Community NHS Trust [2005] UKHL 23,
[2005] 2 AC 373 .... 100, 103, 105, 158, 190
Jebson v Ministry of Defence [2000] 1 WLR 2055 (CA) 125
John Munroe (Acrylics) Ltd v London Fire and Civil Defence
Authority [1997] QB 983 (QBD) 116
Johnson v BJW Property Developments Ltd [2002] EWHC 1131 (TCC),
[2002] 3 All ER 574 309
JJD SA v Avon Tyres Ltd (CA, 23 February 2000) 179
Jolley v Sutton LBC [2000] 1 WLR 1082 (HL) 52
Jones v Boyce (1816) 1 Stark 493, 171 ER 540 358
Jones v Festiniog Rly Co (1868) LR 3 QB 733 (QBD) 306, 318
Jones v Kaney [2011] UKSC 13, [2011] 2 AC 398 40
Jones v Llanwrst Urban Council [1911] 1 Ch 393 (Ch D) 315
Jones v Vernon Pools Ltd [1938] 2 All ER 626 (KBD) 136
Jones (Insurance Brokers) Ltd v Portsmouth City Council [2002]
EWCA Civ 1723, [2003] 1 WLR 427 319
Joyce v O'Brien & Tradex Insurance Co Ltd [2012] EWHC 1324 (QB),
[2012] PIQR P18 42

Kapfunde v Abbey National plc [1998] IRLR 583 (CA) 132
Kelsen v Imperial Tobacco Co [1957] 2 QB 334 (QBD) 276
Kennaway v Thompson [1981] QB 88 (CA) 265, 277
Kent v East Suffolk Rivers Catchment Board [1940]
    1 KB 319 (CA) 109, 115, 121
Kent v Griffiths [2001] QB 36 (CA) 101, 102–3, 105,
                                                                108, 115, 116, 117,
                                                                    118, 132, 186
Kent v London Ambulance Service [1999] Lloyd's Rep Med 58 (CA) 116
KH Enterprise (cargo owners) v Pioneer Container (owners)
    (The Pioneer Container) [1994] 2 AC 324 (HL) 137
Khatun v United Kingdom (1998) 26 EHRR CD 212 (ECommHR) 272
Khorasandjian v Bush [1993] QB 727 (CA) 262, 268
Kine v Jolly [1905] 1 Ch 480 (CA) 297
Kirk v London Borough of Brent [2005] EWCA Civ 1701, [2006]
    Env LR D7 358
Kirkham v Chief Constable of the Greater Manchester Police
    [1990] 2 QB 283 (CA) 141
Kitchen v RAF Association [1958] 1 WLR 563 (CA) 245
Knightley v Johns [1982] 1 WLR 349 (CA) 40, 74
Knox v Mackinnon (1888) 15 R 83 (HL) 87 176
Kommunar (No 3), The [1997] 1 Lloyd's Rep 22 (QBD) 180
Kraemers v A-G of Tasmania [1966] Tas SR 113 (Tas SC) 270
L v M [1979] 2 NZLR 519 (NZCA) 209
Lamb v Camden LBC [1981] QB 625 (CA) 49, 50
Larner v Solihull Metropolitan Borough Council [2001]
    BLGR 255 (CA) 97, 101
Law Society v Sephton & Co [2006] UKHL 22, [2006]
    2 AC 543 .... 193, 380, 386
Lawrence v Fen Tigers Ltd [2011] EWHC 360 (QB), [2011]
    4 All ER 1314 272
Lawrence v Pembrokeshire CC [2007] EWCA Civ 446, [2007]
    1 WLR 2991 190
Laws v Florinplace Ltd [1981] 1 All ER 659 (Ch D) 260, 290, 291, 297
Lawson v Laferriere [1991] 1 SCR 541 (SCC) 227
Leach v Chief Constable of Gloucestershire Constabulary [1999]
    1 All ER 215 (CA) 75
Leakey v National Trust [1980] QB 485 (CA) 162, 163, 175,
                                                                    176, 177, 281,
                                                                        319, 322, 323
Leigh & Sillivan Ltd v Aliakmon Shipping Co Ltd (The Aliakmon)
    [1985] QB 350 (CA) 5, 30, 36, 56
Leigh & Sillivan Ltd v Aliakmon Shipping Co Ltd (The Aliakmon)
    [1986] AC 785 (HL) 268, 387

Lejonvarn v Burgess [2017] EWCA Civ 254, [2017] BLR 277 .... 126, 138
Lemmon v Webb [1894] 3 Ch 1 (CA) 300
Lennon v Metropolitan Police Commissioner [2004] EWCA Civ 130,
    [2004] 1 WLR 2594 150
Lester-Travers v City of Frankston [1970] VR 2 (VSC).............................. 300
Letang v Cooper [1965] 1 QB 232 (CA)..202, 204
Lethbridge v Phillips (1819) 2 Stark 544, 171 ER 731 140
Lindsay v Berkeley Homes (Capital) plc [2018] EWHC 2042 (TCC)..............20
Lippiatt v South Gloucestershire Council [2000] QB 51 (CA) 270
Lockett v A & M Charles Ltd [1938] 4 All ER 170 (KBD)........................... 418
Losinjska Plovidba v Transco Overseas (The Orjula) [1995] 2 Lloyd's
    Rep 395 (QBD) 342, 343,
                                                                            350–1, 390
Malone v Laskey [1907] 2 KB 141 (CA)... 275
Mann v Saulnier (1959) 19 DLR (2d) 130 (New Brunswick CA)............276, 300
Marc Rich & Co v Bishop Rock Marine Co [1996] AC 211 (HL) 69
Marcic v Thames Water Utilities Ltd [2001] 3 All ER 698 (QBD)................ 309
Marsh v Baxter [2014] WASC 187, 46 WAR 377; affirmed [2015]
    WASCA 169, 49 WAR 1 290
Martin v Reynolds Metals Co 342 P 2d 790 (Or 1959) 299
Mason v Levy Auto Parts of England Ltd [1967] 2 QB 530
    (Winchester Assizes) 327
Mason v Hill (1833) 5 B & Ad 1, 110 ER 692 297
Matania v National Provincial Bank Ltd [1936] 2 All ER 633 (CA) 320
Maynard v West Midlands RHA [1984] 1 WLR 634 (HL)............................ 138
McCullagh v Lane Fox & Partners Ltd [1996] PNLR 205 (CA)................... 136
McCulloch v Murray [1942] SCR 141 (SCC) 145..................................... 183
McDonogh v Commonwealth of Australia (1985) 73 ALR 148 (FCA) 110
McFarlane v Tayside Health Board 1997 SLT 211 (CSOH) 208
McFarlane v Tayside Health Board [2000] 2 AC 59 (HL) 42, 43, 206,
                                                                       207, 208, 209,
                                                                       211, 213, 214
McGhee v National Coal Board [1973] 1 WLR 1 (HL) 14, 228, 229–30,
                                                                       232, 233, 234,
                                                                       236, 239, 250
McKenna v British Aluminium Ltd [2002] Env LR 30 (Ch D) 309
McKew v Holland & Hannen & Cubitts (Scotland) Ltd [1969]
    3 All ER 1621 (HL) 40
McKinnon Industries Ltd v Walker [1951] 3 DLR 577 (PC) 266
McLane v Northwest Natural Gas Co 467 P 2d 635 (Or 1970).................... 332
McLoughlin v Jones [2001] EWCA Civ 1743, [2002] QB 1312.............. 199, 203
McLoughlin v O'Brian [1983] 1 AC 410 (HL)..41
McMullin v ICI Australia Operations Pty Ltd (1997) 72 FCR 1 (FCA) 388
Meadows v Khan [2021] UKSC 21, [2022] AC 852.....................................13

Mercer v South Eastern and Chatham Railway Companies Managing
    Committee [1922] 2 KB 549 (KBD)..109–10
Mersey Docks and Harbour Board Trustees v Gibbs (1866)
    LR 1 HL 93 (HL) 72
Merthyr Tydfill County Borough Council v C [2010] EWHC 62 (QB),
    [2010] 1 FLR 1640..100
Messick v General Motors Corpn 460 F 2d 485 (5th Cir 1972)....................354
Metro-North Commuter RR Co v Buckley 521 US 424 (1997)....................355
Metropolitan Properties Ltd v Jones [1939] 2 All ER 202 (KBD)..................265
Michael v Chief Constable of South Wales Police [2015] UKSC 2,
    [2015] AC 1732 ....8, 9, 66, 67, 68,
                                                         69, 70, 71, 73, 77,
                                                         80, 84, 88, 91, 132,
                                                         134, 141, 155
Midland Bank plc v Bardgrove Property Services (1992) 65 P &
    CR 153 (CA)..346, 358
Midwood & Co Ltd v Manchester Corpn [1905] 2 KB 597 (CA).............. 322–3
Miles v Forest Rock Granite Co (1918) 34 TLR 500 (CA) 19, 317
Miller v Jackson [1977] QB 966 (CA)................................... 265, 271, 277, 300
Miller v Miller [2011] HCA 9, 242 CLR 446 42
Ministry of Housing and Local Government v Sharp [1970]
    2 QB 223 (CA) 120
Miranda v Shell Oil Co 17 Cal App 4th 1651 (Cal Ct App 1993).................365
Mitchell v Glasgow City Council [2009] UKHL 11, [2009]
    1 AC 874..41, 57, 58, 79,
                                                         141, 142, 168, 171
Mitchell v Ontario (2004) 242 DLR (4th) 560 (Ont SCJ)............................ 102
Modbury Triangle Shopping Centre Pty Ltd v Anzil [2000] HCA 61,
    205 CLR 254.. 41, 52
Morrison Steamship Co v Greystoke Castle (Cargo Owners)
    (The Greystoke Castle) [1947] AC 265 (HL)..369
Morse v Barratt (Leeds) Ltd (1992) 9 Const LJ 158 (Ch D) 353
Motherwell v Motherwell (1976) 73 DLR (3d) 62 (Alta CA) 262, 269
Moy v Stoop (1909) 25 TLR 262 (KBD) 260, 265
Muirhead v Industrial Tank Specialities Ltd [1986] QB 507 (CA) 134, 417
Mulcahy v Ministry of Defence [1996] QB 732 (CA) 40
Mullin v Richards [1998] 1 WLR 1304 (CA).. 160
Murphy v Brentwood DC [1991] 1 AC 398 (HL) 40, 52, 56, 90,
                                                         160, 169, 340, 349,
                                                         351, 352–3, 360
Murray v Ministry of Defence [1988] 1 WLR 692 (HL) 201
Mutual Life & Citizens' Assurance Co Ltd v Evatt [1971]
    AC 793 (HL)...143, 149
N v Poole BC [2019] UKSC 25, [2020] AC 780.................................. 8, 9, 10

National Telephone Co v Baker [1893] 2 Ch 186 (Ch D)..............................306
Neil Martin Ltd v Revenue and Customs Commissioners [2006]
EWHC 2425 (Ch), [2007] STC 823 119
Neil Martin Ltd v Customs and Revenue Commissioners [2007]
EWCA Civ 1041, [2007] STC 1802...99, 119
Neindorf v Junkovic [2005] HCA 75, 222 ALR 631 ....51, 52
Nettleship v Weston [1971] 2 QB 691 (CA) 42, 139
Network Rail Infrastructure Ltd v Morris [2004] EWCA Civ 172,
[2004] Env LR 41 ....279, 291
Network Rail Infrastructure Ltd v Williams [2018] EWCA Civ 1514,
[2019] QB 601..287, 288
New Zealand Forest Products v O'Sullivan [1974] 2 NZLR 80
(NZHC) 342, 343,
344–5, 361, 362
Nichols v Marsland (1875) LR 10 Exch 255 (Exch)..................313, 321, 329
Nor-Video Services Ltd v Ontario Hydro (1978) 84 DLR (3d) 221
(Ont HCJ) 263, 298
Norges Høyesterett (Hr) 2 June 2006, Retstidende 2006, 691
(Norwegian Supreme Ct) 347
North Shore CC v Body Corporate 188529 [2010] NZSC 158,
[2011] 2 NZLR 289...351
Northern Counties of England Fire Insurance Co v Whipp (1884)
26 Ch D 482 (CA) 181
Northampton Borough Council v Lovatt (1997) 96 LGR 548 (CA) 270
Northwestern Utilities Ltd v London Guarantee and Accident Co
[1936] AC 108 (PC) 310, 320
Norwich City Council v Harvey [1989] 1 WLR 828 (CA) 42
NRAM Ltd v Steel [2018] UKSC 13, [2018] 1 WLR 1190.....................142, 152
Nykredit Mortgage Bank plc v Edward Erdman Group Ltd (No 2)
[1997] 1 WLR 1627 (HL)...379, 386
OGH 16 May 2001, ZVR 2001/73...183
Ogopogo, The [1970] 1 Lloyd's Rep 257 (Ont CA) 118, 119
OLL Ltd v Secretary of State for Transport [1997] 3 All ER 897
(QBD) 103, 106, 107,
108, 112, 117
Olotu v Home Office [1997] 1 WLR 328 (CA)..197
Orange v CC of West Yorkshire Police [2001] EWCA Civ 611,
[2002] QB 347..51
Orchard v Lee [2009] EWCA Civ 295, [2009] PIQR P16 160
Orjula, The. See Losinjska Plovidba v Transco Overseas (The Orjula)
Oropesa, The [1943] P 32 (CA)..31
O'Rourke v Camden London Borough Council [1988]
AC 188 (HL)..103, 104
Orr-Ewing v Colquhoun (1877) 2 App Cas 839 (HL)...............................297

Osman v United Kingdom [1999] 1 FLR 193 (ECtHR) 104–5, 185
Overseas Tankship (UK) v Miller Steamship Co Pty [1967]
    1 AC 617 (PC) 170
Overseas Tankship (UK) v Morts Dock and Engineering Co
    (The Wagon Mound) [1961] AC 388 (PC) 41, 44
Page v Smith [1996] AC 155 (HL) 86
Palmer v Tees Health Authority [1999] Lloyd's Rep Med 351 (CA) 177
Palsgraf v Long Island Railroad Co 162 NE 99 (NY 1928) 34, 53, 240
Paradis Honey Ltd v Canada [2015] FCA 89, [2016] 1 FCR 446 9
Parkinson v St James and Seacroft University Hospital NHS Trust
    [2001] EWCA Civ 530, [2002] QB 266 .... 43, 209, 214
Parramatta City Council v Lutz (1988) 12 NSWLR 293 (NSWCA) 112
Pentecost v London District Auditor [1951] 2 KB 759 (KBD) 177
People (The) ex rel Hoogasian v Sears, Roebuck & Co 287 NE
    2d 677 (Ill 1972) 261
Percy v Hall [1997] QB 924 (CA) 197
Perry v Kendricks Transport Co Ltd [1956] 1 WLR 85 (CA) 317, 318, 329
Peter W v San Francisco Unified School District 60 Cal App 3d 814
    (Cal Ct App 1976) 221
Pett v Sims Paving and Road Construction Co Pty Ltd [1928]
    VR 247 (VSC) 320
Phelps v Hillingdon LBC [1999] 1 WLR 500 (CA) 218, 221
Phelps v London Borough of Hillingdon [2001] 2 AC 619 (HL) 100, 114,
                                                                              120, 166, 167,
                                                                              168, 216–7, 218,
                                                                              219, 220, 221, 222
Phillips v William Whiteley Ltd [1938] 1 All ER 566 (KBD) 138
Pierce v Doncaster Metropolitan Borough Council [2007]
    EWHC 2968 (QB), 100 BMLR 76 100
Pioneer Container, The. See KH Enterprise (cargo owners) v
    Pioneer Container (owners) (The Pioneer Container)
Pippin v Sheppard (1822) 11 Price 400, 147 ER 512 141
Pirelli General Cable Works v Oscar Faber [1983] 2 AC 1 (HL) 30, 193
Pitts v Hunt [1991] 1 QB 24 (CA) 42, 45
Polemis and Furness, Withy & Co Ltd, Re [1921] 3 KB 560 (CA) 44
Port Victoria, The [1902] P 25 (PD) 345
Possfund Custodian Trustee Ltd v Diamond [1996] 1 WLR 1351 (Ch D) 53
Potter v Firestone Tire & Rubber Co 863 P 2d 795 (Cal 1993) 355
Powell v Fall (1880) 5 QBD 597 (CA) 306, 320
Precision Products (NSW) Pty Ltd v Hawkesbury CC [2008]
    NSWCA 278, 74 NSWLR 102 172
Pyrenees Shire Council v Day [1998] HCA 3, 192 CLR 330 .... 98, 102,
                                                                              112, 113, 165

Qualcast (Wolverhampton) Ltd v Haynes [1959] AC 743 (HL)................51, 185
Quinland v Governor of Swaleside Prison [2002] EWCA Civ 174,
    [2003] QB 306...197
R v Adomako [1995] 1 AC 171 (HL) 181
R v Bournewood Community and Mental Health NHS Trust,
    ex p L [1998] 2 WLR 764 (CA); reversed [1999] AC 458 (HL) 201
R v Croydon Health Authority (1997) 40 BMLR 40 (CA) 210
R v Governor of Brockhill Prison, ex p Evans (No 2) [2001]
    2 AC 19 (HL) 197
R v Secretary of State for Transport, ex p Factortame Ltd (No 5)
    [2000] 1 AC 524 (HL)...172
R v Whiteley (1991) 93 Cr App R 25 (CA)...389
Ranicar v Frigmobile Pty Ltd [1983] Tas R 113 (Tas SC) 116 390
Read v J Lyons & Co Ltd [1945] KB 216 (CA) 306, 315
Read v J Lyons & Co Ltd [1947] AC 156 (HL) 305, 306, 315, 316–7,
                                                                       320, 326, 331, 332
Redland Bricks Ltd v Morris [1970] AC 652 (HL).........................343, 357, 358
Rees v Darlington Memorial Hospital NHS Trust [2003] UKHL 52,
    [2004] 1 AC 309 .... 43, 47, 206,
                                                                            213, 214–6
Reeves v Commissioner of Police of the Metropolis [1999] QB 169 (CA) 39
Reeves v Commissioner of Police of the Metropolis [2000]
    1 AC 360 (HL) 39, 41, 141
Regan v Paul Properties Ltd [2006] EWCA Civ 1319, [2007] Ch 135 277
Reilly v Merseyside Regional Health Authority (1995)
    6 Med LR 246 (CA) 196, 199, 387
Renslow v Mennonite Hospital 351 NE 2d 870 (Ill App Ct, 1976) 30
Re-Source American International Ltd v Platt Service Ltd [2003]
    EWHC 1142 (TCC), 90 Con LR 139...309
Reynolds v Clarke (1725) 1 Str 634, 93 ER 747 275
Ribee v Norrie [2001] PIQR P8 (CA) 309
Rice v Secretary of State for Trade and Industry [2007] EWCA Civ 289,
    [2007] PIQR P23..101
Richardson v LRC Products [2000] Lloyd's Rep Med 280 (QBD) 207
Rickards v Lothian [1913] AC 263 (PC) 314, 326
Ricket v Metropolitan Railway Co (1865) 5 B & S 156, 122 ER 790
    (Exch Ch); affirmed (1867) LR 2 HL 175 (HL) 288
Rigby v Chief Constable of Northamptonshire [1985] 1 WLR 1242
    (QBD) 74, 276, 320
Rivtow Marine Ltd v Washington Iron Works Ltd [1974] SCR 1189
    (SCC) 349, 352,
                                                                          362, 363, 367

RM Turton & Co Ltd (in liq) v Kerslake and Partners [2000]
    3 NZLR 406 (NZCA) 134
Robert Addie & Sons (Collieries) Ltd v Dumbreck [1929]
    AC 358 (HL) 162, 174
Robinson v Chief Constable of West Yorkshire Police [2014] EWCA
    Civ 15, [2014] PIQR P14 64–66
Robinson v Chief Constable of West Yorkshire Police [2018]
    UKSC 4, [2018] AC 736 .... 6, 8, 63, 68–81, 126
Robinson v Kilvert (1889) LR 41 Ch D 88 (CA) 266
Robinson v National Bank of Scotland 1916 SC (HL) 154 133
Robinson v PE Jones (Contractors) Ltd [2011] EWCA Civ 9,
    [2012] QB 44 .... 125, 134
Robinson v St Helens Metropolitan Borough Council [2002]
    EWCA Civ 1099, [2002] ELR 681 .... 218, 219
Rogers v Elliott 15 NE 768 (Mass 1888) 267
Rondel v Worsley [1969] 1 AC 191 (HL) 135
Ross v Fedden (1872) 26 LT 966 (QBD) 313
Rothwell v Chemical and Insulating Co Ltd [2007] UKHL 39,
    [2008] AC 281 .... 30, 239,
                                                                                 372, 374
Rowley v Secretary of State for Work and Pensions [2007]
    EWCA Civ 598, [2007] 1 WLR 2861 119
Rufo v Hosking [2004] NSWCA 391, 61 NSWLR 678 227
Rushmer v Polsue & Alfieri Ltd [1906] 1 Ch 234 (CA); affirmed
    [1907] AC 121 (HL) 267
Russell Transport Ltd v Ontario Malleable Iron Co Ltd [1952]
    4 DLR 719 (Ont HC) 265
Rust v Victoria Graving Dock Co (1887) LR 36 Ch D 113 (CA) 274
Rutherford v Attorney-General [1976] 1 NZLR 403 (NZHC) 349
Rylands v Fletcher (1868) LR 3 HL 330 (HL) 313
S v Distillers Co (Biochemicals) [1970] 1 WLR 114 (QBD) 343
S v Gloucestershire CC [2001] Fam 313 (CA) 59, 167, 186, 187
Saadati v Moorhead 2017 SCC 28, [2017] 1 SCR 543 13
Sack v Jones [1925] Ch 235 (Ch D) 281
Saint v Jenner [1973] Ch 275 (CA) 262
St Anne's Well Brewery Co v Roberts (1928) 140 LT 1 (CA) 300
St Helen's Smelting Co v Tipping (1865) 11 HL Cas 642, 11 ER 1483 .... 267, 269
Sandhar v Department of Transport, Environment and the
    Regions [2004] EWCA Civ 1440, [2005] 1 WLR 1632 .... 99, 111,
                                                                                 113, 115
Sandford v London Borough of Waltham Forest [2008] EWHC 1106 (QB),
    [2008] BLGR 816 119
Sanix Ace, The [1987] 1 Lloyd's Rep 465 (QBD) 387

Sayers v Harlow UDC [1958] 1 WLR 623 (CA)......................................196, 197
Scullion v Bank of Scotland plc [2011] EWCA Civ 693, [2011]
   1 WLR 3212 133
Secretary of State for the Home Department v Adiukwu [2020]
   CSIH 47, 2021 SC 38..9
Sedleigh-Denfield v O'Callaghan [1940] AC 880 (HL) 271, 310, 323
Seaway Hotels Ltd v Cragg (Canada) Ltd (1959) 21 DLR (3d)
   264 (Ont CA)..348
Segal v Derrick Golf & Winter Club (1977) 76 DLR (3d) 746 (Alta SC) 300
Sellars v Adelaide Petroleum NL (1994) 179 CLR 332 (HCA) 245
Selwood v Durham County Council [2012] EWCA Civ 979, [2012]
   PIQR P20 53
Shelfer v City of London Electric Lighting Co [1895] 1 Ch 287 (CA) 277
Sherratt v Chief Constable of Greater Manchester Police [2018]
   EWHC 1746 (QB), [2019] PIQR P1 ....132, 153, 155
Shiffman v Order of St John [1936] 1 All ER 557 (KBD)....................317, 320
Shogunn Investments Pty Ltd v Public Transport Authority
   of Western Australia [2016] WASC 42 ....285, 289
Shore v Sedgwick Financial Services Ltd [2008] EWCA Civ 863,
   [2008] PNLR 37 380
Shoreham-by-Sea Urban District Council v Dolphin Canadian
   Proteins Ltd (1972) 71 LGR 261 (QBD) 267
Sienkiewicz v Greif (UK) Ltd [2011] UKSC 10, [2011] 2 AC 229 15
Shaw v Kovac [2017] EWCA Civ 1028, [2017] 1 WLR 4773...........................13
Sheppard v Glossop Corpn [1921] 3 KB 132 (CA) 95
Simaan General Contracting Co v Pilkington Glass Ltd (No 2)
   [1988] QB 758 (CA) 134
Smith v Chief Constable of Sussex Police [2008] EWCA Civ 39,
   [2008] PIQR P232 105
Smith v Chief Constable of Sussex Police [2008] UKHL 50, [2009]
   1 AC 225..74
Smith v Eric S Bush [1990] 1 AC 831 (HL)..133
Smith v Inco Ltd [2011] ONCA 628, 107 OR (3d) 321 ....289, 390
Smith v Jenkins (1970) 119 CLR 397 (HCA)...42
Smith v Littlewoods Organisation Ltd 1986 SLT 272 (CSIH) 170
Smith v Littlewoods Organisation Ltd [1987] AC 241 (HL) 33, 41, 49,
     168–70, 189
Smith v Ministry of Defence [2013] UKSC 41, [2014] AC 52...............69, 79, 84
Soltau v De Held (1851) 2 Sim (NS) 133, 61 ER 291.....................................288
South Australia Asset Management Corp v York Montague Ltd
   [1997] AC 191 (HL) 52
Southern Portland Cement Ltd v Cooper [1974] AC 623 (PC)............. 163, 174,
     177, 188

Southport Corp v Esso Petroleum Co Ltd [1953] 2 All ER 1204
  (Liverpool Assizes)..270, 275, 300
Southwark London Borough Council v Tanner [2001]
  1 AC 1 (HL)...266, 321
Spartan Steel and Alloys Ltd v Martin & Co (Contractors) Ltd
  [1973] 1 QB 27 (CA) 31, 40, 222,
                                                                                322, 347
Spicer v Smee [1946] 1 All ER 489 (KBD)...322
Spread Trustee Co Ltd v Hutcheson [2011] UKPC 13, [2012]
  2 AC 194...181, 182, 184
Spring v Guardian Assurance plc [1995] 2 AC 296 (HL)...............120, 133, 135,
                                                                                148, 150, 153
Stansbie v Troman [1948] 2 KB 48 (CA) 141
Starsin, The. See Homburg Houtimport BV v Agrosin Private Ltd
  (The Starsin)
Stovin v Wise (Norfolk County Council, third party) [1996]
  AC 923 (HL) 73, 95, 96, 97, 98,
                                                                                100, 101, 106, 110,
                                                                                112–3, 120, 188
Stubbings v Webb [1993] AC 498 (HL)...204
Sullivan v Moody [2001] HCA 59, 207 CLR 562.............................190
Summers v Tice 199 P 2d 1 (Cal 1948) 230, 235, 236, 238
Sutherland Shire Council v Heyman (1985) 157 CLR 424 (HCA) 40, 83, 95,
                                                                                104, 110,
                                                                                112, 113
Sutradhar v National Environment Research Council [2006] UKHL 33,
  [2006] 4 All ER 490...54
Swain v Nat Ram Puri [1996] PIQR P442 (CA) 164
Swinney v Chief Constable of Northumbria Police [1997]
  QB 464 (CA)..115, 141
Tabet v Gett [2010] HCA 12, 240 CLR 537 372
Tapling v Jones (1865) 11 HL Cas 290, 11 ER 1344......................261
Tenant v Goldwin (1703) 2 Ld Raym 1089, 91 ER 314 ....312, 315
Thames Trains Ltd v Health & Safety Executive [2003]
  EWCA Civ 720 ....100, 112
Thompson v Commissioner of Police of the Metropolis [1998]
  QB 498 (CA)..224
Thompson v Gibson (1841) 7 M & W 456, 151 ER 845 270
Thompson v Schmidt (1892) 56 JP 212 (CA) 198
Thompson-Schwab v Costaki [1956] 1 WLR 335 (CA) 260, 291, 296, 301
Tindall v Chief Constable of Thames Valley Police [2022] EWCA Civ 25,
  [2022] 4 WLR 104...9
Tomlinson v Congleton BC [2003] UKHL 47, [2004] 1 AC 46 164

Toronto Transit Commission v Swansea (Village) [1935] SCR 455 (SCC) 297
TP and KM v United Kingdom [2001] ECHR 332 (ECommHR) 186
Transco plc v Stockport Metropolitan Borough Council [2003]
    UKHL 61, [2004] 2 AC 1 .... 19, 271, 305, 306,
                                          309–10, 319, 320,
                                        323, 324, 325, 326,
                                        327, 329, 330, 331,
                                        333, 335, 345–6
Trevor Ivory Ltd v Anderson [1992] 2 NZLR 517 (NZCA) 137
Troppi v Scarf 187 NW 2d 511 (Mich 1971) 207
Trustee in Bankruptcy of Sir John Poulton v Ministry of Justice
    [2010] EWCA Civ 392, [2010] 4 All ER 600....................................... 99, 102
University College Cork v Electricity Supply Board [2020] IESC 38.................7
Uren v First National Home Finance Ltd [2005] EWHC 2529 (Ch) 55
Vairy v Wyong Shire Council [2005] HCA 62, 223 CLR 422......................... 52
Van Colle v Chief Constable of Hertfordshire [2008] UKHL 50,
    [2009] 1 AC 225 .... 84, 105,
                                          115, 123, 177
Vellino v Chief Constable of Greater Manchester [2001]
    EWCA Civ 1249, [2002] 1 WLR 218 .... 42, 47
VI v KRONE–Verlag Gesellschaft mbH & Co KG (Case C-65/20),
    EU:C:2021:471.. 399
Victoria Park Racing and Recreation Grounds Co Ltd v Taylor (1937)
    58 CLR 479 (HCA) 260, 261,
                                          288–9, 296
W v Essex County Council [2000] UKHL 17, [2001] 2 AC 592 (HL)............. 186
W v Home Office [1997] Imm AR 302 (CA).. 195, 197,
                                          199, 200
Wagon Mound, The. See Overseas Tankship (UK) v Morts Dock
    and Engineering Co (The Wagon Mound)
Wainwright v Home Office [2001] EWCA Civ 2081, [2002] QB 1334 202
Wainwright v Home Office [2003] UKHL 53, [2004] 2 AC 406..................... 105
Walkin v South Manchester Health Authority [1995]
    1 WLR 1543 (CA) 207, 208, 210, 211
Waters v Commissioner of Police of the Metropolis [2000]
    1 WLR 1607 (HL) 186
Watkins v Secretary of State for the Home Department [2004]
    EWCA Civ 966, [2005] QB 883.. 194
Watkins v Secretary of State for the Home Department [2006]
    UKHL 17, [2006] 2 AC 395 (HL) 194, 205, 391
Watson v British Boxing Board of Control [2001] QB 1134 (CA) 112, 114,
                                          115, 116, 131,
                                          134, 141, 153

Watson v Croft Promosport Ltd [2009] EWCA Civ 15, [2009]
3 All ER 249 277
Watt v Hertfordshire CC [1954] 1 WLR 835 (CA) 161
Wattleworth v Goodwood Road Racing Co Ltd [2004]
EWHC 140 (QB), [2004] PIQR 25 137
Webb v Bird (1862) 13 CBNS 841, 143 ER 332....................................261, 263
Weldon v Home Office [1990] 3 WLR 465 (CA) 201
Welsh v Chief Constable of the Merseyside Police [1993]
1 All ER 692 (QBD) 141, 198, 199, 203
Wheeler v JJ Saunders Ltd [1996] Ch 19 (CA) 284
White v Chief Constable of South Yorkshire Police [1999]
2 AC 455 (HL) 36
White v Jones [1995] 2 AC 207 (HL) 131–2, 133, 142,
148, 152, 380, 383
Wilkes v DePuy International Ltd [2016] EWHC 3096 (QB),
[2018] QB 627..396
Wilkinson v Coverdale (1793) 1 Esp 75, 170 ER 284....................................133
Wilks v Cheltenham Cycle Club [1971] 1 WLR 668 (CA)............................ 162
Williams v Natural Life Health Foods [1998] 1 WLR 830 (HL) 133,
136–7, 146
Williams v Network Rail Infrastructure Ltd [2018] EWCA Civ 1514,
[2019] QB 601... 16, 18
Williams v Peel River Land and Mineral Co (1886) 55 LT 689 (QBD) 194
Willies-Williams v National Trust (199) 65 P & CR 359 (CA) 259
Wilsher v Essex AHA [1987] QB 730 (CA) 160, 232, 234,
236, 239, 243, 250
Wilson v Brett (1843) 11 M & W 113, 152 ER 737 177
Wilson v Pringle [1987] QB 237 (CA)..202
Winkfield, The [1902] P 42 (CA) 387
Winnipeg Condominium Corp No 36 v Bird Construction Co
[1995] 1 SCR 85 (SCC)...352, 362,
363, 367
Woodland v Essex County Council [2013] UKSC 66, [2014] AC 537 137
Woolcock Street Investments Ltd v CDG Pty Ltd [2004] HCA 16,
216 CLR 515..351
Wooldridge v Sumner [1963] 2 QB 43 (CA)..161
Worsley v Tambrands Ltd [2000] PIQR P95 (QBD) 395
Wright v Dunlop Rubber Co Ltd (1972) 13 KIR 255 (CA)............................368
X (minors) v Bedfordshire County Council [1995] 2 AC 633 (HL)........ 103, 132,
165, 166,
186, 216, 217
X and Y v London Borough of Hounslow [2009] EWCA Civ 286,
[2009] 2 FLR 262 ....99, 115
X and Y (by her tutor X) v PAL (1991) 23 NSWLR 26 (NSWCA) 30

Yearworth v North Bristol NHS Trust [2009] EWCA Civ 37, [2010] QB 1.... 149
Yetkin v London Borough of Newham [2010] EWCA Civ 776, [2011]
    QB 827 106
Yorkshire Water Services Ltd v Sun Alliance & London Insurance plc
    [1998] Env LR 204 (QBD) 346
Z v United Kingdom [2001] 2 FCR 246 (ECtHR) 104
Z v United Kingdom (1999) 28 EHRR CD 65 (ECommHR) 186
Zelenko v Gimbel Bros 287 NYS 134 (NY 1935) 107

Table of Legislation

Australia

Commonwealth

Australian Consumer Law (Competition and Consumer Act 2010 (Cth)
  Sch 2 423

Australian Capital Territory

Civil Law (Wrongs) Act 2002 (ACT)
  pt 2.1 .... 159, 174

New South Wales

Civil Liability Act 2002 (NSW)
  s 43A 171, 191
  s 45(1) 175
  s 57 159

Queensland

Law Reform Act 1995 (Qld)
  pt 5 159

South Australia

Civil Liability Act 1936 (SA)
  s 74 .... 159, 174

Tasmania

Civil Liability Act 2002 (Tas)
  pt 8A 159, 174

Victoria

Road Management Act 2004 (Vic)
  s 39 172
  s 103 172
Wrongs Act 1958 (Vic)
  s 31B 159

Western Australia

Civil Liability Act 2002 (WA)
    s 5AD 159, 174
    S 5X 158, 171

Austria

§ 1324 ABGB 183

Canada

Alberta

Emergency Medical Aid Act 2000 (Alta) 158

British Columbia

Good Samaritan Act 1996 (BC) 158

Quebec

Quebec Civil Code
    art 1471 ....
    158

Ontario

Good Samaritan Act 2001 (Ont) 158

Saskatchewan

Consumer Protection and Business Practices Act 2013 (Sask)
    s 35 423
Emergency Medical Aid Act 1979 (Sask) 158

Council of Europe

European Convention on Human Rights 105
    Art 2 105
    Art 3 104
    Art 8 105

Czech Republic

Civil Code
  Art 419 340

European Union

Council Directive 85/374/EEC on Liability for Defective Products........392, 393,
398, 403, 404,
405, 416, 421,
422, 424

France

Code Civil
  art 1240 (formerly art 1382) 3, 382

Germany

BGB (Civil Code)
  § 249 340
  § 521 183
  § 599 183
  § 680 158
  § 687(1) 366
  § 823(1) 46
  § 906 264
  § 906(1) 286

Guernsey

Trusts (Guernsey) Law 1989
  s 34(7) 182

India

Civil Wrongs Bill (draft)
  cl 68 330

Italy

Civil Code
  Art 844 280

Jersey

Trusts (Jersey) Law 1984
  art 26(9) 182

New Zealand

Consumer Guarantees Act 1993 (NZ)
  s 24 423
Crimes Act 1961 (NZ)
  s 150A 181, 183
Crimes Amendment Act 1997 (NZ) 181

Spain

Civil Code
  Art 168.2 183

United Kingdom

Automated and Electric Vehicles Act 2018 423
Child Support Act 1991 119
Children Act 1989 100
  s 17(1) 102
  Sch 2, para 4(1) 102
Civil Procedure Rules 1998, SI 1998/3132 .... 186, 187, 225
  r 24.2 .... 186, 187
  r 24.5 187
  r 32.6 187
Compensation Act 2006
  s 3 .... 235, 239
Competition Act 1998
  s 47A 382

Consumer Protection Act 1987 .... 22, 207, 392, 393,
394, 395, 396, 397,
398, 399, 400, 401,
402, 404, 405, 406,
409, 412, 418, 421,
423, 424, 426
  Pt I 22, 392, 425
  s 1(2) 398
  s 1(2)(a) 402
  s 2(2)(b), (c) 397
  s 2(3) 397
  s 3(1) 395
  s 4(1)(b) 401
  s 4(1)(c) 409
  s 4(1)(d) 399, 401, 402
  s 4(1)(e) 394, 396, 405, 412
  s 5(1) 225
  s 45(1) 210
Contracts (Rights of Third Parties) Act 1999 ....401, 418
Corporate Manslaughter and Corporate Homicide Act 2007
  s 1(1)(b) 181
  s 1(4)(b) 183
Crown Proceedings Act 1947 72
Education Act 1981 165
Environmental Protection Act 1990
  s 73(6) 331
Fatal Accidents Act 1976 215
Financial Services and Markets Act 2000
  s 150 382
Gas Act 1965
  s 14 331
Health and Safety at Work Act 1974 54
Highways Act 1980 96
  s 41 97
  s 41(1) 97
  s 79 ....73, 95
Human Rights Act 1998 ....9, 66, 94, 105,
122, 224, 273
Latent Damage Act 1986
  s 3(1) 388
Law of Property Act 1925
  s 205(1)(ix) 259, 286

Limitation Act 1980
  s 2 204
  s 11 .... 204, 225
  s 38(1) 207, 210
Lunatic Act 1890
  s 16 198
Merchant Shipping Act 1995
  s 153(1)(b) 345
Nuclear Installations Act 1965
  s 12 331
Occupiers' Liability Act 1957 57
Occupiers' Liability Act 1984 .... 162, 163, 164
  s 1(3), (4) 164
Road Traffic Act 1988
  s 2A(1) 181, 183
  s 39 .... 73, 97, 98, 101, 103
  s 39(2) 97
Senior Courts Act 1981 (formerly Supreme Court Act 1981)
  s 32A 365
  s 33 218
  s 33(2) 225
Trustee Act 2000
  Sch 1, para 7 181
Unfair Contract Terms Act 1977
  s 2(1) 189, 225
  s 14 210
Vaccine Damage Payments Act 1979 423
Water Resources Act 1991
  Pt II 263
  s 209 331

United States

Aviation Medical Assistance Act 1998 158
Federal Employers' Liability Act 355
Uniform Commercial Code
  § 2-318 423
Volunteer Protection Act 1997 158

1

Introduction

THIS VOLUME CONSISTS of a selection of my previously published work on tort law, along with a new chapter in which I argue for the repeal of the UK's strict product liability regime (chapter 14). The essays selected for inclusion are organised into three parts: 'Negligence' (seven chapters); 'Nuisance and *Rylands v Fletcher*' (three chapters); and 'Tort in General' (three chapters). They are reproduced as originally published, save for the removal of abstracts and acknowledgements, the addition of the page numbers from the original publication in bold square brackets and the use of Hart Publishing's style throughout.[1] In this chapter I provide an introductory overview, along with brief summaries of the chapters that follow and some reflections on the previously published essays.

I. OVERVIEW

The chapters in this collection all concern liability in the law of tort. Tort sets the basic ground rules for our interactions with other people in the communities in which we live. There is in my view no area of law more fundamental, nor more obviously grounded in the lived reality of human co-existence. It is my belief that tort scholars can best understand and evaluate these ground rules by the study of, and creative reflection on, the rules themselves, the explanations provided for them by the judges who laid them down, and the efforts of our scholarly predecessors and contemporaries. Such scholarship benefits from a deep understanding of the common law and its history, coupled with close attention to earlier writings and the experience of other legal systems wrestling with the same fundamental questions.

I was careful to say in the previous paragraph that the chapters in this book concern *liability* in tort. None concern remedies. This focus (which is reflected in the title of the collection) is deliberate. Although remedial questions are vitally

---

[1] Since I used the final Word versions of the essays as a starting point, it may be that in some instances minor changes made at the proof stage have not been carried over to the versions published here. However, this should not be the case with regard to the more recent essays, where I still had the corrected proofs on file and so was able to make the necessary amendments.

important, in my opinion the balance of scholarship in this field has become somewhat skewed towards remedies, with the result that fundamental issues relating to liability have been neglected. An additional point that I should make about the articles and book chapters that follow is that they are all (to my mind, at least) examples of what Lord Burrows has recently labelled 'practical legal scholarship', intended for an audience of other academics, students and legal practitioners.[2] In particular, they are not envisaged as works of tort theory. Again, while there is much valuable work currently being done in the field of private law theory, Lord Burrows is in my view correct to question whether in private law the right balance is currently being struck between work of a theoretical persuasion and the more traditional doctrinal scholarship which he considers to be in decline. And it is worth emphasising in this connection that it can be difficult to develop a convincing theory of any area of law (assuming that such a theory can be developed[3]) without a proper understanding of the law itself,[4] an understanding which must be grounded in sustained study of the relevant legal rules and principles, as well as the accompanying academic literature.

An area of law that sets the basic ground rules for our interactions with others in organised society is bound to be a large and complex one, and the common law of tort certainly fits that description. The current edition of the practitioner work *Clerk & Lindsell on Torts*[5] runs to some 2400 pages, and the tables of cases and legislation alone take up over 350 pages, making them longer than many monographs. Although in the past there were tort scholars who achieved mastery over the entirety of the subject, such as Sir John Salmond, Sir Percy Winfield, William Prosser and John Fleming, the proliferation of case law and secondary literature makes such mastery extremely difficult to achieve in modern times. As a result, contemporary tort scholars usually focus their scholarship on particular areas of tort law, and general works on the subject tend to be divided up between co-authors. Furthermore, for quite understandable reasons, books on tort law directed at students for the most part deal only with those aspects of the subject that are generally covered in tort modules in English law schools. The process of modularisation has seen some key aspects of the law

---

[2] A Burrows, 'Professor Sir Guenter Treitel (1928–2019)' in J Goudkamp and D Nolan, *Scholars of Contract Law* (Oxford, Hart Publishing, 2022) 284 ff. One might quibble with the precise terminology that Burrows uses (I would probably say 'doctrinal', rather than 'practical'), but not much turns on this.

[3] Tony Weir famously thought that it could not be, at least in the case of tort, describing an enquiry from the Dean of an American law school as to Weir's 'normative theory of tort law' as 'a very stupid question': T Weir, *An Introduction to Tort Law*, 2nd edn (Oxford, OUP, 2006) ix.

[4] See ibid: 'In any event, before producing a "normative theory" or even discussing the purpose of "tort", it is surely desirable to become familiar with what that ragbag [the law of tort] actually contains: otherwise we shall be like adolescents spending all night discussing the meaning of life – before, perhaps instead of, experiencing it.'

[5] MA Jones (ed), *Clerk & Lindsell on Torts*, 20th edn (London, Sweet & Maxwell, 2020).

of tort pushed out of tort courses and into other subjects, so that, for example, the law of defamation is now often to be found in courses on media law, and the intentional torts in courses on civil liberties or medical law.

Much of the focus of my own work in this area has been on topics that do still form the nucleus of the subject as now taught, namely the law of negligence and the law of nuisance. By contrast, I have not published on areas of tort law that are of huge practical and theoretical significance, but which are now more marginal to the teaching of tort law in many law schools, such as defamation, personal property torts and the economic torts. This was not a deliberate choice on my part, but was the result of an enduring fascination with the negligence cause of action, and work that I was asked to do early in my career on nuisance and *Rylands v Fletcher*.[6] The consequences of that focus can be seen in the chapters that follow.

II. NEGLIGENCE

Over half the chapters in this collection are concerned with the law of negligence. I make no apology for that fact. For negligence is not just another tort. On the contrary, what we refer to as the 'tort' of negligence is really the common law equivalent of the general clause found in many civilian legal systems, and epitomised by the famous article 1382 (now article 1240) of the French *Code Civil*. As I have argued elsewhere,[7] the modern common law of tort is a hybrid system, which combines a general cause of action defined by reference to the nature of the defendant's conduct (negligence) with a series of mostly older, so-called 'nominate' torts, the scope of which is defined by the interests that they protect (such as defamation, protecting reputation, or private nuisance and trespass to land, protecting real property interests). As a de facto general clause, negligence has a very broad sweep, and can easily adapt to new problems thrown up by societal and technological change. Furthermore, its practical significance far exceeds that of other torts, with roughly a million negligence claims being brought in the UK every year. The breadth of the cause of action for negligence, and the range of situations to which it responds, mean that negligence law inevitably relies on a set of relatively abstract concepts, such as 'duty of care', 'fault', 'damage' and 'causation'. Abstract concepts are in their nature more malleable than concrete ones, but they are also more difficult to pin down. This generates high levels of conceptual instability, and makes negligence fascinating, but also challenging, to study.

---

[6] See my chapters on these two topics in A Grubb (ed), *The Law of Tort* (London, Butterworths, 2002).

[7] See D Nolan, 'Damage in the English Law of Negligence' (2013) 4 *Journal of European Tort Law* 259, 260.

As a negligence scholar, I have tried to meet those challenges by focusing on what I see as being the three foundation stones of the cause of action, namely fault, damage and causation. The role of each of these three concepts is clear. Fault singles out the defendant. Damage singles out the claimant. And causation connects the fault and the damage. These concepts represent the irreducible core of negligence, and by placing them front and centre of the analysis the essential structure of the cause of action is revealed. It is of course no coincidence that these are also the three foundations of the French general clause, which states with admirable simplicity and elegance that 'Any act whatever of man, which causes damage to another, obliges the one by whose fault it occurred, to compensate it'. As the common law's general clause, it is not surprising that negligence can best be understood in similar terms, but unfortunately this simple conceptual structure is overlain in the common law world with a good deal of unnecessary complexity and obfuscation.

The most obvious problem in this regard is the existence within common law systems of the so-called 'duty of care'. In 'Deconstructing the Duty of Care' (chapter 2), I subjected the orthodoxy that the duty of care is an essential component of the common law of negligence to critical review, and argued that the duty of care concept was obscuring understanding of negligence law and hindering its rational development. I therefore proposed the 'deconstruction' of the duty of care, a process whereby the disparate issues currently subsumed under the duty umbrella would be separated out and reclassified under the other components of the negligence enquiry. I also argued that scepticism about the duty of care was not incompatible with a rights-based approach to negligence law, and that deconstructing duty would improve the quality of judicial reasoning in negligence cases, give a sharper edge to scholarship in the field and improve the understanding of those coming to negligence law for the first time.

I stand by the claims that I made in this essay, although I am happy to accept that in some ways the piece is best understood as a thought experiment, demonstrating how common law systems could if they wished dispense with the duty element, rather than a realistic proposal for the future development of the law. Nevertheless, I am convinced that, if we were designing a law of negligence for common law systems from a clean slate, we would be better off focusing on the three key elements of fault, damage and causation, and doing without the duty concept, except in cases where negligence liability is dependent on the existence of a particular relationship between the parties which arose prior to the allegedly negligent conduct.[8]

One of the things that you notice about the reception of your own scholarly writing is that aspects of a publication that you did not think were particularly controversial or novel sometimes attract more attention than you had

---

[8] A qualification I made in the original article: see ch 2 at p 61.

anticipated. In the case of 'Deconstructing the Duty of Care', this has happened with a short section of the essay in which I argued that the duty of care is not a duty at all.[9] Although I regarded this as mere ground-clearing (and reasonably obvious), the claim has been criticised on various grounds, such as that, in making it, I wrongly assumed that 'A cannot be said to have a legal duty to *x* if A's failure to do *x* does not attract any significant legal sanction'.[10] However, I made no such assumption. Any serious tort scholar must reject such a notion out of hand. Clearly if I trespass on your land, I breach a duty I owe you not to do so even if I cause you no harm, and hence am liable only for nominal damages.[11] But negligence is of course different, since – unlike the wrong of trespass to land – the wrong of negligence requires that the defendant's unreasonable conduct cause the claimant damage. Nor is it to the point that courts sometimes bend the rules of causation so as to impose liability on defendants who have 'breached a duty of care';[12] or that 'in theory, exemplary damages may be available in a case where someone has deliberately breached a duty of care owed to another';[13] or that 'someone can be convicted of the criminal offence of gross negligence manslaughter if their breach of a duty of care owed to another results in that other's death'.[14] I am perfectly happy to admit that the courts would like us to act with reasonable care for the interests of others. Indeed, that seems rather obvious. But it does not follow that we are under a legal duty to those potentially affected by our conduct, which is breached simply by our acting unreasonably, in circumstances where they might end up suffering damage as a result. To argue (as I did) that we are *not* in fact under such a duty is a technical claim about the way that negligence law actually works. It has nothing to do with how the courts would like us to behave.

In making the point that duties of care are not really duties, I was simply reflecting the positive law, according to which the occurrence of damage is an essential element of the wrong of negligence, and not (as some have argued)[15] a mere condition of the actionability of a prior wrong completed by the negligence conduct itself. That is why one of the leading English judges of the late twentieth century observed that the 'true duty is not a duty to be careful, but a duty not to cause damage by carelessness',[16] and another said that '[a] person who acts without reasonable care does no wrong in law; he commits no tort'.[17]

---

[9] See ch 2 at pp 29–32.

[10] N McBride and S Steel, *Great Debates in Jurisprudence* (Oxford, Hart Publishing, 2018) 36.

[11] *Jacque v Steenberg Homes* 563 NW 2d 154 (Wis 1997).

[12] More accurately, 'exposed others to unreasonable risks of injury in circumstances in which such conduct can give rise to negligence liability'.

[13] The words 'in theory' are quite telling here.

[14] NJ McBride and R Bagshaw, *Tort Law*, 6th edn (Harlow, Pearson Education, 2018) 102.

[15] See ibid ch 9.

[16] *Leigh & Sillivan Ltd v Aliakmon Shipping Co Ltd* [1985] QB 350 (CA) 375 (Oliver LJ).

[17] *Browning v War Office* [1963] 1 QB 750 (CA) 765 (Diplock LJ). This is also the view of a leading Australian judge of the current era: see M Leeming, *The Statutory Foundations of Negligence* (Alexandria, NSW, Federation Press, 2015) 17–18.

And it is also why a negligent person who causes another both personal injury and property damage commits two torts, and not one.[18] Finally, it explains the liability of a manufacturer of poisonous baby food to a baby conceived after its manufacture. Or do the scholars who believe that the duty of care really is a duty also think that it is possible to wrong a person who does not exist?[19]

Since we are stuck with the duty concept, we need to make it work as well as it can, and to minimise the difficulties that it causes. The decision of the UK Supreme Court in *Robinson v Chief Constable of West Yorkshire Police*[20] represented a significant step in the right direction in this respect, for reasons that I set out in 'The Duty of Care After *Robinson v Chief Constable of West Yorkshire Police*' (chapter 3). In this essay I argued that the unequivocal rejection of the so-called *Caparo* three-stage test in Lord Reed's leading judgment in *Robinson* amounted to a clear signal from the Supreme Court to courts at all levels that the test should no longer be used to determine the existence of a duty of care in any negligence case. I also argued that the approach to the duty question taken by Lord Reed was not only the best of the alternatives available, but the only approach consistent with common law method and the rule of law. The legal nature of the duty of care issue requires the courts to do as Lord Reed says they should, and to work with the relevant authorities to determine whether the case is covered by binding precedent, and, if not, to reason by analogy and by reference to relevant considerations in order to determine whether a duty of care is owed. In this essay, I also sought to explain why exactly it is that general tests of duty, such as the '*Caparo* test', inevitably fail. My overall conclusion was that the decision in *Robinson* had the potential to usher in a new era in the troubled history of the duty of care, marked by greater transparency, predictability and consistency.

As is so often the case, the great leap forward that *Robinson* represents has not been welcomed by everyone. At least two dissenting strands of opinion can be identified. The first is associated with those who are unable to let go of the idea that the duty enquiry can be reduced to a simple formula, as if we were making ice cream rather than determining the extent of negligence liability across a limitless range of potential circumstances. Those who take this view have not responded to the arguments that I and others have made as to the impossibility of a meaningful general duty test, but have instead tended to downplay the significance of the *Robinson* decision, or to argue that their favoured test has somehow succeeded in transcending the problems that beset other general tests.[21] For the reasons given in my essay, I regard this approach as

---

[18] *Brunsden v Humphrey* (1884) 14 QBD 141 (CA) 150–51.

[19] For a more even-handed account of this debate than I am capable of, see J Morgan, *Great Debates in Tort Law* (Oxford, Hart Publishing, 2022) ch 6.

[20] [2018] UKSC 4, [2018] AC 736.

[21] See, eg, K Chng, G Chan and Y Goh, 'A Novel Development of Tort Law: *Robinson v Chief Constable of West Yorkshire Police*' (2019) 25 *Torts Law Journal* 184.

fundamentally misguided. It is not a question of finding the 'right' general test, since no general test will ever provide a satisfactory methodology for resolving duty of care questions. As Lord Oliver said some decades ago, such a formula is a 'will-o-the-wisp'.[22] It is therefore gratifying to see that at least one other common law apex court, the Supreme Court of Ireland, has embraced the methodology adopted in *Robinson* and abandoned the use of general formulae as 'question-begging'.[23] My prediction is that it is only a matter of time before other common law courts which remain wedded to a general formula come to abandon it.

The other strand of dissenting opinion sides with Lord Mance in *Robinson*, arguing that Lord Reed's approach to the duty question downplays the significance of so-called 'policy reasoning', which (according to this view) should be front and centre of the duty of care analysis.[24] Setting aside the fact that it is often unclear what these commentators mean by the word 'policy', this approach has a rather dated look, reminiscent as it is of realist and post-realist scholarship from the 1960s and 1970s in the United States and beyond. The argument is also rather slippery, as it starts from the false assumption that all duty of care determinations are based on 'policy' considerations in any case, so that the only issue is whether the policy arguments should be debated openly, or instead hidden under the cloak of an approach along the lines of that set out in *Robinson*. The truth is, however, that, as Lord Reed pointed out in *Robinson*, most duty of care decisions rest on considerations of interpersonal justice, rather than community welfare considerations (which is the only meaning of 'policy' in this context that has any concrete meaning). It is also important to note that Lord Reed explicitly rejected the 'policy minimalist'[25] view that community welfare considerations have no place in the duty of care enquiry. On the contrary, he was perfectly happy to accept that they could play a role in novel duty cases where appropriate. It seems to follow that this second strand of criticism of the *Robinson* approach to duty is rooted not only in the belief that the courts should be willing to take account of policy concerns in duty cases (which they still are), but that they should base the determination of whether a duty of care is owed on a laundry list of 'policy factors', an approach that has generated disastrous levels of complexity, inconsistency and uncertainty in Australia, the only jurisdiction in which it has been adopted.[26]

Many of the ideas that are found in the first two essays in this collection are consistent with the approach to the duty question and to duty methodology

---

[22] *Caparo Industries plc v Dickman* [1990] 2 AC 605 (HL) 616 (Lord Oliver).

[23] See *University College Cork v Electricity Supply Board* [2020] IESC 38 [8.6]–[8.12] (Clarke CJ and MacMenamin J).

[24] See, eg, J Morgan, 'Nonfeasance and the End of Policy? Reflections on the Revolution in Public Authority Liability' (2019) 35 *Professional Negligence* 32.

[25] McBride and Bagshaw (n 14) 82.

[26] This is the so-called 'salient features' approach, as encapsulated in the influential judgment of Allsop J in *Caltex Refineries (Qld) Pty Ltd v Stavar* [2009] NSWCA 258, 75 NSWLR 649 (for the non-exhaustive list of 17 'salient features' in that judgment, see [103]).

in the first monograph on the duty of care for many decades, which was published by my former research student James Plunkett in 2018.[27] Plunkett's book provides a comprehensive analysis of the duty of care in modern Commonwealth systems, and I would recommend it to anyone who wishes to delve more deeply into the issues explored in chapters 2 and 3.

In 'The Liability of Public Authorities for Failing to Confer Benefits' (chapter 4), I considered the circumstances in which a public authority could be held liable in negligence for failing to confer a benefit. I gave close consideration to the implications of the decision in *Gorringe v Calderdale MBC*[28] for the English law in this area and subjected the law after *Gorringe* to critical analysis. The essay was divided into three main parts. In the first part, I considered whether negligence liability for failure to confer a benefit could ever be based on the existence of a statutory duty or power imposed or conferred on a public authority defendant. In the second part, I switched focus to the application of ordinary private law principles to public authority defendants in cases involving failures to confer benefits. And in the third and final part, I asked whether the current state of the law in this area was satisfactory.

The analysis in this essay, which was published in 2011, has been largely vindicated by subsequent developments. In *Michael v Chief Constable of South Wales Police*,[29] *Robinson v Chief Constable of West Yorkshire Police*[30] and *N v Poole BC*[31] the Supreme Court has repeatedly reiterated that a common law duty of care cannot be founded on a statutory duty or power, with the result that the negligence liability of public authorities for omissions is based on ordinary private law principles.[32] Furthermore, in the *Poole* case, Lord Reed expressly adopted the terminology that was used in the essay, acknowledging that the issue in so-called 'omissions' cases is whether the defendant was under a positive duty to confer a benefit on the claimant.[33] Admittedly, the section of

---

[27] J Plunkett, *The Duty of Care in Negligence* (Oxford, Hart Publishing, 2018).

[28] [2004] UKHL 15, [2004] 1 WLR 1057.

[29] [2015] UKSC 2, [2015] AC 1732.

[30] *Robinson* (n 20).

[31] *N v Poole BC* [2019] UKSC 25, [2020] AC 780.

[32] See, eg, *Robinson* (n 20) [40] (Lord Reed): '[T]he law of negligence generally applies to public authorities in the same way that it applies to private individuals and bodies.'

[33] It has been objected that this language is misleading, but the objection rests on a mere assertion, namely that 'we cannot divorce the question of whether someone is improving or worsening another's situation from the question of what that other person is entitled to expect' (T Cornford, 'The Negligence Liability of Public Authorities for Omissions' [2019] *CLJ* 545, 554 fn). It is not clear to me why we 'cannot' do this. Furthermore, I think that the distinction I drew chimes with ordinary intuitions about the act/omission dichotomy. We talk, for example, of a 'benefits' system of social security payments, even though the payments that are made through this system are ones that the recipients are entitled to as a matter of law. Cornford accuses those who use the language of 'failing to confer a benefit' of trying to skew the substantive debate about omissions liability in their favour. I can honestly say that that was not my intention. My use of this language was simply born of frustration at what I saw as being somewhat pointless arguments about why it was that, for example, a driver who failed to apply the brakes and hit a pedestrian was not being sued for an omission.

the essay in which I considered whether there might be some limits on the scope of the *Gorringe* decision is now of mostly historical interest, since the case law since 2011 has clarified that no such limits exist. By contrast, the central section of the essay, which considers the application of private law principles in public authority omissions cases, remains highly pertinent, since the courts are now wrestling with precisely this issue on a regular basis.[34] And while the scope of what I called the 'additional damage' principle is I think reasonably clear, much uncertainty still surrounds the circumstances in which a public authority will be considered to have assumed a responsibility to exercise its statutory functions in a reasonable manner, even after the consideration of this issue in cases such as *Michael* and *Poole*. This part of the essay should now be read in the light of the fuller discussion of the assumption of responsibility concept in the later article republished in chapter 5.

One point that I would make about my essay on public authority omissions liability is that it sometimes seems to have been assumed that my primary goal was to defend the approach taken to the liability of public authorities in *Gorringe*,[35] when in fact my main aim was to draw attention to the *Gorringe* decision and to explore its implications. The analysis was therefore mostly descriptive rather than normative, albeit that right at the end of the essay I expressed the tentative view that the *Gorringe* approach was preferable to the previous position, in which a statutory power or duty was capable of generating a private law duty of care. Later developments have in any case confirmed me in that view. In particular, while I can see an argument for compensating those who suffer loss or damage as a result of the negligent failure to confer a benefit on a person who is entitled to that benefit as a matter of public law, in my opinion any such compensation is a matter for public law, whether in the form of a damages award under the Human Rights Act 1998 or some other form of public law damages remedy.[36] The difficulties that stand in the way of fashioning a monetary remedy for cases of this kind out of the law of negligence seem to me to be insuperable, as is suggested by the fact that the common law systems

---

[34] For recent examples, see *Secretary of State for the Home Department v Adiukwu* [2020] CSIH 47, 2021 SC 38; *Tindall v Chief Constable of Thames Valley Police* [2022] EWCA Civ 25, [2022] 4 WLR 104; and *HXA v Surrey County Council* [2022] EWCA Civ 1196, [2023] 1 WLR 116.

[35] See, eg, Cornford (n 33). Cornford claims, for example, that I insist 'that the omissions principle must always apply in the same way whether the defendant is public or private' (at 560). I leave it to the reader of chapter 4 to decide whether I make any such claim in that essay. He also quotes me as saying that 'there is no justification for distinguishing between public authorities and private parties when it comes to failures to confer benefits' (ibid 562), when what I actually wrote was that, *if* either of two particular justifications for the omissions principle were accepted, *then* 'we are drawn to the conclusion that *in private law terms* there is no justification for distinguishing between public authorities and private parties when it comes to failures to confer benefits': see ch 4 at p 121 (emphasis added).

[36] I therefore agree with a Canadian judge who remarked that '[t]he law of liability for public authorities should be governed by principles on the public law side of the divide, not the private law side': *Paradis Honey Ltd v Canada* [2015] FCA 89, [2016] 1 FCR 446 [130] (Stratas JA).

that persist in trying to do so have failed to establish a coherent and defensible framework for determining when liability will be imposed.[37]

My aim in 'Assumption of Responsibility: Four Questions' (chapter 5) was to try to bring some clarity to the controversies surrounding the concept of assumption of responsibility as used in negligence cases. Four questions framed the analysis. *What* does assumption of responsibility mean? *When* does it matter? *Why* do we need it? And *where* does it belong? Although my answers to some of those questions were necessarily tentative, at least one conclusion seemed to me to be clear, namely that assumption of responsibility is a meaningful and distinctive basis on which to impose negligence liability.

This essay was written before the decision of the Supreme Court in the *Poole* case, but the approach to the assumption of responsibility doctrine there was broadly consistent with my analysis. In particular, Lord Reed observed that:

> [T]he principle [of assumption of responsibility] has been applied in a variety of situations in which the defendant provided information or advice to the claimant with an undertaking that reasonable care would be taken as to its reliability (either express or implied, usually from the reasonable foreseeability of the claimant's reliance upon the exercise of such care) ... or undertook the performance of some other task or service for the claimant with an undertaking (express or implied) that reasonable care would be taken.[38]

This formula echoes the distinction I drew in my essay between the undertaking to provide information or advice or to perform a task or service for the claimant and the (separate) undertaking to exercise reasonable care when providing the information or advice or rendering the task or service.[39] As Lord Reed makes clear, it is this second undertaking that generates the duty of care, rather than the undertaking to provide the information or advice or to perform the task or service. Where Lord Reed's formula departs from the analysis in the essay is in the emphasis which he places on the reasonable foreseeability of the claimant's reliance on the exercise of reasonable care as the usual basis on which to imply an undertaking to exercise such care. For the reasons I give in the essay, I respectfully consider that this emphasis on reliance is problematic. Nevertheless, to the extent that reliance is to play a role in determining whether a duty of care arises out of an assumption of responsibility, it is better that the *foreseeability* of reliance should be determinative, rather than the *existence* of reliance, since requiring the latter effectively eliminates assumption of responsibility

---

[37] For criticism of the Canadian law in this area from public and private law perspectives respectively, see P Daly, 'The Policy/Operational Distinction: A View from Administrative Law' (2015) 69 *Supreme Court Law Review (2d)* 17 and B Feldthusen, 'Unique Public Duties of Care: Judicial Activism in the Supreme Court of Canada' (2013) 53 *Alberta Law Review* 955. And for the knots into which the Australian law in this area has become tied, see J Bell-James and K Barker, 'Public Authority Liability for Negligence in the Post-*Ipp* Era: Sceptical Reflections on the "Policy Defence"' (2016) 40 *Melbourne University Law Review* 1.

[38] *N v Poole* (n 31) [68] (Lord Reed).

[39] See ch 5 at p 134.

as a separate source of legal obligation,[40] and also gives rise to the paradox that whether a duty of care was owed at a particular moment is dependent on whether the claimant relied on the defendant at a later time.[41]

One final point that should be made about this essay is that the UK courts are clearly now wedded to the assumption of responsibility concept, and yet there remains considerable uncertainty as to how the doctrine will play out, especially in public authority cases. Although I put forward some strongly held opinions about the concept in the essay, it is a complex idea which would clearly benefit from further sustained academic analysis. And while commentators who continue to dismiss it as essentially meaningless are of course entitled to their opinion, they are unlikely to have much influence on the development of the law in this regard. Furthermore, if they persist in dismissing a doctrine that the courts now use as a key determinant of the duty of care enquiry in a wide range of cases then any claims they make that their approach to tort law takes what the judges say more seriously than other approaches must be taken with a large pinch of salt, as must their criticisms of tort scholars of a different theoretical persuasion for dismissing court decisions with which those scholars disagree as 'wrong'. After all, any tort scholar will tend (to some extent, at least) to pick and choose the decisions and reasoning that suit their broader interpretation of the law, and if a scholar disagrees with a particular decision then it is surely better to say so openly.

One of the symptoms of the common lawyers' obsession with the duty of care is that the more fundamental notion of fault has been rather neglected in scholarly analysis of negligence. In 'Varying the Standard of Care in Negligence' (chapter 6), I sought to demonstrate the potential reach of this concept, and in particular to identify the ways in which the standard of care in negligence could be modified so as to protect potential defendants from liability. This is an issue of considerable practical significance, which had not previously been the subject of systematic analysis. By shining a spotlight on the question I hoped to show that varying the standard of care in this way was a useful technique, which is and could be used in several types of case to achieve an appropriate balance between liability and non-liability. The structure of the analysis was centred on three core questions. First, to what extent has English negligence law already varied the standard of care to favour defendants? Second, if the standard of care is to be varied, how should this be done? And third, when and why might the use of a modified standard of care be desirable?

Although this article was published in 2013, I had begun work on the project almost a decade earlier, when there was much talk in the case law and literature of a shift from duty to breach in certain areas of negligence, such as the liability of public authorities. In the end, not much came of that talk, and, for better or worse, the duty concept remains in rude health, as is shown by the more recent

---

[40] See ch 5 at p 154.
[41] See ch 5 at p 152.

decisions on public authority liability referred to earlier. It is interesting to note, however, that recently academic commentaries have once again begun to question whether breach might not be a better tool for limiting liability in certain types of case than duty.[42] In any case, I hope that my essay serves as a helpful reminder of the potential of the fault concept to serve as a moderating influence on the extent of liability in negligence, which is capable of operating in a more nuanced manner than the duty of care – a dimmer switch, rather than an on/off switch, as it were. The article also highlighted the extent to which common law systems already use graduated levels of fault, and, even if the more prescriptive aspect of the essay is not accepted, its catalogue of the ways in which the standard of care is varied to favour defendants, and the circumstances in which this is done, may be a useful one. It is also important to emphasise that, as I argue in the essay, if this technique is to be employed there are some ways of varying the standard of care which are preferable to others.

Sticking with the three basic building blocks of negligence, we come next to damage, which is the subject of 'New Forms of Damage in Negligence' (chapter 7). If fault has tended to be under-emphasised by common law scholars, damage has generally been ignored altogether. I argued in this essay that although damage was an essential component of negligence liability, important extensions of the categories of actionable damage occurred with little or no analysis or even acknowledgement of the fact. In particular, I drew attention in the essay to a number of new forms of actionable damage which appeared either to have received recognition by the courts in recent years, or to be close to receiving such recognition. The essay is divided into three core sections, dealing with negligent imprisonment, wrongful conception and educational negligence. The principal conclusions were that redress for negligent imprisonment is best achieved through recognition of imprisonment as actionable damage in negligence; that an unwanted pregnancy is a form of personal injury, albeit an unusual one; that the conventional sum award in wrongful conception cases is best analysed as compensation for a diminution in the parents' autonomy; and that while untreated learning disorders are now treated by the courts as a form of personal injury, in the absence of such a disorder educational under-development ought not to be recognised as actionable damage in its own right.

This essay was first published in 2007, and since then there has been an upsurge in academic interest in the damage concept, largely spearheaded by young scholars.[43] Nor has my own interest in the subject abated. In 2013

---

[42] See, eg, J Morgan, 'A Riddle Wrapped in An Enigma: Assumption of Responsibility, Again' [2022] *CLJ* 449, 452.

[43] For recent contributions to the literature, see, eg, M Fordham, 'The Protection of Personal Interests: Evolving Forms of Damage in Negligence' (2015) 27 *Singapore Academy of Law Journal* 643; C Purshouse, 'Judicial Reasoning and the Concept of Damage: Rethinking Medical Negligence Cases' (2015) 15 *Medical Law International* 155; C Purshouse, 'Liability for Lost Autonomy in Negligence: Undermining the Coherence of Tort Law?' (2015) 22 *Torts Law Journal* 226; J Huang, 'The Boundaries of Actionable Damage' (2019) 82 *MLR* 737; H Cooper, 'The Minimum

I published a general overview of the damage requirement in the English law of negligence[44] and in 2017 I explored the relationship between rights, damage and loss (see chapter 13). More recently, I have homed in on particular issues relating to damage, namely whether loss of autonomy should be recognised as damage in the negligence context,[45] and the precise dividing line between property damage and pure economic loss.[46] There has also been a steady stream of recent Commonwealth case law squarely addressing the question of damage as an issue in its own right.[47]

It is an important conceptual advance that common law scholars are now addressing the fundamental question of what sort of interference with a person's protected interests is capable of grounding a negligence action, although the field remains a young one, and there is much more work to be done. Furthermore, there is still much truth in the observation that I made in my essay that issues relating to the damage requirement tend to be repackaged as issues of causation or duty.[48] The result is that the discussion of the damage question tends even now to be dispersed throughout books on tort, rather than being addressed in a systematic way, in a section of the work specifically devoted to the problem. To give just three examples, the loss of a chance issue in medical negligence is not an issue going to causation (where discussion of the question is usually located in the books) but to damage; much of the discussion of the pure economic loss question in negligence is actually concerned with the boundaries of property damage, and with who can bring a property damage claim; and the controversial requirement that a claimant must have suffered a recognised psychiatric illness to bring a claim for pure mental harm in negligence is also properly understood as going to the damage question, in particular what forms of mental disturbance should count as a personal injury.[49]

Actionable Physical Damage in Negligence' (2019) 25 *Torts Law Journal* 128; S Fulham-McQuillan, 'Infringement of Autonomy as Damage in Medical Negligence' (2023) 139 *LQR* 126. And for an overview of the recent academic debates on the damage requirement, see Morgan, *Great Debates in Tort Law* (n 19) ch 8.

[44] Nolan, 'Damage in the English Law of Negligence' (n 7).

[45] D Nolan, 'Negligence and Autonomy' [2022] *Singapore Journal of Legal Studies* 356, 361–74.

[46] D Nolan, 'Damage to "Other Property": Exploring the Boundary Between Property Damage and Pure Economic Loss' (forthcoming, 2023).

[47] See, eg, *Alcan Gove Pty Ltd v Zabic* [2015] HCA 33, 257 CLR 1; *Shaw v Kovac* [2017] EWCA Civ 1028, [2017] 1 WLR 4773; *ACB v Thomson Medical Pte Ltd* [2017] SGCA 20, [2017] 1 SLR 918; *Dryden v Johnson Matthey plc* [2018] UKSC 18, [2019] AC 403.

[48] Though a plurality of the UK Supreme Court recently rejected the suggestion that the damage question could be subsumed into the duty of care enquiry, instead affirming its status as an independent element of the negligence analysis: see *Meadows v Khan* [2021] UKSC 21, [2022] AC 852 [28] (Lord Hodge and Lord Sales). The suggestion was made by Lord Burrows in the same case, at [80].

[49] For recent analysis of this question, see *Saadati v Moorhead* 2017 SCC 28, [2017] 1 SCR 543; R Mulheron, 'Rewriting the Requirement for a "Recognized Psychiatric Injury" in Negligence Claims' (2012) 32 *OJLS* 77; R Orr, 'Speaking with Different Voices: The Problems with English Law and Psychiatric Injury' (2016) 36 *LS* 547; and L Bélanger-Hardy, 'Canada's Common Law,

Finally, we reach the third of the fundamental building blocks of negligence, which is causation, or the link between fault and damage. In 'Causation and the Goals of Tort Law' (chapter 8), I argued that it was impossible to understand or resolve difficult questions concerning causation unless it was appreciated that these issues go to the heart of what tort law is about. The essay is divided into three parts. In the first part, I considered the problem of causal indeterminacy in tort law by reference to the leading English cases on the subject. In the second part, I looked at the loss of a chance theory, according to which some cases of causal indeterminacy in tort law can be resolved by re-characterising the claimant's injury as the loss of a chance of avoiding injury, as opposed to the injury itself. And in the third and final part of the essay, I looked at the relationship between causal indeterminacy and the 'goals' of deterrence and compensation. In particular, I argued that recent developments in the English law on causation were explicable only by reference to these two goals, and that they also underlay the push towards recovery for lost chances. I concluded the essay by identifying some of the drawbacks of modifying tort law in this way in response to instrumentalist concerns.[50]

I again mostly stand by the arguments I made in this essay, although I am prepared to accept now that there is a case grounded in interpersonal justice considerations (as opposed to instrumentalist goals) for carving out a narrowly tailored exception to the but-for test in cases where we know that the claimant's injury was the result of someone else's negligence, but we cannot tell *who* that person is. In such a case, for reasons given by my colleague Sandy Steel,[51] I believe that it is right to bar the different people who were at fault and might be responsible from escaping liability by pointing the finger at the other possible wrongdoers. It is important to note, however, that while this principle would provide an explanation for the decision of the House of Lords in *Fairchild v Glenhaven Funeral Services Ltd*,[52] a case that I discuss at some length in my essay, it does not provide an explanation for the broader *Fairchild* exception to the but-for test, which is not limited to cases in which it is known that the damage was the result of the negligence of someone other than the claimant themselves.[53]

Quebec's Civil Law and the Threshold of Actionable Mental Harm Following Tortious Conduct' in A Robertson and M Tilbury (eds), *Divergences in Private Law* (Oxford, Hart Publishing, 2016).

[50] For a subsequent monograph on causation which takes a similar approach, but which explores the issues in much greater depth, and with more sophistication, see G Turton, *Evidential Uncertainty in Causation in Negligence* (Oxford, Hart Publishing, 2016). Many of the assumptions that underlie my analysis seem also to be shared by Morgan, *Great Debates in Tort Law* (n 19) ch 4.

[51] S Steel, 'Justifying Exceptions to Proof of Causation in Tort Law' (2015) 78 *MLR* 729. This narrower principle was endorsed in *Clements v Clements* 2012 SCC 32, [2012] 2 SCR 181 [46] (McLachlin CJ).

[52] [2002] UKHL 22, [2003] 1 AC 32.

[53] See, eg, *Barker v Corus (UK) Ltd* [2006] UKHL 20, [2006] 2 AC 572, and *McGhee v National Coal Board* [1973] 1 WLR 1 (HL), which latter decision was explained in *Fairchild* as an example of the application of the *Fairchild* exception *avant la lettre*.

As I pointed out in my essay, one of the problems with the broader *Fairchild* exception is that its limits are rationally indefensible. The result has been that the exception has generated much uncertainty, while the departure from the but-for test has also had unexpected knock-on effects in other areas of law, such as insurance and reinsurance.[54] Although in my essay I was careful to limit myself to the claim that departures from the but-for test could only be justified by social goals of deterrence and compensation (and not that they were necessarily a mistake), events since the publication of the essay have shown that, in the words of Lord Brown, 'the law tampers with the but-for test of causation at its peril'.[55] It now seems to me that there is much force in the point that Lord Hoffmann, one of the Law Lords who sat in *Fairchild*, made extra-judicially some 10 years later, when he argued that with the benefit of hindsight it might have been better had the House of Lords decided *Fairchild* against the claimants, and Parliament then legislated to provide a statutory solution to the problem, which it almost certainly would have done.[56]

III. NUISANCE AND *RYLANDS v FLETCHER*

If negligence is the most important tort, private nuisance is arguably the next most significant, and a second main strand of my research relates to this tort and to the related liability for damage caused by the escape of dangerous things known as the 'rule in *Rylands v Fletcher*'. In two book chapters that I wrote early in my career for a practitioner treatise, I provided a detailed account of these two causes of action,[57] and I have been able to draw on the extensive research that went into those chapters in my subsequent work in this area.

In '"A Tort Against Land": Private Nuisance as a Property Tort' (chapter 9), I argued that private nuisance could only properly be understood as a tort which protects rights in land, and that, understood in this way, it was a thoroughly coherent cause of action. I began the essay (which was first published in 2012) by introducing this 'property tort analysis' of private nuisance and by providing a definition of the tort. The bulk of the essay was then devoted to showing that the central doctrines of private nuisance law were consistent with the property tort analysis. I also looked at the relationship between private nuisance and trespass

---

[54] See, eg, *International Energy Group Ltd v Zurich Insurance plc* [2015] UKSC 33, [2016] AC 509, where Lord Neuberger and Lord Reed described the effect of *Fairchild* as a 'sort of juridical version of chaos theory' (at [191]). See also *Equitas Insurance Ltd v Municipal Mutual Insurance Ltd* [2019] EWCA Civ 718, [2020] QB 418 [90] (Males LJ).

[55] *Sienkiewicz v Greif (UK) Ltd* [2011] UKSC 10, [2011] 2 AC 229 [186] (Lord Brown).

[56] L Hoffmann, '*Fairchild* and After' in A Burrows et al (eds), *Judge and Jurist: Essays in Memory of Lord Rodger of Earlsferry* (Oxford, OUP, 2013).

[57] See the chapters on 'Nuisance' and '*Rylands v Fletcher* and Fire' in Grubb (n 6). The most recent versions of these chapters can be found in K Oliphant (ed), *The Law of Tort*, 3rd edn (London, LexisNexis Butterworths, 2015).

to land, identified some sources of confusion which had served to obscure the underlying coherence of private nuisance, and considered the implications of the property tort analysis for the traditional distinction between property and obligations. I concluded the essay by making some more general observations about the value of a rights-based approach to tort law.

Moving on from that analysis, in 'The Essence of Private Nuisance' (chapter 10) I argued that the essence of the tort of private nuisance – by which I meant its defining characteristic – was interference with, or impairment of, the usability of the claimant's land. Although this claim was merely a clarification of the orthodox definition or conception of the tort as centrally concerned with the claimant's use and enjoyment of their land, I argued that the clarification was a significant one. Furthermore, while this central defining feature of private nuisance is well-established, it has been the subject of little sustained analysis, and one of the aims of this essay was to begin the task of plugging that gap. Finally, the orthodox conception of private nuisance had been coming under attack, and there was a danger that without a robust defence of it the coherence and utility of the tort would be compromised. In this essay (which was first published in 2019) I therefore sought to provide such a defence.

The property tort analysis of private nuisance has recently been endorsed by the English courts in decisions such as *Williams v Network Rail Infrastructure Ltd*[58] and *Fearn v Tate Gallery*.[59] In the former case, Sir Terence Etherton MR remarked that '[i]n recent times a number of decisions at the highest level have introduced greater coherence and consistency to the legal principles governing the cause of action for private nuisance',[60] an assessment with which I respectfully agree. It is encouraging, for example, that the courts are increasingly emphasising the explanatory force of the property tort analysis, which they now acknowledge provides a straightforward explanation for the principle that the gravity of the interference is assessed objectively, with no allowance being made for any sensitivity or insensitivity of the claimant or their use,[61] a point that I made in my 2012 essay.[62] Furthermore, in the *Fearn* case, Lord Leggatt explicitly rejected the idea that the unlawfulness of the interference is to be determined by some sort of weighing of the interests of the parties, or cost/benefit analysis, an approach against which I also argued in that essay.[63] And since one of my

---

[58] *Williams v Network Rail Infrastructure Ltd* [2018] EWCA Civ 1514, [2019] QB 601 [40].

[59] *Fearn v Board of Trustees of the Tate Gallery* [2023] UKSC 4, [2023] 2 WLR 339 [9]–[11].

[60] *Williams* (n 58) [31].

[61] ibid [43]; *Fearn* (n 59) [23] (Lord Leggatt) ('The objective nature of the test reflects the fact that the interest protected by the law of private nuisance is the utility of land').

[62] See ch 9 at pp 266–67. For a recent analysis of the implications of understanding private nuisance as a property tort, see Morgan, *Great Debates in Tort Law* (n 19) ch 10.

[63] See ch 9 at pp 264–65. See also Richard Wright's chapter in the collection in which that essay was first published: RW Wright, 'Private Nuisance Law: A Window on Substantive Justice' in D Nolan and A Robertson (eds), *Rights and Private Law* (Oxford, Hart Publishing, 2012) 502–508.

main goals in publishing the 2019 essay was to refute what I called the 'physical invasion' view of nuisance, it was pleasing to see that that view was also dismissed as mistaken by the Supreme Court in *Fearn*.[64]

One argument that I made in the 2012 essay is, however, inconsistent with the reasoning of the majority in *Fearn*, namely that there are certain types of interference with the use and enjoyment of land that are never actionable in nuisance, no matter how severe the interference on the facts.[65] In *Fearn*, Lord Leggatt appears clearly to reject this idea, saying that 'there is no conceptual or a priori limit to what can constitute a nuisance'[66] and that anything short of trespass 'that materially interferes with the claimant's enjoyment of rights in land is capable of being a nuisance'.[67] Instead, he rationalises the decisions in what I called 'no rights' cases in other ways, so that, for example, the rule that no action lies for interference with a view, or for interference with television reception caused by a building, can be explained by a common law liberty to build on one's own land. Although I am still inclined to prefer the explanation that I put forward for the decisions in question in my essay, I am not sure that a great deal turns on which approach is adopted. Having said that, it is not clear where Lord Leggatt's analysis leaves the famous nineteenth-century decision in *Bradford Corporation v Pickles*,[68] in which the House of Lords held that the appropriation of water percolating in undefined channels over or under the claimant's property is incapable of being a nuisance.

An alternative view of private nuisance to that put forward in my 2019 essay has recently been proposed by James Penner, who conceives of nuisance as a form of indirect, or constructive, dispossession.[69] Penner's contribution to the debate is a thoughtful one, and the distance between our two accounts is perhaps not great. Nevertheless, in my view there are some clear difficulties with conceiving of private nuisance as a kind of de facto dispossession. An obvious one is that dispossession or ouster seems to me to be an all-or-nothing concept, and yet in many nuisance cases the claimant can still make a good deal of use of their land, despite the fact that the defendant is causing a substantial interference with that use. For example, the nuisance may consist of unreasonable noise interference for a few hours a day, while not affecting the property at other times at all. In such a case is it not hyperbole to say that the defendant is in effect dispossessing the claimant? Surely a person who is dispossessed cannot use their land at all? Similarly, it seems to me to be rather odd to conceive of substantial interference

---

[64] *Fearn* (n 59) [13] (citing my essay, as well as C Essert, 'Nuisance and the Normative Boundaries of Ownership' (2016) 52 *Tulsa Law Review* 85, in which strong objections were also made to the physical invasion view).

[65] See ch 9 at pp 260–63.

[66] *Fearn* (n 59) [12].

[67] ibid.

[68] *Bradford Corporation v Pickles* [1895] AC 587 (HL).

[69] JE Penner, *Property Rights: A Re-Examination* (Oxford, OUP, 2020) ch 7.

with the natural light reaching a property, or relatively trivial property damage which is nonetheless sufficient to ground a nuisance action – such as the killing of shrubs and flowers on the claimant's land – as forms of *dispossession*.

Penner says with regard to the argument in my 2019 essay that he has difficulty in understanding the conceptual work which the notion of 'usability' is supposed to be doing.[70] However, I made it clear in the essay that in my view the notion of usability provides the best explanation for what nuisance is concerned with, as well as marking out the definitional boundaries of the tort. On that analysis, the conceptual work it is doing seems to me to be obvious. Penner also argues that that none of the cases, as far as he can see, 'make any reference to such a notion [ie, 'usability'] in terms'.[71] But even if it is true that the English courts have not used this particular term,[72] nuisance cases are replete with references to interference with the utility of the claimant's land, including most recently Lord Leggatt's majority judgment in the *Fearn* case,[73] and that surely amounts to the same thing. This is in any case an odd objection for Penner to make, since judges in nuisance cases also do not refer to the 'dispossession' of the claimant. Finally, Penner says that I defend the need for 'damage' in nuisance cases, and that I define 'damage' for these purposes as a diminution in the 'usability' of the land.[74] He provides no citation for this supposed claim of mine, which is not surprising as I am not sure I have ever made it. I only introduce the concept of 'usability' in the 2019 essay, where I do not discuss the damage requirement at all. And in the 2012 essay I am dismissive of damage as a prerequisite of nuisance liability, arguing that it is synonymous with the requirement of a substantial interference with use and enjoyment, and hence adds nothing to that requirement.[75] It follows that Penner and I agree that the concept of 'damage' can effectively be dispensed with in the nuisance context, a position that seems to me to be consistent with the analysis of the Court of Appeal in the *Williams* decision.[76] I am however unable to accept Penner's claim that damage in nuisance is conventionally understood as meaning 'physical damage to the land of some kind'.[77] This is simply not true, as *Williams* confirms.[78]

The final essay in the second part of the collection is 'The Distinctiveness of *Rylands v Fletcher*' (chapter 11). The primary purpose of this essay was to

---

[70] ibid 146.

[71] ibid.

[72] cf *Restatement, Second, Torts* (1977) § 821D, comment b.

[73] *Fearn* (n 59) [11] (Lord Leggatt): 'It follows from the nature of the tort of private nuisance that the harm from which the law protects a claimant is diminution in the utility and amenity value of the claimant's land'.

[74] Penner (n 69) 154.

[75] See ch 9 at p 276.

[76] See *Williams* (n 58) [42] (Sir Terence Etherton MR) (referring to 'the artificiality and elasticity of any requirement of damage for the purpose of establishing nuisance').

[77] Penner (n 69) 154.

[78] There is nothing 'artificial' or 'elastic' (see above, n 76) about physical damage to land.

challenge the proposition that the rule in *Rylands v Fletcher* is best regarded as an offshoot of the tort of private nuisance, being an extension of that cause of action to isolated escapes. This offshoot theory was endorsed by the House of Lords in *Transco Plc v Stockport MBC*,[79] but I argued in the essay that the theory should be rejected, for four reasons. First, that analysis of the *Rylands v Fletcher* case provided little support for the theory. Second, that there were well-established distinctions between the rule in *Rylands v Fletcher* and private nuisance. Third, that merger with the rule would be bad for nuisance. And finally, that the version of the strict liability rule to which the offshoot theory had given rise was unappealing. I also gave consideration in the essay to *Burnie Port Authority v General Jones Pty Ltd*,[80] where the High Court of Australia held that the rule in *Rylands v Fletcher* should be treated as having been absorbed by the principles of ordinary negligence, as well as to the desirability of a strict liability rule independent of nuisance. My conclusion was that the rule in *Rylands v Fletcher* no longer served any useful purpose and should be abolished.

Nothing has happened since this essay was first published in 2005 to cause me to change my mind on the issues discussed, and if anything developments have tended to bear out the arguments made. Very little has been heard of the *Rylands* rule in the intervening years, although there is one case in which liability to some claimants under the rule was admitted by the defendants.[81] It is noteworthy that the most important decision on the rule since 2005, that of the Court of Appeal in *Gore v Stannard (t/a Wyvern Tyres)*,[82] has stripped it of any practical significance it previously had in the fire context. Prior to this decision, it had been thought that in cases involving fire, it was not the flammable material collected by the defendant that must escape for possible liability under the rule to arise, but the fire it caused. However, it was held in *Gore v Stannard* that the thing that escaped and caused the damage must also be the dangerous thing accumulated by the defendant. This analysis emasculates the *Rylands* rule in cases of fire, and it also raises questions about the reliance placed on the rule where, for example, an accumulation of explosive materials caused a blast that damaged the claimant's nearby property.[83] In such a scenario, does it now follow that the claimant can recover only for any damage caused by the impact of the materials themselves, and not by the force of the blast? All in all,

---

[79] [2003] UKHL 61, [2004] 2 AC 1.

[80] (1994) 179 CLR 520 (HCA).

[81] See *Color Quest Ltd v Total Downstream UK plc* [2009] EWHC 540 (Comm), which concerned massive explosions at an oil storage depot. The issue was not considered on appeal: [2011] QB 86 (CA).

[82] [2014] QB 1 (CA). For commentary on this decision, see J Steele and R Merkin, 'Insurance between Neighbours: *Stannard v Gore* and Common Law Liability for Fire' (2013) 25 *Journal of Environmental Law* 305.

[83] See, eg, *Miles v Forest Rock Granite Co* (1918) 34 TLR 500 (KBD) (recovery under the *Rylands* rule for damage done by a rock thrown out of a quarry during blasting).

the assessment of the judge who recently dismissed *Rylands v Fletcher* as 'a rule of limited utility' seems a fair one,[84] which is consistent with the general thrust of my essay.[85]

IV. TORT IN GENERAL

The other two previously published essays in this collection are concerned with the law of tort more generally, while the final essay is a new paper on product liability, a topic which I have long found fascinating.[86]

'Preventive Damages' (chapter 12) was an examination of the damages that are awarded to compensate a claimant for expenditure incurred to prevent anticipated damage arising from another's wrongful conduct. The analysis was a tentative one, with the emphasis on identifying the problems and possible solutions to them, rather than putting forward firmly held views as to how cases of this kind should be resolved. In the essay, I considered the circumstances in which preventive damages were and should be available, and discussed several example cases that squarely raised this issue. In some of these cases, the argument for recovery seemed stronger than in others. I also gave consideration to possible limitations on the recovery of preventive damages, such as a test of reasonableness of the expenditure. Finally, I highlighted the conceptual difficulties posed by claims for preventive damages, and explored some possible doctrinal bases for their recovery.

I remain of the view that the issues discussed in this essay are important ones, with which the English courts will at some stage need to grapple. The reception of this essay by other academics has been positive, and in his excellent recent book *Great Debates in Tort Law*, Jonathan Morgan devotes a section to the issue of preventive damages, in which he engages with my essay and other writings on the subject, including John Fleming's seminal early analysis.[87] Since I published my essay, I have also become aware of various research projects on the same issue in civilian jurisdictions. The recent spate of climate change litigation raises interesting questions in this regard, such as whether a South American farmer who has been forced to incur significant costs to mitigate the consequences of climate change on his business can recover a proportion of these costs from large-scale greenhouse gas emitters, such as European power companies.[88]

---

[84] *Lindsay v Berkeley Homes (Capital) plc* [2018] EWHC 2042 (TCC) [38] (Jefford J).

[85] My view that the rule should be abolished is shared by Anthony Gray: see A Gray, *The Evolution from Strict Liability to Fault in the Law of Torts* (Oxford, Hart Publishing, 2021) ch 3.

[86] This again dates back to early work for the Grubb/Oliphant treatise: see my chapter on the subject in Grubb (n 6). The current version of this chapter can be found in Oliphant (n 57).

[87] Morgan, *Great Debates in Tort Law* (n 19) 202–206. Fleming's essay is JG Fleming, 'Preventive Damages' in NJ Mullany (ed), *Torts in the Nineties* (Sydney, Law Book Co, 1997).

[88] See http://climatecasechart.com/non-us-case/lliuya-v-rwe-ag/.

Similarly, one can easily envisage that flat owners forced by their circumstances to live in high-rise buildings made unsafe by flammable cladding might wish to bring preventive damages claims for the cost of paying for 'waking watches' to mitigate the risk of fire in the aftermath of the Grenfell Tower disaster.[89] Finally, some commentators on the decision in *Dryden v Johnson Matthey plc*[90] were critical of the Supreme Court for not considering the possibility that the employees in that case could have recovered on a preventive damages basis.[91] And although I argued in my essay that this was not a situation where preventive damages were appropriate,[92] I agree that it would have been preferable if the court had at least considered the possibility of such an award on the rather unusual facts of that case.

In 'Rights, Damage and Loss' (chapter 13) I explored the relationship between the concepts of rights, damage and loss. The focus of the analysis was mainly on the law of negligence, although some of the claims had wider ramifications. The essay is divided into three main parts, with each part centred on a different relationship: first, the relationship between rights and damage; second, the relationship between rights and loss; and third, the relationship between damage and loss. In each of these three parts, a separate, but related, claim was made: (1) that a concept of damage was a necessary component of a plausible rights-based conception of negligence law; (2) that a right not to suffer loss was conceptually impossible; and (3) that damage and loss were fundamentally different concepts.

As I mentioned before, the reception of your work can sometimes surprise you, and in the case of this particular essay I have been impressed by the fact that my argument that damage and loss are fundamentally different concepts has frequently been emphasised by other commentators, since I thought this was the least controversial of the three central claims made in the paper. It was also gratifying to see that the distinction played a key role in Iain Field's recent article on the difficult relationship between the contributory negligence doctrine and the mitigation rule concerning avoidable losses.[93]

The claim that a right not to suffer loss is a conceptual impossibility was always likely to be controversial, however, and although the argument seems to have been accepted by a plurality of the Supreme Court of Canada,[94] I am not surprised to see that there has already been a degree of pushback in the literature.

---

[89] See www.gov.uk/government/publications/building-safety-programme-waking-watch-costs/ building-safety-programme-waking-watch-costs.

[90] *Dryden* (n 47).

[91] See, eg, Huang (n 43) 748–49; J Morgan, 'The Outer Limits of Personal Injury' [2018] *CLJ* 461, 463.

[92] See ch 12 at p 350 fn (referring to the first instance decision in *Dryden*).

[93] I Field, 'Contributory Negligence and the Rule of Avoidable Losses' (2018) 38 *OJLS* 475.

[94] *1688782 Ontario Inc v Maple Leaf Foods Inc* 2020 SCC 35, 450 DLR (4th) 181 [19] (Brown and Martin JJ).

In that same article of Field's, for example, the author questions my claim that a person who has, for example, invested money in response to negligent financial advice suffers no damage when the value of the shares declines.[95] In truth, what I actually argued was that in such a case it was not possible to say definitively at any moment in time that the buyer of the shares was worse off as a result, and hence had suffered 'loss' on the definition of that concept that I use in the essay. Nor do I accept that we can easily circumvent the implications of this analysis by saying that as soon as the shares dip in value the claimant suffers 'damage', since the common law notion of damage in negligence cases cannot, for reasons which I explain in my paper, be equated with notions of being 'worse off', whether financially or otherwise.

The final essay in this collection is the only one that has not previously been published. In 'Against Strict Product Liability' (chapter 14) I argue that the experiment with strict product liability in tort has been a failure, and that Parliament should take the opportunity afforded to it by the UK's withdrawal from the European Union to repeal Part I of the Consumer Protection Act 1987. The argument I make for repeal of the 1987 Act is primarily grounded on the conclusion that the justifications that have been put forward for imposing strict tort liability for damage caused by defective products do not hold up to scrutiny. There is, however, a second string to the argument, which is that the imposition of strict product liability in a tort system primarily based on fault requires lines to be drawn that were always hard to justify and which technological change is making unsustainable.

The essay is divided into four main parts. In the first part, I consider the differences between negligence liability and the strict liability regime established by the 1987 Act. In the second part, I set out the difficulties to which strict product liability has given rise. In the third part, I identify the principal arguments that have been made for strict product liability in tort and subject them to critical examination. My conclusion is that none stand up to scrutiny. And in the final part of the essay, I consider various mitigating measures that could be taken if it were thought necessary to soften the blow of repealing the 1987 Act.

Two connections can be made between this essay and the others in the collection. The first is that one of the main goals of my scholarship in tort law has been to try to simplify the law as much as possible, while of course trying not to over-simplify it. Examples are chapter 2, the argument in which is driven by the conviction that the duty of care concept unnecessarily complicates the common law of negligence, and chapter 9, where I seek to demonstrate that treating private nuisance as a property tort results in a more coherent and streamlined cause of action. However, it is only in chapter 14 that I expressly rely on simplification of the law as a positive argument for legal change. The other link is that

---

[95] Field (n 93) 482.

in both chapter 14 and chapter 11 I argue for the abolition of a strict liability cause of action in favour of fault-based liability. Although this is not the place to expand on my preference for fault liability over strict liability, some of the reasons will become apparent from reading those two chapters. In a nutshell I generally find the arguments that are put forward for strict liability unconvincing, and I also believe that such liability tends to make the law more complex than it needs to be. By contrast, negligence law has an attractive simplicity when compared to systems of strict liability, and also chimes with our basic intuitions about responsibility.[96] I should make it clear, however, that these are merely reasons why in my opinion fault liability should be the default rule in the law of tort, and that I am quite happy to accept that in certain scenarios the case for strict liability may be so strong that this default rule should be displaced. It is just that I do not believe that these scenarios include instances of damage caused by the escape of dangerous things (as a general category), nor cases of damage caused by defective products.

V. CONCLUSION

Were the Dean of an American law school to ask me what my normative theory of tort law is, I would be just as nonplussed as Tony Weir.[97] As Weir pointed out, the common law of tort is a ragbag of different causes of action, united only by what they are not (namely breaches of contract or equitable wrongs).[98] And it would be rather surprising if it were possible to produce a coherent overall theory to explain the contents of the bag. Nor is it entirely clear why we would want to do so, since tort law has done just fine for centuries without any such overarching theory. A more useful and realistic endeavour, I would suggest, is to study the contents of the bag and to try to make the best sense that we can of the individual causes of action, as well as of the general principles that apply across the law of tort. In the essays in this collection that is all that I have tried to do. And if the reader feels that they have a better understanding of the law of tort after reading these essays then I will have succeeded in achieving my goal.

---

[96] 'Ethically regarded, the idea of liability for harm caused by one's unexcused errors and mistakes is both straightforward and intuitive': GT Schwartz, 'The Vitality of Negligence and the Ethics of Strict Liability' (1981) 15 *Georgia Law Review* 963, 1003.

[97] See above, n 3.

[98] Weir (n 3) ix.

Part I

Negligence

2

Deconstructing the Duty of Care

(2013) 129 *Law Quarterly Review* 559–588

[559] I. INTRODUCTION

THE EXISTENCE OF what is termed a 'duty of care' is generally regarded as a fundamental building block of the common law of negligence, a 'core ingredient'[1] or 'foundational element'[2] of the cause of action. Furthermore, duty is commonly seen as the logical starting point of the negligence enquiry, analytically anterior to the other building blocks of fault (or 'breach of duty'), damage, causation, remoteness and defences. When I studied tort as an undergraduate, for example, week 1 of the reading list was entitled simply 'Duty of Care', and most English tort textbooks begin their analysis of negligence with one or more chapters on duty. The orthodox perception of the duty of care as a central element of the negligence enquiry analytically anterior to the other elements is neatly summed up by the statement in one of those textbooks that 'Negligence as a tort is a breach of a legal duty to take care which results in damage to the claimant'.[3]

This duty orthodoxy is deeply ingrained in the mindset of common lawyers, and profoundly affects the way in which judges decide negligence cases, and lawyers more generally think about negligence law. Nevertheless, one of the functions of legal scholarship is to challenge such orthodoxies, in the hope that critical review may further understanding of the subject by exposing a wrong turning in our collective thinking about the law, and identifying a more fruitful way forward. In this article, I subject the duty orthodoxy to such critical review, and conclude that the duty of care concept is now obscuring understanding of negligence law and hindering its rational development. I therefore propose the 'deconstruction' of duty, a process whereby the disparate issues currently subsumed under the duty umbrella are separated out and reclassified under the other components of the negligence enquiry.

---

[1] WVH Rogers, *Winfield and Jolowicz on Tort*, 18th edn (London, Sweet and Maxwell, 2010) para 5-2.

[2] D Owen, 'Duty Rules' (2001) 54 *Vanderbilt Law Review* 767, 767–68.

[3] *Winfield and Jolowicz* (n 1) para 5-1.

The duty orthodoxy has of course been challenged before. As long ago as 1934, PH Winfield said of the 'duty idea' that 'in theory it might well be eliminated from the tort of negligence, for it got there only by a historical accident and it seems to be superfluous',[4] and the same year the first US *Restatement of Torts* dispensed with duty in its 'Statement of the Elements of a Cause of Action for Negligence'.[5] Shortly afterwards the Roman lawyer WW Buckland launched a sustained attack on the duty of care, which he famously described as an [560] 'unnecessary fifth wheel on the coach, incapable of sound analysis and possibly productive of injustice'.[6] At the back end of the 1960s, both PS Atiyah and the Canadian scholar R Dale Gibson renewed the assault on the duty concept,[7] and a decade later another Canadian, JC Smith, argued in an essay entitled 'The Mystery of Duty' that the concept was 'confusing and ambiguous':

> It is so because it is not entailed by or assumed in the concept of negligence, nor does it refer to a particular step in reaching a conclusion as to whether a person has been negligent and what his liability will be. Rather, it is often used as equivalent to a number of the notions or ideas related to the concept of negligence, and as well, is used to refer to several of the different steps in a negligence action.[8]

Finally, in the 1990s, the duty concept came under attack once again from both David Howarth and Bob Hepple, with Howarth describing it as 'troublesome, confusing and probably superfluous',[9] and arguing that there was 'nothing in the concept of the duty-situation' that could not be 'dealt with quite adequately under the headings of fault, cause or damage',[10] and Hepple similarly advocating a new framework for negligence in which the 'redundant and incoherent' concept of a notional duty of care was abandoned.[11]

Perceptive though the critics of duty have been, their challenges to the duty orthodoxy have essentially failed. In Buckland's case, this was because his critique was radically incomplete, since it was directed only at the factual duty question, which asks whether damage to someone in the claimant's position was a reasonably foreseeable consequence of the defendant's faulty conduct, and

---

[4] PH Winfield, 'Duty in Tortious Negligence' (1934) 34 *Columbia Law Review* 41, 66.

[5] *Restatement, Torts* (1934) § 281. See also *Restatement, Second, Torts* (1965) § 281.

[6] WW Buckland, 'The Duty to Take Care' (1935) 51 *LQR* 637. See also WW Buckland, *Some Reflections on Jurisprudence* (London, CUP, 1945) 110–15. For a scathing attack on the concept from a scholar steeped in the Roman-Dutch law of South Africa, see TW Price, 'The Conception of the "Duty of Care" in the *Actio Legis Aquiliae*' (1949) 66 *South African Law Journal* 171 (describing the duty of care as variously a 'fetish', a 'will-o'-the-wisp' and a 'red herring').

[7] RD Gibson, 'A New Alphabet of Negligence' in AM Linden (ed), *Studies in Canadian Tort Law* (Toronto, Butterworths, 1968); PS Atiyah, *Accidents, Compensation and the Law* (London, Wiedenfeld and Nicolson, 1970) 45–49.

[8] JC Smith, 'The Mystery of Duty' in L Klar (ed), *Studies in Canadian Tort Law* (Toronto, Butterworths, 1977) 3–4.

[9] D Howarth, *Textbook on Tort* (London, Butterworths, 1995) 158.

[10] D Howarth, 'Negligence after *Murphy*: Time to Re-think' [1991] *CLJ* 67, 68.

[11] B Hepple, 'Negligence: The Search for Coherence' (1997) 50 *CLP* 69, 93.

not at the notional duty question, which asks whether as a matter of law liability in negligence is countenanced in this category of case.[12] Because subsequent critics of duty have addressed both aspects of the duty question, their arguments have been more persuasive, but they have nevertheless failed to loosen the grip which the duty orthodoxy holds over common lawyers' thinking about negligence law. I would suggest that there are two reasons for this failure. The first is that they have failed to set out a sufficiently systematic critique of the duty concept; in particular, the recurrent claim that the duty of care is superfluous has not been supported by a detailed demonstration of the way in which the issues currently considered under the duty umbrella could be accommodated within other stages of the negligence enquiry. And the other reason is that, although the critics of the duty of care have rightly described the concept as confusing and incoherent, they have largely failed [561] to make good this claim by showing how the use of the duty device has detrimentally affected the quality of reasoning in negligence cases and negligence scholarship. In this article, I hope to mount a more powerful attack on the duty concept by keeping in mind these likely explanations for the failure of earlier critiques. Hence I seek to demonstrate exactly how the plethora of issues currently dealt with under the duty heading could be dealt with under other headings of the negligence enquiry, and to show how deconstructing duty in this way would improve our collective understanding. Before I begin those two tasks, however, a number of preliminary points should be made.

II. FOUR PRELIMINARY POINTS

A. Duties of Care Are Not Duties

The first and most important of those preliminary points is that the so-called 'duty of care' is not a duty after all, so that the term is a confusing misnomer. A moment's reflection shows us that this is true. A duty is an obligation, and in private law (of which the law of negligence is a part) duties are obligations owed to other persons. As WN Hohfeld told us, a duty owed to another person correlates with a claim right which that person has against the duty-holder.[13] It follows that if the duty of care were really a duty, then we would all have rights good against everyone else that they not create unreasonable risks of certain kinds of interference with our bodily integrity, property and so forth.

---

[12] For this criticism of Buckland's thesis, see FH Lawson, 'The Duty of Care: A Comparative Study' (1947) 22 *Tulane Law Review* 111; and MA Millner, *Negligence in Modern Law* (London, Butterworths, 1967) 27.

[13] WN Hohfeld, 'Some Fundamental Legal Conceptions as Applied in Judicial Reasoning' (1913) 23 *Yale Law Journal* 16, 32.

Since a violation of a claim right constitutes a wrong to the holder of the right, this would make the wrong underlying actions for negligence unreasonably exposing others to risks of personal injury, property damage and the like. However, we know that this is not in fact the wrong underlying negligence actions because such actions arise only if and when the defendant's unreasonable risk creation results in interference with a legally protected interest of the claimant, such as a broken limb or a dented rear bumper. Damage is the 'gist' of negligence, 'an essential ingredient not merely of recoverability but of the cause of action itself',[14] so that time starts to run for limitation purposes not from the moment of the defendant's 'breach of duty', but from the moment the claimant suffers damage recognised by law,[15] and disputes about the causation of such damage go to liability not quantum. It follows that '[t]he legal wrong in negligence is the negligent injuring of the plaintiff, not the failure of the defendant to conform his conduct to a standard of reasonable risk taking',[16] and that the 'duty' of care is therefore, as Buckland pointed out, 'a myth, with no corresponding right'.[17]

Further considerations point to the same conclusion. Firstly, a 'duty' of care is normatively unconvincing, since a right not to be exposed to risk is both [562] counter-intuitive (do we really believe that a motorist who careers down Piccadilly at 60 miles an hour[18] has violated the rights of all those he *could have* hit?) and philosophically problematic.[19] Secondly, examples can be given which show that the duty of care cannot be a duty owed to others, at least if we accept the Hohfeldian correlation of such duties with claim rights. Suppose that A, a baby of six months, falls ill after eating a tin of baby food negligently manufactured by B 18 months previously. A has a claim in negligence against B in such a case,[20] but how could B have breached a duty he owed A, and how could A's rights therefore have been violated, before A had even been conceived?[21]

---

[14] *Leigh and Sillivan Ltd v Aliakmon Shipping Co Ltd* [1985] QB 350 (CA) 375 (Oliver LJ). See also *Harriton v Stephens* [2006] HCA 15, 226 CLR 52 [161] (Hayne J); and *Rothwell v Chemical and Insulating Co Ltd* [2007] UKHL 39, [2008] AC 281 [2], [7] (Lord Hoffmann).

[15] See, eg, *Pirelli General Cable Works v Oscar Faber* [1983] 2 AC 1 (HL).

[16] BC Zipursky, 'Foreseeability in Breach, Duty, and Proximate Cause' (2009) 44 *Wake Forest Law Review* 1247, 1272. See also *Leigh and Sillivan* (n 14) 375 (Oliver LJ) (that the duty of care is not a duty to be careful but a duty not to cause damage by carelessness is a 'truism').

[17] Buckland, 'The Duty to Take Care' (n 6) 648.

[18] See Buckland, *Some Reflections on Jurisprudence* (n 6) 114.

[19] For an overview of the philosophical difficulties, see S Perry, 'The Role of Duty of Care in a Rights-Based Theory of Negligence Law' in A Robertson and Tang HW (eds), *The Goals of Private Law* (Oxford, Hart Publishing, 2009) 92–96.

[20] See, eg, *Renslow v Mennonite Hospital* 351 NE 2d 870 (Ill App Ct, 1976), allowing a negligence claim by a child for an injury attributable to a blood transfusion given to the child's mother eight years before the child's conception. See also *X and Y (by her tutor X) v PAL* (1991) 23 NSWLR 26 (NSWCA) 30 (Mahoney JA), 41 (Clarke JA).

[21] Nicholas McBride, who argues that duties of care are really duties, responds to this conundrum by saying that B's duty was owed to 'whoever eats the tin of baby food in the future' (NJ McBride, 'Duties of Care: Do They Really Exist?' (2004) 24 *OJLS* 417, 434), but fails to explain how A's rights

Thirdly, there are cases which indirectly demonstrate that duties of care are not really duties. In *Spartan Steel and Alloys Ltd v Martin & Co (Contractors) Ltd*,[22] for example, the same act of negligence by B caused A both property damage and pure economic loss. Had the wrong in the case been the act of negligence itself, then all the loss A suffered as a result of that act should have been recoverable, but as it was the Court of Appeal allowed A to recover only for the property damage, and not the pure economic loss. Similarly, where the same act of negligence by B has caused A both personal injury and property damage, the rule is that there are two causes of action rather than one, and in the leading case – where the plaintiff was allowed to bring a claim for personal injury despite having previously recovered for damage to his cab arising out of the same negligent conduct – Bowen LJ explained this rule in terms wholly incompatible with the idea of a 'duty' of care:

> Two separate kinds of injury were in fact inflicted, and two wrongs done. The mere negligent driving in itself, if accompanied by no injury to the plaintiff, was not actionable at all, for it was not a wrongful act at all till a wrong arose out of the damage which it caused. One wrong was done as soon as the plaintiff's enjoyment of his property was substantially interfered with. A further wrong arose as soon as the driving also caused injury to the plaintiff's person.[23]

In the light of the overwhelming evidence against the proposition that duties of care are really duties, it is worth asking why common lawyers nevertheless use the misnomer 'duty of care' without batting an eyelid. Two explanations present themselves. The first is that a defendant can only ensure that his actions do not lead to liability in negligence by complying with the standard of care in the first place, since once he has unreasonably exposed others to the risk of injury, whether [563] or not injury then materialises is usually out of his control. It follows that on a practical level the basic message conveyed by the law of negligence is 'do not act negligently in relation to the protected interests of others', as it is only by complying with that basic message that a defendant can avoid the possibility of violating its norms. This gives the idea of a 'duty of care' a certain superficial plausibility, despite its analytical incoherence. And the second explanation is that there may well be a *moral* duty to take care of the vital interests of others[24] – we might well, for example, describe the behaviour of the motorist careering down Piccadilly at twice the speed limit as immoral, regardless of its

---

can have been violated before A was conceived, even though elsewhere he accepts the correlativity of duties owed to others and claim rights (or 'coercive rights'): see NJ McBride, 'Rights and the Basis of Tort Law' in D Nolan and A Robertson (eds), *Rights and Private Law* (Oxford, Hart Publishing, 2012) 352. McBride also fails to reconcile his position with the fact that damage is required to complete the cause of action in negligence.

[22] *Spartan Steel and Alloys Ltd v Martin & Co (Contractors) Ltd* [1973] 1 QB 27 (CA).

[23] *Brunsden v Humphrey* (1884) 14 QBD 141 (CA) 150–51. See also *The Oropesa* [1943] P 32 (CA); and (for commentary) EA Machin, 'Negligence and Interest' (1954) 17 *MLR* 405, 405–407.

[24] See Buckland, *Some Reflections on Jurisprudence* (n 6) 111–12.

consequences – albeit that even a moral duty of this kind is unlikely to be an agent-relative duty owed to those others, since a moral right not to be exposed to risk is almost as implausible as a legal right not to be. Again, however, the possible existence of a moral 'duty of care' lends superficial plausibility to the legal language employed.

Nevertheless, it is confusing and inappropriate to label one element of the negligence cause of action 'duty', and this misnomer has served both to conceal the true nature of the duty of care concept and to encourage the unhelpful tendency to pull more and more issues under the umbrella of notional duty, as WL Morison pointed out in a letter to John Fleming published in the *Sydney Law Review* in 1953:

> I would claim that duty as one element only in the cause of action in negligence must have a quite artificial, non-Hohfeldian sense. If it were used in its scientific sense it would have to embrace all the elements in the cause of action in so far as there were rules of law about them at all, and every defence which could be raised to the action would also have to enter into the statement of the duty. But nobody would contend that all this should come under the duty head in negligence. The law abstracts certain issues for convenience and considers only them under the duty head. What I suspect is happening in some of the decisions is that this is being lost sight of in particular sets of circumstances, and the scope of the duty head is therefore tending to grow.[25]

B. Duty of Care Scepticism Is Not Inconsistent with a Rights-Based Analysis of Negligence Law

The second preliminary point is that it is a fallacy to argue, as some scholars have,[26] that scepticism as to the utility of the duty of care concept entails endorsement of a Holmesian conception of negligence liability as a primary obligation to make recompense for loss caused, as opposed to a secondary obligation arising out of a violation of a primary right of the claimant. After all, the vast majority of commentators who have argued that a duty/right relation underlies negligence law accept that the duties in question are not duties of care but duties not to negligently [564] injure others, which correlate with primary rights in those others not to be negligently injured.[27] And since

---

[25] WL Morison, 'Letter' (1953) 1 *Sydney Law Review* 70–71.

[26] See, eg, JCP Goldberg and BC Zipursky, 'The Moral of *McPherson*' (1998) 146 *University of Pennsylvania Law Review* 1733; JCP Goldberg and BC Zipursky, 'The *Restatement (Third)* and the Place of Duty in Negligence Law' (2001) 54 *Vanderbilt Law Review* 657, 629 ff; Owen, 'Duty Rules' (n 2) 785; McBride, 'Duties of Care' (n 21).

[27] The most developed analysis along these lines is to be found in Perry (n 19). Other proponents of the view that negligence law imposes duties not to negligently injure are Buckland, 'The Duty to Take Care' (n 6) 641; Lawson, 'The Duty of Care: A Comparative Study' (n 12) 112; RWM Dias, 'The Duty Problem in Negligence' [1955] *CLJ* 198, 203–204; EJ Weinrib, 'The Disintegration of Duty'

(as Morison pointed out) such duties not to negligently injure others would by definition have to encompass all the elements of the negligence enquiry, it is difficult to see why scepticism as to the utility of the duty of care concept (which is merely one element of the negligence enquiry) should be thought to entail rejection of a primary duty/right model of negligence liability, any more than scepticism as to the utility of a particular element of the tort of battery would entail rejection of a primary duty/right conception of that tort.

The failure of many proponents of a rights-based conception of negligence to distinguish between the 'duty of care' and the global primary obligations which they believe are imposed by negligence law[28] is a good example of the confusion sown by the duty of care concept, and a reminder of the oddity and incoherence of separating out one element of a cause of action and labelling it 'duty'. Be that as it may, what matters for present purposes is that the argument in this article is certainly not premised on a rejection of a duty/right model of negligence liability. On the contrary, it seems to me that in practice the duty of care concept has served to obscure what Allan Beever terms the 'rights base' of the law of negligence,[29] and has encouraged precisely the kind of open-ended policy reasoning which advocates of a rights-based conception of negligence law so strongly deprecate.[30]

C. The Duty of Care Concept Has a Dual Role in Negligence Law

The third preliminary point is that the duty of care device plays a dual role in the modern law of negligence, in that there are two different duty of care questions: first, whether damage to someone in the claimant's position was a reasonably foreseeable consequence of the defendant's negligence (the factual duty question); and second, whether there is a rule of law that either allows or bars recovery in this category of case (the legal, or 'notional', duty question). (I say 'either allows or bars' because although it is commonly asserted that notional duty is essentially negative or exclusionary,[31] the claim seems to be controversial, and it is not clear what, if anything, turns on it.[32])

---

in MS Madden (ed), *Exploring Tort Law* (New York, CUP, 2005) 149; and R Stevens, 'Rights and Other Things' in Nolan and Robertson (n 21) 118. *cf* McBride, 'Duties of Care' (n 21).

[28] For an example of slippage between the two, see Stevens, 'Rights and Other Things' (n 27) 121.

[29] A Beever, *Rediscovering the Law of Negligence* (Oxford, Hart Publishing, 2007) 210 ff.

[30] For a powerful such critique, see ibid, esp ch 5.

[31] See, eg, *Smith v Littlewoods Organisation Ltd* [1987] AC 241 (HL) 280 (Lord Goff); and A Mullis and K Oliphant, *Torts*, 4th edn (Basingstoke, Palgrave Macmillan, 2011) 17.

[32] It is however fair to say that when explaining to students how the notional duty device operates in practice, the most helpful approach seems to be to point out first that the existence of a duty in law is taken as read in run-of-the-mill cases concerning positive conduct leading to physical damage, and that it is only in more difficult areas like liability for omissions and pure economic loss that the notional duty question comes alive.

[565] More sophisticated discussions of the duty concept emphasise this dual role, even if that duality is not always expressed in terms of factual and notional duty.[33] In his essay on 'The Disintegration of Duty', for example, Ernest Weinrib says that the duty of care concept performs two functions:

> The first function is to establish whether the plaintiff's damaged interest has the status of a right, because it is only to a right that the defendant's duty can be correlative. The second function is to establish whether correlativity obtains in the case at hand, that is, whether the defendant breached a duty correlative to that right by creating an unreasonable risk to persons such as the plaintiff.[34]

Similarly, in his 1952 article on the duty of care in South African law, RG McKerron wrote that:

> To appreciate the true import of the [duty of care] concept it is essential to realize that it serves a twofold purpose. In the first place, it serves to determine whether the plaintiff was within the risk of harm created by the defendant's conduct; in other words, whether the plaintiff was sufficiently within the reasonable contemplation of the defendant for the damage done to the plaintiff to be imputable to the defendant. Secondly, it serves to determine whether the defendant's conduct was not merely careless but also constituted a wrong to the plaintiff; in other words, whether the situation is one in which the plaintiff should be afforded a remedy.[35]

Nevertheless, modern commentaries on the duty concept tend to be characterised by an undue emphasis on one or other of its two roles, with the result that at times the protagonists in debates about duty seem to be arguing at cross-purposes. Scholars advocating an approach to negligence law centred on concerns of interpersonal justice tend to emphasise the factual duty component of the duty of care, which they argue demonstrates that negligence is a 'relational concept', as claimed by Cardozo CJ in the leading American case on the foreseeable claimant issue, *Palsgraf v Long Island Railroad Co*.[36] A good example is the treatment of duty in Beever's corrective-justice based account of the law of negligence, where he analyses it solely in terms of the factual duty issue, altogether ignoring the notional duty question.[37] Conversely, adherents

---

[33] See, eg, FH Lawson, *Negligence in the Civil Law* (Oxford, OUP, 1950) 34 ('two entirely different purposes'); Dias, 'The Duty Problem in Negligence' (n 27); Millner, *Negligence in Modern Law* (n 12) 230; PQR Boberg, *The Law of Delict*, vol 1 (Cape Town, Juta, 1984) 31; *Winfield and Jolowicz* (n 1) para 5-3; MA Jones (ed), *Clerk and Lindsell on Torts*, 20th edn (London, Sweet and Maxwell, 2010) para 8-06; and S Deakin, A Johnston and B Markesinis, *Markesinis and Deakin's Tort Law*, 7th edn (Oxford, OUP, 2013) 104–105.

[34] Weinrib, 'The Disintegration of Duty' (n 27) 156.

[35] RG McKerron, 'The Duty of Care in South African Law' (1952) 69 *South African Law Journal* 189, 190.

[36] *Palsgraf v Long Island Railroad Co* 162 NE 99 (NY 1928).

[37] Beever, *Rediscovering the Law of Negligence* (n 29) ch 4. See also EJ Weinrib, *The Idea of Private Law* (Cambridge, Mass, Harvard UP, 1995) 158, 164–65 (but compare the more balanced analysis in Weinrib's more recent essay on the subject, as reflected in the quotation in the text to n 34); and

of a more instrumentalist or policy-focused conception of negligence tend to emphasise the notional duty element, which they characterise as a 'control device' employed to limit the scope of negligence liability. The *locus classicus* of this approach to duty is Fleming's 1952 article 'Remoteness and Duty: The Control Devices in Liability for [566] Negligence',[38] in which he argued that the basic problem raised by negligence law was limitation of liability, and that the duty concept was 'nothing more or less' than a control device 'fashioned by the courts to achieve that purpose'.[39] This idea of the duty of care as a control mechanism has achieved popularity among judges and commentators,[40] as has Fleming's related claim that decisions on notional duty are wholly or largely determined by policy considerations militating in favour of or against liability,[41] with the result that for some the duty of care enquiry is now little more than 'shorthand for a laundry list of policy factors bearing on whether liability should be permitted or barred in some class of cases'.[42]

Unfortunately, both of these competing orthodoxies have in their own ways hindered rational debate about the practical utility of the duty concept. Adherents of the relational view of duty, with its emphasis on the factual duty question, have wrongly assumed that any attack on the duty concept is by definition an attack on a relational or rights-based conception of negligence law, despite the fact that the relational aspect of the duty question (factual duty) could easily be accommodated within another stage of the negligence enquiry, most obviously alongside remoteness of damage as part of an overarching 'scope of the risk' enquiry. Similarly, the characterisation of duty of care as a policy-driven control device has tended both to conceal the extent to which notional duty questions raise important issues of principle, and to imply that the duty of care stage of the enquiry is somehow uniquely suited to the determination of core questions of policy raised by negligence litigation, and is for that

---

JCP Goldberg and BC Zipursky, 'Seeing Tort Law from the Internal Point of View: Holmes and Hart on Legal Duties' (2006) 75 *Fordham Law Review* 1563, 1582–85.

[38] JG Fleming, 'Remoteness and Duty: The Control Devices in Liability for Negligence' (1953) 31 *Canadian Bar Review* 471.

[39] ibid 474.

[40] See, eg, *Cattanach v Melchior* [2003] HCA 38, 215 CLR 1 [238] (Hayne J); S Todd (ed), *The Law of Torts in New Zealand*, 5th edn (Wellington, Brookers, 2009) 135; *Winfield and Jolowicz* (n 1) para 5-2; Mullis and Oliphant (n 31) 10, 17; and K Barker et al, *The Law of Torts in Australia*, 5th edn (Melbourne, OUP Australia and New Zealand, 2012) 456.

[41] Fleming, 'Remoteness and Duty' (n 38) 485. See, eg, *Cooper v Hobart* [2001] 3 SCR 537 (SCC) 551 (McLachlin CJC and Major J); Millner, *Negligence in Modern Law* (n 12) 26–27, 230; FH Lawson and BS Markesinis, *Tortious Liability for Unintentional Harm in the Common Law and Civil Law*, vol 1 (Cambridge, CUP, 1982) 73 ('once we start talking of duty we really start thinking in terms of policy'); Todd (n 40) 135; Mullis and Oliphant (n 31) 23; and *Markesinis and Deakin's Tort Law* (n 33) 102.

[42] Goldberg and Zipursky, 'The Moral of *McPherson*' (n 26) 1846. For an example of such a list, see J Stapleton, 'Duty of Care Factors: A Selection from the Judicial Menus' in P Cane and J Stapleton (eds), *The Law of Obligations: Essays in Celebration of John Fleming* (Oxford, Clarendon Press, 1998).

reason indispensable.[43] By contrast, highlighting the dual role which the duty of care concept plays in the modern law of negligence paves the way for a rational exploration of its utility.

D. The Duty of Care Question Is Not Analytically Anterior to the Question of Fault

The final preliminary point is that the duty of care question is not analytically anterior to the question of fault. The orthodox assumption that '[d]uty comes *first*',[44] [567] in the sense that it takes 'logical or conceptual priority'[45] in the claimant's prima facie case, is both reflected in, and reinforced by, the labelling of the fault issue as 'breach of duty', even though it of course follows from the fact that the duty of care is not a duty that faulty conduct is not a breach of duty either. Again, this mislabelling of an element of the negligence enquiry obscures important truths. One is that in many instances events that take place after the faulty conduct of the defendant determine whether or not a duty of care is imposed.[46] This is frequently so, for example, in cases concerning secondary victims of nervous shock, where the existence of a duty of care may depend on things like the time gap between a traumatic event caused by the defendant's negligence and the claimant's arrival at the scene,[47] or on whether the claimant was in danger when trying to rescue those injured or imperilled by the defendant's negligent conduct.[48] And another important truth obscured by the 'breach of duty' label is that sometimes the existence of a duty will depend on what precisely the 'breach of duty' is, so that the judge must identify the alleged fault of the defendant before he or she can decide the duty question. Indeed, this is always the case when it comes to duty in fact, since there the question is whether the risk of injury to this particular claimant was one of the risks that made the defendant's conduct negligent,[49] a question which cannot be answered until we

---

[43] According to John Bell, for example, the duty concept 'has value as an organizational concept through which the policy questions about the limits of the extent of the [negligence] tort are discussed': J Bell, *Policy Arguments in Judicial Decisions* (Oxford, Clarendon Press, 1983) 43.

[44] NJ McBride and R Bagshaw, *Tort Law*, 4th edn (Harlow, Pearson Education, 2012) 92 (emphasis in original).

[45] DA Esper and GC Keating, 'Abusing 'Duty'' (2005) 79 *Southern California Law Review* 265, 266. See also Goldberg and Zipursky, 'The Moral of *McPherson*' (n 26) 1828; and Owen, 'Duty Rules' (n 2) 786.

[46] There is a sense in which this is *always* the case, since 'the duty of care itself ... can only be defined by reference to the consequences of breach': *Leigh and Sillivan* (n 14) 375 (Oliver LJ). See text to n 67.

[47] *Alcock v Chief Constable of South Yorkshire Police* [1992] 1 AC 310 (HL); *Hunter v British Coal Corp* [1999] QB 140 (CA).

[48] *White v Chief Constable of South Yorkshire Police* [1999] 2 AC 455 (HL).

[49] Weinrib, 'The Disintegration of Duty' (n 27) 152; M Lunney and K Oliphant, *Tort Law: Text and Materials*, 4th edn (Oxford, OUP, 2010) 128.

know what the allegedly negligent conduct was.[50] It can also be true of duty in law, however. A clear example is the rule that a negligence claim against a public authority will fail if the question of whether or not the decision of the authority under attack was negligent is unsuitable for judicial resolution.[51] Again, although this 'justiciability' rule is commonly regarded as a notional duty limit on the liability of public authorities, the alleged fault of the authority must be identified with some precision before the rule can be applied. Appreciating that duty questions are not analytically anterior to the issue of fault paves the way for a deconstruction of duty in which those questions can if appropriate be reallocated to other stages of the negligence enquiry, including not only the fault stage itself but also the stages which logically follow it, namely damage, causation, remoteness and defences.

III. THE OPERATION OF NOTIONAL DUTY

That task of deconstructing duty cannot be undertaken until we have first had a closer look at the notional duty of care. One of the two defining characteristics of [568] notional duty is that it is a question of law.[52] From this, important consequences flow. At the procedural level, the classification of notional duty as a question of law means that if juries sit in negligence cases, then the duty issue falls to be decided by the judge. In nineteenth-century England, this made duty a vital instrument of judicial control, since 'the more that issues could be framed in terms of the duty situation, the more they were removed from the sphere of jury discretion',[53] and this remains the case in the United States, where civil juries are still going strong.[54] As David Ibbetson has pointed out,[55] the demise of the English civil jury in the early twentieth century opened the way for the general test of duty formulated in *Donoghue v Stevenson*,[56] since the maintenance of judicial control over the incidence of negligence liability no longer required

---

[50] Hence Beever, who defines the duty of care stage of the negligence enquiry in purely factual duty terms, deals with it after the standard of care (or fault) stage: see Beever, *Rediscovering the Law of Negligence* (n 29) esp 73.

[51] See K Oliphant (ed), *The Law of Tort*, 2nd edn (London, LexisNexis Butterworths, 2007) paras 17.10–17.13.

[52] MJ Prichard points out that in the commonplace book compiled by Parke B the heading 'Duty' 'contains the solitary entry that it is a matter of law': MJ Prichard, *Scott v Shepherd (1773) and the Emergence of the Tort of Negligence* (London, Selden Society, 1976) 43.

[53] D Ibbetson, *A Historical Introduction to the Law of Obligations* (Oxford, OUP, 1999) 173. See further D Ibbetson, '"The Law of Business Rome": Foundations of the Anglo-American Tort of Negligence' (1999) 52 CLP 74, 89–92.

[54] 'The most significant identity of limited or no-duty rules and immunity rules is that they are determined by judges and legislatures, not by juries': DB Dobbs, *The Law of Torts* (St Paul, Minn, West Publishing, 2000) 577.

[55] Ibbetson, *A Historical Introduction* (n 53) 188–91.

[56] *Donoghue v Stevenson* [1932] AC 562 (HL) 580 (Lord Atkin).

fragmentation of duty into a multiplicity of highly particularised duty rules. But although Lord Atkin's 'neighbour principle' effectively killed off notional duty as an issue in the paradigm scenario of misfeasance causing physical harm, it retained its practical significance in less straightforward cases involving, for example, liability for omissions and psychiatric injury. And the explanation for the continued vitality of notional duty is the same as the explanation for the rise of duty in the nineteenth century: its classification as a question of law. This characteristic has given notional duty two perceived advantages as a component of the conceptual armoury employed in negligence litigation. The first is that framing an issue as one of notional duty enables the defendant to seek its determination on a strike out application, or as a preliminary issue, and hence to dispose of an unmeritorious claim on the pleadings, without the cost and inconvenience of a full trial. And the second is that notional duty determinations are binding precedents, so that through decisions on duty appellate courts can exercise effective control over the boundaries of negligence liability and provide prospective litigants, trial lawyers and lower court judges with clear guidance as to where those boundaries lie.[57]

The other defining characteristic of notional duty is that notional duty questions are always framed – or at least *should* always be framed – in general, or 'categorical', terms. As an American textbook puts it, 'duty rules are classically categorical and abstract; they cover a class or category of cases'.[58] By definition, then, notional duty decisions 'transcend the particular dispute and concern whether, and if so how far, the law of negligence should operate in a situation of a particular [569] type';[59] they are not 'tickets good only for a single ride'.[60] Crucially, however, as long as an issue arising in a negligence case is capable of being framed in such 'categorical' terms, it is capable of being classified as a duty question, regardless of its substantive content. Hence the failure of attempts to identify the particular substantive function which the concept performs in negligence law. Such attempts typically assert that the duty concept fixes or marks out the boundaries of negligence liability: David Owen argues, for example, that the duty concept 'defines the scope and outer limits of the law of negligence' and provides 'negligence law with borders'.[61] However, since *any* element of *any* cause of action serves to mark out its boundaries, statements of

---

[57] See Mullis and Oliphant (n 31) 13.

[58] Dobbs (n 54) 450. See also JG Fleming, *An Introduction to the Law of Torts* (Oxford, Clarendon Press, 1967) 43–44; J Stapleton, 'Duty of Care: Peripheral Parties and Alternative Opportunities for Deterrence' (1995) 111 *LQR* 301, 303; Owen, 'Abusing Duty' (n 2) 777–78; Esper and Keating (n 45) 268; and *Restatement, Third, Torts: Liability for Physical and Emotional Harm* (2010) § 7, comment a.

[59] *Winfield and Jolowicz* (n 1) para 5-3. See also *Clerk and Lindsell* (n 33) para 8-06; and *Markesinis and Deakin's Tort Law* (n 33) 102.

[60] WJ Cardi and MD Green, 'Duty Wars' (2007) 81 *Southern California Law Review* 671, 732.

[61] Owen, 'Duty Rules' (n 2) 777. See also KM Stanton, *The Modern Law of Tort* (London, Sweet and Maxwell, 1994) 27; and P Cane, *Atiyah's Accidents, Compensation and the Law*, 7th edn (Cambridge, CUP, 2006) 69.

this kind identify nothing distinctive about the substantive content of notional duty, precisely because there is nothing distinctive to identify. In the words of the late Tony Weir, '"[d]uty" is an operator, not a real number'.[62]

Weir drew that brilliant mathematical analogy in a note on *Reeves v Commissioner of Police of the Metropolis*,[63] a case which provides an excellent illustration of the open-endedness of notional duty. *Reeves* concerned the suicide of a man while in police custody, which his widow alleged was the fault of the police for failing to take certain precautions despite knowing that he was a suicide risk. At first instance, the judge held that the police owed the deceased a duty to take reasonable steps to prevent him from committing suicide, and before the House of Lords the police conceded the existence of a duty of care framed in this way (and breach of that duty), but nevertheless argued that they were not liable because (a) the act of suicide was a novus actus interveniens, which broke the chain of causation between their negligence and the deceased's death; and (b) the defence of *volenti* applied. As their Lordships pointed out, however, this made no sense, since if the police owed the deceased a duty to take reasonable care to prevent him from committing suicide, then the mere fact of the suicide could not absolve them from legal responsibility for their failure to take reasonable care. By framing the notional duty issue in the way that he did, the trial judge had subsumed any arguments from legal causation and *volenti* raised by the suicide into the duty question,[64] with the result that if the defendants wished to rely on those arguments, they had no choice but to attack the judge's decision on duty. As it was, the position they adopted was self-contradictory, and they were held liable (albeit that the damages were halved for contributory negligence).

The open-ended quality of the notional duty question, coupled with its perceived procedural advantages and its apparent effectiveness as a mechanism of judicial control, has inevitably meant that over time more and more of the issues raised by negligence litigation have come to be dealt with under its rubric.[65] Traditionally, the core of the notional duty question has been the issue of protected interests: which human interests are given general protection by the law of negligence, which [570] limited protection, and which no protection at all.[66] This issue is accommodated within the duty framework by formulating

---

[62] T Weir, 'Suicide in Custody' [1998] *CLJ* 241, 243.

[63] *Reeves v Commissioner of Police of the Metropolis* [2000] 1 AC 360 (HL). Weir's note was on the decision of the Court of Appeal: [1999] QB 169 (CA).

[64] See the perceptive analysis of Morritt LJ in the Court of Appeal: [1999] QB 169 (CA) 190–91.

[65] See Smith, 'The Mystery of Duty' (n 8) 9–10.

[66] This aspect of notional duty is particularly emphasised by comparative lawyers: see, eg, Lawson and Markesinis, *Tortious Liability for Unintentional Harm* (n 41) 99; C von Bar, *The Common European Law of Torts*, vol 1 (Oxford, OUP, 1998) 303; H Koziol, 'Conclusions' in H Koziol (ed), *Unification of Tort Law: Wrongfulness* (The Hague, Kluwer Law International, 1998) 130; and G Wagner, 'Comparative Tort Law' in M Reimann and R Zimmermann (eds), *The Oxford Handbook of Comparative Law*, revised edn (Oxford, OUP, 2006) 1014 (wrongly implying that this is the sole function of the duty concept). For domestic commentaries stressing the centrality of protected

the duty in terms of the nature of the interest invaded, and so considering the existence of a duty separately in respect of each kind of damage suffered by the claimant.[67] It follows that a finding that the defendant owed the claimant a duty of care in respect of one kind of damage does not entail that there was a duty in respect of a different kind of damage, which explains why in the *Spartan Steel* case the claimant company was unable to recover for its pure economic loss, even though the defendants' negligence also caused it actionable property damage.[68] In addition to this core role of delimiting our protected interests, notional duty has also been the repository of the various immunities or special protective rules recognised by the law of negligence over the years. Most of these immunities have now passed into history,[69] but in earlier times providing a home for them was seen as an important function of the duty concept, and in the few genuine cases of immunity which survive, the rule against liability is still generally expressed in terms of the absence of a duty of care, as in *Mulcahy v Ministry of Defence*, where it was held that soldiers did not owe a duty of care to each other when engaging the enemy in the course of hostilities.[70]

Moving beyond the questions of protected interests and special immunities, we come upon issues which have been dealt with both under the heading of notional duty and also at other stages of the negligence enquiry. A good example is the effect of deliberate intervening conduct of a third party or the claimant himself. The obvious home for this issue is legal causation, since traditionally the doctrine of novus actus interveniens determines whether or not intervening conduct 'breaks the chain of causation' and thereby absolves the defendant from legal responsibility for the claimant's damage. However, while cases of non-deliberate intervening conduct are still dealt with under the legal causation heading,[71] in recent years judges faced with instances of deliberate intervening

interests to notional duty, see, eg, Millner, *Negligence in Modern Law* (n 12) 27; and Lunney and Oliphant (n 49) 123. Note also that included within this 'protected interests' idea is the question of liability for failure to confer a benefit (or 'omissions'), since unlike in cases concerning positive conduct causing physical harm, the interest protected by such liability is not our core security interest in the safety of our persons and property but a weaker interest in the expectation of improvement: see Weinrib, 'The Disintegration of Duty' (n 27) 158.

[67] Lunney and Oliphant (n 49) 122. See also *Sutherland Shire Council v Heyman* (1985) 157 CLR 424 (HCA) 481 (Brennan J); *Caparo Industries plc v Dickman* [1990] 2 AC 605 (HL) 627 (Lord Bridge); *Murphy v Brentwood DC* [1991] 1 AC 398 (HL) 485–86 (Lord Oliver).

[68] *Spartan Steel* (n 22). See also *Informer v Chief Constable* [2012] EWCA Civ 197, [2013] QB 579 (police owed informer duty of care in respect of his physical safety but not in respect of pure economic loss).

[69] Recent casualties have been the immunity of advocates in respect of the conduct of civil proceedings (abolished in *Arthur JS Hall & Co (a firm) v Simons* [2002] 1 AC 615 (HL)) and the similar immunity enjoyed by expert witnesses (abolished in *Jones v Kaney* [2011] UKSC 13, [2011] 2 AC 398). For a list of earlier casualties, see MA Millner, 'Growth and Obsolescence in Negligence' (1973) 26 *CLP* 260, 261.

[70] *Mulcahy v Ministry of Defence* [1996] QB 732 (CA).

[71] See, eg, *McKew v Holland & Hannen & Cubitts (Scotland) Ltd* [1969] 3 All ER 1621 (HL); and *Knightley v Johns* [1982] 1 WLR 349 (CA).

conduct have generally dealt with the issue by asking whether the defendant owed the claimant a duty of care [571] which extended to protection against conduct of this kind.[72] The harbinger of this approach was the speech of Lord Diplock in *Home Office v Dorset Yacht Co Ltd*,[73] where the Home Office was sued for damage done to yachts by borstal inmates escaping from custody, allegedly as the result of negligence on the part of the prison officers guarding them. While Lord Reid described the issue of the inmates' intervening acts as one of 'remoteness of damage' pertaining to the extent to which the act of a third party should be regarded as breaking the chain of causation,[74] Lord Diplock characterised the question before the House of Lords as whether 'any duty of care to prevent the escape of a Borstal trainee from custody' was owed 'by the Home Office to persons whose property would be likely to be damaged by the tortious acts of the Borstal trainee if he escaped',[75] a question he then resolved by a notional duty analysis of great sophistication. In the later case of *Smith v Littlewoods Organisation Ltd*,[76] Lord Goff of Chieveley said more generally that in English law the problem of intervening criminal conduct was 'dealt with by means of the mechanism of the duty of care',[77] and more recent House of Lords authority indicates that the notional duty approach is now the favoured conceptual framework for resolving deliberate intervening conduct cases.[78]

Although deliberate intervening conduct cases provide a particularly clear example of the way in which an issue that could be dealt with by another element of the negligence enquiry can be packaged in terms of notional duty, other examples can be given. In *McLoughlin v O'Brian*,[79] for instance, the House of Lords divided over whether claims brought by secondary victims of psychiatric injury should be dealt with by simply asking whether on the facts psychiatric injury to the particular claimant had been reasonably foreseeable (duty in fact), or whether such cases should be subject to special notional duty restrictions for reasons of legal policy,[80] with a definitive ruling in favour of the

---

[72] This conceptual shift seems to have been triggered by the misperception that following the decision in *Overseas Tankship (UK) v Morts Dock and Engineering Co (The Wagon Mound)* [1961] AC 388 (PC), questions pertaining to remoteness and legal causation could be answered only by reference to foreseeability, with the result that liability for foreseeable deliberate interventions could be averted only by formulating limited duty rules in third party cases: see Howarth, *Textbook on Tort* (n 9) 117.

[73] *Home Office v Dorset Yacht Co Ltd* [1970] AC 1004 (HL).

[74] ibid 1027.

[75] ibid 1057–58.

[76] *Smith v Littlewoods Organisation Ltd* [1987] AC 241 (HL).

[77] ibid 280.

[78] See *Hill v CC of West Yorkshire* [1989] AC 53 (HL); *Reeves* (n 63); and *Mitchell v Glasgow CC* [2009] UKHL 11, [2009] 1 AC 874. A notional duty analysis was also adopted by Hayne J in the leading Australian decision on liability for third party acts, *Modbury Triangle Shopping Centre Pty Ltd v Anzil* [2000] HCA 61, 205 CLR 254.

[79] *McLoughlin v O'Brian* [1983] 1 AC 410 (HL).

[80] See the discussion in D Nolan, '*Alcock v Chief Constable of South Yorkshire Police* (1991)' in C Mitchell and P Mitchell (eds), *Landmark Cases in the Law of Tort* (Oxford, Hart Publishing, 2010) 280–84.

latter approach coming only in the later case of *Alcock v CC of South Yorkshire Police*.[81] And the same phenomenon is observable in the case of defences. A negligence action brought by a claimant who was engaged in criminal activity at the time of the alleged tort may be met by a defence of illegality (or *ex turpi causa*), but the courts have also dismissed such actions on the grounds that the illegal conduct prevented a duty of care from arising in the first place. Hence a duty analysis has been employed in a number of cases barring negligence claims between joint participants in criminal activity,[82] and in [572] *Vellino v CC of Greater Manchester*,[83] where the claimant sued the police officers who had come to arrest him in his second-floor flat for not preventing him from trying to escape by jumping out the window, a majority of the Court of Appeal held that since escaping from custody was a sufficiently serious criminal offence to attract the operation of the *ex turpi causa* principle, the police did not owe an arrested person a duty to take care that he was not injured in an escape attempt. Similarly, a duty analysis has also sometimes been used as an alternative to a defence of *volenti non fit injuria*, on the basis that in cases where that doctrine applies, a claimant cannot reasonably expect that the defendant would be under an obligation to exercise care for his safety.[84]

Indeed, despite the fact that notional duty is an element of the cause of action for negligence, apparently it can even be used to determine the quantum of damages in cases where liability is not in doubt.[85] This rather surprising employment of the duty mechanism is observable in the case law on wrongful conception, where the courts have held that the cost of bringing up a healthy child cannot be recovered in proceedings brought against a medical practitioner whose negligence has resulted in an unwanted pregnancy. In *McFarlane v Tayside Health Board*,[86] Lord Slynn of Hadley said that this rule concerned

---

[81] *Alcock v CC of South Yorkshire Police* [1992] 1 AC 310 (HL).

[82] See, eg, *Ashton v Turner* [1981] QB 137 (QBD); *Smith v Jenkins* (1970) 119 CLR 397 (HCA); *Pitts v Hunt* [1991] 1 QB 24 (CA) 51 (Balcombe LJ); *Gala v Preston* (1991) 172 CLR 243 (HCA) 254 (Mason CJ), 263 (Brennan J); and *Joyce v Tradex Insurance Co Ltd* [2012] EWHC 1324 (QB) [46] (Cooke J). This approach to the illegality issue was also endorsed by Sopinka J in *Hall v Hebert* [1993] 2 SCR 159 (SCC) 191–94 and in the recent decision of the High Court of Australia in *Miller v Miller* [2011] HCA 9, 242 CLR 446, but has not escaped judicial criticism: see *Pitts v Hunt* [1991] 1 QB 24 (CA) 46–47 (Beldam LJ); and *Hall v Hebert* [1993] 2 SCR 159 (SCC) 180–85 (McLachlin J).

[83] *Vellino v CC of Greater Manchester* [2002] 1 WLR 218 (CA).

[84] *Hall* (n 82) 191–93 (Sopinka J). See, eg, *Nettleship v Weston* [1971] 2 QB 691 (CA) 704 (Salmon LJ); *Norwich CC v Harvey* [1989] 1 WLR 828 (CA); and *Geary v JD Wetherspoon plc* [2011] EWHC 1506 (QB). For critical discussion of American authorities which have subsumed the *volenti* doctrine into duty, see Esper and Keating (n 45) 290–312; and JCP Goldberg and BC Zipursky, 'Shielding Duty: How Attending to Assumption of Risk, Attractive Nuisance, and Other "Quaint" Doctrines Can Improve Decision-making in Negligence Cases' (2006) 79 *Southern California Law Review* 329.

[85] *cf Hall* (n 82) 184 (McLachlin J) ('the duty of care approach is an all or nothing approach, and cannot be applied selectively to discrete heads of damages').

[86] *McFarlane v Tayside Health Board* [2000] 2 AC 59 (HL).

'the extent of the duty of care' owed by the doctor, and that a duty of care with regard to 'the prevention of pregnancy' did not necessarily extend to 'avoiding the costs of rearing the child', which he described as 'economic loss'.[87] Similarly, Lord Hope of Craighead described those costs as economic loss which fell outside the scope of the duty of care owed.[88] However, since in *McFarlane* the House of Lords awarded damages for the unwanted pregnancy itself, on the basis that it was a species of personal injury, and since obviously the costs of bringing up the child were a consequence of that personal injury, it is difficult to see in the case of the mother's claim why those costs should be treated as a form of 'pure economic loss'[89] in respect of which a particular duty of care had to be established.[90] For this reason, Lord Clyde rejected the duty analysis of the *McFarlane* rule, saying that the issue in the case was 'not properly one of the existence or non-existence of a duty of care', but rather the [573] extent of the losses recoverable in respect of a recognised right of action,[91] a view echoed by Lord Millett both in *McFarlane*[92] and in the later case of *Rees v Darlington Memorial Hospital NHS Trust*, where he described it as 'impossible' to say that consequential loss fell outside the scope of the duty owed.[93]

IV. DECONSTRUCTING DUTY

We can now turn our attention to the task of deconstructing the duty of care. An obvious starting place is the separation out of duty in fact and duty in law. It seems that the question of whether a person in the claimant's position was foreseeably endangered by the defendant's negligent conduct came to be treated as a duty issue because this classification was a way of limiting the power of civil juries,[94] and the classification probably survived the demise of the civil jury only because it would have been difficult to move it into the remoteness stage

---

[87] ibid 75–76.

[88] ibid 97. See also *Parkinson v St James and Seacroft University Hospital NHS Trust* [2001] EWCA Civ 530, [2002] QB 266 [26], [32] (Brooke LJ); *Rees v Darlington Memorial Hospital NHS Trust* [2003] UKHL 52, [2004] 1 AC 309 [52] (Lord Hope).

[89] As held by Lord Steyn: *McFarlane* (n 86) 79.

[90] In *McFarlane*, unlike in the two later cases of *Parkinson* (n 88) and *Rees* (n 88), the father was also a party to the action, but even though in his case the losses were purely economic, on ordinary principles the defenders owed him a relevant duty of care, since in the circumstances there was clearly a relevant assumption of responsibility towards him.

[91] *McFarlane* (n 86) 102.

[92] *McFarlane* (n 86) 107–108.

[93] *Rees* (n 88) [108]. See also *Parkinson* (n 88) [90] (Hale LJ); and *Cattanach* (n 40) [59] (McHugh and Gummow JJ), [188]–[194] (Hayne J).

[94] Ibbetson, *A Historical Introduction* (n 53) 176–77; GE White, *Tort Law in America: An Intellectual History*, expanded edn (New York, OUP, 2003) 184.

of the negligence enquiry at a time when the test of remoteness was directness rather than foreseeability.[95] Following the decision in *The Wagon Mound*,[96] however, the remoteness or 'scope of liability' stage is the most obvious home for the foreseeable claimant question, where it would form one part of the larger question of whether the damage that occurred represented the materialisation of one of the risks that made the defendant's conduct negligent.[97] Far from being an original suggestion, the reclassification of factual duty along these lines is pretty much academic orthodoxy. The issue is generally dealt with in the chapter on proximate cause in American tort textbooks, for example,[98] and a broad range of tort scholars have expressly endorsed the categorisation of factual duty as a question of remoteness or proximate cause,[99] while others have accepted that the two concepts perform the same function within the negligence enquiry and are 'frequently interchangeable',[100] or agreed that the foreseeable claimant issue is not a question of duty, but classified it as going to breach rather than remoteness, thereby introducing a relational aspect into the fault question.[101]

To a certain extent the deconstruction of notional duty is also straightforward. As we have seen, there are a number of issues which have sometimes been treated [574] as going to notional duty and sometimes been dealt with at other stages of the negligence enquiry. Here, deconstructing duty simply requires allocating the issue to that alternative heading, so that deliberate intervening conduct goes to legal causation, secondary victim 'nervous shock' claims are dealt with under factual duty/remoteness, illegality and *volenti* are analysed as defences, and so on. Furthermore, there are also notional duty issues which could be dealt with under the fault heading. One example is the 'justiciability' rule mentioned earlier,[102] since a holding that the conduct of a public authority is not justiciable is a holding that as a matter of law the claimant cannot establish that that conduct was negligent. And another is the argument sometimes

---

[95] *Re Polemis and Furness, Withy & Co Ltd* [1921] 3 KB 560 (CA). The difficulties this decision posed for eradication of the duty of care are adverted to by Buckland, 'The Duty to Take Care' (n 6) 644.

[96] *The Wagon Mound* (n 72).

[97] As Weinrib puts it, the concepts of duty in fact and proximate cause (remoteness) follow through on the idea of unreasonable risk creation underlying negligence law by addressing, respectively, 'the questions of risk to whom and risk of what': Weinrib, *The Idea of Private Law* (n 37) 158.

[98] See, eg, WP Keeton et al, *Prosser and Keeton on Torts*, 5th edn (St Paul, Minn, West Publishing, 1984) 284–90; Dobbs (n 54) 455, 585.

[99] See, eg, Buckland, 'The Duty to Take Care' (n 6) 643–44; Lawson, *Negligence in the Civil Law* (n 33) 34; Price (n 6) 185–86; Fleming, 'Duty and Remoteness' (n 38) 496; Smith (n 8) 14–15, 24; Howarth, *Textbook on Tort* (n 9) 116; *Winfield and Jolowicz* (n 1) para 5-23; *Markesinis and Deakin's Tort Law* (n 33) 104.

[100] Weinrib, *The Idea of Private Law* (n 37) 158–59.

[101] RWM Dias, 'The Breach Problem and the Duty of Care' (1956) 30 *Tulane Law Review* 376, 379; JCP Goldberg and BC Zipursky, *The Oxford Introductions to US Law: Torts* (New York, OUP, 2010) 100–101.

[102] Text to n 51.

made against recognition of a duty of care that in the circumstances it would be impossible to set a standard of care.[103]

That leaves only the core questions of notional duty, namely the issue of protected interests and the existence of certain special immunities which are generally justified on grounds of public policy. It will be helpful to deal with the latter first, since they are less problematic. The key to the reclassification of these immunity rules is that it is up to the defendant to establish that the case for such a rule is made out. Hence where a general multi-stage test for the existence of a duty of care is employed, as in the two-stage *Anns* test[104] and the three-stage *Caparo* test,[105] these rules are generally considered to belong to the final stage, which Andrew Robertson has convincingly argued is best understood as the repository of community welfare arguments which may negative a prima facie duty of care arising solely out of considerations of interpersonal justice.[106] And since, as Robertson points out,[107] the burden of proof at this stage is firmly on the defendant, such rules are best understood as defences to negligence liability which at the moment are wrongly classified as going to the existence of an element of the cause of action.[108] Furthermore, it is clearly appropriate that the burden of proof should lie on the defendant here, since an immunity of this kind operates in derogation of general negligence principles, and the onus of establishing that such an exceptional rule is justified ought surely to rest on the person claiming its protection.[109] As part of the process of deconstructing duty these immunities should therefore be recognised as defences, which the defendant must establish in the usual way.[110] Examples of such defences would be the combat immunity mentioned earlier,[111] and the rule that where a public authority acts pursuant to a statutory duty or power designed for the benefit of a particular class of persons, it cannot [575] be liable in negligence to others whose interests are adversely affected by that action.[112]

Finally, then, we are left with the question of protected interests, the heartland of notional duty, and the greatest challenge to the process of deconstructing the concept. The first important step here is to separate out negligence cases

---

[103] This argument is sometimes used to justify barring recovery in cases where the two parties were engaged in a joint illegal enterprise at the time of the alleged tort: see, eg, *Jackson v Harrison* (1978) 138 CLR 438 (HCA) 455–56 (Mason J), 457–58 (Jacobs J); *Pitts v Hunt* (n 82) 50 (Balcombe LJ).

[104] *Anns v Merton London Borough* [1978] AC 728 (HL) 751–52 (Lord Wilberforce).

[105] *Caparo Industries plc v Dickman* [1990] 2 AC 605 (HL) 617–18 (Lord Bridge).

[106] A Robertson, 'Rights, Pluralism and the Duty of Care' in Nolan and Robertson (n 21) 446. See also *Cooper v Hobart* (n 41) 551 (McLachlin CJC and Major J).

[107] Robertson, 'Rights, Pluralism and the Duty of Care' (n 106) 447. See also Ibbetson, *A Historical Introduction* (n 53) 194.

[108] In the United States, some courts have treated special immunity rules as affirmative defences in this way: see, eg, *Conques v Hardy* 337 So 2d 627 (LA Ct App 1976) (judicial immunity).

[109] See *Hall* (n 82) 184 (McLachlin J) (discussing the burden of proof in illegality cases).

[110] See also RHS Tur, 'Defeasibilism' (2001) 21 *OJLS* 355, 365 (recommending such a relocation).

[111] Text to n 70.

[112] *Jain v Trent SHA* [2009] UKHL 4, [2009] 1 AC 853 [28] (Lord Scott).

concerning core rights held against the whole world, and those concerning acquired rights held only against particular individuals. The law of negligence has occasionally lost sight of this historically important distinction between what Hohfeld termed 'paucital' and 'multitial' rights,[113] but it has been given renewed emphasis by the revival of the assumption of responsibility concept in the fifty years since *Hedley Byrne & Co Ltd v Heller & Partners Ltd.*[114] Because a relevant contract, fiduciary relationship or assumption of responsibility may enlarge the range of interests protected against negligent interference to encompass (for example) pure economic loss[115] and the interest in having one's default position improved which lies behind actions for negligent omissions,[116] analysis of the protected interests issue in negligence law would be more focused were a clearer line to be drawn between core and acquired rights as part of the process of deconstructing notional duty. Indeed, the separation of the two types of case might have even more profound consequences for the conceptual structure of negligence law, since I suggest below that even if the duty of care concept were disposed of in cases involving core rights there would be a strong argument for retaining it in acquired rights cases, which would in effect entail a partial deconstruction of negligence law itself.

While the separation out of cases involving a relevant assumption of responsibility would help to clarify the protected interests issue in core rights cases, the question remains of where that issue would be dealt with in a negligence framework without the duty of care. One possibility would be to develop a new element of the cause of action focused entirely on this question of 'wrongfulness', analogous to the list of protected interests in paragraph 823(1) of the German Civil Code. However, since a new concept along these lines might cause confusion, it is suggested that a better solution would be to accommodate the issue within the damage element of the negligence enquiry. Damage is the least analysed element of the cause of action for negligence,[117] but its potential significance should not be underestimated. Properly understood, damage is a term of legal art which connotes the violation of a right rather than 'loss',[118] and hence its role in the negligence enquiry could if necessary be expanded to encompass the protected interests question, so that for example in the absence of an acquired right pure economic loss would not be recognised as a form of damage for the purposes of negligence liability. It is noteworthy in this regard that the protected interests question is dealt with under the heading of damage in the

---

[113] WN Hohfeld, 'Fundamental Legal Conceptions as Applied in Judicial Reasoning' (1917) 26 *Yale Law Journal* 710, 716.

[114] *Hedley Byrne & Co Ltd v Heller & Partners Ltd* [1964] AC 465 (HL).

[115] See, eg, *Henderson v Merrett Syndicates Ltd* [1995] 2 AC 145 (HL).

[116] See, eg, *Barrett v Ministry of Defence* [1995] 1 WLR 1217 (CA).

[117] See generally D Nolan, 'New Forms of Damage in Negligence' (2007) 70 *MLR* 59.

[118] See further R Stevens, *Torts and Rights* (Oxford, OUP, 2007) 116–21; and D Nolan, 'Damage in the English Law of Negligence' (2013) 4 *Journal of European Tort Law* 259.

two sets of common European principles of tort law, neither of which features the duty of care concept. According to [576] article 2:101 of the *Principles of European Tort Law*,[119] for example, '[d]amage requires material or immaterial harm to a legally protected interest', while the 'basic rule' of delictual liability in art 1:101(1) of the *Principles of European Law on Non-Contractual Liability Arising Out of Damage Caused to Another*[120] is centred around a concept of 'legally relevant damage' which draws upon the Italian idea of *danno ingiusto*, or infringement of a legally protected interest.[121]

V. WHY DECONSTRUCT DUTY?

Although I hope to have shown in the previous section that common law systems could dispense with the duty of care concept (at least in negligence cases which do not depend on a prior relationship between the parties), there remains the question of why we would be better off without it. After all, does it really matter how we choose to package up the substantive issues which arise in negligence litigation? Were the judges in *Vellino v CC of Greater Manchester* not right to agree that it was immaterial whether, when the *ex turpi causa* maxim applied, the correct analysis was that no duty of care was owed or that the maxim afforded a freestanding reason for holding that the action failed?[122] Similarly, was Lord Steyn not justified in saying in *Rees v Darlington Memorial Hospital NHS Trust* that, provided the different concepts yield the same results, 'the difference in method is not of great importance'?[123] The short answer is no. For a start, the classification question may have concrete consequences. Whether *ex turpi causa* is a defence or goes to the existence of a duty of care will determine where the burden of proof lies, for example, and a duty analysis will lead to procedural complications where a claim is brought in both tort and contract, since in contract the doctrine is clearly a defence.[124] Similarly, in the wrongful conception cases the chosen mode of analysis will determine whether it is up to the claimant to establish that a duty of care was owed in respect of pure economic loss, or up to the defendant to show that a head of damages should be excluded for an

---

[119] European Group on Tort Law, *Principles of European Tort Law* (Vienna, Springer, 2005).

[120] C von Bar, *Principles of European Law on Non-Contractual Liability Arising Out of Damage Caused to Another* (Oxford, OUP, 2009).

[121] ibid art 2:101, note 1. See further on *danno ingiusto*, von Bar, *The Common European Law of Torts* (n 66) para 20.

[122] *Vellino* (n 83) [62] (Sir Murray Stuart-Smith).

[123] *Rees* (n 88) [30]. See also [85] (Lord Hutton) ('a point in the area of conceptualist thinking'). By contrast, Lord Millett ([108]) felt that the classification of the issue was important.

[124] *Hall* (n 82) 185 (McLachlin J). For a full list of the consequences that might attend classification of a rule as a defence as opposed to an element of a tort, see J Goudkamp, 'A Taxonomy of Tort Law Defences' in S Degeling et al (eds), *Torts in Commercial Law* (Sydney, Thomson Reuters Australia, 2012) 494–500.

admitted wrong. More generally, however, the answer to this conceptual scepticism lies in Fleming's observation that the respective suitability of the differing concepts employed in negligence cases 'can be assessed only by reference to the degree to which they impair or assist forthright adversion to the real issue before the court'.[125] With this observation in mind, I put forward in this section of the article a number of reasons why deconstructing duty would improve the quality of reasoning in negligence cases, and indeed our understanding of negligence law more generally. The arguments [577] being made essentially concern judicial methodology, but are no less important for that.

A. Deconstructing Duty Would Produce a More Structured and Focused Enquiry on Any Matters of Law Arising

The first argument for deconstructing duty is that separating out the wide variety of different issues currently dealt with under the duty umbrella would give more shape and structure to negligence law, and so better enable the courts to address the central questions of law arising on the facts of a case. Framing disparate issues in the language of duty means that different problems get muddled.[126] If, for example, a policy objection is put forward against liability in a certain type of case, then asking whether the objection should be recognised as a defence to a cause of action that would otherwise arise on ordinary negligence principles requires the court to decide whether the argument is sufficiently powerful to outweigh the considerations of interpersonal justice which would ordinarily ground negligence liability in that scenario.[127] By contrast, mixing the objection in with those other concerns under the rubric of the duty head produces a 'melange of justice and policy considerations'[128] which may cause a court to lose sight of the essential nature of the decision it faces. Doctrinal clarity, in other words, 'focuses attention on what is at stake'.[129]

Suppose for instance that a case involves deliberate intervening conduct of a third party and that policy objections are also raised against liability. In such a case, it surely makes sense to deal with the third-party issue first, and then, if it is concluded that the third party's intervention does not bar the claim, to proceed to ask whether the policy arguments outweigh the prima facie case for liability. At the moment, however, the fact that the two issues are dealt with under the overarching rubric of notional duty means that they may not be properly separated out.[130] Similarly, if a case involves both an omission and the deliberate

---

[125] Fleming, 'Remoteness and Duty' (n 38) 498.
[126] Smith, 'The Mystery of Duty' (n 8) 9. See similarly J Stapleton, 'Reflections on Common Sense Causation in Australia' in Degeling et al (n 124) 337.
[127] See also Tur (n 110) 365.
[128] Weinrib, 'The Disintegration of Duty' (n 27) 166.
[129] RL Rabin, 'The Duty Concept in Negligence Law' (2001) 54 *Vanderbilt Law Review* 787, 792.
[130] See, eg, *Mitchell* (n 78) [28]–[29] (Lord Hope).

intervening conduct of a third party, it is more likely that those two distinct issues will be addressed directly if they are dealt with at different stages of the negligence enquiry than if they are classified under the duty head and then dealt with jointly by reference to a formless concept of 'proximity', while the use of the open-ended notional duty concept may also obscure the circumstances in which an assumption of responsibility is a prerequisite of negligence liability.

Furthermore, the deconstruction of notional duty would make it easier for the courts to identify the most pertinent earlier decisions, and so produce better analogical reasoning on what are by definition questions of law. The difficulty at the moment is that so many different matters are subsumed under the heading of notional duty that it can be difficult for a court to work out which authorities bear most heavily on the legal issues arising on the facts. [578]

B. Deconstructing Duty Would Mean That Similar Issues Could Be Dealt with Alongside Each Other

Deconstructing duty would also allow similar issues which currently arise at different stages of the negligence enquiry to be dealt with alongside each other, thereby promoting consistency and facilitating the drawing of appropriate analogies.[131] Three examples can be given. Firstly, separating out the factual duty and notional duty questions would enable the former issue to be considered alongside the analogous questions (arising at the remoteness stage) of whether the type of damage suffered and the manner of its infliction were foreseeable consequences of the defendant's negligence, as connected components of an overarching 'scope of the risk' enquiry. Secondly, if it were to be recognised that the recoverability of the cost of bringing up a child arising out of an unwanted pregnancy went to damages rather than duty, this might enable illuminating comparisons to be made with other types of case in which a particular head of damages has been excluded for policy reasons, for example those involving claims for compensation in respect of a sentence imposed for a criminal act.[132] The final example concerns the question of deliberate intervening conduct. The relevance of such intervening conduct may go either to liability, as in *Smith v Littlewoods Organisation Ltd*,[133] or to the quantum of damages, as in *Lamb v Camden LBC*,[134] where the foundations of the claimant's house were undermined following an escape of water for which the defendants were responsible,

---

[131] In some instances, such as illegality and *volenti*, taking an issue out of duty may also help to achieve consistency with the position elsewhere in the law of tort, where the duty of care is not an available concept.

[132] *Clunis v Camden and Islington HA* [1998] QB 978 (CA); *Gray v Thames Trains Ltd* [2009] UKHL 33, [2009] 1 AC 1339.

[133] *Smith v Littlewoods Organisation Ltd* [1987] AC 241 (HL).

[134] *Lamb v Camden LBC* [1981] QB 625 (CA).

and the question was whether in addition to recovering for that damage she could also recover for the additional damage done by squatters who invaded the house when it was left unoccupied pending repair. As we have seen,[135] in cases of the former kind, the intervening conduct question is commonly packaged as a matter of duty, but this is difficult to do in a case such as *Lamb*, where liability is not disputed, with the result that precisely the same issue tends to be dealt with there as a matter of legal causation (or, less satisfactorily, remoteness). By contrast, deconstructing duty would ensure that the same questions were always dealt with under the same heading.

C. Deconstructing Duty Would Make it Less Likely that Important Issues are Missed or Under-Analysed

One of the consequences of the potential breadth of the notional duty enquiry is that it may result in a court missing an important issue raised by the facts of a case. In particular, the fact that both policy objections to liability and the issue of protected interests are dealt with under notional duty means that sometimes courts decide cases on policy grounds without even noticing that in the circumstances no duty of care would ordinarily arise in respect of the kind of damage suffered. As a result, time and energy is wasted on the assessment of often highly contested [579] policy arguments when a more straightforward route to the resolution of the case is available. In *Jain v Trent SHA*,[136] for example, the House of Lords held that a regulatory authority exercising its statutory power to apply for an order cancelling the registration of a nursing home owed no duty of care to the home's owners, because (inter alia) such a duty might damage the interests of the nursing home residents the power was designed to protect. Surprisingly, however, at no point did the House advert to the fact that the nursing home owners had suffered only pure economic loss in circumstances in which it would be difficult to establish any assumption of responsibility towards them by the defendant authority.

Furthermore, using an overarching notional duty concept to soak up so many of the issues of law raised by negligence litigation inevitably tends to mean that other important questions are under-analysed. An obvious example is the concept of damage, which is rarely considered as a separate issue in textbook treatments of negligence, and which courts sometimes overlook in their eagerness to address other issues pleaded under duty.[137] Deconstructing duty

---

[135] Text following n 70.

[136] *Jain v Trent SHA* [2009] UKHL 4, [2009] 1 AC 853.

[137] See, eg, *Cowan v CC of Avon and Somerset Constabulary* [2001] EWCA Civ 1699, [2002] HLR 44, where the Court of Appeal held that the police did not owe a duty of care to a tenant unlawfully evicted in their presence, but failed to advert to the fact that the claimant appeared to have suffered no actionable damage.

would pave the way for fuller consideration of the important question of what does and does not amount to damage for the purposes of a negligence action, with the result that for example books on tort law might at least attempt to provide answers to questions such as whether the irretrievable loss of property constitutes damage for negligence purposes.[138]

D. Deconstructing Duty Would Avoid the Unhelpful Confusion of Issues of Law and Fact

A further unfortunate consequence of the duty of care mechanism is the well-known phenomenon of factual questions of fault being subsumed into the duty analysis by an over-specific formulation of the duty question. An example of this phenomenon is the statement in a leading textbook that 'the courts will not find that A owed B a duty of care not to do *x* if it was reasonable for A to act in that way', from which it is concluded that the reasonableness of the defendant's conduct is a factor to be taken into account in the duty of care enquiry.[139] Similarly, in *Orange v CC of West Yorkshire Police*,[140] the Court of Appeal held that the obligation on the police to take reasonable care to prevent a prisoner in their custody from committing suicide only arose where they knew or ought to have known that the prisoner presented a suicide risk, and that since on the facts the police had been justified in concluding that the deceased did not present such a risk, they had not owed him a duty of care to prevent him from taking his own life. If we ask why the police were not liable in this case, the answer is that they were not at fault, so this is a decision on 'breach' dressed up as one on duty.[141]

[580] We have seen that the two defining characteristics of notional duty are that it is a question of law, and that rulings on notional duty apply not only to the facts of the case in hand, but to a category of cases of which the case in hand is but an example. By contrast, fault is a question of fact, so that a decision on whether or not a particular defendant has been negligent has no precedential force,[142] and is subject to different principles of appellate review than a decision on a question of law.[143] It follows that the fault issue cannot legitimately be subsumed into notional duty, and the confusion of issues of fault and notional

---

[138] As to which, see R Bagshaw, 'The Edges of Tort Law's Rights' in Nolan and Robertson (n 21) 425–26.

[139] McBride and Bagshaw (n 44) 108.

[140] *Orange v CC of West Yorkshire Police* [2001] EWCA Civ 611, [2002] QB 347.

[141] For other examples of the conflation of duty and breach, see *AG of the British Virgin Islands v Hartwell* [2004] UKPC 12, [2004] 1 WLR 1273 [25] (Lord Nicholls); and *Bhamra v Dubb (t/a Lucky Caterers)* [2010] EWCA Civ 13 [19], [25] (Moore-Bick LJ).

[142] *Qualcast (Wolverhampton) Ltd v Haynes* [1959] AC 743 (HL).

[143] *Neindorf v Junkovic* [2005] HCA 75, 222 ALR 631 [54] (Kirby J).

duty has rightly been condemned as an error.[144] Within the existing negligence framework, the error can of course be avoided by formulating duties of care at an appropriately general level, so that we speak, for example, of a motorist's duty to take reasonable care for the safety of other road users, and not of a duty of care 'to keep a proper lookout or sound a warning or to keep a safe distance away from the car in front'.[145] Nevertheless, it is the inherent ambiguity of the duty concept which produces this error, and only the deconstruction of that concept can ensure its elimination.

Another similar error is to characterise factual issues of remoteness in duty terms. On a global level, this can be done by the unhelpful and pointless reformulation of the remoteness issue as whether or not a particular consequence of the defendant's negligence fell within the scope of the duty of care owed, manipulation of the so-called 'scope of the duty' being one of the favoured techniques for subsuming inappropriate issues into the notional duty enquiry.[146] This approach to the remoteness question is particularly associated with the speech of Lord Hoffmann in *South Australia Asset Management Corp v York Montague Ltd*,[147] albeit that he later disavowed it extra-judicially.[148] Since here the 'scope of the duty' idea amounts to little more than a relabelling of the remoteness issue, it is less objectionable than another way of reformulating the remoteness question, which is to ask whether the defendant owed the claimant a duty of care in respect of a particular risk (or consequence). An example of this latter reformulation is found in Lord Nicholls' opinion in *AG of the British Virgin Islands v Hartwell*,[149] where he described remoteness cases such as *Doughty v Turner*[150] and *Jolley v Sutton LBC*[151] as turning on whether a duty of care had been owed in respect of the particular risk that had materialised in the claimant's injury.[152] As with the [581] conflation of fault

---

[144] See, eg, *Modbury* (n 78) [109] (Hayne J); *Neindorf* (n 143) [50]–[55] (Kirby J); and Howarth, 'Negligence after *Murphy*' (n 9) 72–79. The error is also common in the United States, where the result is the judge's usurpation of the jury's prerogative of determining the reasonableness of the defendant's conduct: see further Esper and Keating (n 45); and Goldberg and Zipursky, 'The *Restatement (Third)* and the Place of Duty in Negligence Law' (n 26) 712–17.

[145] See *Vairy v Wyong SC* [2005] HCA 62, 223 CLR 422 [26] (McHugh J) (advocating the more general formulation).

[146] See, eg, the way in which this terminology has been used to turn the quantum of damages for an admitted wrong into a duty issue in the wrongful conception cases (text following n 85); and see also *Calvert v William Hill Credit Ltd* [2008] EWCA Civ 1427, [2009] Ch 330 [46]–[47] (Sir Anthony May P) where a straightforward question of factual causation was complicated by references to the 'scope of the duty'. For criticism of the use of phrases such as 'the scope and content of the duty' to convert questions of fact into questions of law, see *Vairy* (n 145) [29] (McHugh J).

[147] *South Australia Asset Management Corp v York Montague Ltd* [1997] AC 191 (HL).

[148] Lord Hoffmann, 'Causation' (2005) 121 LQR 592, 596.

[149] *AG of the British Virgin Islands v Hartwell* [2004] UKPC 12, [2004] 1 WLR 1273.

[150] *Doughty v Turner* [1964] 1 QB 518 (CA).

[151] *Jolley v Sutton LBC* [2000] 1 WLR 1082 (HL).

[152] *Hartwell* (n 149) [28]–[29].

and duty, allowing duty to swallow up remoteness in this way turns an issue of fact into one of law, an error once again attributable to the ambiguity of the duty concept.

Finally, the conflation of factual duty and notional duty into one overarching duty enquiry can itself bring about the confusion of issues of fact and law, since there is a risk that the legal question of notional duty will be skewed by the foreseeability of the risk to the claimant, even though the two concepts perform completely different functions within the negligence analysis. This danger was particularly acute when the two-stage *Anns* test[153] was used to determine the duty issue, since on one view of that test a prima facie notional duty of care arose out of the foreseeability of injury alone, but even following the separation out of (factual) foreseeability and (legal) proximity under the tripartite *Caparo* test[154] the risk of confusion remains, since judges frequently say that the three components of this test are not entirely separate but infuse each other.[155]

E. The Malleability of the Duty Question Causes Confusion and Incoherence

One of the difficulties with the duty of care concept is that duty questions can be framed at very different levels of generality. This is because the only limit on the formulation of a duty question is that it must encompass a category of cases, and there is nothing to say how broadly or narrowly that category is drawn.[156] To give a flavour of the malleability of the duty enquiry, consider the following formulations of the notional duty question, all taken from English cases decided since 1995:

- Do those responsible for issuing a company's prospectus owe a duty of care to persons who rely upon it by subsequently buying shares of that company in the market?[157]

---

[153] *Anns* (n 104) 751–52 (Lord Wilberforce).

[154] *Caparo* (n 105) 618 (Lord Bridge).

[155] See, eg, *Caparo* (n 105) 633 (Lord Oliver); *Selwood v Durham CC* [2012] EWCA Civ 979 [53] (Smith LJ).

[156] An extreme example of a narrow category is the following (humorous) characterisation of the rule of law established by the *Palsgraf* case (n 36):

> [A] railroad does not owe to an intending passenger the duty to refrain from permitting its guards to push upon a moving train another passenger carrying a package which, though innocent in appearance, contains fireworks, and which, if joggled from the boarding passenger's arm, will fall to the tracks, explode, shake the platform, knock down the scales, and thus injure the intending passenger.

(TA Cowan, 'The Riddle of the *Palsgraf* Case' (1938) 23 *Minnesota Law Review* 46, 56).

[157] *Possfund Custodian Trustee Ltd v Diamond* [1996] 1 WLR 1351 (Ch D).

- Does the fire brigade owe a duty of care to an owner of property if they respond to an emergency call about a fire at the property, arrive at the scene and start to fight the fire?[158]
- Does a health and safety inspector owe a duty of care to a business in respect of economic loss caused by a notice issued on his advice under the Health and Safety at Work Act 1974?[159]
- Does an insurance company which advises a customer on insurance provision for pension and life cover owe a duty of care to dependants of the customer whose interests are fundamental to the transaction [582] in question not to give the customer negligent advice which will adversely affect their interests as the customer intended them to be?[160]
- Do the professionals involved in compiling reports for adoption agencies on children up for adoption owe a duty of care to prospective adopters?[161]
- Did the British Geological Survey owe a duty of care to the population of Bangladesh not to publish a report which implied by its silence that it believed that the presence of arsenic in the water in that country was so unlikely that it was not necessary to test for it?[162]

The extraordinary malleability of the duty question as revealed by these examples is a disadvantage of the duty concept for three reasons: (1) because it makes it difficult to summarise the law in a given field of negligence with any precision; (2) because it creates a danger that a court will overlook an earlier duty decision which has either resolved or is at least closely analogous to the central question of law raised by the facts of the case; and (3) because the tendency revealed by at least some of these examples to formulate the duty question in an overly specific manner threatens to return negligence law to the 'wilderness of single instances'[163] which characterised the field before the great generalising decision in *Donoghue v Stevenson*.[164] The result is inevitably confusion and uncertainty, and occasionally incoherence. Indeed, one could go further, and argue that the malleability of the duty enquiry raises the spectre – perhaps already a reality in some Commonwealth jurisdictions – of a departure from the rule of law itself, with the ad hoc nature of duty adjudication meaning that

---

[158] *Capital and Counties plc v Hampshire CC* [1997] QB 1004 (CA).

[159] *Harris v Evans* [1998] 1 WLR 1285 (CA).

[160] *Gorham v British Telecommunications plc* [2000] 1 WLR 2129 (CA).

[161] *A v Essex CC* [2003] EWCA Civ 1848, [2004] 1 FLR 749.

[162] *Sutradhar v National Environment Research Council* [2006] UKHL 33, [2006] 4 All ER 490.

[163] 'The Duty of Care Towards One's Neighbour' (1883) 18 *Law Journal* 618, 619 (after Alfred, Lord Tennyson, *Aylmer's Field* (1863)).

[164] *Donoghue v Stevenson* [1932] AC 562 (HL). For a powerful critique of this tendency, see *Harriton* (n 14) [69]–[70] (Kirby J).

negligence law ceases to 'give definite guidance to actors before the fact or to judges after the fact'.[165]

F. The Search for a General Test of Duty Obscures and Confuses

A final disadvantage of treating the duty of care as an element of the cause of action for negligence is that it fosters the belief that it is possible to come up with a meaningful general test for duty, even though the open-endedness of notional duty is such that any general formula will inevitably be so abstract as to be devoid of practical utility. This 'futile quest'[166] for a 'will-o'-the-wisp'[167] soaks up time and energy which would be better employed in considering the substantive questions which fall under the duty heading, while the use of the general tests which have been put forward frequently masks a failure to address those questions in a meaningful way. As a result, the standard of judicial reasoning in some duty cases is now so low that parts of the judgments are little more than gobbledygook.

[583] Hence we find judges (a) applying an 'incremental' test for the existence of duty (and commentators attacking them for doing so),[168] when 'incrementalism' is nothing more than the analogical reasoning employed in a common law system to decide *any* novel question of law;[169] (b) describing the process of deciding a duty question as involving 'an evaluative judgment which includes normative considerations as to the appropriateness of the imputation of legal responsibility and the extent thereof'[170] (what else could it possibly involve?); (c) asking whether it is 'fair, just and reasonable' to impose negligence liability,[171] as if the blatant tautology will somehow obscure the emptiness of the formula; (d) treating 'assumption of responsibility' as a possible *general* test of duty, even though, for example, road users clearly owe each other duties of care despite having had no previous dealings whatsoever; and (e) arguing that in novel cases each of the various different tests for the existence of a duty of care is best regarded as a check on the conclusion provisionally reached upon

---

[165] PJ Kelley, 'Restating Duty, Breach, and Proximate Cause in Negligence Law: Descriptive Theory and the Rule of Law' (2001) 54 *Vanderbilt Law Review* 1039, 1052.

[166] Fleming, 'Remoteness and Duty' (n 38) 495.

[167] *Caparo* (n 105) 633 (Lord Oliver).

[168] See generally KM Stanton, 'Incremental Approaches to the Duty of Care' in NJ Mullany (ed), *Torts in the Nineties* (Sydney, LBC Information Services, 1997).

[169] Hence, for example, in determining whether an enrichment is 'unjust' for the purposes of the law of restitution, it must be shown that the case falls 'within or close to some established category or factual recovery situation' (*Uren v First National Home Finance Ltd* [2005] EWHC 2529 (Ch) [18] (Mann J)).

[170] *Caltex Refineries (Qld) Pty Ltd v Stavar* [2009] NSWCA 258, 75 NSWLR 649 [106] (Allsop P).

[171] *Caparo* (n 105) 618 (Lord Bridge).

the application of the others, so that a test can 'safely be taken to be reliable' only when it 'has been verified as correctly conducted by a finding that it leads to the same conclusion' as the others.[172] The fact that an authoritative textbook can state that to the extent that there is an approved Australian approach to the duty issue in novel cases it involves 'analysis of the relevant facts of individual cases ... in terms of "principles" (or "legal policies")',[173] and that this 'approach' is apparently *controversial*, says all that needs to be said about the morass into which the duty concept has now sunk.

The meaningless abstraction of general duty formulae is exemplified by the use of the 'Delphic criterion'[174] of 'proximity' to try to encapsulate a wide range of notional duty issues, including core questions of protected interests (economic loss, omissions, etc) and the problem of deliberate intervening conduct. The proximity concept derives from the old law on remoteness, where it connoted a sufficiently direct link between the defendant's fault and the claimant's damage,[175] and it was in that sense that Lord Atkin used the word in his speech in *Donoghue v Stevenson*.[176] The unlikely transposition of proximity into a test (or partial test) of notional duty is explained by its extreme abstraction. It is important to understand that it is precisely because it is 'blatantly meaningless'[177] in this context that proximity has proven so popular; no meaningful concept would be capable of [584] capturing so wide a range of the issues which can be accommodated within the notional duty enquiry. In this sense, the criticism that the concept is vacuous, though entirely valid, misses the point.[178]

---

[172] *Customs and Excise Commissioners v Barclays Bank plc* [2004] EWCA Civ 1555, [2005] 1 WLR 2082 [52] (Lindsay J).

[173] Barker et al (n 41) 459–60.

[174] *Hawkins v Clayton* (1988) 164 CLR 539 (HCA) 555 (Brennan J).

[175] See Howarth, 'Negligence after *Murphy*' (n 9) 82; Hepple (n 11) 78; Lord Oliver of Aylmerton, 'Judicial Legislation: Retreat from *Anns*' in V Sinnadurai (ed), *The Sultan Azlan Shah Law Lectures: Judges on the Common Law* (Kuala Lumpur, Professional Law Books, 2004) 64. The most sophisticated attempts to give meaning to the proximity concept have interpreted it as a test of 'directness' in this sense: see C Witting, 'Negligent Inspectors and Flying Machines' [2000] *CLJ* 544, 559–60; and A Kramer, 'Proximity as Principles: Directness, Community Norms and the Tort of Negligence' (2003) 11 *Tort Law Review* 70, 103 (proximity is 'really a question of proximate cause' and hence 'largely redundant').

[176] *Donoghue v Stevenson* [1932] AC 562 (HL) 581–82. See also *Grant v Australian Knitting Mills Ltd* [1936] AC 85 (PC) 104 (Lord Wright).

[177] J Stone, *Precedent and Law: Dynamics of Common Law Growth* (Sydney, Butterworths, 1985) 216.

[178] For a particularly telling critique of proximity, see *Gala* (n 82) 259–63 (Brennan J). See also *Leigh and Sillivan* (n 14) 395 (Robert Goff LJ); MH McHugh, 'Neighbourhood, Proximity and Reliance' in PD Finn (ed), *Essays on Torts* (Sydney, Law Book Co, 1989) 36–39; Howarth, 'Negligence after *Murphy*' (n 9) 71–72; and Hepple (n 11) 80. And for criticism of the three-stage *Caparo* test of which proximity is the second stage, see, eg, Weinrib, 'The Disintegration of Duty' (n 27) 171 (a 'ramshackle enquiry'); J Morgan, 'The Rise and Fall of the General Duty of Care' (2006) 22 *Professional Negligence* 206, 209–11.

More generally, the fact that faith in the utility of general tests of duty has survived the scepticism of eminent judges[179] and distinguished commentators[180] suggests that the problem here is the duty concept itself. After all, it is not unreasonable to think that it should be possible to devise a general test for a discrete element of a cause of action, and the search for such a test (and the use of tests previously put forward) is an understandable response to the formlessness of the notional duty enquiry. It is therefore the duty concept which should be in our sights, not the fruitless search for a general duty formula which is its inevitable concomitant.

VI. AN EXAMPLE

Some of the difficulties which the duty concept is causing in modern negligence law are illustrated by a recent Court of Appeal decision on liability for the deliberate acts of third parties. In *Everett v Comojo (UK) Ltd (t/a The Metropolitan)*,[181] the victims of a knife attack in a London bar brought a negligence claim against the company which managed the bar on the grounds that it had failed to take appropriate steps to protect its guests. Smith LJ held that the management of such establishments owe their guests a duty of care in respect of deliberate third-party acts on the premises, while concluding that on the facts the defendants had not been at fault. Surprisingly, however, she made no reference in her judgment to the leading House of Lords case on liability in negligence for the deliberate acts of third parties, *Mitchell v Glasgow CC*,[182] choosing instead to apply the *Caparo* three-stage test of foreseeability, proximity and 'fair, just and reasonableness'.[183] As usual, the use of this general test of duty, and particularly the vague 'proximity' concept, deflected attention away from the question of whether the duty of care argued for was consistent with principle and previous authority. Furthermore, the dangers of such an approach were made apparent in a passage of Smith LJ's judgment in which she attached significance to the fact that the defendant clearly owed the claimants a duty of care in relation to the state of the premises by virtue of the Occupiers' Liability Act 1957, saying that it would be 'surprising if management could be liable to a guest who tripped over a worn carpet, and yet escape liability for injuries inflicted by a fellow guest who was a foreseeable [585] danger'.[184]

---

[179] See, eg, *Caparo* (n 105) 628 (Lord Roskill), 633 (Lord Oliver); and McHugh (n 178) 20.

[180] See, eg, Fleming, 'Remoteness and Duty' (n 38) 495; and Stapleton, 'Duty of Care Factors' (n 42) 60 ('There *can* be no "duty test" given what it is that judges do under the cloak of this analytical label').

[181] *Everett v Comojo (UK) Ltd (t/a The Metropolitan)* [2011] EWCA Civ 13, [2012] 1 WLR 150.

[182] *Mitchell v Glasgow CC* [2009] UKHL 11, [2009] 1 AC 874.

[183] See text to n 171.

[184] *Everett* (n 181) [33].

This was despite the fact that in *Mitchell* their Lordships emphasised the general principle that the law does not normally impose a duty on one person to protect against the deliberate acts of a legally responsible third party, a principle which would clearly justify differentiating between these two scenarios in an appropriate case.

The deconstruction of duty would have ensured that the critical question of deliberate third-party conduct in *Everett* would have been addressed more directly as a matter of legal causation and also made it more likely that reference would have been made to relevant authorities like *Mitchell*. Moreover, while the malleability of the duty concept enabled the court to formulate a highly specific rule about the duties owed by the management of a nightclub to its guests – a rule with such fuzzy boundaries that it is bound to lead to further litigation – a legal causation analysis informed by the relevant authorities would have seen the case for what it was, namely an application of the more general principle highlighted in *Mitchell* that the deliberate conduct of a third party will not operate to bar a negligence action where the defendant has assumed a responsibility towards the claimant which encompasses such conduct.[185]

VII. WHAT WOULD BE LOST?

What, if anything, would be lost if the duty stage of the negligence enquiry were to be dispensed with? Defences of the concept generally focus on the characterisation of notional duty as a question of law.[186] Hence it is argued that deciding cases on notional duty grounds is productive of greater legal certainty, because such decisions have precedential force and can be expressed in categorical, 'bright line' rules of general application, and that duty cases may involve 'choices among fundamental values and policies' which are best determined by general rules rather than on an ad hoc, case-by-case basis.[187] Furthermore, it is argued, characterising an issue as one of notional duty enables it to be dealt with as a preliminary issue, without a detailed examination of the facts.[188] On closer inspection, however, these supposed advantages of the duty mechanism turn out to be largely illusory, and they certainly provide no justification for rejecting the argument for the deconstruction of duty being put forward here.

---

[185] *Mitchell* (n 182) [23] (Lord Hope), [76] (Lady Hale), [82] (Lord Brown).
[186] See, eg, J Stapleton, 'Controlling the Future of the Common Law by Restatement' in Madden (n 27) 270, 287 ('language of duty' required for 'systematic restraint on the growth of future liability'); Morgan, 'The Rise and Fall of the General Duty of Care' (n 178) 218–19; T Weir, *An Introduction to Tort Law*, 2nd edn (Oxford, OUP, 2006) 31–32; Mullis and Oliphant (n 31) 10–11.
[187] Owen, 'Duty Rules' (n 2) 779.
[188] See text to n 57.

The key reason for this conclusion is that even if we were to deconstruct duty along the lines advocated, the issues which are currently dealt with under the notional duty heading could still where appropriate be treated as questions of law, with all the potential advantages that that characterisation offers. Hence, for example, the protected interests issue would surely remain an issue of law even if repackaged under the damage heading, and the same could be true of the relevance of deliberate intervening conduct if that were to be dealt with under the rubric of [586] legal causation.[189] Furthermore, it is arguable that the malleability of the duty concept has actually undermined the effectiveness of notional duty as a source of bright-line rules with strong precedential force, since (as the *Everett* case shows) notional duty questions can be formulated in such a way as effectively to bypass a previous decision governing the substantive issue before the court, with the result that instead of a clear set of principles emerging, the law descends into a tangled web of overlapping rules pitched at differing levels of generality.

Nor should dealing with issues currently falling under the heading of notional duty at other stages of the negligence enquiry necessarily require closer examination of the facts than is the case currently. The extent to which the court must delve into the factual background in order to determine an issue of law depends not on the classification of the issue but on the particular issue under scrutiny. And as the Chief Justice of New Zealand recently pointed out, the decision whether to recognise a duty of care in novel circumstances will frequently be 'intensely fact-specific', so that in many cases 'duty of care is no more suitable for peremptory assessment on assumed facts than questions of breach or damage'.[190] For instance, the complex set of duty rules which regulate secondary victim psychiatric injury claims are couched in such terms that a detailed factual inquiry – into, for example, whether there was a close tie of love and affection between the claimant and the primary victim, or whether the claimant arrived at the scene in the 'immediate aftermath' of the accident – will often be required before the duty question can be answered.[191] Similarly, when applying the justiciability 'duty' rule in a public authority negligence case, the court needs to know why the decision under attack was made before it can determine whether it is in a position to evaluate whether or not it was negligent, and this may in turn require that the court delve into the factual background.[192]

---

[189] For the same reason, the deconstruction of duty need not affect the functional separation of judge and jury in jurisdictions retaining civil juries.

[190] *Couch v A-G* [2008] NZSC 45, [2008] 3 NZLR 725 [53], [43] (Elias CJ).

[191] The leading case is *Alcock* (n 47).

[192] See *S v Gloucestershire CC* [2001] Fam 313 (CA) 338 (May LJ); D Fairgrieve, *State Liability in Tort: A Comparative Law Study* (Oxford, OUP, 2003) 62.

Finally, Jane Stapleton's defence of notional duty on the grounds that it 'provides the opportunity to signal systemic concerns' such as the concern with individual autonomy which she claims underlies the general no-duty-to-rescue doctrine,[193] is also unconvincing. After all, even if we assume that it is part of the role of the law of negligence to give 'signals' of this kind, these could still be given out by bright-line rules following a deconstruction of the duty concept. Furthermore, it is likely that any signals that the law of negligence does currently send out are being obscured by the mixing together of different issues under the umbrella of notional duty. Hence, for example, by treating illegality as a defence to a negligence action, the courts make it clear that 'the defendant has acted wrongly in negligently causing harm' and that liability is not imposed only out of concern for 'the integrity of the legal system',[194] a message which may become blurred if the illegality issue is submerged into the more general duty enquiry. [587]

VIII. CONCLUSION

I have argued in this article that the duty of care concept should be deconstructed, and the issues with which it deals reallocated to other stages of the negligence enquiry. Duty reasoning obscures more than it clarifies, and the deficiencies of the duty concept are in large part responsible for the conceptual confusion in which negligence law is now mired. Deconstructing duty would improve the quality of judicial reasoning in negligence cases, give a sharper edge to scholarship in the field, and improve the understanding of those coming to negligence law for the first time.

Nevertheless, because the duty of care concept currently plays such a central role in the common law of negligence, a call to dispense with it is likely to encounter considerable resistance. Those who are minded to defend the concept would however do well to remember two things. One is that, with the exception of 'relationship negligence',[195] the duty of care concept was 'quite unknown' in early negligence law,[196] and it emerged in the nineteenth century only because of a series of historical accidents.[197] And the other is that no

---

[193] Stapleton, 'Reflections on Common Sense Causation in Australia' (n 126) 337. See also the similar argument in the *Restatement, Torts, Third: Liability for Physical and Emotional Harm* (2010) that duty 'is usefully employed when a court seeks to make a telling pronouncement about when actors may or, on the other hand, may not be held liable' (§ 29, comment f).

[194] *Hall* (n 82) 181 (McLachlin J).

[195] Prichard (n 52) 30.

[196] Winfield, 'Duty in Tortious Negligence' (n 4) 65.

[197] ibid 66. See also Dias, 'The Breach Problem and the Duty of Care' (n 101) 401. On the reasons for its emergence, see Winfield, 'Duty in Tortious Negligence' (n 4) 44–58; Prichard (n 52) 30–33; and Ibbetson, '"The Law of Business Rome"' (n 53) 87–92.

equivalent to the duty of care as it has developed in the common law world exists in most civil law systems.[198] If others can do just fine without the duty of care, it is hard to believe that it is really indispensable.

Two final points should be made. The first is that, even after the deconstruction of the duty of care which I have argued for here, there might still be a residual role for the concept in 'acquired rights' cases where negligence liability is dependent on the existence of a particular relationship between the parties which arose prior to the negligent conduct. I have in mind here contractual relationships, fiduciary relationships, and also relationships created by an assumption of responsibility by the defendant towards the claimant. In cases of this kind, it is necessary to demonstrate that a relationship was formed between the parties which put the defendant under an obligation to take care of the claimant's interests going beyond the core duty not to negligently cause damage, and this obligation could usefully be labelled a 'duty of care'. Furthermore, it is arguable that in acquired rights cases (unlike in core rights cases) this label would not be a misnomer, on the grounds that in such cases the defendant really is under an obligation to take care, and not merely an obligation not to negligently injure. This is clearly the position when it comes to contractual duties of care, which (like other contractual obligations) are actionable per se, and the same may be true of other duties of care arising out of particular relationships as well.

And the second point is that although I have argued in this article for the complete deconstruction of duty, such that outside the prior relationship context the concept is dispensed with altogether, the case for deconstructing duty is not [588] an all-or-nothing one, as even a less dramatic move away from dependence on the duty concept would have beneficial effects. A less drastic deconstruction of duty would I suggest require three steps to be taken. First, the question of factual duty should be separated out from legal or notional duty and dealt with as part of a wider enquiry into the 'scope of the risk'. Second, where another existing element of the negligence enquiry – such as legal causation, damage, or the illegality defence – has previously been used to deal with the question of law arising in a negligence case, the issue should if possible be dealt with under that heading, rather than under notional duty. And finally, the core notional duty issues of protected interests and special immunity rules should be properly identified and classified, so that the notional duty enquiry which remains has a commonly agreed structure, within which notional duty questions are dealt with at a consistent level of generality, a step which demands of judges that they not

---

[198] Although Winfield described the duty of care as 'a conception wholly alien to Roman Law and of which there is no trace in the modern Continental systems' ('Duty in Tortious Negligence' (n 4) 58), German tort law does now employ the concept to a certain extent, if not always in the same way as common law systems: see BS Markesinis and H Unberath, *The German Law of Torts: A Comparative Treatise*, 4th edn (Oxford, Hart Publishing, 2002) 79 ff.

simply accept the duty question as formulated in the pleadings, but themselves dictate the structure of the analysis by framing that question in an appropriate way. Although the disadvantages of the duty concept are such that it would be preferable to abandon it altogether, these three less radical changes would in themselves considerably enhance both the quality of reasoning in negligence cases, and the general understanding of negligence law.

3

The Duty of Care After Robinson v Chief Constable of West Yorkshire Police

D Clarry (ed), *The UK Supreme Court Yearbook, Volume 9: 2017–2018 Legal Year* (London, Appellate Press, 2019) 174–205

[174] I. INTRODUCTION

HOW A COURT determines whether a duty of care was owed in a negligence case is a question that continues to attract considerable judicial and academic attention. On the one hand, this is not altogether surprising. After all, negligence is by far the most important cause of action in tort, and the duty of care element plays a central role in negligence law, marking out as it does the limits of liability for negligent conduct that causes damage. Furthermore, the approach the courts take to the determination of the duty question has important implications not only for the scope of negligence liability – with some approaches tending towards expansionist outcomes, and others more restrictive ones – but also for the extent to which the courts higher up in the hierarchy can exercise control over those lower down. On the other hand, it will be argued in this chapter that the approach that the courts ought to take to deciding duty cases is really quite straightforward, and can best be understood as the application of ordinary common law reasoning to the issues such cases raise. This insight clears the path towards a more predictable and more coherent law of negligence, in which duty questions are resolved in a reasoned and transparent way.

The focus of this chapter is on the recent decision of the UK Supreme Court ('the Supreme Court') in *Robinson v Chief Constable of West Yorkshire Police* ('*Robinson*'),[1] where Lord Reed gave a leading judgment that represents a golden opportunity to place future duty of care reasoning on a secure, settled and defensible footing. An attempt will be made in this chapter to demonstrate

---

[1] *Robinson v Chief Constable of West Yorkshire Police* [2018] UKSC 4, [2018] AC 736.

that Lord Reed's approach to the duty question is not only the [175] best of the alternatives available, but the only approach that is consistent with common law method and the rule of law. The real question, it will be argued, is not whether the decision in *Robinson* marks a welcome return to orthodoxy, but whether courts at all levels will be prepared to abandon other ways of reasoning that in recent years have become embedded in the thinking of judges, practitioners and academics, with regrettable results. As Lord Reed said in the opening paragraphs of his judgment in *Robinson*:

> Most of [the issues raised in these proceedings] can be decided by applying long-established principles of the law of negligence. The fact that the issues have reached this court reflects the extent to which those principles have been eroded in recent times by uncertainty and confusion.[2]

II. THE FACTS OF *ROBINSON* AND THE DECISIONS BELOW

The litigation in *Robinson* arose out of a routine drug bust on the streets of Huddersfield. One of the police officers involved had seen the suspect apparently dealing drugs in a park and called for backup with a view to making an arrest. By the time the backup arrived, the suspect was standing in a busy street in front of a bookmakers he had just visited. Two of the four officers now on the scene attempted to effect an arrest, but the suspect resisted, and in the ensuing tussle, the claimant passer-by, a 'relatively frail' woman of 76, was knocked over and injured.[3]

The claimant brought a negligence claim for her personal injuries against the police, which was dismissed by the Recorder. The Recorder found that the officers' conduct had exposed the claimant to a foreseeable risk of injury, and also that the officers had acted negligently in carrying out the arrest. Nevertheless, the Recorder held that the police were not liable, since the decision of the House of Lords in *Hill v Chief Constable of West Yorkshire* ('*Hill*')[4] had conferred on them an immunity from suit in negligence, which extended to the facts of this case.

The claimant's appeal was dismissed by the Court of Appeal. Hallett LJ applied the so-called '*Caparo* test', derived from the speech of Lord Bridge in *Caparo Industries plc v Dickman* ('*Caparo*'),[5] on the footing that this test should be used in all negligence claims. The third stage of that test (requiring that it be 'fair, just and reasonable'[6] to impose a duty of care) [176] meant,

---

[2] ibid [3].
[3] ibid [1].
[4] *Hill v Chief Constable of West Yorkshire* [1989] AC 53 (HL).
[5] *Caparo Industries plc v Dickman* [1990] 2 AC 605 (HL) 617–18.
[6] ibid 618 (Lord Bridge).

Hallett LJ said, that a court would 'only impose a duty where it considers it right to do so on the facts'.[7] And this would rarely be the case where the police were sued for negligence in respect of their conduct 'in the course of investigating and suppressing crime and apprehending offenders', since the courts had concluded that the interests of the public would not be best served by the imposition of a duty of care in such cases.[8] Furthermore, Hallett LJ argued, 'provided the police act within reason, the public would prefer to see them doing their job and taking drug dealers off the street', and any risk thereby imposed on passers-by such as the claimant was 'trumped by the risk to society as a whole'.[9]

It is worth pausing at this point to notice two things about the core reasoning of Hallett LJ in the Court of Appeal. The first is that the *Caparo* test is used to justify what appears to be an untrammelled negative discretion, whereby a court (seemingly at any level) can simply refuse to impose a duty of care on the grounds that it considers it 'right to do so' on the facts. Where, we might ask, does this leave the doctrine of precedent? And the other thing that we can observe in this reasoning is the use of an appeal to public sentiment, albeit one that does not seem to be based on any empirical evidence. It should immediately be apparent that something has gone very wrong here. A law-abiding citizen injured through the alleged negligence of police officers while going about her daily business is, in effect, told that she is not entitled to compensation since the court takes the view that imposing liability on the facts would be a bad thing to do, and that the court of public opinion would (if asked, though it has not been) take the same view.

Naturally, this is an over-simplification of Hallett LJ's reasoning and, in reality, the Court of Appeal also appealed to precedent in support of their conclusion that no duty of care was owed, relying, as had the Recorder, on a supposed 'immunity' for the police from negligence liability recognised in the *Hill* case. Hallett LJ accepted that there were a number of possible exceptions to the no-duty rule laid down in *Hill* – namely, cases of outrageous negligence, cases which did not relate to core police functions, and cases where the police had assumed a responsibility towards the claimant – but considered that none of them applied on the facts, which she described as a 'paradigm' case for the application of the immunity rule.[10]

In addition to the alleged immunity based on the *Hill* decision, the Court of Appeal also prayed in aid a number of supplementary arguments to justify [177] their conclusion that the claimant's appeal should be dismissed. One was that the claimant had in fact been hurt by the suspect, and that any fault of

---

[7] *Robinson v Chief Constable of West Yorkshire Police* [2014] EWCA Civ 15 [40].
[8] ibid [46].
[9] ibid [47].
[10] ibid [51].

the officers lay in their failing to prevent him from injuring her, so that in reality this was an omissions case, rather than a positive conduct case. Another was that there was no 'proximity' between the officers and the claimant (this being a reference to the second stage of the *Caparo* test[11]), notwithstanding the court's acceptance of the Recorder's finding that injury to the claimant had been a reasonably foreseeable risk of the officers' decision to effect an arrest. And finally, the Court of Appeal disagreed with the Recorder on the issue of breach of duty, taking the view that the officers had acted reasonably in attempting to arrest the suspect at the time and place in question.

III. *MICHAEL v CHIEF CONSTABLE OF SOUTH WALES POLICE*

A considerable time elapsed between the decision of the Court of Appeal in *Robinson* and the hearing of the claimant's appeal from that decision by the Supreme Court. In the meantime, the Supreme Court decided another police negligence case of great significance, namely *Michael v Chief Constable of South Wales Police*.[12] The claim in *Michael* arose out of the murder of a young woman by her former partner, which it was alleged could have been prevented if the police had responded appropriately to an emergency call the deceased had made shortly before she died. The Supreme Court agreed with the Court of Appeal in *Michael* that a negligence claim against the police forces involved should be struck out, although an alternative claim under the Human Rights Act 1998 was allowed to proceed to trial. Although the facts of the two cases were very different, the reasoning in *Michael* cast significant doubt on the Court of Appeal's decision in *Robinson*, for two main reasons.

The first reason was that in the majority judgment in *Michael* the late Lord Toulson poured cold water on the idea that duty of care questions could be resolved by the application of a general formula or test, saying:

> From time to time the courts have looked for some universal formula or yardstick [for determining duty of care issues], but the quest has been elusive. And from time to time a court has used an expression in explaining its reasons for reaching a particular decision which has then been squashed and squeezed in other cases where it does not fit so aptly.[13] [178]

Furthermore, after referring to the passage in the speech of Lord Bridge in *Caparo* from which the 'three-stage test' is said to be derived, Lord Toulson commented that '[p]aradoxically, this passage in Lord Bridge's speech has sometimes come to be treated as a blueprint for deciding cases, despite the pains which

---

[11] *Caparo* (n 5) 618.
[12] *Michael v Chief Constable of South Wales Police* [2015] UKSC 2, [2015] AC 1732.
[13] ibid [103].

the author took to make clear that it was not intended to be any such thing'.[14] By explicitly repudiating the use of the three-stage test to determine the existence of a duty of care, Lord Toulson had completely undermined the foundations of the Court of Appeal's decision in *Robinson*.

The second reason that *Michael* cast doubt on the Court of Appeal's dismissal of the *Robinson* appeal was that the decision that no duty of care had been owed in *Michael* was premised on the assumption that as far as the law of negligence was concerned, public defendants and private defendants were essentially subject to the same liability regime. In *Michael*, this approach had favoured the defendants, the reasoning being that (applying the omissions rule) no liability would attach to a private individual for not helping the murdered woman, and hence no liability attached to the police either, at least in the absence of an assumption of responsibility. However, this 'equality principle' cuts both ways, and on the facts of *Robinson* it appeared to favour the claimant – assuming it was a positive conduct case – since of course a private citizen who carelessly collided with a passer-by in the street would potentially be subject to negligence liability for any injury that resulted. What is more, while Hallett LJ had relied on the idea that in *Hill* the House of Lords had conferred on the police a broad immunity from negligence liability, in *Michael* Lord Toulson expressly denied this. On the contrary, Lord Toulson said that in *Hill* Lord Keith had 'recognised that the general law of tort applies as much to the police as to anyone else',[15] and that although he had admittedly used the language of 'immunity', this turn of phrase had been 'not only unnecessary but unfortunate'.[16] This was because:

> The refusal of the courts to impose a private law duty on the police to exercise reasonable care to safeguard victims or potential victims of crime … does not involve giving special treatment to the police. It is consistent with the way in which the common law has been applied to other authorities vested with powers or duties as a matter of public law for the protection of the public … The question is therefore not whether the police should have a special immunity, but whether an exception should be made to the ordinary application of com- [179] mon law principles which would cover the facts of the present case.[17]

Following *Michael*, a successful appeal to the Supreme Court in *Robinson* therefore looked to be on the cards, but it was by no means a foregone conclusion. After all, the decision to strike out the negligence claim in *Michael* was made by only a 5-2 majority, and in his dissenting judgment Lord Kerr had used the *Caparo* test to reach the conclusion that a duty of care had been owed, and had said that in the context of the appeal he did 'not consider it particularly

---

[14] ibid [106].
[15] ibid [37].
[16] ibid [44].
[17] ibid [115]–[116].

relevant' whether any finding that the police were not liable was based on an immunity or not.[18] Although Lord Kerr's analysis was geared towards making the police accountable in negligence for their mistakes, there was at least a possibility that on the facts of *Robinson* an approach along similar lines would generate a very different kind of outcome.

IV. DUTY OF CARE IN GENERAL

In general terms, the principal significance of the *Robinson* decision undoubtedly lies in Lord Reed's analysis of the method a court should use to determine whether a duty of care was owed in a negligence case. Although, as we have seen, Lord Toulson touched upon this issue in *Michael*, the discussion in *Robinson* of the correct approach to duty questions is both more sustained and more forceful. Indeed, I would go so far as to claim that it is the most important case on this question since the decision in *Caparo* almost three decades ago.

Lord Reed distinguished in his analysis of the duty question between cases covered by established principles and novel cases. With regard to cases of the former type, he said that 'there are many situations in which it has been clearly established that a duty of care is or is not owed', giving as examples the duties of care owed by 'motorists to other road users, by manufacturers to consumers, by employers to their employees, and by doctors to their patients'.[19] In such cases, once the decision has been made that a duty of care is owed, then that decision will apply to all future cases of the same kind. Furthermore, since in cases of this type 'a consideration of justice and reasonableness forms part of the basis on which the law has arrived at the relevant principles' it is 'unnecessary and inappropriate to reconsider [180] whether the existence of the duty is fair, just and reasonable', unless, that is, the court has been invited to depart from an established precedent.[20]

> Nor, a fortiori, can justice and reasonableness constitute a basis for discarding established principles and deciding each case according to what the court may regard as its broader merits. Such an approach would be a recipe for inconsistency and uncertainty ....[21]

As for novel cases, where the courts must go beyond established principles to determine whether a duty of care was owed:

> Following the *Caparo* case, the characteristic approach of the common law in such situations is to develop incrementally and by analogy with established authority.

---

[18] ibid [151].
[19] *Robinson* (n 1) [26].
[20] ibid.
[21] ibid.

The drawing of an analogy depends on identifying the legally significant features of the situations with which the earlier authorities were concerned. The courts also have to exercise judgement when deciding whether a duty of care should be recognised in a novel type of case.[22]

Taking the two types of case together, then, the overall approach that the courts should take in deciding whether or not a duty of care was owed is as follows:

In the ordinary run of cases, courts consider what has been decided previously and follow the precedents (unless it is necessary to consider whether the precedents should be departed from). In cases where the question whether a duty of care arises has not previously been decided, the courts will consider the closest analogies in the existing law, with a view to maintaining the coherence of the law and the avoidance of inappropriate distinctions. They will also weigh up the reasons for and against imposing liability, in order to decide whether the existence of a duty of care would be just and reasonable.[23] [181]

Furthermore, Lord Reed could not have been clearer in his rejection of the idea that the courts should use a three-stage test of foreseeability, proximity and 'fair, just and reasonableness' based on Lord Bridge's speech in *Caparo*:

The proposition that there is a *Caparo* test which applies to all claims in the modern law of negligence, and that in consequence the court will only impose a duty of care where it considers it fair, just and reasonable to do so on the particular facts, is mistaken. As Lord Toulson pointed out in his landmark judgment in [*Michael*], that understanding of the case mistakes the whole point of *Caparo*, which was to repudiate the idea that there is a single test which can be applied in all cases in order to determine whether a duty of care exists, and instead to adopt an approach based, in the manner characteristic of the common law, on precedent, and on the development of the law incrementally and by analogy with established authorities.[24]

The popularity of the *Caparo* test means that it is important to emphasise that Lord Reed was not merely rejecting the notion that (as Hallett LJ had held in the Court of Appeal) the three-stage test should be used to decide all duty cases. Rather, Lord Reed made it crystal clear, drawing on the judgment of Lord Toulson in *Michael*, that he disapproved of the very idea that Lord Bridge had intended to lay down a 'test' at all, or that the supposed test could be of use in deciding *any* duty case. For example, in response to the fact that Hallett LJ had relied on the use of the three-stage test by the Supreme Court in *Smith v Ministry of Defence*[25] and by Lord Steyn in *Marc Rich & Co v Bishop Rock Marine Co*,[26] Lord Reed pointed out that these cases had raised novel or contentious duty questions, but added that '[i]t was *in any event* made clear in

---

[22] ibid [27].
[23] ibid [29].
[24] ibid [21].
[25] *Smith v Ministry of Defence* [2013] UKSC 41, [2014] AC 52.
[26] *Marc Rich & Co v Bishop Rock Marine Co* [1996] AC 211 (HL).

Michael that the idea that *Caparo* established a tripartite case is mistaken'.[27] Like Lord Toulson in *Michael*, Lord Reed pointed to the fact that in *Caparo* Lord Bridge had been at pains to deny that a single general principle could provide a practical test to determine whether a duty of care was owed, and considered it 'ironic that ... Lord Bridge's speech has been treated as laying down such a test'.[28] On the contrary, Lord Bridge had adopted 'an incremental approach, based on the use of established authorities to provide guidance as to how [182] novel questions should be decided', and 'it was that approach, and not a supposed tripartite test' which Lord Bridge had then used to decide the case.[29] Incremental reasoning, by analogy from existing authority, was the *true Caparo* approach, and 'the existence of a duty of care does not depend on the application of a "*Caparo* test" to the facts of the particular case'.[30]

In a commentary on the *Michael* decision, James Goudkamp stated that the case 'arguably signals a major shift in the approach to determining when a duty of care exists generally',[31] but expressed doubts as to the implications of Lord Toulson's analysis for the continued use of the *Caparo* test:

> It is rather difficult to know what to make of Lord Toulson's remarks [about the *Caparo* 'test'], which are extremely brief. One possibility is that his Lordship thought that the *Caparo* test should be abandoned. A less radical way of reading Lord Toulson is as saying that the *Caparo* test should be applied much more cautiously than it has been to date. Either way, Lord Toulson's comments in this regard ... have given the *Caparo* test a very significant knock.[32]

While I agree with Goudkamp that the brevity of Lord Toulson's comments limits their impact, it seems clear to me from the force with which he expressed himself on the issue that the more radical interpretation of those comments is the correct one. Be that as it may, what is surely beyond doubt is the import of Lord Reed's more extended, but equally forceful, observations in *Robinson*. To adapt Goudkamp's metaphor, even if in *Michael* Lord Toulson only put the *Caparo* test on the ropes, in *Robinson* Lord Reed has surely delivered the knockout blow.

Lady Hale and Lord Hodge agreed with Lord Reed in *Robinson*, while Lord Mance and Lord Hughes delivered concurring judgments. In his judgment, Lord Mance was notably less dismissive of the *Caparo* three-stage test than Lord Reed. He accepted that it was 'unnecessary in every claim of negligence to resort to the three-stage analysis', but said that this was because there were 'well-established categories, including (generally) liability for causing

[27] *Robinson* (n 1) [28] (emphasis added).
[28] ibid [24].
[29] ibid [25].
[30] ibid [30].
[31] J Goudkamp, 'A Revolution in Duty of Care?' (2015) 131 *LQR* 519, 520.
[32] ibid 521–22.

physical injury by positive act', where the elements of proximity and 'fair, just and reasonableness' are 'at least assumed'.[33] And while Lord Mance agreed with Lord Reed that outside these categories [183] the law proceeded 'incrementally', he tied this process of incremental development to the *Caparo* test, saying that in such cases 'all three stages of the *Caparo* analysis will be material'.[34] In his concurring judgment, Lord Hughes was more ambivalent, for while he expressed his agreement with Lord Reed's discussion of the *Caparo* decision, the gist of his analysis is conveyed in relatively conservative terms, as limited to excluding the use of the three-stage test in cases covered by established precedent (an interpretation that, with respect, I have argued is unsustainable).[35]

Nevertheless, it is submitted that the unequivocal rejection of the *Caparo* test in the leading judgment in *Robinson*, particularly when considered alongside the critical remarks of Lord Toulson in *Michael*, amounts to a clear signal from the Supreme Court to courts at all levels that the three-stage test should no longer be used to determine the existence of a duty of care in any negligence case.

V. PUBLIC AUTHORITY NEGLIGENCE LIABILITY IN GENERAL

Robinson is a less significant case on public authority negligence liability than it is on the determination of the duty of care, since Lord Reed's analysis of the former question closely tracks earlier case law, and in particular the *Michael* decision. Then again, *Robinson* represents yet another strong endorsement by the UK's highest court of the equality principle in the negligence context and is also significant for clarifying that that principle cuts both ways. Earlier cases applying the principle – such as *Gorringe v Calderdale Metropolitan Borough Council* ('*Gorringe*')[36] and *Michael* – concerned omissions, so that the import of the principle was *against* the imposition of a duty of care, on the footing that since a private party would not be subject to negligence liability for failing to act in the circumstances in question, a public authority should not be so liable either. However, *Robinson* was a positive conduct case, and so here the equality principle *favoured* the imposition of a duty, with the reasoning being that since this time a private party *would* be liable in negligence, the police should be liable as well. Although in recent times this positive aspect of the equality principle has been less prominent than its negative aspect, it is a well-established implication of the ideal of equal treatment of public and private parties, and its powerful reiteration by the Supreme Court is to be welcomed. [184]

---

[33] *Robinson* (n 1) [83].
[34] ibid.
[35] ibid [100].
[36] *Gorringe v Calderdale Metropolitan Borough Council* [2004] UKHL 15, [2004] 1 WLR 1057.

The equality principle itself is usually traced back to the writings of AV Dicey, who considered it to be one of the three pillars of the rule of law. According to Dicey:

> [W]hen we speak of the 'rule of law' as a characteristic of our country, [we mean] not only that with us no man is above the law, but (what is a different thing) that here every man, whatever be his rank or condition, is subject to the ordinary law of the realm and amenable to the jurisdiction of the ordinary tribunals.[37]

For a good example of the operation of that principle, we need look no further than *Mersey Docks and Harbour Board Trustees v Gibbs*,[38] where a ship had been damaged when it collided with a mud bank at the entrance to the defendants' dock. The defendants were held liable for the damage in negligence and appealed to the House of Lords on the ground that they were a public body entrusted by Parliament with the task of maintaining the docks. The House held that the defendants' status did not absolve them from their common law duty to exercise reasonable care. According to Blackburn J, who delivered the opinion of the learned judges advising the House:

> [T]he proper rule of construction of such statutes is that, in the absence of something to shew a contrary intention, the Legislature intends that the body, the creature of the statute, shall have the same duties, and that its funds shall be rendered subject to the same liabilities as the general law would impose on a private person doing the same things.[39]

In *Robinson*, Lord Reed began his discussion of public authority liability with a forthright expression of the positive aspect of the equality principle:

> At common law, public authorities are generally subject to the same liabilities in tort as private individuals and bodies ... Accordingly, if conduct would be tortious if committed by a private person or body, it is generally equally tortious [185] if committed by a public authority ... It follows that public authorities are generally under a duty of care to avoid causing actionable harm in situations where a duty of care would arise under ordinary principles of the law of negligence, unless the law provides otherwise.[40]

This positive aspect of the equality principle went hand in hand with its negative aspect, however, with the result that 'public authorities, like private individuals and bodies, are generally under no duty of care to prevent the occurrence of harm',[41] and in the absence of circumstances in which *any* party would

---

[37] AV Dicey, *Introduction to the Study of the Law of the Constitution*, 8th edn (London, Macmillan, 1915) 114.

[38] *Mersey Docks and Harbour Board Trustees v Gibbs* (1866) LR 1 HL 93 (HL).

[39] ibid 110. Of course, there were exceptions to the positive aspect of the equality principle, most notably Crown immunity, but even that immunity was largely abrogated by the Crown Proceedings Act 1947.

[40] *Robinson* (n 1) [32]–[33].

[41] ibid [34].

come under a duty of care to prevent the occurrence of harm – such as cases where the defendant has created the danger, or assumed a responsibility for the claimant's safety – 'public authorities generally owe no duty of care towards individuals to confer a benefit upon them by protecting them from harm, any more than would a private individual or body'.[42] And this same principle of equal treatment of public defendants applied even where a public authority had statutory powers or duties 'enabling or requiring it to prevent the harm in question',[43] unless, that is, the statute in question gave rise to a private right of action in the tort of breach of statutory duty. As Lord Reed pointed out, after what he termed a 'period of confusion' following the decision of the House of Lords in *Anns v Merton London Borough Council* ('*Anns*'),[44] there had been a 'return to orthodoxy' in this respect in *Stovin v Wise*[45] and then, 'more fully and clearly', in the *Gorringe* case.[46] The end result of applying both aspects of the equality principle in this context was a simple rule, namely that 'the law of negligence generally applies to public authorities in the same way that it applies to private individuals and bodies'.[47] [186]

VI. POLICE LIABILITY IN NEGLIGENCE

Turning to the negligence liability of the police in particular, Lord Reed again reiterated that the equality principle applied, so that 'as one would expect, given the general position of public authorities' as he had explained it, 'the police are subject to liability for causing personal injury in accordance with the general law of tort'.[48] It followed, with reference to negligence in particular, that the police were 'generally under a duty of care to avoid causing personal injury where such a duty would arise according to ordinary principles of the law of negligence',[49] a conclusion that he considered to be consistent not only with Lord Toulson's judgment in *Michael* but also with the *Hill* case, where Lord Keith had said that there was no question that a police officer 'like

---

[42] ibid [35].

[43] ibid [36].

[44] *Anns v Merton London Borough Council* [1978] AC 728 (HL).

[45] *Stovin v Wise* [1996] AC 923 (HL).

[46] *Robinson* (n 1) [31]. For discussion of the 'return to orthodoxy', with particular reference to the *Gorringe* decision and its implications, see D Nolan, 'The Liability of Public Authorities for Failing to Confer Benefits' (2011) 127 *LQR* 260. It should be noted (though nothing really turns on it) that in his discussion of these developments, Lord Reed fell into error when he said (at [39]) that in *Gorringe* it was made clear that 'the principle which had been applied in *Stovin v Wise* in relation to a statutory duty was also applicable to statutory powers', since in fact it was the other way round: *Stovin* concerned a statutory power (Highways Act 1980, s 79), whereas *Gorringe* concerned a statutory duty (Road Traffic Act 1988, s 39).

[47] *Robinson* (n 1) [40].

[48] ibid [45].

[49] ibid [67].

anyone else, may be liable in tort to a person who is injured as a direct result of his acts or omissions'.[50] Hence, the police could be liable in negligence where by their positive conduct they had caused reasonably foreseeable personal injury or property damage, as in, for example, *Knightley v Johns*,[51] *Rigby v Chief Constable of Northamptonshire*[52] and *Attorney General of the British Virgin Islands v Hartwell*.[53]

Then again, here as elsewhere the equality principle cut both ways, and so it followed that in the absence of special circumstances (such as an assumption of responsibility) the police's public duty to enforce the law and investigate crime did not generate a private law duty to protect individual members of the public from the criminal conduct of third parties. Furthermore, it was this rule, generated by the combination of the equality principle and the general negligence law governing omissions, that explained the ruling in the *Hill* case that the officers investigating a serial killer had not owed a duty of care to his potential future victims to take reasonable care to catch him. Lord Keith's endorsement of public policy objections to liability in *Hill* had therefore been unnecessary to the decision in the case, which Lord Reed observed had 'now to be understood in the light of the later authorities' reiterating the equality principle.[54] It followed that *Hill* was not 'authority for the proposition that the police enjoy a general immunity from suit in respect of anything done by them in the course of investigating or preventing crime'.[55] Lord Reed summed up his discussion of the negligence liability of the police as follows: [187]

> [T]here is no general rule that the police are not under any duty of care when discharging their function of preventing and investigating crime. They generally owe a duty of care when such a duty arises under ordinary principles of the law of negligence, unless statute or the common law provides otherwise.[56]

The principle that, as far as the law of negligence is concerned, the police are subject to the same liabilities as everyone else is a simple one, but reconciling it with all the earlier case law was less straightforward. *Hill* can indeed readily be explained as an omissions case, and the same is true of *Smith v Chief Constable of Sussex Police*,[57] where the House of Lords held that the police did not owe a duty of care to a person who had informed them that he had received threats of violence, in circumstances where it seems the House took the view that there had been no assumption of responsibility.[58] However, another House of

---

[50] *Hill* (n 4) 59.

[51] *Knightley v Johns* [1982] 1 WLR 349 (CA).

[52] *Rigby v Chief Constable of Northamptonshire* [1985] 1 WLR 1242 (QBD).

[53] *Attorney General of the British Virgin Islands v Hartwell* [2004] UKPC 12, [2004] 1 WLR 1273.

[54] *Robinson* (n 1) [54].

[55] ibid [55].

[56] ibid [70].

[57] *Smith v Chief Constable of Sussex Police* [2008] UKHL 50, [2009] 1 AC 225.

[58] See ibid [122] (Lord Brown).

Lords decision, *Brooks v Commissioner of Police of the Metropolis* ('*Brooks*'),[59] posed more difficulties. The claimant in *Brooks* had brought a negligence action for psychiatric harm he had allegedly suffered as a result of his insensitive treatment by the police officers investigating a notorious racist attack in which he had been assaulted and his friend had been killed. The House of Lords held that on these facts it was not arguable that the police had owed the claimant a duty of care, relying on the public policy objections to police liability that had been articulated by Lord Keith in *Hill*. Lord Reed's attempt in *Robinson* to explain this decision by reference to ordinary negligence principles was, with respect, unpersuasive. According to Lord Reed, even though *Brooks* was a positive conduct case, and not an omissions case,[60] the police had owed the claimant no duty of care because '[o]n ordinary principles, behaviour which is merely insensitive is not normally actionable, even if it results in a psychiatric illness'.[61] However, while this might seem like a sensible rule, it is unclear what the authority for it is. Two subsequent passages in Lord Reed's judgment strongly suggest that in his eyes the explanation for the *Brooks* ruling lay in the fact that the harm was psychiatric rather than physical. First of all, he denied that Lord Steyn had said anything in his judgment in *Brooks* to cast doubt on the proposition that the police owed potential claimants 'a duty of care to avoid causing *physical* [188] harm'[62] in accordance with ordinary negligence principles. And secondly, he said that in *Brooks* the claimant had 'sought to have the police held liable for a mental illness which they had caused by treating him inconsiderately'.[63] But again it is unclear what the authority is for distinguishing between mental and physical harm in a case of this kind. Of course, the courts have since *Alcock v Chief Constable of South Yorkshire Police* ('*Alcock*')[64] applied special restrictions to negligence claims for psychiatric illness brought by so-called 'secondary victims', but the claimant in *Brooks* was not a secondary victim in this sense, and although the issue is not beyond doubt, the general understanding seems to be that in other types of case the courts do not subject psychiatric injury claims to special rules at the duty stage of the negligence enquiry.[65] Furthermore, as Lord Mance pointed out in *Robinson*, the House in *Brooks* clearly did not decide the case on the basis of the distinction between physical and psychiatric injury,[66] and indeed there is no mention of that distinction in Lord Steyn's judgment in that case.

---

[59] *Brooks v Commissioner of Police of the Metropolis* [2005] UKHL 24, [2005] 1 WLR 1495.
[60] See *Robinson* (n 1) [69].
[61] ibid [60].
[62] ibid [62] (emphasis added).
[63] ibid [69].
[64] *Alcock v Chief Constable of South Yorkshire Police* [1992] 1 AC 310 (HL).
[65] See, for example, the cases on stress at work, such as *Barber v Somerset CC* [2004] UKHL 13, [2004] 1 WLR 1089. For a useful discussion of the general issue flagged in the text, see *Leach v Chief Constable of Gloucestershire Constabulary* [1999] 1 All ER 215 (CA) 227–29 (Brooke LJ).
[66] *Robinson* (n 1) [93].

VII. DISPOSAL OF THE APPEAL ON THE FACTS
AND THE CONCURRING JUDGMENTS

Application of the principles that Lord Reed had identified to the facts of *Robinson* led to the conclusion that the police were liable to the claimant for her injuries. Although the Court of Appeal had taken the view that the case was concerned with an omission rather than a positive act, Lord Reed disagreed. The claimant's argument was 'not that the police officers failed to protect her against the risk of being injured, but that their actions resulted in her being injured'.[67] This clearly seems right. A rule of thumb that is useful in identifying a true omissions case is to ask whether, if the defendant were removed from the situation altogether, the claimant would still have suffered the damage. Clearly that test was not satisfied here: had the officers not sought to arrest the suspect, the tussle would not have happened, and the claimant would not have been hurt. Furthermore, it was reasonably foreseeable that the suspect would try to evade arrest and that in the course of his doing so passers-by such as the claimant might be knocked into and injured. And as this was a case of positive action causing physical injury that [189] was sufficient, applying orthodox negligence principles, to establish that the officers had owed pedestrians in the immediate vicinity a duty of care. As for the breach of duty question, Lord Reed agreed with the Recorder that this was made out, on the basis that the officers should have noticed the claimant walking past and delayed the arrest until she was out of harm's way.[68]

Lord Mance and Lord Hughes agreed with Lord Reed that the appeal should be allowed, although as we shall see some important differences of emphasis are observable in their judgments. Lord Mance said that a duty of care was owed because:

> [W]e should now recognise the direct physical interface between the police and the public, in the course of an arrest placing an innocent passer-by or bystander at risk, as falling within a now established area of general police liability for positive negligent conduct which foreseeably and directly inflicts physical injury on the public.[69]

As for Lord Hughes, he was sceptical of Lord Reed's assumption that the case could be disposed of by reference to the act/omission distinction and considered that the *Hill* case was good authority for a policy-based rule that police officers engaged in the investigation and prevention of crime owed no duty of care towards victims, suspects or witnesses. However, the present case did not fall within this rule, and since there remained 'a duty of care imposed on police officers not by positive action to occasion physical harm or damage to

---

[67] ibid [73].
[68] ibid [79]–[80].
[69] ibid [97].

property which ought reasonably to be avoided',[70] on the facts a duty of care had been owed to the claimant. On the question of breach, both Lord Mance and Lord Hughes were more inclined towards the Court of Appeal's view than Lord Reed, but both ultimately deferred to the Recorder's finding that the police had been careless. Lord Hughes said that he had 'pondered hard' about the breach issue but emphasised the importance of appellate courts not second-guessing 'trial judges who have had the opportunity to hear the witnesses in person'.[71] Lord Mance also confessed to doubts about the Recorder's conclusion but did not on balance consider that this was a case where an appellate court should interfere.[72] [190]

VIII. THE ROLE OF PUBLIC POLICY

The discussion that follows will primarily be concerned with the general question of how the courts should determine whether a duty of care is owed in a particular case. However, before I turn to consider that question there are some other aspects of Lord Reed's duty of care analysis in *Robinson* that ought to be highlighted, the first of which is the way that Lord Reed downplays the role of public policy arguments in the duty enquiry.

Although the *Hill* case had widely been interpreted as laying down a policy-based immunity for the police in negligence cases concerned with the prevention and investigation of crime, Lord Reed instead chose to explain that decision (as had Lord Toulson in *Michael*) as a simple application of the omissions rule, so that resort to policy was not required to justify the outcome. Once it was understood that public authority defendants were to be treated the same as private parties in negligence, there was no need to have recourse to public policy to justify their non-liability, and since *Gorringe* 'a public authority's non-liability for the consequences of an omission' could generally be justified by reference to the omissions principle.[73] And in a section of his judgment in which Lord Reed responded to some of Lord Hughes's observations, he made some more general comments about the role of policy in negligence adjudication:

> [I]t is important to understand that [discussions of policy considerations] are not a routine aspect of deciding cases in the law of negligence, and are unnecessary when existing principles provide a clear basis for the decision, as in the present appeal ... The absence of a duty towards victims of crime, for example, does not depend merely on a policy devised by a recent generation of judges in relation to policing: it is based on the application of a general and long-established principle that the

---

[70] ibid [120].
[71] ibid [123].
[72] ibid [82].
[73] ibid [40].

common law imposes no liability to protect persons against harm caused by third parties, in the absence of a recognised exception such as a voluntary assumption of responsibility.[74]

At the same time, Lord Reed made it clear that he was not saying that policy concerns had no place in the duty of care enquiry: on the contrary, while the courts were not 'policy-making bodies in the sense in which that can be said of the Law Commission or government departments', he accepted that [191] 'the exercise of judgement about the potential consequences of a decision' had a part to play when a court was asked to decide whether a novel duty of care existed,[75] at least where 'established principles' did not provide a clear answer to the duty question.[76] We can, therefore, extrapolate from Lord Reed's discussion of policy three separate, but related, points:

(1) although policy considerations do have a role to play in the duty enquiry, this is limited to novel cases;
(2) the role of policy arguments in novel cases is secondary to the role of established principles; and
(3) many existing authorities which have been justified on policy grounds are better explained as applications of those established principles.

It was this aspect of Lord Reed's analysis that provoked the strongest reactions from Lord Mance and Lord Hughes. According to Lord Mance, it would be 'unrealistic to suggest that, when recognising and developing an established category [of negligence liability], the courts are not influenced by policy considerations', and the reality was that 'in recognising the existence of any generalised duty in particular circumstances they are making policy choices'.[77] Furthermore, in the particular context of this case, close consideration of the existing authorities showed that it was 'not possible to state absolutely that policy considerations may not shape police or [Crown Prosecution Service] liability in a context where the conduct of the police may perfectly well be analysed as positive, rather than simply as involving some form of omission'.[78] Similarly, Lord Hughes said that earlier judicial reliance on policy considerations was 'simply too considered, too powerful and too authoritative in law to be consigned to history', and that it was not possible to treat such considerations as 'no more than supporting arguments'.[79]

When considering the tensions between Lord Reed's approach to the role of policy and that of the two concurring justices, we can distinguish the 'is' question

---

[74] ibid [69].
[75] ibid.
[76] ibid [42].
[77] ibid [84].
[78] ibid [94].
[79] ibid [113].

of the extent to which the courts have in fact relied on policy considerations to decide duty cases, and the 'ought' question of the extent to which it is appropriate for them to base duty decisions on such [192] considerations. On the 'is' question, my view is that Lord Reed's take on the authorities is more convincing overall, but that on occasion it would have been better to concede that a given case was decided on policy grounds than to seek an explanation for it in 'established principles'. The particular significance of Lord Reed's analysis of the authorities lies in his acknowledgment that many of the cases in which policy considerations were mentioned by the judges either were, or could have been, decided in the same way by reference to general negligence principles, so that the discussion of policy was otiose. This is an important insight, which is borne out by recent empirical research by James Plunkett into the use of policy reasoning by the House of Lords/Supreme Court in the period 1985–2015, which shows that only in a small minority of duty of care cases in which reliance was placed upon policy considerations were they solely determinative of the outcome of the duty enquiry.[80] Perhaps the best example of this phenomenon is the *Hill* case itself, which is easily explicable by reference both to the omissions principle and to the separate principle that 'A is not ordinarily liable to victim B for injuries … deliberately inflicted by third party C',[81] and where the discussion of policy in Lord Keith's speech consists of one paragraph, which begins with the words '[t]hat is sufficient for the disposal of the appeal'.[82] On the other hand, Plunkett's research also accords with Lord Mance's observation in *Robinson* that there are undoubtedly *some* earlier cases at the highest level where it was accepted that a duty of care could be denied on policy grounds, even if established principles pointed to the existence of a duty. A good example of such a decision is *Smith v Ministry of Defence*,[83] where all the seven Law Lords who sat in the case upheld the existence of a 'combat immunity' applicable to anything done in the course of military operations against an enemy, an immunity justified on the grounds that the existence of a duty of care might hamper the conduct of the military in wartime. This immunity means that even in cases where a defendant combatant causes foreseeable physical injury or physical damage to property by their positive conduct (and where one would therefore expect there to be a duty of care in accordance with the general principles upheld in *Robinson*) no liability in negligence can arise. With respect, therefore, Lord Reed's dismissal of *Smith* as a case that raised 'a novel legal issue' and which 'did not concern an established category of liability'[84] rings rather hollow. As for the 'ought' question, Lord Reed's treatment of policy concerns as legitimate, but of secondary significance,

---

[80] J Plunkett, *The Duty of Care in Negligence* (Oxford, Hart Publishing, 2018) 203 (Table 13).
[81] *Mitchell v Glasgow CC* [2009] UKHL 11, [2009] 1 AC 874 [81] (Lord Brown).
[82] *Hill* (n 4) 63.
[83] *Smith v Ministry of Defence* (n 25).
[84] *Robinson* (n 1) [28].

accords with much current academic thinking on [193] that question,[85] and although the concurring justices clearly considered that a more significant role for policy was appropriate, in the case of Lord Mance the strength of this argument was perhaps undermined by the very expansive meaning that he seemed to attach to the concept of 'policy'.[86]

IX. TWO FURTHER ISSUES

Two further issues raised by the judgments in *Robinson* should also be noted. The first is that, while Lord Reed downplayed the importance of policy in the duty of care enquiry, he played up the distinction between acts and omissions. He said:

> The distinction between careless acts causing personal injury, for which the law generally imposes liability, and careless omissions to prevent acts (by other agencies) causing personal injury, for which the common law generally imposes no liability, is not a mere alternative to policy-based reasoning, but is inherent in the nature of the tort of negligence. For the same reason, although the distinction, like any other distinction, can be difficult to draw in borderline cases, it is of fundamental importance. The central point is that the law of negligence generally imposes duties not to cause harm to other people or their property: it does not generally impose duties to provide them with benefits (including the prevention of harm caused by other agencies).[87]

As with other parts of his judgment, this focus on the act/omission distinction was consistent with Lord Toulson's approach in *Michael*, albeit that there the focus on the distinction had militated against liability, whereas here it militated in its favour. This time it was Lord Hughes who reacted the more strongly against Lord Reed's analysis. In particular, while Lord [194] Hughes acknowledged the significance of the act/omission distinction, he considered that it could not explain the absence of a duty of care in a case like *Hill* for two reasons: first, because there were exceptions to the no-liability for omissions rule; and, second, because 'there is no firm line capable of determination between a case of omission and of commission'.[88] With respect, however, these

---

[85] See, eg, S Perry, 'The Role of Duty of Care in a Rights-Based Theory of Negligence Law' in A Robertson and Tang HW (eds), *The Goals of Private Law* (Oxford, Hart Publishing, 2009) 83–91; A Robertson, 'Justice, Community Welfare and the Duty of Care' (2011) 127 *LQR* 370 and A Robertson, 'Rights, Pluralism and the Duty of Care' in D Nolan and A Robertson (eds), *Rights and Private Law* (Oxford, Hart Publishing, 2012); NJ McBride and R Bagshaw, *Tort Law*, 6th edn (Harlow, Pearson Education, 2018) 83. For the contrasting view that it is illegitimate to take policy considerations into account at all, see R Stevens, *Torts and Rights* (Oxford, OUP, 2007) ch 14; and A Beever, *Rediscovering the Law of Negligence* (Oxford, Hart Publishing, 2007). And for a helpful overview of the issue, see Plunkett (n 80) 151–64.

[86] See, in particular, *Robinson* (n 1) [84].

[87] ibid [69].

[88] ibid [117].

are not convincing objections. The existence of exceptions to a no-liability rule does not necessarily (or even presumptively) rob the rule of force in cases which do not fall within the exceptions. For example, the outcome of a case can plausibly be explained by reference to the general rule against recovery of pure economic loss in negligence even though the rule is not absolute. And the idea that there is not a workable distinction between positive conduct cases and omissions cases, and that 'the great majority of cases can be analysed in terms of either'[89] is, with respect, simply implausible. On the contrary, once it is understood that the distinction in play here is between making things worse for the claimant and not making them better, the distinction works perfectly well in the vast majority of cases.[90]

The other issue that deserves a mention is the idea bubbling beneath the surface in *Robinson* that victims of psychiatric injury may not be as well protected by negligence law as those who have suffered injury of a physical kind, even outside the category of so-called 'secondary victims' whose claims are subject to the restrictions imposed in *Alcock*.[91] As *Robinson* was not itself a psychiatric injury case, it would be a mistake to read too much into these runes, but it is nevertheless noteworthy that in all three judgments significance seems to have been attached to the distinction between the two different types of harm, either in the discussion of the earlier authorities or in the formulation of general liability principles.[92] Lord Hughes was particularly explicit on this point when he said that 'no duty of care towards victims of crime, witnesses or suspects' could be 'erected on the back of foreseeability of psychiatric harm' for policy reasons.[93] [195]

X. DETERMINATION OF THE DUTY OF CARE: BACK TO BASICS

The chief importance of the *Robinson* decision lies in the approach that the Supreme Court lays down for the determination of the duty of care issue. As Lord Bridge pointed out in *Caparo*, 'there has for long been a tension between two different approaches' to this question.[94] Under what he called the traditional approach, 'the law finds the existence of the duty in different specific situations each exhibiting its own particular characteristics', whereas under

---

[89] ibid.
[90] See further, Nolan, 'The Liability of Public Authorities for Failing to Confer Benefits' (n 46).
[91] *Alcock* (n 64).
[92] See *Robinson* (n 1) [69] (Lord Reed, discussing *Brooks* (n 59)), [94] (Lord Mance, stating that 'any otherwise generally established category' of negligence liability concerning the police or Crown Prosecution Service did not encompass 'extended detention and psychiatric injury'), [101] (Lord Hughes, limiting the scope of police liability to positive negligent acts causing *physical* harm to individuals or damage to property).
[93] ibid [119].
[94] *Caparo* (n 5) 616.

'the more modern approach', a single general principle is sought 'which may be applied in all circumstances to determine the existence of a duty of care'.[95] Unsurprisingly Lord Bridge traced the 'modern approach' to the speech of Lord Atkin in *Donoghue v Stevenson*,[96] and indeed the enunciation of Lord Atkin's famous 'neighbour principle' can (and has been) interpreted as a 'single general principle' of this kind. In truth, however, it seems unlikely that Lord Atkin meant the principle to operate as a general duty test, and in the decades that followed *Donoghue* the courts do not seem to have treated it as such. The real significance of *Donoghue* lay elsewhere, namely:

(1)   in the clear judicial recognition of negligence as a tort, rather than simply a means of committing one, a proposition that (though controversial) gained swift general acceptance; and

(2)   in the fact that over time *Donoghue* came to stand for the proposition that there was a presumption that a duty of care was owed in cases where a negligent *act* of the defendant had caused physical injury to the claimant or their property – precisely the 'established principle' on which Lord Reed based the duty of care in *Robinson*.

By contrast, the broader proposition that the neighbour principle could operate as a general test of duty was really untenable, since it was impossible to square with established authorities limiting liability for, among other things, omissions and pure economic loss.[97]

Nevertheless, the seed of the general duty test had been sown and in the 1970s it began to germinate. The first clear sign came in *Home Office v Dorset Yacht Co*, where Lord Reid said that the time had come 'when we can [196] and should say that [the neighbour principle] ought to apply unless there is some justification or valid explanation for its exclusion'.[98] Although in the same case Lord Diplock gave a classic exposition of the more traditional approach, focused on the 'kinds of conduct and relationships which have been held in previous decisions ... to give rise to a duty of care',[99] eight years later, in *Anns v Merton LBC*, Lord Wilberforce drew upon Lord Reid's dictum when he laid down a general two-stage test for the determination of the duty issue which marked the high point of the 'modern approach' to the duty enquiry.[100] Unfortunately, the *Anns* test was interpreted (doubtless wrongly) to mean that the lower courts were no longer constrained by precedent, but were instead

---

[95] ibid.

[96] *Donoghue v Stevenson* [1932] AC 562 (HL).

[97] See WE Peel and J Goudkamp, *Winfield & Jolowicz on Tort*, 19th edn (London, Sweet & Maxwell, 2014) para 5-016 ('little reliance was placed upon this generalised concept'). See also Plunkett (n 80) 39.

[98] *Home Office v Dorset Yacht Co Ltd* [1970] AC 1004 (HL) 1027. See also at 1054 (Lord Pearson).

[99] ibid 1058.

[100] *Anns* (n 44) 751–52.

free to expand the boundaries of negligence law as and how they wished.[101] It did not take long for the House of Lords to realise that the genie needed to be put firmly back in the bottle, and so began the 'retreat from *Anns*', which culminated in the abandonment of the *Anns* test in *Caparo* and the reaffirmation of the orthodox approach (now christened 'incrementalism', following the influential judgment of Brennan J in *Sutherland Shire Council v Heyman*[102]).

However, even in *Caparo* the tension between the two approaches was evident. On the one hand, both Lord Bridge and Lord Oliver emphasised that the key to the duty question lay in what Lord Bridge called 'the more traditional categorisation of distinct and recognisable situations',[103] and that the search for a general duty test was pointless and detrimental – a pursuit of a 'will-o'-the wisp', according to Lord Oliver, which served 'not to clarify the law but merely to bedevil its development in a way which corresponds with practicality and common sense'.[104] And yet at the same time Lord Bridge could not resist the temptation to identify three 'necessary ingredients' for a duty of care to arise, namely foreseeability, 'proximity' and that it be 'fair, just and reasonable' for a duty of care to be imposed.[105] Despite the fact that Lord Bridge *specifically denied* that the latter two concepts were 'susceptible of any such precise definition as would be necessary to give them utility as practical tests',[106] these three ingredients led in time to the resurrection of the general test approach, under the guise of a so-called 'three-stage test' named (paradoxically) after the case which had so forcefully sought to restore the traditional approach. Unlike the *Anns* two-stage test, the *Caparo* [197] three-stage test was a slow burner, as one can see from the way it only gradually insinuated itself into the standard textbook discussions of the duty question in the years that followed the *Caparo* decision.[107] And also unlike *Anns*, the three-stage test failed to achieve real dominance, particularly at the level of the House of Lords/Supreme Court, where it was used in only 30 per cent of duty of care determinations in the quarter century after *Caparo* was decided.[108] Nevertheless, the *Caparo* test was

---

[101] See Plunkett (n 80) 45.

[102] 'It is preferable, in my view, that the law should develop novel categories of negligence incrementally and by analogy with established categories' (*Sutherland Shire Council v Heyman* (1985) 157 CLR 424 (HCA) 481).

[103] *Caparo* (n 5) 618. See also at 628 (Lord Roskill).

[104] ibid 633.

[105] ibid 617–18.

[106] ibid 618.

[107] Compare WVH Rogers, *Winfield & Jolowicz on Tort*, 14th edn (London, Sweet & Maxwell, 1994) 86–87 (a fleeting reference to what 'one member of the House of Lords' has said, which focuses on Lord Bridge's denial of the utility of the concepts as tests); WVH Rogers, *Winfield & Jolowicz on Tort*, 15th edn (London, Sweet & Maxwell, 1998) 97 ff (an extended discussion of the three – or possibly four – separate steps that 'seem' to make up the duty enquiry); and WVH Rogers, *Winfield & Jolowicz on Tort*, 16th edn (London, Sweet & Maxwell, 2002) 112 ('The leading case [on duty of care] is now [*Caparo*] ... There are now three separate steps or issues in the [duty] enquiry').

[108] See Plunkett (n 80) 186. See also K Stanton, 'Decision-making in the Tort of Negligence in the House of Lords' (2007) 15 *Tort Law Review* 93, 99 ('scarcely any use' made by the House of Lords of the *Caparo* test in the early years of this century).

widely relied upon lower down the judicial hierarchy, and even at the ultimate appellate level the test was described as '[c]urrently ... the most favoured test of liability'[109] and 'the starting point' for determination of the duty question,[110] a view shared by the authors of *Clerk & Lindsell on Torts*.[111]

Although this story is well-known, it is worth repeating it in order properly to contextualise the very strong reaction against the *Caparo* 'test' in *Michael* and *Robinson*. Only for a few years after *Anns* has our highest court thrown its full weight behind any general test for the determination of the duty of care, and yet the tendency towards reliance on this approach in the courts below has been persistent, with the ultimate irony being that a House of Lords decision that explicitly disavowed general tests came itself to be regarded as the source of such a test. *Robinson* in particular seems to represent a concerted effort to stamp out the general test approach once and for all, and it will surely be very hard for the lower courts to ignore it, not least because the Supreme Court has unanimously endorsed Lord Reed's analysis in two subsequent cases.[112] Indeed, arguably for a lower court to employ the *Caparo* test after *Robinson* would amount to nothing short of *lèse-majesté*. [198]

XI. WHY GENERAL TESTS OF DUTY ARE DOOMED TO FAIL

It seems to me to be no coincidence that it is the ultimate appellate court that has been so resistant to the use of a general test of duty, and that the use of such tests has been more prevalent in lower-level courts. In this section of my chapter I will seek to show why it is that general tests of duty inevitably fail, and why, therefore, the only plausible approach to the duty of care question is the traditional one.

The key to understanding the superiority of the traditional approach lies in the recollection that the notional duty question is a question of law,[113] and that this marks a critical difference between the duty enquiry and, say, the breach or factual causation enquiries, which are of course questions of fact. Where the court in a negligence case is faced with a question of fact, it makes perfect sense for that question to be resolved by a one-size-fits-all test, which asks, for example, whether the conduct of the defendant fell below the standard of the

---

[109] *Van Colle v Chief Constable of Hertfordshire* [2008] UKHL 50, [2009] 1 AC 225 [42] (Lord Bingham).

[110] *Smith v Ministry of Defence* (n 25) [162] (Lord Carnwath).

[111] '[T]he accepted test for the existence of a notional duty' (MA Jones (ed), *Clerk & Lindsell on Torts*, 22nd edn (London, Sweet & Maxwell, 2018) para 8-16).

[112] See *James-Bowen v Commissioner of Police of the Metropolis* [2018] UKSC 40, [2018] 1 WLR 4021 [23] (Lord Lloyd-Jones); and *Darnley v Croydon Health Services NHS Trust* [2018] UKSC 50, [2019] AC 831 [15]–[16] (Lord Lloyd-Jones).

[113] Indeed, I have previously argued that this is one of only two defining characteristics of the concept: see D Nolan, 'Deconstructing the Duty of Care' (2013) 129 *LQR* 559, 567–69.

reasonable person, or whether the defendant's fault was a but-for cause of the claimant's injury. Indeed, how else could a court decide such a question, when by definition earlier decisions on questions of fact are not precedents, and so cannot be followed? By contrast, when it comes to notional duty, earlier decisions are binding on the court, and hence a quite different kind of reasoning is required. The reasoning in question is standard common law reasoning,[114] working with the relevant authorities to determine whether the case is covered by binding precedent, and, if not, reasoning by analogy and by reference to relevant considerations in order to decide whether or not a duty of care is owed.[115] While that process may be more or less straightforward in a particular case, and there may be legitimate disagreement about the considerations a court should take into account, there is nothing remotely mysterious about what ought to be going on. In truth, the approach that courts take to determining the duty of care question should be thoroughly predictable, and really rather uninteresting. It is a sad reflection of how unsophisticated common law thinking on negligence remains that pages and pages of the textbooks are devoted to what ought to be a routine issue, and that our highest court should have had yet again to remind other judges and practitioners of what needs to be done.

The same 'poverty of thought'[116] is responsible for the widespread belief [199] that a satisfactory answer to the notional duty question can be arrived at by the use of a general test of the kind used to determine questions of fact. There are two reasons why such a general test cannot work. The first is that in order to encompass the very wide range of different issues that fall under the notional duty umbrella, the concepts that make up a general duty test must by definition be so abstract ('neighbourhood', 'proximity' etc) that in themselves they provide little or no guidance to the court as to whether a duty of care ought to be recognised. And the other reason why such tests inevitably fail is that their relationship with precedent is problematic and obscure. Taken literally, they seem to leave no room for the doctrine of precedent at all. The judge simply applies the test to the facts, or the 'duty situation', and the test itself produces the right answer. Earlier authority simply goes by the board, as in the worst excesses of the *Anns* era. In practice, of course, a more nuanced approach is taken, but the basic question of how the general test is to be reconciled with the doctrine of precedent never receives a satisfactory answer, because no such answer can be given. Hence the use of a general test in combination with traditional precedent-based reasoning necessarily generates irresolvable tensions and the law inevitably becomes unclear and incoherent.

---

[114] See K Stanton, 'Incremental Approaches to the Duty of Care' in NJ Mullany (ed), *Torts in the Nineties* (Sydney, LBC Information Services, 1997) 39 ('incrementalism may be regarded as restoring a traditional method of adjudication to the tort of negligence').

[115] See also Plunkett (n 80) 71.

[116] See RFV Heuston, '*Donoghue v Stevenson* in Retrospect' (1957) 20 *MLR* 1, 23.

Suppose, for example, that we take seriously the proposition put forward by the Court of Appeal in *Robinson* that the *Caparo* three-stage test be used in every duty case. Where would this leave the complex web of duty rules that have developed to govern liability for psychiatric injury in cases like *Alcock*[117] and *Page v Smith*[118] ? Does the court simply ignore these decisions, despite the fact that they appear to govern the claim in question, and apply the *Caparo* test instead? And if the answer is no, that in that type of case the precedents must be followed, then why not always do so, in which case the *Caparo* analysis in fact plays no role in the decision-making process, and is rendered superfluous? Nor is it an adequate response to this critique to say that the *Caparo* test is only to be used in 'novel' cases, whatever that might mean. Precedent-based reasoning is not some sort of on-off switch, whereby either the case is determined by precedent or precedent is irrelevant. Under the traditional approach to the duty question, the extent of the judge's discretion in deciding whether or not to recognise a duty of care is of course determined by the pertinence of the relevant authorities, but there always *are* relevant authorities. In an advanced system of precedent-based rules, there is simply no such thing as a jurisprudential vacuum, where a court is completely unconstrained by earlier case law. Analogies *always* exist.

[200] Needless to say, when the theoretical underpinnings of general duty tests are this weak, their use inevitably leads to fundamental problems. Three in particular can be identified. The first is that the weakening of precedent and the increasing number of *ad hoc* decisions applying the test render the law uncertain and unstable. The outcome of cases becomes less predictable,[119] which in turn generates more litigation. With respect, Lord Bingham's suggestion (if that is what it was) that a general test of duty is required if the law is not to become a 'morass of single instances'[120] gets it precisely wrong: on the contrary, that is exactly what use of such a general test will produce.

A second shortcoming of general duty tests is that a judge who is both freed from the constraints of precedent and asked to apply a test made up of concepts so abstract as to be meaningless is essentially given *carte blanche* to decide the case however he or she wishes. Although this does not necessarily result in bad outcomes in individual cases, such an approach is antithetical to the philosophy of the common law and weakens the authority of the decisions that are made. As Lord Diplock pointed out in *Dorset Yacht*:

> The justification of the courts' role in giving the effect of law to the judges' conception of the public interest in the field of negligence is based upon the cumulative

---

[117] *Alcock* (n 64).

[118] *Page v Smith* [1996] AC 155 (HL).

[119] See S Deakin, A Johnston and B Markesinis, *Markesinis and Deakin's Tort Law*, 7th edn (Oxford, OUP, 2012) 114 (commenting on the difficulty of predicting the outcome of applying the *Caparo* three-stage test, and the 'conceptual uncertainty' that surrounds it). See also J Morgan, 'The Rise and Fall of the General Duty of Care' (2006) 22 *Professional Negligence* 206, 217–18.

[120] *Customs and Excise Commissioners v Barclays Bank plc* [2006] UKHL 28, [2007] 1 AC 181 [8].

experience of the judiciary of the actual consequences of lack of care in particular instances.[121]

Disregard that 'cumulative experience' by abandoning precedent-based reasoning for an *ad hoc* approach, and the justification falls away.

And a third difficulty caused by the use of a general test of duty is that it is likely to become impossible to reconcile the case law into a coherent body of rules. To give an example, in an earlier article on the duty of care concept, I showed how the Court of Appeal's reliance on the *Caparo* test in *Everett v Comojo (UK) Ltd (t/a The Metropolitan)*,[122] led to it deciding the case without reference to highly pertinent House of Lords authority on the question of negligence liability for the deliberate criminal acts of third parties.[123] [201] Although in this instance the outcome of the case was probably consistent with that earlier authority, one can easily imagine scenarios where a ruling made with the use of a general duty test is impossible rationally to reconcile with an earlier decision of a higher court, with the result that the law becomes incoherent, in the sense that it is not possible to expound or explain the law in an internally consistent way.

By way of contrast, the traditional approach of applying precedent and reasoning by analogy promotes consistency and predictability, restores authority to decisions on duty, and is at least capable of bringing about a high level of internal coherence. By reducing and constraining the degree of individual judgment involved in deciding cases, the traditional approach brings the law of negligence closer to the 'rule of law ideal where the outcome of the case does not depend upon the individual views of the particular decision-maker, but upon the common understanding of what the law requires'.[124] And by providing 'specific guidance for specific types of problem', the traditional approach is 'of considerably more use' to lower-level courts and practitioners.[125]

Faced with the overwhelmingly strong case against general tests of duty, one is forced to ask why they have proven so attractive to the lower courts. The most plausible answer is threefold: first, that the existence of general tests for questions of fact such as breach of duty and causation generates an expectation that the duty of care issue can be approached in the same way; second, that 'a judge may find it reassuring to be able to identify a general governing standard and explain his decision by reference to its terms';[126] and, third, that it is simply *easier* for an overworked and time-poor judge to decide such an issue by reference to an open-ended general test than by a careful analysis of the existing

---

[121] *Dorset Yacht* (n 98) 1058.

[122] *Everett v Comojo (UK) Ltd (t/a The Metropolitan)* [2011] EWCA Civ 13, [2012] 1 WLR 150.

[123] Nolan, 'Deconstructing the Duty of Care' (n 113) 584–85.

[124] G Lamond, 'Analogical Reasoning in the Common Law' (2014) 34 *OJLS* 567, 576.

[125] Plunkett (n 80) 77.

[126] JA Smillie, 'Principle, Policy and Negligence' (1984) 11 *New Zealand Universities Law Review* 111, 144.

precedents and (where appropriate) policy considerations.[127] When considering the impact of the *Robinson* decision, it is important to bear these three considerations in mind. For while there is nothing remotely ambiguous about Lord Reed's disavowal of the *Caparo* test, the allure of general duty tests is such that some resistance to his message is to be expected. [202]

XII. APPLYING THE TRADITIONAL APPROACH POST-*ROBINSON*

To finish, it may be useful to consider how the courts should apply the traditional approach to duty in a particular case, and to dispel some myths about it.[128] If the general test approach represents a move away from precedent, the traditional approach puts it centre stage, so that the arguments of the parties, and the reasoning of the court, are firmly located within the context of the existing authorities. Hence, Lord Devlin's observation in *Hedley Byrne & Co v Heller & Partners Ltd* ('*Hedley Byrne*') that the first step in the duty enquiry 'is to see how far the authorities have gone',[129] and Lord Bridge's statement in *Caparo* that applying the traditional approach it was to the authorities 'directly relevant to this relatively narrow corner of the field' that the court should look to determine the duty question in that case.[130] In *Michael*, Lord Toulson summed up the approach to be taken in the following words:

> The established method of the court involves examining the decided cases to see how far the law has gone and where it has refrained from going. From that analysis it looks to see whether there is an argument by analogy for extending liability to a new situation, or whether an earlier limitation is no longer logically or socially justifiable. In doing so it pays regard to the need for overall coherence. Often there will be a mixture of policy considerations to take into account.[131]

The breadth of the negligence cause of action means that the authorities must be organised into categories for this process to operate effectively.[132] To understand how the process of categorisation works, it is useful to think in terms of a number of key case types that fall outside the *Donoghue v Stevenson*

---

[127] As one commentator pointed out in the aftermath of *Anns*, an attraction of the general test approach is that 'the judge is spared the hard task of distinguishing or supplying convincing reasons for refusing to follow inconvenient precedents', and of identifying and weighing all the relevant arguments for and against liability: ibid 145.

[128] For a not dissimilar approach to the one advocated here, see Plunkett (n 80) 139–48.

[129] *Hedley Byrne & Co v Heller & Partners Ltd* [1964] AC 465 (HL) 525.

[130] *Caparo* (n 5) 619.

[131] *Michael* (n 12) [102].

[132] See the reference by Lord Bridge in *Caparo* (n 5) 618 to the 'categorisation of distinct and recognisable situations as guides to the existence, the scope and the limits' of the duties of care the law imposes. And see also *Markesinis and Deakin's Tort Law* (n 119) 116 (the courts 'approach the application of the law relating to duty of care by breaking it down into a series of categories, which give rise to distinct issues').

paradigm of positive conduct directly causing physical harm (where a duty of care is presumed).[133] These key case types [203] concern omissions, deliberate intervening acts, psychiatric injury and pure economic loss. Although these four case types give rise to the most general categories of earlier authority, the process of categorisation does not stop there. In a psychiatric injury case, for example, different rules apply to primary victims, secondary victims, victims of work stress and so on. And where a case raises a duty issue that does not fall within any of the four key case types (such as the 'combat immunity' question), then a narrower line of authority relating to that particular problem will constitute the relevant body of case law. Like the law itself, the categories are dynamic. For example, if claims against public authorities are subject to special rules at the duty stage, a public authority category (or categories) is required, but if the equality principle is applied, as it now is, no such category is needed. Similarly, if the Supreme Court decided to abolish the duty-level limitations that currently govern claims for psychiatric injury, then cases that would previously have fallen into the psychiatric injury category would subsequently be encompassed by the *Donoghue v Stevenson* paradigm, and so the category would disappear.

Once the relevant category or sub-category has been identified, the judge turns to the case law in that category and the usual process of reasoning from precedent, and by the use of analogy, takes place. If a case falls into more than one category (for example, because it concerns an omission *and* pure economic loss), then the precedents in each category must be considered before a duty determination can be made. As McHugh J said in *Crimmins v Stevedoring Industry Finance Committee*, '[i]n determining whether the instant case is analogous to existing precedents, the reasons why the material facts in the precedent cases did or did not found a duty will ordinarily be controlling', and 'the precedent cases have to be examined to reveal their bases in principle and policy'.[134] To the extent that the precedents do not show the way forward, an exercise of judgment will need to be made as to whether negligence liability ought to be extended to the new situation. The result of employing this approach is that 'decisions in new cases can be more confidently predicted, by reference to a limited number of principles capable of application throughout the category'.[135] Other benefits of analogical reasoning include encouraging settlements, discouraging appeals

---

[133] See *Dorset Yacht* (n 98) 1061, where Lord Diplock identified 'two special characteristics' that differentiated the facts of the case from the facts of *Donoghue*, and then started his analysis of the duty question 'with an examination of the previous cases in which both or one of these special characteristics' was present.

[134] *Crimmins v Stevedoring Industry Finance Committee* (1999) 200 CLR 1 (HCA) [72]–[73]. See also Stanton, 'Incremental Approaches to the Duty of Care' (n 114) 46 ('The underlying logic and policies of the recognised category of duty of care are identified in order to decide whether the case in issue is truly analogous').

[135] *Crimmins* (n 134) [77].

and narrowing the range of evidentiary materials, thereby reducing the cost of litigation.[136] As is so often the case, an abstract exposition is less useful than looking at the best examples of the method **[204]** in action, such as the speeches of Lord Diplock in *Dorset Yacht* and Lord Bridge in *Caparo*. And since there is nothing particularly distinctive about the method as it is employed in the duty of care context, guidance can also be sought from more general discussions of analogical reasoning in the common law tradition.[137]

Three further points should be made. First, on the traditional approach to the duty question no sharp distinction can be drawn between novel cases and cases covered by authority, as the use of analogical reasoning blurs the boundary. Besides, it is only after the authorities have been fully considered that any assessment of the novelty of the claim before the court can be made, so the idea that a different approach (such as a general test) can be used *ab initio* in a 'novel case' makes little sense. Second, the idea that the traditional approach is just another 'test' for the existence of a duty of care (viz, the 'incremental test'[138]) is completely misguided, since the whole point of the traditional approach is that there is, and can be, no such thing.[139] And finally, the argument that is sometimes made against the traditional approach that it is stultifying and does not allow negligence to develop[140] is a caricature apparently borne of the failure to appreciate that this approach is just standard common law reasoning. After all, no-one could seriously suppose that the common law itself is incapable of development just because it is a system of rules based on precedent and reasoning by analogy. The label 'incrementalism' may be partly to blame for this misapprehension and is perhaps best avoided. In truth, analogical reasoning does not preclude radical decisions that significantly expand the boundaries of negligence liability.[141] *Hedley Byrne*[142] was such a decision, as was *Henderson v Merrett Syndicates* ('*Henderson*'),[143] where that case was extended from negligent statements to negligent services. Both are exemplars of the kind of common law reasoning that is being advocated, which (needless to say) focuses not just on the rules laid down in earlier cases, but also on the principles that underlie those rules, a point that comes through particularly clearly in Lord Goff's speech in *Henderson*. **[205]**

---

[136] ibid [76].

[137] See, eg, Lamond (n 124).

[138] See, eg, *Customs and Excise Commissioners* (n 120) [7] (Lord Bingham). See also Stanton 'Incremental Approaches to the Duty of Care' (n 114) 50 (the 'test of incrementalism').

[139] See *Crimmins* (n 134) [73] (McHugh J): 'The policy of developing novel cases incrementally by reference to analogous cases acknowledges that there is no general test for determining whether a duty of care exists'. See also Stanton, 'Incremental Approaches to the Duty of Care' (n 114) 34 (describing 'incrementalism' as the 'antithesis' of a general duty test).

[140] See, eg, D Howarth, 'Negligence after *Murphy*: Time to Re-think' [1991] *CLJ* 58, 71.

[141] See Stanton, 'Incremental Approaches to the Duty of Care' (n 114) 54 ('incrementalism has not prevented the English courts from achieving more radical results than those which are found elsewhere').

[142] *Hedley Byrne* (n 129).

[143] *Henderson v Merrett Syndicates* [1995] 2 AC 145 (HL).

XIII. CONCLUSION

The decisions of the Supreme Court in *Michael* and *Robinson* have the potential to usher in a new era in the troubled history of the duty of care in negligence, an era marked by greater transparency, predictability and consistency. Four common themes run through the leading judgments in the cases, two more specific and two more general. The two more specific themes are the fundamental nature of the act/omission dichotomy, and the idea that no distinction ought generally to be drawn between private and public defendants at the duty of care stage of the negligence enquiry. The first more general theme is that, while policy arguments have a legitimate role to play in the duty enquiry, they are very much subsidiary to arguments from principle and precedent. And the second more general theme is that, when faced with duty of care issues, the courts should eschew the 'beguiling simplicity'[144] of general duty tests, and instead employ traditional common law methods, using analogical reasoning and reasoned argumentation to produce a 'pattern of liability as diversified as befits the complex society which [the law of negligence] serves'.[145] In this final respect, the message coming from the Supreme Court could hardly be clearer. It remains to be seen whether the rest of the profession is listening.

---

[144] MA Millner, *Negligence in Modern Law* (London, Butterworths, 1967) 236.
[145] ibid 237.

4

The Liability of Public Authorities for Failing to Confer Benefits

(2011) 127 *Law Quarterly Review* 260–287

[260] I. INTRODUCTION

IN THIS ARTICLE I consider the circumstances in which a public authority may be held liable in negligence for failing to confer a benefit. Although the question of liability for failure to confer benefits is often framed in terms of liability for 'omissions', the use of the term 'omission' is open to the objection that an omission presupposes a duty to act, and can lead to unnecessary handwringing about the difficulties of distinguishing between acts and omissions, difficulties which are largely bypassed when the issue is framed in terms of whether the defendant has made things worse for the claimant or simply failed to confer a benefit on her.[1] The question of liability for failure to confer benefits is of course one of general importance in the law of negligence, but in practice it most frequently crops up in cases involving public authority defendants. Similarly, while the difficulties surrounding public authority liability in negligence are by no means limited to this issue, in a good proportion of the relevant case law the defendant authority was sued not for making things worse, but for not making things better.[2]

Surprisingly, however, discussions of public authority negligence liability frequently downplay or ignore the question of liability for failure to confer benefits, focusing instead on other issues raised by public authority cases, such as the utility of public law principles in this context and the validity of policy arguments against recognition of a duty of care in particular types of case. There are, for example, only very brief discussions of the issue in

---

[1] For use of the language of failure to confer benefits, see, eg, MJ Bowman and SH Bailey, 'Negligence in Public Law: A Positive Obligation to Rescue?' [1984] *PL* 277, 283; A Beever, *Rediscovering the Law of Negligence* (Oxford, Hart Publishing, 2007) 211; and R Stevens, *Torts and Rights* (Oxford, OUP, 2007) 9.

[2] See C Harlow, *State Liability: Tort Law and Beyond* (Oxford, OUP, 2004) 16.

Fairgrieve's comparative study of state liability,[3] and in the Law Commission's consultation paper on administrative redress.[4] It is also noteworthy that the most important English case on the liability of public authorities for failing to confer benefits, *Gorringe v Calderdale Metropolitan Borough Council*,[5] met with a somewhat muted reaction. As we shall see, *Gorringe* was in many respects a radically restrictive decision, which called into question the validity of a number of cases in which public bodies had apparently been made liable for [**261**] failing to exercise a statutory duty or power. And yet, as an early commentator on the decision pointed out, initially *Gorringe* was the subject of 'remarkably little wider consideration'.[6] Moreover, even when consideration was given to the case, there was a tendency to downplay its implications. A good example is a note on *Gorringe* by Howarth in the *Cambridge Law Journal*,[7] in which he consistently sought to undermine the significance of the decision, and described it as 'eminently distinguishable', since it could have been decided on grounds different from those on which it was in fact decided, and because it was a 'case about roads'. And although the significance of the decision in *Gorringe* does appear increasingly to be appreciated by the judiciary and academic commentators, the decision has still not been subjected to comprehensive review.[8]

My aim in this article is to redress the balance somewhat, by providing a considered analysis of the issue of public authority liability for failure to confer benefits, in particular by looking closely at the implications of the *Gorringe* decision for the English law in this area, and by subjecting the law after *Gorringe* to critical analysis. The article is divided into three main parts. In the first part, I consider whether negligence liability for failure to confer a benefit can ever be based on the existence of a statutory duty or power imposed or conferred on a public authority defendant. In the second part, I consider the application of ordinary private law principles to public authority defendants in cases involving failures to confer benefits. And in the third and final part, I ask whether the current state of the law in this area is satisfactory. I should point out that although my focus is solely on the question of failure to confer benefits, a public authority defendant may of course argue against the imposition of a duty of

---

[3] D Fairgrieve, *State Liability in Tort: A Comparative Law Study* (Oxford, OUP, 2003). The discussion of omissions liability is limited to less than two pages (128–29).

[4] Law Commission, *Administrative Redress: Public Bodies and the Citizen* (Law Com CP No 187, 2008). The Commission devotes a mere four paragraphs to the issue (paras 3.160–3.163).

[5] *Gorringe v Calderdale Metropolitan Borough Council* [2004] UKHL 15, [2004] 1 WLR 1057.

[6] AR Keene, 'Negligence Claims Against Public Bodies' (2005) 155 *New Law Journal* 86, 86.

[7] D Howarth, 'Public Authority Non-Liability: Spinning Out of Control?' [2004] *CLJ* 546. For a more balanced account, see J Morgan, 'Slowing the Expansion of Public Authorities' Liability' (2005) 121 *LQR* 43.

[8] Perhaps the most considered analysis of *Gorringe* is to be found in C Booth and D Squires, *The Negligence Liability of Public Authorities* (Oxford, OUP, 2006) paras 3.104–3.134.

care for other reasons, and that some of these arguments may not be available to private parties.[9] I should also point out that my focus throughout is on the law of negligence, and that I am not therefore concerned (directly, at any rate) with the circumstances in which public authorities may be held liable for failing to confer benefits in other torts, or under the Human Rights Act 1998.

II. STATUTORY DUTIES AND POWERS AS SOURCES OF OBLIGATIONS TO CONFER BENEFITS

The issue under consideration in this part of the article is whether liability in negligence for failure to confer a benefit can ever be based on the existence of a statutory duty or power imposed or conferred on the defendant. Although in *Gorringe v Calderdale Metropolitan Borough Council*,[10] the House of Lords seems to have answered 'no' to this question, the issue nevertheless merits close consideration, for two reasons: first, because there are various ways in which it might be argued that the scope of that negative response might be limited; and, second, because that response is difficult to reconcile with a number of cases in which public authorities have [262] apparently been held liable for failing to confer benefits in circumstances in which it seems unlikely that such liability would have arisen on ordinary common law principles. Although the bulk of the discussion will be focused on the *Gorringe* decision and its implications, it will be helpful to begin with a brief survey of the development of the law before *Gorringe*.

A. Developments Before *Gorringe*

Before *Gorringe*, the case law on the negligence liability of public authorities for omissions centred on failure to exercise statutory powers, and for a long time the rule was a simple one, as laid down by the House of Lords in *East Suffolk Rivers Catchment Board v Kent County Council*.[11] In *East Suffolk*, the claimants' lands had been flooded when a protective wall partially collapsed. The defendant catchment board tried to repair the breach, but as a result of various mistakes on their part, the work was unsuccessful, and the land remained flooded for some considerable time longer than it would have been had they exercised reasonable care. It was held that in these circumstances an action would lie only if the

---

[9] See further, D Nolan, 'Government Liability' in K Oliphant (ed), *The Law of Tort*, 2nd edn (London, LexisNexis Butterworths, 2007) paras 17.10–17.22.
[10] *Gorringe* (n 5).
[11] *East Suffolk Rivers Catchment Board v Kent County Council* [1941] AC 74 (HL).

defendants' intervention had inflicted fresh injury on the claimants.[12] In Lord Romer's words:

> Where a statutory authority is entrusted with a mere power, it cannot be made liable for any damage sustained by a member of the public by reason of a failure to exercise that power. If in the exercise of their discretion they embark upon an execution of the power, the only duty they owe to any member of the public is not thereby to add to the damages which he would have suffered had they done nothing.[13]

This longstanding rule was however abandoned in *Anns v Merton London Borough Council*,[14] where the House of Lords founded a duty of care in negligence on statutory powers a local authority had been given to inspect the foundations of buildings under construction. Lord Wilberforce said that in determining whether a public authority was liable in negligence it was irrelevant to the existence of a duty of care whether what was created by the statute was a duty or a power – a common law duty could exist in either case.[15] In *Sutherland Shire Council v Heyman*,[16] the High Court of Australia agreed. According to Mason J, there was no reason why a public authority should not be subject to a common law duty of care in appropriate circumstances in relation to the performance or non-performance of its statutory powers.[17]

Eight years before *Gorringe* a majority of the House of Lords backtracked from *Anns* in *Stovin v Wise (Norfolk County Council, third party)*.[18] The claimant in *Stovin* had been injured when his motorbike collided with a car which was emerging from a side road. He sought damages from the driver of the car in negligence, and the defendant then joined the local highway authority as third party, arguing that the accident had in part been caused by a bank of earth on land adjacent to the junction, which obscured the view of those turning [**263**] out of the side road. Under section 79 of the Highways Act 1980, the authority had a statutory power to order the removal of the bank, and the defendant contended that the failure to exercise that power had been negligent, and gave rise to a common law claim for damages on the part of those who suffered injury as a result. The House of Lords (Lord Slynn of Hadley and Lord Nicholls of Birkenhead dissenting) held that the council did not owe the claimant a duty of care.

Lord Hoffmann, who spoke for the majority, said that the fact that Parliament had chosen to confer a power rather than to impose a duty was an indication

---

[12] *East Suffolk* was consistent with an earlier Court of Appeal decision, *Sheppard v Glossop Corpn* [1921] 3 KB 132 (CA), where it was held that a local authority could not be liable for failing to exercise a power to light the streets.

[13] *East Suffolk* (n 11) 102.

[14] *Anns v Merton London Borough Council* [1978] AC 728 (HL).

[15] ibid 758.

[16] *Sutherland Shire Council v Heyman* (1985) 157 CLR 424 (HCA).

[17] ibid 457–58.

[18] *Stovin v Wise (Norfolk County Council, third party)* [1996] AC 923 (HL).

'that the policy of the Act conferring the power was not to create a right to compensation',[19] and that although it was possible that a statutory 'may' could give rise to a common law 'ought', the need to have regard to the policy of the statute meant that any such exceptions to the *East Suffolk* principle would be rare. In any case, for this to happen, two preconditions would have to be met: first, that in the circumstances it would have been irrational not to have exercised the power; and, second, that there were 'exceptional grounds' for holding that the policy of the statute required compensation to be paid to those who suffered loss as a result of the failure to exercise the power.[20] As regards the second precondition, Lord Hoffmann indicated that this requirement would be met only if 'a widespread assumption that a statutory power will be exercised' had affected 'the general pattern of social and economic behaviour';[21] his Lordship referred to this basis for the imposition of a duty of care as 'general reliance'.[22] The application of these two preconditions to the authority's omission in *Stovin* led Lord Hoffmann to conclude that a duty of care did not arise. The failure to ensure removal of the bank of earth had not been irrational, since resources were limited, and the junction was not an accident black spot. Furthermore, the circumstances fell outside the general reliance doctrine. There was no question of reliance on the council having improved the junction, or of the claimant having been denied a benefit which was routinely provided to others, and the case did not concern 'provision of a uniform identifiable benefit or service'.[23]

B. The *Gorringe* Decision

The claimant in *Gorringe* suffered serious injuries when the car she was driving collided with a bus on a country road in Yorkshire. The evidence indicated that she had braked sharply just short of a crest in the road, that her brakes had then locked, and that she had skidded into the side of the bus, which was travelling in the opposite direction. It was common ground that the claimant had been driving too fast, and that the driver of the bus was free from blame, but the claimant argued that the responsibility for the accident lay with the local highway authority, since it had not painted the word SLOW on the road surface below the crest. The judge held that the highway authority was liable, and refused to make a deduction for contributory negligence. The Court of Appeal disagreed, holding by a majority [264] (Potter LJ dissenting) that in these circumstances no duty of

---

[19] ibid 953.
[20] ibid 953.
[21] ibid 954.
[22] See further on 'general reliance', text following n 105.
[23] *Stovin* (n 18) 957.

care was owed to the claimant.[24] That decision to dismiss her claim was unanimously upheld by the House of Lords.

The claimant relied on two statutory duties imposed on the authority: the duty to maintain the highway in section 41(1) of the Highways Act 1980, and the duty to promote road safety in section 39 of the Road Traffic Act 1988. Her section 41 argument, framed in terms of the tort of breach of statutory duty, was rejected on the grounds that the duty to maintain was limited to keeping the highway in repair, and did not extend to the provision of information, whether by street furniture or painted signs.[25] The section 39 issue was more involved. Although the claimant accepted that breach of a local authority's duty 'to prepare and carry out a programme of measures designed to promote road safety'[26] did not directly give rise to a private law cause of action via the tort of breach of statutory duty, none the less she argued that the existence of the statutory duty in question could serve as the foundation for a common law duty of care in certain circumstances. In particular, she relied upon *Larner v Solihull Metropolitan Borough Council*,[27] where Lord Woolf CJ had drawn upon Lord Hoffmann's reasoning in *Stovin* in holding that common law liability could arise out of section 39 in 'circumstances of an exceptional nature', as where an authority had acted 'wholly unreasonably'.[28]

However, Lord Hoffmann now felt that it might have been 'ill-advised' to advert to possible exceptions in *Stovin*,[29] and he expressly disapproved the analysis of Lord Woolf in *Larner*. He found it 'difficult to imagine a case in which a common law duty [could] be founded simply upon the failure (however irrational) to provide some benefit which a public authority has power (or a public law duty) to provide'.[30] Lord Scott of Foscote was even more forthright. It was common ground that damages could not be recovered in an action for breach of the statutory duty imposed by section 39, because the provision did 'not impose a duty owed to any individual', but rather 'a duty owed to the public as a whole'.[31] And yet, if that was the case, then how could section 39 give rise to a duty of care that the common law would not impose in its absence? The policy of the statute that precluded claims for breach of statutory duty also precluded claims for negligence, and it followed that a common law duty could not 'grow parasitically out of a statutory duty not intended to be owed to individuals'.[32] This reasoning led Lord Scott to conclude that 'if a statutory duty does not give

---

[24] *Gorringe v Calderdale Metropolitan Borough Council* [2002] EWCA Civ 595, [2002] RTR 446.

[25] *Gorringe* (n 5) [14]–[15] (Lord Hoffmann), [52] (Lord Scott). See also *Goodes v East Sussex County Council* [2000] 1 WLR 1356 (HL).

[26] Road Traffic Act 1988, s 39(2).

[27] *Larner v Solihull Metropolitan Borough Council* [2001] BLGR 255 (CA).

[28] ibid 260.

[29] *Gorringe* (n 5) [26].

[30] ibid [32]. At [90], Lord Rodger expressly endorsed this aspect of Lord Hoffmann's analysis.

[31] ibid [70].

[32] ibid [71].

rise to a private right to sue for breach, then the duty cannot create a duty of care that would not have been owed at common law if the statute were not there'.[33] [265] It followed from their Lordships' analysis that if a duty of care was to be imposed on a public authority, it could only be by reference to ordinary private law principles, as where it had assumed a responsibility towards the claimant, or created a source of danger by positive conduct.[34] It might be that in such a case the public authority had acted pursuant to a statutory power or duty, but this would not in itself negative the existence of a common law duty of care, though there might be circumstances in which the terms of the statute would serve to do so.[35] In any case, on the facts there had been no assumption of responsibility by the authority, and nor had it created a source of danger by positive conduct. It followed that the claimant's argument on section 39 failed, and that her claim failed with it.

C. The Implications of *Gorringe*

There can be no doubt that *Gorringe* was a very restrictive decision. Whereas the majority in *Stovin* limited their analysis to the failure to exercise a statutory *power*, in *Gorringe* the House of Lords dealt both with the failure to exercise a statutory power and the failure to exercise a statutory *duty*. Furthermore, Lord Scott said that there were no circumstances in which the failure to exercise such a power or duty would in itself give rise to negligence liability, while Lord Hoffmann said that he found it 'difficult to imagine' circumstances in which this would take place. This can be contrasted with Lord Hoffmann's speech in *Stovin*, where he accepted that it was possible that this could happen. It would appear, therefore, that the law has reverted to the position adopted in *East Suffolk*, with the qualification that the *East Suffolk* analysis has now also been extended to failure to exercise statutory duties.[36] This interpretation of their Lordships' reasoning is consistent with a number of subsequent Court of Appeal decisions in which *Gorringe* has been taken as authority for the proposition that in the absence of circumstances that would generally give rise to an obligation to take positive action at common law, a public body will never be liable in negligence

---

[33] ibid [70].

[34] ibid [38] (Lord Hoffmann), [73] (Lord Scott).

[35] ibid [38] (Lord Hoffmann).

[36] The restrictive nature of the decision in *Gorringe* is also evident if a comparison is made with the position in other jurisdictions. See, eg, *Pyrenees Shire Council v Day* [1998] HCA 3, 192 CLR 330 (Australia); *City of Kamloops v Nielsen* (1984) 10 DLR (4th) 641 (SCC) (Canada), and *Invercargill City Council v Hamlin* [1994] 3 NZLR 513 (NZCA) (affirmed [1996] AC 624 (PC)) (New Zealand), all cases in which liability was imposed for failure to exercise a statutory power. See also *Couch v Attorney-General* [2008] NZSC 45, [2008] NZLR 725 [62]–[65] (Elias CJ and Anderson J) (the proximity sufficient to give rise to a duty of care 'can arise by reason of statutory obligations and powers').

for a failure to confer a benefit, no matter how irrational. A particularly clear statement to this effect can be found in the judgment of May LJ in *Sandhar v Department of Transport, Environment and the Regions*:

> Although statutory duties or powers which do not give rise to a private law right of action may constitute part of the relevant factual background, the existence of those duties or powers cannot reinforce parasitically the existence of a common law duty of care in the public authority. In short, unless a statute [266] on its proper construction provides a private law right of action or conversely unless the statute excludes it, the existence of a common law duty of care depends on unvarnished common law principles.[37]

Furthermore, the Court of Appeal has given the lie to early suggestions that somehow the impact of *Gorringe* might be limited to the highways context[38] by applying *Gorringe* in cases concerning alleged educational malpractice,[39] the liability of the Inland Revenue,[40] an allegedly culpable failure by a local authority to protect vulnerable council tenants from abuse by local youths,[41] and a failure by a court official to send notice of the filing of a bankruptcy petition to the Chief Land Registrar.[42]

It would seem, then, that the implications of *Gorringe* are clear: as Lord Hoffmann himself put it in a lecture on public authority negligence, unless the statute confers an immunity on a public authority defendant, 'its statutory powers and duties are irrelevant' in determining whether a public body owes a duty of care at common law, and it owes such a duty 'in such circumstances, and only in such circumstances, as a private body would have owed a duty'.[43] However, beneath the surface lies a complication, which is that this apparently simple rule is difficult to reconcile with other cases in which it does seem to have been accepted that a common law duty of care can be founded on the existence of a statutory duty or power. This raises the question of whether the position is in fact more complex, and whether these apparently inconsistent authorities can be reconciled with *Gorringe* by applying limits to the scope of that decision.

---

[37] *Sandhar v Department of Transport, Environment and the Regions* [2004] EWCA Civ 1440, [2005] 1 WLR 1632 [37]. See similarly, *Carty v Croydon London Borough Council* [2005] EWCA Civ 19, [2005] 1 WLR 2312 [21] (Dyson LJ), [84] (Mummery LJ); and *Trustee in Bankruptcy of Sir John Poulton v Ministry of Justice* [2010] EWCA Civ 392, [2010] 4 All ER 600 [93] (Lloyd LJ).

[38] See, eg, Howarth (n 7).

[39] See *Carty* (n 37) [42] (Dyson LJ).

[40] *Neil Martin Ltd v Customs and Revenue Commissioners* [2007] EWCA Civ 1041, [2007] STC 1802.

[41] *X and Y v London Borough of Hounslow* [2009] EWCA Civ 286, [2009] 2 FLR 262.

[42] *Trustee in Bankruptcy of Sir John Poulton* (n 37).

[43] Lord Hoffmann, 'Reforming the Law of Public Authority Negligence' (Bar Law Reform Committee Lecture, 19 November 2009) paras 6 and 12. See also at para 13 ('you cannot get a common law duty out of a statutory power or public law duty') and para 15 ('public bodies owe no duty of care by virtue only of the fact that they have statutory duties or powers').

D. Can *Gorringe* Be Limited?

i. The Apparently Inconsistent Authorities

Many of the leading cases in which liability has been imposed on public bodies are perfectly consistent with the proposition that such liability arises only on the application of ordinary common law principles. In *Home Office v Dorset Yacht Co Ltd*,[44] for example, the Home Office created the danger by bringing young offenders to an island and then letting them escape, while both *Barrett v Enfield London Borough Council*[45] – where a local social services department was held liable for neglecting a boy who had been taken into care – and the educational negligence case of *Phelps v London Borough of Hillingdon*[46] can plausibly be explained on the grounds that there was an assumption of responsibility by the defendant, and were so explained by Lord [267] Hoffmann in *Gorringe*.[47] However, *Gorringe* is more difficult to reconcile with two other cases in which it seems that public bodies have been made liable for failing to confer a benefit, despite the apparent absence of an assumption of responsibility.[48]

The first of these cases is *JD v East Berkshire Community NHS Trust*,[49] where the Court of Appeal held that it was no longer legitimate to rule, as a matter of law, that no common law duty of care was owed to a child in relation to the investigation of child abuse and the initiation of care proceedings, a view apparently endorsed by the House of Lords when the case went on appeal.[50] Since in at least some such cases a duty of care would have to be founded on the defendant's statutory duties under the Children Act 1989, it is difficult to see how this decision can be reconciled with the reasoning in *Gorringe*. And the

---

[44] *Home Office v Dorset Yacht Co Ltd* [1970] AC 1004 (HL).

[45] *Barrett v Enfield London Borough Council* [2001] 2 AC 550 (HL).

[46] *Phelps v London Borough of Hillingdon* [2001] 2 AC 619 (HL).

[47] *Gorringe* (n 5) [39]–[40].

[48] Another decision that might be thought to be inconsistent with *Gorringe* is *Thames Trains Ltd v Health & Safety Executive* [2003] EWCA Civ 720, where the Court of Appeal held that it was arguable that the Railway Inspectorate had breached a common law duty of care owed to the victims of the Ladbroke Grove rail crash by failing to take measures in respect of the signalling system and infrastructure in the Paddington area. However, the decision not to strike out the claim in *Thames Trains* is of limited general significance, since on the facts there may well have been an assumption of responsibility by the Inspectorate, and the refusal to rule out omissions liability was based on the possible exceptions to the no-liability rule adverted to by Lord Hoffmann in *Stovin v Wise* (n 18), which were later disavowed in *Gorringe*.

[49] *JD v East Berkshire Community NHS Trust* [2003] EWCA Civ 1151, [2004] QB 558.

[50] Although this aspect of the Court of Appeal's decision was not the subject of the appeal to the House of Lords, since the defendants had by then conceded that a duty of care was owed to the child in this type of case, their Lordships appeared to regard that concession as having been correctly made: see [2005] UKHL 23, [2005] 2 AC 373 [30] (Lord Bingham), [82] (Lord Nicholls). See also the first instance decisions in *Pierce v Doncaster Metropolitan Borough Council* [2007] EWHC 2968 (QB), 100 BMLR 76 and *Merthyr Tydfil County Borough Council v C* [2010] EWHC 62 (QB), in both of which it was simply assumed that in the light of *JD* a local authority would generally owe a duty of care to a child at foreseeable risk of abuse in its locality.

second problem case is *Kent v Griffiths*,[51] where the Court of Appeal held an ambulance service liable for not responding reasonably promptly to a 999 call, a decision which appeared to depend in part on the suggestion of an irrationality exception in *Stovin v Wise*,[52] a suggestion specifically disavowed by Lord Hoffmann in *Gorringe*.

ii. 'Target' or 'Public' Duties

Is there any way in which these apparently inconsistent authorities can be reconciled with the reasoning in *Gorringe*, or, more generally, any way in which the apparent breadth of the statements in *Gorringe* can be limited? One possibility is to focus on the emphasis certain of their Lordships placed on the fact that the statutory duty at issue in *Gorringe*, the duty to promote road safety, was a broad, or 'target', duty. According to Lord Scott, the section 39 duty was 'an entirely general one', which imposed 'a "target duty" and no more than that',[53] while Lord Rodger of Earlsferry described it as 'the kind of target duty that gives rise to no right to damages for [268] its breach at the suit of an individual'.[54] This language was also used in a subsequent Court of Appeal decision, *Rice v Secretary of State for Trade and Industry*, in which May LJ said that the authorities stood for the proposition that 'a statute containing broad target duties owed to the public at large ... is unlikely to give rise to a common law duty of care'.[55] There would appear to be two rather different ways of defining such a 'target duty'. The first is to say that a target duty is a general duty, which gives a public authority a good deal of discretion, rather than telling it precisely what to do; for example, in the *Larner* case Lord Woolf said that the section 39 duty could be described as a target duty because it did 'no more than require the council to exercise its powers in the manner' it considered appropriate.[56] However, if this interpretation of the target duty concept is correct, then it would appear to be of little utility in the present context, since the statutory duties at issue in negligence cases are generally of this kind – the duty to safeguard the welfare of children, for example, which lay at the heart of the *JD v East Berkshire* case,[57] is couched in terms that confer a considerable discretion on local authorities, and

---

[51] *Kent v Griffiths* [2001] QB 36 (CA).

[52] ibid 52 (Lord Woolf MR) ('This case is one in which it would have been irrational not to have accepted the request to provide an ambulance and this can alter the situation').

[53] *Gorringe* (n 5) [72].

[54] ibid [90]. Lord Hoffmann also remarked (at [38]) that the case was concerned only 'with an attempt to impose upon a local authority a common law duty to act based solely on the existence of a *broad* public duty' (emphasis added), though the context suggests that this statement was simply intended to differentiate the situation under consideration from one in which a duty of care would arise on ordinary private law principles.

[55] *Rice v Secretary of State for Trade and Industry* [2007] EWCA Civ 289, [2007] PIQR P23 [42].

[56] *Larner* (n 27) 258.

[57] *JD v East Berkshire* (n 49).

is in this sense a 'target duty'.[58] It follows that emphasising the breadth of the duty involved in the *Gorringe* case is unlikely significantly to limit the impact of the decision. Furthermore, *Gorringe* has recently been applied by the Court of Appeal in a case involving the statutory duty of a court official to inform the Chief Land Registrar of the filing of a bankruptcy petition, even though Lloyd LJ acknowledged that this duty was a 'narrow and specific' one.[59]

An alternative definition of a target duty is a duty that is 'not intended to be owed to individuals as a matter of public law'.[60] This raises the possibility that the impact of *Gorringe* might be limited by drawing a distinction between statutory powers and duties which are designed to benefit the public as a whole, and those that are designed to benefit particular individuals. Such a distinction is certainly relied upon in other jurisdictions. Courts in the United States, for example, have frequently dismissed negligence actions against public bodies on the grounds that the duty in question was owed to the public generally,[61] and similar reasoning was employed by the Supreme Court of Canada to dismiss an action against a financial regulator in *Cooper v Hobart*.[62] In Australia, too, Brennan CJ said in *Pyrenees* [269] *Shire Council v Day* that no duty breach of which sounds in damages can be imposed when a statutory power is intended to be exercised for the benefit of the public generally and not for the protection of the person or property of members of a particular class.[63] Furthermore, a public/private benefit approach would go a long way towards explaining the two decisions apparently inconsistent with *Gorringe*, *Kent v Griffiths*[64] and *JD v East Berkshire*.[65] In *Kent v Griffiths*, Lord Woolf MR used precisely this kind of reasoning to distinguish cases in which it had been held that neither the police nor the fire brigade were liable for negligently failing to respond in an emergency situation: while the primary obligation of the other two emergency

---

[58] See the Children Act 1989, s 17(1): 'It shall be the general duty of every local authority ... to safeguard and promote the welfare of children within their area who are in need'. And even the more specific duties that arise out of this general duty give local authorities considerable leeway: see, eg, sch 2, para 4(1): 'Every local authority shall take reasonable steps ... to prevent children within their area suffering ill-treatment or neglect.'

[59] *Trustee in Bankruptcy of Sir John Poulton* [2010] EWCA Civ 392, [2010] 4 All ER 600 [88].

[60] S Bailey, 'Public Authority Liability in Negligence: The Continued Search for Coherence' (2006) 26 *Legal Studies* 155, 173. See also C Callaghan, 'What is a "Target Duty"?' [2000] *Judicial Review* 184, 185 ('broadly framed duties which are owed to the public at large, not to an individual').

[61] See DB Dobbs, *The Law of Torts* (St Paul, Minn, West Publishing, 2000) 723–27; *Restatement, Third, Torts: Liability for Physical Harm* (Proposed Final Draft No 1, 2005) § 7, comment g.

[62] *Cooper v Hobart* [2001] 3 SCR 537 (SCC). See also *Mitchell v Ontario* (2004) 242 DLR (4th) 560 (Ont SCJ) (ministerial duties relating to the provision of health services owed to the public as a whole, not particular individuals).

[63] *Pyrenees* (n 36) [26]. See also *Crimmins v Stevedoring Industry Financing Committee* (1999) 200 CLR 1 (HCA) [93] (McHugh J); *Graham Barclay Oysters Pty Ltd v Ryan* [2002] HCA 54, 211 CLR 540 [32], [39] (Gleeson CJ). In German law, a similar approach is evident, based on the concept of the 'duty towards the individual' (*drittbezogene Amtspflicht*): see further, BS Markesinis et al, *Tortious Liability of Statutory Bodies* (Oxford, Hart Publishing, 1999) 23–27.

[64] *Kent* (n 51).

[65] *JD* (n 49).

services was owed to the public at large, he argued, on the facts of *Kent* the only person who could be adversely affected by a failure on the part of the ambulance service was the claimant.[66] Similarly, it could be argued that the duty to intervene in child abuse cases – the duty involved in the *JD v East Berkshire* case – is primarily for the benefit of vulnerable children, rather than the public in general.[67]

There are, however, three difficulties with relying on a public/private benefit distinction to limit the scope of the *Gorringe* decision. The first is that there is very little support for such a distinction in *Gorringe* itself, or in the subsequent case law, except for the rather vague references to 'target duties' and the fact that Lord Hoffmann pointed out that it was in the wider public interest that local authorities should take steps to promote road safety, and drew a parallel between the section 39 duty and the duty to house the homeless, which had previously been held to be for the benefit of the public as a whole, and not merely for the private benefit of homeless people.[68]

The second difficulty with this approach is that, as Dobbs points out, 'whether the statutory duty is public or special is largely in the eye of the beholder'.[69] It could be argued, for example, that statutory child protection duties are based on public interest considerations – since abused children are more likely to suffer psychiatric illness, or to commit crime in later life – and in a leading case on negligence liability in the child protection context, *X (minors) v Bedfordshire County Council*, Lord Browne-Wilkinson said that regulatory or welfare legislation was not to be treated as being passed for the benefit of those individuals particularly affected, [270] 'but for the benefit of society in general'.[70] Conversely, an Australian judge has said that '[w]here powers are given for the removal of risks to person or property, it will usually be difficult to exclude a duty on the ground that there is no specific [protected] class',[71] a formulation so broad that it would appear to encompass the statutory duty in *Gorringe* itself.

---

[66] *Kent* (n 51) 52–53. The authorities in question were *Alexandrou v Oxford* [1993] 4 All ER 328 (CA) (police), and *Capital and Counties plc v Hampshire County Council* [1997] QB 1004 (CA) (fire brigade). However, recovery was also denied in a case concerning the coastguard, *OLL Ltd v Secretary of State for Transport* [1997] 3 All ER 897 (QBD), where the primary obligation is presumably owed not to the public but to those in peril.

[67] In New Zealand, the equivalent duty has been held to be for the benefit of the child at risk (*AG v Prince* [1998] 1 NZLR 262 (NZCA)), an analysis which influenced the reasoning of the Privy Council in *B v AG of New Zealand* [2003] UKPC 61, [2003] 4 All ER 833, reasoning in turn endorsed by Lord Brown in the House of Lords in *JD v East Berkshire* (n 50) [125].

[68] *Gorringe* (n 5) [35]. One explanation for these comments may be that their Lordships were confusing the principles applicable in negligence with the position in the tort of breach of statutory duty, where the public/private benefit distinction is well established. This explanation is consistent with the fact that in the homelessness case referred to by Lord Hoffmann, *O'Rourke v Camden London Borough Council* [1988] AC 188 (HL), the action was for breach of statutory duty.

[69] Dobbs (n 61) 724.

[70] *X (minors) v Bedfordshire County Council* [1995] 2 AC 633, 731–32.

[71] *Crimmins* (n 63) [99] (McHugh J).

The third difficulty with this approach is that it would overlap with the approach traditionally taken to the discernment of legislative intent in the tort of breach of statutory duty,[72] although it would be needed only in cases where it was clear that no direct action on the statute would lie. It would seem paradoxical if a claimant who was unable to establish that a particular statutory duty was intended for the benefit of a particular class for the purposes of a breach of statutory duty claim could then argue that the duty gave rise to a duty of care in negligence for precisely that reason (though there are of course significant differences between the two causes of action, not least that – unless the duty in question requires only the exercise of reasonable care – breach of statutory duty is a tort of strict liability).

All in all, it is difficult to disagree with the conclusion that in the negligence context 'the distinction between powers exercisable for the benefit of the public generally and those exercisable for individuals or a class of individuals is of dubious value',[73] although it does not follow that there is no role at all for such a distinction in negligence litigation, and it will be suggested below that it may be helpful in discerning whether or not the acceptance of a 999 call should be held to amount to an assumption of responsibility by the emergency service in question.[74]

iii. Human Rights

Another possible way of limiting the effect of *Gorringe* is by arguing that where possible claimants should be afforded a remedy in negligence if they have suffered damage as a result of a breach of their human rights, and that therefore where there has been such a violation, the *Gorringe* principle should not apply, and it should be possible to found a common law duty of care on a statutory duty or power. An argument along these lines works quite well as an explanation for the common law duty to a child at risk of abuse recognised in *JD v East Berkshire*, since the European Court of Human Rights has held that the state's failure to put a stop to child abuse may amount to a breach of the victim's right under Article 3 of the European Convention not to be subjected to inhuman or degrading treatment.[75] Indeed that ruling influenced the decision in the *JD* case, albeit only in a roundabout way (the Court of Appeal reasoned that the possibility of a direct action based on the violation of Article 3 had pulled the rug out from under the public policy arguments used to justify the earlier refusal to impose a duty of care). Human rights issues may also be in play in cases involving the emergency services, since [271] in *Osman v United Kingdom* the

---

[72] See, eg, *O'Rourke* (n 68); *Gorringe* (n 5) [70] (Lord Scott).
[73] *Sutherland* (n 16) 465 (Mason J).
[74] See text following n 133.
[75] *Z v United Kingdom* [2001] 2 FCR 246 (ECtHR).

Strasbourg court held that there could be a violation of the Article 2 right to life if the authorities failed to take reasonable protective steps when they 'knew or ought to have known ... of the existence of a real and immediate risk to the life of an identified individual or individuals from the criminal acts of a third party'.[76] If this positive obligation on the part of the state were to be extended beyond criminal conduct to encompass natural events and accidents, and also extended – via Article 8 of the Convention, which has been held to protect bodily integrity – to include cases of personal injury as well as death, then it would appear to be directly in point in the *Kent v Griffiths* scenario.

There are, however, two difficulties with this human rights argument. The first is that it does not explain why the ambulance service can be held liable in negligence for failing to respond to a 999 call, but the police and fire brigade cannot.[77] And the second objection is that the argument obviously only works if the fact that there has been a violation of the claimant's Convention rights is thought to militate in favour of negligence liability, and yet the senior judiciary seems increasingly to be rejecting this view, and arguing that if anything the human rights violation *weakens* the case for extending the protection of the law of negligence, since the claimant will have a direct remedy under the Human Rights Act in any case.[78] It follows that although in some situations failure to exercise a statutory duty or power may give rise to a claim for damages under the Human Rights Act, the impact of the *Gorringe* decision on the position of public authority defendants in negligence is unlikely to be limited by reference to human rights arguments.

The conclusion to be drawn from this analysis seems to be that the impact of the *Gorringe* decision cannot in fact be limited, and that liability in negligence for failure to confer a benefit can never be grounded on the mere existence of a statutory duty or power. Instead, it seems that any such liability will have to be based on the application of ordinary private law principles.

---

[76] *Osman v United Kingdom* [1999] 1 FLR 193 (ECtHR) 223 [116]. For further discussion of this principle, see *Van Colle v Chief Constable of Hertfordshire Police* [2008] UKHL 50, [2009] 1 AC 225.

[77] One possible distinction is that, unlike the ambulance service, the fire brigade and police are frequently called upon to protect property interests (see J Wright, *Tort Law and Human Rights* (Oxford, Hart Publishing, 2001) 139; see also *Smith v Chief Constable of Sussex Police* [2008] EWCA Civ 39 [31], where Sedley LJ said that there might be a distinction to be made at common law, as there is in the Convention, between the protection of property and the protection of life). However, there is no suggestion in the case law on these services that a duty would be owed where the threat is to life or limb (although on the facts of the cases themselves, it appears that only property interests were at risk).

[78] See *Wainwright v Home Office* [2003] UKHL 53, [2004] 2 AC 406 [34] (Lord Hoffmann) (discussing privacy); *Van Colle* (n 76) [82] (Lord Hope), [136]–[139] (Lord Brown); and *Jain v Trent Strategic Health Authority* [2009] UKHL 4, [2009] 1 AC 853 [39] (Lord Scott). cf *JD v East Berkshire* (n 50) [50] and *Van Colle* (n 76) [58] (Lord Bingham). Note also the views to the contrary of two members of the Court of Appeal in *Smith* (n 77) (see [45] (Rimer LJ) and [53]–[58] (Pill LJ)), one of the two cases considered by the House of Lords in *Van Colle*.

III. THE APPLICATION OF ORDINARY PRIVATE LAW PRINCIPLES

On the application of ordinary private law principles, there are two principal circumstances in which a public authority may be held liable in negligence: first, where by its positive conduct it caused the claimant additional damage; and, [272] second, where it failed to confer a benefit on a person towards whom it had assumed a responsibility.[79] For the purposes of analysis, the first category of case can be sub-divided into cases where the public authority's actions induced reliance on the claimant's part, which then left the claimant worse off when her expectations were disappointed, and cases where the harm to the claimant came about in some other way. The end result is three categories: ordinary 'additional damage' cases; cases of claimant reliance; and cases involving assumptions of responsibility. In this part of the article, I consider the application of ordinary private law principles to public authority defendants in these three categories of case.

A. Additional Damage Cases

A public authority may be liable for positive conduct that causes damage, just as a private party would be.[80] In such a case, the authority may have acted pursuant to a statutory duty or power, but according to Lord Hoffmann in *Gorringe* this would negative the existence of a common law duty of care only if that was the import of the terms of the statute in question.[81] The additional damage category includes cases where the public authority has created a source of danger which it has then negligently failed to control, as in *Home Office v Dorset Yacht Co Ltd*,[82] where the defendant had taken young offenders to an island, and then inadequately supervised them, thereby enabling the boys to attempt to escape on the claimants' yachts. As *Dorset Yacht* makes clear, it is not necessary that the creation of the source of danger itself have been negligent, provided the authority subsequently fails to take reasonable steps to prevent it causing harm; hence a local authority which exercised its statutory power to build an air-raid shelter on a highway during the war was liable for not lighting the structure after a ban on street lighting turned it into a hazard.[83]

---

[79] There are other situations in which a public authority can be held liable for failing to confer a benefit on ordinary private law principles, as where a duty of positive action arises out of the authority's occupation of land. However, since these types of case raise no particular issues with regard to the public nature of the defendant's activities, there is no need to consider them further.

[80] See *East Suffolk* (n 11) 84 (Viscount Simon LC), 97 (Lord Romer), 104–105 (Lord Porter); *Stovin* (n 18) 947 (Lord Hoffmann); *Capital and Counties* (n 66) 1031 (Stuart-Smith LJ); and *OLL* (n 66) 907 (May J). For a recent example, see *Yetkin v London Borough of Newham* [2010] EWCA Civ 776, where it was held that a highway authority could be liable for planting shrubs and bushes in a central reservation which obscured the view pedestrians had of the carriageway.

[81] *Gorringe* (n 5) [38].

[82] *Dorset Yacht* (n 44).

[83] *Fisher v Ruislip-Northwood UDC* [1945] KB 584 (CA).

By and large, the application of this 'additional damage' idea to public authority defendants seems straightforward, but there are a couple of points that should be made. The first is that when considering the actions of a public body, the court needs to remember that the appropriate question is whether the negligent conduct of the defendant has left the claimant in a worse position than she would have been in if the public authority *had not intervened at all*.[84] This point is well illustrated by the leading case on the liability of the fire brigade, *Capital and* [273] *Counties plc v Hampshire County Council*.[85] In one of the appeals heard in *Capital and Counties*, the *Hampshire* case, the judge at first instance had found as a fact that the fire brigade had not simply failed to confer a benefit on the claimants by extinguishing the fire at their factory, but had actually made the situation worse by turning off sprinklers that were helping to prevent the fire rampaging through the roof space. In what looks at first blush like a straightforward application of the additional damage principle, the Court of Appeal held that this action on the defendants' part was sufficient to establish liability. However, it seems that the sprinklers would have prevented the spread of the fire only in tandem with the efforts of the fire crews at the scene, in which case overall the intervention of the fire brigade did *not* make things worse, and it follows that liability ought not to have been imposed.[86]

The second point is that sometimes the additional damage comes about because the defendant's conduct dissuades or prevents a third party from going to the claimant's assistance. Suppose, for example, that a swimmer gets into difficulties off a crowded beach. An onlooker dives into the surf, giving the others on the beach the impression that he is going to the rescue. And suppose that in fact he then does not assist the drowning man, but callously swims past him, and that by the time this happens, it is too late for the other onlookers to help. On the assumption that another onlooker would have acted if the 'rescuer' had stayed put, this is a case of additional damage covered by what McBride and Bagshaw describe as the 'interference principle'. Under this principle, if A knows or ought to know that B is in danger, and that she has done something which has had the effect of either dissuading or preventing someone else from helping B, then A herself comes under an obligation to take reasonable steps to assist B.[87] The same authors have suggested that this principle provides an explanation for

---

[84] See *OLL* (n 66) 905 (May J) (coastguard liable only if 'their negligence amounted to a positive act which directly caused greater injury than would have occurred if they had not intervened at all').

[85] *Capital and Counties* (n 66).

[86] See further, A Mullis and D Nolan, 'Tort' in the *All England Law Reports Annual Review 1997* (London, Butterworths, 1998) 501–502.

[87] NJ McBride and R Bagshaw, *Tort Law*, 3rd edn (Harlow, Pearson Education, 2008) 160–64. See also EJ Weinrib, 'The Case for a Duty to Rescue' (1980) 90 *Yale Law Journal* 247, 258; WP Keeton et al, *Prosser and Keeton on Torts*, 5th edn (St Paul, Minn, West Publishing, 1984) 382. See, eg, *Zelenko v Gimbel Bros* 287 NYS 134 (NY 1935), where it was held that a department store which moved an ill customer to its infirmary was then obliged to treat her, since by doing so it had prevented others from helping her.

Kent v Griffiths,[88] on the basis that if it had not been for repeated assurances as to the timely arrival of an ambulance, the claimant would have been taken to hospital more quickly by her husband or the doctor attending her.[89] However, the only support for this explanation in the judgment of Lord Woolf MR in the Court of Appeal is a seemingly throwaway line in which his Lordship observed that if misleading information about the ambulance's likely arrival time had not been given, 'other means of transport could have been used',[90] and the scope of the decision has not generally been considered to be limited to the causing of additional damage. Nevertheless, there is no reason why the interference principle should not be applied where another emergency service – such as the police or the fire brigade – is under no common law duty to respond but makes the claimant's position worse by indicating that it will do so.

[274] Two further points should be made about the application of the interference principle in public authority cases. The first is that, as McBride and Bagshaw point out,[91] the principle applies only where the defendant dissuades or prevents a *third party* from helping the claimant, and there may be cases where it is not immediately apparent whether or not the alternative rescuer should be so characterised. It is submitted that the alternative rescuer should be treated as a third party for these purposes if she is a legally distinct entity, unless she and the defendant are employees of the same employer. If this is the correct test, then it follows that in *OLL Ltd v Secretary of State for Transport*[92] May J ought not to have refused to differentiate between the different rescue agencies where the coastguard had misdirected a lifeboat and a Royal Navy helicopter searching for a party of stricken canoeists.

The second point is that the fact that a particular state agency has been assigned the task of intervening in certain situations may cause private parties or other state agencies not to act in a given case, in the belief that the agency in question will take care of the matter. In these circumstances, if the agency then fails to intervene, or does so ineffectively, the person it ought to have protected may be left worse off than if the agency had not taken on the task in the first place. Precisely this argument was made by Brennan J in his dissenting opinion in *DeShaney v Winnebago County Department of Social Services*,[93] where a majority of the United States Supreme Court held that a local social services departments was under no constitutional duty to protect a child after they received complaints of physical abuse by the boy's father. According to Brennan J:

> Wisconsin law invites – indeed directs – citizens and other governmental entities to depend on local departments of social services [DSS] ... to protect children from

[88] *Kent* (n 51).
[89] McBride and Bagshaw (n 87) 160–61.
[90] *Kent* (n 51) 54.
[91] McBride and Bagshaw (n 87) 161–62.
[92] *OLL* (n 66).
[93] *DeShaney v Winnebago County Department of Social Services* 489 US 189 (1989).

abuse ... In these circumstances, a private citizen or even a person working in a government agency other than DSS, would doubtless feel that her job was done as soon as she had reported her suspicions of child abuse to DSS. Through its child-welfare program, in other words, the State of Wisconsin has relieved ordinary citizens and governmental bodies other than [DSS] of any sense of obligation to do anything more than report their suspicions of child abuse to DSS. If DSS ignores or dismisses these suspicions, no one will step in to fill the gap ... Conceivably, then, children like Joshua are made worse off by the existence of this program when the persons and entities charged with carrying it out fail to do their jobs.[94]

Powerful though the logic of this argument undoubtedly is, it is questionable whether in practice it could be used to justify the imposition of negligence liability in cases of public authority inaction, as it would be difficult to prove in a particular case that the existence of the state agency in question had made the claimant's position worse. This difficulty will be compounded where the relevant legal framework confers unique powers of intervention on the agency – such as the ability to remove a child at risk from the family unit – as in these circumstances those who would have felt inclined to intervene had the agency not existed might [275] have lacked the legal powers to do so effectively. Nevertheless, like the 'general reliance' doctrine which is explored in the next section of this article, Brennan J's argument raises the question of whether some kind of redress ought to be available in at least some cases of state inaction, even if no remedy is available on a strict application of ordinary private law principles.

B. Claimant Reliance

One particular form of additional damage case is where the claimant has relied to her detriment on an express or implied representation by the defendant that a benefit will be conferred on her; in the case of the stricken swimmer, for example, the apparent 'rescuer' could be held liable if in response to his entering the water the swimmer in difficulties had started to swim towards him instead of a sandbank in the other direction. Claimant reliance may also take the form of failing to take measures to help oneself in the reasonable belief that the defendant is going to provide assistance; in the Court of Appeal in the *East Suffolk* case, for example, du Parcq LJ was prepared to assume that 'some cause of action could be based on the allegation that the plaintiffs were induced or compelled to abstain from helping themselves by the futile and misguided attempts of the defendant board to help the community'.[95]

Furthermore, it is clear that a representation can be implied from the general pattern of the defendant's conduct, as is shown by *Mercer v South Eastern and*

---

[94] ibid 208–10.
[95] *Kent v East Suffolk Rivers Catchment Board* [1940] 1 KB 319 (CA) 339.

Chatham Railway Companies Managing Committee,[96] where Lush J held that a railway company which habitually locked a gate on a level crossing when trains were passing was liable to a pedestrian who had wrongly assumed that it was safe to cross when he found that the gate was open. As the learned judge said:

> It may seem a hardship on a railway company to hold them responsible for the omission to do something which they were under no legal obligation to do, and which they only did for the protection of the public. They ought, however, to have contemplated that if a self-imposed duty is ordinarily performed, those who know of it will draw an inference if on a given occasion it is not performed.[97]

The same reasoning can be applied where a public authority has, by inducing reliance on the continued performance of its statutory functions, created or increased the risk of damage should such performance be discontinued without notice.[98] If, for example, a lighthouse authority operates a lighthouse, and thereby creates an expectation in mariners that the light will alert them to danger, the authority will [276] be liable if harm results from its negligent failure to provide the expected warning.[99] In *Gorringe*, Lord Hoffmann acknowledged that in this type of case a public authority might come under a duty to act:

> I would certainly accept the principle that if a highway authority conducts itself so as to create a reasonable expectation about the state of the highway, it will be under a duty to ensure that it does not thereby create a trap for the careful motorist who drives in reliance upon such an expectation.[100]

However, their Lordships did not make the scope of this 'entrapment' idea very clear. Lord Rodger seems to have thought, for example, that it might justify the decision in *Bird v Pearce (Somerset CC, third party)*,[101] where the Court of Appeal held that by painting white lines indicating priority at a series of junctions along a road, and then failing to repaint lines that had been obliterated at one junction, a highway authority had itself created a source of danger that

---

[96] *Mercer v South Eastern and Chatham Railway Companies Managing Committee* [1922] 2 KB 549 (KBD).

[97] ibid 554.

[98] See *Sutherland* (n 16) 486 (Brennan J). See also 461 (Mason J) and *Stovin* (n 18) 935 (Lord Nicholls).

[99] *Stovin* (n 18) 953 (Lord Hoffmann). An illustrative American authority is *Florence v Goldberg* 375 NE 2d 763 (NY 1978), where a mother noticed that the local council was providing crossing guards on her child's route to school, and so stopped accompanying the child to school herself. The New York Court of Appeals imposed liability when the child was run over on a day on which the council negligently failed to provide a crossing guard, on the basis that the regular provision of such guards meant that the failure to provide one on that occasion left the child worse off than if no guards had ever been laid on. See also the draft *Restatement, Third, Torts: Liability for Physical Harm* (n 61) § 42, illustration 6.

[100] *Gorringe* (n 5) [43]. For an example of the successful deployment of this entrapment argument in the highways context, see *McDonogh v Commonwealth of Australia* (1985) 73 ALR 148 (FCA), where the Federal Court of Australia held that by grading and levelling a road, but compacting only some of the fill, a highway authority had given it an appearance of safety which could mislead drivers.

[101] *Bird v Pearce (Somerset CC, third party)* (1979) 77 LGR 753 (CA).

would not have existed had no lines been painted at all.[102] By contrast, Lord Hoffmann chose to express no view as to the correctness of that decision, while Lord Scott suggested that there were some difficulties in applying the entrapment principle to the facts of that case, and Lord Brown of Eaton-under-Heywood said that he expected entrapment cases to be 'few and far between', and that *Bird v Pearce* was certainly not one of them.[103] Besides, it is not clear why this sort of reasoning could not have been used to justify the opposite result in *Gorringe* itself, on the grounds that by routinely warning motorists when to slow down, and then not doing so on a particular occasion, a highway authority can in effect create a 'trap'. After all, the road on which the accident happened in *Gorringe* was a fairly significant country road of the kind where it would be usual for motorists to be alerted by a 'SLOW' warning to the existence of an impending hazard, such as an intersection or a sharp bend. In those circumstances, it could be argued that the failure by the authority in *Gorringe* to paint such a warning on the road below the crest 'broke the pattern',[104] and thereby entrapped the claimant.

The entrapment idea discussed in *Gorringe* was in issue in *Sandhar v Department of Transport, Environment and the Regions*,[105] where the claimant argued that the defendant government department had created a trap by fostering a public expectation that major roads would be salted in frosty conditions, and then failing to salt one. On the facts, however, the Court of Appeal held that there was no evidence that the driver involved had relied on any such expectation. As *Sandhar* illustrates, it will often be difficult for a claimant to prove that he or she [277] relied on the exercise of a given statutory power or duty, and it was this difficulty which led to the development of the doctrine of 'general reliance', whereby the focus shifted from reliance by the claimant to reliance by the community as a whole. The point of this doctrine was that the state habitually takes it upon itself to provide particular benefits to its citizens, and this inevitably creates expectations on the part of those citizens, which in turn give rise to reliance, so that, for example, individuals do not contract for fire or ambulance services, because they rely upon public authorities to lay them on, and drivers perhaps fail to take precautions which they would take if they were not habitually warned of upcoming hazards.[106] This element of general

---

[102] *Gorringe* (n 5) [85].

[103] ibid [43], [65] and [102] respectively.

[104] ibid [85] (Lord Rodger).

[105] *Sandhar* (n 37).

[106] In *Gorringe* (n 5), Lord Brown warned drivers that they were not entitled to suppose that the need for care would 'generally be highlighted so as to protect them from their own negligence' (at [101]), but drivers might argue that the prevalence of warning signs means that they are *not* negligent if they assume that they will be alerted to prospective dangers. Lord Rodger also remarked (at [93]) that drivers could not rely on highway authorities having warned them against hazards, and that the common law insisted that they look out for dangers themselves and not rely on others, but this seems to be a conclusion derived from the result in *Gorringe* as opposed to a justification for it (see similarly *Sandhar* (n 37) [43] (May LJ)).

reliance was then used to justify imposing tort liability when in a particular case the relevant service was not provided, and the claimant suffered harm as a result. An Australian judge described general reliance as 'a legitimate analogical development of the established category of specific reliance' in the public authority liability context,[107] and the doctrine was also defended by Bagshaw, who argued that the situations in which general reliance was invoked could be said to involve a generalised form of 'additional damage':

> If the State routinely provides a subsidised service and thus stifles private initiatives to provide similar protective services it is arguable that the State should owe the same duties as such private service providers would have done.[108]

However, in spite of its logical appeal, the general reliance doctrine seems now to have fallen from favour. Although the *locus classicus* of the doctrine is the judgment of Mason J in *Sutherland Shire Council v Heyman*,[109] the High Court of Australia has since abandoned it,[110] and notwithstanding its apparent endorsement by Lord Hoffmann in *Stovin v Wise*,[111] general reliance never really took root in English law.[112] Responsibility for the failure of the doctrine to take hold can in part be laid at the door of its judicial proponents, who to some extent failed to encapsulate its logical force. Mason J, for example, seemed unsure as to whether [278] an alteration in community behaviour was required, or whether instead a more general 'dependence' on the authority's exercise of its power was sufficient. By contrast, while Lord Hoffmann did make it clear that 'a widespread assumption that a statutory power will be exercised' must have affected 'the general pattern of social and economic behaviour',[113] his Lordship added the unnecessary gloss that the benefit provided by the exercise of the statutory power must be of 'a uniform

---

[107] *Parramatta City Council v Lutz* (1988) 12 NSWLR 293 (NSWCA) 330 (McHugh JA).

[108] R Bagshaw, 'The Duties of Care of Emergency Service Providers' [1999] *Lloyd's Maritime and Commercial Law Quarterly* 71, 81.

[109] *Heyman* (n 16).

[110] See *Pyrenees* (n 36) [19] (Brennan CJ), [157]–[165] (Gummow J), [225]–[232] (Kirby J); *Brodie v Singleton Shire Council* [2001] HCA 29, 206 CLR 512 [307]–[308] (Hayne J). By contrast, in *Pyrenees*, Toohey J (at [58]–[72]) and McHugh J (at [103]–[110]) still felt that the doctrine had a role to play, and the door has not yet been closed on it in New Zealand: see *Couch* (n 36) [64] (Elias CJ and Anderson J).

[111] *Stovin* (n 18) 953–55.

[112] See *Capital and Counties* (n 66) 1027 (Stuart-Smith LJ) ('the doctrine [of general reliance] has received little if any support in English law'); *OLL* (n 66) 907 (May J) ('in English law no duty of care arises in cases such as this from a general expectation'); *Watson v British Boxing Board of Control* [2001] QB 1134 (CA) 1151 (Lord Phillips MR). cf *Thames Trains* (n 48) [25] (Waller LJ), who however drew upon aspects of Lord Hoffmann's speech in *Stovin* which do not survive *Gorringe*. Surprisingly, Lord Hoffmann's discussion of general reliance in *Stovin* was also invoked in a case decided after *Gorringe*: see *A v Secretary of State for the Home Department* [2004] EWHC 1585 (Admin) [36] (Keith J).

[113] *Stovin* (n 18) 954.

and routine nature', such that it would be 'irrational for a public authority to provide it in one case and arbitrarily withhold it in another',[114] an invocation of a public law-style entitlement theory of little obvious relevance to the law of negligence.[115] Nor did it advance the cause of general reliance for Lord Hoffmann to say that it would be easier to infer a right to compensation for non-exercise of a power where it was designed to protect individuals from risks they could not guard against in other ways,[116] when what power the doctrine has derives from the very fact that the public would have sought alternative means of protection had it not been assumed that dependence could be placed on the state.

These weaknesses of exposition gave the opponents of general reliance an easier target at which to aim, but even so their criticisms were noticeably flimsy. It was said, for example, that general reliance rested on a fiction,[117] when in fact the whole point of the doctrine was that claimant reliance (which might well be fictional) was not necessary, and was replaced by a perfectly real requirement of community reliance. Nor was there much merit in the argument that proof of such general reliance was likely to be particularly difficult;[118] would it really be so far-fetched for a court to conclude, for example, that in the absence of a fire service provided by the state, the public would contract for similar protection from private companies?[119] On the other hand, there were undoubtedly practical difficulties in applying a doctrine based on general community expectations in negligence litigation, and my purpose in calling attention to the logic of the general reliance doctrine is not to recommend its resurrection, but rather to emphasise the complexities of applying the private law concept of claimant reliance in certain types of public authority case. In any case, the rejection of the doctrine has left the law of negligence without a specific response to the 'communal expectations that public authorities will act in certain ways and around which people shape their behaviour';[120] instead, the claimant will have to argue that she personally had such an expectation, and that she relied to her detriment upon it. The outcome in *Sandhar*, and the failure of their Lordships even to advert to the possibility of such 'specific reliance' on the facts of *Gorringe*, indicate that in practice this argument is unlikely to succeed.

---

[114] ibid 954.

[115] See B Feldthusen, 'Discretionary Public Benefits: The Case for Complete Negligence Immunity' (1997) 5 *Tort Law Review* 17, 27. For such a theory, see D Cohen and JC Smith, 'Entitlement and the Body Politic: Rethinking Negligence in Public Law' (1986) 64 *Canadian Bar Review* 1.

[116] *Stovin* (n 18) 954, drawing upon *Sutherland* (n 16) 464 (Mason J) (a risk 'of such magnitude or complexity that individuals cannot, or may not, take adequate steps for their own protection').

[117] See, eg, *Pyrenees* (n 36) [230]–[232] (Kirby J); *Brodie* (n 110) [307]–[308] (Hayne J).

[118] See, eg, *Pyrenees* (n 36) [19] (Brennan CJ).

[119] See Booth and Squires (n 8) para 3.134.

[120] Booth and Squires (n 8) para 3.129.

[279] C. Assumption of Responsibility

Unlike claimant reliance – where liability arises out of the causing of additional damage – an undertaking or assumption of responsibility by the defendant may give rise to a genuine instance of liability for failure to confer a benefit. In such cases, the obligation to confer the benefit has been voluntarily incurred by the defendant, and the imposition of liability is explained by this element of consent.[121] It follows that, although in practice an assumption of responsibility may give rise to reliance – either by the claimant or by a third party, to the claimant's detriment[122] – no such reliance is necessary: the passing doctor who takes charge of a heart attack victim owes her a duty of care even if the victim is unconscious and the street deserted.[123] This example also shows us that there can be an assumption of responsibility of which the claimant is unaware.[124] Finally, it is important to note that in this example, the doctor's duty is the usual duty to take reasonable care of his patient, and that this duty requires him to take reasonable steps to improve the situation; his duty is not limited to not making things worse. If it were so limited, the assumption of responsibility would be adding nothing to the background duty we all owe each other not carelessly to inflict additional damage.

i. When Is There an Assumption of Responsibility in Public Authority Cases?

Subject to a concern discussed below about the 'voluntariness' of some of their undertakings, it seems generally to be accepted that, like a private individual, a public authority which takes upon itself a positive obligation to act may be liable if it negligently fails to carry through on its undertaking. In *Gorringe*, for example, Lord Hoffmann explained both *Barrett v Enfield London Borough Council*[125] and *Phelps v London Borough of Hillingdon*[126] as involving such an assumption of responsibility by the defendant,[127] and in a number of cases the police have been held liable for failing to confer a benefit on the claimant

---

[121] Indeed, strictly speaking, the basis of the liability is not the failure to confer the benefit at all, but the breach of the undertaking (see Beever (n 1) 222). As to whether the consent of the defendant must be the result of a free choice, see text following n 154.

[122] See further the draft *Restatement, Third, Torts: Liability for Physical Harm* (n 61) § 42.

[123] Stevens (n 1) 14. See, eg, *Barrett v Ministry of Defence* [1995] 1 WLR 1217 (CA), where it was held that a naval officer who took charge of an unconscious airman had assumed a responsibility towards him, and that this grounded a duty of care. See also *Watson* (n 112) 1151 (Lord Phillips MR) (a duty of care would be owed to an unconscious road accident victim by the hospital where she is accepted for treatment).

[124] Stevens (n 1) 10–12.

[125] *Barrett* (n 45).

[126] *Phelps* (n 46).

[127] *Gorringe* (n 5) [39]–[40].

because of a prior assumption of responsibility.[128] However, these were all relatively clear-cut cases, and it may not always be so easy to tell whether or not liability should be imposed on a public authority on the grounds that it has assumed a responsibility towards the claimant.[129]

[280] In *East Suffolk*,[130] for example, why could it not have been said that the defendant catchment board had assumed a responsibility towards the claimant landowners by taking upon itself the task of repairing the sea defences? Clearly, the House of Lords did not believe that it had, as they held that the only duty which it owed when it chose to exercise its statutory powers was not to add to the damage which would have been suffered had it done nothing.[131] The answer may lie in the dissenting judgment of du Parcq LJ in the Court of Appeal (where the majority held that the defendant was liable). In response to MacKinnon LJ's assertion that the defendant had assumed a responsibility towards the claimants,[132] du Parcq LJ said:

> All that need be said on this point is that it was neither proved nor alleged that the defendants ever undertook any obligation to the plaintiffs. *The defendants were acting not for the plaintiffs, but, it must be assumed, for the common good.*[133]

This distinction between acting for a particular individual, and acting for the common good, may also provide the explanation for the apparently inconsistent treatment of the different emergency services in the English case law. As we have seen, in *Kent v Griffiths*[134] an ambulance service was held liable for not responding effectively to a 999 call, but on the authorities no such liability attaches to the police and the fire brigade.[135] In the light of *Gorringe*, only an assumption of responsibility analysis can explain the ambulance service's obligation to confer a benefit, and this explanation – which is consistent with the fact that the duty seems to arise only when the emergency call has been accepted[136] – has been expressly adopted in two later Court of Appeal decisions.[137] However, this raises

---

[128] *Swinney v Chief Constable of Northumbria Police* [1997] QB 464 (CA); *Costello v Chief Constable of the Northumbria Police* [1999] 1 All ER 550 (CA). See also *Van Colle* (n 76) [135] (Lord Brown).

[129] For a recent example of a case where no such responsibility was held to have been assumed, see *X and Y* (n 41).

[130] *East Suffolk* (n 11).

[131] ibid 102 (Lord Romer).

[132] *East Suffolk Rivers Catchment Board v Kent* [1940] 1 KB 319 (CA) 334.

[133] ibid 340 (emphasis added).

[134] *Kent* (n 51).

[135] See respectively, *Alexandrou* and *Capital and Counties* (n 66).

[136] *Kent* (n 51) 54 (Lord Woolf MR). See also at 43 ('once a call has been accepted, the service is dealing with a named individual upon whom the duty becomes focused').

[137] See *Watson* (n 112) 1152 (Lord Phillips MR) (the duty of care in *Kent* 'turned upon the acceptance by the ambulance service of the request to provide an ambulance and thus the acceptance of responsibility for the care of the particular patient'); and *Sandhar* (n 37) [47] (May LJ) (in *Kent* 'the defendants … assumed responsibility to a particular [claimant]').

the question of why the same analysis cannot be used to justify imposition of a duty of care when a call to the police or the fire brigade is accepted. One possible answer is that while the ambulance service acts for the benefit of individuals in need of medical care, the police and the fire brigade do not act for the benefit of particular individuals, but the public as a whole,[138] and hence that while it is plausible to interpret the acceptance of a call by the ambulance service as an assumption of responsibility towards the person on behalf of whom it is made, the same is not true of the acceptance of a call by the police or the fire service. Such a distinction is consistent with the fact that the ambulance service is simply one component of [281] the wider health service (a point emphasised by Lord Woolf MR in *Kent*[139]), since it is clearly established that the acceptance of someone as a patient by the health service carries it with an implicit undertaking to care for the patient's needs.[140] Furthermore, this analysis derives support from the reasoning in the leading fire brigade case, *Capital and Counties*, where Stuart-Smith LJ held that by turning up at the scene of a fire and taking control, the fire brigade had not assumed any responsibility towards those affected by their operations because their primary duty was to the public at large – a duty which might conflict with the interests of particular property owners – and because it would be difficult to pin down to whom exactly the defendants would be taken to have assumed responsibility.[141]

Attractive though this public/private benefit analysis is, it is not free from difficulty. The first difficulty is that this distinction only provides an explanation for the *English* case law on the emergency services: in a number of Scottish cases, obligations to confer benefits have been imposed on the police and the fire service.[142] The second difficulty is that while many of the tasks carried out by the police and the fire service would appear to be for the benefit of the public as a whole, in other cases, it seems artificial to distinguish between these services and the ambulance service in this way: an example would be the aftermath of

---

[138] See, eg, P Giliker, '*Osman* and Police Immunity in the English Law of Torts' (2000) 20 *Legal Studies* 372, 384 (police); and *John Munroe (Acrylics) Ltd v London Fire and Civil Defence Authority* [1997] QB 983 (QBD) 996 (Rougier J) (fire brigade). cf *Burnett v Grampian Fire and Rescue Services* [2007] CSOH 3, 2007 SLT 61 [52] (Lord Macphail) (arguable that when fighting a fire, the fire brigade owes a duty to those whose lives or property are endangered).

[139] *Kent* (n 51) 52.

[140] *Watson* (n 112) 1150 (Lord Phillips MR). See, eg, *Barnett v Chelsea and Kensington Hospital Management Committee* [1969] 1 QB 428 (QBD).

[141] *Capital and Counties* (n 66) 1036. Note also that when the claim in *Kent v Griffiths* first came before the Court of Appeal in strike-out proceedings, precisely this argument was used to distinguish *Capital and Counties*: see *Kent v London Ambulance Service* [1999] Lloyd's Rep Med 58, 62–63 (Kennedy LJ), 64 (Schiemann LJ). The public duty/private duty distinction is also drawn by Lord Phillips MR in *Watson* (n 112) 1151. cf *Burnett* (n 138) [70] (Lord Macphail) (denying that the ambulance service can be distinguished from the police and fire brigade in this way).

[142] *Duff v Highland and Islands Fire Board* 1995 SLT 1362 (CSOH) and *Burnett* (n 138) (fire brigade); *Gibson v Orr* 1999 SC 420 (CSOH) (police). See further, D Brodie, 'Public Authority Liability: The Scottish Approach' (2007) 11 *Edinburgh Law Review* 254.

a road accident, where police officers and fire crews extricate the victims from their vehicles, and ambulance crews then provide emergency medical care.[143] And the final difficulty is that this public/private benefit distinction is hard to reconcile with the decision in *OLL Ltd v Secretary of State for Transport*[144] that in an emergency situation no duty of care is owed by the coastguard to those in peril, since they would appear to act for the specific benefit of individuals in difficulties at sea, and so their position would seem to be more analogous to that of the ambulance service than to that of the police and fire brigade.[145]

Another justification for distinguishing on an assumption of responsibility analysis between the ambulance service, on the one hand, and the police and fire brigade on the other, is that although detrimental reliance is not a prerequisite of an assumption of responsibility, the *foreseeable possibility* of such reliance (whether by the claimant or a third party) may determine whether or not the defendant has implicitly assumed a responsibility towards the claimant.[146] In particular, [282] 'where the undertaking of a task means that it will not be undertaken by anyone else, this supports a finding that there is an implied assumption of responsibility in carrying it out'.[147] If this argument is accepted, then an undertaking by the ambulance service to respond to an emergency call could be interpreted as an assumption of responsibility because the effect of such an undertaking is likely to be that alternative means of transportation are not employed. Conversely, the acceptance of an emergency call by the police or fire brigade should not be interpreted as an assumption of responsibility because it is less likely to induce detrimental reliance, alternative avenues of protection not generally being available in such cases.

ii. *When Precisely Is Responsibility Assumed, and Can an Assumption of Responsibility be Revoked?*

Even where an assumption of responsibility analysis looks plausible, there remains the question of when precisely it is that responsibility is assumed, and whether once there has been an assumption of responsibility, it can be revoked.[148] The problems can be illustrated by returning to our example of the stricken swimmer. Suppose that this time the onlooker enters the sea with the intention of helping, but turns around and returns to the beach when he realises that the drowning man is his mortal enemy. And suppose that this time there is no-one

---

[143] K Williams, 'Litigation Against English NHS Ambulance Services and the Rule in *Kent v Griffiths*' [2007] *Medical Law Review* 153, 161 fn.

[144] *OLL Ltd v Secretary of State for Transport* [1997] 3 All ER 897 (QBD).

[145] The same would appear to be true of the mountain rescue service.

[146] Stevens (n 1) 14.

[147] Stevens (n 1) 14.

[148] See generally, A Burrows, *Understanding the Law of Obligations* (Oxford, Hart Publishing, 1998) 34–40.

else on the beach, so that it cannot be argued that the onlooker's actions have caused the swimmer additional damage. Clearly, the onlooker was not under any obligation to assist in the first place, but does the very fact that he began a rescue amount to an assumption of responsibility, with the result that he could be held liable for discontinuing his efforts without good reason? And what if he had reached the stricken swimmer, and begun to help him to safety, but had then inexplicably abandoned him on the way back to shore?

It is submitted that in this type of case the onlooker assumes a responsibility not when he sets off from the beach, but when he reaches the stricken swimmer, and *takes control* of the situation;[149] until then, therefore, he is free to discontinue his rescue attempt at any time, provided he has not induced any reliance. Furthermore, there seems to be no good reason why a rescuer who has taken control of a situation and thereby assumed a responsibility should not be free to relinquish control, revoking the assumption of responsibility (again, as long as his actions [283] have not induced reliance).[150] It follows that, in the absence of reliance, the onlooker would not be liable to the stricken swimmer if he callously chose to abandon him halfway through the rescue.[151]

One final point is that some of the authorities seem to go further than this, and to hold that a rescuer who was under no obligation to attempt a rescue in the first place does not come under any duty to be careful in effecting a rescue if he undertakes the attempt.[152] This position amounts to denying that the rescuer's assumption of responsibility gives rise to an obligation to confer a benefit at all, by limiting the liability of the rescuer to the causing of additional damage.

---

[149] See, eg, *Restatement, Second, Torts* (1977) § 324 ('takes charge of another'); ER Alexander, 'One Rescuer's Obligation to Another: The "Ogopogo" Lands in the Supreme Court of Canada' (1972) 2 *University of Toronto Law Journal* 98, 105 (has the volunteer 'gone so far in what he has done as to have taken charge of the situation?'); and *Prosser and Keeton* (n 87) 378 ('takes charge and control of the situation'). This analysis is also consistent with the Scottish cases in which the police and the fire brigade have been held to have assumed responsibilities in emergency situations, since the duty of care has been held to arise when the defendants took control of the situation: see *Gibson* (n 142) and *Burnett* (n 138). It is doubtful whether this test of 'taking control' was satisfied by the mere acceptance of the 999 call in *Kent v Griffiths* (n 51), but this test is merely a rule of thumb, and it does not follow that the Court of Appeal should have held that the ambulance service assumes no responsibility until a crew arrives at the scene and begins to treat the patient. In the medical context, it seems generally to be considered that responsibility is assumed when someone is accepted as a patient, even if treatment does not immediately follow, and the acceptance of an emergency call by the ambulance service is arguably equivalent to the initial processing of a patient arriving at an accident and emergency department.

[150] See *Prosser on Torts* (St Paul, Minn, West Publishing, 1941) 195 fn.

[151] 'Even if a person embarks on a rescue and does not carry it through, he is not under any liability to the person whose aid he has come so long as discontinuance of his efforts did not leave the other in a worse condition than when he took charge' (*The Ogopogo* [1970] 1 Lloyd's Rep 257 (Ont CA) 263 (Schroeder JA); see also 267 (Jessup JA)). *cf* Alexander (n 149), who argues (at 105) that once the rescuer has taken control, he must take reasonable steps to carry the rescue through, and the draft *Restatement, Third, Torts: Liability for Physical Harm* (n 61) § 44, comment h. The point was left open in the *Restatement, Second, Torts* (1977): see the caveat to § 324.

[152] *Capital and Counties* (n 66) 1037 (Stuart-Smith LJ). This would also appear to be Burrows's position (n 148) 35.

Although such a rule would be inconsistent with the general principles governing assumptions of responsibility, it could perhaps be justified in rescue cases on
the policy ground that imposing liability on a volunteer for failing to confer a
benefit might discourage altruistic behaviour,[153] although this policy argument
would obviously not be available to a public authority charged by Parliament
with a duty to intervene.[154]

iii. Does a Public Authority Acting Pursuant to a Statutory Duty Voluntarily Assume Responsibility?

The final issue which arises with regard to assumptions of responsibility is
whether a public authority acting pursuant to a statutory duty can be said
to have *voluntarily* assumed a responsibility when, as a matter of public law,
the authority had no choice but to act. The view that it cannot derives some
support from *Customs and Excise Commissioners v Barclays Bank plc*, where
the House of Lords held that a bank which had been served with a freez-
ing order prohibiting the disposal of a client's funds had not assumed any
responsibility towards the party which had obtained the order, and where
Lord Bingham of Cornhill and Lord Mance reasoned that since the bank was
bound to comply with the order, any assumption of responsibility was not
voluntary, and hence could not give rise to a duty of care.[155] Similarly, in the
first instance decision in *Neil Martin Ltd v Commissioners of Her Majesty's
Revenue and Customs*, Andrew Simmonds QC held that a tax officer processing an application for a certificate under a scheme for construction industry
subcontractors had not assumed any responsibility to the applicant, since the
Revenue was bound by statute to deal with the application,[156] and in *Rowley
v Secretary of State for Work and Pensions*, Dyson LJ argued that by making
a maintenance assessment [284] under the Child Support Act 1991, the Child
Support Agency did not assume a responsibility towards those foreseeably
affected by the assessment, since the statute required that such an assessment
be made.[157]

It is submitted, however, that this approach is based on a misinterpretation
of the word 'voluntary' in this context. The better view, which was expressed
by Lord Walker of Gestingthorpe in the *Customs and Excise Commissioners*

---

[153] See *The Ogopogo* (n 151) 267 (Jessup JA). See also *Prosser and Keeton* (n 87) 378 ('a real, and serious, deterrent to the giving of needed aid').

[154] See *Burnett* (n 138) [64] (Lord Macphail) (fire officers on duty not 'Good Samaritans').

[155] *Customs and Excise Commissioners v Barclays Bank plc* [2006] UKHL 28, [2007] 1 AC 181 [14] (Lord Bingham), [94] (Lord Mance).

[156] *Neil Martin Ltd v Revenue and Customs Commissioners* [2006] EWHC 2425 (Ch) [97]. The point as to voluntariness was not discussed on appeal: [2007] EWCA Civ 1041, [2007] STC 1802.

[157] *Rowley v Secretary of State for Work and Pensions* [2007] EWCA Civ 598, [2007] 1 WLR 2861 [54]. See also *Sandford v London Borough of Waltham Forest* [2008] EWHC 1106 (QB), [2008] BLGR 816 [36]–[38] (Judge Richard Seymour QC).

case, is that the undertaking is voluntary because it is 'conscious', 'considered' or 'deliberate', and not because it is the result of a free choice whether or not to act.[158] After all, no-one would suggest that a public authority is not bound by a contract because it was under a public law duty to enter into it, and in a number of negligence cases in which public bodies have been held to have assumed a responsibility towards the claimant, including *Barrett v Enfield London Borough Council*[159] and *Phelps v London Borough of Hillingdon*,[160] the defendant's actions were pursuant to duties imposed on it by Parliament.[161] Furthermore, the idea that an assumption of responsibility must have been freely undertaken is difficult to square with cases outside the public authorities context in which conduct pursuant to a contractual obligation owed to a third party or required under the rules of a self-regulatory body has been held to amount to an assumption of responsibility.[162]

IV. EVALUATING *GORRINGE*

Finally, we should consider whether *Gorringe* is a welcome development, and whether it is right that the rules governing negligence liability for failure to confer benefits should be the same for public authority defendants as for private parties. The answer to this question depends on which of the suggested justifications for the general rule against liability for 'omissions' one chooses to adopt.[163] It is certainly true that, as Lord Hoffmann himself accepted in *Stovin*,[164] some of the justifications put forward for this rule do not apply where the defendant is a public authority.[165] For example, the difficulty of singling out a particular defendant for failing to act when there were many others in the same position (the 'why pick on me?' argument) disappears, since the existence of the statutory duty or power in question singles the authority out. Similarly, whereas requiring a private individual to confer a benefit may be burdensome, and hence threaten her autonomy, no such concern arises when a public

---

[158] *Customs and Excise Commissioners* (n 155) [73] (see also at [38], where Lord Hoffmann made it clear that in his view action pursuant to a statutory duty could amount to an assumption of responsibility). Lord Walker's interpretation was preferred by Briggs J in *Calvert v William Hill Credit Ltd* [2008] EWHC 454 (Ch), [2009] Ch 330 [177].

[159] *Barrett* (n 45).

[160] *Phelps* (n 46).

[161] See also *Ministry of Housing and Local Government v Sharp* [1970] 2 QB 223 (CA).

[162] See respectively *Henderson v Merrett Syndicates Ltd* [1995] 2 AC 145 (HL) and *Spring v Guardian Assurance plc* [1995] 2 AC 296 (HL).

[163] For a helpful survey of the possible justifications for distinguishing between acts and omissions, see J Kortmann, *Altruism in Private Law: Liability for Nonfeasance and Negotiorum Gestio* (Oxford, OUP, 2005) ch 3.

[164] *Stovin* (n 18) 946. See also 935 (Lord Nicholls).

[165] See also Brodie (n 142) 255; Law Com CP No 187 (n 4) para 3.161; and M Aronson, 'Government Liability in Negligence' (2008) 32 *Melbourne University Law Review* 44, 69.

authority is involved (particularly when the authority is under a public law duty to act in any case) and concerns about the [285] cost of imposing affirmative duties of action on private parties carry less weight when the full resources of the state can be brought to bear. These are not, however, particularly convincing arguments for the general rule against omissions liability, not least because they do not explain why the rule is general, and not limited to cases where there are in fact multiple possible defendants, or where intervention would indeed be burdensome or costly.[166]

There are, however, more convincing justifications for distinguishing between making things worse and not making them better, and these apply just as forcefully to public bodies as to private parties. One such justification is provided by Honoré, who argues that in general harmful abstentions are less culpable than wrongful acts, because while the latter constitute inroads on security, the former threaten only the expectation of improvement, a different and secondary value.[167] Similarly, the 'omissions rule' is defended by those who argue that tort law is concerned with the secondary obligations generated by the infringement of primary rights, on the grounds that we do not have a right good against the whole world that others confer benefits on us, and that therefore such a right can arise only as a result of an undertaking, whether contractual or otherwise, or where a statute has conferred the right on the claimant (in which case there will be an action for breach of statutory duty).[168] If we accept the force of either of these rationales of the general no-liability rule, then we are drawn to the conclusion that in private law terms there is no justification for distinguishing between public authorities and private parties when it comes to failures to confer benefits, and that therefore *Gorringe* represents a welcome rationalisation of the law.

This conclusion is reinforced by two other considerations. The first is that, as Simmonds has observed, '[t]he more extensive the protective scope of the state's authority, the less we will be inclined to regard tragedies as the result of ill-fortune, and the more we will seek to ascribe blame',[169] and yet it seems paradoxical that the more things that governments do, and the more measures which they take to protect the public, the more likely it is that they will be criticised

---

[166] See Beever (n 1) 210 ('The non-existence of a duty to rescue is not easily explicable in terms of policy'). The 'why pick on me?' argument is particularly weak, and is demolished by Weinrib (n 87) 262.

[167] T Honoré, 'Are Omissions Less Culpable?' in P Cane and J Stapleton (eds), *Essays for Patrick Atiyah* (Oxford, Clarendon Press, 1991) 48–51.

[168] See Stevens (n 1) 9 ('the failure to confer a benefit on someone else does not, alone, constitute the infringement of a right'); and Beever (n 1) ch 9. For an example of judicial reliance on rights-based reasoning in his context, see the dissenting judgment of du Parcq LJ in the Court of Appeal in *Kent v East Suffolk* (n 95) 337–39.

[169] NE Simmonds, 'Justice, Causation and Private Law' in M D'Entrèves and U Vogel, *Public and Private: Legal, Political and Philosophical Perspectives* (London, Routledge, 2000) 171.

(and possibly sued) for not doing more.[170] Indeed it has been argued that this paradox is a potentially dangerous one, since attaching liability to government attempts to protect citizens may deter the state from involving itself in such matters,[171] though obviously this danger would not arise if the withdrawal of state protection would be politically unacceptable, as it obviously would be in areas such as policing and social services.[172]

[286] The second consideration is that, while there is clearly a need for public authorities to be held accountable for their mistakes, negligence liability is not the only mechanism through which such accountability can be achieved, and other avenues of redress – including Ombudsman procedures, actions under the Human Rights Act, and statutory or administrative compensation – may prove both more effective and more efficient.[173] After all, the very characteristics of the state which make the application of ordinary private law principles so potentially complex in public authority cases also call into question the wisdom of using a cause of action developed with private parties in mind to regulate liability issues arising out of the performance (or non-performance) of uniquely governmental functions. Beever captures this point well:

> The problem as identified concerns the state's obligations to its citizens. Accordingly, the appropriate place to deal with this problem, if it can be dealt with in law at all, is in the area of law that controls the relationship between the state and its citizens: public law. It may be that, for instance, the state possesses special obligations to rescue its citizens from harm that private persons do not possess. If these obligations exist, their justification lies in the nature of the state, not in the structure of tort law. Moreover, if these obligations exist, it is not necessarily the case that tort law ought to protect them. Perhaps it would be better to institute or strengthen a separate public law area of accountability ... The point is ... that, if the state has special obligations, those are a product of the kind (or kinds) of legal entity it is and not of the law of negligence ... [T]ort law should not be used as the law's

---

[170] See PS Atiyah, *The Damages Lottery* (Oxford, Hart Publishing, 1997) 86.

[171] See *Clemente v United States* 567 F 2d 1140 (1st Cir 1977) 1150 (Coffin CJ).

[172] We should also note the counter-argument that holding public authorities liable for negligent interventions, but not for negligent failures to intervene, may have the effect of distorting their priorities in sensitive contexts such as child protection (see Booth and Squires (n 8) para 8.40). Indeed, it could be argued that the need to avoid creating perverse incentives is in itself sufficient justification for the positive obligation to intervene to protect children recognised in *JD v East Berkshire* (n 49), though any such incentives created by the negligence liability rules would now be moderated by the possibility that a failure to intervene will give rise to a claim under the Human Rights Act.

[173] Harlow (n 2) 8. See also Feldthusen (n 115) 32, arguing that other avenues, such as public audits and formalised complaint mechanisms, are needed to secure policy accountability; Cohen and Smith (n 115), who argue that it is impossible for negligence principles to furnish a basis for state liability for failure to confer benefits, and that instead this should be done via a public law principle of 'entitlement'; and Hoffmann (n 43) para 15, commending the use of Ombudsman procedures. *cf* T Cornford, *Towards a Public Law of Tort* (Aldershot, Ashgate Publishing, 2008), arguing that negligence law is an appropriate vehicle for holding public authorities to account.

Swiss Army knife to fix potential inadequacies in public law. It has a structure of its own.[174]

V. CONCLUSION

By way of conclusion, two observations of more general significance can be made, both of which call into question the current predominance of policy reasoning in negligence adjudication. The first is that the law's insistence that public authorities are liable for failing to confer benefits only when private parties would be casts doubt on the common assumption that the general no-liability rule in omissions cases is based on policy concerns such as the autonomy objection and the 'Why pick on me?' argument. The fact that these arguments have little or no force where [287] public authority defendants are concerned, but that such defendants are still shielded by the no-liability rule, suggests that the reasons why negligence law distinguishes between making things worse and not making things better lie elsewhere.

The second observation concerns the apparent inability of at least some judges and commentators to 'join the dots' in this area. An example can be found in the speech of Lord Scott in *Jain v Trent Strategic Health Authority*, where his Lordship said that while it would be problematic to hold that a regulatory authority owed a duty of care to the owner of a registered nursing home when performing its supervisory functions, it might be fair and reasonable to conclude that an authority owed such a duty to the residents of a home if conditions warranting the exercise of the authority's statutory powers came to its attention but nothing was then done.[175] Is it not strange that the judge who was most forthright in *Gorringe* about the impossibility of founding a common law duty of care on the mere existence of a statutory duty or power should have been so amenable to the possibility of just such a duty being imposed when it came to the supervision of nursing homes? Similarly, is it not surprising that courts at all levels now seem to assume that social services departments owe a duty of care to children at risk of abuse, even though no attempt has been made to reconcile this assumption with the *Gorringe* decision, and that there was no mention of *Gorringe* in a subsequent House of Lords case in which the police were sued in negligence for failing to protect the claimant from a dangerous ex-partner?[176] The most likely explanation for these apparent discontinuities

---

[174] Beever (n 1) 340. See also Hoffmann (n 43) para 18, arguing that the duty of care concept is a 'primitive and individualist template' which 'fits awkwardly upon questions involving the administration of public bodies'.

[175] *Jain* (n 78) [20].

[176] *Van Colle* (n 76). The House held that no duty of care was owed for public policy reasons.

is the fact that judicial reasoning in duty of care cases is increasingly dominated by arguments of public policy. Naturally, this focus on policy is bound
to distract judges from issues of principle such as the act/omission distinction,
but because the policy arguments in question are generally context-specific, it
also serves to fragment negligence law into contextual compartments, so that
increasingly judges and commentators think in terms of police cases, social
services cases, highways cases and so forth, rather than conceiving of negligence law – or even the negligence liability of public authorities – as a unified
whole. In these circumstances, it is hardly surprising if vital connections are
missed, and the conceptual unity of the law undermined. The obvious conclusion to draw is that only if arguments from principle return to their rightful
place at the heart of judicial reasoning in negligence cases can consistency and
coherence be maintained.

5

Assumption of Responsibility: Four Questions

(2019) 72 *Current Legal Problems* 123–158

[123] I. INTRODUCTION

THE PHRASE 'ASSUMPTION of responsibility' should be familiar to anyone with even a passing knowledge of the modern law of negligence. The underlying principle is an ancient one,[1] though it is only since the seminal [124] decision of the House of Lords in *Hedley Byrne & Co v Heller and Partners*[2] in 1963 that our courts have imposed negligence liability explicitly on the grounds that the defendant had assumed a responsibility towards the claimant. The tendency of the courts to do this is now more pronounced than ever. The Court of Appeal has, since the turn of the century, employed the concept to justify imposing negligence liability on a parent company for an asbestos-related disease suffered by an employee of a subsidiary,[3] on the Ministry of Defence for injuries suffered by a soldier who fell off the back of a lorry after a drunken night on the town,[4] and on a householder whose friend had fallen out of the householder's loft while working on the entry hatch cover.[5] And the concept is also of central importance in the law of professional liability,[6] as is shown by another, very recent, decision of the Court of Appeal in which it was held that an architect's provision of her expertise free of charge to a couple

---

[1] 'It is ancient learning that one who assumes to act, even though gratuitously, may thereby become subject to the duty of acting carefully, if he acts at all' (*Glanzer v Shepard* 135 NE 275 (NY 1922) 276 (Cardozo J)). On the historical underpinnings of the concept, see P Mitchell, '*Hedley Byrne & Co Ltd v Heller & Partners Ltd* (1963)' in C Mitchell and P Mitchell (eds), *Landmark Cases in the Law of Tort* (Oxford, Hart Publishing, 2010). See also JH Beale, 'Gratuitous Undertakings' (1891–92) 5 *Harvard Law Review* 222.

[2] *Hedley Byrne & Co v Heller and Partners* [1963] AC 465 (HL).

[3] *Chandler v Cape plc* [2012] EWCA Civ 525, [2012] 1 WLR 3111.

[4] *Jebson v Ministry of Defence* [2000] 1 WLR 2055 (CA).

[5] *Biddick (decd) v Morcom* [2014] EWCA Civ 182.

[6] See *Robinson v PE Jones (Contractors) Ltd* [2011] EWCA Civ 9, [2012] QB 44 [74] (Jackson LJ). It is also worth remembering that the liability of health professionals who provide healthcare free of charge under the National Health Service is partly grounded on assumption of responsibility.

who were her friends had given rise to a duty of care in respect of their purely economic interests.[7] Furthermore, the recent demise of the general three-stage test for the existence of a duty of care said to be derived from the speech of Lord Bridge in *Caparo Industries plc v Dickman*[8] enhances the significance of the concept, by removing from the armoury of the courts a rival approach to the determination of the duty of care issue in the types of case in which it has been used.[9] [125]

But despite the frequency with which the courts invoke the assumption of responsibility concept, it is difficult to be sure what they mean by it, as different judges seem to have quite different things in mind when they employ the phrase. Judicial ambivalence is mirrored by academic disagreement, as was graphically illustrated by the recent publication of a collection of essays commemorating the fiftieth anniversary of *Hedley Byrne*.[10] At least four different schools of thought are discernible in the academic writings on assumption of responsibility, in that collection and elsewhere: (1) that the concept as employed by the courts[11] is essentially meaningless, and either a foil for policy arguments

[7] *Lejonvarn v Burgess* [2017] EWCA Civ 254, [2017] BLR 277.

[8] *Caparo Industries plc v Dickman* [1990] 2 AC 605 (HL). I have argued elsewhere that the continued use of the three-stage test is clearly inconsistent with the approach to the duty of care question laid down by Lord Reed in *Robinson v Chief Constable of West Yorkshire Police* [2018] UKSC 4, [2018] AC 736 and subsequently confirmed in later Supreme Court decisions: see D Nolan, 'The Duty of Care After *Robinson v Chief Constable of West Yorkshire Police*' in D Clarry (ed), *The UK Supreme Court Yearbook, Volume 9: 2017–2018 Legal Year* (London, Appellate Press, 2019).

[9] The tension between the two approaches was particularly apparent in *Customs and Excise Commissioners v Barclays Bank plc* [2006] UKHL 28, [2007] 1 AC 181. Nor is it an accident that some of the most vocal academic critics of assumption of responsibility are also supporters of the *Caparo* test, and its central component of 'proximity'. Again, the fact that it is now clear that – at least as far as English law is concerned – those sceptics backed the wrong horse is likely only to strengthen the assumption of responsibility concept in years to come. For particularly explicit comparisons of assumption of responsibility and the *Caparo* test (favouring the latter), see K Barker, 'Wielding Occam's Razor: Pruning Strategies for Economic Loss' (2006) 26 *OJLS* 289; and J Hartshorne, 'Contemporary Approaches Towards Pure Economic Loss in the Law of Negligence' [2014] *Journal of Business Law* 425. Note, however, that there are at least two alternative approaches to the relationship between assumption of responsibility and general duty tests. One is to try to integrate the two, by making the presence of an assumption of responsibility determinative of an element of the general test, such as proximity: see, eg, *Brownie Wills v Shrimpton* [1998] 2 NZLR 320 (NZCA) 329 (Tipping J); *Deloitte & Touche v Livent Inc (Receiver of)* [2017] SCC 63, [2017] 2 SCR 855. And the other is to dismiss assumption of responsibility as yet another vacuous duty concept, along with 'proximity', 'neighbourhood' and the like: see, eg, *Caparo* (n 8) 627–29 (Lord Roskill). The former approach has the advantage of reducing the uncertainty and incoherence that always results from the use of a general duty test, but it would be far preferable to abandon the general test altogether. As for the latter, it is the central message of this article that assumption of responsibility is, unlike, say, 'proximity', a perfectly meaningful notion.

[10] K Barker et al (eds), *The Law of Misstatements: 50 Years on from Hedley Byrne v Heller* (Oxford, Hart Publishing, 2015).

[11] I am grateful to James Plunkett for alerting me to the need for the qualifying words 'as employed by the courts'. As he himself has pointed out (J Plunkett, *The Duty of Care in Negligence* (Oxford, Hart Publishing, 2018) 137) critics of assumption of responsibility generally accept that there are some, very limited, circumstances in which the concept can serve as an independent justification for negligence liability. However, their critique rests on the claim that the courts routinely abuse the concept by employing it in circumstances where it cannot so serve.

or for an alternative, allegedly more meaningful concept, such as 'proximity'; (2) that cases of assumption of responsibility are really just instances of liability in contract, minus consideration; (3) that in the cases where the assumption of responsibility concept is employed no liability should have been imposed at all; and (4) that assumption of responsibility is a distinctive sui generis basis of legal obligation, separate from both core negligence law and the law of contract. Furthermore, as the essays in the anniversary collection make clear, the academic disputation over assumption of responsibility runs deep. There is quite simply no common ground on this issue between scholars such as Bob Hepple, who described assumption of responsibility as 'a discredited fiction' in a *Current Legal Problems* lecture in [126] 1997,[12] and scholars such as Robert Stevens, who treats assumption of responsibility as an important source of rights in his book *Torts and Rights*.[13]

In this article, my goal is to step back from this maelstrom and to try to bring some clarity to the controversies surrounding assumption of responsibility. Four questions frame the analysis. *What* does assumption of responsibility mean? *When* does it matter? *Why* do we need it? And *where* does it belong? After trying to answer those four questions, I will also highlight three red herrings that in my view have clouded analysis of the concept. The scope of the article is broad: my concern is with all duties of care that arise out of assumptions of responsibility, including in cases of gratuitous bailment and gratuitous agency.[14] And I should make it clear at the outset that the breadth of the subject-matter and constraints of space mean that I am unable to explore all of the interesting questions that are raised by cases of this kind, or to engage in detailed critique of alternative positions. Instead I have chosen to put forward a positive vision of the assumption of responsibility concept, at a relatively high level of generality.

II. A TRIP TO THE BEACH

Before I turn to the first of the four questions I want to consider, it will be instructive for us to go on a little journey. Tony Weir famously said of the House of Lords in *Hedley Byrne* that 'one almost has the feeling that their Lordships had been on a trip to Mount Olympus and perhaps smoked a

---

[12] B Hepple, 'Negligence: The Search for Coherence' [1997] *CLP* 87, 88.

[13] R Stevens, *Torts and Rights* (Oxford, OUP, 2007).

[14] Needless to say, other kinds of obligations can also arise out of an assumption of responsibility, but since this article is concerned with negligence they are not relevant here. For discussion of these kinds of obligation in relation to bailment, see A Bell, 'The Place of Bailment in the Modern Law of Obligations' in N Palmer and E McKendrick (eds), *Interests in Goods*, 2nd edn (London, LLP, 1998) 484.

joint on the bus'.[15] However, since I know virtually nothing about Greek law, ancient or modern, I am afraid that our trip will need to be within the jurisdiction, and, as we will need our wits about us, no intoxicating substances will be involved.

So let us imagine instead that you take a trip to the English seaside at the height of summer. It is the middle of a heatwave, and the beach is crowded. You settle down for the afternoon, accompanied by your young son and, naturally, your mobile phone. After a few minutes, you fall into [127] conversation with a couple who are sunbathing nearby. A young man wearing a t-shirt that says 'Lifeguard' then appears. He hoists a flag that indicates his presence to those on the beach and takes up a vantage point on a platform from which he can survey the surf. Reassured by this, you then decide that you would like to cool off with a bracing swim (this is England remember). Since the couple you are talking to seem nice, and sensible, you ask them if they would mind keeping an eye on your son and looking after your phone for a few minutes, and they agree to do so. You enter the water, and swim out from the beach until you are well out of your depth. At that point, you have a severe attack of cramp and get into difficulties. You sink beneath the surface, and eventually lose consciousness. An observer on the beach raises the alarm, and another swimmer pulls your head out of the water and begins to bring you back to the shore. Soon the lifeguard arrives and between them they haul you up onto the beach. You are still unconscious, and have stopped breathing. An off-duty doctor who is nearby comes to their assistance and resuscitates you. Someone has called an ambulance, which arrives on the scene within minutes. You have swallowed so much water that the ambulance crew decide to take you to the nearest hospital, where you are admitted as a patient and make a full and rapid recovery. You are eventually reunited with your son and your phone.

Now the first thing that will strike a seasoned negligence hand about this story is that nobody (apart, possibly, from you yourself) has done anything wrong. The couple did not let a stranger steal your phone and kidnap your child. The other swimmer did not abandon the rescue halfway through for no good reason and let you drown. The lifeguard did not ignore your plight because he was busy updating his status on Facebook. The doctor did not break your ribs while trying to get you breathing again. And the ambulance crew did not go to the wrong beach and turn up an hour late. Indeed, the facts would make for a truly terrible exam question, since no torts whatsoever appear to have been committed.

Nevertheless, the story is instructive, since a number of things happen in it which could amount to 'assumptions of responsibility' that alter the legal relationships between those involved. Hence the story of the trip to the beach

---

[15] T Weir, 'Errare Humanum Est' in P Birks (ed), *The Frontiers of Liability*, vol 2 (Oxford, OUP, 1994) 105 fn.

should be of interest to a tort lawyer even though everybody involved acts impeccably and the ending is, most unusually for tort law, a happy one.[16] Unfortunately, we will have to leave the beach for now, [128] but we will be returning to it at various points in the remainder of the article.

III. WHAT DOES ASSUMPTION OF RESPONSIBILITY MEAN?

My first question is also the most difficult to answer, because the meaning of the phrase 'assumption of responsibility' is wreathed in doubt. Two central ambiguities can be identified. The first relates to the word 'responsibility', which has a number of quite distinct meanings, as HLA Hart pointed out in an article entitled 'Varieties of Responsibility'.[17] In the present context, the two meanings of interest to us are what Hart called 'role responsibility' and 'legal liability-responsibility' (hereafter 'legal responsibility'). By the former, Hart meant the (non-legal) responsibility that attaches to a role or the taking on of a task or job. Suppose for example that I agree with my wife that I will put the bins out tomorrow. I am now 'responsible' for putting out the bins, and she is not. This sense of the word need have nothing to do with the law at all. By contrast, what Hart meant by 'legal responsibility' was legal accountability, or exposure to liability. This is what we mean, for example, when we say that an employer is 'responsible' for the torts of its employees. Clearly, when we talk about 'responsibility' in these two senses, we are talking about two quite different things. And yet it is often difficult to know which of these two meanings of the word is intended when judges and scholars talk of 'assumption of responsibility'.

   The second ambiguity is apparent not so much from the phrase 'assumption of responsibility' itself, but from the word 'undertaking', which is often used as a synonym for it.[18] The problem here is that the word undertaking can mean either to promise or give an assurance that you will do something, or to tackle or begin doing something. Hence *having undertaken to put the bins out, I am now undertaking the task*. Unfortunately, however, it is again sometimes unclear which of these two senses of the word is intended when it is said that negligence liability is based on an undertaking, with the result that it is unclear whether

---

[16] And therein lies an important truth about the nature of tort law, and indeed private law more generally. Naturally, tort lawyers are inclined to focus on liability and litigation, as it is when these are in issue that their services tend to be required. But that can cause us to forget that tort law is in the background of our lives all the time, setting many of the rules by which people in a civilised community co-exist. It would be strange to think of the rules of chess only in terms of their violation. And similarly, it is strange (though also, for various reasons, perfectly understandable) to think of tort law only in terms of wrongs.

[17] HLA Hart, 'Varieties of Responsibility' (1967) 83 *LQR* 346.

[18] Both the noun 'undertaking' and the verb 'undertake' feature frequently in *Hedley Byrne* (n 2): for the noun, see 492 (Lord Reid), 529–30, 532–33 (Lord Devlin); and for the verb, see, eg, 495, 497, 502–503 (Lord Morris), 528 (Lord Devlin).

the [129] duty of care arises out of an express or implied promise or assurance which the defendant has made, or simply out of the fact that the defendant has begun performing a task or job of some kind, and has thereby assumed responsibility in the role responsibility sense.[19]

The end result is that when a negligence lawyer talks about an 'assumption of responsibility', she could mean any of three different things: (1) the taking on of a task, including by beginning performance of it ('role' responsibility, and the second sense of 'undertaking'); (2) the acceptance of a legal duty (which is to say, an acceptance of responsibility in the 'legal responsibility' sense); or (3) the giving of a promise or assurance (the first sense of 'undertaking'). Furthermore, it seems to me from reading the cases that judges have ascribed all three of these possible meanings to the phrase, and indeed sometimes have ascribed more than one of these meanings to it in the same judgment.

Matters are complicated further by the fact that although the different meanings are distinct, the same action can amount to an assumption of responsibility in more than one of these senses. So, for example, when I tell my wife that I will take the bins out tomorrow, I am both taking upon myself the task of doing so (meaning one), and also giving her an assurance that I will do so (meaning three). Similarly, when I become a trustee of a charity, I am both taking on a task (meaning one again) and accepting a legal duty (meaning two).

Although it looks at this point as though there may be no clear answer to my first question, the deadlock can be broken if we switch our focus to the results of the cases, and ask ourselves what conduct it is that triggers the judicial conclusion that an assumption of responsibility has taken place ('the conduct that engenders the relation', as Cardozo CJ put it[20]). And looking at the cases, it seems clear that by far the most plausible way of characterising the conduct that, at least prima facie, triggers that conclusion is that *A has taken on a task or job for B* (ie, meaning one).[21] And it [130] follows that unless A has taken on a task or job for B, there is no assumption of responsibility, and any legal duty that the court recognises must rest on a different foundation.

---

[19] Highlighting the historical significance of the ambiguity, see JH Baker, *An Introduction to English Legal History*, 4th edn (London, Butterworths LexisNexis, 2002) 334. And see also PH Winfield, 'Duty in Tortious Negligence' (1934) 34 *Columbia Law Review* 41, 55 ('a conveniently ambiguous word').

[20] *HR Moch Co Inc v Rensselaer Water Co* 159 NE 896 (NY 1928) 898.

[21] See, eg, *Hedley Byrne* (n 2) 497 (Lord Morris) (referring to 'situations in which one person voluntarily or gratuitously undertakes to do something for another person'); and *Henderson v Merrett Syndicates Ltd* [1995] 2 AC 145 (HL) 186 (Lord Goff) (*Hedley Byrne* established 'the principle upon which liability may arise in tortious negligence in respect of services (including advice) which are rendered for another'). For a particularly clear judicial use of this test, predating *Hedley Byrne*, see *Davis v Foots* [1940] 1 KB 116 (CA) 122, 124 (MacKinnon LJ) ('I do not think there was any undertaking to do work for the plaintiff', 'there is no question of doing a service for the plaintiff or her husband at all'). Note also the parallel with the old *assumpsit* action, which lay 'where one party undertook to act for the benefit of another and carelessly misperformed' (Mitchell (n 1) 173).

A few examples will help us to see what I mean by this claim. In *Henderson v Merrett Syndicates Ltd*,[22] the defendant underwriting agents took on the task of managing the insurance syndicates of which the claimants were members. In *Barrett v Enfield London Borough Council*[23] the local authority took on the task of looking after the claimant when they took him into their care as a baby. In *Watson v British Boxing Board of Control*[24] the British Boxing Board of Control took on for the participants the task of ensuring that there were adequate medical facilities at an approved title bout. In *Biddick v Morcom*[25] (the case about the loft hatch cover), the defendant took on the task of ensuring that the cover remained locked. In bailment cases, the bailee takes on the task of looking after the goods of the bailor. And so on and so forth.

Perhaps even more illuminating are the cases where this requirement that A took on a task or job for B was *not* satisfied, so that there was no assumption of responsibility. The best such example is *White v Jones*,[26] a decision which, properly understood, is arguably the single most illuminating case on the assumption of responsibility concept.[27] In *White*, a majority of the House of Lords held that an intended beneficiary under a will was entitled to recover damages from the testator's solicitor, if, by reason of his negligence, the testator's intention to benefit the claimant had not been carried into effect. Now it seems perfectly clear that the liability in *White* does not rest on an assumption of responsibility basis, since although the defendant had agreed to prepare the will, he had not taken on this task *for* the beneficiaries (the claimants), but *for* the testator. What is more, both Lord Goff, in the leading majority speech, and Lord Mustill in the leading dissenting speech, make this point quite explicitly. According to Lord Goff, there was 'great difficulty' in holding that a solicitor assumed any responsibility towards the intended beneficiary of [131] a will since 'in the absence of special circumstances', the relevant work 'cannot be said to have been undertaken for the intended beneficiary'.[28] Hence his conclusion that the assumption of responsibility towards the testator in the case should be 'held in law' to extend to the intended beneficiaries[29] (in other words, although in fact there was no assumption of responsibility towards the claimants, there should be 'deemed' to be one). Similarly, Lord Mustill emphasised the fact that the solicitor had not undertaken the task of

---

[22] *Henderson* (n 21).

[23] *Barrett v Enfield London Borough Council* [2000] 2 AC 550 (HL).

[24] *Watson v British Boxing Board of Control* [2001] QB 1134 (CA).

[25] *Biddick* (n 5).

[26] *White v Jones* [1995] 2 AC 207 (HL).

[27] Other useful negative examples include *Customs and Excise Commissioners* (n 9), where, as Lord Mance said (at [94]), it was 'difficult in any meaningful sense to speak of the bank as having voluntarily assumed responsibility even for the task in relation to which it was allegedly negligent, let alone responsibility towards the commissioners for the task'.

[28] *White* (n 26) 262. See also at 268.

[29] ibid 268.

drawing up the will '*for* the beneficiaries' (his emphasis), but for the testator, and said that the 'cardinal feature' of the *Hedley Byrne* case was that 'the defendants undertook the job [in that case, of providing a credit reference] for the plaintiffs'.[30]

A recent decision of the Supreme Court, *Banca Nazionale del Lavoro SPA v Playboy Club London Ltd*,[31] rests on precisely the same kind of reasoning. In this case a bank provided a credit reference in respect of one Hassan Barakat to a company called Burlington Street Services. The company was acting on behalf of the Playboy Club, a casino frequented by Barakat, but the bank did not know this. Since the bank did not assume any responsibility to the *Playboy Club*,[32] no duty of care was owed to the club in respect of the reference.[33] This reasoning also explains why a doctor carrying out a pre-employment health assessment for a company, or instructed by an insurer to examine an applicant for life insurance, owes no duty of care to the subject of the assessment or examination beyond the core *Donoghue v Stevenson*[34] duty not negligently to injure through positive conduct.[35] And it may even explain why it is that, unlike the ambulance service,[36] the police[37] and fire [132] brigade[38] generally owe no duty of care to individuals in emergency situations, on the footing that when responding to an emergency call they act not for the benefit of particular individuals, but the public as a whole.[39]

Although I am wary of becoming mired in the case law, I should acknowledge that there are at least two important decisions at the highest level which are

---

[30] ibid 290. See also at 251 (Lord Keith).
[31] *Banca Nazionale del Lavoro SPA v Playboy Club London Ltd* [2018] UKSC 43, [2018] 1 WLR 4041.
[32] See ibid [16] (Lord Sumption).
[33] For criticism of some aspects of the Supreme Court's reasoning, albeit within an overall framework similar to mine, see JAW Grower and OF Sherman, 'Equivalent to Contract? Confronting the Nature of the Duty Arising under *Hedley Byrne v Heller*' (2019) 135 LQR 177. Of course, there will be borderline cases where opinions can reasonably differ on the question of for whom the work was taken on. For a helpful discussion, see K Stanton, '*Hedley Byrne and Heller*: The Relationship Factor' [2007] *Professional Negligence* 94.
[34] *Donoghue v Stevenson* [1932] AC 562 (HL).
[35] See *X (minors) v Bedfordshire County Council* [1995] 2 AC 633 (HL) 752 (Lord Browne-Wilkinson) (life insurance example); *Kapfunde v Abbey National plc* [1998] IRLR 583 (CA) (pre-employment health check). See also the decision in *X (minors)* that social workers and psychiatrists instructed by a local authority to report on suspected victims of child sexual abuse did not assume any general professional duty of care to the children in question.
[36] *Kent v Griffiths* [2001] QB 36 (CA).
[37] *Michael v Chief Constable of South Wales Police* [2015] UKSC 2, [2015] AC 1732.
[38] *Capital and Counties plc v Hampshire CC* [1997] QB 1004 (CA).
[39] For general discussion, see D Nolan, 'The Liability of Public Authorities for Failing to Confer Benefits' (2011) 127 LQR 260, 280–81. A distinction along these lines was adverted to by Stuart-Smith LJ in *Capital and Counties* (n 38) 1036–37, and by Lord Woolf MR in *Kent* (n 36) 52–53, and was explicitly endorsed and employed in *Furnell v Flaherty* [2013] EWHC 377 (QB) [64] (Turner J). However, its application is not always straightforward: see, eg, *Sherratt v Chief Constable of Greater Manchester Police* [2018] EWHC 1746 (QB), [2019] PIQR P1 [83] (King J) (arguing that in some circumstances the police, like the ambulance service, act for the benefit of a particular individual).

difficult to reconcile with this analysis. The first is *Smith v Eric S Bush*,[40] which was not decided on an assumption of responsibility basis, but which is nevertheless now considered to be a possible application of the *Hedley Byrne* principle. In the first of the two appeals in this case (*Smith*), it was arguable that the surveyor had in fact taken on the job of surveying the property both for the bank *and* for the claimants (the prospective purchasers of the house), not least because the surveyor knew that the claimants had paid for the survey, and that a copy of his report would be passed on to them by the bank. However, in the second of the two appeals (*Harris v Wyre Forest District Council*), it was not really plausible to say that the council surveyor assumed any responsibility towards the prospective purchasers, since the mortgage application form stated that the valuation was intended solely for the information of the local authority lender, and it was never intended that it be shown to the claimants (as indeed it was not).[41] If I am correct in my evaluation of the two appeals, then it follows that while the outcomes in the Court of Appeal in both cases were consistent with an assumption of responsibility analysis, this was not so in the House of Lords in relation to the second appeal.[42] [133]

And the other case that is difficult to explain on my view of the law is *Spring v Guardian Assurance*,[43] for while in general I think that it is plausible to say that an employer who undertakes to provide a reference for a former employee is taking on the task for the employee,[44] on the facts of *Spring* the request came from the prospective employer, rather than the former employee, and there was no suggestion that the provision of a reference was something that the defendant had agreed to do on the employee's behalf.[45] Hence it seems to me that the decision to impose liability in *Spring* may better be explained on an alternative basis (such as an implied term of the contract of employment).

Returning to the three different possible meanings of the phrase 'assumption of responsibility', in cases where A has taken on a task or job for B, A may or may not have done so by making a promise or giving an assurance to B,[46] but for present purposes that seems to me to be irrelevant. What matters is that

---

[40] *Smith v Eric S Bush* [1990] 1 AC 831 (HL).

[41] A comparison of the facts of the *Wyre Forest* appeal with the discussion of *Robinson v National Bank of Scotland* 1916 SC (HL) 154 in Lord Devlin's speech in *Hedley Byrne* (n 2) at 532–33 is particularly revealing.

[42] In *Williams v Natural Life Health Foods* [1998] 1 WLR 830 (HL), Lord Steyn said (at 837), in a section of his speech defending the assumption of responsibility concept against academic criticism, that both *Smith v Bush* and *White v Jones* had been 'decided on special facts'. And for implicit disapproval of the decision in the *Wyre Forest* appeal in particular, see also *Scullion v Bank of Scotland plc* [2011] EWCA 693, [2011] 1 WLR 3212 [48] (Lord Neuberger MR).

[43] *Spring v Guardian Assurance* [1995] 2 AC 296 (HL).

[44] See the analysis of Lord Goff in *Spring* (n 43) 319.

[45] See similarly, A Beever, *Rediscovering the Law of Negligence* (Oxford, Hart Publishing, 2007) 316–19.

[46] This would, for example, have been the case in *Wilkinson v Coverdale* (1793) 1 Esp 75, 170 ER 284, had the defendant in fact promised to procure insurance cover for the plaintiff.

A has taken on the task, not how A has done so.[47] It follows that an assumption of responsibility does not necessarily involve any communication from A to B, and hence that the off-duty doctor may be assuming a responsibility to you on the beach (and thereby coming under a positive obligation to assist you[48]) even though you are unconscious. The apparent equation of assumption of responsibility with a 'promise' or 'assurance' in Lord Toulson's brief discussion of the concept in *Michael v Chief Constable of South Wales Police* was therefore contrary to principle.[49] [134]

The resolution of the ambiguity between the two meanings of *responsibility* is more challenging. Here the best interpretation of the cases is that although in theory *both* are required, when A takes on the task or job for B (role responsibility), A will be presumed to be implicitly taking on the duty to perform that task with due care, and that the law generally attaches legal responsibility to that implicit undertaking to take care, unless there is a good reason why it should not do so.[50] And there are at least five reasons that the courts have given for not recognising a legal duty of care in such a case: (1) that A took on the task or job in an informal or social context;[51] (2) that A expressly disclaimed legal responsibility (as in *Hedley Byrne* itself); (3) that the recognition of legal responsibility would be inconsistent with the terms of a contract between A and B;[52] (4) that A and B deliberately structured their commercial relationship in such a way as to avoid direct liability inter se, so that an assumed duty of care would have the effect of 'short-circuiting' this contractual structure;[53] and (5) that recognition

---

[47] Much depends on the context, it seems. The obligations of a gratuitous bailee arise only when A actually takes possession of B's property; a promise to look after it is not enough. Conversely, in gratuitous agency cases, the agent's obligations may arise simply by virtue of A saying that he will arrange the insurance, etc for B. In the latter situation, attaching significance to the promise/assurance may seem to contradict the principle that promises are not binding without consideration, but this is not the case. The law is not saying here that A must *keep the promise*: rather, that he must exercise reasonable care in carrying out the task he promised to perform. And besides, the better view is that in such a case A is free to renege on the promised performance altogether, as long as B is left no worse off: see, eg, *Restatement, Second, Agency* (1958) § 378, comment b.

[48] Though *cf* the claim by Stuart-Smith LJ in *Capital and Counties* (n 38) 1035 that in the absence of a doctor-patient relationship no special duty is assumed, so that the only obligation of an off-duty doctor who assists a road accident victim is not to make things worse (and see similarly *Watson* (n 24) [47] (Lord Phillips MR)).

[49] *Michael* (n 37) [138].

[50] The assumption of legal responsibility is therefore 'an explanatory construction, not a fact which must be separately found' (JA Weir, 'Liability for Syntax' [1963] *CLJ* 216, 217). As to why the law might approach the issue in this way, see AJE Jaffey, 'Contract in Tort's Clothing' (1985) 5 *Legal Studies* 77, 102. And for a similar analysis to that in the text, see B Feldthusen, *Economic Negligence*, 6th edn (Toronto, Carswell, 2012) 57–62.

[51] See *Hedley Byrne* (n 2) 482–83 (Lord Reid).

[52] *Henderson* (n 21) 194–95 (Lord Goff). See, eg, *Robinson v PE Jones (Contractors) Ltd* (n 6) [84] (Jackson LJ).

[53] *Henderson* (n 21) 195 (Lord Goff). See also *Muirhead v Industrial Tank Specialities Ltd* [1986] QB 507 (CA); *Simaan General Contracting Co v Pilkington Glass Ltd (No 2)* [1988] QB 758 (CA) 781 (Bingham LJ), 785 (Dillon LJ); and *RM Turton & Co Ltd (in liq) v Kerslake and Partners* [2000] 3 NZLR 406 (NZCA). For a defence of this principle, see Jaffey (n 50) 92, but compare Thomas J's powerful dissenting judgment in the New Zealand case.

of a legal duty of care would be contrary to public policy.[54] Note that these reasons are not necessarily exhaustive, and that they do not necessarily have equal force in all contexts: the informal nature of the undertaking, for instance, seems not to be a bar to an assumption of legal responsibility in personal injury cases.[55]

The analysis here is consistent with the fact that the cases abound with statements to the effect that 'the assumption of the task ... was the assumption of a duty [of care]'.[56] In *Hedley Byrne* itself, for example, Lord Reid repeatedly used the language of inference, as when he said [135] that 'in this case the question is whether an undertaking to assume a duty to take care can be inferred',[57] while Lord Devlin repeatedly used the terminology of implication.[58] For the law to treat the taking on a task for another as impliedly involving an undertaking to perform that task with due care is hardly controversial. By saying that they will look after your phone and child it is clear that the couple on the beach are implicitly undertaking to exercise due care in doing so. And indeed such an interpretation of their conduct is consistent with the way in which terms are implied into contracts; hence the duties of care that are routinely implied into professional services contracts, employment contracts and so forth.[59]

And as for the law attaching legal responsibility to the implicit undertaking to exercise reasonable care unless there is a good reason not to do so, this defeasibility analysis is consistent with the statement by Lord Goff in the *Spring* case that 'in the context under consideration, there is no question of the circumstances ... being, for example, so informal *as to negative* an assumption of responsibility by the employer'.[60]

---

[54] Hence the immunity that barristers used to enjoy in respect of their conduct of litigation (*Rondel v Worsley* [1969] 1 AC 191 (HL)), abolished in *Arthur JS Hall & Co Ltd v Simons* [2002] 1 AC 615 (HL).

[55] See, eg, *Biddick* (n 5), where the assumption of responsibility was in a very informal context.

[56] *Glanzer* (n 1) 276 (Cardozo J). See similarly *Cassidy v Ministry of Health* [1951] 2 KB 343 (CA) 359–60 (Denning LJ); *Gilchrist Watt & Sanderson Pty Ltd v York Products Pty Ltd* [1970] 1 WLR 1262 (PC) 1267–68 (Lord Pearson) (discussing bailment); *Henderson* (n 21) 205 (Lord Browne-Wilkinson); and *Biddick* (n 5) [53] (McCombe LJ).

[57] *Hedley Byrne* (n 2) 492.

[58] See, eg, ibid 532 ('an implied undertaking to accept responsibility').

[59] See also Plunkett (n 11) 137 (referring to the 'officious bystander' test). And for an argument to similar effect with regard to fiduciary duties, see J Edelman, 'When do Fiduciary Duties Arise?' (2010) 126 LQR 302. On implication in general, see J Raz, 'Promises in Morality and Law' (1982) 95 *Harvard Law Review* 916, 932. In theory it is possible for A to make it clear to B that he is not undertaking to exercise reasonable care, in which case clearly no special duty of care (legal or moral) will arise, although the relevant words or conduct might instead be understood as merely lowering the implied standard of care. This seems to me to be conceptually distinct from a disclaimer of legal responsibility – where a moral duty of care may nonetheless arise – though legally nothing turns on the distinction, and it is not clearly articulated in the case law.

[60] *Spring* (n 43) 319 (emphasis added).

Again, the analogy of contract law is helpful, since the best way of understanding what is going on with regard to legal responsibility here is to consider
the contract doctrine of 'intention to create legal relations'.[61] Although in
theory that doctrine is a positive requirement of a binding contract, in practice it operates as a negative condition, such that an agreement supported by
consideration will be held to be legally binding unless either the parties have
expressly said that it was not intended to be,[62] or it was made in an informal
or domestic setting.[63] This analogy [136] also helps us to understand why it is
that these countervailing considerations prevent any legal duty from arising,
rather than excluding a duty that already exists, as was emphasised in *Hedley
Byrne*[64] and has been confirmed in later judicial analysis of disclaimers in this
type of case.[65]

Although that concludes the core of my answer to the first question, before
I move on I want to identify some further distinctive features of the assumption
of responsibility concept, and then to respond to two possible objections to my
analysis of it.

Enough has I hope been said to demonstrate that the obligations of care
which flow from an assumption of responsibility are distinguishable from
what we might call 'core negligence' obligations – which is to say those
that we automatically owe to others simply by virtue of our presence in the
jurisdiction – since they come into being only if we take on a task for another
person. There are at least three other distinct features of these obligations.
The first is that they are not owed by all of us to everyone else. Rather, the
assumption of responsibility doctrine comes with its own form of privity rule,
which, like the contractual privity rule, cuts both ways. Hence, only those *for
whom* the task or job is undertaken can rely on the assumption of responsibility, as the *Banca Nazionale del Lavoro* case illustrates. But equally, only
those who in fact undertake the task or job for the claimant are burdened by
the assumption of responsibility. This explains, for example, why the managing director of the company in *Williams v Natural Life Health Foods*[66] owed

---

[61] See also S Whittaker, 'The Application of the "Broad Principle of *Hedley Byrne*" as Between
Parties to a Contract' (1997) 17 *Legal Studies* 169, 176; Beever, *Rediscovering the Law of Negligence*
(n 45) 291.

[62] See, eg, *Jones v Vernon Pools Ltd* [1938] 2 All ER 626 (KBD).

[63] See, eg, *Balfour v Balfour* [1919] 2 KB 571 (CA). In language strongly reminiscent of that used
in the contract context, Stocker LJ said in the assumption of responsibility case of *Chaudhry
v Prabhakar* [1989] 1 WLR 29 (CA) (at 36) that 'in the absence of other factors giving rise to [a duty
of care], the giving of advice sought in the context of family, domestic or social relationships will not
in itself give rise to any duty in respect of such advice'.

[64] *Hedley Byrne* (n 2) 492 (Lord Reid), 504 (Lord Morris), 511 (Lord Hodson), 533 (Lord Devlin),
540 (Lord Pearce).

[65] See, eg, *McCullagh v Lane Fox & Partners Ltd* [1996] PNLR 205 (CA) 223 (Hobhouse LJ);
Barclays Bank plc v Grant Thornton UK LLP [2015] EWHC 320 (Comm), [2015] 2 BCLC 537 [41]
(Cooke J). It follows that, as their Lordships made clear in *Hedley Byrne*, such a disclaimer should
not necessarily be subject to the same restrictions as are operative where a defendant seeks to exclude
or limit a core negligence duty, such as interpretation *contra proferentem*.

[66] *Williams v Natural Life Health Foods* [1998] 1 WLR 830 (HL).

no duty of care to the claimant franchisees, since it was the company that had taken on the task for the franchisees and not the director personally.[67] And it also explains why it is that a sub-bailee only comes under a positive obligation to the original bailor if the sub-bailee has notice of the head bailment.[68] As was rightly [137] said by Lord Sumption in the *Banca Nazionale del Lavoro* case, the relational aspect of the duties that arise out of an assumption of responsibility is one of the concept's fundamental characteristics.[69]

The second distinctive feature of the obligations that flow from an assumption of responsibility is that the duty in question is in general not merely a duty to take care, but a *duty to ensure that care is taken*, or in other words a 'non-delegable duty'. This is apparent from the leading case on non-delegable duties, *Woodland v Essex County Council*,[70] where Baroness Hale said that the reason why a hospital or school is liable for the negligence of a nurse or teacher, regardless of whether they are an employee of the hospital or school, is that 'the hospital has undertaken to take care for the patient, and the school has undertaken to teach the pupil'.[71] And the same rule applies in other types of case where assumed duties of care are recognised, such as employment and bailment relationships.[72] It is also important to note the way in which in these cases the defendant's liability for the negligence of a third party connects back to the idea of assumption of responsibility as taking on a task or job for another person. For liability attaches *only* to negligence in the performance of the task undertaken by the defendant and delegated to the third party,[73] and the non-delegable duty is owed *only* to the person for whom the task was undertaken.

And the final distinctive feature of the obligations of care that arise out of assumptions of responsibility is the fact that, unlike in core negligence law, the defendant can expressly or impliedly tailor the scope or content of the duty, in three different ways: (1) by making it clear for whom the task or job is being done; (2) by delimiting the scope of the task or job itself;[74] [138] and (3) by

---

[67] See also the illuminating discussion in *Trevor Ivory Ltd v Anderson* [1992] 2 NZLR 517 (NZCA).

[68] See *KH Enterprise (cargo owners) v Pioneer Container (owners) (The Pioneer Container)* [1994] 2 AC 324 (HL) 341 (Lord Goff). Hence, for example, in the beach story, if after taking possession of your phone the couple had asked another beachgoer to look at it, then the other beachgoer would only come under a positive obligation *to you* if he was told that it was your phone (and that therefore, in a sense, he was taking on the task of minding the phone *for* you).

[69] *Banca Nazionale del Lavoro* (n 31) [7].

[70] *Woodland v Essex County Council* [2013] UKSC 66, [2014] AC 537.

[71] ibid [34].

[72] See further, Stevens, *Torts and Rights* (n 13) 114–23.

[73] *Woodland* (n 70) [23] (Lord Sumption).

[74] See, eg, *Wattleworth v Goodwood Road Racing Co Ltd* [2004] EWHC 140 (QB), [2004] PIQR 25 (assumption of responsibility by Motor Sports Association limited to structure of course, safety barriers etc); *Calvert v William Hill Credit Ltd* [2008] EWCA 1427, [2009] Ch 330 [47] (Sir Anthony May P) (responsibility assumed by defendants was not to prevent the claimant from gambling, but 'not to allow him to place telephone bets with them'); *Biddick* (n 5) [42] (the defendant 'assumed responsibility, not for bearing [the claimant's] weight if he happened to fall on the latch cover, but in

calibrating the standard of care against which the defendant's performance of the job or task will be measured, which is determined, as the cases show us, by the skill or expertise that she 'holds herself out' as possessing.[75] Any such tailoring of the scope or content of the duty is based on an objective interpretation of A's words or conduct,[76] taking into account all the circumstances of the case.[77]

The ability of the person assuming responsibility to tailor the scope of their obligation provides a straightforward explanation for the rule laid down in *Caparo Industries v Dickman* that in a negligent misstatement case, it must be shown that A knew that his statement would be communicated to B, 'either as an individual or as a member of an identifiable class, specifically in connection with a particular transaction or transactions of a particular kind'.[78] Suppose that B asks A, an expert on white goods, which dishwasher B should buy, and A replies that B should buy a model manufactured by Bosch. In so doing, A is taking on the task of advising B about dishwasher purchase, and any duty of care is so limited. If B subsequently passes on A's advice to C, C is owed no duty by A, as A did not take on the task for C, but for B. And if B buys shares in Bosch as a result of A's advice, A's duty to B does not extend to the investment decision, since A did not take on the task of giving B investment advice. Elaborate policy-based explanations of the *Caparo* limits in terms of indeterminate liability and so forth are unnecessary.[79] They are inherent [139] in the concept of assumption of responsibility itself.[80] Similarly, the failure to appreciate the significance of the distinction between core and assumed obligations

---

undertaking to ensure that the latch remained closed'). See also the very particular formulation of the scope of the duty in *Lejonvarn* (n 7) [111]. Where the parties are in a contractual relationship, the scope of the task or job will usually be discernible from the contract (for example, a solicitor's retainer).

[75] See, eg, *Phillips v William Whiteley Ltd* [1938] 1 All ER 566 (KBD). See also the calibration of the standard of care by reference to the different types of medical practitioner (eg, *Maynard v West Midlands RHA* [1984] 1 WLR 634 (HL)). The same principle applies in cases of gratuitous agency (see GHL Fridman, *The Law of Agency*, 7th edn (London, Butterworths, 1996) 160–61), and in gratuitous bailment cases, the standard of care is calibrated by reference to 'all the circumstances of the deposit' (A Burrows (ed), *English Private Law*, 3rd edn (Oxford, OUP, 2013) para 16.36; see further, Bell (n 14) 475–77). The different manners of limitation of the duty may blend into each other. Suppose that in the beach example, a person in a wheelchair had agreed to look after your child. The obvious fact of the person's disability could be interpreted as (implicitly) limiting the scope of the task or alternatively as bearing on the calibration of the standard of care. And the same could be said of the off-duty doctor who intervenes in an emergency situation, and who obviously lacks adequate equipment, may have limited expertise and so on.

[76] See, eg, *Banca Nazionale del Lavoro* (n 31) [24] (Lord Mance).

[77] See *Gold v Essex County Council* [1942] 2 KB 293 (CA) 301 (Lord Greene MR).

[78] *Caparo* (n 8) 621 (Lord Bridge). See similarly at 637–38 (Lord Oliver).

[79] See, eg, *Hercules Managements Ltd v Ernst & Young* [1997] 2 SCR 165 (SCC) [28] (La Forest J). An alternative justification sometimes given for such limits is that reliance on a statement made for a different purpose, or to a different person, is for that reason unreasonable. However, as Beever points out, this claim is as misguided as the similar arguments criticised below, text following n 119: A Beever, 'The Basis of the *Hedley Byrne* Action', in Barker et al (n 10) 108.

[80] See *Customs and Excise Commissioners* (n 9) [35] (Lord Hoffmann).

causes commentators to tie themselves into knots when trying to reconcile
the refusal to lower the standard of care for a learner driver in *Nettleship v
Weston*[81] (a core *Donoghue v Stevenson* case) with the standards of care of
those who hold themselves out as having special skills – such as doctors – in
cases where the duty arises out of an undertaking. Again, a proper appreciation
of the significance of assumption of responsibility offers a simple explanation
for the approaches adopted by the courts in the two different types of case.

Let us finally turn to two possible objections to my analysis. The first is that
if ultimately it is the law that decides whether legal responsibility arises, then
the liability is in truth imposed by law, rather than assumed by the defendant,
and so the idea that it rests on an assumption of responsibility is a 'fiction'.[82]
This objection can be dismissed quickly. All legal obligations are ultimately
imposed by law; otherwise they would not be *legal* obligations. So this in no
way undermines the claim that assumption of responsibility is a distinctive
source of obligation, or at least no more so than it does the claim that contractual obligations are.

The second objection is that, if by 'assumption of responsibility' the law
means only 'taking on a task', then the concept is not a distinctive source of
legal obligation, since (it is said) we could just as easily say that a car driver's
duty of care towards other road users is grounded in their taking on the task of
driving their car.[83] This objection also fails, for three reasons. First, my claim is
not that assumption of responsibility means *only* taking on a task, but that, by
taking on a task for B, A is in general treated as assuming a legal responsibility
to exercise due care in the performance of that task (although, unlike in the car
case, this responsibility can be avoided by a disclaimer etc). Secondly, the three
additional distinctive features of assumption of responsibility that I have identified – its relational quality, the non-delegable nature of the duty, and the ability
of the defendant expressly or impliedly tailor the scope of the obligation – are
all missing in the case of the car driver's duty. And thirdly, and most fundamentally, the objection rests on a mistaken premise, which is that it is only when
the driver gets behind the wheel of the car that their duty of [140] care towards
other road users arises. In fact, with one or two very narrow exceptions, each
and every one of us owes a general duty not to cause others personal injury or
property damage through our negligent positive conduct, an obligation which
arises either when we are born, or when we move into the jurisdiction. By getting
into my car and driving down the street, I may make it more likely that I will
breach that duty than if I stay at home and watch *Eastenders*, but the duty is not

---

[81] *Nettleship v Weston* [1971] 2 QB 691 (CA).
[82] See, eg, Hepple (n 12).
[83] For examples of this kind of argument, see, eg, *Customs and Excise Commissioners* (n 9)
[37]–[38] (Lord Hoffmann); and K Barker, 'Unreliable Assumptions in the Law of Negligence' (1993)
109 *LQR* 461, 474.

the result of my action, any more than my duty not to lie (as imposed by the tort of deceit) is the result of my deciding to speak.

By contrast, when a duty of care is based on an assumption of responsibility it *is* the result of something that the defendant has done, namely taking on a task or job for the claimant. And the fact that the duty is not automatic, but the result of *something the defendant has done* is one of the things that marks out assumption of responsibility as a distinctive basis for the imposition of negligence liability. Had the couple in the beach story refused to accept responsibility for your child, or refused to take possession of your phone, their legal obligations would have remained the same as before. They could have been liable for injuring your child, or smashing your phone, but they would have owed no duty to protect either. And this would also have been the case if, for example, you had slipped your phone into their beach bag without their consent.[84] Having taken on those tasks, however, their obligations changed. It was their conduct that brought into being the new legal relation.

IV. WHEN DOES ASSUMPTION OF RESPONSIBILITY MATTER?

Happily, my second question is a good deal more straightforward to answer than the first, although not without its own controversies. Resolving those controversies would require a closer study of the case law than is possible here, so instead I will content myself with flagging up the situations in which the courts have employed the assumption of responsibility concept to justify imposing a duty of care in negligence. There are three distinct[85] types of case where this phenomenon is observable: cases involving pure economic loss, omissions cases and deliberate [141] intervening conduct cases. In all these categories of case, the general rule in English law is that there is no duty of care, but such a duty will be owed if there is a relevant assumption of responsibility of the defendant towards the claimant.[86]

Hence, in the beach story, although the doctor who helped to resuscitate you was free (as a matter of tort law anyway) to do nothing to help you, because he chose to intervene a duty of care arose, which was not limited to not making things worse, but which required him to take reasonable steps

---

[84] A person cannot, 'without his knowledge and consent, be considered as a bailee [of property]': *Lethbridge v Phillips* (1819) 2 Stark 544, 545; 171 ER 731, 731 (Abbott CJ). An 'involuntary bailment' is therefore 'a contradiction in terms': Bell (n 14) 468.

[85] I emphasise this because of the unfortunate tendency not to distinguish properly (or even at all) between the omissions question and the intervening conduct question. The fact that the two issues often arise on the same facts does not make them the same issue.

[86] For a helpful discussion of the interaction between the assumption of responsibility concept and the category-based approach our courts generally take when dealing with notional duty questions, see Plunkett (n 11) 139–44.

to improve your situation.[87] In the case of an established doctor-patient relationship, the same is of course also true, quite regardless of contract,[88] and more generally the assumption of responsibility principle has been said to embrace the relationships 'in which a duty to take positive action typically arises', including school and pupil and employer and employee.[89]

Similarly, before they took possession of your phone, the couple had no duty to protect it from the criminal activity of third parties. Had they seen a thief steal it from your bag while you were looking the other way, they would have been at liberty to do and say nothing. However, when they took possession of the phone from you, an obligation to safeguard it arose.[90] And note that this obligation to protect the claimant against deliberately harmful conduct can even extend to the conduct of the claimant herself, which is the best explanation for the decision in *Reeves v Commissioner of Police of the Metropolis*[91] that the police were liable for negligently failing to prevent a vulnerable prisoner from committing suicide. [142]

As for economic loss, ever since *Hedley Byrne* it has been clear that pure economic loss may be recoverable in negligence where there was a prior assumption of responsibility by the defendant towards the claimant. In the years following *Hedley Byrne*, assumption of responsibility was thought to be limited in this context to cases of negligent misstatement, but one consequence of Lord Goff's reformulation of the doctrine in the 1990s was its extension to the negligent performance of a service in the *Henderson* case. This generalisation of the principle helped to put our law of professional negligence on a more rational footing, which can be contrasted with the way in which some other common law systems continue, for no good reason that I can see, to treat negligent misstatements as a separate category of duty case.[92]

---

[87] For the general principle that an assumption of responsibility may give rise to positive obligations, see, eg, *Gorringe v Calderdale MBC* [2004] UKHL 15, [2004] 1 WLR 1057. Good examples include *Welsh v Chief Constable of the Merseyside Police* [1993] 1 All ER 692 (QBD); *Barrett v Ministry of Defence* [1995] 1 WLR 1217 (CA); *Costello v Chief Constable of the Northumbria Police* [1999] 1 All ER 550 (CA); *Watson* (n 24); *Chandler* (n 3); and *Biddick* (n 5).

[88] Hence a wife or child could historically sue for the negligence of a surgeon employed by a husband/father: see, eg, *Pippin v Sheppard* (1822) 11 Price 400, 147 ER 512 (wife); *Gladwell v Steggall* (1839) 5 Bing NC 733, 132 ER 1283 (daughter). As Erskine J said in the latter case (at 737, 1284), 'the substance of the issue is, that the Defendant was employed to cure the Plaintiff; not, that he was employed by the Plaintiff'.

[89] *Michael* (n 37) [100] (Lord Toulson).

[90] See *Mitchell v Glasgow City Council* [2009] UKHL 11, [2009] 1 AC 874 [23] (Lord Hope), [76] (Lady Hale), [82] (Lord Brown). See, eg, *Stansbie v Troman* [1948] 2 KB 48 (CA); and *Swinney v Chief Constable of the Northumbria Police* [1997] QB 464 (CA).

[91] *Reeves v Metropolitan Police Commissioner* [2001] AC 360 (HL). See also *Kirkham v Chief Constable of the Greater Manchester Police* [1990] 2 QB 283 (CA), a case where, unlike in *Reeves*, liability was expressly founded on an assumption of responsibility analysis.

[92] As Tony Honoré said in his brilliant 1965 article on *Hedley Byrne*, 'the distinction between verbal and non-verbal means of doing mischief is not of fundamental importance': AM Honoré, 'Hedley Byrne & Co Ltd v Heller & Partners Ltd' (1965) 8 *Journal of the Society of Public Teachers of Law (ns)* 284, 298. The tendency to treat negligent misstatement as a distinct category of

While there is surely no doubt that assumption of responsibility plays an important role in the duty enquiry in these three types of case, there is less agreement about the extent of its significance. The better view seems to be that Lord Goff was right to say in *White v Jones* that 'as a general rule', no action lies in negligence for pure economic loss apart from cases of assumption of responsibility.[93] Admittedly, that statement is difficult to square with the speeches in the House of Lords in *Customs and Excise Commissioners v Barclays Bank*,[94] but there was precious little consistency in the analysis of the significance of assumption of responsibility in that case,[95] and in recent Supreme Court decisions on economic loss the concept has been regarded as determinative of the duty issue,[96] and [143] described as 'the foundation of this area of law'.[97] As for omissions and intervening conduct cases, there is no doubt that positive obligations can arise in negligence without an assumption of responsibility,[98] and while I am attracted to the simplicity of Baroness Hale's suggestion (if that is what it was) in *Mitchell v Glasgow City Council* that the *only* exception to the general principle of non-liability for the consequences of the deliberate conduct of others should be assumption of responsibility,[99] it is difficult to square that proposition with cases such as *Home Office v Dorset Yacht Co*,[100] where the Home Office was held liable for the damage done to the yachts by the escaping borstal boys even though it had not taken on a task of any kind for the yacht owners.

Overall, my sense is that in the economic loss context, the *results* of the cases (if not necessarily the reasoning) are broadly consistent with Lord Goff's claim that assumption of responsibility is generally the determinant of whether a duty of care exists, whereas in the other two types of case assumption of responsibility is only one of a number of broad brush exceptions to the general no-liability rule.

---

negligence case is particularly apparent in the United States, but judges and commentators in the Commonwealth also frequently do this: see, eg, the title of the anniversary collection (Barker et al (n 10)), and of some of the chapters in it; *Customs and Excise Commissioners* (n 9) [35] (Lord Hoffmann); and *NRAM Ltd v Steel* [2018] UKSC 13, [2018] 1 WLR 1190. This tendency is best understood as a vestige of older, more primitive, ways of thinking about negligence, where the focus was on how the damage or loss came about, rather than questions of more fundamental significance, such as the nature of the damage, the difference between nonfeasance and misfeasance etc. But the misstatement category is not only an unsophisticated throwback (like 'liability for animals'), it is also incoherent as employed, since many routine negligence cases that are not treated as misstatement cases, including *Donoghue v Stevenson*, can in fact be analysed in those terms: see Beever, 'The Basis of the *Hedley Byrne* Action' (n 79) 89.

[93] *White* (n 26) 257.
[94] *Customs and Excise Commissioners* (n 9).
[95] Indeed the case provides so little clarity on the general question of liability for economic loss that it is best largely to ignore it in that connection.
[96] See *NRAM* (n 92); *Banca Nazionale del Lavoro* (n 31).
[97] *Banca Nazionale del Lavoro* (n 31) [7] (Lord Sumption).
[98] See, eg, *Goldman v Hargrave* [1967] 1 AC 645 (PC).
[99] [2009] UKHL 11, [2009] 1 AC 874 [76].
[100] [1970] AC 1004 (HL).

V. WHY DO WE NEED ASSUMPTION OF RESPONSIBILITY?

A more neutral framing of my third question would be '*Do* we need assumption of responsibility?', but as well as ruining the alliteration in my four questions, I am content to forego neutrality from the off, as I am firmly of the opinion that our law of negligence does indeed need the concept (or at least something like it).

I would make three arguments in defence of the concept. First, in these cases it seems to me that the law is tracking morality. While the couple on the beach are under a moral obligation to protect your child from danger, even before they agree to look after him, that moral obligation is clearly considerably strengthened by their having taken on the responsibility of doing so.[101] For the law to translate that stronger moral duty into a legal one seems entirely defensible.[102] [144]

The second argument is closely connected to the first. Although I deny below that reliance is a prerequisite of an assumption of responsibility,[103] the fact that assumptions of responsibility frequently and foreseeably induce reliance – whether on the part of the person to whom responsibility is assumed or a third party – is undoubtedly one of the reasons why they create moral, and legal, obligations. Suppose that having agreed to look after your phone the couple on the beach had failed to safeguard it, and it had been stolen. You could legitimately complain that had they not assumed the responsibility of looking after it – and, implicitly, of doing this with due care – then you would either have foregone your swim, or asked another person, who most likely would have taken better care of it. As a result of your reliance on them, you are therefore left worse off than you would have been had they not assumed responsibility. In theory, the law could respond to this concern in such a case not by recognising the assumption of responsibility as itself the source of an obligation, but instead by requiring you to demonstrate that you or a third party did in fact rely on the assumption of responsibility to your detriment. However, it again seems perfectly sensible for the law *not* to require this, but instead to treat the assumption of responsibility as a freestanding source of obligation, albeit one justified, in part, by the fact that such assumptions of responsibility are often accompanied by reliance.

The third argument rests on the fact that the most important reason for limiting our core negligence obligations is to protect our freedom of action.

---

[101] Imagine, for example, that a friend of theirs arrived, and proposed that they go to the beach café for a drink. While before undertaking their protective task, they were completely free to do so, now one can readily imagine them saying that they cannot, as they are looking after your child and your phone for you.

[102] See Lord Reid and Lord Morris's reference to 'moral obligation' in the *Hedley Byrne* context in *Mutual Life & Citizens' Assurance Co Ltd v Evatt* [1971] AC 793 (HL) 812.

[103] See text following n 146.

A generalised obligation to take reasonable steps to confer benefits on others or to safeguard their economic interests is a much greater threat to our autonomy than a minimalist duty not to injure them or their property through our positive conduct. However, much of the force of this concern is lost in cases where we have chosen to assume a responsibility to another person,[104] particularly since we have seen that the law allows us to make clear that no liability is to attach to such an assumption of responsibility, and also to limit its scope in three different respects (for whom we undertake it, what we undertake to do, and the standard of care to be expected of us in undertaking it).

Now, none of these arguments in defence of the assumption of responsibility concept is definitive, and of course it can be argued that, unless B has provided consideration, then A should owe no legal obligation in respect of B's economic interests and so forth. This is essentially the view [145] of Tony Weir, who heartily disapproved of *Hedley Byrne*,[105] and is also the position adopted by David Campbell in the anniversary collection.[106] This position essentially rests on the assertion (for that is all it really is) that unless one has oneself paid for information, advice or a service, one should have no legal right to care in its provision. As Tony Honoré pointed out, faced with such a claim, there is no right or wrong answer – 'one can merely make a declaration of faith'.[107] However, it seems to me (as it did to Honoré) that, all in all, the rule of liability is preferable.[108] Furthermore, that seems also to be the view taken in all legal systems of which I have a passing knowledge. And nor should we forget that this kind of contractual libertarianism is also impossible to reconcile with a raft of other deeply embedded private law institutions, including fiduciary obligation and the trust.

Another line of attack on the assumption of responsibility concept is to argue that while liability should perhaps be imposed in some or all of the cases in question, this should be done on a different basis. One possible alternative ground of liability might be thought to be contract, but it will become apparent from my response to the fourth question that that is not a plausible solution. A second alternative is to try to integrate such cases into the tort mainstream, by renouncing assumption of responsibility and instead determining the duty issue by reference to an approach of universal application. Two such approaches have been suggested in the academic commentary. One rests on proximity, and is associated with the so-called *Caparo* 'three-stage test'. The other is a multi-factorial policy-based approach, in which the policy arguments for and against liability are weighed in the balance. Both approaches find their supporters in the

---

[104] See also S Steel, 'Rationalising Omissions Liability in Negligence' (2019) 135 *LQR* 484, 499–500.
[105] See Weir, 'Liability for Syntax' (n 50) 218.
[106] D Campbell, 'The Curious Incident of the Dog that did Bark in the Night-Time: What Mischief does *Hedley Byrne v Heller* Correct?' in Barker et al (n 10).
[107] Honoré (n 92) 299.
[108] ibid.

anniversary collection on *Hedley Byrne*,[109] and both rest on the premise that assumption of responsibility as used by the courts is a mere 'foil' or 'veil' for something else (either 'proximity', or alternatively policy considerations) that supposedly provides the real explanation for the results [146] in the cases.[110] Needless to say that premise is sharply at odds with my argument in this article that, properly understood, assumption of responsibility is a perfectly meaningful concept.

Quite apart from being based on a false premise, these alternatives have little to commend them, as Allan Beever demonstrates in his merciless attack on them in the anniversary collection.[111] Unlike assumption of responsibility, proximity is a genuinely meaningless concept in this context, with the result that its use to determine duty of care questions is a recipe for ad hoc decision-making unconstrained by principle or precedent. And a multi-factorial policy-based approach is subject to the same objection, with the added disadvantage that the spurious and frequently ill-informed 'policy' argumentation that it generates serves only to make the litigation created by the resultant uncertainty longer and more expensive to resolve.[112] Anyone who believes that these approaches are preferable to the use of the assumption of responsibility doctrine should read the chapters in the anniversary collection on the law of negligent misstatements in Australia, Canada and New Zealand, all of which have succumbed to varieties of these alternatives, and in all of which the result seems to be an unholy mess.

VI. WHERE DOES ASSUMPTION OF RESPONSIBILITY BELONG?

That brings me to my final question, which is perhaps the most intriguing of all. Its importance lies not in the quest for taxonomical order per se, but in the fact that a proper appreciation of the place of assumption of responsibility within private law will better enable us to understand the concept and its implications.

---

[109] In support of the proximity/three-stage test approach, see A Robertson and J Wang, 'The Assumption of Responsibility', and C Witting, 'What are We Doing Here? The Relationship Between Negligence in General and Misstatements in English Law', both in Barker et al (n 10). And in favour of a multi-factorial policy analysis, see K Barker, 'Negligent Misstatement in Australia – Resolving the Uncertain Legacy of *Esanda*' in the same collection.

[110] See, eg, Barker, 'Unreliable Assumptions in the Law of Negligence' (n 83) 483 (policy concerns).

[111] Beever, 'The Basis of the *Hedley Byrne* Action' (n 79) 91–98. Little is to be gained from my repeating Beever's critique, but there is no doubt that the positive case for assumption of responsibility I put forward here is considerably strengthened by the reasons he gives for rejecting the core negligence analysis.

[112] In his chapter in the anniversary collection, Barker lists no fewer than nine separate policy concerns that he believes the courts should take into account when determining the duty question in negligent misstatement cases, and doubtless there are others the courts could add to the mix: Barker, 'Negligent Misstatement in Australia' (n 109) 324.

If we turn to the academic commentary on this question for help, the first thing we notice is the extent to which the reductive contract/tort dichotomy continues to exert a quite extraordinary hold over the [147] common law imagination. The continuing tendency to assume that common law obligations must fall into the categories of contract or tort is apparent in the efforts of commentators to explain away assumption of responsibility cases as either core negligence cases, or as contract cases in disguise. Unfortunately this makes it harder to 'extract its rules and peculiarities untrammelled by false equations and superficial resemblances to other concepts'.[113]

On the tort front, the 'core negligence' view of assumption of responsibility holds that there is no fundamental difference between these cases and negligence cases where liability is based on *Donoghue v Stevenson*.[114] This view is encapsulated in Andrew Robertson and Julia Wang's conclusion in their essay in the anniversary collection that 'assumption of responsibility is not a distinctive category of obligation, but simply a particular manifestation of [Lord Atkin's] neighbour principle'.[115] Since I have already identified a number of distinctive features of assumption of responsibility as the foundation of duties of care, it will be readily apparent why I regard this view as untenable.

That is not, however, the only difficulty that the core negligence view faces. There is also the question of fit with the case law. Proponents of the core negligence view have argued that the results in the cases in this area are explicable in proximity terms, but the argument is unpersuasive.[116] Why, for example, was there no 'proximity' in *Caparo v Dickman*,[117] or in *Williams v Natural Life Health Foods*,[118] or in *Customs and Excise Commissioners v Barclays Bank*?[119] Efforts to explain away key features of the case law in core negligence terms, such as the ability of a defendant to avoid legal liability by an appropriate disclaimer, are also unconvincing. It has been argued, for example, that this can be explained on the [148] basis that in a negligent misstatement case the fact of a disclaimer makes the claimant's reliance unreasonable,[120] but this is

---

[113] N Palmer, 'Gratuitous Bailment – Contract or Tort?' (1975) 24 *ICLQ* 565, 572 (writing of bailment). See also WL Shattuck, 'Gratuitous Promises – A New Writ' (1937) 35 *Michigan Law Review* 908, 942 fn ('Mere misbranding is of itself unimportant. It matters little what a thing is called so long as its characteristics are understood and it is handled accordingly. But all too frequently a misnomer covers a failure to so understand and a long train of mischief results.').

[114] *Donoghue* (n 34).

[115] Robertson and Wang (n 109) 82. This view is not new, but is observable in the early commentary on *Hedley Byrne*: see Mitchell (n 1) 187.

[116] For a convincing critique, see Beever, 'The Basis of the *Hedley Byrne* Action' (n 79) 91–94.

[117] *Caparo* (n 8).

[118] *Williams* (n 42).

[119] According to Longmore LJ in the Court of Appeal in *Customs and Excise Commissioners*, the relationship between the parties was 'about as proximate as one can envisage' ([2004] EWCA Civ 1555, [2005] 1 WLR 2082 (CA) [30]).

[120] See, eg, Robertson and Wang (n 109) 63–64.

utterly unconvincing. The claimants in *Hedley Byrne* were hard-headed business people who enquired about the creditworthiness of a client from the client's bankers and who *themselves* made clear (through their agents) that the enquiry was 'without responsibility'. It is very odd to suppose that it was *for that reason* unreasonable of them to have relied on any information or advice the bankers provided. If that were true, then only an idiot would have made the enquiry in those terms in the first place.[121] And the attempt to explain away in the same manner the exclusion from the scope of the *Hedley Byrne* principle of advice given on a social or informal occasion is open to the same objection. There is nothing 'unreasonable' about relying on advice given on such occasions. If there were, why would people routinely ask for and offer it? Nearly half a century ago Joseph Raz gave an example that reveals how misguided these kinds of argument are.[122]

In his essay in the anniversary collection, Beever leaves the core negligence view of assumption of responsibility in a heap of smoking ruins. However, he falls into the opposite trap of trying to force assumption of responsibility into a contractual straightjacket, an approach I also find unpersuasive (albeit less damaging).[123] The 'contract view' of assumption of responsibility conceives the concept as contract minus consideration, and for scholars – such as Beever – who see no need for consideration, the conclusion that cases of this kind should be assimilated into contract naturally follows. However, the exclusive focus on consideration is unwarranted, since this is by no means the only problem with a contract analysis. On the contrary, there is another, arguably more fundamental, objection to the contract view of assumption of responsibility, which is that while a contract is an *agreement* formed by communicative acts ('offer' and 'acceptance'), an assumption of responsibility does not [149] require any kind of communication between the parties at all, and can generate new duties without the beneficiary of those duties even being aware of it.[124] (Was there really a 'contract' in any possible sense, for example, with the ten-month-old baby who was taken into care in *Barrett v Enfield*?) Nor are the differences between contract and assumption of responsibility limited to the circumstances in which

---

[121] The same point can be made in response to Kit Barker's claim that the presence of a disclaimer indicates that the defendant did not intend the claimant to rely on the statement (Barker, 'Negligent Misstatement in Australia' (n 109) 338). This is quite simply a non-sequitur. And again, if it were true, why make the statement at all?

[122] J Raz, 'Voluntary Obligations and Normative Powers' (1972) 46 *Proceedings of the Aristotelian Society, Supplementary Volumes* 79, 99.

[123] The contract minus consideration analysis is particularly associated with Lord Devlin's speech in *Hedley Byrne*, where he famously referred to relationships 'equivalent to contract' (*Hedley Byrne* (n 2) 530), a German concept (see Honoré (n 92) 295–96) not well suited to the common law. However, the intellectual origins of the contract view pre-date *Hedley Byrne*: see Mitchell (n 1) 194–95.

[124] Beever's position is at least consistent, since he believes (wrongly, in my view) that assumption of responsibility necessarily involves a communication from the defendant to the claimant: Beever, *Rediscovering the Law of Negligence* (n 45) 308.

the new obligations arise. There are also different defences, different privity rules, different remedies and so on.[125]

There is no doubt that the case law in this area is shot through with ideas that we tend to associate with contract, such as the avoidability of the obligation, notions of privity, intention to create legal relations, disclaimers, non-delegable duties and the like. Furthermore, as we have seen, analogies with contract are frequently illuminating in this context. But that is a far cry from the conclusion that the liability in question is best understood as contractual in nature. As Lord Sumption said in the *Banca Nazionale del Lavoro* case, it 'does not follow from the fact that a non-contractual relationship ... is as proximate as a contractual relationship, that it is legally the same as a contractual relationship or involves all of the same legal incidents'.[126]

One consequence of contract/tort reductionism in this context is the tendency to miss the connections between assumption of responsibility and the law relating to fiduciaries. Those connections were emphasised by Lord Reid in *Hedley Byrne*, and by Lord Browne-Wilkinson in *Henderson* and *White*. And the similarity between Lord Goff's reformulation of the assumption of responsibility concept and standard definitions of fiduciary relationships is certainly striking.[127] But, as with contract, the resemblances between these concepts should not be mistaken for equivalence, nor the differences between them ignored.[128] [150]

The truth is that, as Paul Mitchell has pointed out, 'assumption of responsibility [predates] categorisation into contract and tort, and [cannot] sensibly forced into either category'.[129] The concept should instead be understood as a sui generis source of legal obligation, connected to, but distinct from, core tort, contract and fiduciary duty.[130] Such an understanding of gratuitous undertakings and bailment was commonplace among scholars of earlier generations, such as Joseph Beale[131] and Percy Winfield.[132] And in more recent times, similar

---

[125] See Stevens, *Torts and Rights* (n 13) 33.

[126] *Banca Nazionale del Lavoro* (n 31) [13] (Lord Sumption).

[127] Compare *Spring* (n 43) 318 (Lord Goff) with, for example, the definitions cited by R Flannigan, 'The Fiduciary Obligation' (1989) 9 *OJLS* 285, 306–307.

[128] At a definitional level, the key difference seems to be that, while both concepts involve 'A taking on a task for or on behalf of B', in the case of fiduciary obligation there is the important added element that in the performance of that task A must exercise a power or discretion the exercise of which will affect B's interests. This also has the effect of making B particularly vulnerable in the fiduciary situation. The law responds to these distinctive features of fiduciary relations by imposing a stringent set of duties on the fiduciary over and above a duty of care, and by backing these up with some equally stringent remedies.

[129] Mitchell (n 1) 195.

[130] For an early suggestion that *Hedley Byrne* (n 2) might best be understood in these terms, see R Stevens, '*Hedley Byrne v Heller*: Judicial Creativity and Doctrinal Possibility' (1964) 27 *MLR* 121, 161.

[131] Beale (n 1) 225 ('another division of personal rights, co-ordinate with torts and contracts'). See also Shattuck (n 113) 942.

[132] PH Winfield, *The Province of the Law of Tort* (Cambridge, CUP, 1931) ch 5.

views have been expressed in respect of bailment by Norman Palmer.[133] It is no coincidence that the works of these scholars are informed by a deep knowledge of our legal history, since, as Winfield pointed out, the nineteenth-century contract/tort dichotomy 'deliberately ignore[d]' that history.[134] By contrast, much of the recent scholarship on assumption of responsibility is sorely lacking in historical perspective, and misunderstands *Hedley Byrne* because it views the case against 'an oversimplified, reductive and unhistorical background of the law of obligations'.[135]

VII. THREE RED HERRINGS

That concludes my discussion of the four questions I have posed about assumption of responsibility, but I would now like to highlight three distractions which have served to obscure the real meaning and significance of the concept.

A. Special Skill or Knowledge

The first red herring is the idea that the defendant must have some special skill or knowledge for the assumption of responsibility analysis to hold. **[151]** The origins of this meme lie deep in our legal history,[136] and it is clearly observable in the speeches in *Hedley Byrne*. But it seems to me that in the modern law the defendant's skill and knowledge is really of relevance at the *breach* stage of the negligence enquiry, rather than the duty stage.[137] When it comes to deciding whether the defendant has been negligent in an assumption of responsibility case, we have seen that any special skill or knowledge that he held herself out as having is relevant in determining the standard of care against which his conduct will be measured. However, apart from its possible second-order significance as a consideration in the 'intention to create legal relations' enquiry,[138] there is no reason why the defendant's specialist expertise should be relevant to the question of whether there was an assumption of responsibility in the first place. In any case, this requirement need not concern

---

[133] Palmer (n 113). See also *Yearworth v North Bristol NHS Trust* [2009] EWCA Civ 37, [2010] QB 1 [48] (Lord Judge CJ); CHS Fifoot, *History and Sources of the Common Law* (London, Stevens & Sons, 1949) 24; GW Paton, *Bailment in the Common Law* (London, Stevens & Sons, 1952) 3, 29; and Bell (n 14).

[134] Winfield, *The Province of the Law of Tort* (n 132) 64.

[135] Mitchell (n 1) 197.

[136] See AWB Simpson, *A History of the Common Law of Contract* (Oxford, Clarendon Press, 1975) 229, 233.

[137] For judicial analysis of the issue consistent with this claim, see, eg, *Mutual Life* (n 102) 803–804 (Lord Diplock). And for a similar argument, see Whittaker (n 61) 178–79.

[138] See *Hedley Byrne* (n 2) 531 (Lord Devlin).

us unduly since in *Spring v Guardian Assurance* Lord Goff watered it down to such an extent[139] that it no longer seems to operate as a substantive limit on the scope of the assumption of responsibility concept, even in economic loss cases.[140]

B. Voluntariness

Much ink has been spilt on the question of whether or not the obligations to which an assumption of responsibility gives rise are properly described as *voluntary* obligations, but the debate is not particularly illuminating, both because the protagonists clearly have very different ideas of what a voluntary obligation is, and because it is not entirely clear why it matters anyway.

One of the reasons why the debate has arisen is that critics of the assumption of responsibility concept seem to assume that if they can show that the obligations to which assumptions of responsibility give rise are not (in their terms) 'voluntary' then they have demonstrated both that there is no meaningful distinction between those obligations and those imposed by core negligence law, and that there is no good reason for the law to impose obligations on an assumption of responsibility [152] basis.[141] But neither claim is correct. We have already seen that there are many quite concrete distinctions between the duties of care that arise out of assumptions of responsibility and those that are imposed by core negligence law, and the existence of those distinctions does not depend on the former being voluntary obligations and the latter not. (It may be that some of those distinctions point to the conclusion that the former are indeed properly described as voluntary obligations, but that is of course a very different question.) Furthermore, in answer to my third question, I identified three good reasons why the law is justified in employing the assumption of responsibility concept to determine whether duties of care exist, none of which rests on the premise that the obligations to which an assumption of responsibility give rise are correctly described as voluntary (though again, the third reason points to the conclusion that they are). Once again, the analogy with contract is helpful. Contractual obligations may or may not be properly described as voluntary, but if (according to the definition of voluntary we are employing) we arrive at the conclusion that they are not, it does not follow either that there is no meaningful distinction between contract and tort, nor that there is no there is no good reason for the law to impose obligations on the basis that they arise out of a contract between the parties.

---

[139] *Spring* (n 43) 320. See also *Henderson* (n 21) 180 (Lord Goff).
[140] See, eg, *Lennon v Metropolitan Police Commissioner* [2004] EWCA Civ 130, [2004] 1 WLR 2594.
[141] See, eg, Robertson and Wang (n 109) 56–57.

The focus on voluntariness has also given rise to the very damaging idea that an assumption of responsibility must be the result of a free choice on the defendant's part. While I am happy to accept that no duty of care would arise out of an assumption of responsibility that was the result of, say, duress, it is a serious error to suppose that for the concept to apply A must have a free choice whether to take on a task or job for B, unconstrained by A's existing obligations. It is therefore most unfortunate that the contrary has sometimes been assumed by commentators seeking to undermine the concept,[142] and by judges who have held that the conduct of a public authority which is acting pursuant to a statutory duty cannot constitute an assumption of responsibility since it was obliged so to act as a matter of public law.[143] Not only is this argument impossible to square with the case law – see, for example, *Barrett v Enfield* – but it also rests on a false premise about the nature and significance of assumed obligations. A's decision to buy the last remaining bottle of Dow's 1871 Vintage Port [153] from B is still binding even if A has previously contracted to sell such a bottle to C, and so has no real choice but to enter the transaction. And a public authority that argued that it could renege on its contractual commitments because they were entered into in pursuance of its statutory obligations would rightly be laughed out of court.

Although I regard discussions of the voluntariness of assumed obligations as largely a distraction, I should emphasise that I am perfectly content to describe these obligations as voluntary, while recognising that of course it all depends on what we mean by such a claim.[144] At a basic level, such a description is consistent with the fact that the obligations arise out of the defendant's taking on the task or job in question, so that, unlike core negligence obligations, they are the avoidable result of A's voluntary conduct. And if we want to employ a more sophisticated analysis, we can turn to the work of Raz, who identifies three characteristics of voluntary obligations properly so called: (1) that the person undertaking the obligation is aware of its normative implications; (2) that the person can avoid those implications; and (3) that the person's belief that he will incur an obligation by his action is a positive reason for holding him bound by it.[145] Since all three of those conditions would appear to be satisfied in this context, it follows that the obligations to which an assumption of responsibility

---

[142] See, eg, ibid 59, 65.

[143] See Nolan, 'The Liability of Public Authorities for Failing to Confer Benefits' (n 39) 283–84 (and cases there cited). See also the criticism of this idea by T Cornford, 'Assumption of Responsibility by Public Authorities' (2018) 30 *Denning Law Journal* 55, 78–79.

[144] Critics of assumption of responsibility tend to employ definitions of voluntary obligation so narrow that they would not even encompass contractual obligations. Hence the claim that an obligation is only voluntary 'in a meaningful sense' if it represents the manifestation of a person's subjective will or intention (see, eg, Barker, 'Negligent Misstatement in Australia' (n 109) 323–24; Witting (n 109) 236 fn), which smacks of the long discredited will theory of contract.

[145] Raz, 'Promises in Morality and Law' (n 59) 929.

gives rise can properly be described as voluntary in the Razian sense. And note that, if that is right, then it provides us with another distinction between these obligations and core negligence obligations (which are clearly not voluntary in this sense), as well as with a fourth possible reason for recognising assumption of responsibility as a source of obligations, namely Raz's argument that by enforcing voluntary obligations the law both recognises and reinforces the social practice of undertaking them.[146]

C. Reliance

Finally, I come to the most pervasive and significant of the three red herrings, which is the idea that an assumption of responsibility requires [154] some sort of reliance on the part of the claimant. The specific origins of this idea lie in the fact that the modern concept of assumption of responsibility derives from the decision in *Hedley Byrne*, a case concerned with a statement made by the defendant (A) to the claimant (B). In cases of this kind, B's reliance on the statement is of course required for it to cause her the loss necessary to render the statement actionable in negligence. However, the fact of B's reliance (in this sense) cannot determine the question of whether there was a prior assumption of responsibility by A towards B, since by definition such reliance occurs after the statement is made, and therefore, after the assumption of responsibility takes place.[147] Rather, reliance plays a primarily causal role in misstatement cases of this kind, with the caveat that the foreseeability of reliance by B is also necessary for A to have breached any duty owed to B.[148]

In assumption of responsibility cases not involving negligent misstatements, reliance in this straightforward, causal, sense, is of course unnecessary. And yet when Lord Goff sought to extend the *Hedley Byrne* principle beyond misstatements in the 1990s, he tried to hold on to the connection with reliance by using the word in its weaker, more passive sense of 'hope or expectation', as when he spoke of the claimant's relying 'on the defendant to exercise due

---

[146] ibid 933.

[147] For the same reason, whether the reliance was *reasonable* cannot logically be relevant to whether a duty of care arose, though it may have a bearing on issues of legal causation and contributory negligence. Nevertheless, courts and commentators sometimes fall into the trap of asserting that the existence of a duty is or should be dependent on the reasonableness of the claimant's reliance: see, eg, *NRAM* (n 92) [32], [35] (Lord Wilson); Barker, 'Negligent Misstatement in Australia' (n 109) 338. Note that I am not denying that a reliance-based test can serve as the touchstone of duty in the negligent misstatement context; on the contrary, this is (unfortunately, in my view) the position in many common law jurisdictions. But such a test must logically be founded not on the fact of (reasonable) reliance, but on the fact that A *intended* B to rely, *invited* B to rely, should have *foreseen* that B would rely, etc.

[148] These points are made very clearly by Lord Browne-Wilkinson in *White* (n 26) 272.

care and skill'.[149] This was an unhelpful distraction, not least because in this weaker sense, reliance appears to have no normative significance.[150] Then again, it seems not to cause a great deal of trouble in practice in the professional negligence context, where there is usually a degree of mutuality between the parties, with the result that this weak requirement of reliance rarely poses much of a problem for claimants. [155]

However, in recent times, the focus on reliance in the professional negligence context has increasingly begun to influence judicial reasoning in assumption of responsibility cases involving omissions and third parties. In such cases, the better view is that no reliance, in any sense, is required. Hence in the beach story, the doctor owes you a duty of care by virtue of his assumption of responsibility even though you are unconscious and completely unaware of his involvement.[151] This view is consistent with both of the *Barrett* cases, one of which (*Barrett v Ministry of Defence*[152]) involved assistance given to a serviceman rendered insensible by drink, and the other of which (*Barrett v Enfield*) involved, as we have seen, the taking into care of a ten-month old baby.[153] And – as Robert Stevens points out[154] – it is also consistent with the authorities on sub-bailment, and the obligations that attach to finders of property. In neither case need the owner of the property even be aware of the sub-bailment or finding for the obligations owed to her to arise. Indeed, as Stevens also points out, it is a general characteristic of the rights created by non-contractual undertakings that the beneficiary need have no knowledge of the right.[155]

---

[149] *Spring* (n 43) 318 (Lord Goff). See also *Henderson* (n 21) 180, where Lord Goff highlights the shift in meaning.

[150] As Weir wrote, the change of meaning 'rob[s] the idea of all utility': T Weir, *An Introduction to Tort Law*, 2nd edn (Oxford, OUP, 2006) 38. See also Whittaker (n 61) 181 (reliance plays 'no real restrictive role' outside the misstatement context).

[151] *Banbury v Bank of Montreal* [1918] AC 626 (HL) 689 (Lord Atkinson). See also *Hedley Byrne* (n 2) 495 (Lord Morris); and *Watson* (n 24) [48] (Lord Phillips MR) (accepting that reliance was not required for a doctor-patient relationship – and the positive obligations entailed by it – to come into existence. The fact is that every day of the year hospitals come under positive obligations to unconscious persons whom they accept as patients.

[152] *Barrett v Ministry of Defence* (n 87).

[153] See also *Chandler* (n 3), where there was no evidence of reliance either by the claimant or the subsidiary; and (more emphatically) *Biddick* (n 5). And for explicit judicial acknowledgement of the distinction between negligent misrepresentation cases and omissions cases in this regard, see *Sherratt* (n 39) [82] (King J). Commentators reluctant to accept that assumption of responsibility alone can give rise to positive obligations sometimes attempt to explain the outcomes in such cases by arguing that *in fact* there was some form of reliance by B or a third party, and that this explains why A is liable: see, eg, NJ McBride and R Bagshaw, *Tort Law*, 6th edn (Harlow, Pearson, 2018) 213–15. The trouble with this is, first, that the argument is speculative (there might have been reliance, but this cannot actually be demonstrated), and secondly, that this is clearly not the basis on which liability was imposed in these cases.

[154] Stevens, *Torts and Rights* (n 13) 11.

[155] ibid 10.

It is worth emphasising what is at stake here. The idea that reliance is some-how required for an assumption of responsibility analysis to hold in, say, a rescue case is not a minor gloss on the concept but threatens completely to undermine its significance as a distinctive source of legal obligation in this context. This is because, if the ground of liability is not the defendant's undertaking, but the fact that the claimant or a third party has relied on it to the claimant's detriment, then the case ceases to be a true [156] omissions case at all, and the defend-ant's liability can readily be explained under the core *Donoghue v Stevenson* principle.[156] And so it is precisely in the case where there is *no* reliance that the assumption of responsibility concept assumes its greatest importance.

Finally, note that the rejection of reliance as a prerequisite of an assump-tion of responsibility analysis is not inconsistent with my earlier claim that the likelihood of reliance (either by the claimant or a third party) is a good reason for the law to attach significance to assumptions of responsibility in the first instance. After all, I also argued that there were other reasons for the law to do that, and besides there are lots of possible justifications for the law choosing to relieve the claimant of the burden of establishing reliance on the facts of each particular case.[157]

VIII. CONCLUSION

To conclude I wish to make five additional observations about a topic the complexity and significance of which I have been unable to do justice to in the space available.

The first observation is that I believe that our courts will soon be required to address the question of whether it is possible for a defendant to assume a responsibility not just to an identifiable individual or group – such as, perhaps, all those on the beach in the case of the lifeguard – but to the entire community (what Blackstone called a 'general undertaking'[158]). There is a clear connec-tion here with the ancient idea of the common calling.[159] For example, there is

---

[156] See Nolan, 'The Liability of Public Authorities for Failing to Confer Benefits' (n 39) 273–78.

[157] I should make it clear that I would not wish to exclude the possibility that, like special skill or knowledge, reliance may have a second-order significance in this context. It is possible, for example, that the vexed question of when A can withdraw from a prior assumption of responsibility towards B could be resolved by making the withdrawal contingent on A either establishing that neither B nor a third party had relied on it to B's detriment, or compensating B for any loss suffered as a result of such reliance: see ibid 282–83.

[158] III Bl Comm 164 (also referring to a 'universal assumpsit'). See also R Bagshaw, 'The Duties of Care of Emergency Service Providers' [1999] *Lloyd's Maritime and Commercial Law Quarterly* 71, 82–85.

[159] For useful discussion of the common calling idea, see CK Burdick, 'The Origin of the Peculiar Duties of Public Service Companies: Part I' (1911) 11 *Columbia Law Review* 514. As Burdick points out, by holding himself out to serve the public generally, a person assumed two obligations: 'to serve all who should apply and to serve with care' (at 522).

arguably an analogy between the brightly lit signs announcing the presence of an Accident & Emergency Department in an NHS hospital and the signs still hung [157] outside inns, which for centuries the courts have interpreted as representing a commitment to provide shelter and sustenance to passing travellers.[160] An analysis along these lines might provide a suitable solution to the vexed question of emergency services liability, which currently threatens to collapse into a case-by-case scrutiny of the precise words used by 999 call handlers,[161] a development which could result in those handlers being instructed by their employers to say as little as possible, to the potential detriment of the distressed individuals on the other end of the line.[162]

Secondly, I stand by my suggestion in an earlier article that in cases of acquired rights arising out of an assumption of responsibility, the defendant really is under a legal obligation to take care, so that the negligence is itself the wrong.[163] This can be contrasted with the position in core rights cases – which is to say those where negligence liability is not based on a prior relationship between the parties – where there is in fact no legal 'duty of care' at all, but rather a duty not to negligently injure. If that is correct, then it follows that in assumption of responsibility cases the wrong is done not when loss or damage is suffered, but when the negligent conduct takes place. Were the courts to accept this, they would rid themselves of the impossible task of pinpointing the moment at which 'damage' occurs in economic loss cases,[164] as well as eliminating at a stroke the absurdity of applying different limitation rules to the same breach of the same obligation in professional negligence cases, depending on whether the claim is framed in contract or tort.

Thirdly, while I have attempted in this article to identify general principles of assumption of responsibility that apply in all types of case, I am conscious that in doing so I may have succumbed to what Lord Goff called 'the temptation of elegance',[165] and that assumption of [158] responsibility may better be understood as a looser, more flexible concept, which, though underpinned by some common essentials, plays out differently in different contexts. It may well be, for example, that while reliance is not relevant in omissions and third

---

[160] See, eg, *Constantine v Imperial Hotels Ltd* [1944] KB 693 (KBD). For the analogy, see also Stevens, *Torts and Rights* (n 13) 11.

[161] See, eg, *Sherratt* (n 39).

[162] See *Michael* (n 37) [165], [167] (Lord Kerr); and Cornford (n 143) 72 (both arguing that it makes no sense to rest liability on such niceties). Cornford appears to be supportive of what would in effect be a 'general undertaking' approach in all public authority cases (67–68).

[163] D Nolan, 'Deconstructing the Duty of Care' (2013) 129 *LQR* 559, 587. This was the understanding in the early nineteenth century: see, eg, *Howell v Young* (1826) 5 B & C 259, 108 ER 97 (the negligence of an attorney was the gist of the action, from when time began to run for limitation purposes, regardless of whether the claim was brought in contract or tort).

[164] As to which, see D Nolan, 'Rights, Damage and Loss' (2017) 37 *OJLS* 255, 263–64 (and authorities there cited).

[165] R Goff, 'The Search for Principle' (1983) 69 *Proceedings of the British Academy* 169, 174.

party cases, it is (in some form) a prerequisite of liability in the economic loss context, and that conversely the ability of a potential defendant to disclaim legal responsibility, and to tailor the scope of the obligation, is more pronounced in economic loss cases than in other situations. Furthermore, the duty of care in bailment may be better understood as resting on principles that are distinct, albeit closely analogous to those in play in other assumption of responsibility cases.[166] But Honoré was surely right to say that the common law should 'aim at a certain generality',[167] and it is that aspiration which explains my reluctance to adopt a more fine-grained or context-specific approach than is obviously necessary.

My fourth observation is that our judges deserve considerable credit for sticking with the assumption of responsibility concept in the face of fairly consistent hostility directed at it by academic commentators. The House of Lords in *Hedley Byrne* may only have 'seen through a glass, darkly', but they saw nonetheless, and Lord Goff did our law of negligence a great service by rescuing the concept when it was imperilled, and by clearing away much of the grime on the glass. What is more, the modern vitality of the concept demonstrates that our judiciary continue to recognise its explanatory and normative force, and experience in jurisdictions that have renounced it in favour of alternative approaches strongly suggests that they are right to do so.

Finally, as that last observation suggests, I have to admit to a certain degree of frustration with much of the recent scholarship on this question, which to my mind takes a somewhat narrow and blinkered view of the law, and lacks a broader perspective informed by legal history and the work of our scholarly predecessors. Were the blinkers to be removed, and the perspective broadened, I firmly believe that scholars would stop arguing about whether or not assumption of responsibility is a meaningful and distinctive basis of legal obligation, and instead move on to a more productive discussion as to what exactly it means and why precisely it is distinct.

---

[166] That negligence liability has some distinctive features in the case of bailment is undeniable, the most obvious being the reversal of the burden of proof as to fault. See further, Bell (n 14) 474–84 (though many of the examples he gives are characteristic of assumed duties of care generally).
[167] Honoré (n 92) 299.

6

Varying the Standard of Care in Negligence

[2013] *Cambridge Law Journal* 651–688

[651] I. INTRODUCTION

IN THE SWIRLING seas of the modern law of negligence, there seems to be only one fixed point, an apparently invulnerable rock lying right in the eye of the storm. The objective standard of the reasonable person – the yardstick against which the defendant's conduct has been [652] measured for over 150 years[1] – has been left largely unscathed by the controversies which have engulfed the other elements of the cause of action for negligence. By and large, the disputes about the appropriate boundaries of negligence liability have been played out elsewhere. There is evidence, however, that the force of the waves is beginning to chip away at the edges of the reasonable person standard, and it seems likely that the process of erosion will accelerate in the future. For while the core standard is not itself under threat, there is discernible movement towards the use of standards more favourable to defendants in certain peripheral types of case. In English law, these moves have in the main been rather tentative, and some have been rebuffed. However, legislatures in other jurisdictions have taken more decisive measures along these lines, and there is every prospect that at some point ours will follow suit.

The most high-profile recent example of an assault on the objective standard of reasonable care in English law has been in the public authority liability context.[2] In the not-so-distant past, public authorities' liability for negligence in the exercise of discretionary statutory duties and powers was conditional on proof that the conduct in question was irrational (or *Wednesbury* unreasonable[3]), and while that restriction has now been abandoned, certain

---

[1] *Blyth v Birmingham Waterworks Co* (1856) 11 Exch 781, 784; 156 ER 1047, 1049 (Alderson B).
[2] The common law developments are discussed below, text following n 51.
[3] *Associated Provincial Picture Houses v Wednesbury Corp* [1948] 1 KB 223 (CA).

judges have more recently advocated a move away from duty of care restrictions in such cases in favour of tracing 'the contours of liability' by the use of a 'modulated' standard of care.[4] Another front of the attack on the ordinary standard of care in this context was opened by the Law Commission, which suggested in its consultation paper on *Administrative Redress* that where a public body was engaged in a 'truly public' activity, its liability in negligence should be governed not by the standard of reasonable care, but by a 'serious fault' test which would require the claimant to establish that the authority's conduct fell 'far below' the standard to be expected of it in the circumstances.[5] The Commission's proposals were heavily criticised, and have now been abandoned,[6] but the centrality of the test of serious fault to those proposals,[7] coupled with the fact that the Western Australian legislature has replaced the standard of reasonable care with a standard of *Wednesbury* [653] unreasonableness for claims based on policy decisions taken in the exercise of public functions,[8] suggests that the possibility of Parliament altering the standard of care in public authority negligence cases cannot be ruled out.

Another context in which Parliament might choose to lower the standard of care is voluntary emergency assistance. In many jurisdictions, the concern that potential good Samaritans might refrain from helping others for fear of liability has led to the replacement of the standard of reasonable care with a lesser standard of gross negligence or recklessness where one person causes harm to another while seeking to protect that other from an imminent danger.[9] German law, for example, employs a standard of gross negligence in such cases,[10] and in the United States,[11] Canada[12]

---

[4] *JD v East Berkshire Community Health NHS Trust* [2005] UKHL 23, [2005] 2 AC 373 [92]–[94] (Lord Nicholls). See also [49] (Lord Bingham).

[5] Law Commission, *Administrative Redress: Public Bodies and the Citizen* (Law Com CP No 187, 2008).

[6] Law Commission, *Administrative Redress: Public Bodies and the Citizen* (Law Com No 322, 2010) para 3.75.

[7] The Commission described the test as 'the key' to its proposals: Law Com CP No 187 (n 5) para 4.152.

[8] Civil Liability Act 2002 (WA), s 5X. For other examples from Australian state legislation, see n 94.

[9] For examples of incidents along these lines in the US and China respectively, see 'Hospital Refused to Help Shot Boy of 15 Dying in the Street' *The Times* (London, 19 May 1998); and 'Chinese City Poised to Introduce Country's First Good Samaritan Rules' *The Guardian* (London, 30 November 2011). For a sceptical view of such protection in the case of professional medical assistance, see K Williams, 'Medical Samaritans: Is There a Duty to Treat?' (2001) 21 *OJLS* 393, 411.

[10] § 680 BGB.

[11] In the majority of US states, 'good Samaritan' statutes confer immunity on those who provide emergency medical care without the expectation of remuneration unless gross negligence or wilful misconduct is established. For an example at federal level, see the Aviation Medical Assistance Act 1998. See also the federal Volunteer Protection Act 1997, which gives similar protection to volunteers engaged in the activities of non-profit organisations and government entities.

[12] See, eg, Emergency Medical Aid Act 1979 (Sask); Good Samaritan Act 1996 (BC); Emergency Medical Aid Act 2000 (Alta); Good Samaritan Act 2001 (Ont); Quebec Civil Code, art 1471. All this legislation sets the standard at gross negligence (or in the case of Quebec, 'gross fault').

and Australia,[13] there is now extensive legislative protection of good Samaritans along these lines, albeit sometimes limited to off-duty medical personnel providing emergency medical help. Furthermore, the Irish Law Reform Commission recently recommended a gross negligence standard for individual good Samaritans and volunteers in its report on the *Civil Liability of Good Samaritans and Volunteers*.[14] According to the Commission:

> [T]he imposition of a gross negligence test succeeds in striking a balance between the policy of encouraging altruistic behaviours [and] the public's right to redress. With regard to encouraging altruistic behaviour, the leniency of the gross negligence test may be understood as a reward for good behaviour. Furthermore, it militates against the deterrent effect that the fear of litigation may cause ... The application of the ordinary negligence test, on the [654] other hand, would be to impose too heavy a burden that would threaten the continuation of such benevolent activities.[15]

In England, the use of a modified standard of care to protect good Samaritans was rejected when a claim was brought against the St John's Ambulance Brigade for alleged failures in the treatment of a schoolboy injured in a motor cycle race,[16] but the possibility of legislation to clarify the law on the issue was mooted in Lord Young's report for the current Government on health and safety and the compensation culture,[17] and it is conceivable that such legislation would go beyond clarification of the existing position and limit liability to instances of gross negligence or recklessness.

With these and other scenarios in mind, this article is an exploration of the variation of the standard of care in negligence to favour defendants, an issue of considerable practical significance which has not previously been the subject of systematic analysis. By shining a spotlight on this issue I hope to show that varying the standard of care in this way is a useful technique, which is and could be used in a number of types of case to achieve an appropriate balance between liability and non-liability. I also hope to show that if this technique is employed there are some ways of varying the standard of care which are preferable to others. The structure of my analysis is centred around three core questions. First, to what extent has English negligence law already varied the standard of care to favour defendants? Secondly, if the standard of care is to be varied, how should this be done? And thirdly, when and why might the use of a modified standard of care be desirable?

---

[13] For protection of good Samaritans acting in good faith and without recklessness, see Civil Liability Act 1936 (SA), s 74; Civil Law (Wrongs) Act 2002 (ACT), pt 2.1; Civil Liability Act 2002 (Tas), pt 8A; Civil Liability Act 2002 (WA), s 5AD. In Queensland, the standard is one of gross negligence: Law Reform Act 1995 (Qld), pt 5. In the two most populous states, even greater protection is given: Wrongs Act 1958 (Vic), s 31B; Civil Liability Act 2002 (NSW), s 57.

[14] Law Reform Commission, *Civil Liability of Good Samaritans and Volunteers* (LRC 93, 2009).

[15] ibid para 4.81.

[16] *Cattley v St John's Ambulance Brigade* (QBD, 25 November 1988).

[17] Lord Young of Graffham, *Common Sense, Common Safety* (2010) www.gov.uk/government/uploads/system/uploads/attachment_data/file/60905/402906_CommonSense_acc.pdf.

Before we turn to the first of those questions, however, the scope of the analysis should be clarified. My concern is with any deviation from the objective standard of reasonable care which could favour defendants, such as the use of a standard of care tailored to the defendant as an individual,[18] or the use of a gross negligence standard.[19] I do not consider cases where the objective standard of reasonable care is employed, but simply adapted to a particular class of defendants, as where the conduct of a child is assessed by reference to the standard of a [655] reasonable child of the same age,[20] or that of a hospital doctor by reference to the standard of a reasonable person holding that particular post.[21] Nor do I consider the *Bolam* test, according to which a professional is not guilty of negligence if she acted in accordance with a practice accepted as proper by a responsible body of relevant professional opinion,[22] since (although the contrary is sometimes implied[23]) that test does not represent a departure from the ordinary standard of the reasonable person, but is merely an attempt to apply that standard in the light of the fact that judges lack the knowledge and expertise usually required to choose between competing professional opinions.[24]

II. TO WHAT EXTENT HAS ENGLISH NEGLIGENCE LAW ALREADY VARIED THE STANDARD OF CARE TO FAVOUR DEFENDANTS?

My first task is to identify the areas of negligence law where Parliament or the courts have deviated from the ordinary objective standard of the reasonable person in a way which favours defendants. This is not entirely straightforward, because it is sometimes difficult to tell whether the standard of care has been varied, or whether an apparently more lenient approach is in fact just the way that the ordinary standard of care is playing out in a particular context. After all, the standard of reasonable care is of necessity a very flexible one, since it must be applied in a wide variety of different circumstances. To drive at 60 miles per hour on a motorway will not generally be negligent, for example, but to

---

[18] Of course, the use of a subjective standard of care might favour the claimant in a particular case, but because it represents a departure from the objective standard which *could* favour defendants it falls within the scope of my enquiry.

[19] Another, neater, way of expressing this idea would be to refer to 'lowering the standard of care', but this formulation has been avoided since it can give rise to confusion. The reason for the confusion seems to be that although in these cases the standard of care is lowered, the hurdle which the claimant must clear to establish breach of duty is raised, and it is from the claimant's perspective that we tend to view the elements of a negligence action.

[20] *Mullin v Richards* [1998] 1 WLR 1304 (CA); *Orchard v Lee* [2009] EWCA Civ 295, [2009] PIQR P16.

[21] *Wilsher v Essex AHA* [1987] QB 730 (CA).

[22] *Bolam v Friern Hospital Management Committee* [1957] 1 WLR 582 (QBD) 587 (McNair J).

[23] See, eg, P Cane, *The Anatomy of Tort Law* (Oxford, OUP, 1997) 41. The test has been described as a 'partial immunity rule': D Howarth, 'Negligence After *Murphy*: Time to Re-think' [1991] *CLJ* 58, 96.

[24] See *Connor v Surrey CC* [2010] EWCA Civ 286, [2011] QB 429 [66] (Laws LJ).

do so in an urban high street almost always will be, not because the standard is varied for the motorway motorist, but simply because the conditions are so very different. Similarly, while a driver who jumps a red light or breaks the speed limit will generally be considered to be negligent, the same may not be true of an ambulance driver who takes these and other risks when responding to an emergency call, not because he is subject to a different standard of care,[25] but because the application of the ordinary standard of care takes into account the exceptional circumstances of the case.[26]

While these examples are straightforward, other types of case are less so. Consider for instance the standard of care applied to those [**656**] taking part in sport and related physical activities, such as 'horseplay'. The nature of these activities is such that, when one participant injures another (or a spectator), it can be difficult to decide whether to attribute the injury to negligence, or to the inherent risks of the activity in question. The courts' response to this difficulty has typically been to stipulate that in such cases liability will not be imposed for a mere error of judgment or lapse of skill, but only where the defendant's conduct was such as to evince a reckless disregard of the claimant's safety.[27] Does this approach represent a varying of the standard of care, or should it instead be interpreted as the application of the ordinary standard in a somewhat unusual context? The better view is that in this type of case the standard of care has not been varied. There is, after all, no reason why it *should* be varied in this category of case.[28] Moreover, it is clear from the relevant authorities that the courts' own justification for this approach is the need to take account of the circumstances when applying the ordinary negligence standard. In the leading case of *Wooldridge v Sumner*, for example, Diplock LJ said that 'the law of negligence has always recognised that the standard of care which a reasonable man will exercise depends on the conditions under which the decision to avoid the act or omission relied on as negligence has to be taken',[29] and described the test of 'reckless disregard' as 'the practical result of this analysis' in the sporting context.[30] Similarly, in *Blake v Galloway*, where the Court of Appeal expanded the reckless disregard test to include 'a very high degree of carelessness', Dyson LJ said that the participants in horseplay owed each other a duty to take

---

[25] As suggested by R Kidner, 'The Variable Standard of Care' (1991) 11 *Legal Studies* 1, 16.

[26] See *Daborn v Bath Tramways Motor Co Ltd* [1946] 2 All ER 333 (CA); *Watt v Hertfordshire CC* [1954] 1 WLR 835 (CA).

[27] See *Wooldridge v Sumner* [1963] 2 QB 43 (CA) 68–69 (Diplock LJ) (and see similarly 56–57 (Sellers LJ)).

[28] Although there are occasionally references to *volenti*-type arguments in the case law, these cannot furnish a justification for a lower standard of care, since there is no reason to suppose that the participants in such activities impliedly consent to *negligence* (as determined by the ordinary standard of care) on the part of others involved. They can be said to impliedly consent to the inherent risks of the activity, but that just goes to show that the *volenti* analysis is superfluous, since by definition those risks are not the result of negligent conduct.

[29] *Wooldridge* (n 27) 68.

[30] ibid.

reasonable care not to cause injury, and made it clear that the issue was what that meant 'in the context of play of this kind'.[31]

But even if in the end we conclude that no modification of the standard of care has taken place in the sporting context, the example shows that discerning such modifications is not always an easy task. Bearing that caveat in mind, we can turn to three areas in which the standard of care may already have been varied. In two of these areas – the liability of occupiers and of public authorities – it seems clear that this has occurred. In the other – liability for the deliberate [657] conduct of third parties – there are indications that a modified standard of care may have been used, but the evidence is less conclusive.

A. The Liability of Occupiers

There are two types of case where a varied standard of care has been applied to occupiers. The first relates to the obligations occupiers owe trespassers and other non-visitors. It used to be that an occupier was liable to a trespasser only for harm arising out of a reckless disregard for the latter's safety.[32] This restriction was abandoned in *British Railways Board v Herrington*,[33] but the House of Lords imposed a lesser duty of 'common humanity' instead of the ordinary duty of reasonable care, and this lesser duty was then put on a statutory footing in the Occupiers' Liability Act 1984. The other type of case where a modified standard has been employed is where the occupier is sued for 'continuing' a nuisance which emanates from his land but which he did not himself create, as in *Leakey v National Trust*,[34] where the Court of Appeal held that the defendants had to meet the cost of the measures required to prevent soil and rocks slipping onto neighbouring properties from a hill in their occupation.[35] In cases of this kind, the fact that the harm results from an omission rather than a positive act has been taken into account by making the standard of care partly subjective.

Precisely how has the standard of care been varied in these two types of case? The *Leakey* category will be dealt with first, since here the answer is more straightforward. Where an occupier is sued for continuing a nuisance, he will be liable only if, after he became – or should have become – aware of the danger the state of affairs posed to neighbouring property, he omitted to take reasonable

---

[31] *Blake v Galloway* [2004] EWCA Civ 814, [2004] 1 WLR 2844 [15]. See also *Wilks v Cheltenham Cycle Club* [1971] 1 WLR 668 (CA) 670 (Lord Denning MR), 674 (Edmund Davies LJ), 676 (Phillimore LJ); *Condon v Basi* [1985] 1 WLR 866 (CA) 867–68 (Sir John Donaldson MR).

[32] *Robert Addie & Sons (Collieries) Ltd v Dumbreck* [1929] AC 358 (HL).

[33] *British Railways Board v Herrington* [1972] AC 877 (HL).

[34] *Leakey v National Trust* [1980] QB 485 (CA).

[35] Although the claim in *Leakey* was brought in private nuisance, the analogous case of *Goldman v Hargrave* [1967] 1 AC 645 (PC) was pleaded in negligence, and it has been said that in cases of this kind '[t]he label nuisance or negligence is treated as of no real significance' (*Delaware Mansions Ltd v Westminster CC* [2002] 1 AC 321 (HL) [31] (Lord Cooke)).

steps to remove or reduce the threat.[36] So far, this is just the ordinary reasonableness approach, but there are two important caveats. First, the danger must be patent and not latent, so that liability may be imposed if the occupier saw or should have seen the problem on his land, but not if the threat to neighbouring property was discoverable only by further investigation.[37] And secondly, even when the occupier does have actual or presumed knowledge of the danger in this sense, his duty is to do only what it is reasonable to expect of him in his individual circumstances, [658] so that if physical effort is required to avert the danger, account is taken of the occupier's age and physical condition,[38] and, if expenditure of money is required, of his means.[39]

The precise nature of the duty owed by occupiers to trespassers and other non-visitors is more complex. Although no clear rule emerged from the speeches in *Herrington*, three general themes were discernible. The first was that the duty did not arise until the occupier had actual knowledge 'either of the presence of the trespasser upon his land or of facts which make it likely that the trespasser will come on to his land' and of 'facts as to the condition of his land or of activities carried out upon it' which were likely to cause personal injury to a trespasser unaware of the danger.[40] Moreover, the occupier was under no duty to make any inquiry or inspection to ascertain whether or not such facts did exist.[41] Secondly, if the duty did arise, it was subjective, so that the defendant's knowledge, skill and resources would be taken into account when assessing whether it had been discharged.[42] And finally, it was also said that the duty owed was a lesser one than the general duty of care, this lower level of obligation being described as a duty of 'common' or 'ordinary' humanity.[43] Overall it was clear that in the case of a trespasser an occupier was not subject (as Lord Reid later put it) to the 'full obligations' arising out of a relationship of neighbourhood in the *Donoghue v Stevenson* sense,[44] since that relationship had been 'forced on him against his will'.[45]

Under the 1984 Act, an occupier owes a duty of reasonable care to a trespasser or other non-visitor in respect of a particular danger on his land if (a) he is aware of the danger, or has reasonable grounds to believe it exists; (b) he knows, or has reasonable grounds to believe, that the other is, or is likely

---

[36] See *Holbeck Hall Hotel Ltd v Scarborough BC* [2000] QB 836 (CA) 852–53 (Stuart-Smith LJ).

[37] ibid 857–58 (Stuart-Smith LJ).

[38] 'Less must be expected of the infirm than of the able-bodied' (*Goldman* (n 35) (Lord Wilberforce)).

[39] *Leakey* (n 34) 526 (Megaw LJ).

[40] *Herrington* (n 33) 941–42 (Lord Diplock).

[41] ibid.

[42] ibid 898–99 (Lord Reid). See also 920 (Lord Wilberforce), 941–42 (Lord Diplock).

[43] ibid 909 (Lord Morris), 926–27 (Lord Pearson) respectively.

[44] *Donoghue v Stevenson* [1932] AC 562 (HL) 580 (Lord Atkin).

[45] *Southern Portland Cement Ltd v Cooper* [1974] AC 623 (PC) 642–44. See also *Herrington* (n 33) 898–99 (Lord Reid), 936 (Lord Diplock). It is therefore surprising that some commentators maintain that the duty of common humanity was simply an application of the ordinary standard of care: see, eg, D Ibbetson, *A Historical Introduction to the Law of Obligations* (Oxford, OUP, 1999) 192.

to come into, the vicinity of the danger; and (c) the risk is one against which he may reasonably be expected to offer the other some protection.[46] Although it could be argued that this duty is simply an application of the ordinary standard of care in the peculiar circumstances of unauthorised entry, the better view is that here too the standard of care has been varied because the relationship from which [659] the duty flows has been forced upon the occupier. For while the draft Bill in the Law Commission report which preceded the Act simply laid down the ordinary standard of reasonable care,[47] the Act itself requires that the occupier either knew or had reasonable grounds to believe that the danger existed and that the claimant was in, or was likely to come into, the vicinity of that danger. And since the phrase 'reasonable grounds to believe' has been held to require actual knowledge of facts that would have led a reasonable person to the conclusion in question (so that it is not enough to show that a reasonable occupier would have been aware of the danger, and of the claimant's proximity to it),[48] it is clear that there is a subjective element to the standard laid down by the Act, which therefore represents a departure from the ordinary, objective, standard of care. Hence Lord Hoffmann's statement that the duty under the 1984 Act was 'intended to be a lesser duty, as to both incidence and scope' than the duty to lawful visitors,[49] and Lord Phillips MR's description of the former as 'significantly less exacting' than the latter.[50]

This survey of the law relating to the liability of occupiers reveals that at various times the standard of care has been varied in two different ways. First, the duty to take precautionary measures has not been assessed (as it normally would be) in the light of the risks that would be apparent to a reasonable person: in the case of trespassers, actual knowledge of the risk – or of facts from which a reasonable person would identify the risk – is required, and in the nuisance scenario, the danger must be patent and not latent. And secondly, the occupier's personal circumstances have been taken into account when deciding what steps he ought to have taken to reduce or eliminate the risk.

B. The Liability of Public Authorities

The second context in which the standard of care has been varied is the liability of public authorities. Formerly, it was held that a negligence action

---

[46] Occupiers' Liability Act 1984, ss 1(3) and 1(4).

[47] Law Commission, *Report on Liability for Damage or Injury to Trespassers and Related Questions of Occupiers' Liability* (Law Com No 75, 1976).

[48] *Swain v Nat Ram Puri* [1996] PIQR P442 (CA). This would appear to be the correct interpretation: see MA Jones, 'The Occupiers' Liability Act 1984' (1984) 47 *MLR* 713, 718. In the US, similar formulae requiring actual knowledge have been used to limit the duty owed to trespassers (see *Restatement, Second, Torts* (1977) §§ 334–39; WP Keeton et al, *Prosser and Keeton on Torts*, 5th edn (St Paul, Minn, West Publishing, 1984) 398).

[49] *Tomlinson v Congleton BC* [2003] UKHL 47, [2004] 1 AC 46 [13]. See also [68] (Lord Hobhouse).

[50] *Donoghue v Folkestone Properties Ltd* [2003] EWCA Civ 231, [2003] QB 1008 [31].

could succeed only if the decision of the public authority under attack was *Wednesbury* unreasonable – that is, if it was so unreasonable that no reasonable authority could have made it. Latterly, the courts have moved away from this express dependence on public law [660] concepts towards a private law approach, under which the problems surrounding discretionary decision-making are accommodated at the breach of duty stage of the negligence enquiry. Although on the former approach the *Wednesbury* unreasonableness hurdle appeared at the duty stage, in effect it meant that public authorities exercising a statutory discretion were subject to a modified standard of care. On the latter approach, public authorities are notionally subject to the application of ordinary negligence principles, but there is evidence to suggest that in practice a modified standard of care is still being applied.

Where Parliament has conferred a discretion on a public authority, the judiciary are naturally disinclined to tread on the authority's toes by imposing liability for conduct that falls within the ambit of that discretion. However, the precise mechanics by which the courts give effect to this inhibition have varied over the years. Previously, reliance was placed on public law concepts, in particular *Wednesbury* unreasonableness. According to Lord Reid in *Home Office v Dorset Yacht Co Ltd*, a decision of a public authority could ground liability in negligence only if it was so careless or unreasonable that it did not amount to a real exercise of the statutory discretion at all.[51] Similarly, in *X (minors) v Bedfordshire CC*,[52] the House of Lords held that the first requirement in such cases was to show that the decision under attack was so unreasonable that it fell outside the ambit of the discretion altogether.[53] Since it is 'significantly more difficult'[54] to establish that a public authority has fallen foul of the public law *Wednesbury* unreasonable standard than it is to show that it has fallen foul of the private law standard of negligence, the use of this concept amounted in effect to the use of a modified standard of care in such cases. This was confirmed by Lord Browne-Wilkinson in *X (minors)* when he said that it followed from the *Wednesbury* unreasonableness precondition that a claim against a local education authority in respect of a statement of special educational needs it made under the Education Act 1981 could not succeed merely because the relevant decisions were made carelessly, but that it would have to be shown that they were so 'grossly delinquent' that no reasonable education authority could have reached the same decisions.[55]

---

[51] *Home Office v Dorset Yacht Co Ltd* [1970] AC 1004 (HL) 1031.

[52] *X (minors) v Bedfordshire CC* [1995] 2 AC 633 (HL).

[53] ibid 736–38 (Lord Browne-Wilkinson).

[54] C Booth and D Squires, *The Negligence Liability of Public Authorities* (Oxford, OUP, 2006) para 2.27. See also *Pyrenees Shire Council v Day* [1998] HCA 3, 192 CLR 330 [253] (Kirby J) (requiring the plaintiff to satisfy the public law irrationality test imposes a more onerous burden than proof of ordinary negligence).

[55] *X (minors)* (n 52) 761.

In *Barrett v Enfield LBC*,[56] however, the House of Lords abandoned the *Wednesbury* unreasonableness requirement. According to [661] Lord Hutton, provided the decision under attack was justiciable – in other words, suitable for scrutiny by a court in a private law action – it was preferable for the courts to resolve the liability issue by direct application of the negligence concept, rather than by applying *Wednesbury* unreasonableness as a preliminary test.[57] The abandonment of the *Wednesbury* requirement was confirmed in *Phelps v London Borough of Hillingdon*, where Lord Slynn said that the fact that acts claimed to be negligent were carried out within the ambit of a statutory discretion was not in itself a reason why it should be held that no claim for negligence could be brought in respect of them.[58] It did not however follow that the discretionary nature of a public authority's decision-making was to be ignored altogether, for it would instead be taken into account at the breach of duty stage. Hence, in *Barrett*, where a local authority was being sued for alleged defects in its foster care provision, Lord Hutton said that the standard of care expected of the defendant would have to be determined against the background that it was 'given discretions to exercise by statute in a sphere involving difficult decisions in relation to the welfare of children'.[59]

Another development which occurred in *Barratt* and *Phelps* concerned an argument which had previously proved influential when it came to deciding whether it would be fair, just and reasonable to impose a duty of care on a public authority. In *X (minors)*, one of the reasons which Lord Browne-Wilkinson gave for his conclusion that no duty of care was owed by local authorities in respect of their child protection functions was that 'the task of the local authority and its servant in dealing with children at risk' was 'extraordinarily delicate'.[60] However, when this point was made by counsel for the defendants in *Barrett*, it met with a rather different response, for while Lord Slynn accepted that the provision of foster care involved the balancing of delicate and difficult factors, he clearly felt that, rather than ruling out liability altogether, this should instead be taken into account at the breach of duty stage.[61] Similarly, in *Phelps*, which concerned four different cases of alleged educational malpractice, Lord Clyde recognised that educational psychologists and other professionals had to make difficult decisions concerning diagnosis of dyslexia and the like, but considered that the *Bolam* test gave those involved sufficient protection.[62]

---

[56] *Barrett v Enfield LBC* [2001] 2 AC 550 (HL).
[57] ibid 586.
[58] *Phelps v London Borough of Hillingdon* [2001] 2 AC 619 (HL) 652–53.
[59] *Barrett* (n 56) 591.
[60] *X (minors)* (n 52) 750.
[61] *Barrett* (n 56) 572–73. Lord Hutton dismissed the argument on the ground that the provision of foster care (the issue in *Barrett*) was not as delicate as the task of the defendants in *X (minors)*: ibid 589.
[62] *Phelps* (n 58) 672.

[**662**] Whether in the aftermath of these developments a modified standard of care is still being used in certain types of public authority negligence cases is open to question. What is clear is that the judiciary have emphasised that it will be difficult to establish breach of duty in this context. In *Barrett*, Lord Slynn said that in the child protection and foster care context 'the courts should not be too ready to find ... that there has been negligence by staff who largely are skilled and dedicated',[63] and he made a similar statement about findings of negligence in education cases in *Phelps*,[64] where Lord Nicholls also remarked that claims for educational malpractice should be limited to instances of 'manifest incompetence or negligence comprising specific, identifiable mistakes'.[65] These observations were echoed in subsequent Court of Appeal decisions. In *S v Gloucestershire CC*, for example, May LJ interpreted *Barrett* as laying down that 'in considering whether a discretionary decision was negligent, the court will not substitute its view for that of the local authority upon whom the statute has placed the power to exercise the discretion, unless the discretionary decision was plainly wrong',[66] while in *Carty v Croydon LBC*, Dyson LJ said that in the light of the nature of the statutory function and the difficulty of the decisions involved, in the educational malpractice sphere the courts will usually only hold that there is a duty to avoid decisions that are 'plainly and obviously wrong'.[67]

Two points can be made. The first is that although some commentators have linked the leeway that is now given to discretionary decision-makers in public authority cases with the *Bolam* test of professional negligence,[68] the analogy is not convincing. Although an institutional competence problem similar to the one underlying the *Bolam* test may arise in public authority cases,[69] it is dealt with at the justiciability stage. It follows that by the time the breach issue falls to be considered, the court has already determined that it is capable of assessing the reasonableness of the decision under attack, and hence any special latitude or 'margin of appreciation' that the authority is accorded must be based on considerations different from those which underlie the *Bolam* test. This lends support to the view that a modified standard of care is being applied in this context. And the second point [**663**] is that although in this context the judiciary have refrained from laying down a special standard of care along the lines of the occupiers' liability standard, they do seem to be saying that a discretionary decision will

---

[63] *Barrett* (n 56) 572. See also 591 (Lord Hutton).

[64] *Phelps* (n 58) 655.

[65] ibid 667.

[66] *S v Gloucestershire CC* [2001] Fam 313 (CA) 338.

[67] *Carty v Croydon LBC* [2005] EWCA Civ 19, [2005] 1 WLR 2312 [43].

[68] See, eg, MJ Bowman and SH Bailey, 'Negligence in the Realms of Public Law: A Positive Obligation to Rescue?' [1984] *Public Law* 277, 306–307; S Todd, 'Liability in Tort of Public Bodies' in NJ Mullany and AM Linden (eds), *Torts Tomorrow: A Tribute to John Fleming* (Sydney, LBC Information Services, 1998) 46–47.

[69] See J Doyle and J Redwood, 'The Common Law Liability of Public Authorities: The Interface Between Public and Private Law' (1997) 7 *Tort Law Review* 30, 34.

be deemed negligent only if it was 'manifestly' or 'plainly' mistaken. And since it is argued below that a test of manifest or obvious fault may amount in effect to a gross negligence standard,[70] this also lends support to the conclusion that the breach test which has emerged from the case law on public authorities does represent a deviation – albeit a minor one – from the ordinary standard of care. This conclusion is consistent with the statements in the leading work on public authority negligence liability that in *Barrett* and *Phelps* the House of Lords set 'a high hurdle for establishing negligence' in such cases, which was designed to catch only 'particularly egregious failings'.[71]

C. Liability for the Deliberate Acts of Third Parties

Finally, there is some evidence that a modified standard of care has previously been used in cases where the claimant seeks to hold the defendant liable for the consequences of the deliberate act of a third party, albeit that this approach is now on the wane. Cases of this kind have given rise to enormous conceptual difficulties, and the courts have resorted to three different elements of the negligence cause of action to deal with them: (1) factual duty (the question of whether damage to someone in the claimant's position was a reasonably foreseeable consequence of the defendant's negligence), or, where the defendant caused some initial damage to the claimant before the third party intervened, remoteness of damage; (2) notional duty (the question of whether there is a rule of law that either allows or bars recovery in this category of case); and (3) breach of duty. Although there is some heavyweight judicial support for the factual duty/remoteness approach,[72] it will not be discussed further, since it received no backing in either of the two most recent House of Lords decisions on the subject, *Smith v Littlewoods Organisation Ltd*[73] and *Mitchell v Glasgow CC*[74] That leaves notional duty and breach. Analysis in terms of notional duty was preferred by Lord Diplock in *Home Office v Dorset Yacht*[75] and by Lord Goff in *Smith v Littlewoods*, and is currently in the ascendant following the House of Lords' endorsement in *Mitchell* of Lord Goff's approach in *Smith*. However, the breach approach has [**664**] also proven influential, and since it seems to involve the application of a modified standard of care, it is worth taking a closer look at it.

The key decision is *Smith v Littlewoods*.[76] The defenders purchased a disused cinema, intending to turn it into a supermarket. Before they got a chance to do

---

[70] See text to n 185.
[71] Booth and Squires (n 54) para 1.35 (including footnote). See also para 1.37.
[72] Notably Lord Reid in *Dorset Yacht* (n 51).
[73] *Smith v Littlewoods Organisation Ltd* [1987] AC 241 (HL).
[74] *Mitchell v Glasgow CC* [2009] UKHL 11, [2009] 1 AC 874.
[75] *Dorset Yacht* (n 51).
[76] *Smith* (n 73).

so, vandals set it on fire, and the fire spread to the pursuer's premises nearby. Were the defenders liable for not having anticipated and guarded against the vandals' conduct? Lord Goff dealt with the problem by reference to the duty of care concept.[77] There was 'no general duty at common law to prevent persons from harming others by their deliberate wrongdoing, however foreseeable such harm may be if the defender does not take steps to prevent it',[78] and although there were a number of exceptions to this general no-liability rule, on the facts none of them applied. Both Lord Griffiths and Lord Brandon, on the other hand, held that the defenders had owed the pursuers a duty of care, but that they were not in breach of that duty, although the latter made the common mistake of framing the breach question in terms of a specific 'duty' (as in 'Was the motorist under a duty to slow down as she approached the junction?').[79]

For present purposes, however, the most important speech is that of Lord Mackay.[80] Although his reasoning is somewhat opaque, the better view is that in effect he agreed with Lords Griffiths and Brandon: there was a duty, but it was not breached.[81] However, while Lord Griffiths based the duty in *Smith v Littlewoods* on *Goldman v Hargrave*,[82] Lord Mackay did not limit it in this way. His opinion can therefore be interpreted as doing away with duty restrictions in third party cases, in favour of regulation by breach. Moreover, the following passage suggests that he may have been endorsing the employment in such cases of a modified standard of care:

> [W]here the only possible source of the type of damage or injury which is in question is agency of a human being for whom the person against whom the claim is made has no responsibility, it may not be easy to find that as a reasonable person he was bound to anticipate that type of damage as a consequence of his act or omission. The more unpredictable the conduct in question, the less easy to affirm that any particular result from it is probable and in many circumstances the only way in which a judge could properly be persuaded to come to the conclusion that the result was not only possible but reasonably foreseeable as probable would [665] be to convince him that, in the circumstances, it was highly likely ... Unless the judge can be satisfied that the result of the human action is highly probable or very likely he may have to conclude that all that the reasonable man could say was that it was a mere possibility. Unless the needle that measures the probability of a particular result flowing from the conduct of a human agent is near the top of the scale it may be hard to conclude that it has risen sufficiently from the bottom to create the duty reasonably to foresee it.[83]

---

[77] See ibid 280 ('Problems such as these are solved in Scotland, as in England, by means of the mechanism of the duty of care').

[78] ibid 279.

[79] A point highlighted by Howarth, 'Negligence After *Murphy*' (n 23) 73.

[80] Lord Keith agreed with Lord Mackay and Lord Goff.

[81] See BS Markesinis, 'Negligence, Nuisance and Affirmative Duties of Action' (1989) 105 *LQR* 104, 108–11.

[82] *Smith* (n 73) 206–207. See also 273 (Lord Goff).

[83] ibid 261.

Two points can be made. The first is that, although the language used here is redolent of the factual duty/remoteness approach favoured by Lord Reid in *Dorset Yacht*, in essence Lord Mackay's analysis seems to be centred on breach of duty. This is consistent with the fact that in the immediately preceding passage Lord Mackay cites extensively from *Glasgow Corporation v Muir*,[84] where the defenders were held not to have breached the duty of care they owed the pursuer because the risk of negligence by the third parties who were the immediate cause of the harm was not sufficiently foreseeable. Furthermore, in her careful analysis of *Smith v Littlewoods*, Elspeth Reid argues that Lord Mackay 'drew upon substantially the same framework' as the Inner House of the Court of Session,[85] which she interprets as resting on breach, a duty of care being assumed.[86] And the second point is that, while Lord Mackay presented his analysis as an application of ordinary breach principles, in truth he was stacking the odds heavily against the claimant, since the degree of required foreseeability was set extremely high, and nothing was said (at this point[87]) about the other side of the equation, namely the cost of the precautions necessary to eliminate the risk. This goes against breach of duty orthodoxy, whereby even the running of a minor risk may be negligent if the burden of precautions is low.[88] Similarly, there is no justification in breach terms for Lord Griffiths' statement that for an occupier to have to take precautions against the criminal activity of third parties on their premises the circumstances 'would surely have to be extreme indeed'[89] – what if, for example, the occupier knew that vandals were messing about in a warehouse full of inflammable materials, and that a simple padlock would keep them out?

[666] It is therefore plausible to conclude that the majority in *Smith v Littlewoods* favoured the determination of third party cases by the application of a modified standard of care, rather than by reference to the duty restrictions favoured by Lord Goff, a conclusion fortified by two later first-instance decisions, in both of which a modified standard of care seems to have been applied to defendants who were sued for the consequences of deliberate third party conduct.[90] Whether there is much of a future for the use of a modified standard

---

[84] *Glasgow Corporation v Muir* [1943] AC 448 (HL).

[85] E Reid, '*Smith v Littlewoods Organisation Ltd* (1985)' in C Mitchell and P Mitchell (eds), *Landmark Cases in the Law of Tort* (Oxford, Hart Publishing, 2010) 263.

[86] ibid 259–60. The decision of the Inner House can be found at *Smith v Littlewoods Organisation Ltd* 1986 SLT 272 (CSIH). Other commentators who have interpreted Lord Mackay's reasoning as breach-oriented include Markesinis (n 81) and D Howarth, 'My Brother's Keeper? Liability for Acts of Third Parties' (1994) 14 *Legal Studies* 88, 94–95.

[87] cf *Smith* (n 73) 268–69.

[88] See *Overseas Tankship (UK) v Miller Steamship Co Pty* [1967] 1 AC 617 (PC) 642 (Lord Reid).

[89] *Smith* (n 73) 251.

[90] See *Dickinson v Cornwall CC* (QBD, 10 December 1999), where Steel J said that '[a]n affirmative duty to prevent deliberate wrongdoing by a third party will only arise where the action is not merely foreseeable but likely to happen'; and *Crosby v Regency Security Services Ltd* (Colchester CC, 18 May 2006), where HHJ Yelton said that a nightclub doorman could only be held liable for an assault by one patron on another if it was 'highly probable' that such an assault would take place.

of care in this context is doubtful, however. In the most recent House of Lords decision on the topic, *Mitchell v Glasgow CC*, the House clearly preferred Lord Goff's duty approach,[91] albeit that Lord Hope, who gave the leading speech, limited his approval of that approach to cases in which the alleged negligence consisted of a failure 'to prevent the risk of harm being caused to the [pursuer] by the criminal act of a third party which they did not create and had not undertaken to avert',[92] thereby leaving open the possibility that the standard of care approach may continue to be employed in cases where the defendant has created a source of danger exploited by a third party or assumed a responsibility towards the claimant to protect her from third party conduct. There was however little in the other speeches to suggest approval of such a qualification on the use of duty analysis.

III. IF THE STANDARD OF CARE IS TO BE VARIED, HOW SHOULD THIS BE DONE?

There are a number of ways in which the ordinary standard of care can be varied in a way which could favour the defendant, and in this section of the article I evaluate the different possibilities. The primary focus will be on the two most obvious possibilities, subjectivising the standard of care and using a standard of gross negligence. Before we turn to these, however, it will be helpful to consider two alternative approaches which involve abandoning a negligence standard altogether.

A. Abandoning a Negligence Standard Altogether

There are at least two ways in which the scales can be tipped in favour of the defendant at the breach of duty stage which effectively involve abandoning the negligence standard altogether, namely the use of [667] tests originating in public law, and the use of a recklessness or wilful misconduct standard.

i. Public Law Standards

We have seen that in the past the English courts employed the public law test of *Wednesbury* unreasonableness as a preliminary filter in cases involving alleged negligence in the exercise of a statutory discretion, and some recent Australian state legislation uses the same test.[93] There has also been

---

[91] *Mitchell* (n 74) [20] (Lord Hope), [56] (Lord Rodger), [76] (Lady Hale).
[92] ibid [20].
[93] See Civil Liability Act 2002 (WA), s 5X (applying a *Wednesbury* unreasonableness standard where a negligence claim arises out of a policy decision taken in the performance or non-performance of a public function); Civil Liability Act 2002 (NSW), s 43A (applying the test to claims based on the

considerable interest in the use of tests originating in the European law context to regulate the liability of public authorities in domestic law. It has been suggested, for example, that the test of a sufficiently serious breach used to determine state liability in European law could also be used to regulate the domestic liability of public authorities,[94] while the Law Commission has advocated the use in this context of a test of 'serious fault' heavily influenced by the sufficiently serious breach approach.[95] Although strictly speaking public law tests of this kind do not lay down 'standards of care' at all, in a general sense their effect is to modify the standard of care in favour of the defendant, as was acknowledged in the Australian report which led to the adoption of the *Wednesbury* standard in some state legislation:

> The effect of the test [of *Wednesbury* unreasonableness] is to lower the standard of care. It ... [gives] the defendant more leeway for choice in deciding how to exercise its functions than would the normal definition of negligence (in terms of reasonable care).[96]

The use of public law tests of this kind is not however a helpful means of modifying the standard of care, since they have been developed to perform specifically public law functions and are ill-suited to the task [668] of setting standards of conduct in the private law context. Many of the factors taken into account in determining whether a state's breach of an EU legal norm is 'sufficiently serious' to justify the award of compensation would, for example, be irrelevant to the question of breach in a negligence case, relating as they do to matters such as the importance of the norm in question, its clarity and precision, the method chosen by the national authorities to implement the unlawful policy, and the steps taken by them after it became clear an infringement had occurred.[97] Indeed, so far removed are these factors from a negligence analysis

exercise or non-exercise of a 'special statutory power'); and Road Management Act 2004 (Vic), ss 39, 103 (applying the test to policy decisions of road authorities). Legislation in five Australian states also adopts the *Wednesbury* standard for breach of statutory duty cases involving public authority defendants. See further, E Carroll, '*Wednesbury* Unreasonableness as a Limit on the Civil Liability of Public Authorities' (2007) 15 *Tort Law Review* 77.

[94] See P Craig, 'The Domestic Liability of Public Authorities in Damages: Lessons from the European Community?' in J Beatson and T Tridimas (eds), *New Directions in European Public Law* (Oxford, Hart Publishing, 1998). See also M Andenas and D Fairgrieve, 'Sufficiently Serious? Judicial Restraint in Tortious Liability of Public Authorities and the European Influence' in M Andenas (ed), *English Public Law and the Common Law of Europe* (London, Key Haven, 1998).

[95] Law Com CP No 187 (n 5).

[96] *Review of the Law of Negligence: Final Report* (Commonwealth of Australia, 2002) para 10.27. See also *Precision Products (NSW) Pty Ltd v Hawkesbury CC* [2008] NSWCA 278, 74 NSWLR 102 [176]–[177] (Allsop P); M Aronson, 'Government Liability in Negligence' (2008) 32 *Melbourne University Law Review* 44, 76.

[97] See *R v Secretary of State for Transport, ex p Factortame Ltd (No 5)* [2000] 1 AC 524 (HL) 550–51 (Lord Hope); PP Craig, 'Once More Unto the Breach: Community, State and Damages Liability' (1997) 113 *LQR* 67, 73.

that it has been questioned whether the test is really a test of fault at all.[98] Nor is this disparity surprising if it is borne in mind that the EU law test is a component of a member state liability regime the primary purpose of which has been described as ensuring 'the uniform application of EU law throughout the Union'.[99]

Similar observations can be made about the Law Commission's serious fault test, which the Commission acknowledged was greatly influenced by the sufficiently serious breach test.[100] Although the definition of serious fault as conduct falling '*far* below the standard expected in the circumstances'[101] reads as a simple standard of gross negligence,[102] some of the factors which the Commission argued should be taken into account when applying the test – such as the seriousness of the harm caused, and the extent to which senior officials were implicated in the failures in question[103] – were again alien to orthodox private law approaches to the fault issue.[104] Here the difficulty was that the serious fault test was designed to straddle public and private law, since under the Commission's proposals it would have been used to determine the availability of damages not only in certain types of public authority negligence case, but in judicial review proceedings as well.[105]

[**669**] Finally, the use of the *Wednesbury* unreasonableness standard to protect public authorities from liability in recent Australian state legislation has been criticised by commentators on the grounds that it is a public law concept ill-suited to operating as a fault standard in negligence adjudication. According to Mark Aronson, for example, 'transplanting *Wednesbury* into negligence soil' gives it a 'wholly different operation', since in its original public law context it 'had nothing to say to decision-makers about being careful to avoid harming others'.[106] The central difficulty with the use of the

---

[98] Law Commission, *Administrative Redress: Public Bodies and the Citizen* (n 6) para 3.34 (comment of Professor C Harlow). See also F du Bois, 'Human Rights and the Tort Liability of Public Authorities' (2011) 127 *LQR* 588, 604.

[99] T Cornford, 'Administrative Redress: The Law Commission's Consultation Paper' [2009] *Public Law* 70, 82.

[100] Law Com CP No 187 (n 5) para 4.143. See also the factors listed as having been taken into account in the application of the serious fault test to past judicial review cases (Appendix C, note 4), which closely mirror those taken into account in the application of the EU law test.

[101] ibid para 4.145 (emphasis in original).

[102] See text following n 176, where it is argued that this is in fact the best definition of gross negligence.

[103] Law Com CP No 187 (n 5) para 4.146, points (2) and (7).

[104] The *likely* gravity of the harm is of course a factor in an orthodox negligence analysis, but not the *actual* harm caused, which appeared to be the Commission's focus (and which is also taken into account when applying the EU law test of sufficiently serious breach).

[105] It is telling that all the Commission's examples of the test's operation were drawn from public law, and that the test provoked much more, mostly adverse, comment in relation to its proposed operation in private law (Law Com No 322 (n 7) para 2.80).

[106] Aronson (n 96) 80. See also Carroll (n 93) 87 (*Wednesbury* unreasonableness not an appropriate substitute for the standard of care in negligence, because it 'removes the concept from its context … and disregards its function within public law').

Wednesbury approach is that it was developed as a test of the rationality of a *decision*, whereas the private law standard of negligence is concerned not with whether a decision of the defendant was rational, but with whether the defendant's *conduct* created unreasonable risks of harm to others. The English courts' abandonment of the use of public law concepts in negligence was therefore a welcome development, and it would be ill-advised of Parliament to follow the Australian example of employing them as a mechanism for modifying the standard of care in public authority negligence cases.

ii. Recklessness or Wilful Misconduct

Another possibility which should be rejected is to replace the ordinary standard of reasonable care with a test of recklessness or wilful misconduct in certain contexts. Although recklessness plays an important role in English criminal law, the concept has only occasionally surfaced in our law of tort, examples being the tort of deceit, the old law on an occupier's duty towards a trespasser,[107] and the illegality limb of the tort of misfeasance in public office.[108] However, a 'wilful, wanton or reckless' standard has been extensively employed in American tort law as a condition of awarding punitive damages or watering down the causation requirement; to extend duties of care to new situations (such as liability for the sale of alcohol to an intoxicated patron); and to exclude the defence of contributory negligence.[109] Similarly, legislation in a number of Australian states protects good Samaritans from liability if they acted in good faith and without recklessness.[110] There is though little merit in such an approach, since replacing a standard of care of whatever stripe with a test of recklessness or wilful misconduct [670] substitutes for an assessment of a person's behaviour a much more difficult enquiry into the state of his mind,[111] thereby adding uncertainty and complexity to the law.

---

[107] *Dumbreck* (n 32).

[108] See K Oliphant (ed), *The Law of Tort*, 2nd edn (London, LexisNexis Butterworths, 2007) para 17.53.

[109] See *Prosser and Keeton on Torts* (n 48) 212–14; *Restatement, Second, Torts* (1977) § 501(2) (causation), § 503 (contributory negligence), § 908 (punitive damages).

[110] Civil Liability Act 1936 (SA), s 74; Civil Law (Wrongs) Act 2002 (ACT), pt 2.1; Civil Liability Act 2002 (Tas), pt 8A; Civil Liability Act 2002 (WA), s 5AD.

[111] Hence 'recklessness differs in kind from lack of care' (*Southern Portland Cement* (n 45) 642 (Lord Reid)). See further on the relationship between the two concepts, H Edgerton, 'Negligence, Inadvertence and Indifference: The Relation of Mental States to Negligence' (1926) 39 *Harvard Law Review* 849; P Cane, 'Mens Rea in Tort Law' (2000) 20 *OJLS* 533, 535–38; A Merry and A McCall Smith, *Errors, Medicine and the Law* (Cambridge, CUP, 2001) ch 5. Of course, this assumes a test of subjective recklessness (or 'conscious indifference'), but since objective recklessness (or 'non-conscious indifference') and negligence are practically indistinguishable it is difficult to see any reason to import the latter form into tort law: Cane (ibid) 553–54.

B. Subjectivising the Standard of Care

It is trite law that the standard of care in negligence is generally objective. There is, however, nothing inevitable about this objective approach. In Roman law, for example, reliance was placed on a standard of *culpa levis in concreto*, meaning the failure to use the care the particular defendant ordinarily employed in his own affairs.[112] Furthermore, we have seen that in English law the standard of care has been partly subjectivised when occupiers of land have been sued by trespassers, or in respect of nuisances they have not themselves created. This subjectivisation has manifested itself in two main ways: (1) assessing the duty to take precautions in the light of the occupier's actual – as opposed to constructive – knowledge of the risk (or of facts from which a reasonable person would identify the risk); and (2) assessing the steps the occupier ought to have taken to deal with the risk in the light of his personal circumstances, and in particular the resources on which he can draw.

The first of these methods of subjectivising the standard appears to be unobjectionable, though it will be more difficult to adduce evidence that the occupier was aware of the danger than to adduce evidence that he should have been.[113] Taking into account the occupier's personal circumstances is more controversial, however. As we have seen, this approach has already been abandoned in the context of an occupier's liability to trespassers, and it has also come under attack in the nuisance context as well. In *Abbahall Ltd v Smee*,[114] the roof of a mews property had fallen into disrepair, with the result that water was leaking into the claimant's ground-floor flat. Pursuant to a court order, the claimant entered the flat above, which was owned by the defendant, to carry out repairs. The Court of Appeal held that the defendant owed [671] the claimant a duty under the *Leakey* principle to take reasonable steps to prevent the disrepair of the roof causing damage to the claimant's property, but that in a case like this – where the roof served equally to protect both premises – the cost of such remedial action should be shared equally. Significantly, however, Munby J (who gave the only substantive judgment) also held that in a case of this type the relative means of the parties ought not to be taken into account in apportioning the cost of the work. The judge at first instance had limited the defendant's contribution to a quarter of the cost, on the ground that she was less well off than the defendant, but Munby J felt that this was both odd and impractical: odd, because it would for example follow that the claimant's share would depend on whether the defendant was idle or hard-working; and impractical,

---

[112] See WW Buckland, *Textbook of Roman Law*, 2nd edn (Cambridge, CUP, 1932) 556.

[113] This technique has been employed in Australian state legislation to limit the liability of highway authorities for nonfeasance: see, eg, Civil Liability Act 2002 (NSW), s 45(1), which requires that the authority had 'actual knowledge of the particular risk the materialisation of which resulted in the harm'.

[114] *Abbahall Ltd v Smee* [2002] EWCA Civ 1831, [2003] 1 WLR 1472.

because the respective liabilities would be difficult to assess and liable to change frequently. This latter objection to a subjective standard of care was also forcefully expressed by Lord Watson in response to the contention that in Scots law trustees were held only to a subjective standard of care. Such a rule, he said, would be 'highly inconvenient in practice' because:

> In every case where neglect of duty is imputed to a body of trustees it would necessitate an exhaustive inquiry into the private transactions of each individual member, the interest of the trustee being to shew that he was a stupid fellow, careless in money matters, and that of his opponents to prove that he was a man of superior intelligence and exceptional shrewdness.[115]

The answer to these two objections is that the duty ought only to be subjectivised a little. In the *Leakey* case, for example, Megaw LJ said that it was not contemplated that there would be 'discovery of the defendant's bank account or any detailed examination of his financial resources'.[116] Although the defendant's means were to be considered if substantial expenditure were required, and his age and physical condition if physical effort were needed, this could only 'be in the way of a broad, and not a detailed, assessment', and if this caveat were borne in mind, any difficulties were likely to be 'more theoretical than practical'.[117] Provided the degree of 'subjectivisation' is limited in this way, then it seems that this method of modifying the standard of care can provide a useful and workable mechanism for limiting the burden on potential defendants who are subject to duties of affirmative action.

A more fundamental objection to the use of a subjective standard has been made by Richard Wright. According to Wright, the [672] external exercise of freedom depends on sufficient security against interference by others with one's person and property. And the use of a subjective approach makes such security impossible, 'since the risks to which one could permissibly be exposed by others would depend on the subjective capacities of the particular others with whom one happens (often unpredictably) to interact'.[118] An objective standard is therefore required if our expectations are to be sufficiently secure. But even if this argument is accepted in general terms, it would appear not to apply in the contexts in which English law has in fact employed a subjectivised approach. After all, a trespasser can hardly complain that the risks to which he is permissibly exposed depend on the subjective capacities of the occupier with whom he 'happens to interact', since that interaction is something he has (wittingly or unwittingly) forced on the unwilling defendant, and Wright himself accepts that in this context a subjective approach is appropriate.[119] What is more, Wright's

---

[115] *Knox v Mackinnon* (1888) 15 R 83 (HL) 87.
[116] *Leakey* (n 34) 526.
[117] ibid.
[118] RW Wright, 'The Standards of Care in Negligence Law' in DG Owen (ed), *Philosophical Foundations of Tort Law* (Oxford, Clarendon Press, 1995) 258–59.
[119] ibid 265.

argument would appear not to cover omissions of the kind involved in the *Leakey* category of nuisance case, since (as Tony Honoré has pointed out) in nonfeasance cases the defendant threatens not the claimant's security so much as his expectation of improvement, a different but secondary value.[120] The import of Wright's analysis is not therefore that a subjective approach should be ruled out altogether, but that, while it may be unacceptable in most instances of positive conduct, a subjective standard of care may be peculiarly appropriate when it comes to liability for omissions.[121]

C. The Use of a Gross Negligence Standard[122]

Although the term negligence covers a multitude of sins, from momentary inadvertence to wilful disregard for the safety of others,[123] English tort law recognises only one standard of care – that of the reasonable person. At the liability stage, degrees of negligence are not distinguished, and ever since Rolfe B famously dismissed it as negligence 'with the addition of a vituperative epithet',[124] it has been orthodox stoutly to deny that gross negligence does or should play any [673] part in the civil law. A good example of this scepticism is Millett LJ's remark that 'English lawyers have always had a healthy disrespect' for the distinction between different degrees of negligence.[125] However, there are also examples of English judges defending the gross negligence concept,[126] and it has been suggested that dispensing with it was a mistake.[127]

The utility of the gross negligence concept has most recently been considered in debates on the permissible scope of trustee exemption clauses, a context

---

[120] T Honoré, 'Are Omissions Less Culpable?' in P Cane and J Stapleton (eds), *Essays for Patrick Atiyah* (Oxford, Clarendon Press, 1991) 51. Indeed, Wright himself goes on to argue that in nonfeasance cases a subjective approach may not only be permitted, but required: Wright (n 118) 274 (discussing a duty to rescue).

[121] See also R Stevens, *Torts and Rights* (Oxford, OUP, 2007) 124.

[122] SD Elliott, 'Degrees of Negligence' (1933) *Southern California Law Review* 92; CA Wright, 'Gross Negligence' (1983) 33 *University of Toronto Law Journal* 184 (written in 1927).

[123] A Tunc, 'Fault: A Common Name for Different Misdeeds' (1974) 49 *Tulane Law Review* 279. For an illuminating account of the different levels of negligent behaviour that can be found in a medical context, see Merry and McCall Smith (n 111).

[124] *Wilson v Brett* (1843) 11 M & W 113, 116; 152 ER 737, 739.

[125] *Armitage v Nurse* [1998] Ch 241 (CA) 254. See also *Pentecost v London District Auditor* [1951] 2 KB 759 (KBD) 764 (Lynskey J), 766–67 (Lord Goddard CJ); *Herrington v British Railways Board* [1971] 2 QB 107 (CA) 125 (Salmon LJ); *Southern Portland Cement* (n 45) 642 (Lord Reid); *Palmer v Tees HA* [1999] Lloyd's Rep Med 351 (CA) 356 (Stuart-Smith LJ); *Van Colle v CC of Hertfordshire Police* [2008] UKHL 50, [2009] 1 AC 225 [109] (Lord Carswell).

[126] See, eg, *Giblin v McMullen* (1868) LR 2 PC 317 (PC) 336 (Lord Chelmsford).

[127] T Weir, *An Introduction to Tort Law*, 2nd edn (Oxford, OUP, 2015) 67–68. Other defenders of gross negligence include OW Holmes, *The Common Law* (Boston, Little, Brown, 1881) 120 (though deprecating its use in jury trials), and NE Palmer (ed), *Palmer on Bailment*, 3rd edn (London, Sweet & Maxwell, 2009) para 10-025. For academic criticism of the concept, see Elliott (n 122), Wright (n 122) and F Green, 'High Care and Gross Negligence' (1928) 62 *American Law Review* 545.

in which some jurisdictions draw a distinction between ordinary negligence by a trustee, which is excludable, and gross negligence, which is not. In its report on trustee exemption clauses the Law Commission rejected the use of this distinction on certainty grounds,[128] but the Trust Law Committee defended the concept, arguing that there was 'a long and respectable line of authority ... dealing with the concept of gross negligence in the common law, and distinguishing it from ordinary negligence',[129] and the Scottish Law Commission concluded in its discussion paper on *Breach of Trust* that gross negligence was a 'workable concept',[130] and recommended its continued use in this context in Scottish law. According to the Scottish Law Commission:

> The courts in Scotland have been using gross negligence in the field of trust law for well over a century without it having caused difficulties ... It has to be acknowledged that it is impossible to draw a hard and fast line between negligence and gross negligence, but difficulties in establishing boundaries occur throughout the law.[131]

In this part of the article it will be argued that gross negligence is a meaningful concept which could usefully be employed in negligence law where for some reason a modified standard of care is considered desirable. The discussion is divided into three sections, which consider (1) the nineteenth-century reaction against the use of gross negligence in English tort law; (2) the way that gross negligence is currently [674] employed in other areas of English law, and in the law of other jurisdictions; and (3) the definition of gross negligence.

i. The Nineteenth-Century Reaction Against the Use of Gross Negligence in English Tort Law

Gross negligence (or *crassa negligentia*) is generally thought to have come to English law from Roman law via Bracton[132] and the law of bailment, where it was used to minimise the obligations of gratuitous bailees.[133] The concept was then extended to other gratuitous undertakings, so that, for example, it came to

---

[128] Law Commission, *Trustee Exemption Clauses* (Law Com No 301, 2006) paras A.43–A.48.
[129] Trust Law Committee, *Trustee Exemption Clauses* (1999) para 2.8.
[130] Scottish Law Commission, *Breach of Trust* (Scot Law Com DP No 123, 2003) para 3.30.
[131] ibid.
[132] Bracton lib 3, c 2, 99b. Though Elliott points out that Bracton did not refer in terms either to gross negligence, or to its Roman equivalent, *culpa lata*: Elliott (n 122) 107.
[133] *Coggs v Barnard* (1703) 2 Ld Raym 909, 92 ER 107; Sir W Jones, *An Essay on the Law of Bailments* (London, J Nichols, 1781); J Story, *Commentaries on the Law of Bailments* (Cambridge, Mass, Hilliard and Brown, 1832). There are suggestions of a threefold classification of negligence (gross, ordinary and slight) in *Coggs v Barnard*, though it was only in Jones's *Essay* that these three degrees of fault were clearly articulated. Jones claimed that Roman law recognised the same three degrees of negligence – *culpa lata*, *culpa levis*, and *culpa levissima* – but it is now generally accepted that *culpa levissima* was not a separate standard: Elliott (n 122) 100. On the bailment angle generally, see Elliott (n 122) 107–12; D Ibbetson, '"The Law of Business Rome": Foundations of the Anglo-American Tort of Negligence' [1999] *CLP* 74, 80–84; and J Getzler, 'Duty of Care' in P Birks and A Pretto (eds), *Breach of Trust* (Oxford, Hart Publishing, 2002) 45–50.

determine the personal liability of charitable trustees.[134] The language of gross negligence was also employed in a number of other contexts, though in some it may have meant no more than the failure to take reasonable care.[135] Examples included the liability of a lawyer to his client, or of a doctor to his patient; whether the holder of a bill of exchange would be affected by a defect in the bill; and whether a tenant was barred from relief against forfeiture.[136] Towards the middle of the nineteenth century, however, the courts began to turn against gross negligence. Influential judicial criticism of the concept came in 1842, when Denman CJ doubted whether any intelligible distinction existed between gross and ordinary negligence,[137] and – famously – from Rolfe B a year later.[138] There was also a decisive move against gross negligence on the ground.[139] In 1856, for example, the rule that an innkeeper was liable for the loss of a guest's property unless he could establish gross negligence on the guest's part was abolished, with an ordinary negligence standard being employed instead.[140] As far as tort law was [675] concerned, the killer blow came in the same year, with Alderson B's classic definition of negligence as 'the omission to do something which a reasonable man, guided upon those considerations which ordinarily regulate the conduct of human affairs, would do, or doing something which a prudent and reasonable man would not do'.[141] The advent of the reasonable man condemned gross negligence to an (at best) marginal role in the modern law of obligations.[142]

It would however be a mistake to regard the nineteenth-century reaction against gross negligence as evidence that the concept lacks validity or utility, since the origins of that reaction lay elsewhere.[143] First, gross negligence

---

[134] *Charitable Corporation v Sutton* (1742) 2 Atk 400, 405 406; 26 ER 642, 644–45 (Lord Hardwicke LC). Similarly, in Roman law a person who did not benefit from the transaction was liable only for *dolus* (intentional conduct) or, according to some texts, *culpa lata*: Buckland (n 112) 556.

[135] See Getzler (n 133) 53–57, who argues that gross negligence at times referred to the breach of a specifically defined duty – such as falling below the standard of one's profession or calling – and that this was 'only distantly connected to the plainer meaning of "great" or "exorbitant" negligence'.

[136] See Ibbetson, 'The Law of Business Rome' (n 133) 92–95.

[137] *Hinton v Dibbin* (1842) 2 QB 646, 661; 114 ER 253, 258.

[138] See n 124.

[139] See Ibbetson, 'The Law of Business Rome' (n 133) 97–98.

[140] *Cashill v Wright* (1856) 6 El & Bl 891, 119 ER 1096.

[141] *Blyth* (n 1) 784.

[142] Gross negligence lingered on in the law of bailment, but even there it has now been almost completely abandoned in England, though perhaps not yet in Australia: see *Palmer on Bailment* (n 127) para 10-008. (I say 'almost completely' because of the suggestion that an involuntary bailee of uncollected goods may be liable for damage to them only if grossly negligent: *JJD SA v Avon Tyres Ltd* (CA, 23 February 2000) [54]–[55] (Lord Bingham of Cornhill LCJ)). In many, if not most, US jurisdictions a gross negligence standard is still applied in cases where the bailment was gratuitous, and for the sole benefit of the bailor: *Prosser and Keeton on Torts* (n 48) 210n.

[143] In addition to the three causes of the decline of gross negligence identified here, Ibbetson has also argued that the common law's 'substantial if ragged abandonment' of degrees of negligence may have been influenced by a similar trend in continental European practice at the time, coupled with revisionist analysis of the phenomenon's Roman law roots: Ibbetson, 'The Law of Business Rome' (n 133) 99–109.

was often used to protect those who performed services gratuitously[144] (on the basis that the recipient of such a service could not reasonably expect the same level of care as one who had paid), but the historical trend was then – and has since been – away from special treatment of this kind.[145] Secondly, gross negligence may have fallen into disfavour because, up until the mid-nineteenth century, it was rather chameleonic.[146] This meant that it was not always clear what the term meant in a particular context, so that while at times it seems in effect to have been a synonym for fraud, recklessness or wilful default, at others it suggested a subjective standard of care, or was indistinguishable from ordinary negligence.[147] And finally, in the early nineteenth century gross negligence was used somewhat disingenuously as a way of circumventing exclusion clauses in contracts of carriage and such like: it was held that clauses excluding liability for negligence could not have been intended to cover gross negligence, but then when it came to instructing the jury, gross negligence was described as [676] the failure to take reasonable care.[148] Although an effective way of neutralising exclusions of liability, this ruse devalued gross negligence and called its distinctiveness into question – it is noteworthy, for example, that *Hinton v Dibbin*,[149] the case in which Denman CJ questioned whether there was any intelligible distinction between gross and ordinary negligence, was a case of this kind.

ii. Current Usage of Gross Negligence and Similar Concepts

Although gross negligence has now been almost completely abandoned by the English law of tort,[150] gross negligence and related concepts are commonly employed in other areas of English law, and in the tort law of other jurisdictions. This widespread reliance on the distinction between gross and ordinary negligence would suggest that the distinction is perfectly intelligible, and that its application in practice is not particularly problematic. Moreover, it lends support to the contention that one size does not invariably fit all, and that there

---

[144] 'Throughout its checkered career, gross negligence under one form or another has been a series of attempts to express more or less coherently an idea of less care in gratuitous undertakings' (Wright (n 122) 213).

[145] *Palmer on Bailment* (n 127) para 10–010.

[146] See Ibbetson, 'The Law of Business Rome' (n 133) 94 ('the range of meanings was positively anarchic').

[147] ibid 94–95; Wright (n 122) passim. See also *Palmer on Bailment* (n 127) para 10-010 for examples from the law of bailment; and WR Cornish et al, *The Oxford History of the Laws of England: Volume XII* (Oxford, OUP, 2010) 916 (attorneys' liability). Getzler has argued that sometimes judges used a gross negligence test to 'guide juries towards a desired finding of fact' (Getzler (n 133) 51).

[148] MJ Prichard, *Scott v Shepherd (1773) and the Emergence of the Tort of Negligence* (London, Selden Society, 1976) 29–30. See also Wright (n 122) 230–33; Cornish et al (n 147) 914–15.

[149] *Hinton v Dibbin* (1842) 2 QB 646, 114 ER 253.

[150] Though it remains the case that damages are available for the wrongful arrest of a vessel only if there was bad faith or gross negligence (see, eg, *The Kommunar (No 3)* [1997] 1 Lloyd's Rep 22 (QBD)).

are contexts where a gross negligence standard can usefully provide additional flexibility.

In English criminal law, it is well established that manslaughter can be committed by gross negligence,[151] and the concept is used (in effect) to distinguish dangerous driving from the lesser offence of careless driving.[152] [677] Gross negligence is also a central pillar of the offence of corporate manslaughter.[153] Nor is our criminal law unusual in its reliance on the concept; New Zealand has, for example, moved from a position in which certain types of manslaughter case were governed by an ordinary negligence standard to an across-the-board test of gross negligence.[154] What is more, criminal lawyers seem perfectly comfortable with the concept. According to a leading textbook:

> If negligence is regarded as non-attainment of a required standard of conduct then it is clear that there are degrees of it. One person may fall just short of the required standard, another may fall far short.[155]

Gross negligence is also widely used in other areas of English law. In the law of mortgages, for example, a legal mortgagee will be postponed on the ground of his conduct only if he is guilty of fraud or such gross negligence that it would be unjust to deprive a prior equitable incumbrancer of his priority.[156] And in *Re D' Jan of London Ltd*,[157] it was held that a director of an insolvent company who had negligently signed an insurance proposal without reading it should be relieved of full liability to compensate the company for its resultant loss because his negligence had not been gross. Gross negligence is also frequently used to limit the scope of exclusions of liability. Contract parties often stipulate that an exclusion clause does not cover gross negligence,[158] for example, and on one view, trustees used to lose the protection of exemption clauses if they were grossly negligent[159] (this is still the case in many

---

[151] See, eg, *R v Adomako* [1995] 1 AC 171 (HL).

[152] Road Traffic Act 1988, s 2A(1) (a person drives dangerously if, inter alia, 'the way he drives falls far below what would be expected of a competent and careful driver').

[153] See the Corporate Manslaughter and Corporate Homicide Act 2007, s 1(1)(b).

[154] Crimes Amendment Act 1997 (NZ), inserting s 150A into the Crimes Act 1961 (NZ).

[155] D Ormerod, *Smith & Hogan's Criminal Law*, 13th edn (Oxford, OUP, 2011) 153. For a defence of the use of a gross negligence standard in crimes *mala in se*, see J Horder, 'Gross Negligence and Criminal Culpability' (1997) 47 *University of Toronto Law Journal* 495.

[156] *Northern Counties of England Fire Insurance Co v Whipp* (1884) 26 Ch D 482 (CA).

[157] *Re D' Jan of London Ltd* [1994] 1 BCLC 561 (Ch D).

[158] See, eg, the extended discussion of gross negligence in this context in *The Hellespont Ardent* [1997] 2 Lloyd's Rep 547 (QBD), and *Camarata Property Inc v Credit Suisse Securities (Europe) Ltd* [2011] EWHC 479 (Comm), [2011] 2 BCLC 54, where the terms of an agreement to provide investment advice limited liability to cases where the adviser was grossly negligent.

[159] See P Matthews, 'The Efficacy of Trustee Exemption Clauses in English Law' [1989] *Conveyancer* 42 and (more tentatively) Law Commission, *Fiduciary Duties and Regulatory Rules* (Law Com CP No 124, 1992) para 3.3.41; *Spread Trustee Co Ltd v Hutcheson* [2011] UKPC 13, [2012] 2 AC 194 [137] (Lady Hale). cf *Armitage* (n 125); *Spread Trustee* [57] (Lord Clarke), [106] (Lord Mance). The Trustee Act 2000, sch 1, para 7 now permits any exclusion of the trustee's duty of care, no matter how sweeping.

other jurisdictions,[160] including Scotland[161]). These examples show that, as Lord Clarke remarked in a recent Privy Council decision on trustee exemption clauses, English law does recognise 'the difference in legal principle between negligence and gross negligence'.[162]

Nor is English law alone in this, for (as Tony Weir pointed out) 'other systems operate quite nicely' with the gross negligence concept.[163] In the United States, for example, gross negligence has been used to limit the liability of emergency vehicle operators, public bodies such as parole boards, volunteer athletic coaches and occupiers vis-à-vis recreational users of their land,[164] and in the past both US and Canadian legislation frequently dictated that non-paying passengers could only sue car drivers if they established gross negligence or some other form of aggravated misconduct,[165] though the reasoning behind [678] these 'automobile guest statutes' has fallen out of favour, and most such legislation has now been repealed. French law has also long recognised the distinction between gross and ordinary fault. Under the *Loi* Badinter governing road traffic accidents, for example, a car driver can plead the defence of victim fault against a non-driver victim only if the fault was inexcusable (*faute inexcusable*).[166] Meanwhile, the French administrative courts have employed a standard of grave fault (*faute lourde*) to shield public authorities engaged in particularly complex, difficult or sensitive tasks, such as police activities and the exercise of regulatory functions,[167] and, although there has been a decline in the use of *faute lourde* in recent years, the move to ordinary fault (*faute simple*) appears mainly to have occurred in contexts – such as taxation, and the emergency and postal services – where special protection was arguably never appropriate in the first place.[168] There is extensive reliance on gross negligence in German civil law as well. If, for example, an object gratuitously given or lent to another causes him injury, the donor is liable only for

---

[160] See J Mowbray et al, *Lewin on Trusts*, 18th edn (London, Sweet & Maxwell, 2008) para 39-124.

[161] See Scottish Law Commission, *Breach of Trust* (Scot Law Com DP No 123, 2003) paras 3.13–3.16. See also Trusts (Guernsey) Law 1989, s 34(7); Trusts (Jersey) Law 1984, art 26(9).

[162] *Spread Trustee* (n 159) [51].

[163] Weir (n 127) 68.

[164] DB Dobbs, *The Law of Torts* (St Paul, Minn, West Publishing, 2000) 350. On the proliferation of 'recreational use' statutes, see *Prosser and Keeton on Torts* (n 48) 415–16, and on degrees of care in US tort law more generally, see FV Harper, F James and OS Gray, *Harper, James and Gray on Torts*, 3rd edn (New York, Aspen Publishers, 2006) vol 3, paras 16.13–16.15.

[165] US: *Prosser and Keeton on Torts* (n 48) 215–17; *Harper, James and Gray on Torts* (n 164) vol 3, para 16.15. Canada: WG MacArthur, 'Gross Negligence and the Guest Passenger' (1938) 60 *Canadian Bar Review* 47; JR Singleton, 'Gross Negligence and the Guest Passenger' (1973) 11 *Alberta Law Review* 165.

[166] W van Gerven, J Lever and P Larouche, *Cases, Materials and Text on National, Supranational and International Tort Law* (Oxford, Hart Publishing, 2000) 591.

[167] See D Fairgrieve, *State Liability in Tort: A Comparative Law Study* (Oxford, OUP, 2003) 106–20.

[168] On the decline of *faute lourde*, see ibid 117–18.

wilful default or gross negligence,[169] while where an employee causes loss in the course of his employment, this is generally apportioned between employer and employee if the worker's fault was 'normal', but borne entirely by the worker in the case of gross negligence.[170] Other civil law countries also rely on the concept.[171] In Austria, for example, a wrongdoer guilty of gross negligence may have to pay more extensive compensation than one who is not,[172] and the presence of gross negligence or intention gives rise to action where emotional disturbance falling short of damage to health is caused by the death of a close relative,[173] while in Spain parents are jointly and severally liable for damage they cause to the property of a minor child if they acted intentionally or were grossly negligent.[174]

iii. Defining Gross Negligence

The simpler the definition of gross negligence, the better, particularly since historically its meaning was notoriously elusive.[175] The most [679] straight-forward meaning that can be attached to the concept is 'conduct that falls far below the standard of the reasonable person'. This is in effect the test laid down for the offence of corporate manslaughter,[176] and was also the definition given for the concept of 'serious fault' in the Law Commission's consultation paper on *Administrative Redress*.[177] Nor should this test pose great problems in practice, for it has been said to be 'no more difficult to say whether a person fell far below the acceptable standard than whether he fell below it at all'.[178] Another way of encapsulating the same idea is to say that there must have been a 'very marked' or 'major' departure from the expected standard of care.[179]

---

[169] §§ 521, 599 BGB.

[170] See BS Markesinis and H Unberath, *The German Law of Torts*, 4th edn (Oxford, Hart Publishing, 2002) 707–708.

[171] For an overview, see C von Bar, *The Common European Law of Torts* (Oxford, OUP, 2000) vol 2, paras 242–43. Exemption clauses are generally not valid where the harm is caused intentionally or through gross negligence, for example, and where one party (such as an employer or the State) has been held liable for the acts of another (such as an employee or agent), the right of the former to recoup its losses from the latter frequently depends on proof of intention or gross negligence.

[172] § 1324 ABGB.

[173] OGH 16 May 2001, ZVR 2001/73.

[174] Civil Code, art 168.2.

[175] For some of its different meanings, see Getzler (n 133) 50–57.

[176] Corporate Manslaughter and Corporate Homicide Act 2007, s 1(4)(b). See also the definition of dangerous driving in section 2A(1) of the Road Traffic Act 1988.

[177] Law Com CP No 187 (n 5) para 4.145.

[178] Weir (n 127) 68.

[179] For 'very marked', see, eg, *McCulloch v Murray* [1942] SCR 141 (SCC) 145 (Duff CJ); for 'major', see, eg, the offence of gross negligence manslaughter as defined in the Crimes Act 1961 (NZ), s 150A.

Two further points should be made on the definition issue. The first is that it is not the fact that risk-taking is conscious that distinguishes gross negligence from ordinary negligence. Hence, although there may be an overlap between the two, gross negligence is not to be equated with recklessness, since recklessness is a state of mind, while negligence (of any kind) is a failure to comply with a particular standard of conduct. Similarly, because '[g]ross negligence, like negligence not so qualified, may be committed in good faith and, therefore, without dishonesty or wilfulness',[180] it is not to be equated with fraud or wilful misconduct. The difference between negligence and gross negligence is one of degree, not kind.[181] And the second point is that an alternative workable test of gross negligence would focus not on the degree of the departure from the reasonable person standard, but on whether it was a clear or obvious departure. Some of the definitions of the French *faute lourde* standard have this flavour to them, referring to fault that is 'flagrant', or which 'jumps out at you',[182] and we have seen that this kind of language can also be found in some of the recent English case law concerning the liability of public authorities.[183] A test along these lines might be particularly appealing where there are overkill concerns, to the extent that this objection to negligence liability is predicated on potential defendants misreading the standard of care required of them.[184] **[680]**

IV. WHEN AND WHY MIGHT THE USE OF A MODIFIED STANDARD OF CARE BE DESIRABLE?

The final issue to be considered is when and why the use of a modified standard of care might be desirable. My primary concern here is with situations in which for some reason it is felt to be inappropriate to recognise a duty of care accompanied by the usual objective standard of care of the reasonable person, and where a choice must therefore be made between refusing to impose a duty of care at all (or imposing a duty only in certain limited circumstances), and imposing a duty, but modifying the standard of care. My analysis of this issue is divided into two parts. First I identify some general advantages and disadvantages of these two possible responses to liability concerns, and then I consider the choice between the two approaches in particular types of case (as well as touching upon some other possible uses of a modified standard of care).

---

[180] *Spread Trustee* (n 159) [117] (Sir Robin Auld). See also [51] (Lord Clarke) ('To describe negligence as gross does not change its nature so as to make it fraudulent or wilful misconduct').
[181] ibid [117] (Sir Robin Auld).
[182] See Fairgrieve (n 167) 113–14.
[183] Text to n 70.
[184] See text following n 215.

A. General Advantages and Disadvantages of the Two Approaches

Although I have argued elsewhere that the duty of care concept has outlived its usefulness and should now be done away with,[185] it would be foolish not to acknowledge that the denial of a duty of care does offer some advantages over the recognition of a duty accompanied by a modification of the standard of care. Because notional duty – the question of whether there is a rule of law that either allows or bars recovery in this category of case – is by definition a question of law, no-duty (or restricted-duty) rules are binding precedents, which should enable appellate courts to exercise effective control over the boundaries of negligence liability and provide potential litigants and lower court judges with clear guidance as to where those boundaries lie. By contrast, breach of duty is of course a question of fact, and it follows that decisions on breach do not create precedents, and provide no more than useful guidance to judges in future cases.[186] Furthermore, even though juries in negligence cases are long gone, breach is still essentially a 'jury' question, 'a matter of impression resulting from the consideration and weighing-up of lots of different factors'.[187] The result is that recognising a duty but applying a modified standard of care inevitably results in less certainty than a bright-line no-duty rule.[188]

[681] The other side of the coin, however, is that the discretionary and particularistic nature of the breach inquiry means that lowering the standard of care may produce a more proportionate response to the liability concern in question than a blunt no-duty rule. We might note, for example, the criticisms levelled at English negligence law in *Osman v United Kingdom*,[189] where the European Court of Human Rights expressed its concern that the no-duty rule under scrutiny applied across the board, without reference either to the gravity of the harm suffered by the claimant or to the gravity of the defendant's alleged negligence:

> In [the Court's] view, it must be open to a domestic court to have regard to the presence of other public interest considerations which pull in the opposite direction to the application of the [no-duty] rule. Failing this, there will be no distinction made between degrees of negligence or of harm suffered or any consideration of the justice of a particular case.[190]

---

[185] D Nolan, 'Deconstructing the Duty of Care' (2013) 129 *LQR* 558.

[186] *Qualcast (Wolverhampton) Ltd v Haynes* [1959] AC 743 (HL) is the leading authority.

[187] Weir (n 127) 55.

[188] Hence the criticism of the shift of focus from duty to breach in the occupiers' liability context on the grounds that it made the outcome of disputes less predictable and would therefore lead to an increase in litigation: JC Smith and P Burns, '*Donoghue v Stevenson*: The Not So Golden Anniversary' (1983) 46 *MLR* 147, 162.

[189] *Osman v United Kingdom* [1999] 1 FLR 193 (ECtHR).

[190] ibid 232–33.

The failure of no-duty rules to take any account of the gravity of the alleged negligence was also emphasised in the reports of the European Commission of Human Rights in *Z v United Kingdom* and *TP and KM v United Kingdom*. Referring this time to the no-duty rule laid down by the House of Lords in the child abuse context,[191] the Commission acknowledged that the exclusionary rule furthered a legitimate aim, but was not satisfied that it amounted to a proportionate response, noting that it 'gave no consideration to the seriousness or otherwise of the damage or the nature or degree of the negligence alleged'.[192]

In the past, an additional advantage of the no-duty route was that it enabled the defendant to seek to dispose of a claim on a strike-out application, or as a preliminary issue, and hence to dispose of an unmeritorious claim on the pleadings, and without the cost and inconvenience of a trial. This advantage has however been undermined by two developments at the procedural level. The first is that the courts in at least some duty cases have discouraged the use of these mechanisms, and insisted that where the law is less than crystal clear, the duty question should generally be answered in the light of the actual facts as revealed at trial. In *S v Gloucestershire CC*, for example, May LJ said that in difficult duty cases, it 'will often not be possible to determine by an abstract inquiry which does not address the detailed facts of a [682] particular case that a claim in negligence is bound to fail',[193] while according to Lord Browne-Wilkinson in *Barrett v Enfield LBC*:

> [I]n an area of the law which [is] uncertain and developing ... it is not normally appropriate to strike out. In my judgment it is of great importance that such development should be on the basis of actual facts found at trial not on hypothetical facts assumed (possibly wrongly) to be true for the purpose of the strike out.[194]

The second relevant development was the passage of the Civil Procedure Rules 1998 (CPR). For whereas under the old rules the defendant had to show on a striking out application that the claim must plainly fail as a matter of law, the summary judgment procedure under CPR 24.2 is not so limited, and it follows that a defendant can apply for summary judgment on a question of fact, such as breach of duty.[195] Moreover, because the parties are now able to

---

[191] *X (minors)* (n 52).

[192] *Z v United Kingdom* (1999) 28 EHRR CD 65 (ECommHR) [114]; *TP and KM v United Kingdom* [2001] ECHR 332 (ECommHR) [91].

[193] *S* (n 66) 338.

[194] *Barrett* (n 56) 557–58. See also the remarks of Lord Slynn in *Barrett* at 574–75, in *Waters v Commissioner of Police of the Metropolis* [2000] 1 WLR 1607 (HL) at 1613–14, and in *W v Essex CC* [2001] 2 AC 592 (HL) at 598; *Godden v Kent & Medway SHA* [2004] EWHC 1629 (QB), [2004] Lloyd's Rep Med 521; and *Brooks v Metropolitan Police Commissioner* [2005] UKHL 24, [2005] 1 WLR 1495 [3] (Lord Bingham). *cf Kent v Griffiths* [2001] QB 36 (CA) 51 (Lord Woolf) (if the legal position is clear, and an investigation of the facts would provide no assistance, then courts should still dismiss claims which have no real prospect of success).

[195] CPR 24.2. Summary judgment will be given against a party only if the court considers that that party has no real prospect of succeeding, and there is no compelling reason why the matter should

bring forward evidence in preliminary proceedings of this kind,[196] the court may well be in a position to decide the breach issue on such an application. The possibilities thrown up by the CPR are illustrated by the *S v Gloucestershire CC* case,[197] where the two appeals concerned allegations that the claimants had been sexually abused by foster parents assigned to them by the defendant local authorities. At first instance, both claims were struck out as disclosing no cause of action, and the defendants were asking the Court of Appeal either to uphold those decisions, or to determine the appeals as applications for summary judgment under CPR 24.2. On the summary judgment issue, the court held that while one of the claims should proceed to trial, in the other summary judgment should be given against the claimant, since the evidence produced by the local authority – which consisted of contemporary notes from the relevant social services files – indicated that she had no real prospect of establishing negligence. Although this decision shows how the current procedural regime reduces the advantages offered by the use of [683] no-duty rules to limit liability, of course it remains true that even if a modified standard of care is employed many cases will still need to proceed to trial on breach, so that no-duty rules will continue to provide defendants like public authorities with greater security than a modified standard of care.[198] The question, however, is whether the greater certainty offered by blanket prohibitions justifies excluding liability in even the most egregious instances of negligence.

B. The Choice Between the Two Approaches in Particular Types of Case

Turning to the choice between the two approaches in particular types of case, I will first consider the areas in which a varied standard of care may already have been used in English negligence law, and then consider whether there are other contexts where a modified standard might usefully be employed. Once again, the assumption underlying the analysis is that the alternative to modifying the standard of care is either a no-duty or a restricted-duty rule.

i. Areas Where a Modified Standard of Care May Already Have Been Used

We have seen that there are three areas where a modified standard of care may already have been used in English negligence law: occupiers' liability, the liability

---

be disposed of at a trial. Although summary judgment procedures pre-date the CPR, they were previously available only to claimants.

[196] CPR 24.5. The applicant can rely on any written evidence contained in her statement of case or application notice, or in a witness statement, but oral evidence cannot be adduced unless the court allows it (CPR 32.6).

[197] *S* (n 66).

[198] See Booth and Squires (n 54) para 4.94.

of public authorities, and liability for deliberate third party acts. The use of a [684] subjectivised standard in the occupiers' liability context has been justified on the ground that the obligations in question are not voluntarily incurred, but thrust upon the defendant against his will.[199] And, although there are admittedly some difficulties with the use of a subjective standard of care,[200] it does seem to be a reasonable response to the peculiarly coercive nature of positive obligations, particularly if these require expenditure on the defendant's part.[201] In particular, the otherwise reasonable argument that a person who cannot afford to take necessary precautions against the risks of an activity should not engage in that activity[202] carries no weight where the defendant is sued for *failing to do* something, provided there was no earlier assumption of responsibility on his part. It follows that if it were considered desirable to extend omissions liability – so as, for example, to impose a general duty to rescue – then the use of a reduced or subjectivised standard of care would be an obvious way of softening the blow.[203]

In the public authority liability context, the abandonment of a public law filter which amounted to a modified standard of care but notionally operated at the duty stage was described by Duncan Fairgrieve as a 'welcomed rationalization of this area of law'.[204] This seems right. While there may have been some practical advantages in categorising what was effectively a breach issue as one of duty under the old procedural regime, it was difficult to see any rationale for it once a claim could be disposed of at a preliminary stage on breach grounds. As for ruling out a duty of care on the ground that the decision in question was a difficult and delicate one, this was surely a case of using a sledgehammer to crack a nut, and taking account of the difficulty and sensitivity of the decisions public bodies must make at the breach stage seems a more proportionate response to the problem. Of course, it may be questioned whether any special protection is required at all in this context, but on the assumption that it is, it

---

[199] See *Goldman v Hargrave* (n 35) 663 (Lord Wilberforce); *Herrington* (n 33) 898–99 (Lord Reid), 936 (Lord Diplock); *Southern Portland Cement* (n 45) 642 (Lord Reid).

[200] See text following n 113.

[201] See *Stovin v Wise (Norfolk CC, third party)* [1996] AC 923 (HL) 933 (Lord Nicholls); J Kortmann, *Altruism in Private Law: Liability for Nonfeasance and Negotiorum Gestio* (Oxford, OUP, 2005) 77.

[202] Cane, *The Anatomy of Tort Law* (n 23) 43.

[203] See Bowman and Bailey (n 68) 303. In France, where criminal sanctions attach to those who fail to assist others, the standard is set very low: see FH Lawson and BS Markesinis, *Tortious Liability for Unintentional Harm in the Common Law and the Civil Law* (Cambridge, CUP, 1982) vol 1, 74–75.

[204] Fairgrieve (n 167) 50. See also BS Markesinis et al, *Tortious Liability of Statutory Bodies* (Oxford, Hart Publishing, 1999) 121; *Crimmins v Stevedoring Industry Financing Committee* (1999) 200 CLR 1 (HCA) [87] (McHugh J); and SH Bailey and MJ Bowman, 'Public Authority Negligence Revisited' [2000] *CLJ* 85, 130 (by acknowledging that the discretionary nature of the decision-making in question should rightly be taken into account at the breach stage, Lord Hutton in *Barrett* provided 'clear testimony to the flexibility and sophistication of the breach of duty mechanism').

seems preferable that it take the form of a modified standard of care operating at the breach stage, rather than no-duty or restricted-duty rules.

Finally, there is the difficult question of liability for the consequences of deliberate third party conduct. We have seen that some judges have preferred to deal with this issue by means of a notional duty analysis, while others have recognised a duty, but apparently varied the standard of care. Commentators also disagree as to which approach is preferable.[205] The arguments seem evenly balanced. In favour of duty restrictions is the fact that this is an area where duty is capable of operating at a categorical level, with recognised exceptions to a general no-duty rule,[206] and so this approach is likely to provide better guidance to potential litigants than use of the breach mechanism. Furthermore, there is a risk that under a breach approach, judges reluctant to impose liability will simply conclude (rightly or wrongly) that the foreseeability of the third party behaviour was very low, in which case a set of clear [685] duty limits would not in practice lead to different outcomes but would offer advantages in terms of efficiency and transparency. On the other hand, the breach approach would as ever offer greater flexibility and a more fact-sensitive approach in an area which has proved resistant to attempts at generalisation.

ii. Other Contexts Where a Modified Standard of Care Could Usefully be Employed

There are also other contexts in which the technique of lowering the standard of care could usefully be employed. At a general level, we might think for example of the uses to which the gross negligence concept is put in the tort law of other jurisdictions. Hence, a modified standard of care could be employed in cases where good Samaritans and volunteers are sued for negligence; to govern the right of redress of an employer against an employee for whom the employer is vicariously liable; and to determine the availability of certain types of damages, or of damages for certain types of harm. And rather than the all-or-nothing approach which currently governs the exclusion of liability for negligence causing personal injury and death under section 2(1) of the Unfair Contract Terms Act 1977 (*no exclusion* of business liability; *no limit* on exclusion of non-business liability), a gross negligence standard could be used as part of a more nuanced approach, or alternatively the exclusion of liability for gross negligence could simply be made impermissible in all cases.

There are at least three further examples of liability concerns which could be met with a modified standard of care. The first is the concern that recognition

---

[205] Compare J Stapleton, 'Duty of Care: Peripheral Parties and Alternative Opportunities for Deterrence' (1995) 111 *LQR* 301, favouring duty limits, and Howarth, 'My Brother's Keeper?' (n 86) favouring a breach approach.

[206] Indeed, Lord Goff's analysis in *Smith v Littlewoods* is a classic example of this kind of duty reasoning.

of a duty of care would create an undesirable conflict of interest, as where it is argued that a public authority's performance of its statutory child protection duties might be undermined by a duty of care owed to those it wrongly accuses of abuse.[207] Elizabeth Handley has argued that rather than simply refusing to recognise a duty of care in such situations, the courts should consider the use of a modified standard of care, which would ensure that at least the 'more egregious cases' could be dealt with.[208] Similarly, in his dissenting speech in one of the leading cases on the issue, Lord Bingham favoured the imposition of a duty of care, but with the caveat that liability would require proof of 'a very clear departure from ordinary standards of skill and care',[209] a restriction seemingly intended to be analogous [**686**] to the French *faute lourde* standard.[210] On the other hand, in *Lawrence v Pembrokeshire CC*, Auld LJ specifically rejected the possibility of using breach rather than duty to deal with cases of this kind on the grounds that it would put

> to one side the mischief at which the … exclusion of a general duty of care … is based, namely the potential conflict of interests … creating the imperative, whilst the truth is still unknown, for social workers to do all that they reasonably can and should to secure the welfare of the child.[211]

While it seems clear, therefore, that the recognition of a duty of care in cases of this kind would be less inhibiting if tempered by the application of a standard of gross negligence or the like, it may be that the welfare of the suspected victim is so paramount a consideration that no degree of inhibition can be countenanced at all.

The second liability concern which could be met with a modified standard of care is the so-called 'overkill' argument, that is to say the argument – deployed most frequently to protect public authorities – that the threat of liability may lead potential defendants to go about their activities in an excessively cautious (or 'defensive') manner, or even to curtail them altogether.[212] If we assume that this is a valid concern, then whether varying the standard of care is an appropriate response to it depends on why it is that potential defendants are over-deterred in this way. If the reason is that they simply do not want to have to fight negligence claims at all, because of the cost and trouble of doing so, then a modified standard of care is a less effective response to the concern than a no-duty rule,

---

[207] JD (n 4). On the conflict of interest argument more generally, see Oliphant (n 108) para 17.22.

[208] E Handley, '*Sullivan v Moody*: Foreseeability of Injury is Not Enough to Found a Duty of Care in Negligence – But Should It Be?' (2003) 11 *Torts Law Journal* 1, 9. Another commentator apparently sympathetic to such an approach is S Bailey, 'Public Authority Liability in Negligence: The Continued Search for Coherence' (2006) 26 *Legal Studies* 155, 181–82.

[209] JD (n 4) [49].

[210] 'It should be no easier to succeed here than in France or Germany' (ibid).

[211] *Lawrence v Pembrokeshire CC* [2007] EWCA Civ 446, [2007] 1 WLR 2991 [50] (Auld LJ). See also JD (n 4) [137], where Lord Brown specifically rejected the adjustment of the standard of care as a response to the concern in this type of case.

[212] See Oliphant (n 108) para 17.20.

since they will still face *a* threat of liability, albeit a reduced one. On the other hand, if the overkill concern rests on the assumption that potential defendants may misread the standard of conduct required of them, or be uncertain as to that standard, then it may be peculiarly appropriate to respond to it by varying the standard of care, since this makes it much less likely that defendants will take inefficient precautions,[213] while at the same time affording claimants the possibility of redress in egregious cases.

It is noteworthy in this connection that in France application of the *faute lourde* standard has been justified by reference to overkill [687] concerns,[214] while one of the reasons given for employing the sufficiently serious breach test in European law has been that otherwise the relevant institutions would be unduly hampered in the performance of their functions.[215] It is also worth noting that a gross negligence standard is used in a number of European countries to protect those charged with the supervision of financial institutions from liability to third-party depositors and investors, primarily out of fear that untrammelled fault liability could distort priorities and distract supervisory authorities from their core function of promoting financial stability.[216] And while other jurisdictions have responded to the same concern by laying down an even more lenient standard of bad faith (as in the UK) or by immunising such authorities from third-party liability altogether (as in Germany), the use of a gross negligence approach has been endorsed by commentators on the grounds that it is sufficient to allay fears of defensive supervision, while at the same time affording depositors and investors redress in more egregious cases of supervisory failure.[217]

And finally, varying the standard of care might be considered (as in the French law of administrative responsibility[218]) to be an appropriate response to the connected concern that the task in question is particularly delicate or difficult, though here a sufficiently robust application of the ordinary negligence standard ought to be enough to allay the concern.

---

[213] For the view that in conditions of uncertainty, a gross negligence standard may generate much the same incentives as would be generated by an ordinary negligence standard in the absence of uncertainty, so that if uncertainty is unavoidable a gross negligence standard may be preferable to an ordinary negligence standard in deterrence terms, see R Craswell and JE Calfee, 'Deterrence and Uncertain Legal Standards' (1986) 2 *Journal of Law, Economics and Organisation* 279, 285.

[214] Fairgrieve (n 167) 115–16; Markesinis et al (n 204) 53.

[215] Craig, 'Once More Unto the Breach' (n 97) 72.

[216] See D Nolan, 'The Liability of Financial Supervisory Authorities' (2013) 4 *Journal of European Tort Law* 188, esp 198–200.

[217] See F Rossi, 'Tort Liability of Financial Regulators: A Comparative Study of Italian and English Law in a European Context' [2003] *European Business Law Review* 643, 671; AP Scarso, 'Tortious Liability of Regulatory Authorities', in H Koziol and BC Steininger (eds), *European Tort Law 2005* (Vienna, Verlag Österreich, 2006) 102, 116.

[218] See text to n 167. This would also appear to have been the motivation for the use of a gross negligence standard in section 43A of the Civil Liability Act 2002 (NSW) to protect those exercising 'special statutory powers', such as doctors performing certification roles under mental health legislation: see Aronson (n 96) 78.

V. CONCLUSION

This article has been concerned with the varying of the standard of care in negligence to protect defendants. It has been argued that English negligence law may already have varied the standard of care in three categories of case: the liability of occupiers for omissions; the liability of public authorities; and liability for the consequences of deliberate third party acts. It has also been argued that where the varying of the standard of care is thought to be desirable, two particular modifications can usefully be employed: one is to subjectivise [688] the standard, though only to a limited degree; the other is to make liability conditional on proof of gross negligence. Finally, consideration has been given to when and why a modified standard of care might be used.

Two final points should be made. The first is that, while the judiciary have already indicated a willingness to vary the standard of care in certain contexts, future reliance on this technique is perhaps more likely to be the product of legislative intervention, as it generally has been in other common law jurisdictions. This is particularly the case when it comes to the use of a gross negligence standard. And the second point is that drawing attention to the potential advantages of this technique is perfectly neutral as far as debates regarding the appropriate boundaries of negligence liability are concerned. Of course, if the standard of care is varied in existing duty situations, the effect is restrictive, but equally a modified breach test can be and has been used to justify the extension of negligence law into new areas.[219] My primary purpose has been to draw attention to the tool available, rather than to advocate its use for any particular task.

---

[219] Hence the irony that, while the French *faute lourde* standard was initially welcomed by liberal commentators as a tool with which to chip away at the immunity of the administration, in recent years it has come under attack as an unnecessary limitation on the state's liability: Fairgrieve (n 167) 114.

7

New Forms of Damage in Negligence

(2007) 70 *Modern Law Review* 59–88

[59] [T]ort law can be employed to protect whatever interests are deemed worthy of protection in any particular society: the list of protected interests is not set in stone.[1]

I. INTRODUCTION

T HAT DAMAGE IS an element of the tort of negligence is not in doubt: actionable injury completes the cause of action, so that time begins to run for limitation purposes only from the moment it occurs.[2] It seems strange, therefore, that this essential component of negligence liability should be so widely ignored. Issues concerning actionable damage are frequently repackaged as questions of duty or causation, and important extensions of the categories of actionable damage take place with little or no analysis or even acknowledgement of the fact.[3] The causes of this neglect are not altogether clear, but Ibbetson has provided two important clues. The first is that because the substantive tort of negligence developed out of [60] the action on the case, 'right from the start there were no inherent boundaries as to what constituted a recoverable loss', and nor were any provided by the natural lawyers whose works provided the intellectual background to the new cause of action.[4] The other clue may lie in Ibbetson's observation that it was only in the latter part of the twentieth century that lawyers began to focus on the type of loss suffered in negligence cases: their forebears were more concerned with the way in which that loss had come about.[5] Since those same forebears wrote the textbooks that established

---

[1] K Oliphant, 'The Nature of Tortious Liability' in A Grubb (ed), *The Law of Tort* (London, Butterworths, 2002) para 1.12.

[2] See, eg, *Pirelli General Cable Works v Oscar Faber* [1983] 2 AC 1 (HL); *Law Society v Sephton & Co* [2006] UKHL 22, [2006] 2 AC 543.

[3] See, eg, *Cowan v Chief Constable of Avon and Somerset Constabulary* [2001] EWCA Civ 1699, [2002] HLR 44, where, although the Court of Appeal held that the police owed no duty of care to a tenant unlawfully evicted in their presence, no mention was made of the fact that the claimant appeared to have suffered no actionable damage.

[4] D Ibbetson, 'How the Romans Did for Us: Ancient Roots of the Tort of Negligence' (2003) 26 *University of New South Wales Law Journal* 475, 488.

[5] D Ibbetson, *A Historical Introduction to the Law of Obligations* (Oxford, OUP, 1999) 194–95.

the analytical structure of the negligence tort, and since that structure is still in use today, it is perhaps not surprising that even though lawyers are now more alert to the type of harm the claimant has suffered there has still not been – with a few notable exceptions[6] – a great deal of academic analysis of the damage concept.[7]

Although one consequence of the academic neglect of the actionable damage issue is the absence of an established framework of governing principles, it is not my purpose in this article to construct a framework of this kind. Instead, my more modest aim is to focus attention on a number of new forms of actionable damage which appear either to have received recognition by the courts in recent years, or to be close to receiving such recognition. In so doing, I hope both to identify and to analyse some developments of significance for particular areas of negligence law, and also to advance understanding of the actionable damage concept as a whole. Before we turn to those developments, however, a few general observations concerning the actionable damage requirement will be in order. The first is the rather obvious observation that some torts are actionable per se and some are actionable only on proof of damage. There is a correlation between this distinction and the historical distinction between actions in trespass and actions on the case, though the correlation is not now a precise one, since certain actions on the case have been held to be actionable in the absence of proven harm.[8] The second [61] point is that where damage is required, what qualifies as actionable varies with different torts:[9] substantial inconvenience and discomfort constitute damage in private nuisance, for example, but not in negligence. The third point is that a distinction should be made between forms of harm which are never

---

[6] See particularly, J Stapleton, 'The Gist of Negligence' (1988) 104 *LQR* 213, 389; C Witting, 'Physical Damage in Negligence' [2002] *CLJ* 189; and (from a comparative law perspective) C von Bar, 'Damage Without Loss' in W Swadling and G Jones (eds), *The Search for Principle* (Oxford, OUP, 1999). For a useful example of the scrutiny of the damage issue in a particular context, see CAR Weston, 'Suing in Tort for Loss of Computer Data' [1999] *CLJ* 67.

[7] Ibbetson ('How the Romans Did for Us' (n 4) 488 fn) remarks that historically the principal textbooks showed 'a near-cavalier disregard for the question', and of the leading contemporary works, only J Fleming, *The Law of Torts*, 9th edn (Sydney, LBC Information Services, 1998) devotes a chapter to the subject, all but two pages of which (216–18) deal with causation. The neglect of the damage issue in negligence has parallels with the tendency on the part of legal theorists to under-theorise the concept of harm, on which see R West, *Caring for Justice* (New York, New York UP, 1997) ch 2.

[8] See, eg, *Williams v Peel River Land and Mineral Co* (1886) 55 LT 689 (QBD) (conversion); *Constantine v Imperial London Hotels Ltd* [1944] KB 693 (KBD) (wrongful exclusion from an inn). In *Watkins v Secretary of State for the Home Department* [2004] EWCA Civ 966, [2005] QB 883, the Court of Appeal held that the same was true of the tort of misfeasance in public office, but that decision has now been reversed by the House of Lords ([2006] UKHL 17, [2006] 2 AC 395), where Lord Carswell incorrectly suggested (at [79]) that a claimant will always fail in an action on the case if he cannot prove damage. The action on the case for libel is also actionable *per se* (as are certain forms of slander), though here the reasoning seems to be that damage is presumed, rather than that damage is not required: see *Constantine* at 699 (Birkett J). It has been argued that nuisance may also be actionable without proof of damage where the interference is with a servitude of the claimant, but the better view is that damage is in fact required: see Grubb (n 1) para 22.14.

[9] See *E (a minor) v Dorset County Council* [1994] 3 WLR 853 (CA) 876 (Evans LJ).

actionable in negligence, and those which are actionable only in certain limited circumstances. Emotional harm falling short of a recognised psychiatric illness is in the former category; recognised psychiatric illnesses themselves are in the latter (along with pure economic loss). Furthermore, it seems preferable to deal with the question of whether a given harm is *ever* actionable under the heading of actionable damage, and to deal with the question of whether a sometimes actionable harm is actionable in this particular case under the separate heading of duty of care, since doing so draws attention to the distinction we have identified, and makes it more likely that the important issues raised by the former question will be addressed openly and comprehensively. Unfortunately, however, there is a tendency to subsume the damage issue into the duty of care question,[10] though the practice of the courts in this regard has not been consistent: in the psychiatric injury context, for example, the actionable damage issue has been dealt with at the duty of care stage, but in other types of case it has frequently been treated as an independent element of the negligence inquiry.[11] The fourth point is that physical harm to the claimant's person or property clearly constitutes actionable damage for negligence purposes, though the boundaries of the concept of physical damage are not always clear.[12] And the final, rather elementary, point is that the issue of the damage sufficient to establish a cause of action should not be confused with the harms for which recovery is permitted once the cause of action has been established.[13] Hence while distress or upset do not themselves ground a negligence claim, if they are brought about by a harm that does – such as a broken leg – then compensation will generally be payable in respect of them.

The article is divided into three core sections. In the first section, I consider whether imprisonment is, and ought to be, recognised as a form of actionable damage in negligence. The normative element of this inquiry entails, among other things, an assessment of the relative merits of negligence and false imprisonment as modes of redress for negligent imprisonment. In the second section, I look at issues concerning actionable damage raised by the case law on wrongful conception. In particular, I consider the characterisation of pregnancy as personal [62] injury, and the form of damage, if any, which underlies the conventional sum that is now awarded to the parents in such cases. And finally, in the

---

[10] See RWM Dias, 'The Duty Problem in Negligence' [1955] *CLJ* 198, 202; Oliphant (n 1) para 1.11.

[11] See, eg, *Hotson v East Berkshire Area Health Authority* [1987] 2 WLR 287 (CA) 295 (Sir John Donaldson MR); *E (a minor)* (n 9) 874 (Sir Thomas Bingham MR); *Hunter v Canary Wharf Ltd* [1996] 2 WLR 348 (CA) 365–67 (Pill LJ); *W v Home Office* [1997] Imm AR 302 (CA) 312 (Lord Woolf MR). In *Harriton v Stephens* [2006] HCA 15, 226 CLR 52, Hayne J specifically commented (at [161]) that the question of what was recognised as actionable damage in negligence was 'separate and distinct from questions of duty or causation'.

[12] See further the articles by Stapleton and Witting (n 6).

[13] Nor should the concept of actionable damage be confused with the pleader's term 'special damage': see G Williams and BA Hepple, *Foundations of the Law of Tort* (London, Butterworths, 1976) 59–61.

third section of the article I turn my attention to the law concerning liability for educational negligence, and I ask whether failure to ameliorate a specific learning disorder is, and ought to be, classified as actionable damage, and also whether, in the absence of such a disorder, impaired intellectual development can and should be capable of constituting the gist of a negligence action.

II. NEGLIGENT IMPRISONMENT

On 3 January 1990, an elderly couple went to the maternity hospital in Liverpool to visit their new-born grandson. The lift they took to the second floor was overloaded, and came to a standstill between floors; it was an hour and twenty minutes before the occupants were released. The couple sued the health authority in negligence for the mental distress this experience caused them, but their claim was dismissed. Although the trial judge found that the defendants had been negligent in not installing a cut-out device which would have prevented the lift from moving when overloaded, the Court of Appeal held that, in the absence of a recognisable psychiatric illness, the claimants had suffered no actionable damage.[14] Suppose, however, that the claimants had taken a different tack, and argued that the imprisonment was *itself* a form of actionable damage (regardless of its consequences)? Would this argument have succeeded? More generally, do such instances of negligent imprisonment merit redress, and, if so, should this be via the tort of negligence or instead by the extension of the tort of false imprisonment to cover negligent conduct?

Two different categories of 'negligent imprisonment' case should be distinguished. In the first, the imprisonment is not intended, but comes about by accident. Examples include people being trapped in malfunctioning lifts and toilet cubicles;[15] people being accidentally locked into libraries, bank vaults[16] and department store wash rooms;[17] and Street's example of a new chaplain visiting a prisoner in his cell, who is not warned that the cell door locks automatically.[18] In the second category of case, the imprisonment is intended, but the decision to imprison is arrived at as a result of a mistake. Instances of this type of case include the confinement of a patient under mental health legislation after an inaccurate diagnosis,[19] a delay in the release of a prisoner caused by an administrative error,[20] and the detention of an asylum seeker by immigration officials who had

---

[14] *Reilly v Merseyside Regional Health Authority* (1995) 6 Med LR 246 (CA).

[15] See *Sayers v Harlow UDC* [1958] 1 WLR 623 (CA).

[16] See AJ Harding and T Keng Feng, 'Negligent False Imprisonment – A Problem in the Law of Trespass' (1980) 22 *Malaya Law Review* 29, 29.

[17] See FA Trindade, 'The Modern Tort of False Imprisonment' in NJ Mullany (ed), *Torts in the Nineties* (Sydney, LBC Information Services, 1997) 254.

[18] H Street, *The Law of Torts* (London, Butterworths, 1955) 22.

[19] See, eg, *Everett v Griffiths* [1920] 3 KB 163 (CA).

[20] See, eg, *Clarke v Crew* (1999) 149 NLJ 899 (CA).

mixed up his file with someone else's.[21] Although the gist of the wrong is the same in both [63] cases, in the first category the imprisonment will generally be brief and often trivial, and the likelihood of litigation will therefore be low. (If the accidental confinement causes the claimant to suffer personal injury, then recovery for this in negligence should be straightforward, subject to arguments from remoteness and contributory fault.[22]) In the second category, by contrast, the loss of liberty is likely to be much more serious, as regards both its duration and its consequences, and hence the claimant is more likely to seek redress. Two other points should be made about the second category of case. One is that cases of deliberate imprisonment may give rise to public policy concerns that will militate against the imposition of liability. The other is that, where the imprisonment is intentional, a straightforward claim for false imprisonment will lie if the mistake in question renders the detention unlawful (since the requisite intention is to imprison, not to imprison *unlawfully*). A complication is that the defendant in such an action will usually not be the person responsible for the mistake. In theory, this should not matter, but the courts are now inclined to extend the defence of lawful authority to protect defendants who have themselves acted reasonably,[23] and this tendency to shield the innocent gaoler from liability forces the claimant to look to the party at fault for redress. This shift of focus means that in practice liability for negligent imprisonment has become more important than was previously the case.

In the discussion that follows I will consider whether liability for negligent imprisonment is best brought about through recognition of loss of liberty as actionable damage in the tort of negligence or through extending the tort of false imprisonment to cover negligent conduct. Each option will be considered in turn, and its advantages and disadvantages will be assessed. Of course it could be argued that neither option need be adopted, since negligent imprisonment does not warrant redress unless personal injury results. However, if we bear in mind the importance of freedom of movement as an interest in its own right, and also the many negative consequences to which detention can give rise, then it seems reasonable to proceed on the basis that some form of liability is appropriate for negligent imprisonment, at least in serious cases.[24] This conclusion is

---

[21] W (n 11).

[22] See, eg, *Sayers* (n 15) where a woman trapped in a public toilet injured herself in the course of an escape attempt. The Court of Appeal held that the damage was not too remote, but reduced the claimant's damages by one quarter for contributory negligence. See also the example given in the *Restatement, Second, Torts* (1965) § 42, comment b, of a boy whose health suffers after he spends two days locked in a bank vault without food or water.

[23] See, eg, *Percy v Hall* [1997] QB 924 (CA); *Olotu v Home Office* [1997] 1 WLR 328 (CA); *Quinland v Governor of Swaleside Prison* [2002] EWCA Civ 174, [2003] QB 306. But *cf R v Governor of Brockhill, ex p Evans (No 2)* [2001] 2 AC 19 (HL).

[24] See Harding and Tan (n 16) 30; FA Trindade, 'Some Curiosities of Negligent Trespass to the Person: A Comparative Study' (1971) 20 *ICLQ* 706, 711–12 (drawing attention to the humiliation, mental suffering and disgrace which a negligent imprisonment may cause).

reinforced by the fact that freedom of movement is an interest protected against negligent conduct in most civil law systems.[25] **[64]**

A. Liability for Imprisonment in Negligence

The first route to recovery for negligent imprisonment is recognition of imprisonment as a form of actionable damage in negligence. A significant advantage of this option is that it would not require any change in the law, as there is already a body of authority in which the actionability of imprisonment appears to have been assumed. Most of the relevant cases are from the last decade or so, but there is also an older line of authority dealing with negligent certification of lunacy. In *De Freville v Dill*,[26] for example, liability was imposed on a doctor who had negligently issued a medical certificate which led to the claimant's detention under section 16 of the Lunatic Act 1890. The claim was described by McCardie J as 'an action on the case for negligence'.[27] Furthermore, the actionability of imprisonment was not questioned in two other cases in which the Court of Appeal dismissed similar claims on the grounds of lack of duty or legal causation, *Thompson v Schmidt*[28] and *Everett v Griffiths*.[29]

The first of the more recent authorities was *Welsh v Chief Constable of the Merseyside Police*,[30] where the Crown Prosecution Service (CPS) had failed to inform a magistrates' court that two of the claimant's offences had already been taken into consideration in the Crown Court. As a result, a warrant was issued for the claimant's arrest when he failed to turn up at the magistrates' court, and he spent two days in police custody before the mistake was discovered. Tudor Evans J refused to accede to the defendant's request that he strike out the claim on the ground that the CPS did not owe a duty of care to the claimant. No mention was made of the damage issue. The CPS was also the defendant in *Elguzouli-Daf v Commissioner of Police of the Metropolis*,[31] where the two claimants complained that their pre-trial detention had been unnecessarily prolonged by the negligent failure to discontinue their prosecutions at an earlier stage. This time the Court of Appeal upheld the trial judge's decision to strike out the claim on the ground that no duty of care was owed for public policy

---

[25] C von Bar, *The Common European Law of Torts*, vol 2 (Munich, CH Beck, 2000) para 76.

[26] *De Freville v Dill* (1927) 96 LJKB 1056 (KBD).

[27] ibid 1060.

[28] *Thompson v Schmidt* (1892) 56 JP 212 (CA).

[29] *Everett v Griffiths* [1920] 3 KB 163 (CA). Atkin LJ dissented, but the decision was affirmed by the House of Lords: [1921] 1 AC 631 (HL).

[30] *Welsh v Chief Constable of the Merseyside Police* [1993] 1 All ER 692 (QBD).

[31] *Elguzouli-Daf v Commissioner of Police of the Metropolis* [1995] QB 335 (CA).

reasons. There was no need for the court to consider the damage issue,[32] but the fact that both Steyn LJ and Morritt LJ appeared to agree with the result in *Welsh*[33] is an indication that they were prepared to accept the actionability of detention in an appropriate case.[34]

[65] However, perhaps the two most significant authorities on imprisonment as damage are *W v Home Office*[35] and *McLoughlin v Jones*.[36] In *W* the claimant was an asylum seeker whose detention had been extended as a result of an administrative error on the part of the immigration authorities. Two preliminary points came before the Court of Appeal: whether the defendant owed the claimant a duty of care in respect of the length of time for which he was detained, and whether the prolongation of the claimant's detention constituted loss or damage in respect of which a negligence action would lie. Although the Court decided the first point in favour of the defendant, it would have backed the claimant on the second. Lord Woolf MR cited the negligent certification cases, as well as *Welsh* and *Eguzouli-Daf*, and concluded that detention was a recognised form of damage.[37] The claimant in *McLoughlin* alleged that his solicitor's incompetence had caused him to be wrongfully convicted of causing grievous bodily harm and robbery. He spent three months in prison before his convictions were quashed, and sought redress for, among other things, a psychiatric illness caused by this experience. The Court of Appeal held that he was a primary victim for the purposes of the law governing psychiatric injury, and hence that he could recover for the illness if it had been reasonably foreseeable. In the course of her reasoning on this issue, Hale LJ made clear that in her view imprisonment was a serious harm, akin to physical injury: 'Loss of liberty', she remarked, 'is just as much an interference in bodily integrity as is loss of a limb'.[38] Since it would follow from this that the tort of negligence ought to give as much protection to freedom of movement as it does to physical integrity, her Ladyship's comments, coupled with the reasoning in *W*, are a strong indication that the courts will continue to recognise imprisonment as the gist of a negligence action in appropriate cases.[39]

Academic writers have endorsed the courts' recognition of imprisonment as damage, and argued that this represents the optimal solution to the problem

---

[32] Morritt LJ assumed in favour of the claimants that they had 'suffered damage of the type relevant to a claim in negligence' (ibid 351).

[33] ibid 350, 352.

[34] See also *Clarke* (n 20) where the Court of Appeal upheld the trial judge's decision to award compensation to a man imprisoned for 32 hours as a result of the negligent endorsement of a warrant by a police officer. Simon Brown LJ did not address the question of actionable damage in terms, though he did point out that incarceration seriously affects a prisoner's well-being.

[35] *W* (n 11).

[36] *McLoughlin v Jones* [2001] EWCA Civ 1743, [2002] QB 1312.

[37] *W* (n 11) 312–13.

[38] *McLoughlin* (n 36) [57].

[39] The only case that casts doubt on this conclusion is the hospital lift case, *Reilly v Merseyside Regional Health Authority* (discussed above, text preceding n 14), but there the imprisonment point

of negligent imprisonment. Hence Heffey, the most prominent advocate of this approach, has remarked that:

> Freedom of movement is certainly an interest which the law of torts protects and there does not seem to be any conceptual reason why the violation of this … interest should not be regarded as damage [in negligence]. Loss of personal liberty is almost as grave a deprivation as loss of life itself.[40]

[66] It is also noteworthy in this connection that imprisonment constitutes damage for the purposes of another action on the case, the tort of malicious prosecution.[41] An objection to this course of action is that it could lead to the imposition of liability in very trivial cases, as where the claimant is locked in a room for only thirty seconds before the defendant realises her mistake. And although this difficulty could be avoided by requiring that the imprisonment be 'substantial', such a requirement would itself be problematic: how long, for example, would a claimant have to be stuck in a lift for her imprisonment to count as substantial? In truth, however, there is nothing unique about imprisonment in this respect – the smallest of scratches, whether to me or to my car, presumably grounds a negligence action – and it must be assumed that either a person who suffers trivial injury will not bother to litigate, or that the court will punish her with an order for costs if she does. Similarly, the fact that the claimant's loss would ordinarily not be pecuniary in nature is no objection to negligence liability. The same is true of claims for pain and suffering and loss of amenity in personal injury cases, and, as there, the courts would somehow have to translate a non-pecuniary loss into money's worth for the purposes of compensation. Account should of course be taken of the duration of the imprisonment, and of any humiliation or distress suffered. If the claimant's confinement leads to consequential harm, such as physical injury or economic loss, then this should also be compensated, provided it was reasonably foreseeable.

A more significant difficulty with the negligence route to redress arises in cases where the claimant is unaware of her imprisonment, or, although aware of it, would not have left the place of her confinement even had she been able to do so. It might be thought that the latter scenario is the more straightforward, since it could be argued that to interfere with a person's freedom of movement

---

was neither taken nor considered. In W (n 11) Lord Woolf MR commented (at 313) that in any case there was 'an obvious distinction between being detained in a lift and being detained in a prison', though query whether this distinction should affect the actionability of the harm.

[40] PG Heffey, 'Negligent Infliction of Imprisonment: Actionable "Per Se" or "Cum Damno"?' (1983) 14 *Melbourne University Law Review* 53. See also MA Millner, *Negligence in Modern Law* (London, Butterworths, 1967) 210 ('There is no reason in principle, why deprivation of freedom should not be a category of negligence'). Other supporters of the negligence route include L Klar, *Tort Law*, 3rd edn (Toronto, Thomson Carswell, 2003) 54 (discussing battery), and, more tentatively, D Howarth, *Textbook on Tort* (London, Butterworths, 1995) 462 and WVH Rogers, *Winfield & Jolowicz on Tort*, 16th edn (London, Sweet & Maxwell, 2002) 97.

[41] Fleming (n 7) 686.

is to deprive that person of the *opportunity* to move around, in which case such an interference occurs regardless of whether the person wishes to do so or not. This was accepted by the Court of Appeal in *Weldon v Home Office*, where Ralph Gibson LJ said that an action in false imprisonment would lie in such a case,[42] while adding that the fact that the imprisoned person did not wish to leave would be relevant to the assessment of damages.[43] In such a scenario, it would also be possible to hold that there was actionable damage for the purposes of negligence, although it would then follow that the claimant would be entitled to substantial (as opposed to nominal) damages. If the claimant is entirely unaware of her confinement, then the case for liability seems weaker, although here too it has been accepted that liability could be imposed in false imprisonment, with the caveat that in such a scenario the claimant could 'normally expect to recover no more than nominal damages'.[44] From the negligence point of view, however, this caveat is [67] problematic, since nominal damages cannot logically be awarded where a cause of action can only be established on proof of damage. It follows that if negligence liability were to be imposed in this scenario, substantial damages would have to be awarded in both causes of action (since it would surely be unacceptable if the remedy in negligence were to be better than the remedy in false imprisonment), and it might be concluded, therefore, that imprisonment ought only to qualify as actionable damage where the claimant is aware of it, thereby ruling out redress in negligence in this type of case.

B. Negligent False Imprisonment

Some commentators have argued that the problem of negligent confinement should be dealt with by imposing liability in the tort of false imprisonment.[45] False imprisonment can be defined as the unlawful and direct imprisonment of another person, with imprisonment meaning a total restraint of that other's freedom of movement. This cause of action is a form of trespass to the person, and hence actionable per se. The obvious advantage of dealing with negligent confinement cases in false imprisonment would therefore be that difficulties surrounding the characterisation of imprisonment as 'damage' would fall

---

[42] *Weldon v Home Office* [1990] 3 WLR 465 (CA) 470 (and that this would be so even if the claimant had been obliged – under a contract, for example – to remain in the place of confinement).

[43] ibid.

[44] *Murray v Ministry of Defence* [1988] 1 WLR 692 (HL) 703 (Lord Griffiths). The Court of Appeal made an award of nominal damages in a case of this kind, *R v Bournewood Community and Mental Health NHS Trust, ex p L* [1998] 2 WLR 764 (CA) 778 (Lord Woolf MR), but was then reversed on liability by the House of Lords: [1999] AC 458 (HL). According to the *Restatement, Second, Torts* (1965) § 42, either consciousness of the confinement or resultant harm is required for an action in false imprisonment to lie.

[45] Harding and Tan (n 16); Trindade, 'The Modern Tort of False Imprisonment' (n 17) 252–56; U Burnham, 'Negligent False Imprisonment – Scope for Re-emergence?' (1998) 61 *MLR* 573.

away.[46] However, there is an equally obvious objection to this approach, which is that, as English law stands, liability in trespass to the person requires intention – carelessness is not enough. The authority for this proposition is the judgment of Lord Denning MR (with whom Danckwerts LJ agreed) in *Letang v Cooper*:

> If one man intentionally applies force directly to another, the plaintiff has a cause of action in assault and battery, or, if you so please to describe it, in trespass to the person ... If he does not inflict injury intentionally, but only unintentionally, the plaintiff has no cause of action today in trespass. His only cause of action is in negligence.[47]

The proponents of negligent false imprisonment have attempted to sideline *Letang v Cooper* in various ways. It has been pointed out, for example, that the courts have not yet closed the door on actions for negligent trespass in Australia[48] [68] and Canada[49] (though they have in the United States[50]), but while this may be significant when it comes to the discussion of the issue in those jurisdictions, it is of little relevance to claimants in this country.[51] A stronger point is that *Letang* was concerned with battery, not false imprisonment, and that there is an important distinction between the two, since while negligent batteries or assaults do not merit compensation unless bodily or psychiatric injury results,[52] a negligent imprisonment may well do so.[53] This distinction suggests that while *Letang v Cooper* is a significant obstacle to recovery for negligent false imprisonment, it may not be an insuperable one.

There is, however, a further difficulty with the false imprisonment route, which is that recovery for negligent confinement would depend on the existence of a direct link between the defendant's conduct and the claimant's confinement. As Pollock CB once remarked, 'a person ought not to be held responsible in trespass, unless he directly and immediately causes the imprisonment'.[54] This

---

[46] F Trindade and P Cane, *The Law of Torts in Australia*, 3rd edn (Melbourne, OUP, 1999) 332.

[47] *Letang v Cooper* [1965] 1 QB 232 (CA) 239. See also *Wilson v Pringle* [1987] QB 237 (CA) 247 (Croom-Johnson LJ); *Wainwright v Home Office* [2001] EWCA Civ 2081, [2002] QB 1334 [71] (Buxton LJ). Diplock LJ took a slightly different approach in *Letang*, though one leading to the same results. In particular, while his Lordship was prepared to countenance an unintentional trespass, he made it clear that for liability to arise for an unintentional trespass, actual damage would have to ensue. For a convincing critique of his reasoning, see JA Jolowicz [1964] *CLJ* 200, 201–202.

[48] See Trindade and Cane (n 46) 328–30.

[49] See AM Linden, *Canadian Tort Law*, 5th edn (Toronto, Butterworths, 1993) 252–54.

[50] *Restatement, Second, Torts* (1965) §§ 13, 18 (battery), 21 (assault), 35 (false imprisonment).

[51] For a comparative overview of negligent trespass, see Trindade, 'Some Curiosities of Negligent Trespass to the Person' (n 24).

[52] The strongest counter-example would perhaps be if X unintentionally spat in the face of Y (PG Heffey and H Glasbeek, 'Trespass: High Court Versus Court of Appeal' (1966) 5 *Melbourne University Law Review* 158, 163), but even here the absence of intention undermines an argument based on Y's dignity interest, and the mere unpleasantness of the experience does not itself justify legal redress.

[53] Harding and Tan (n 16) 30. For this reason, *Winfield & Jolowicz* (n 40) 96–97 approves *Letang v Cooper* in the battery/assault context, but has reservations in the case of false imprisonment.

[54] *Grinham v Willey* (1859) 4 H & N 496, 499; 157 ER 934, 935.

element of directness may be missing both in the case where the imprisonment is accidental, and where it is intentional but attributable to a mistake of the defendant. As to the former, if it is accepted that the element of directness is missing where the defendant digs a pit into which the claimant falls,[55] then the same must presumably be true when the entrapment results from the careless failure to repair a lift or a toilet door. As to the latter, where (as is usually the case) the defendant is not the claimant's gaoler, the presence of a sufficiently direct link is unlikely.[56] Consider, for example, the facts of *Welsh v Chief Constable of the Merseyside Police*,[57] discussed above, where the claimant spent two days in police custody as a result of the failure of the CPS to inform a magistrates' court that two of his offences had already been taken into consideration by another court. A claim against the CPS in negligent false imprisonment would almost certainly have failed on these facts for lack of directness. It is also unlikely that the directness requirement would be satisfied where, for example, the defendant negligently certifies that a patient's mental health requires her involuntary hospitalisation,[58] where the incompetence of a solicitor causes her client to be imprisoned for an offence he did not [69] commit,[59] or where a mistake by a store detective leads a police officer to arrest the claimant.[60]

The result is that the extension of false imprisonment to negligent conduct would catch only a narrow band of negligent imprisonment cases, of the kind where the defendant accidentally locks the claimant into a library, bank vault and so forth. Not only would this limit the effectiveness of this liability route, it would also foster arbitrary distinctions: why should a student locked in the college library for half an hour have a remedy, and an asylum seeker locked in a detention centre for two months as a result of an administrative error have none? To give the trespass tort more bite, and to eliminate such arbitrary distinctions, would require abrogation of the directness requirement, a move taken by the drafters of the *Second Restatement of Torts*.[61] Such a move could be defended on the ground that it would put the modern law of trespass to the person on a more rational footing, but it would be a radical step, since the connection

---

[55] The classic example: see Trindade, 'The Modern Tort of False Imprisonment' (n 17) 231.

[56] Where the mistake is by the gaoler, then an orthodox false imprisonment claim will lie, subject to the defence of lawful authority: 'negligent' false imprisonment would add nothing.

[57] *Welsh* (n 30).

[58] Hence the false imprisonment claim was withdrawn in *De Freville v Dill* (n 26) a case of this kind. See also *Everett v Griffiths* (n 29) 219 (Atkins LJ) ('Had the action been framed for false imprisonment only, I could have appreciated the ground of the decision on the principle of cases where the prosecutor has been held not to be liable for imprisonment ordered by the judicial decision of the Court').

[59] See, eg, *McLoughlin v Jones* (n 36) (litigated in negligence).

[60] See *Davidson v Chief Constable of North Wales* [1994] 2 All ER 597 (CA). Here the action was in false imprisonment, but it failed on directness grounds, since the police officer exercised an independent discretion.

[61] See *Restatement, Second, Torts* (1965) § 13(b) (contact caused indirectly a battery), § 35(1)(b) (confinement caused indirectly a false imprisonment).

between trespass and directness goes back a long way. And it would surely be too much to ask the courts to couple this step with a departure from *Letang v Cooper*, so as to allow actions in trespass for confinement caused both indirectly and negligently. The conclusion must be that while theoretically there is scope for expanding false imprisonment to deal with the problem of negligent imprisonment, it is unlikely that the courts will take the steps required, particularly when an alternative route to liability is readily available.

Before we dismiss the option of imposing liability in false imprisonment for careless confinement, however, the arguments put forward by the supporters of this approach must be addressed. Not infrequently, the case for the false imprisonment route is a negative one: redress should be available, and imprisonment is not actionable in negligence, so extension of the nominate tort is required.[62] Since we have seen that the assumption which underlies this argument is mistaken, it need not detain us further. More important are the positive arguments Trindade and Burnham have put forward for preferring the false imprisonment approach to the negligence one. Trindade has drawn attention to what he considers to be the possible advantages to the claimant of bringing an action in negligent trespass.[63] However, his principal focus is Australian law, and it would seem that a claimant in this country would today only rarely benefit from framing her action in this way. Unlike in Australia and Canada, where the burden of proof as to fault shifts in trespass cases once direct interference has been established,[64] in English law it remains with the claimant.[65] Nor would a claimant generally benefit from a longer limitation period in false imprisonment. A negligence claim for imprisonment per se would presumably not be an action for 'personal injury' under section 11 of the [70] Limitation Act 1980, and hence would be subject to the ordinary tort limit of six years laid down in section 2 – as would a false imprisonment claim.[66] Only if the claimant were to seek damages for personal injury suffered as a result of her confinement would there be a distinction: in negligence, the three-year limit would presumably apply, but in false imprisonment the limit would still be six years.[67] And since it would appear that the defence of contributory negligence is available even in cases of intentional trespass to the person,[68] it can scarcely be doubted (*pace*

---

[62] See, eg, Harding and Tan (n 16); Trindade and Cane (n 46) 331–32.

[63] Trindade, 'The Modern Tort of False Imprisonment' (n 17) *passim*.

[64] See Trindade and Cane (n 46) 332–36 (Australia); Klar (n 40) 47–48 (Canada). The rule does not apply in highway cases.

[65] *Fowler v Lanning* [1959] 1 QB 426 (QBD).

[66] Trindade, 'Some Curiosities of Negligent Trespass to the Person' (n 24) seems to assume that a negligence action for imprisonment would be caught by the shorter period (at 725), but it is difficult to see why the words 'personal injuries' should be thought to cover confinement *per se*.

[67] Following *Stubbings v Webb* [1993] AC 498 (HL).

[68] *Winfield & Jolowicz* (n 40) 249.

Trindade[69]) that a defendant in a negligent false imprisonment claim would be able to invoke it if appropriate. Finally, although in theory a claimant who sued in negligent false imprisonment would benefit from the more generous trespass rules as to remoteness – so that the test would be one of directness of the consequence, rather than its foreseeability – it is perfectly possible that the courts would decide that such a distinction was untenable, and hence would apply the foreseeability principle in cases of negligent trespass as well as in cases of negligence proper.

Burnham, meanwhile, objects to the way in which the courts have refused to impose duties of care in negligent imprisonment cases for policy reasons,[70] and envisages actions in negligent false imprisonment as a way round the problem.[71] But in truth this draws attention to an additional *advantage* of the negligence approach. Where, as in all the litigated cases, the decision to imprison is deliberately arrived at, there may well be public policy objections to the imposition of liability. And unlike false imprisonment, the tort of negligence has a device tailor-made to deal with such arguments: the duty of care mechanism. We may disagree with particular duty decisions that the courts have made in this area, but it seems odd to use that as an argument for putting it out of their power to make any such determinations in future. Nor is Burnham's argument that careless imprisonment is a violation of a 'constitutional right' which the law of tort should 'vindicate' a convincing objection to the imposition of duty limits in negligence. Suppose that two prisoners are held on remand for six months before trial. In prisoner A's case the CPS should have realised that he was innocent early on, and dropped the case; in prisoner B's case, his innocence emerged only during the trial. Are we to believe that A's constitutional rights have been violated, but that B's have not? The only difference between the two is that in A's case the CPS were careless, and in B's they were not, but this should at most ground a negligence claim against the CPS for the damage they have done to A's interest in freedom of movement. That is a weighty interest, and the courts should be slow to dismiss such a claim for policy reasons, but it is submitted that the invocation of A's constitutional rights adds nothing to our understanding of the issues involved.[72] [71]

---

[69] *cf* Trindade, 'The Modern Tort of False Imprisonment' (n 17) 256; Trindade, 'Some Curiosities of Negligent Trespass to the Person' (n 24) 729–30.

[70] See, eg, *Elguzouli-Daf* (n 31); *W* (n 21).

[71] Burnham (n 45).

[72] It is noteworthy in this regard that the House of Lords was dismissive of recognition of a particular category of 'constitutional rights' in the tort context in *Watkins v Secretary of State for the Home Department* (n 8). According to Lord Rodger (at [62]), 'At least within the realm of tort law, questions about the availability of a remedy are best answered by looking at the substance of the supposed wrong rather than by reference to a somewhat imprecise label which lawyers might attach to it in another connection'.

III. WRONGFUL CONCEPTION

An action for wrongful conception is founded either on the failure of a doctor correctly to carry out a sterilisation or vasectomy operation, or on her failure to warn the subject of such an operation that a small risk of conception remains. In *McFarlane v Tayside Health Board*,[73] the House of Lords held that for policy reasons a couple were unable to recover the cost of bringing up a child born to the wife after allegedly negligent advice as to the effect of a vasectomy on the husband. A majority of their Lordships were, however, prepared to allow the mother damages for the pain and distress caused by the pregnancy itself, and also for its direct financial consequences. The *McFarlane* decision was upheld by a seven-strong panel of the House of Lords in *Rees v Darlington Memorial Hospital NHS Trust*,[74] where the majority ruled that no exception to the exclusion of child-rearing costs should be recognised in the case of a disabled mother, but that in all wrongful conception cases the parents were entitled to a conventional sum award of £15,000 (on top of the mother's pregnancy claim) for the denial of an important aspect of their personal autonomy, namely 'the right to limit the size of their family'.[75]

For the most part, the discussion in these cases, and in the equivalent authorities in other common law countries, has centred on arguments against the recovery of child-rearing costs based on the dignity or commodification of the child, the impossibility of assessing the damages, and distributive justice concerns. By contrast, the issue of actionable damage has received relatively little attention. The general perception seems to be that the mother's pregnancy claim is a straightforward personal injury action, and that the claim for the cost of upkeep is for either a pure or a consequential economic loss. Both these propositions are plausible, but there are two complications which bring the wrongful conception cases within the scope of this article. The first is that some judges and commentators have argued that an unwanted pregnancy is not a physical injury (at least in the 'orthodox' sense). The second is that the form of actionable damage which underlies the conventional sum awarded in *Rees* seems to represent a significant departure from previous categories of recognised harm. These two issues will be considered in turn.

A. Pregnancy as Personal Injury

Where a procedure is carried out in order to avoid a particular event (here, pregnancy), the defendant is clearly in no position to turn around afterwards and deny that that event constitutes actionable damage. This explains why there is

---

[73] *McFarlane v Tayside Health Board* [2000] 2 AC 59 (HL).
[74] *Rees v Darlington Memorial Hospital NHS Trust* [2003] UKHL 52, [2004] 1 AC 309.
[75] ibid [122] (Lord Millett).

such broad acceptance that the mother in a wrongful conception case is the victim of a legal wrong, and why almost all the judges who have looked at the issue have agreed that she is entitled to damages at least in respect of the pregnancy and [72] birth.[76] It would, however, be a mistake to conclude from this that the appropriate classification of the damage caused is irrelevant. In the first place, there could be analogous cases where the characterisation of the harm might make a difference. Suppose, for example, that the claimant became pregnant after having sex with a man whose vasectomy was carried out before her relationship with him began. If her injury is considered not to be physical, but (say) economic, then she is unlikely to recover, as the doctor will probably be held not to have assumed any responsibility towards her when he undertook the procedure.[77] Similarly, an assumption of responsibility is unlikely to exist if the defendant is, for example, a manufacturer of faulty condoms,[78] or a pharmacist who mistakenly dispenses tranquillisers instead of contraceptives.[79] Furthermore, the way in which the harm of unwanted pregnancy is classified raises a number of interesting issues, and calls into question the utility of a general test of physical damage in the law of negligence. Broader lessons can therefore be learned.

In general, judges and commentators have been happy to accept that an unwanted pregnancy is a form of personal injury. Indeed, the point was effectively conceded in *Walkin v South Manchester Health Authority*,[80] where the issue was whether a wrongful conception claim limited to the economic losses caused by an unwanted pregnancy and birth was none the less an action 'in respect of personal injuries' within the meaning of section 38(1) of the Limitation Act 1980. Similarly, in *Richardson v LRC Products*,[81] Kennedy J seems to have assumed that an unwanted pregnancy amounted to personal injury and hence was actionable damage under the Consumer Protection Act 1987, and academic endorsement of this analysis has been provided by, among others, Rogers[82] and Mullis.[83] Furthermore, a similar approach is apparent in so-called 'wrongful

---

[76] Lord Millett in *McFarlane* is a notable exception, but his conclusion was based on policy arguments, not a denial of the existence of damage. In the leading Australian case on wrongful conception, *Cattanach v Melchior* [2003] HCA 38, 215 CLR 1, there was no appeal from the award of damages to the mother for the pregnancy and birth (see [14] (Gleeson CJ)), and von Bar states that 'nearly all' European systems allow the mother to recover for loss of earnings arising out of pregnancy: C von Bar, *The Common European Law of Torts*, vol 1 (Oxford, OUP, 1998) para 583.

[77] See *Goodwill v British Pregnancy Advisory Service* [1996] 1 WLR 1397 (CA). Note, though, the argument that even if the harm is characterised as physical in a case of this kind, liability should still be limited to those within the 'zone of knowledge' of the doctor at the time the treatment was given: I Kennedy and A Grubb, *Medical Law*, 3rd edn (London, Butterworths, 2000) 1585.

[78] See *Richardson v LRC Products* [2000] Lloyd's Rep Med 280 (QBD) (though here the condom was found not to have been defective).

[79] As in *Troppi v Scarf* 187 NW 2d 511 (Mich 1971).

[80] *Walkin v South Manchester Health Authority* [1995] 1 WLR 1543 (CA).

[81] *Richardson* (n 78).

[82] H Rogers, 'Legal Implications of Ineffective Sterilization' (1985) 5 *Legal Studies* 296, 310.

[83] A Mullis, 'Wrongful Conception Unravelled' (1993) 1 *Medical Law Review* 320, 325.

birth' actions, where the alleged negligence relates not to the prevention of the pregnancy in the first place, but to its continuation through to birth; in this type of case, the unwanted continuation of the pregnancy has been treated as a form of personal injury.[84] There have, however, been some dissenting voices. In *Walkin* itself, Roch LJ had [73] difficulty with the classification of pregnancy as a personal injury in cases where the motivation for the sterilisation or vasectomy was financial,[85] while both Cooke J (in the New Zealand Court of Appeal)[86] and the Lord Ordinary, Lord Gill (in the Outer House of the Court of Session) have disavowed such a characterisation altogether. Lord Gill, sitting at first instance in *McFarlane*, remarked:

> In my view, a pregnancy occurring in the circumstances of this case cannot be equiperated with a physical injury. Pregnancy causes discomfort, pain and sickness. Labour is acutely painful and distressing. But these are natural processes resulting in a happy outcome. They are the natural sequelae of conception, and that is an event that in this case can hardly be considered as a physical injury per se. I do not consider that a normal pregnancy, even if undesired ... can properly be described as a personal injury.[87]

Moreover, although this analysis was not endorsed when *McFarlane* reached the House of Lords, their Lordships were by no means agreed that pregnancy constituted personal injury in what might be termed the 'orthodox' sense. It is true that Lord Steyn specifically rejected a submission from counsel for the defenders that the 'natural processes of conception and childbirth cannot in law amount to personal injury', and that Lord Millett described an unwanted pregnancy as 'an invasion of [the woman's] bodily integrity' which 'threatened further damage both physical and financial',[88] but on the other hand Lord Hope described the mother's claim only as 'analogous' to that which might be made in a case of personal injury,[89] while Lord Slynn felt that nothing was to be gained by considering the events in terms of harm or injury in the ordinary sense: it was enough that the pregnancy was unwanted, and that the purpose of the vasectomy was to prevent it from taking place.[90] Similar ambivalence can be detected in Witting's article 'Physical Damage in Negligence'.[91] Although Witting accepts that pregnancy is physical damage of a 'socially constructed' kind, he denies that it amounts to physical damage of an orthodox kind. In *McFarlane*, he comments, 'the mother's conception was an entirely natural event that her

---

[84] *Anderson v Forth Valley Health Board* (1997) 44 BMLR 108 (CSOH) 137 (Lord Nimmo Smith); *Das v Ganju* [1999] PIQR P260 (CA); *Godfrey v Gloucestershire Royal Infirmary NHS Trust* [2003] EWHC 549, [2003] Lloyd's Rep Med 398.

[85] *Walkin* (n 80) 1554.

[86] *L v M* [1979] 2 NZLR 519 (NZCA) 529–30.

[87] *McFarlane v Tayside Health Board* 1997 SLT 211 (CSOH) 214.

[88] *McFarlane* (n 73) 107.

[89] ibid 86.

[90] ibid 76.

[91] Witting (n 6).

physiological constitution was designed to induce and to accommodate', so that her 'physiological integrity was not compromised'.[92] Moreover, most women were 'only too glad to avail themselves of the opportunity to conceive and to give birth at some stage in their reproductive lives'.[93]

It would appear, then, that the two principal concerns of those who are sceptical about the characterisation of pregnancy as physical damage are that pregnancy is a 'natural' event, and that some (perhaps most) women are pleased when they find out they are pregnant. There are also felt to be difficulties with fitting [74] pregnancy into general tests of personal injury and physical damage respectively. How much weight do these concerns carry? In itself, the fact that pregnancy is a 'natural' event seems irrelevant; after all, so are cancer and arthritis, yet these would undoubtedly qualify as physical damage in an appropriate case.[94] However, what really seems to lie behind the word 'natural' here is the fact that, as Witting puts it, in pregnancy a woman's 'physiological integrity' is not compromised.[95] Now from a medical perspective, this is surely correct: pregnancy is not pathological, while cancer and arthritis are. But does this matter from a legal point of view? I would submit that it does not, except in so far as it helps to explain why some women welcome pregnancy while none welcome cancer, and why pregnancy is difficult to fit within orthodox general tests of personal injury and physical damage. In itself, however, the objection carries little, if any, weight, for the simple reason that it tells us nothing about the nature of an unwanted pregnancy as experienced by the woman herself. From *her* point of view (which is surely the perspective that matters to the law of tort) the pregnancy is unquestionably a violation of her bodily integrity, as Hale LJ forcefully pointed out in *Parkinson v St James and Seacroft University Hospital NHS Trust*. An unwanted pregnancy seriously limits both a woman's physical autonomy – her ability to choose what happens to her own body – and her personal autonomy – '[her] life is no longer just [her] own but also someone else's' – while at the same time subjecting her to considerable pain and discomfort.[96] Scientifically, she may be just as 'healthy' as she was before, but for her there has been a radical change, and a change for the worse. The fact that the process is physiologically 'natural' is unlikely to be of much comfort to her.

Similarly, the difficulty with the objection that some women welcome pregnancy is that the perspective is wrong. What matters is not what some (or even

---

[92] ibid 192, 193.

[93] ibid 192–93.

[94] See *McFarlane* (n 73) 87 (Lord Hope).

[95] Thomas points out that in a number of New Zealand court decisions it has been held that since pregnancy is a natural physiological function, it is not a personal injury caused by accident for the purposes of that country's accident compensation scheme: C Thomas, 'Claims for Wrongful Pregnancy and Damages for the Upbringing of the Child' (2003) 26 *University of New South Wales Law Journal* 125, 131.

[96] *Parkinson v St James and Seacroft University Hospital NHS Trust* [2001] EWCA Civ 530, [2002] QB 266 [63]–[68]. See also West (n 7) 105: 'the physical invasion of the body occasioned by a preg-

most) women think, but what the claimant herself thinks: after all, the question is not whether pregnancy is damage *in general*, but whether it is damage *to this woman*.[97] Having said that, however, it must be admitted that hidden within this objection is an important point about pregnancy as damage. In most cases, something which is damaging to one would be damaging to all, a broken limb being a case in point. With pregnancy this is not so: since a pregnancy which is desired is incapable of amounting to a personal injury,[98] 'pregnancy may be a personal [75] injury in some cases but not in others'.[99] There is no reason why this should affect the classification of an unwanted pregnancy as actionable damage, however, since although this subjective element does give rise to a couple of complications, neither appears to be that serious. Where the existence of damage depends not only on what takes place, but also on the claimant's attitude towards it, there is a possibility that a defendant could be held liable for causing an outcome which the claimant considers harmful, but which the defendant could not reasonably have foreseen would be perceived in such terms.[100] Clearly, though, this line of argument is not open to a doctor who has negligently carried out a sterilisation or a vasectomy, nor to the manufacturer of a defective condom. Nor should it matter *why* the pregnancy is undesired: even if the mother's motivation for not wanting a child is primarily financial, the pregnancy is still unwelcome, and it is difficult to see why a woman in this position should in some way be disentitled from complaining about its effect on her physical and personal autonomy, and the pain and discomfort it causes.[101]

The final concern which seems to underlie scepticism about the classification of pregnancy as physical damage or personal injury is the perceived difficulty of fitting it into general definitions of these concepts. In the Limitation Act 1980, for example, it is said that the term 'personal injuries' 'includes any disease and any impairment of a person's physical or mental condition'.[102] Pregnancy

---

nancy ... when unwanted, is itself a harm: pregnancy is at best uncomfortable, almost always at some point painful, and at worst dangerous and life-threatening'.

[97] See *Harriton v Stephens* (n 11) [168] (Hayne J) (the damage inquiry 'directs attention to the position of the particular plaintiff, not some hypothetical class of persons of which the plaintiff might be said to be a member').

[98] See, eg, *R v Croydon Health Authority* (1997) 40 BMLR 40 (CA), where the claimant was denied recovery for the cost of bringing up a child which she had wanted, but which she would not have borne if a radiologist had detected an abnormality that meant that pregnancy put her health at risk. According to Kennedy LJ (at 47), 'when the mother wants both the pregnancy and the healthy child there is simply no loss which can give rise to a claim for damages in respect of either the normal expenses and trauma of pregnancy or the costs of bringing up the child'. See also *Walkin* (n 80) 1553 (Roch LJ).

[99] Mullis (n 83) 325.

[100] See A Grubb, 'Failed Sterilisation: Limitation and Personal Injury' [1996] *Medical Law Review* 94, 97.

[101] cf *Walkin* (n 80) 1553 (Roch LJ).

[102] s 38(1). See also Consumer Protection Act 1987, s 45(1), which uses the same formulation, though with the word 'other' inserted before the word 'impairment', and Unfair Contract Terms Act 1977, s 14 ('"personal injury" includes any disease and any impairment of physical and mental condition'). Similarly, the *Restatement, Third, Torts: Liability for Physical Harm* (Proposed Final

is obviously not a disease, but is it an 'impairment'?[103] Again, we could answer that, while it might be thought to be inappropriate and inaccurate to label pregnancy an impairment in general terms, from the point of the claimant in a wrongful conception case, it would be experienced as such, and that should be enough. An alternative response would be that the pregnancy example simply shows that this test, while useful in most contexts, cannot cover all instances of personal injury. Indeed this is implicit in the wording of the statute, which says only that personal injury *includes* diseases and impairments – in other words, the test is a guide, rather than an exhaustive definition. Similarly, Witting provides a useful general test of 'physical damage', which, he says, 'most often involves deleterious changes in the physical state or structure of persons or property',[104] and then goes on to remark that 'there was no actual deleterious change in the state of … the claimant's body' in *McFarlane*.[105] [76] The possible two responses are the same: first, that from a physiological point of view, the changes may not be deleterious, but from the claimant's point of view they undoubtedly are; or, alternatively, that the test put forward is not exhaustive – as Witting himself seems to accept, by adding the words 'most often' – and does not cover pregnancy. Either way, the use of such general tests ought not to cause us to apply a formal or scientific 'rationality' which disconnects tort law from the reality of the claimant's experience.

One possible disadvantage of characterising pregnancy as physical injury is that doing so will serve to reinforce what has been described as 'the damaging association of pregnancy with illness and vulnerability', which is in turn related to the conception of women as the 'weaker sex'.[106] In the discrimination law context, this concern led some commentators to object when the courts at one stage compared the treatment of a pregnant woman with the treatment of a sick man for the purposes of the bar on direct sex discrimination. Fredman, for example, responded that 'pregnancy is not an illness, and should not be stigmatised as "unhealthy"'.[107] Such a characterisation would also be at odds with an influential school of thought within modern obstetric medicine which has emphasised the 'natural' quality of pregnancy and childbirth, and criticised the tendency of other obstetricians to treat it as if it were an illness or medical 'condition'. These are important considerations, which might cause us to think twice, for example, before acceding to the description of pregnancy as

---

Draft No. 1, 2005) § 4 defines physical harm as 'the physical impairment of the human body or of real property or tangible personal property', adding (in comment b) that 'a change in the physical condition of a person's body or property must be detrimental for the change to count as a harmful impairment'.

[103] For an affirmative answer to this question, see *Walkin* (n 80) 1550 (Auld LJ).

[104] Witting (n 6) 190.

[105] ibid 196.

[106] J Conaghan, 'Pregnancy and the Workplace: A Question of Strategy?' (1993) 20 *Journal of Law and Society* 71, 75, 82.

[107] S Fredman, 'Pregnancy and Parenthood Reassessed' (1994) 110 *LQR* 106, 113.

an 'impairment' for the purposes of the statutory definition of personal injury. It is submitted, however, that they are not grounds for refusing to classify an unwanted pregnancy as physical damage. This is because *injury* and *illness* are clearly distinct concepts, and so by recognising an unwanted pregnancy as an actionable injury the law is in no way endorsing the stigmatisation of pregnancy as a form of ill health.

Finally, is the analysis here open to one of the criticisms which Conaghan has levelled at Witting's approach, namely that his perspective is underpinned by 'a strict separation of mind and (female) body'[108]? Conaghan goes on to develop the point as follows:

> Locating the injury of wrongful conception in a woman's *perception* of her state in a way which divorces that perception from her 'naturally' pregnant (and thereby harm-less) body, Witting manages to present the injury as non-physical in origin, a truly remarkable feat which is all the more amazing in being widely shared.[109]

My analysis also locates the injury of wrongful conception in the claimant's 'perception of her state', since I have argued that pregnancy is only actionable damage when unwelcome, and also that one possible response to arguments that pregnancy does not fall within 'orthodox' definitions of personal injury or physical damage is that these fail to take into account the subjective experience of the woman involved. In other words – and as Conaghan herself implicitly [77] acknowledges[110] – the harmfulness of pregnancy cannot be separated from the outlook of the woman in question.[111] I have not, however, 'divorced that percep-tion from the claimant's "naturally" pregnant (and thereby harm-less) body', since such a divorce presupposes adoption, on one level, of the 'neutral' or 'scientific' perspective the appropriateness of which I have expressly disavowed. It follows that, on my analysis, although the injury has a subjective aspect to it, the harm is just as 'real' and 'physical' as a broken limb. (Indeed, an unwanted pregnancy is in one respect *more* invasive than any other form of personal injury, since the claimant may be expected to follow a particular diet, and to abstain from particular substances and activities, in order not to harm the foetus. No other form of personal injury requires behaviour that puts another's interests – in this case those of the foetus – above the actor's own in this way.)

---

[108] J Conaghan, 'Tort Law and Feminist Critique' (2003) 56 *CLP* 175, 191.

[109] ibid.

[110] See ibid 204–205, where Conaghan asks whether, if we were to start with an idea of personhood which corresponded with the female rather than the male body, it would be doubted 'even for a moment that a negligently induced, *involuntary* pregnancy would be viewed as invasive' (emphasis added).

[111] Though some radical feminists would disagree: see, eg, S Firestone, *The Dialectic of Sex* (London, Cape, 1970) who argues that pregnancy is *inherently* injurious, and should be treated as such. This appears to presuppose an extraordinary degree of 'false consciousness' on the part of those women who welcome pregnancy, although it may, as Robin West has argued, capture women's own sense of the injury and danger of pregnancy, even where (in a sense) the pregnancy is desired

B. Damage and the Conventional Sum Award

As we have seen, in *Rees v Darlington Memorial Hospital NHS Trust*, a majority of the House of Lords held that in wrongful conception cases the parents were entitled to a conventional sum award of £15,000. This award was in addition to the damages payable to the mother in respect of the pregnancy and the birth. The origins of the conventional sum award lie in Lord Millett's speech in *McFarlane*. His Lordship took a particularly hard line in that case, rejecting the parents' principal claim on the grounds that it would be unfair to allow them to recover the cost of upkeep without offsetting the benefits they would receive, but concluding (unlike the rest of the House) that this argument also applied to the pregnancy and birth, since these were also the 'price of parenthood'.[112] He went on to say:

> It does not, however, follow that [the claimants] should be sent away empty-handed. The rejection of their claim to measure their loss by the consequences of Catherine's conception and birth does not lead to the conclusion that they have suffered none. They have suffered both injury and loss. They have lost the freedom to limit the size of their family. They have been denied an important aspect of their personal autonomy. Their decision to have no more children is one the law should respect and protect. They are entitled to general damages to reflect the true nature of the wrong done to them.[113]

[78] Lord Millett added that the assessment of the conventional sum should be left to the trial judge, but that in a straightforward case like *McFarlane* he would not expect it to exceed £5,000. The majority in *Rees* endorsed the idea of a conventional sum award, but departed from Lord Millett's approach in three ways: first, the award was to be on top of an award to the mother for the pregnancy and birth; secondly, the sum was to be the same in all cases; and thirdly, the sum was to be fixed at £15,000, three times the amount Lord Millett had suggested. None the less, the reasoning behind the conventional sum award was the same. According to Lord Bingham, the parents in such cases were the victims of a legal wrong, and it would be unfair to deny them any recompense at all beyond the award for the pregnancy and birth. The 'real loss' suffered in a case of this kind was the denial of the parent's (particularly the mother's) 'opportunity to live her life in the way that she wished and planned', and the conventional award would 'afford some measure of recognition of the wrong done'.[114] Lord Millett, who also sat in *Rees*, agreed. Compensation for the financial

---

(R West, 'Jurisprudence and Gender' (1988) 55 *University of Chicago Law Review* 1, 30). In any case, in a *legal* context, pregnancy can surely only be considered injurious when unwelcome, as indeed the courts have held (see n 98).

[112] *McFarlane* (n 73) 114.

[113] ibid.

[114] *Rees* (n 74) [8].

consequences of the defendant's negligence was ruled out by *McFarlane*, but 'a modest award' would 'adequately compensate for the very different injury to the parents' autonomy'.[115]

What, though, is the nature of the injury which underlies the award of the conventional sum? Since the award is to the *parents*, and not just the mother, it cannot be parasitical on the pregnancy itself; rather, the gist of the wrong must have been suffered by both the mother and the father. The case law suggests that if the award is for 'damage' at all, then the gist must be the parents' loss of autonomy. In *Cattanach v Melchior*, the leading Australian decision on wrongful conception, McHugh J and Gummow J described the interest protected by the law of negligence in such cases as the parents' interest 'in the planning of their family or, as it has been put in the United States, their reproductive future'.[116] And, as their Honours pointed out, the injury to that interest has 'varied elements'.[117] In particular, there is the physical impact on the mother, which is compensatable under *McFarlane*, and the economic impact on the parents, which is not. In addition, though, the wrongful conception deprives the parents of the ability to lead their lives as they would wish, since the bringing up of a child is an immensely time-consuming responsibility, which also radically reduces the choices the parents have when it comes to social activities, holidays and the like.[118] One way of explaining the conventional sum award would be to say that it is an attempt to compensate the parents for this loss of autonomy.[119]

[79] If that is the correct analysis, then it represents a significant departure from established principles of actionable damage, since loss of autonomy would no longer be merely a compensatable aspect of a more orthodox form of damage (as with loss of amenity and personal injury): it would instead amount to an actionable injury in its own right. There is, however, another possible interpretation of the thinking behind the conventional award, which is that the award is not compensatory at all, but is rather (in Weir's words) 'a token of the court's perception that the parents' rights ... have been infringed'.[120] Aspects of the reasoning of Lord Bingham and Lord Millett in *Rees* are certainly consistent with this rights-vindication analysis. The former remarked, for example, that the conventional award was not, and was not intended to be, 'compensatory':

---

[115] ibid [125].

[116] *Cattanach* (n 76) [66].

[117] ibid. See also [27] (Gleeson CJ) (a parent/child relationship has 'multiple aspects and consequences').

[118] As Hale LJ said in *Parkinson* (n 96), 'The obligation to provide or make acceptable and safe arrangements for the child's care and supervision lasts for 24 hours a day, 7 days a week, all year round, until the child becomes old enough to take care of himself' (at [71]).

[119] In an article written before the House of Lords' decision in *Rees*, Priaulx argued persuasively that 'the loss central to the wrongful conception case is one of reproductive autonomy' (N Priaulx, 'Joy to the World! A (Healthy) Child is Born! Reconceptualising "Harm" in Wrongful Conception' (2004) 13 *Social & Legal Studies* 5, 16).

[120] T Weir, *A Casebook on Tort*, 10th edn (London, Sweet & Maxwell, 2004) 17.

rather, it afforded 'some measure of recognition' of the wrong done.[121] And Lord Millett explicitly invoked the language of rights when justifying the conventional award in *Rees*: the award was for the denial of the parents' 'right to limit the size of their family', and the loss of the parents' opportunity to live their lives in the way they wished, 'whether characterised as a right or a freedom', was 'a proper subject for compensation'.[122]

The rights-vindication analysis of the conventional sum award represents a fundamental challenge to negligence principles, however, since on this view the award does not compensate the claimant for damage she has suffered, but is instead legal recognition of a rights violation, like an award of nominal damages in a trespass case. This challenge must be rebuffed. As we have seen, the damage requirement is central to negligence law, and it follows that, while torts such as battery can vindicate rights in the absence of harm, negligence cannot. The boundaries of actionable damage may be extended if this is thought necessary to give adequate protection to a particular interest (such as personal autonomy), but the requirement of damage cannot simply be done away with altogether. This is not a narrow, conceptualist, argument. The reason why trespass-based torts are actionable per se is that they typically involve direct, intentional conduct of a very particular nature: touching, imprisoning and so forth. Negligence, on the other hand, applies paradigmatically to unintentional conduct, incorporates no requirement of directness, and encompasses a limitless variety of actions or omissions. The damage requirement – coupled with limitations on the kinds of damage which are actionable – is therefore essential if negligence law is not unduly to restrict people's freedom of action. It follows that the compensatory analysis of the conventional sum is to be preferred.

This is almost certainly what the majority in *Rees* had in mind in any case. After all, both Lord Bingham and Lord Millett referred to the 'loss' or 'injury' which the parents had suffered when discussing the conventional sum,[123] and it is possible that when Lord Bingham denied that the award was compensatory, he meant only that the harm in question was not (unlike the cost of upkeep) readily [80] quantifiable in pecuniary terms.[124] As for Lord Millett's 'rights talk', this was probably no more than an unfortunate rhetorical slip.[125] Furthermore, Lord

---

[121] *Rees* (n 74) [8]. Lord Nicholls also said (at [17]) that the award was 'to recognise that in respect of the birth of the child the parent has suffered a legal wrong'.

[122] ibid [123].

[123] See ibid [8] (Lord Bingham) (referring three times to the parents' 'loss', and once to their 'injury') and [125] (Lord Millett) (referring to the 'injury' to the parents' autonomy).

[124] See ibid [8] (emphasis added): 'The conventional award would not be, and would not be intended to be, compensatory. *It would not be the product of calculation*'. It should be emphasised that although a fixed conventional award of this kind is unusual, it is not unique: such a sum is payable as damages for bereavement under the Fatal Accidents Act 1976, and the same technique was employed when damages used to be payable for loss of life expectancy.

[125] In Lord Hope's dissenting speech in *Rees* (n 74), he quite rightly pointed out (at [70]) that to speak of a 'right' to limit the size of one's family was to beg a lot of questions, which Lord Millett had left unanswered. In *Cattanach* (n 76), Gleeson CJ was also critical (at [23]) of this so-called 'right'.

Scott, who agreed with the conventional sum award, clearly considered it to be compensatory, describing it as an attempt 'to put a monetary value on the expected benefit of which [the claimant] was, by the doctor's negligence, deprived',[126] while Lord Hope, dissenting, asked what basis there could be for the award *other* than the compensatory principle.[127] As his Lordship pointed out, the award was not purely nominal, and yet if the purpose was simply to vindicate a rights violation, then such an award – or at most what Lord Hoffmann referred to in another context as a 'modest solatium'[128] – would surely have been sufficient; £15,000, by contrast, is a significant sum of money (roughly three-fifths of the average annual salary), the award of which must have been envisaged as redress for a substantive loss. The obvious conclusion, therefore, is that while Lord Steyn was correct to describe the conventional sum award as a 'radical and most important development' in his dissenting speech in *Rees*,[129] its significance is that it amounts to recognition of diminished autonomy as a form of actionable damage, not that it does away with the requirement of damage altogether.

IV. EDUCATIONAL NEGLIGENCE

Actions against local education authorities for defective educational provision are a relatively recent phenomenon. Claims of this kind began to surface in the law reports in the early 1990s, and the issues they raised were first considered by the House of Lords in *X (minors) v Bedfordshire County Council*,[130] where three of the five appeals concerned alleged defects in the education of children with special educational needs. The actions were brought against the education authorities themselves, and also against employees for whom they would be vicariously liable. The House held that, for public policy reasons, the direct actions based on the authorities' functions under the Education Acts should be struck out as disclosing no reasonable cause of action. However, a direct action arising out of advice provided by a psychology service set up by one authority was allowed to proceed to trial, as were the claims against employees such as educational psychologists and teachers. More generally, Lord Browne-Wilkinson said that 'a school which accepts a pupil assumes responsibility not only for his physical well-being, [81] but also for his educational needs'.[131] A few years later, the issue came before the House again, in *Phelps v London Borough of Hillingdon*.[132] This time, a seven-strong panel held that those employed by a

---

[126] *Rees* (n 74) [148].
[127] ibid [74].
[128] *Chester v Afshar* [2004] UKHL 41, [2005] 1 AC 134 [34].
[129] *Rees* (n 74) [43].
[130] *X (minors) v Bedfordshire County Council* [1995] 2 AC 633 (HL).
[131] ibid 766.
[132] *Phelps v London Borough of Hillingdon* [2001] 2 AC 619 (HL).

local education authority to carry out professional services pursuant to the authority's statutory duties owed a duty of care to the children affected by their work, and that, prima facie, the authority would be vicariously liable for the breach of this duty. Whether a direct action would lie in these circumstances was left open.

Of all the areas of law considered in this paper, it is in the educational negligence case law that the most extended analysis of the actionable damage issue is to be found. Although the House of Lords rather glossed over the point in *X (minors)* and *Phelps*,[133] the Court of Appeal has addressed it more directly, and courts at all levels have been required specifically to consider the nature of the injury in educational negligence cases for limitation purposes. Before we turn to consider these authorities in more detail, two preliminary points should be made. The first is that the actionable damage point is only one issue among many raised by educational negligence cases; hence, even if it is concluded that the type of harm which underpins such claims should be recognised as actionable damage in negligence it does not necessarily follow that recovery should be permitted. The other point is that cases involving allegations of failure to alleviate specific learning disorders (such as dyslexia) must be distinguished from more general claims of impaired intellectual development. Since it is clear that all children are owed duties of care in respect of the educational provision made for them, the issue of damage will be considered in both types of case.

It will be helpful to deal first with the learning disorders issue, since thus far this is where the case law spotlight has fallen. In *X (minors)*, for example, the three education appeals heard by the House of Lords all concerned pupils with learning disorders: one claimant sought recovery for the cost of attending a fee-paying school, an expense allegedly incurred as a result of a failure by the defendant to make provision for his numeracy difficulties, the second also sought to recover the cost of private tuition, as well as damages for impaired intellectual and personal development and distress, and the third claimed damages for diminished employment prospects and behavioural problems, which he blamed on the defendant's failure to diagnose and treat his dyslexia. In *Phelps* too, the appeals involved children with special educational needs: three of the claimants were dyslexic, and the fourth suffered from Duchenne muscular dystrophy. One of the dyslexia cases (*Phelps* itself) had gone to trial, and the claimant had been awarded general damages of £12,500 and damages of just over £30,000 for loss of earnings and the cost of tuition.

The conclusion which has emerged from this case law is that the continuing effects of a failure to ameliorate a condition such as dyslexia are themselves a form of actionable damage. The courts have generally taken the view that

---

[133] In *X (minors)* (n 130), Lord Browne-Wilkinson responded (at 764) to a defendant's submission that the damage claimed was not recoverable by saying that it was not appropriate to decide the issue at the striking-out stage.

dyslexia is a [82] condition of constitutional origin, and that although the underlying physiological causes are untreatable, the adverse consequences of the condition can be substantially mitigated by early diagnosis, followed by appropriate educational provision. Furthermore, while the defendant in these cases is not accused of worsening the claimant's condition, but only of failing to improve it, this has not in itself been seen as a problem, any more than it would be in the medical negligence context.[134] As for the condition itself, when the three education appeals in X *(minors)* came before the Court of Appeal, Evans LJ could see no reason why such a condition 'should not be recognised as a form of injury for which compensation may be awarded',[135] and Lord Slynn said in *Phelps* that 'failure to diagnose a congenital condition [such as dyslexia] and to take appropriate action as a result of which a child's level of achievement is reduced' may constitute 'damage for the purpose of the common law'.[136] We should note, however, that support for this position has not been universal: in the Court of Appeal in *Phelps*, Stuart-Smith LJ said that dyslexia was not itself an injury and that he did not see how failure to ameliorate or mitigate its effects could be an injury either.[137]

Clarification as to the nature of this form of actionable damage has been provided by an overlapping line of authority concerning the classification of educational negligence cases for the purposes of limitation and discovery. In *Phelps*, the House of Lords held that a claim for failure to mitigate the effects of dyslexia was 'a claim in respect of personal injuries' under section 33 of the Supreme Court Act 1981, a provision relating to pre-action disclosure – according to Lord Slynn, having regard to the purpose of the provision it would be wrong to adopt 'an over-legalistic view' of what amounted to personal injuries.[138] The same approach has been taken in the limitation context. In *Robinson v St Helens Metropolitan Borough Council*,[139] the Court of Appeal held that a claim in respect of failure to diagnose and make provision for dyslexia was subject to the three-year limitation period applicable in personal injury cases, and this was subsequently affirmed by the House of Lords in *Adams v Bracknell Forest DC*.[140] The leading speech in *Adams* was given by Lord Hoffmann, who described dyslexia as a congenital condition, presumably of neurological origin, the 'distinctive feature' of which was 'the combination of average or better general mental ability with severe and long-term difficulty in reading, writing and spelling'.[141] His Lordship went on to say that undiagnosed dyslexia had

---

[134] See *E (a minor)* (n 9) 877–78 (Evans LJ).
[135] ibid 877. See also 874 (Sir Thomas Bingham MR).
[136] *Phelps* (n 132) 654.
[137] *Phelps v Hillingdon LBC* [1999] 1 WLR 500 (CA) [44]. It followed that the action was not an action for personal injury, but for economic loss (ibid).
[138] *Phelps* (n 132) 664.
[139] *Robinson v St Helens Metropolitan Borough Council* [2002] EWCA Civ 1099, [2002] ELR 681.
[140] *Adams v Bracknell Forest DC* [2004] UKHL 29, [2005] 1 AC 76.
[141] ibid [2].

been treated by the courts as 'a mental disability (not being able to read and write properly) which ought to have been ameliorated', and that 'in a post-Cartesian world' such a claim was for personal injury.[142] Baroness Hale agreed: undiagnosed dyslexia was 'an impairment of the claimant's mental [83] condition' which could sound in damages for loss of amenity even if the major part of any claim would be for consequential financial loss.[143]

Once again, though, it is noteworthy that the prevailing analysis of the classification issue has met with a degree of scepticism. In *Robinson*, Sir Murray Stuart-Smith came to the conclusion that claims in respect of undiagnosed dyslexia were subject to the limitation rules pertaining to personal injury 'not without considerable hesitation',[144] and Brooke LJ said that while he understood why the House of Lords in *Phelps* wished these cases to fall within the general parameters of the personal injuries limitation regime, they were not concerned with 'vindicating a person's physical or mental integrity in the traditional sense'.[145] Similarly, in *Adams* Lord Scott remarked that although he felt bound by the decision in *Phelps*, he did not himself think that 'the deprivation of the benefit of literacy' fitted comfortably within the concept of a personal injury, since it was not (in his view) 'an impairment of a physical or mental state'.[146] This scepticism appears not to be borne out by the scientific literature, however. Most researchers now seem to accept that dyslexia is a congenital condition characterised by a phonological processing deficit, which in turn arises out of some impairment of the individual's phonological processing ability.[147] Moreover, while it is true that there are a number of dyslexia researchers who might loosely be termed 'sceptics', their scepticism is not so much directed at the idea that dyslexia is a condition of biological origin as at the idea that dyslexia should be defined by reference to a discrepancy between general intelligence and reading ability: in a nutshell, their argument is that there is no pedagogical justification for distinguishing between poor readers with high IQs and other poor readers, not least because there is no reason to expect IQ and reading ability to correlate in the first place.[148] The rights and wrongs of that debate need not concern us here, however – what matters for our purposes is that both sides of the debate seem to agree that poor reading ability is probably the result of a

---

[142] ibid [10].

[143] ibid [80].

[144] *Robinson* (n 139) [24].

[145] ibid [37].

[146] *Adams* (n 140) [68].

[147] See generally, M Snowling, *Dyslexia*, 2nd edn (Oxford, Blackwell, 2000) ch 8. See also U Firth, 'Paradoxes in the Definition of Dyslexia' (1999) 5 *Dyslexia* 192, 211 ('The consensus is emerging that dyslexia is a neuro-developmental disorder with a biological origin, which impacts on speech processing with a range of clinical manifestations'). But *cf* AW Ellis, SJP McDougall and AF Monk, 'Are Dyslexics Different? IV. In Defence of Uncertainty' (1997) 3 *Dyslexia* 12, questioning the phonological deficit hypothesis.

[148] It was an argument along these lines that formed the basis of the much publicised Dispatches television programme 'The Dyslexia Myth' (Channel 4, 8 September 2005). For a summary of the

phonological deficit of some kind, and that this deficit is likely to be of congenital origin. To the extent that there is indeed a scientific consensus along these lines, the legal characterisation of untreated dyslexia as a [84] form of actionable damage – and more particularly, a form of personal injury – would appear to be justified.

What about the second type of case, where the claimant does not suffer from a congenital condition like dyslexia, but is none the less complaining that the education provided by the defendant was in some way inadequate? Although Lord Nicholls made it clear in *Phelps* that teachers owe duties of care to *all* their pupils in the discharge of their educational responsibilities, and not just those with learning disorders,[149] it does not necessarily follow that educational underdevelopment ought to be recognised as a form of actionable damage in the absence of a learning disorder. On the contrary, it is submitted that it would in fact be a mistake to regard intellectual impairment per se as actionable damage, and that this position is consistent with the relevant authorities. In *E (a minor) v Dorset County Council*, for example, Evans LJ expressed the provisional view that a claimant without special educational needs who brought an educational negligence claim would be unable to establish any damage other than economic loss.[150] Furthermore, the reasoning of the House of Lords in *Adams v Bracknell Forest DC* indicates that impaired educational development is not per se a form of 'personal injury'. Consider Lord Hoffmann's analysis of the dyslexia issue:

> [O]n what basis can the lack of the ability to read and write be a personal injury? We know very little about the way the brain works. Some mental disabilities are caused by congenital and irremediable defects in the brain circuitry. But the brain has the most remarkable capacity to compensate for defects or injuries by calling upon other parts of the circuitry. Compare, for example, the recoveries people make from strokes which have irreversibly damaged parts of the brain. Such people, with the aid of physiotherapy and other treatment, appear to get better. Other parts of the brain acquire the ability to do the work of the damaged tissue … It would be drawing too fine a distinction to say that the neglect caused no injury because nothing could be done to repair the congenital damage in the brain circuitry and the other parts of the brain which would have to be trained to compensate had never been injured. What matters is whether one has improved one's ability to read and write. Treating the inability to do so as an untreated injury originally proceeding from other causes produces a sensible practical result.[151]

---

arguments presented in that programme, see J Moorhead, 'Is Dyslexia Just a Myth?', *The Guardian*, 7 September 2005, and for more scientific versions of the argument, see AW Ellis, SJP McDougall and AF Monk, 'Are Dyslexics Different? I. A Comparison Between Dyslexics, Reading Age Controls, Poor Readers and Precocious Readers' (1996) 2 *Dyslexia* 31; and K Stanovich, 'Toward a More Inclusive Definition of Dyslexia' (1999) 5 *Dyslexia* 154. For an overview of the issues, see Snowling (n 147) ch 2.

[149] *Phelps* (n 132) 667.

[150] *E (a minor)* (n 9) 886–87.

[151] *Adams* (n 142) [20].

This passage suggests that the inability to read and write constitutes personal injury only where its origins lie in a 'mental disability' of some kind, and where the defendant has negligently failed to help the claimant to compensate for that disability by providing her with appropriate assistance. It must follow that impaired educational development is not *generally* a form of personal injury.[152] And while this does not necessarily forestall its characterisation as actionable damage, it is difficult to see the case for recognising 'the "injury" of ignorance'[153] [85] as a sui generis category. The 'harm' in question is nebulous in the extreme, not least because while a physically injured person can be contrasted with a healthy one, there is no standard level of educational achievement with which the claimant's can be compared. How, for example, would one go about identifying the time at which the damage occurred for limitation purposes? It will also be very difficult to establish causation in cases of this type, since, as Lord Nicholls pointed out in *Phelps*, a child's ability to learn is determined in part by factors over which a school has no control, such as his emotional health and his home environment.[154] Similar difficulties may of course also arise in the learning disorders context, but they are likely to be less severe, since at least there the court is considering the effect on a child's educational progress of 'an error in diagnosing and treating a specific problem'.[155] A related complication concerns the quantum of damages. If the connection between teaching and educational advancement is murky, so too is the link between the latter and success in one's working life. Awards for loss of earnings will therefore be highly speculative. Again, the problem arises in the learning disorder cases as well,[156] but in those the court has only to consider the impact of a specific learning difficulty, and in that context there is also the option – not, perhaps regrettably, taken up by the courts – of limiting damages to the less speculative cost of remedial tuition.[157] Finally, the reason Lord Nicholls gave for extending the duty of care to all pupils – that it would be 'extraordinary' if teachers owed a duty to some pupils but not others[158] – is (with respect) unconvincing, since his Lordship was making the common mistake of speaking in general terms about a 'duty of care' without

---

[152] This also appears to be the import of Lord Scott's analysis: see especially at [68]. See also von Bar (n 76) para 283 ('It is extremely doubtful whether disruption of personality development can be properly described as personal injury').

[153] *Donohue v Copiague Union Free School District* 407 NYS 2d 874 (NY App Div 1978) 880 (Damiani JP).

[154] *Phelps* (n 132) 668. See also *Peter W v San Francisco Unified School District* 60 Cal App 3d 814 (Cal Ct App 1976) 824: '[There are] a host of factors which affect the pupil subjectively ... They may be physical, neurological, emotional, cultural, environmental'.

[155] D Fairgrieve, 'Pushing Back the Boundaries of Public Authority Liability: Tort Law Enters the Classroom' [2002] *PL* 288, 306.

[156] In the Court of Appeal in *Phelps* (n 137) Stuart-Smith LJ described the task of assessing future loss of earnings and general damages in such a case as 'virtually impossible' (at 526). See also at 530 (Otton LJ).

[157] See Fairgrieve (n 155) 306.

[158] *Phelps* (n 132) 667.

identifying the type of harm in respect of which the duty is owed. Once it is appreciated that the ongoing effects of a congenital learning disorder are a specific form of injury, distinguishable from impairment of educational development generally, any apparent inconsistency falls away: it is no more illogical to say that teachers owe a duty of care in respect of learning disorders, but not educational advancement generally, than it is to say that a construction firm owes a factory owner a duty of care in respect of physical damage to property, but not in respect of pure economic loss.[159] In any case, it is hard to see why the law of tort should not single out children with learning disorders for special treatment when policy makers and educationalists do so as a matter of course.

If, as is suggested, the law ought not to recognise educational under-development as a form of damage, then an educational negligence claimant without a learning disorder would have to bring her claim on the basis of an established head of actionable damage, such as economic loss, or psychiatric harm amounting to a recognised psychiatric illness. The latter is perhaps unlikely, though not out of [86] the question;[160] as for economic loss, the claimant would have to establish that the defendant owed her a duty in respect of economic loss. Although it is questionable whether the pupil/teacher relationship should be construed as giving rise to an assumption of responsibility under the principle in *Hedley Byrne & Co Ltd v Heller & Partners Ltd*,[161] it would be premature to rule out the possibility, particularly in the light of the emphasis the House of Lords placed on the special skills of teachers and other educational professionals in *Phelps*.[162] In any case, such an extension of *Hedley Byrne* is of little significance as regards the subject-matter of this paper, since the gist of the action would then be the pupil's financial loss, as opposed to some novel notion of 'impaired educational development'.

V. CONCLUSION

The conclusions I have arrived at in this paper on new forms of damage in negligence can be summarised as follows. First, negligent imprisonment merits compensation, at least in more serious cases, and the best way to give such redress is through recognition of imprisonment as actionable damage in negligence,

---

[159] As held in *Spartan Steel and Alloys Ltd v Martin & Co (Contractors) Ltd* [1973] QB 27 (CA).
[160] In *Gower v London Brorough of Bromley* [1999] ELR 356 (CA), for example, the claimant attributed his clinical depression to the poor education he had received at the defendant's hands.
[161] *Hedley Byrne & Co Ltd v Heller & Partners Ltd* [1964] AC 465 (HL).
[162] It is perhaps noteworthy in this connection that the example Lord Nicholls gave in *Phelps* (n 132) of an educational failure outside the special needs context was of a teacher teaching the wrong syllabus for an external examination, and thereby causing 'provable financial loss' (at 667). It is also worth noting that in *Phelps* Lord Slynn emphasised (at 653) the professional obligations of teachers, educational psychologists and the like, although his Lordship made no direct reference to the *Hedley Byrne* principle, and these comments were made in the context of what must now be regarded as actions for personal injury.

rather than extension of the tort of false imprisonment. Second, an unwanted pregnancy is a form of personal injury, albeit an unusual one, in that the existence of the injury is contingent on the perspective of the woman involved. Third, the conventional sum awarded in wrongful conception cases is best analysed as compensation for the diminution of the parents' autonomy brought about by the defendant's negligence. And, finally, while an undiagnosed and untreated learning disorder is now treated by the courts as a form of personal injury, in the absence of such a disorder educational under-development ought not to be recognised as actionable damage in its own right.

This survey also enables us to identify a number of general conclusions relating to the recognition of new categories of actionable damage. Some of these can be extrapolated from one of the examples we have looked at, standing alone. The analysis of the negligent imprisonment issue demonstrates, for example, that in some types of case the decision whether to recognise a given harm as actionable damage in negligence may be influenced by consideration of the appropriate boundaries of another cause of action, while the educational negligence example illustrates that it may also be influenced by likely difficulties in establishing causation and in quantifying damages. Meanwhile the pregnancy example indicates that in some types of case characterisation of an occurrence as damage may depend upon the perspective of the individual claimant, though it must be remembered that, while this is perfectly acceptable in the wrongful conception [87] scenario (where the defendant is inevitably aware of the claimant's likely response to pregnancy), a subjective element could give rise to complications in other contexts, where the defendant might not always be in a position accurately to predict the claimant's reaction to the event in question.

Four other general points can be made, this time drawing on more than one of the example areas discussed. The first is that whereas previously autonomy was only protected indirectly by the law of negligence (via claims for personal injury and so forth), increasingly loss of autonomy appears to be being accorded recognition as a form of actionable damage in its own right. The conventional sum award in wrongful conception cases is an example of this phenomenon, as is the case law allowing recovery for negligent imprisonment (a person's freedom of movement being, of course, an aspect of their autonomy). Since autonomy is a very important interest, this development is to be welcomed, although if negligence liability is to be kept within acceptable limits, protection can only be accorded, as at present, to certain derivative autonomy interests – freedom of movement, reproductive autonomy and so forth – rather than to autonomy in the round.[163]

---

[163] Similarly, Raz has argued (J Raz, *The Morality of Freedom* (Oxford, OUP, 1986) 247) that although the moral ideal of personal autonomy may serve to justify and to reinforce various derivative rights, there is no such thing as a right to personal autonomy as such, since it would be unduly burdensome on the members of society at large if they were duty-bound to provide the right-holder with the conditions necessary for an autonomous life.

The second point is that some of the new forms of actionable damage are difficult to quantify in monetary terms. The autonomy-based cases are good examples: it is not easy to arrive at an appropriate sum of compensation for a period of imprisonment, or for the diminished autonomy brought about by an unwanted pregnancy. These problems should not be exaggerated, however. The difficulties are no greater than those involved in assessing damages for pain and suffering or loss of amenity in a physical injury case, or for discomfort or inconvenience in nuisance. Moreover, the courts have long been required to calculate damages for loss of liberty in cases of false imprisonment,[164] while in the wrongful conception scenario the difficulties of quantification have already been resolved by the decision to award a conventional sum. Indeed, if anything, this aspect of the recent expansion of the categories of actionable damage should be welcomed as evidence that the courts are not privileging interests interference with which is readily translated into monetary terms – such as property interests – over equally important interests – such as freedom of movement – of which the same cannot be said.[165]

The third point concerns negligence as a mechanism for the vindication of rights. Hickman has argued that the expansion of the categories of actionable harm 'can be seen as an unstated response to pressures from litigants wanting to vindicate rights through actions in negligence'.[166] There is certainly some truth in [88] this observation: we have seen, for example, that negligence claims have been used to vindicate the claimant's right to freedom of movement, and it could also be argued that educational negligence litigation is designed to vindicate a broad social welfare right, the right to education. On the other hand, the very existence of the requirement of actionable damage limits the utility of negligence as a rights-vindication mechanism. This became apparent in the discussion of the rights-vindication analysis of the conventional sum award in wrongful conception cases, and the same conclusion could be drawn from the difficulties surrounding the imposition of liability for negligent imprisonment in cases in which the claimant was unaware of her imprisonment, or had no wish to leave the place of her confinement, since although in such cases it seems plausible to argue that there has been a technical violation of the claimant's right to freedom of movement, requiring the payment of nominal damages, it seems much less plausible to argue that the claimant has sustained actual damage, and hence deserves a substantial damages award. It follows that if the law's aim is

---

[164] In practice, the award is usually made by a jury, though its discretion is not unlimited: see further, *Thompson v Commissioner of Police of the Metropolis* [1998] QB 498 (CA).

[165] In *Harriton v Stephens* (n 11) Kirby J remarked (at [83]) that 'Merely because the damage is imperfectly translated into monetary terms will not necessarily preclude a court from awarding compensation in respect of that damage. It is a mistake to think otherwise'.

[166] TR Hickman, 'Tort Law, Public Authorities and the Human Rights Act 1998' in D Fairgrieve, M Andenas and J Bell (eds), *Tort Liability of Public Authorities in Comparative Perspective* (London, BIICL, 2002) 37.

to provide a comprehensive mechanism for the vindication of a right, it may be necessary to employ a cause of action other than negligence.

The final point is the importance of flexibility. Both judges and academic commentators have occasionally succumbed to the temptation to shoehorn novel forms of harm into existing categories of actionable damage, by, for example, classifying wrongful conception as a form of pure economic loss. Moreover, the courts have sometimes had little choice but to squeeze a square peg into a round hole, since they have been required to apply statutory provisions that differentiate between 'actions for personal injuries' and actions for other types of harm in cases where it is unclear on which side of that line the damage in question falls.[167] The recent expansion of the categories of actionable damage calls into question this rather unsophisticated statutory distinction, and, more generally, requires that tort lawyers pay heed to Conaghan's warning against an 'excessive deference to coherence', which she describes as 'a strong commitment to maintaining the integrity of those categories and classifications with which tort law is already imbued, and a reluctance to embrace arguments or adopt positions which might undermine tort's basic architecture'.[168] The origins of such inflexibility are no doubt multifaceted, but it seems plausible to suppose that the tendency to think only in terms of well-established categories of actionable damage is to some extent the product of an orthodox analytical framework for negligence in which the issue of actionable damage is all but ignored. By bringing that issue out into the open, therefore, we can help to ensure that in future questions concerning the limits of actionable damage meet with responses that are not only more transparent, but also more imaginative.

---

[167] Examples of such provisions are Limitation Act 1980, s 11; Consumer Protection Act 1987, s 5(1); and Unfair Contract Terms Act 1977, s 2(1). The same distinction used to be drawn in the pre-action disclosure context (see text to n 138), but the provision in question (Supreme Court Act 1981, s 33(2)) was amended when the Civil Procedure Rules were brought in, and now applies to all proceedings, not only those for personal injury and death.

[168] Conaghan (n 108) 208.

8

Causation and the Goals of Tort Law

A Robertson and Tang HW (eds), *The Goals of Private Law*
(Oxford, Hart Publishing, 2009) 165–190

[165] I. INTRODUCTION

IN THIS CHAPTER, I explore the relationship between causation and what
some people think of as the 'goals' of tort law. My contention is that it is
impossible to understand or to resolve difficult questions concerning causation unless it is appreciated that these issues go to the heart of what tort law is
about. The scope of the chapter is quite limited. In the first place, my analysis
is limited to causation in fact – the question of whether or not there is a historical connection between the wrongful conduct of the defendant and the damage
suffered by the claimant. The analytically distinct question of 'legal causation'
(or 'proximate cause') – whether the historical connection between the defendant's wrongful conduct and the damage suffered by the claimant is strong
enough to justify the imposition of liability – gives rise to its own problems,
but to my mind these are less closely connected to the question of what tort law
is about than the issues I explore in this chapter. Secondly, within the realm of
causation in fact, I am concerned only with problems of uncertainty, or proof.
The difficult issue of over-determined causes (or 'multiple causation') therefore
lies outside the scope of the chapter, since in these cases we know everything
there is to know about what happened, and the problems lie elsewhere. Again,
my justification for excluding these types of case is that I think that they tell
us less about the 'goals' of tort law than do cases of evidential uncertainty.[1]

The scope of my chapter is also limited by the supposed goals of tort law
I consider. In his very helpful analysis of the goals of tort law, Allen Linden
[166] lists six,[2] some of which appear more plausible than others, but none
of which appears absurd. Nevertheless, in this chapter, I limit my analysis to
only two of the goals which Linden identifies, compensation and deterrence.

---

[1] Though *cf* LA Alexander, 'Causation and Corrective Justice: Does Tort Law Make Sense?'
(1987) 6 *Law & Philosophy* 1, 12–13 (arguing that the urge to allow recovery in cases of causal over-
determination is grounded in retributive and distributive concerns).

[2] AM Linden, *Canadian Tort Law*, 5th edn (Toronto, Butterworths, 1993) ch 1.

The justification for this is that these are the two goals which are most frequently relied upon by those who adopt an instrumentalist approach to tort law, and that when judicial reasoning in tort cases takes an instrumentalist turn, it is to these two goals that reference is most often made. (As we shall see, this tendency is apparent in causation cases, although in this context judicial reliance on deterrence reasoning tends to be the more transparent.) The idea of tort law as a deterrence mechanism is easy enough to understand, though it should be made clear that in this chapter references to deterrence as a goal of tort law should be taken as referring to 'specific' deterrence rather than 'market' deterrence. A word or two about 'compensation' as a goal of tort law is necessary, however. At first blush it seems odd to think of compensation as an aim of tort law, since compensation is a large part of what tort law *does*. Compensation therefore looks like a means to an end, rather than the end itself, with the result that the claim that compensation is a goal of tort law seems nonsensical: one of the purposes of compensating is to compensate. Needless to say, however, this is not what is meant when compensation is described as a goal of tort law. Rather, 'compensation' is in this context shorthand for the spreading of one person's loss throughout society, this being regarded as a legitimate societal goal because conducive to the overall welfare (the combination of small losses being thought to be less damaging than a single catastrophic one) and consistent with prevailing notions of social solidarity. In other words, for 'compensation' read 'loss-spreading'.

I contrast instrumentalist accounts of tort law with the idea of tort law as a system of corrective justice. When I use the term 'corrective justice' in this chapter, I intend the phrase to encompass any account of tort law which justifies tort obligations by reference to the bipolar relationship between the parties, as opposed to external social goals such as deterrence and compensation. This clearly encompasses the work of corrective justice theorists such as Ernest Weinrib,[3] as well as the important recent rights-based accounts of tort law and negligence law given by Robert Stevens[4] and Allan Beever.[5] There are, of course, many points of disagreement between these writers, but for the purposes of this chapter what they have in common is more important.

The chapter is divided into three parts. In the first part, I consider the problem of causal indeterminacy in tort law by reference to the leading English[6] cases on the subject. I begin by looking at the cases themselves in some [167]

---

[3] EJ Weinrib, *The Idea of Private Law* (Cambridge, Mass, Harvard UP, 1995).
[4] R Stevens, *Torts and Rights* (Oxford, OUP, 2007).
[5] A Beever, *Rediscovering the Law of Negligence* (Oxford, Hart Publishing, 2007).
[6] It so happens that the leading Commonwealth cases on causal indeterminacy have arisen before the English courts, though the Supreme Court of Canada's decisions in *Cook v Lewis* [1951] SCR 830 (SCC) and *Lawson v Laferriere* [1991] 1 SCR 541 (SCC) are also important landmarks, and there is some recent Australian jurisprudence on loss of a chance, including the decision of the New South Wales Court of Appeal in *Rufo v Hosking* [2004] NSWCA 391. In the United States there is of course extensive case law in this area, and reference is made to this where appropriate.

detail, and then ask whether these cases are consistent with accounts of tort law as a system of corrective justice. In the second part of the chapter I look at the loss of a chance theory, according to which some cases of causal indeterminacy in tort law can be resolved by recharacterising the claimant's injury as the loss of a chance of avoiding injury, as opposed to the injury itself. Again, this is done by looking first at the two leading English cases in which this analysis has been put forward, and then by asking whether or not the theory holds water. I should make clear that in my view there is no fundamental distinction between the loss of a chance cases and the other cases of causal indeterminacy which have come before the courts, as is demonstrated by the fact that many of the problems with the loss of chance theory have direct counterparts in other approaches to the resolution of the causal indeterminacy problem. Nevertheless, it is I think convenient to separate out the loss of chance cases for the purposes of analysis. In the third and final part of the chapter, I look at the relationship between causal indeterminacy and the 'goals' of deterrence and compensation. In particular, I argue that recent developments in the English law on causation are only explicable by reference to these two goals, and that they also underlie the push towards recovery for lost chances. I finish by identifying some of the drawbacks of modifying tort law in this way in response to instrumentalist concerns.

II. CAUSAL INDETERMINACY

The cases I consider in this part of the chapter are all cases in which it is impossible to know for certain whether or not there was a causal link between the defendant's negligent conduct and an injury to the claimant which broadly speaking falls within the risks created by that conduct. If, notwithstanding a degree of causal indeterminacy, the claimant can still establish on the balance of probabilities that there is a causal connection, recovery is of course permitted. It is the cases where this is not possible which are problematic. There are now three such cases in which the House of Lords has allowed recovery notwithstanding the claimant's inability to establish causation in the orthodox way: *McGhee v National Coal Board*,[7] *Fairchild v Glenhaven Funeral Services Ltd*[8] and *Barker v Corus (UK) Ltd*.[9] In this part of the chapter, I begin by analysing these three cases in some detail, before asking whether or not these departures from causal orthodoxy can be justified within a framework of corrective justice, or whether instead they can be explained only by reference to external goals of deterrence and compensation. [168]

---

[7] *McGhee v National Coal Board* [1973] 1 WLR 1 (HL).
[8] *Fairchild v Glenhaven Funeral Services Ltd* [2002] UKHL 22, [2003] 1 AC 32.
[9] *Barker v Corus (UK) Ltd* [2006] UKHL 20, [2006] 2 AC 572.

A. The Case Law

The pursuer in *McGhee v National Coal Board*[10] was required by his employers to clean out brick kilns, in the course of which he was exposed to clouds of abrasive brick dust. Had his employers provided adequate washing facilities at his workplace, the pursuer could have washed off this grime at the end of his working day, but instead he remained caked in it during his cycle home from work. After a few days working in the kilns, the pursuer contracted dermatitis, and he sued his employers in negligence. The medical evidence indicated that the dermatitis was caused by the brick dust, and that the risk of contracting dermatitis had been increased by the failure to provide washing facilities. However, while the Court of Session had found that the failure to provide washing facilities had been negligent, it also held that the pursuer had not shown on the balance of probabilities that this would have prevented the dermatitis. The House of Lords allowed the pursuer's appeal, with the majority of their Lordships holding that a finding that the defender's breach of duty had materially increased the risk of injury amounted, for practical purposes, to a finding that it had 'materially contributed' to it, which was itself a sufficient causal connection according to the earlier decision of the House in *Bonnington Castings Ltd v Wardlaw*.[11] This conflation of material increase in risk and material contribution was a fairly blatant judicial sleight of hand, which has since been disapproved.[12] The one member of the House who did not endorse this reasoning was Lord Wilberforce, who described the majority's approach as 'something of a fiction',[13] and relied instead on the 'sound principle' that where a person had negligently created a risk, and injury had occurred within that risk, he should be liable unless he could show that the injury had some other cause.[14] In other words, it was the negligent defendant, rather than the innocent claimant, who should bear the consequences of the 'inherent evidential difficulty'.[15] Clearly, the House of Lords was determined to hold the defenders in *McGhee* liable, even if to do so required either reliance on a fiction or an unprecedented reversal of the burden of proof. Clues as to their Lordships' motivation are provided by Lord Simon and Lord Salmon. According to the former, not to impose liability 'would mean that the respondents were under a legal duty which they could, in the present state of medical knowledge, with impunity ignore'.[16] Lord Salmon expressed himself in almost identical terms: the approach of the courts below 'would mean that in the present state of medical knowledge ... an employer would be permitted by the law to disregard with [169] impunity his duty to take reasonable care for

---

[10] *McGhee* (n 7).
[11] *Bonnington Castings Ltd v Wardlaw* [1956] AC 613 (HL).
[12] See *Fairchild* (n 8) [65] (Lord Hoffmann).
[13] *McGhee* (n 7) 7.
[14] ibid 6.
[15] ibid.
[16] ibid 9.

the safety of his employees'.[17] In the light of these remarks, it seems plausible to suppose that the rationale for the departure from orthodox causation principles in *McGhee* was the perceived need to deter employers from exposing their employees to unreasonable risks in cases where it would be scientifically impossible for an employee to establish a link between that exposure and his or her subsequent injury.

The second of the three cases, *Fairchild v Glenhaven Funeral Services Ltd*,[18] involved a variant on the classic 'two hunters problem' raised by the Californian case of *Summers v Tice*.[19] Each of the two defendants in *Summers* at or about the same time shot at a quail, and in so doing carelessly fired towards the plaintiff, who was struck by shot. Although it was clear that one of the two defendants was responsible, the plaintiff was unable to establish from which of the two guns the shot had come. The Californian Supreme Court held that the plaintiff could recover against either defendant. The burden of proof as to causation should be shifted to the defendants, as otherwise the outcome – to deny liability altogether – would be unacceptable. A couple of years after *Summers v Tice*, the same problem confronted the Supreme Court of Canada in *Cook v Lewis*.[20] The majority of the court agreed that if the jury found themselves unable to decide which of the two hunters had shot the plaintiff because both had shot negligently in his direction, then both defendants should have been found liable. The principle underlying these decisions was subsequently expressed in the *Second Restatement of Torts* in the following terms:

> Where the conduct of two or more actors is tortious, and it is proved that harm has been caused to the plaintiff by only one of them, but there is uncertainty as to which one has caused it, the burden is upon each such actor to prove that he has not caused the harm.[21]

The issue in *Fairchild* was whether if an employee was employed at different times by two employers, both of whom breached their duty to take reasonable care to prevent him inhaling asbestos dust, the employee could recover damages from the employers if he contracted mesothelioma as a result of this exposure, but was unable to establish on the balance of probabilities whether this was due to the exposure caused by one employer, the other employer, or the two together.[22] Before addressing the legal issues raised by this question, Lord Bingham identified precisely what was and was not known about the causal link between the inhalation of asbestos dust and the onset of mesothelioma.[23] The more dust that was inhaled, the more likely it was that mesothelioma

---

[17] ibid 12.
[18] *Fairchild* (n 8).
[19] *Summers v Tice* 199 P 2d 1 (Cal 1948).
[20] *Cook* (n 6).
[21] *Restatement, Second, Torts* (1977) § 433B.
[22] See *Fairchild* (n 8) [2] (Lord Bingham).
[23] ibid [7].

would develop. However, it [170] was equally likely that the condition was caused by a single fibre, by a few fibres, or by many fibres, and the condition, once caused, was not aggravated by further exposure. It followed that, where an employee was exposed to asbestos dust by two employers in succession, his mesothelioma might have been caused by inhalation of a single fibre during one or the other period of employment, or by inhalation of a number of fibres during both periods of employment, and no one of these possibilities was any more probable than the others. The scenario in *Fairchild* was therefore slightly different from the 'two hunters' scenario, the difference being that while in the two hunters case it was definitely only one of the defendants who caused the harm, in *Fairchild* it could have been both.

The House of Lords held that in this situation, the conduct of the two employers in wrongfully exposing the employee to the risk of mesothelioma should be treated as making a material contribution to the contracting of that condition.[24] It did not matter if one of the two wrongdoers was not before the court, and the employee's entitlement against either was to full damages, though the usual contribution rules would apply. According to Lord Hoffmann, the purpose of the causal requirement rules was 'to produce a just result by delimiting the scope of liability in a way which relates to the reasons why liability for the conduct in question exists in the first place'.[25] Although one could generalise about causal requirements to some extent, where the application of such a generalisation would produce a result at odds with the underlying rationale of the liability in question, then an exception to that generalisation should be recognised. In his Lordship's opinion, this was such a situation, since the application of the general but-for rule in this case would rob the duty to protect employees against mesothelioma of all content. In such circumstances, it was therefore sufficient for the claimant to establish that the breach of duty 'contributed substantially to the risk that [he] would contract the disease'.[26]

Lord Hoffmann's policy analysis was echoed in the other speeches. Lord Bingham accepted that it could be said to be unjust to impose liability on a party who had not been shown to have caused the claimant's injury, but felt that this possibility of injustice was outweighed by the fact that otherwise an employer exposing his workers to asbestos dust could ensure his complete immunity from mesothelioma claims by ensuring that he employed only those previously exposed to excessive quantities of asbestos dust.[27] Similarly, Lord Rodger said that if the law imposed a standard of proof that no claimant could ever satisfy, then 'the substantive duty of care would be emptied of all practical content' and employers could negligently expose their employees to the risk of mesothelioma with impunity.[28]

[24] See [34] (Lord Bingham).
[25] ibid [56].
[26] ibid [47].
[27] ibid [33].
[28] ibid [155].

[171] The House of Lords felt that the outcome in *Fairchild* was consistent with that in *McGhee*.[29] It was true that, unlike in *Fairchild*, in *McGhee* the defenders were the only possible wrongdoers, but Lord Rodger did not think the distinction material:

> The important point is that in both cases the state of scientific knowledge makes it impossible for the victim to prove on the balance of probabilities that his injury was caused by the ... defendants' wrongdoing rather than by events of a similar nature which would not constitute wrongdoing on their part.[30]

On the other hand, the House went out of its way to distinguish its decision in *Wilsher v Essex Area Health Authority*,[31] where a doctor had negligently administered excess oxygen to a premature baby who had then developed a serious eye condition. Although the excess oxygen was one possible cause of this condition, on the balance of probabilities it was the result of one of a number of other possible causal agents, none of which were connected to the doctor's negligence. In these circumstances, the House of Lords had applied the but-for test and denied the claimant damages. In *Fairchild*, Lord Bingham distinguished *Wilsher* on the grounds that while in *Fairchild* only a single noxious agent was involved, in *Wilsher* there were a number of noxious agents which could have caused the damage.[32] Lord Rodger agreed that the claimant would usually have to prove that his injury was caused, 'if not by exactly the same agency as was involved in the defendant's wrongdoing, at least by an agency that operated in substantially the same way', since it was essential that the claimant prove that his injury 'was caused by the eventuation of the kind of risk created by the defendant's wrongdoing'.[33] By contrast, Lord Hoffmann believed that no principled distinction could be drawn between a single-agent and a multiple-agent case: why should it matter if the claimant had been exposed to asbestos dust and some other dust, both of which had created the risk of cancer? Nevertheless, his Lordship agreed with the result in *Wilsher* on the ground that that was not a situation in which the duty in question – to take reasonable care of patients – would have been virtually drained of content unless the causal rules had been modified.[34]

It is noteworthy that, once again, several of their Lordships in *Fairchild* expressly relied on what looked very much like a deterrence rationale for the relaxation of the causation rules, namely the argument that in cases of scientific uncertainty a strict application of orthodox causation principles would empty the duty of care owed by the defendant of all substantive content. On the other hand, it also seems fairly clear that the House of Lords considered that to

---

[29] See, eg, ibid [21] (Lord Bingham).
[30] ibid [153].
[31] *Wilsher v Essex Area Health Authority* [1988] AC 1074 (HL).
[32] *Fairchild* (n 8) [22]. See also [118] (Lord Hutton).
[33] ibid [170].
[34] ibid [69].

refuse an employee recovery in these circumstances would be *unjust*, although this position was not really [172] fully articulated, no justification being given for the assertion that irredeemable evidential uncertainty should operate to the detriment of the negligent defendants rather than the blameless employee.

In the third case, *Barker v Corus (UK) Ltd*,[35] the House of Lords was required to tidy up some unfinished business arising out of the *Fairchild* decision. The two issues that fell for decision in *Barker* were (1) whether the *Fairchild* principle applied if one element of the claimant's overall exposure to asbestos came about through a period of self-employment; and (2) whether, if liability were imposed on a defendant under the *Fairchild* principle, he was entitled to an apportionment of his liability to reflect the extent of the overall exposure attributable to his breach of duty. Their Lordships answered both these questions in the affirmative, although Lord Rodger dissented on the second issue, and was only prepared to go along with the majority's reasoning on the first issue in the light of their conclusion on the apportionment question.

The leading opinion for the majority was delivered by Lord Hoffmann, who dealt with the scope of the *Fairchild* ruling first. The significance of the fact that some of the exposure took place during a period of self-employment was that, unlike in *Fairchild*, it could not be said that the mesothelioma was definitely the result of wrongful conduct by *somebody*. However, his Lordship did not believe that the *Fairchild* principle had been intended to be so limited, not least because in *Fairchild* the House had taken the view that the facts of *McGhee* fell within the *Fairchild* principle, despite the fact that in *McGhee* the alternative source of exposure to the brick dust had not been the negligence of a third party, but the non-negligent conduct of the defendant. Instead, Lord Hoffmann considered the real limit on the scope of the *Fairchild* exception to be 'the impossibility of proving that the defendant caused the damage arises out of the existence of another potential causative agent which operated in the same way'.[36] Departing from his position in *Fairchild*, Lord Hoffmann was therefore now prepared to accept the validity of the 'single-agent' limitation, albeit only in the more nuanced form put forward by Lord Rodger, with the result that it did not matter that the alternative potential causal agent differed from the agent for which the defendant was responsible in some causally irrelevant respect, as long as the mechanism by which it could have caused the damage was the same.

The decision on this issue was more or less inevitable once it was accepted – as it had been in *Fairchild* – that *McGhee* fell within the *Fairchild* principle. As we shall see, though, it has been argued that there is a particularly strong case for displacing the normal rules of factual causation where the harm is undoubtedly the result of wrongful conduct, and the extension of the *Fairchild* principle beyond this type of case means that a justification for it must be found elsewhere.

---

[35] *Barker* (n 9).
[36] ibid [24]. See also [64] (Lord Scott).

Furthermore, once it is accepted that the exception is not so limited, there is a [173] danger that it will run out of control, and as a result it was necessary to adopt a different limitation, the 'single-agent' rule. However, it is difficult to see any logic in this limitation, and Lord Hoffmann's criticisms of it in *Fairchild* appear justified. On a practical level, the single-agent limitation does ensure that the *Fairchild* principle will not swallow up the rule to which it forms an exception, but it also seems likely to lead to significant uncertainty, as there are bound to be doubts as to whether or not two different agents have operated 'in the same way'.[37]

The apportionment question in *Barker* arose because mesothelioma is an indivisible injury, with the result that the defendants in a case like *Fairchild* appear to be concurrent joint tortfeasors, who would then, applying well-established principles, be expected to be jointly and severally liable for the entirety of the claimant's damage. Since in asbestos-related litigation many of the defendants are likely to be untraceable or insolvent, there was every likelihood that the combination of the *Fairchild* exception and the principle of joint and several liability would lead to the burdening of a single solvent defendant with a very considerable liability, despite its being responsible for only a small proportion of the claimant's overall exposure to asbestos. In *Barker*, Lord Hoffmann solved this problem by holding that in cases coming within the *Fairchild* principle, the damage which the defendant should be regarded as having caused was not the disease itself, but the creation of a risk of the disease coming about. And since risks are infinitely divisible, this meant that each defendant would be liable only for the share of the claimant's exposure attributable to his negligence. Baroness Hale agreed that liability should be apportioned, but since in her view the damage was the disease (and not the risk of disease), her Ladyship could only arrive at this result by carving out an exception to the rule that liability is *in solidum* where the damage is a single, indivisible injury. Although the majority's desire to apportion the liability in *Barker* was understandable, both the routes taken to arrive at that result were problematic. Baroness Hale's analysis represented a clear departure from well-established principles on joint and several liability, while Lord Hoffmann's recognition of risk imposition as injury is open to a number of objections, and is also difficult to reconcile with the loss of a chance cases discussed in the second part of this chapter. Before we turn to look at these issues in more depth, however, we should note that the decision in *Barker* on the apportionment issue has since been reversed by Parliament, although

---

[37] B Coote, 'Chance and the Burden of Proof in Contract and Tort' (1988) 62 *Australian Law Journal* 761, 765 neatly captures the essence of the single-agent restriction when he distinguishes between *McGhee* and *Wilsher* on the grounds that in *McGhee* the defendant increased the intensity of the risk from a single cause whereas in *Wilsher* the defendant increased the number of potential causes (see also *Accident Compensation Corporation v Ambros* [2007] NZCA 304 [31], where Glazebrook J describes the distinction as being between cases where the breach 'increases an existing risk factor' and cases where it adds a new risk factor). However, we are still left with the difficult task of distinguishing single causes from multiple potential causes in borderline cases.

the relevant provision (section 3 of the Compensation Act 2006) applies only to claims for mesothelioma, and hence the proportional liability approach will continue to apply in other cases. [174]

B. Corrective Justice Explanations

In this part of the chapter, I ask whether these three decisions of the House of Lords can be justified by reference to corrective justice considerations. I group the possible explanations into three categories: straightforward equity-based arguments for the imposition of liability; arguments based on the idea that in these causal indeterminacy cases the defendant has caused the claimant 'evidential damage'; and finally the argument that subjection to an increased risk of injury should itself count as actionable damage in negligence.

Many commentators take the view that in at least some cases of causal indeterminacy justice demands that a negligent defendant be held liable. This is particularly apparent in discussions of the 'two hunters' scenario, where it is frequently said that it would be quite wrong for the claimant to 'fall between two stools' because unable to establish causation against either one or other of the hunters. For example, Jane Stapleton has written that:

> [A]s between the innocent victim and the hunters, both of whom were careless and one of whom must have fired the fatal bullet, it might be said that the injustice to the victim in applying the orthodox common law was very great.[38]

Similarly, John Fleming considered the rationale of *Summers v Tice* to be that 'the equities between an innocent plaintiff and two negligent defendants, each of whom could have caused his injury, favour placing the risk of proof of uncertainty on the latter'.[39] There is no doubt that this position has intuitive appeal, and it seems likely to have had at least some impact on the thinking of the House of Lords in *Fairchild*, even if only Lords Nicholls and Lord Rodger make express reference to the equities as between the parties as a factor in favour of the decision.[40]

The flaw in the argument, however, is that it refers not to each defendant as an individual but to the defendants as a collective entity. And while it seems reasonable to say that, as between the claimant and the *defendants*, the equities favour the claimant, unless there is some good reason why we should 'collectivise' the defendants in this way, we still do not have a justification for the imposition of liability as between the claimant and each individual defendant. Of course, tort law does sometimes treat defendants as a collective entity, under the rubric of the principle of joint liability, but this requires an agreement

---

[38] J Stapleton, 'Lords a'leaping Evidentiary Gaps' (2002) 10 *Torts Law Journal* 276, 289.
[39] J Fleming, 'Probabilistic Causation in Tort Law' (1989) 68 *Canadian Bar Review* 661, 665.
[40] *Fairchild* (n 8) [39] and [155].

to engage in conduct fraught with unreasonable risk, an agreement which was found to be absent in *Summers v Tice*[41] and which was clearly missing on the facts of *Fairchild*. Where two defendants do not act in concert one with the other, they have are entitled to be dealt with as individuals, and it follows that from a corrective justice viewpoint we need an explanation of why *this* defendant ought to be liable to *this* claimant. In the [175] two hunters scenario, such an explanation is difficult to find. From the individual defendant's point of view, it seems irrelevant that the other possible cause of the claimant's injury is the negligence of another person, as opposed to non-negligent conduct or a natural event.[42] And yet unless the fact that all the possible causes of the injury are tortious is significant, there is nothing to distinguish the two hunters scenario from any other case of causal indeterminacy, at least as far as the basic equities between the parties are concerned. In any case, even if the equities do favour the claimant in the two hunters scenario, this explains only one of the three House of Lords decisions we have looked at, the *Fairchild* case. In neither *McGhee* nor *Barker* were all the possible causes of the claimant's injury tortious, and the attempt by the defendants in *Barker* to limit the *Fairchild* decision to such situations failed.

If we turn to look at cases of causal indeterminacy in general, and we set aside for now arguments which reformulate the damage suffered by the claimant, the only remaining justification for the imposition of liability within a corrective justice framework is that as between the innocent claimant and the admittedly negligent defendant, it is the defendant who should lose out when causation is impossible to establish. However, underlying this argument rests the assumption that somehow fault matters more than causation (without this assumption, there is no more reason to say that because the defendant is at fault, the claimant need not prove causation than there is to say that because the defendant admittedly caused the injury the claimant need not prove that the defendant was negligent). And within a corrective justice framework this assumption is simply false, for, as Allan Beever points out, 'from the perspective of corrective justice, the defendant is *entirely innocent* (with respect to the claimant) unless the claimant establishes *all* [the elements of the cause of action] against the defendant'.[43] In any case, this argument once again fails to explain the English case law, since in both *Wilsher*[44] and in *Hotson v East Berkshire Health Authority*[45] (one of the loss of a chance cases discussed below), it was impossible for the claimant to prove that the admittedly negligent doctor had caused his condition, and yet recovery was denied.

---

[41] *Summers* (n 19). It was also held that there had been no such concerted action in *Cook* (n 6).

[42] Stevens (n 4) 151. See also B Hogan, '*Cook v Lewis* Re-examined' (1961) 24 *MLR* 331, 344 (imposing liability in the two hunters scenario 'fails to give to the interests of the defendant the same consideration which it readily accords the plaintiff').

[43] Beever, *Rediscovering the Law of Negligence* (n 5) 446 (emphasis in original).

[44] *Wilsher* (n 31).

[45] *Hotson v East Berkshire Health Authority* [1987] AC 750 (HL).

The only other way of justifying the English cases within a corrective justice framework is by reformulating the damage that the claimant has suffered. Two ways of doing this have been suggested. The first, which we can call 'evidential damage', is best explained by reference to the two hunters scenario. In this scenario, we know that one of the two defendants shot the claimant, but we don't know which one. However, we also know that by his negligent act in shooting in the claimant's direction, the defendant who did not shoot the claimant (D2) obscured the fact that the other defendant (D1) did. In other words, if we take D2's negligent [176] conduct out of the equation, the claimant would have a straightforward claim for damages against D1. It has been argued that D2 has therefore caused the claimant 'evidential damage', and that this fact justifies either imposing liability on both defendants in the two hunters scenario, or at least reversing the burden of proof.[46] This is an ingenious argument, which goes some way towards explaining why we might justly treat a defendant differently where the other possible cause or causes of the claimant's injury are wrongful conduct. Ultimately, however, the argument fails to provide a justification for the English case law. As with the 'between two stools' argument, it works only if all the possible causes of the injury are tortious, and so the only case it might explain is *Fairchild*, but even there it falls down. If we revert for a moment to the two hunters scenario, the evidential damage argument must provide a justification either for reversing the burden of proof or for a stand-alone cause of action against D2. The former works fine if there are indeed two hunters, but if there are more than two it fails, since each defendant will be able to establish on the balance of probabilities that he or she was not responsible, and hence to discharge the reversed burden of proof. But the House of Lords in *Fairchild* did not limit its decision to cases involving only two employers (at least one of the appeals concerned more than two) and nor did it reverse the burden of proof, and hence give each employer the opportunity to exculpate itself. More generally, the fact that reversing the burden of proof works only in cases involving two defendants significantly undermines its utility as a mechanism for achieving just results in this context, there being no obvious distinction in principle between a two-hunter and a three-hunter scenario.[47]

---

[46] See A Porat and A Stein, *Tort Liability Under Uncertainty* (Oxford, OUP, 2001) esp ch VI. A similar argument was relied upon by Rand J in *Cook* (n 6). According to his Honour (at 832–33), the burden of proof should be shifted to the defendants as they had 'violated not only the victim's substantive right to security, but ... also culpably impaired the latter's remedial right of establishing liability'. For related arguments that centre on the creation of uncertainty as the basis of liability, see A Ripstein, *Equality, Responsibility and the Law* (Cambridge, CUP, 1999) 78–80; and A Beever, 'Cause-in-Fact: Two Steps Out of the Mire' (2001) 51 *University of Toronto Law Journal* 327.

[47] A possible way round this would be to require the defendants to discharge the reversed burden of proof without recourse to purely statistical evidence. In other words, it would not be enough for a defendant in a three hunters case to point only to the statistical improbability of his having shot the claimant – he would have to adduce other, more particularistic, evidence (for example, that the markings on the bullet show that it did not come from his gun). Although there is as yet no sign of

Unfortunately, the evidential damage doctrine runs into even greater problems if used to justify a stand-alone cause of action. Let us suppose that in the two hunters case the claimant is able to establish that in the case of both D1 and D2 either the defendant shot him or the defendant caused him evidential damage in such circumstances as would ground a cause of action. Let us suppose further that [177] we are prepared to accept that the damages in the evidential damage action would be the same as the damages in the personal injury claim, as in principle they ought to be. In these circumstances, it seems clear to me that we ought to allow the claimant to recover in full from either defendant, since we know for sure that one way or another he has a valid claim against that defendant of value $£x$.[48] The trouble is, however, that the case for such a stand-alone claim for evidential damage seems weak. As has been pointed out,[49] it is unlikely that a claim would exist for the negligent loss of hospital or police records essential to a cause of action against a third party. This is because evidential damage claims would be for pure economic loss, which is generally only recoverable in English tort law where the defendant has voluntarily assumed a responsibility towards the claimant. Added to this is a remoteness objection, since it is highly unlikely that in the two hunters scenario D2 could reasonably have foreseen that his negligence would cause the claimant to suffer from evidential damage, as opposed to personal injury.[50]

The other way of reformulating the claimant's damage is to describe it as the increased risk of injury rather than the injury itself. As we have seen, this was what Lord Hoffmann did in *Barker* to justify apportioning liability between the tortfeasors in cases falling within the *Fairchild* principle. Clearly

the English courts discounting purely statistical evidence in causation cases, the adoption of such an approach would give more bite to the reversal of the burden of proof technique, an advantage of which is that it may serve to flush out evidence the defendants might otherwise withhold (see *Summers v Tice* (n 19) 4 (Carter J): 'Ordinarily defendants are in a far better position to offer evidence to determine which one caused the injury'). I am grateful to Stephen Perry for alerting me to these possibilities.

[48] *cf* Stevens (n 4) who argues (at 150) that 'it could not be shown on the balance of probabilities against either defendant individually that he had caused a right not to suffer evidential damage to be infringed'.

[49] ibid.

[50] ibid. Stevens also argues that the evidential damage argument suffers from a circularity problem. He accepts that D2's action has obscured the fact that D1 shot the claimant, and so has robbed the claimant of the action he would otherwise have had against D1. However, he argues that if we use this fact to justify imposing liability on *both* defendants (which we must, since of course we do not know which is which) then it is no longer the case that D2 has caused the claimant loss, since the claimant now has a perfectly valid claim against D1. In his words, 'if [the argument] works against both [defendants], it works against neither' (ibid). However, this is not a circularity problem, but an infinite regression, whereby in position x the logic of argument y drives us to position z, but then in position z the logic of argument y no longer applies, so that we are bounced back to position x, where argument y kicks in again, bouncing us back to position z, and so on, ad infinitum. Hence, if we accept the evidential damage argument we are driven to a conclusion which is inconsistent with the argument, but if we abandon that position (and deny recovery), the force of the argument returns. In such cases, we are as a matter of logic free to choose between either of the competing positions.

this approach is consistent with the outcome in *Barker* itself. It is not, however, consistent with the outcome in *McGhee*, where the employer was held liable for the dermatitis, not the increased risk of contracting it brought about by the absence of washing facilities, nor with the outcome in *Fairchild*, where again liability was imposed *in solidum*. Still, we must assume that in future the English courts will apply *Barker* in cases not caught by section 3 of the Compensation Act 2006, and therefore that where liability is imposed in cases of this kind, it will be limited to the degree of additional risk created by the defendant. Unfortunately, however, the reformulation of the damage as the increased risk of injury is no more convincing than the evidential damage doctrine. Four problems can be identified. The first is that in *Barker*, Lord Hoffmann insisted – not surprisingly, bearing in mind the [178] implications of the alternative – that liability would arise only if the claimant did in fact contract mesothelioma,[51] but it is difficult to see why this should be the case if the risk really is the damage.[52] The second is that it is difficult to see why the imposition of risk is itself harmful. Of course, we do not want to be subjected to risks of injury, but that is because we do not want to suffer physical injury; if the risk does not cause us to suffer such injury then it is surely harmless,[53] and of course in these cases the whole point is that the claimant is unable to prove that the risk created by the defendant *has* caused injury.[54] The third problem is that if we accept that the imposition of risk is itself a harm, and that this provides the justification for the results in *McGhee*, *Fairchild* and *Barker*, we then need a good reason for not imposing liability for the imposition of risk in *Wilsher*. As we have seen, the single-agent/multiple-agent distinction does not provide such a reason.

The final objection is that it is assumed in all these cases that we know for certain that each defendant has materially increased the risk of injury to the claimant, but this assumption is questionable. If we take the scenario in *Fairchild*, for example, it is possible that a single asbestos fibre caused the claimant's mesothelioma, and, if this is the case, we have no way of knowing when

---

[51] *Barker* (n 9) [48].

[52] See HM Hurd, 'The Deontology of Negligence' (1996) 76 *Boston University Law Review* 249, 263 fn ('if risk-taking ... is not only culpable, but wrongful, then the requirement that a defendant cause harm is morally irrelevant'); and J Coleman, *Risks and Wrongs* (Cambridge, CUP, 1992) 399.

[53] This may not always be the case. A claimant who knows that he has been exposed to the risk of future harm may suffer anxiety as a result, and in severe cases this might result in psychiatric injury, as was alleged to have happened in one of the appeals heard by the House of Lords in *Rothwell v Chemical & Insulating Co Ltd* [2007] UKHL 39, [2008] AC 281. However, where this happens the actionable damage is not the increased risk, but the psychiatric injury it causes. See further on this and related issues, J Steele, *Risks and Legal Theory* (Oxford, Hart Publishing, 2004) 116–18.

[54] See further Hurd (n 52) 263, arguing that for an unrealised risk to count as a harm, risks would have to possess a moral ontology separate from any physical or psychological harms that materialise from them, 'a highly implausible metaphysical claim'. As she goes on to point out, risks are better understood as 'probabilistic calculations about future events derived inductively from past experience', in other words as epistemic constructs, not ontological entities. As we shall see below, the same is true of the loss of a statistical 'chance' of recovery in the medical negligence context.

that particular fibre was ingested. If in fact it was inhaled before the claimant began working for the defendant, then by the time the defendant negligently exposed the claimant to asbestos, the claimant was already doomed, and the negligence of the defendant not only did not, but *could not*, have made any difference. The argument is even stronger in the two hunters scenario, since here it seems positively unlikely that the hunter who did not in fact shoot the claimant increased the risk of injury to the claimant by negligently firing in his direction. We can test this by asking whether, at the moment the defendant pulled the trigger, there was any possibility of his shot hitting the claimant. Even if we assume a degree of indeterminism in the processes involved, for this to be the case, his gun would still have to be pointing so close to the claimant that in the split second between the defendant pulling the trigger and the bullet reaching the claimant's position the claimant might [179] move directly into the line of fire. If not, then by pulling the trigger the defendant imposes no risk whatsoever on the claimant, since there is no way that by doing so he can cause him injury.

It could be argued that this is to adopt the wrong perspective.[55] From the point of view of the defendant at the time of the breach of duty, a risk *was* imposed on the claimant (as he could not have known that his bullet would miss), and indeed this must always be the case where the defendant has been negligent *towards the claimant*, as he has to be to be liable.[56] But even if we assume that this was the perspective the House of Lords had in mind when they said that in cases falling within the *Fairchild* principle, the defendant was deemed to have caused the injury when he could be shown to have materially increased the risk of its happening, this switch from objective risk to subjective risk cannot rescue the risk as damage idea. This is because even if we accept the premise that an unrealised risk is a form of harm, this claim can surely be sustainable only if the defendant's action did *in fact* create a risk for the claimant; it would be a very strange form of 'damage' that depended for its existence on the knowledge available to the defendant at the time of the breach. As we shall see, a mirror image of this objection to the idea of risk as damage can be found in the debate on loss of a chance, where (as we shall see) it has been argued that only if the *objective* probability of the claimant recovering was greater than zero can the claimant's loss of a 'chance' plausibly be regarded as a form of harm.

---

[55] See eg S Perry, 'Risk, Harm, Interests, and Rights' in T Lewens (ed), *Risk: Philosophical Perspectives* (New York, Routledge, 2007) 197, where it is argued that for many moral purposes 'the most appropriate epistemic perspective for determining what risk one person has imposed on another will be the perspective either of the actor himself/herself or of some idealized agent, such as a reasonable person, who is imagined to be in the actor's situation at the time of acting'.

[56] See *Palsgraf v Long Island Railroad Co* 162 NE 99 (NY 1928); *Bourhill v Young* [1943] AC 92 (HL).

III. LOSS OF A CHANCE

In this part of the chapter, I consider one particular response to the problem of causal indeterminacy that has proven popular in medical negligence cases, the argument that the negligence of the defendant doctor has caused the claimant patient to lose a chance of a positive outcome. The argument is closely related to the argument from risk imposition which we have just looked at, since taking away a chance of a positive outcome and imposing a risk of injury are two sides of the same coin (we usually say that the claimant has lost a chance where the defendant was obliged to take reasonable steps to *improve* her position, and that the claimant has been subjected to a risk of injury where the defendant was under a duty to take reasonable steps not to *worsen* her position). It is not surprising, therefore, to find that the loss of a chance argument is subject to similar [180] objections. However, before we evaluate the argument, it will be helpful to take a look at the two English cases in which it has been most fully considered, *Hotson v East Berkshire Area Health Authority*[57] and *Gregg v Scott*.[58]

A. *Hotson* and *Gregg*

The claimant in *Hotson* was a boy who had fallen from a tree and injured his hip. He was taken to the defendant's hospital, but the injury was not correctly diagnosed, and he was sent home. After five days of serious pain, the claimant returned to the hospital where a proper diagnosis was made, and appropriate emergency treatment given. Unfortunately, the nature of his injury was such that a serious and permanent disability was likely to develop, and this is what eventually happened. The claimant sought damages from the defendant, which admitted that the failure to make a correct diagnosis in the first place had been negligent, but denied that this had been the cause of the disability. At the trial of the action there was a clash of medical evidence on the causation issue, but in the end the judge reached the conclusion that while there was only a one in four probability that the boy would have avoided developing the condition even if he had been given prompt treatment, the defendant's negligence had reduced that probability to zero, and that the defendant should therefore pay the claimant damages for the loss of the chance of recovery, those damages being one quarter of the damages which would have been awarded for the disability itself.

That decision was affirmed by the Court of Appeal,[59] but the House of Lords unanimously allowed the defendant's appeal. In their Lordships' opinion, it was not correct to say that the defendant's breach of duty had deprived the claimant

---

[57] *Hotson* (n 44).
[58] *Gregg v Scott* [2005] UKHL 2, [2005] 2 AC 176.
[59] *Hotson v East Berkshire HA* [1987] 2 WLR 287 (CA).

of a one in four chance of recovery. On the contrary, the evidence was that the state of the claimant's leg when he first arrived at the hospital determined one way or the other whether prompt treatment would have brought about a full recovery or whether it would have made no difference. Since the state of the claimant's leg at that time was a matter of past fact, it was up to the claimant to show on the balance of probabilities that treatment would have made a difference, and since he could not do that, his action failed. In the words of Lord Mackay:

> In the circumstances of this case the probable effect of delay in treatment was deter-
> mined by the state of the facts existing when the plaintiff was first presented to the
> hospital. It is not, in my opinion, correct to say that on arrival at the hospital he had
> a 25 per cent chance of recovery. If insufficient blood vessels were left intact by the
> fall he had no prospect of avoiding complete avascular necrosis whereas if sufficient
> blood vessels [181] were left intact on the judge's findings no further damage to the
> blood supply would have resulted if he had been given immediate treatment, and he
> would not have suffered the avascular necrosis.[60]

Similarly, Lord Ackner said that the loss of a chance issue 'cannot arise where there has been a positive finding that before the duty arose the damage complained of had already been sustained or had become inevitable'.[61] Lord Mackay made it clear that he was not ruling out the possibility that a claimant could succeed by proving loss of a chance in a medical negligence case,[62] and Lord Bridge also left this question open.[63] All that *Hotson* established, therefore, was that the loss of a chance argument will fail where on the balance of probabilities the fate of the claimant was determined at the time of the defendant's breach of duty.

The House of Lords recently revisited the loss of a chance issue in another medical negligence case, *Gregg v Scott*.[64] When the claimant in *Gregg* had visited the defendant general practitioner about a lump under his arm, the defendant assumed it to be benign, and negligently failed to refer the claimant to a specialist for further investigations. The lump turned out to be cancerous, and the defendant's negligence meant that the start of treatment was delayed for nine months. During that nine months, the cancer had spread, and it was estimated that as a result the claimant's chance of being cured (cure being defined as survival for at least 10 years) had been cut from 42 per cent to 25 per cent. The claimant sought damages for the diminution in his prospects attributable to the delay, but both the trial judge and the Court of Appeal dismissed his claim because on the balance of probabilities he would not have survived in any case. By a majority (Lord Nicholls and Lord Hope dissenting), the House of Lords agreed.

---

[60] *Hotson* (n 44) 785.
[61] ibid 792.
[62] ibid 786.
[63] ibid 782.
[64] *Gregg* (n 58).

Lord Hoffmann was not convinced by the claimant's argument that even though he could not prove, on the balance of probabilities, that the defendant's negligence had deprived him of a cure, the loss of the chance of that outcome ought itself to be recognised as a form of actionable damage. The full logical implication of this argument was that damages should be awarded in all cases in which the defendant might have caused an injury and had increased the likelihood of the injury being suffered. Adhering to this position would require the House to abandon a good deal of authority (including *Hotson* and *Wilsher*), and there were 'no new arguments or change of circumstances which could justify such a radical departure from precedent'.[65] Lord Phillips agreed that the appeal should be dismissed. Close analysis of the difficulties surrounding the statistical evidence relied on in the case only served to illustrate that the exercise of assessing the loss of a chance in a clinical negligence case was a difficult one. By contrast, establishing the consequences [182] of a doctor's negligence on the balance of probabilities was likely to be very much easier. This practical consideration was a policy reason for rejecting the loss of a chance approach, since a 'robust test which produces rough justice may be preferable to a test that on occasion will be difficult, if not impossible, to apply with confidence in practice'.[66]

Baroness Hale arrived at the same conclusion. Whether the loss of a chance argument should be accepted was in her view a matter of legal policy, and in the end she concluded that the case for change had not been made out. In particular, she was concerned that it would be unjust if claimants were given a free choice as to whether to formulate the damage as the loss of the chance of a positive outcome, or the loss of the outcome itself, since this would mean that in cases where the balance of probabilities test was satisfied, they would recover full damages, and in cases where it was not they would still recover proportionate damages. And yet if proportionate recovery were introduced across the board, that would 'surely be a case of two steps forward, three steps back for the great majority of straightforward personal injury cases'.[67] Besides, proportionate recovery would add considerably to the complexity of the issues to be resolved, and this would make settlements and trials much more difficult. All in all, the problems to which acceptance of the loss of a chance approach would give rise outweighed any policy advantages it would bring.

Lord Nicholls, dissenting, felt that in cases such as *Fairchild* the courts had demonstrated a willingness to leap an evidentiary gap when overall justice plainly so required. This was not appropriate in cases (such as *Hotson*) where the patient's actual condition at the time of the negligence was determinative of the answer to the hypothetical 'but-for' test of causation, but it was appropriate

---

[65] ibid [85].
[66] ibid [170].
[67] ibid [225].

in less straightforward cases, where the limitations on scientific and medical knowledge meant that a full identification of the patient's condition at the time of the breach of duty would not necessarily provide such an answer. And the present case was of the latter kind, since identifying the nature and extent of the claimant's cancer at the time of the mistaken diagnosis would not provide a simple answer to the question of what the outcome would have been if he had been treated promptly. His Lordship also drew on the 'empty duty' argument which had proved so influential in *Fairchild*: if claims for loss of a chance of recovery were not allowed, then the duty of care of a doctor faced with a patient with a poor prognosis would be 'hollow'.[68] Lord Hope agreed with Lord Nicholls that the appeal should be allowed, and although his reasoning was influenced more by a second argument which the claimant had put forward,[69] he made it clear that he also accepted the loss of a chance argument.

[183] Before a broader assessment of *Hotson* and *Gregg* is made, we should note that *Gregg* was not a case, like *Hotson*, where medical negligence had increased the probability of an adverse outcome *which had then material-ised*, since the claimant in *Gregg* was still alive when the case was heard in the House of Lords. This meant that Lord Phillips was able to leave open the question of whether proportionate recovery should be permitted where an adverse outcome had in fact materialised, and it follows that *Gregg* has not shut the door on claims for loss of a chance, since although no such reserva-tions were apparent in the opinions of Lord Hoffmann and Baroness Hale, the appeal was dismissed by only a bare majority of their Lordships. If we take *Hotson* and *Gregg* together, therefore, all we can say for certain on the English authorities is that a claimant will not be able to recover for a lost chance in a medical negligence case where either on the balance of probabilities his condi-tion was such at the time of the breach of duty that the threatened injury was already inevitable, or where the threatened injury has yet to materialise. Where neither of these conditions is satisfied, recovery for loss of a chance remains an open question.

B. Evaluating the Loss of a Chance Argument

Before we turn to an evaluation of the loss of a chance theory, there are three red herrings which must be dispensed with. The first is the fact that in contract there is no problem with recovery for lost chances, as is shown by the beauty contest

---

[68] ibid [4].

[69] This was that the delay in diagnosis had undoubtedly caused *some* physical injury to the claim-ant – namely the enlargement of the tumour – and that when it came to quantifying the damages for that injury, an award should be made for the effect it had had on the claimant's prospects. The diffi-culty with this argument is that it was *not* obvious that the delayed diagnosis had caused the cancer to spread: it was more likely than not that this would have happened in any case (see NJ McBride and R Bagshaw, *Tort Law*, 3rd edn (Harlow, Pearson Longman, 2008) 563).

case, *Chaplin v Hicks*.[70] The short answer to this is that breach of contract is actionable per se, and hence the claimant does not have to show (as he does in negligence) that on the balance of probabilities the defendant has caused him damage.[71] It follows that in contract cases, recovery for lost chances is a question of quantification, rather than liability, and it is well established that where a hypothetical (as opposed to a past fact) is in issue at the quantification stage, the balance of probabilities test is abandoned, and proportionate recovery permitted. That takes us to the second red herring, which is recovery for lost chances at the quantification stage in personal injury or death cases. Again, the explanation is that this is permitted at this stage where questions of past fact are not in issue.[72] The third red herring is claims for loss of a chance of an economic gain, as in *Allied Maples Group Ltd v Simmons & Simmons (a firm)*,[73] where a solicitor's negligence caused a client to miss out on the opportunity of a favourable business transaction. This [184] time the action is in tort, and the issue goes to liability rather than quantum, but none the less this type of case is of little relevance to the medical negligence context because a chance of economic gain is itself something of economic value, and hence its loss is itself an economic loss. As Tony Weir has written, '[l]osing a chance of [a monetary] gain is a loss like the loss of the gain itself, alike in quality, just less in quantity: losing a chance of not losing a leg is not at all the same kind of thing as losing the leg'.[74]

Since the loss of a chance argument is closely related to the idea of risk imposition as damage, it is not surprising to find that it is subject to similar objections. The first is that if the loss of the chance really is the damage – in Jane Stapleton's terms the 'gist' of the action[75] – then recovery should be allowed whether or not the threatened injury has actually materialised. However, it seems to be widely accepted, even by proponents of the loss of chance theory,[76] that purely speculative claims ought not to be allowed before some physical injury has occurred, and in the end the absence of such an injury was the basis of the rejection of the claim in *Gregg*. Limiting the application of the loss of chance doctrine to cases where

---

[70] *Chaplin v Hicks* [1911] 2 KB 786 (CA). See also *Kitchen v RAF Association* [1958] 1 WLR 563 (CA).

[71] See M Lunney, 'What Price a Chance?' (1995) 15 *Legal Studies* 1, 4. See also *Sellars v Adelaide Petroleum NL* (1994) 179 CLR 332 (HCA) 359 (Brennan J).

[72] See, eg, *Davies v Taylor (No 1)* [1974] AC 207 (HL).

[73] *Allied Maples Group Ltd v Simmons & Simmons (a firm)* [1995] 1 WLR 1602 (CA).

[74] T Weir, *An Introduction to Tort Law*, 2nd edn (Oxford, OUP, 2006) 80. See also Coote (n 37) 772; *Sellars* (n 71) 355 (Mason CJ, Dawson, Toohey and Gaudron JJ) ('in a case such as the present, the applicant shows *some* loss or damage was sustained by demonstrating that the contravening conduct caused the loss of a commercial opportunity which had *some* value … the value being ascertained by reference to the degree of probabilities or possibilities') (emphasis in original).

[75] J Stapleton, 'The Gist of Negligence, Part II: The Relationship between "Damage" and Causation' (1988) 104 *LQR* 389.

[76] See, eg, ibid 395, where Stapleton says that it might be possible to restrict the argument to cases where the outcome has occurred or is certain to occur.

the injury has materialised amounts to a tacit admission that the real damage is the physical injury, rather than the chance of avoiding it, in which case the theory is merely a fiction designed to circumvent the causal indeterminacy problem.[77]

The second objection is that, if recovery is to be allowed on a loss of a chance basis, then the quid pro quo must surely be that the damages of a claimant who can establish on the probabilities that the defendant caused his injury should be discounted to reflect the less than even chance that his injury would have happened anyway. And yet it seems impossible to achieve this outcome since there is nothing to stop the claimant in such a case from saying that the gist of his claim is the injury itself, and that since he can prove causation of that damage, he is entitled to full recovery. Jane Stapleton has argued that under the 'vicissitudes of life' principle a discount would in any case be made to reflect the chance that the claimant would have suffered the injury at some time even without the defendant's breach, and that 'in many cases, if not all, this approach will give a result indistinguishable from that produced had the claim been framed in [185] terms of loss a chance'.[78] With respect, however, it is difficult to see the basis for this claim that the two types of discount are likely to produce anything like the same result. Let us suppose, for example, that the probabilities in *Hotson* were reversed, so that the probability that prompt treatment would have brought about a full recovery was 75 per cent instead of 25 per cent. Full application of the loss of chance idea would require that in these circumstances the boy's damages be discounted by 25 per cent to reflect the probability that the injury would have come about in any case, but clearly any discount under the vicissitudes of life principle to reflect the possibility that even after a full recovery the boy would have developed a similar disability in the future would be far less.

The final objection to the loss of chance theory is the mirror image of the final objection to the 'risk as damage' idea, namely that in some, if not all, of the so-called loss of a chance cases the claimant has not really lost any chance at all. Where the occurrence or otherwise of the physical injury is causally determined at the time of the defendant's breach of duty, the claimant has not lost a personal chance, but only a statistical chance.[79] This was the basis of the decision in *Hotson*, where either the injury sustained in the fall ruptured so many blood vessels that necrosis was inevitable, or it did not. In other words, either the injury was treatable, in which case the breach caused the necrosis, or the injury was not treatable, in which case the breach did not cause any damage at

---

[77] See T Hill, 'A Lost Chance for Compensation in the Tort of Negligence by the House of Lords' (1991) 54 *MLR* 511, 517–18; Lunney (n 71) 5–6.

[78] Stapleton (n 75) 398.

[79] Hill (n 77) provides an excellent exposition of this argument, as does SR Perry, 'Protected Interests and Undertakings in the Law of Negligence' (1992) 42 *University of Toronto Law Journal* 247 and SR Perry, 'Risk, Harm and Responsibility' in DG Owen (ed), *Philosophical Foundations of Tort Law* (Oxford, Clarendon Press, 1995).

all. What the breach did *not* cause was the loss of a 'chance' of avoiding necrosis that the claimant had when he turned up at the hospital. Furthermore, it would be quite misguided to recognise the loss of a mere statistical chance as actionable damage in negligence, since as Stephen Perry has pointed out, it would be very odd to suppose that 'the hypothetical situation of 100 people who are assumed to have independently suffered the 'same' injury could in some sense be an asset possessed by an actual individual who has in fact incurred such an injury'.[80] The same argument against loss of a chance recovery has been put forward by Allan Beever,[81] though Beever refers not to statistical and personal chances, but to objective and epistemological probability. Objective probability, he says, is 'a feature of the world'; an event has an objective probability if 'there really is a chance that it will or will not happen'.[82] By contrast, epistemological probability 'is not a feature of the world but reflects only our understanding of the world'.[83] Suppose, for example, that you negligently [186] destroy my lottery ticket, and that I have no record of the number. If this happens before the draw is made, then it is possible (depending on whether we accept a degree of indeterminism in such matters) that there was an objective probability of, say, one in a million, that my ticket would have been the winning ticket, but if the same thing happens after the draw has been made, this is no longer a possibility. Either it was the winning ticket or it was not; we just don't *know*. If we now say that there was a one in a million 'chance' that it was the winning ticket, this cannot therefore be a reference to an objective chance, but only to an epistemological one. And as Beever says, the loss of an epistemological 'chance' is not a real loss: 'it is simply a form of factual uncertainty'.[84]

It follows that to establish actionable damage, the claimant in a loss of a chance case would have to show that at the time of the defendant's breach the later occurrence of his injury was still 'up in the air', as opposed to determined, one way or the other. Only if this is the case are we in the realms of personal (or objective) chances, as opposed to statistical (or epistemological) ones. This takes us into very deep waters indeed, however, for while in some scenarios – such as Hotson – it will be clear that this is not the case, in others it will be impossible to know either way. On the facts of *Gregg*, for example, was the claimant's fate sealed, one way or the other, when he first went to see his doctor, or could subsequent events have also played a part in the development of the

---

[80] Perry, 'Protected Interests and Undertakings' (n 79) 255. See also Hill (n 77) 516 ('a statistical chance has no real value, it is therefore not a loss and consequently not compensatable').

[81] A Beever, '*Gregg v Scott* and Loss of a Chance' (2005) 24 *University of Queensland Law Journal* 201.

[82] ibid 207.

[83] ibid.

[84] ibid 210. See also at 212 (it cannot be right for the law to compensate for the loss of such a chance, 'as that would be to compensate for the "loss" of something that does not exist').

lymphoma?[85] If, as Beever argues,[86] the law should take a deterministic stance, and assume that in all such cases the outcome was already inevitable, then there is no scope for the loss of a chance theory at all. But even if we do not go this far, the impossibility of knowing whether a subsequent outcome was or was not determined at a particular moment in time makes the distinction unworkable. In any case, since it is up to the claimant to establish that the defendant caused him damage, and since he can do this only by proving the impossible – that the outcome was not determined at the time of the breach – there is nothing to be lost by adopting Beever's position, and hence rejecting the loss of a chance argument in all cases.

One final argument, this time in favour of loss of a chance recovery, should be noted. As we have seen, in contract cases the fact that the claimant does not need to establish actionable damage means that recovery for lost chances is straightforward. It follows that if there is a contractual relationship between the two parties, there is no reason why a patient who has lost a personal chance of recovery as a result of a doctor's negligence should not be able to recover appropriate damages. Robert Stevens has suggested that the same is true whenever the defendant has voluntarily assumed a responsibility towards the claimant – as will commonly be [187] the case in the medical negligence context – since in such cases the lost chance is consequent upon the infringement of a right to careful treatment created by the assumption of responsibility.[87] Superficially, this is an attractive argument, albeit not one yet considered by the English courts. However, it should not be pushed too far. Stevens seems to think that the argument can be applied both to personal and statistical chances, since he refers to the *Hotson* case as one where this reasoning might have been used to justify recovery. The contract cases all concern personal chances, however, and the difficulty in a statistical chance case like *Hotson* is that even if the claim had been made in contract, the court would still have been faced with a question of past fact requiring resolution on the balance of probabilities. And while Stevens points out that even in a case like *Hotson* the provision of careful treatment is something for which the claimant would pay,[88] it does not follow from the fact that careful treatment has a market value that the failure to provide it causes the claimant loss recoverable in tort.[89]

---

[85] In the Court of Appeal in *Gregg*, Mance LJ took the view that subsequent events might also have played a part, and hence that the case was distinguishable from *Hotson*: see *Gregg v Scott* [2002] EWCA Civ 1471, (2003) 71 BMLR 16.

[86] Beever, '*Gregg v Scott* and Loss of a Chance' (n 80). Stephen Perry also seems to incline towards this position: see 'Risk, Harm, and Responsibility' (n 79) 337.

[87] Stevens (n 4) 50.

[88] ibid.

[89] If there were a contract between the parties, and the claimant had paid for careful treatment, then there would be a stronger case for damages, although calculating them would raise difficulties, and there would certainly be no justification for doing so by reference to a fictional lost chance of recovery.

IV. COMPENSATION AND DETERRENCE

In the first two parts of this chapter, I have argued that it is very difficult, if not impossible, to justify a relaxation of the rules in causal indeterminacy cases by reference to arguments rooted in corrective justice. It should come as no surprise that the same difficulties do not emerge if the justification is sought instead in 'goals' of compensation and deterrence. After all, if it were true that the function of tort law is to compensate and to deter, there would be no obvious reason for having a causation requirement at all. A compensation goal looks only to the loss suffered by the claimant, and a deterrence goal only at the defendant's negligent behaviour. Either way, causation, which links the two, is entirely redundant, and indeed positively counter-productive, since the enforcement of a causation requirement will mean that claimants who have suffered losses will go uncompensated, and that defendants who have acted negligently will go unpunished, with the result that tort law will under-deter.[90]

It does not necessarily follow that instrumentalist concerns of this kind lie behind the drive to water down the requirement of factual causation; the motivation might instead be a mistaken belief that doing so will bring about more just outcomes in individual cases. In fact, however, there is considerable evidence from [188] both the case law and academic commentaries that deterrence and compensation have been significant motivating factors in this connection. This claim is more difficult to substantiate in the case of compensation, but it is important to note that the cases in which the causation rules have been relaxed have all involved employees suing for diseases contracted in the workplace, a context in which there has traditionally been a powerful drive to compensate, even when negligence has not been established. Compensation as a goal may also explain the strong intuition that a claimant who can show that his injury is the result of tortious conduct, but who is unable to pinpoint the tortfeasor, ought to be awarded damages. I have argued that from a corrective justice viewpoint, this factor ought not to operate to the detriment of an individual defendant, but it does seem to give the claimant a particularly powerful societal claim to have his loss spread more widely, and of course the easiest way of doing this is via the defendant's liability insurance.[91] This certainly seems to be the view of Parliament, which responded to the decision in *Barker v Corus* by legislating for recovery *in solidum* in mesothelioma cases, thereby making it much more likely that claimants would receive full compensation than under the apportionment approach adopted by the House of Lords.

---

[90] According to two leading lawyer economists, 'the idea of causation can largely be dispensed with in an economic analysis of torts' (WM Landes and RA Posner, *The Economic Structure of Tort Law* (Cambridge, Mass, Harvard UP, 1987) 229).

[91] See *Restatement, Third, Torts: Liability for Physical Harm* (Proposed Final Draft No 1, 2005) § 28, comment o, where it is argued in the context of the American 'market-share doctrine' that a plaintiff who can demonstrate that the marketing and sale of a product was tortious, and that the product caused their harm, has a strong claim for compensation.

It is much easier to show that moves to resolve causal indeterminacy problems in favour of claimants have been motivated at least to some extent by deterrence concerns. As we have seen, in *McGhee* two members of the House of Lords were concerned that unless liability were imposed employers would be able to disregard the duties of care they owed their employees with impunity. Similarly, in *Fairchild*, Lord Bingham, Lord Hoffmann and Lord Rodger all made it apparent that one of their motivations for departing from the general but-for rule was the fact that its application would rob the duty to protect employees against mesothelioma of all content. The concern underlying this 'empty duty' is clearly that in some types of case strict adherence to the usual causation rules would not give employers an incentive to take reasonable care of their employees' interests. Supporters of the loss of a chance theory have also argued that it would produce more effective incentives than the all-or-nothing approach which is currently used in personal injury cases. For example, John Fleming, an early proponent of 'probabilistic causation', wrote that 'insistence on the traditional criteria of proof ... leads to serious under-deterrence of the harmful activity'.[92] Furthermore, a deterrence rationale might also serve to explain why the courts have been more willing to modify the causation rules in employers' negligence cases than in medical negligence cases, since the judiciary may well feel that employers need more incentives to [189] exercise reasonable care than healthcare providers. The 'empty duty' argument, for example, carries a lot more weight where the breach of duty is deliberate as opposed to inadvertent, and deliberate breaches are much more likely to happen in a commercial context where the defendant may save money by not taking the precaution in question. Installing showers in *McGhee* would have cost money; administering less oxygen in *Wilsher* would not.[93]

The wider question of whether compensation and deterrence are best achieved through tort litigation is not my present concern, but it does seem to me to be clear that adapting a mechanism of corrective justice in order to bring about broader social goals of compensation and deterrence will inevitably lead to incoherence. This incoherence is the product of an irreconcilable tension between these two goals and the fundamental nature of the mechanism through which they are sought to be achieved. Both the tension, and the resultant incoherence, are amply demonstrated by the developments in the English law governing factual causation which I have considered in this chapter. The trouble is that the logic of the instrumentalist approach has no obvious stopping

---

[92] Fleming (n 39) 662–63. See also Stapleton (n 75) 390–91, 399; and D Rosenberg, 'The Causal Connection in Mass Exposure Cases: a "Public Law" Vision of the Tort System' (1984) 97 *Harvard Law Review* 851, 866.

[93] Although the courts have been careful to adopt restrictions (such as the single-agent rule) which are superficially neutral as between industrial disease and medical negligence cases, there are clear suggestions in the case law that in practice a distinction is being drawn between the two contexts: see, eg, *Fairchild* (n 8) [69] (Lord Hoffmann).

point. If we really think, for example, that negligence should be turned into a deterrence mechanism, then not only should we do away with the causation requirement, we should do away with the damage requirement as well. But if we do this, then we find ourselves with something that no longer looks like tort law at all, but much more like the criminal law. Similarly, if we want to turn negligence into a compensation mechanism, all that matters is that the claimant has suffered loss; fault and causation are irrelevant. But again this would leave us with something that looked much more like a social security system than tort law. And because there are no logical stopping points – or rather because the logical stopping points are incompatible with the basic idea of tort law – the courts have had to resort to illogical ones instead. Hence the fact that the single-agent/multiple-agent distinction has been used to prevent the *Fairchild* exception from becoming the general rule, despite the fact that no rationale can be given for it. And hence also the fact that in *Gregg v Scott*, Lord Hoffmann ruled out recovery for loss of a chance, but only a year later, in *Barker v Corus*, his Lordship was prepared to recognise the imposition of risk as a form of actionable damage, when, as Tony Weir has pointed out, 'if contribution to the risk of harm is sufficient, it is hard to see why diminishing the chance of avoiding it should not be'.[94]

Writing extra-judicially, Lord Hoffmann has explained that the House of Lords in *Gregg* refused to enlarge the *Fairchild* exception so as to encompass the loss of a chance cases because 'one would not know where to stop. Anyone would be able [190] to sue for the possibility that his damage had been caused by a defendant. This would be a radical change in the law of tort'.[95] However, the need to preserve the essential nature of tort law by the imposition of such arbitrary limitations would never have arisen had the House of Lords resisted the temptation to use tort law as a mechanism of social policy in the first place. Perhaps, therefore, it would have been better if what his Lordship went on to describe as the 'general rule that insuperable evidential problems are the claimant's hard luck'[96] had remained not only the general rule, but the universal one.

---

[94] T Weir, 'All or Nothing?' (2004) 78 *Tulane Law Review* 511, 531. See also Lunney (n 71) 8–9. Note that since only one agent was in play in *Gregg* (the cancer), the single-agent rule cannot be used to distinguish the two cases.
[95] Lord Hoffmann, 'Causation' (2005) 121 *LQR* 592, 600.
[96] ibid 601.

Part II

Nuisance and *Rylands v Fletcher*

9

'A Tort Against Land': Private Nuisance as a Property Tort

D Nolan and A Robertson (eds), *Rights and Private Law*
(Oxford, Hart Publishing, 2012) 459–490

[459] I. INTRODUCTION

T
HE THESIS OF this chapter is that private nuisance can only properly be
understood as a tort which protects rights in land, and that, understood
in this way, it is a thoroughly coherent cause of action. I will term this the
'property tort analysis' of private nuisance. The chapter fits with the theme of
this collection because the property tort analysis of private nuisance is consistent
with the argument of Robert Stevens in his important book *Torts and Rights*
that '[t]he infringement of rights, not the infliction of loss, is the gist of the law
of torts'.[1] I begin by introducing the property tort analysis and by providing a
definition of private nuisance. The bulk of the chapter is then devoted to showing that the central doctrines of private nuisance law are consistent with the
property tort analysis. In the remainder of the chapter, I look at the relationship
between private nuisance and trespass to land, identify some sources of confusion which have served to obscure the underlying coherence of private nuisance
and consider the implications of the property tort analysis for the traditional
distinction between property and obligations. I finish off by making some more
general observations about the value of a rights-based analysis of private law.

Three preliminary points should be made. The first is that there is not the
space to discuss every aspect of the tort of private nuisance, so I have limited
my analysis to those aspects of the cause of action which seem to me to be most
relevant to the property tort analysis. The second point is [460] that my primary
focus is on English law. The basic structure of the private nuisance tort and
the substance of private nuisance law are similar throughout the common law
world, but there are significant differences in some areas, for example when it
comes to the rules on standing and the circumstances in which it is appropriate

---

[1] R Stevens, *Torts and Rights* (Oxford, OUP, 2007) 2.

for a court to award damages in lieu of an injunction. On these, and other, questions, it will be seen that the modern English law is particularly conducive to the property tort analysis, but I hope it will be concluded that despite some inconsistencies such an analysis also provides the best interpretation of the cause of action as it has developed in other common law jurisdictions. That brings me to my final preliminary point, which is that my aim is an interpretive one: to provide the best account of private nuisance law *as it stands*.[2] My claim is not therefore that the tort of private nuisance as it has developed provides the best possible means of protecting interests in the use and enjoyment of land. It may be that if we started from scratch we could devise a cause of action (or causes of action) which would do a better job at protecting these interests than private nuisance does. However, in a common law system, there are few opportunities to start from scratch, and in the case of private nuisance doing so would mean turning our back on over 800 years of legal history,[3] and potentially creating significant incoherence within the wider law of real property. It is unlikely that such an enterprise would be worth the candle.

II. 'A TORT AGAINST LAND'

In the leading modern English authority on private nuisance, *Hunter v Canary Wharf Ltd*, Lord Hoffmann described the cause of action as 'a tort against land'.[4] His Lordship obviously did not mean this literally – torts are always against *persons* – but it was a neat way of expressing the idea that a private nuisance is a violation of real property rights, or (as Dyson LJ put it in a recent public nuisance case) that '[t]he essence of the right that is protected by the tort of private nuisance is the right to enjoy one's property'.[5] Similarly, Lord Hope said in the *Hunter* case that '[t]he tort of nuisance is an invasion of the plaintiff's interest in the possession [461] and enjoyment of land',[6] and in his influential article 'The Boundaries of Nuisance', FH Newark said that private nuisance was 'a tort directed against the plaintiff's enjoyment of rights over land'.[7]

---

[2] On interpretive accounts or theories of law, see SA Smith, *Contract Theory* (Oxford, OUP, 2004) ch 1.

[3] John Baker traces the likely origins of private nuisance to the lost legislation which established the assize of novel disseisin in the reign of Henry II (1154–1189): JH Baker, *An Introduction to English Legal History*, 4th edn (London, LexisNexis Butterworths, 2002) 423.

[4] *Hunter v Canary Wharf Ltd* [1997] AC 655 (HL) 702. See also *Restatement Second, Torts* (1977) ch 40 introductory note (private nuisance is 'always a tort against land').

[5] *Corby Group Litigation Claimants v Corby Borough Council* [2008] EWCA Civ 463, [2009] QB 335 [29].

[6] *Hunter* (n 4) 723. See also at 696 (Lord Lloyd): '[T]he essence of private nuisance is easy enough to identify ... namely interference with land or the enjoyment of land'.

[7] FH Newark, 'The Boundaries of Nuisance' (1949) 65 *LQR* 480, 482. See also *Cunard v Antifyre Ltd* [1933] 1 KB 551 (KBD) 556 (Talbot J) (private nuisance 'is correctly confined to injuries to property'); *Bone v Seale* [1975] 1 WLR 797 (CA) 804 (Scarman LJ) ('Nuisance is a wrong to property').

As Lord Hoffmann went on to point out in *Hunter*, the fact that private nuisance is a violation of real property rights is obvious in cases of physical damage to the claimant's land, but less so when the interference is with the comfort and convenience of those occupying the land.[8] However, the property tort analysis holds with equal force for all types of private nuisance, once it is appreciated that in cases involving noise, smells and so on the gist of the action is not the discomfort of those affected, but the diminished utility of the land on which they live[9] – hence '[a] sulphurous chimney in a residential area is not a nuisance because it makes house-holders cough and splutter but because it prevents them taking their ease in their gardens'.[10] As we shall see, taking this idea seriously is critical to understanding the explanatory power of the property tort analysis.

Superficially, the assertion that private nuisance protects real property rights might seem uncontroversial, but there are a number of reasons why it is important that the property tort analysis be explored and defended. First, I hope to show that this analysis explains more aspects of the cause of action than is generally recognised, as well as reducing the room for manoeuvre when it comes to issues like the standing rules. Secondly, there are commentators who have expressly challenged the property tort analysis. Peter Cane has argued, for example, that unlike trespass to land, which is 'unequivocally a property tort',[11] private nuisance is 'an amalgam of property-based and obligation-based ideas', and that 'undue concentration on its property aspects is bound to produce doctrinal complications'.[12] In particular, there is a reluctance to accept that in cases of interference with comfort and convenience the gist of the action is the diminished utility of the land, with this analysis being variously described as 'odd',[13] [462] 'artificial'[14] and 'strained',[15] and with one textbook writer going so far as to say that it is based upon 'fictions' and barely stands up to scrutiny.[16] Academic criticism of the requirement that a claimant in private nuisance must have an interest in the affected land is also indicative of resistance to the property tort analysis.[17] Finally, the property tort analysis gives the lie to the apparently

---

[8] *Hunter* (n 4) 706.
[9] ibid:

> In the case of nuisances 'productive of sensible personal discomfort', the action is not for causing discomfort to the person but ... for causing injury to the land. True it is that the land has not suffered 'sensible' injury, but its utility has been diminished by the existence of the nuisance.

[10] Newark (n 7) 489.
[11] P Cane, 'What a Nuisance!' (1997) 113 *LQR* 515, 515.
[12] ibid 517–18.
[13] T Weir, *An Introduction to Tort Law*, 2nd edn (Oxford, OUP, 2006) 159 ('It is odd, however, to say that noises and smells affect the land itself, which has neither ears nor nose'). Try telling that to an estate agent tasked with selling a house next to a busy road or a sewage works.
[14] J O'Sullivan, 'Nuisance in the House of Lords: Normal Service Resumed' [1997] *CLJ* 483, 485.
[15] MA Jones, *Textbook on Torts*, 8th edn (Oxford, OUP, 2002) 338.
[16] ibid 337–38.
[17] See pt VI below.

widely held conviction that private nuisance is incoherent. To some extent, this perception seems to be based on a misreading of critical remarks directed not at private nuisance, but at an unholy combination of private and public nuisance loosely termed 'nuisance' or 'the law of nuisance'. Examples of such remarks are William Prosser's famous jibe that '[t]here is perhaps no more impenetrable jungle in the entire law than that which surrounds the word "nuisance"',[18] and Newark's remark that 'the tort of nuisance' is 'the least satisfactory department' of the law of tort.[19] However, even if we set aside remarks of this kind, we find that there is plenty of criticism of private nuisance in isolation as well. In his article on the place of private nuisance in the modern law of torts, for example, Conor Gearty pulled no punches, saying variously that the tort was 'confused and confusing', suffered from a 'poverty of principle', had lost 'all sense of that for which it stands', and lacked definition, any sense of direction and 'any coherent goals or purpose'.[20] Similarly, the authors of one tort textbook say that 'even considered on its own, in isolation from public nuisance, private nuisance suffers from a lack of doctrinal clarity' and that the tort 'has yet to be united under a coherent thread of general principle'.[21] On the contrary, the property tort analysis reveals that private nuisance suffers from no such lack of doctrinal clarity, and that properly understood it is characterised by a high level of internal coherence.

[463] III. DEFINING PRIVATE NUISANCE

Although it has been said that the word 'nuisance' is difficult to define,[22] no such difficulty attaches to the tort of private nuisance, which can be defined as an *unlawful non-trespassory interference with the private use and enjoyment of land*. It is worth taking a closer look at the elements of this definition. Some can be explained briefly. The word 'private', for example, excludes interference with a right over land which is held by members of the public generally, such as obstruction of a highway, which is not a private nuisance, but may be a public nuisance. As for the word 'unlawful', it encapsulates two important limits on the operation of the tort, both of which are explored below. One is that not all types of interference with the private use and enjoyment of land are actionable in private nuisance, but only interferences with 'natural' and 'acquired' rights. The other is that even in the case of natural or acquired rights, only a

---

[18] WL Prosser, *Handbook of the Law of Torts* (St Paul, Minn, West Publishing, 1941) 549.

[19] Newark (n 7) 480. See also JG Fleming, *The Law of Torts*, 9th edn (Sydney, Law Book Co, 1998) 457 ('Few words in the legal vocabulary are bedevilled with so much obscurity and confusion as "nuisance"').

[20] C Gearty, 'The Place of Private Nuisance in a Modern Law of Torts' [1989] *CLJ* 214, 214–16.

[21] A Mullis and K Oliphant, *Torts*, 4th edn (Basingstoke, Palgrave Macmillan, 2011) 247. See also M Lee, 'What Is Private Nuisance?' (2003) 119 *LQR* 298, 298 (the 'difficulty, if not impossibility, of reconciling the decisions on private nuisance need not be emphasised').

[22] See, eg, *Hunter* (n 4) 723 (Lord Hope); PH Winfield, 'Nuisance as a Tort' [1931] *CLJ* 189, 189.

substantial interference with the right amounts to a private nuisance. Finally, the cumbersome word 'non-trespassory' expresses the fact that the torts of trespass to land and private nuisance are mutually exclusive; the precise dividing line between the two is explored below.[23]

More complexity attaches to the phrase 'interference with ... use and enjoyment' and the word 'land'. Taking the latter first, many definitions of private nuisance refer to an interference with a person's use and enjoyment of land 'or some right over, or in connection with [land]'.[24] This qualification helpfully serves to emphasise that private nuisance encompasses interferences with acquired rights or servitudes[25] – easements and profits à prendre – but is strictly unnecessary, since the word 'land' in the definition of private nuisance refers to the legal conception of land, which is usually taken to encompass 'incorporeal hereditaments' of this kind. According to section 205(1)(ix) of the Law of Property Act 1925, for example, 'land' includes

> land of any tenure ... buildings or parts of buildings ... and other corporeal hereditaments; also a manor, an advowson, and a rent and other incorporeal hereditaments, and an easement, right, privilege, or benefit in, over, or derived from land.[26]

[464] Furthermore, since the legal conception of land encompasses not only the surface layer of the land, but also physical things attached to it, such as buildings, other structures, trees, shrubs and crops,[27] all these things rightly fall under the protection of the tort of private nuisance. By contrast, damage to personal property and personal injury are excluded by this definition from the ambit of private nuisance, with the important caveat (explored below[28]) that they could conceivably be recoverable for as consequential loss if they result from an unlawful interference with the claimant's land.

'Interference with ... use and enjoyment' of land is a broad concept: it includes, for example, causing an alteration of the physical condition of land that reduces its utility value, which explains why physical damage to the land falls within the scope of private nuisance. On the other hand, the use of this phrase excludes from the tort certain conduct which in a broad sense 'harms' the claimant's property. Opening a shop next door to a competitor may deprive the latter of much of their custom, for example, but it does not interfere with their use and enjoyment of

---

[23] See pt IX below.

[24] See, eg, WVH Rogers, *Winfield and Jolowicz on Tort*, 18th edn (London, Sweet & Maxwell, 2010) para 14-4.

[25] Gearty (n 20) 216 claims that private nuisance has a definitional problem which can be solved only by recognising that it 'must be seen as distinct ... from interference with servitudes' but as we shall see there is no such distinction, and it is hard to see why the use of private nuisance to protect acquired rights in land should be considered problematic.

[26] See also *Willies-Williams v National Trust* (1993) 65 P & CR 359 (CA) 361 (Hoffmann LJ): 'An easement is ... itself "land" vested in the proprietor of the dominant tenement'.

[27] See also K Gray and SF Gray, *Elements of Land Law*, 5th edn (Oxford, OUP, 2009) ch 1.2.

[28] See pt VIII.

their land.[29] And while diminution in market value may be evidence of substantial interference with the claimant's use and enjoyment of his or her land, it does not itself amount to such an interference[30] – a company which triggers a collapse in house prices in an area by closing down the main source of local employment does not thereby create a nuisance. These examples are illustrative of Allan Beever's statement that tort law 'is not interested in loss per se, but only in losses that flow from a violation of the claimant's primary legal rights',[31] in this case the right to the use and enjoyment of land. In two cases involving interlocutory relief, the English courts sailed rather close to the wind in this respect. By holding in *Laws v Florinplace*[32] that the mere presence of a sex shop in the locality could potentially amount to a nuisance, Vinelott J came close to imposing liability for diminution in value alone, and the same is true of the Court of Appeal's decision to grant an interlocutory injunction in *Thompson-Schwab v Costaki*,[33] which concerned a brothel. These two cases have been subjected to telling criticism by Richard Kidner, who argues that the fact that your neighbours are 'undesirable' and lower the tone of the area [465] should not in itself give you a right of action, even if their mere presence affects the value of your property.[34]

IV. NATURAL RIGHTS, ACQUIRED RIGHTS AND 'NO RIGHTS'

The presence of the word 'unlawful' in the definition of private nuisance reminds us that not every interference with the private use and enjoyment of land is actionable, but it also conceals an important distinction which is frequently overlooked or underplayed. This is the distinction between the *types* of interference with the use and enjoyment of land which are potentially actionable in private nuisance and the question of whether the *particular* interference in question is a substantial one, and so in fact actionable.[35] In this part of the chapter I want to consider the first of these two issues.

The definition of private nuisance tells us that in general terms the right which the tort protects is the right to the private use and enjoyment of land. However, closer inspection of private nuisance law reveals that in fact this umbrella 'right' encompasses a complex substructure of more specific natural rights and acquired rights, and that the tort does not protect against certain kinds of interference

---

[29] *Victoria Park Racing and Recreation Grounds Co Ltd v Taylor* (1937) 58 CLR 479 (HCA) 508 (Dixon J).

[30] *Harrison v Good* (1871) LR 11 Eq 338 (Ch) 351 (Sir James Bacon V-C); *Moy v Stoop* (1909) 25 TLR 262 (KBD) 263 (Channell J).

[31] A Beever, *Rediscovering the Tort of Negligence* (Oxford, Hart Publishing, 2007) 218. See also EJ Weinrib, *The Idea of Private Law* (Cambridge, Mass, Harvard UP, 1995) 132, 134.

[32] *Laws v Florinplace Ltd* [1981] 1 All ER 659 (Ch D).

[33] *Thompson-Schwab v Costaki* [1956] 1 WLR 335 (CA).

[34] R Kidner, 'Nuisance and Rights of Property' [1998] *Conveyancer* 267.

[35] A (perhaps crude) analogy might be drawn between this distinction and the duty/breach distinction in negligence.

with the private use and enjoyment of land at all. This threefold classification of *natural rights* (which attach automatically to the land), *acquired rights* (which the law recognises, but which must be acquired by grant or prescription) and *'no rights'* (which the law does not recognise at all) operates as a preliminary filter in private nuisance cases, which operates independently of, and anterior to, the question of whether on the facts the interference is substantial.

One of the reasons why this threefold distinction is often overlooked is that most private nuisance cases concern natural rights where the existence of protection against the type of interference in question is a given. It would be impossible to list all of these natural rights, but examples are riparian rights, the right not to have your land subjected to intolerable noise and smells, and the right to have the surface of your land supported by neighbouring land.[36] Since these rights are automatic incidents of the ownership or occupation of land, a substantial interference with such a right is actionable in private nuisance without the claimant needing to plead the existence of a servitude. In the case of acquired rights, by contrast, the existence of a servitude (an easement or a profit) must be established [466] before the court turns to consider whether or not the interference is substantial. Examples of such rights are rights of way, rights to light, rights to take wood or turf from another's land and rights to have buildings on your land supported. Finally, 'no rights' are types of interference with the private use and enjoyment of land which are not actionable in private nuisance in any circumstances – as a nineteenth-century judge put it, 'of this species of injury the law takes no cognizance'.[37] There is no natural right to be free from these kinds of interference, and such a right cannot be acquired as an easement. In such cases, the substantial interference issue never arises, with the result that, for example, even malicious interference is lawful.[38] Unlike the almost limitless variety of natural rights, the established list of 'no rights' in English law is short: there is no right to the free and uninterrupted passage of air over neighbouring land,[39] to receive percolating water from a neighbour's property,[40] not to have the view from your land obstructed,[41] not to have your land overlooked,[42] or not to have the television reception on your land interfered with by a nearby building.[43]

---

[36] For a fuller list, see K Oliphant (ed), *The Law of Tort*, 2nd edn (London, LexisNexis Butterworths, 2007) paras 22.30–22.38.

[37] *Tapling v Jones* (1865) 11 HL Cas 290, 317; 11 ER 1344, 1355 (Lord Chelmsford).

[38] See, eg, *Bradford Corp v Pickles* [1895] AC 587 (HL) (malicious appropriation of percolating water not actionable).

[39] *Webb v Bird* (1862) 13 CBNS 841, 143 ER 332.

[40] *Chasemore v Richards* (1859) 7 HL Cas 349, 11 ER 140; *Bradford Corp* (n 38).

[41] See, eg, *Aldred's Case* (1610) 9 Co Rep 57b, 58b; 77 ER 816, 821 (Wray CJ). In the United States, it has also been held that no action lies in respect of the unsightly appearance of neighbouring property: see Oliphant (n 36) para 22.20.

[42] *Tapling* (n 37); *Victoria Park Racing* (n 29).

[43] *Hunter* (n 4). See also *The People ex rel Hoogasian v Sears, Roebuck & Co* 287 NE 2d 677 (Ill 1972).

A number of further points can be made about this threefold classification. The first is that private nuisance affords precisely the same level of protection to acquired rights as it does to natural rights, no more and no less. Hence the requirement that the interference be substantial applies in cases on rights of way and rights to light, just as it does in cases on interference by noise or smell,[44] and once substantial interference has been established the usual nuisance remedies are available.[45] The second point is that the rules which give effect to this three-fold distinction are complex and resistant to attempts at simplification.[46] It is sometimes said, for example, that the list of 'no rights' reflects a wider principle that a private nuisance either always or generally requires some sort of physical intrusion or emanation, and that therefore no action lies where the defendant simply prevents something (such as percolating water or air) from reaching [467] the claimant's property.[47] While superficially neat, this attempt to force private nuisance into a trespass-type straightjacket fails to reflect the complex reality of private nuisance law, which gives an action, inter alia, for the withdrawal of lateral support from the claimant's land, diverting a stream or river away from the claimant's land, obstructing access to the claimant's land,[48] and for interference with acquired rights of way, rights to receive light and rights to receive air through a defined aperture or channel.[49] Similarly, although it is tempting to discern in the 'no rights' in respect of views and television reception a positive common law liberty (in Hohfeldian terms a 'privilege'[50]) to build whatever one likes on one's own land,[51] in English law this liberty may in fact be constrained by acquired rights to light and to the passage of air.

The final point concerns the rationale of the threefold scheme, and the considerations which the courts bring to bear when deciding how to classify a particular type of interference. Perhaps the best that can be said here is that in determining the rights we have against each other, an appropriate balance

---

[44] See Oliphant (n 36) paras 22.53–22.55.

[45] *Saint v Jenner* [1973] Ch 275 (CA) 280 (Stamp LJ).

[46] See also R Bagshaw, 'The Edges of Tort Law's Rights' in D Nolan and A Robertson (eds), *Rights and Private Law* (Oxford, Hart Publishing, 2012) 417–21.

[47] See, eg, *Hunter* (n 4) 685 (Lord Goff); *Anglian Water Services Ltd v Crawshaw Robbins & Co Ltd* [2001] BLR 173 (QBD) 197 (Burnton J); M Taggart, *Private Property and Abuse of Rights in Victorian England* (Oxford, OUP, 2002) 189; RW Wright, 'Private Nuisance Law: A Window on Substantive Justice' in Nolan and Robertson (n 46) 512–14. For a more sophisticated analysis which merely places some weight on the distinction between emanation and obstruction/withdrawal, see NJ McBride and R Bagshaw, *Tort Law*, 3rd edn (Harlow, Pearson Longman, 2008) 371–72.

[48] *J Lyons & Sons v Wilkins* [1899] 1 Ch 255 (CA); *Hubbard v Pitt* [1976] QB 142 (CA).

[49] See also the cases involving persistent phone calls to the claimant's home: *Motherwell v Motherwell* (1976) 73 DLR (3d) 62 (Alta CA); *Khorasandjian v Bush* [1993] QB 727 (CA). Is a phone call an 'emanation'?

[50] WN Hohfeld, 'Some Fundamental Legal Conceptions as Applied in Judicial Reasoning' (1913) 23 *Yale Law Journal* 16, 33.

[51] See, eg, III Bl Comm 217 ('every man may do what he pleases upon the upright or perpendicular of his own soil'). Less forthright (and more accurate): *Hunter* (n 4) 685 (Lord Goff), 709 (Lord Hoffmann).

needs to be struck between our interest in security from harm and our interest in freedom of action,[52] and that in nuisance cases achieving the right balance between the security interests of potential claimants and the liberty interests of potential defendants cannot always be done by determining whether the particular interference is or is not substantial, but requires some form of a priori ranking of interference types. In carrying out that ranking, the courts consider both the gravity of the threat which the type of interference in question poses to potential claimants' security interests, and the extent to which granting protection against this type of interference would threaten the freedom of action of potential defendants, so that for example the 'no right to a view' rule has been justified both by denigrating the threatened security interest as a 'matter only of delight, and not of necessity'[53] and by pointing to the potentially significant [468] impact such a right would have on the freedom to build on land over a 'very large and indefinite area'.[54] Needless to say, precisely where the lines are drawn will vary according to place and time, so that, for example, in the United States there is no acquired right to light,[55] and the existence of a right not to have television reception interfered with by an activity of the defendant was doubted in England in the 1960s,[56] accepted in Canada in the 1970s,[57] and countenanced (if not confirmed) in England in the 1990s.[58] It should of course also be borne in mind that the practical significance of some of the common law rules governing the actionability of different interference types has now been diminished by legislative interventions, such as planning controls and licensing schemes governing the abstraction of water.[59]

V. THE SUBSTANTIAL INTERFERENCE REQUIREMENT

Even where a natural or acquired right is in play, so that the interference type is potentially actionable, it must also be shown that on the facts the particular interference is substantial and therefore unlawful. In the words of a

---

[52] Stevens, *Torts and Rights* (n 1) 107. See further A Ripstein, *Equality, Responsibility, and the Law* (Cambridge, CUP, 1999) ch 3.

[53] *Aldred's Case* (n 41) 58b, 821 (Wray CJ).

[54] *Dalton v Henry Angus & Co* (1881) LR 6 App Cas 740 (HL) 824 (Lord Blackburn). On the threats to freedom posed by a right to the general flow of air, a right to receive percolating water and a general right to television reception, see respectively *Webb v Bird* (1861) 10 CBNS 268, 284; 142 ER 455, 461 (Erle CJ); Taggart (n 47) 65–66; *Hunter* (n 4) 727 (Lord Hope).

[55] *Fontainebleau Hotel Corp v Forty-Five Twenty-Five Inc* 114 So 2d 357 (Fla Dist Ct App 1959) 359 ('the English doctrine of "ancient lights" has been unanimously repudiated in this country').

[56] *Bridlington Relay Ltd v Yorkshire Electricity Board* [1965] Ch 436 (Ch D) 447 (Buckley J).

[57] *Nor-Video Services Ltd v Ontario Hydro* (1978) 84 DLR (3d) 221 (Ont HCJ).

[58] *Hunter* (n 4) 684–85 (Lord Goff), 708 (Lord Hoffmann). Lord Cooke clearly favoured recognition of such a right (at 719).

[59] For an example of the latter, see the Water Resources Act 1991, pt II. In *Hunter* (n 4) at 710, Lord Hoffmann described the planning system as 'a far more appropriate form of control ... than enlarging the right to bring actions for nuisance at common law'.

leading comparative tort lawyer, 'substantial interference represents a breach of a proprietary right which, in the absence of a specific justification, amounts to a wrongful act'.[60] Again, this requirement is necessary in order to achieve an appropriate balance between the claimant's security interests and the legitimate liberty interests of those in the vicinity of the claimant's property. In common law systems, this substantial interference requirement is often referred to as a requirement that there be an 'unreasonable user' of the defendant's land, but this language is [469] best avoided, for two reasons. The first is that it serves to reinforce the common misconception that only the occupier of the land from which the nuisance emanates can be liable for it.[61] And the other reason is that the use of the word 'unreasonable' in this context is apt to be understood as signifying that the *conduct of the defendant* must be unreasonable, when in fact it is the *interference with the claimant's property* which must be unreasonable.[62]

Further confusion over the import of the substantial interference requirement has been generated by commentaries on private nuisance law – most famously the *Second Restatement of Torts* – which imply that this question of substantial interference is to be answered (at least in part) by some kind of cost-benefit analysis, in which the harm the interference causes the claimant is weighed against the utility of the activity of the defendant generating the interference.[63] If this were true, then it would call into question the idea that the tort protects the claimant's real property rights, since determining the question of actionability in such a way would not give property owners and occupiers an objective 'right' at all, just as I would not have a meaningful right to bodily integrity if someone who punched me on the nose were liable in battery only if I could show that the harm thereby caused to me outweighed any gratification or other benefit they received from doing the act. In fact, however, when

---

[60] C von Bar, *The Common European Law of Torts*, vol 1 (Oxford, OUP, 1998) 552–53. See also § 906 BGB (referring to a 'substantial impairment' of the use of the affected property).

[61] See pt VII below.

[62] R Epstein, 'Nuisance Law: Corrective Justice and its Utilitarian Constraints' (1979) 8 *Journal of Legal Studies* 49, 85 ('"reasonableness" in nuisance cases should be ... understood as a synonym for the word "substantial" that directs judicial inquiry into the *level* of the defendant's invasion'). See also Wright (n 47) 507 ('In sum, "unreasonable" refers to the impact on the plaintiff's use and enjoyment of his or her land, rather than to the defendant's conduct'). On the confusion caused by the use of the word 'unreasonable' in this context, see also pt X below.

[63] See *Restatement Second, Torts* (n 4) § 826:

> An intentional invasion of another's interest in the use and enjoyment of land is unreasonable if (a) the gravity of the harm outweighs the utility of the actor's conduct, or (b) the harm caused by the conduct is serious and the financial burden of compensating for this and similar harm to others would not make the continuation of the conduct not feasible.

See also TW Merrill, 'Trespass, Nuisance and the Costs of Determining Property Rights' (1985) 14 *Journal of Legal Studies* 13, 13 ('as a rule the landholder must show that the costs of the intrusion outweigh its benefits'). Note, however, that in 1990 an American commentator claimed that only seven states 'can be said to employ the balance of utilities test as the primary criterion for the determination of nuisance liability': JL Lewin, '*Boomer* and the American Law of Nuisance: Past, Present, and Future' (1990) 54 *Albany Law Review* 189, 234. For a thorough critique of this aspect of the second *Restatement* from an American perspective, see Wright (n 47).

we look at the authorities (certainly in English law) we find no evidence that this kind of cost-benefit analysis is employed in determining liability. On the contrary, ever since *Bamford v Turnley*[64] was decided in the 1860s the courts have consistently held that no matter how beneficial the defendant's activity is, if the interference it produces is intolerable, then a private [470] nuisance action will lie.[65] As that word 'intolerable' makes clear, the true determinant of whether an interference with the use and enjoyment of land is substantial, and so actionable, is whether in all the circumstances the claimant can reasonably be expected to put up with it.[66]

Three further points can be made about this claimant-sided test of substantial interference. The first is that when assessing what the claimant can reasonably be expected to tolerate, account is taken of the force of the defendant's countervailing liberty interest. Where that liberty interest is strong, the claimant can reasonably be expected to put up with a higher level of interference, as Goddard LJ explained in *Metropolitan Properties Ltd v Jones*:

> If my neighbour is going to put up some bookcases in his house, or put in a new fireplace, for a day or two I shall be exposed, no doubt, to a considerable disturbance … but the law does not regard that as a nuisance. A man may be doing that which is necessary for his house, or his own comfort, just as I may do the same thing in my own house the following month. It is one of those things which one has to put up with.[67]

Conversely, where the defendant's liberty interest is weak or non-existent, the *less* the claimant can be expected to put up with it, so that for example where the defendant's activity has no legitimate purpose, but is motivated solely by a desire to injure the claimant, a finding of substantial interference can be expected even if the level of the interference is relatively low.[68] Similarly, the defendant's failure to take reasonable precautions to reduce or eliminate the interference caused by his or her activity will usually lead to the conclusion that it is actionable.[69]

---

[64] *Bamford v Turnley* (1862) 3 B & S 66, 122 ER 27.

[65] See, eg, *Miller v Jackson* [1977] QB 966 (CA); *Kennaway v Thompson* [1981] QB 88 (CA); *Dennis v Ministry of Defence* [2003] EWHC 793 (QB), [2003] Env LR 34. Lord Denning MR dissented on the liability issue in *Miller* but his reasoning has not been followed and is now generally disregarded.

[66] Baker (n 3) 430. See also *Kennaway* (n 65) 94 (Lawton LJ); Weir (n 13) 160; P Cane, *The Anatomy of Tort Law* (Oxford, Hart Publishing, 1997) 142. In Scots law, the standard is aptly described as one of 'reasonable tolerability': see, eg, *The Laws of Scotland: Stair Memorial Encyclopaedia* (Edinburgh, Butterworths, 1988) vol 14, paras 2037 ff; GDL Cameron, 'Neighbourhood Liability in Scotland 1850–2000' in J Gordley (ed), *The Development of Liability Between Neighbours* (Cambridge, CUP, 2010) 132, 139–40.

[67] *Metropolitan Properties Ltd v Jones* [1939] 2 All ER 202 (KBD) 205. This also explains the rule in *Harrison v Southwark and Vauxhall Water Co* [1891] 2 Ch 409 (Ch D) that temporary construction work is not actionable in nuisance if all reasonable precautions are taken to minimise the disturbance caused.

[68] See, eg, *Christie v Davey* [1893] 1 Ch 316 (Ch D); *Hollywood Silver Fox Farm Ltd v Emmett* [1936] 2 KB 468 (KBD).

[69] See, eg, *Moy v Stoop* (1909) 25 TLR 262 (KBD); *Russell Transport Ltd v Ontario Malleable Iron Co Ltd* [1952] 4 DLR 719 (Ont HC).

The second point relates to the important observation made earlier that the property tort analysis of private nuisance entails that the gist of [471] the wrong in cases of interferences with comfort and convenience (as by noise or smell) is the reduction in the utility of the land, rather than the discomfort of the people occupying it. It follows from this that when a court considers whether a particular interference is substantial, the gravity of the interference must be assessed objectively, in terms of its impact on the land itself. Hence the question at the substantial interference stage is not whether the claimant personally considers the discomfort or inconvenience to be intolerable, but whether a reasonable person in the claimant's shoes would see it that way. Famously, this principle extends to the uses to which the claimant puts his or her land,[70] but it is less often pointed out that it also extends to the physical make-up of buildings and other fixtures on the claimant's land, so that for example there is no claim if a factory emits vibrations which cause the collapse of the claimant's house only because it is abnormally decrepit,[71] or produces smoke which kills flowers growing in the claimant's garden only because they are unusually delicate.[72] This explains why private nuisance actions in respect of noises or smells have failed where the problem is attributable to the absence of adequate sound insulation[73] or the permeability of a party wall.[74]

The objective approach to the gravity of the interference is often referred to as the 'abnormal sensitivity' rule, but this is potentially misleading, since the principle should apply with equal force where the claimant or his or her use of land is abnormally *in*sensitive, as where a deaf person is in occupation of land affected by a noise nuisance.[75] Moreover, the fact that even scholars who appear to share the rights-based view of private nuisance have put forward

[70] See, eg, *Robinson v Kilvert* (1889) LR 41 Ch D 88 (CA); *Amphitheaters Inc v Portland Meadows* 198 P 2d 847 (Or 1948). See also the rule in right-to-light cases that the extent of the right 'is neither increased nor diminished by the actual use to which the dominant owner has chosen to put his premises or any of the rooms in them': *Carr-Saunders v Dick McNeil Associates Ltd* [1986] 1 WLR 922 (Ch D) 928 (Millett J).

[71] See, eg, *Cremidas v Fenton* 111 NE 855 (Mass 1916) (vibration damage to old, weak house not actionable).

[72] In *McKinnon Industries Ltd v Walker* [1951] 3 DLR 577 (PC), the Privy Council seemed to assume that damage to sensitive orchids came within the scope of the 'abnormal sensitivity' rule (which did not, however, apply on the facts).

[73] *Southwark London Borough Council v Tanner* [2001] 1 AC 1 (HL) (noise). In dismissing the claim on the grounds that the ordinary use of residential premises was not actionable in nuisance, the House of Lords arrived at the right result for the wrong reason.

[74] *Hirose Electrical UK Ltd v Peak Ingredients Ltd* [2011] EWCA Civ 987, [2011] Env LR 34 (smell).

[75] Although there appears to be no direct authority on the point, the application of an objective approach in these circumstances is approved in the *Restatement, Second, Torts* (n 4) § 821F, comment d. See also WP Keeton et al, *Prosser and Keeton on Torts*, 5th edn (St Paul, Minn, West Publishing, 1984) 628–29; McBride and Bagshaw (n 47) 369. *cf* J Murphy, *Street on Torts*, 12th edn (Oxford, OUP, 2007) 431–33 (interference actionable only if the claimant is subjectively affected). Whether, as the second *Restatement* suggests, the claimant's deafness should affect the damages recoverable is considered in pt VIII below.

ingenious alternative explanations for this principle of objective assessment suggests that the full ramifications [472] of the property tort analysis have not always been understood.[76] This is not to deny that a subjective approach would have unfortunate consequences – such as imposing an undue burden on potential defendants and 'paralysing industrial enterprises'[77] – but rather to emphasise that the courts have not simply chosen to adopt an objective standard because it leads to fairer or more efficient outcomes. On the contrary, the objective approach is an inevitable corollary of the fact that private nuisance is a tort against land.

This brings me to the final point I wish to make about the test of substantial interference, which concerns the 'locality principle', according to which the character of the neighbourhood is a relevant consideration in determining the actionability of the interference.[78] Again, ingenious explanations of this principle have been put forward – some commentators have argued, for example, that it amounts to a common law zoning regime,[79] while critical legal scholars have discerned in it a judicial conspiracy to keep the poor and downtrodden in their place.[80] A more plausible, if prosaic, explanation is that the locality principle is simply a logical concomitant of the reasonable tolerability test of substantial interference. The claimant's reasonable expectations cannot be assessed in the abstract, but must reflect the nature of the area in which he or she has chosen to buy or rent property; as a judge in a nuisance case once sardonically observed, '[T]his is an industrial area. The local inhabitants are not entitled to expect to sit in a sweet-smelling orchard'.[81] Viewing the locality principle through the prism of the reasonable tolerability test in this way explains why it is only one of the factors in the substantial interference inquiry, so that, for example, in *Rushmer v Polsue & Alfieri Ltd*[82] the *only* resident of an area devoted to printing and other noisy trades was granted an injunction where the night noise from printing presses next door represented a substantial addition to the pre-existing noise in the locality. As James Penner observes, cases such as this give the lie

---

[76] See, eg, Weinrib (n 31) 192–94 ('nuisance law disallows claims based on the plaintiff's hypersensitivity because they reflect the less ordinary of the parties' competing uses' and hence would allow 'the particular condition of one party ... to be decisive for the bipolar relationship of equals'). See also Epstein (n 62) 90–94.

[77] *Rogers v Elliott* 15 NE 768 (Mass 1888) 772 (Knowlton J).

[78] See, eg, *St Helen's Smelting Co v Tipping* (1865) 11 HL Cas 642, 11 ER 1483.

[79] See, eg, RC Ellickson, 'Alternatives to Zoning: Covenants, Nuisance Rules, and Fines as Land Use Controls' (1973) 40 *University of Chicago Law Review* 681; JF Brenner, 'Nuisance Law and the Industrial Revolution' (1974) 3 *Journal of Legal Studies* 403.

[80] See, eg, J Conaghan and W Mansell, *The Wrongs of Tort*, 2nd edn (London, Pluto Press, 1999) 137 ('an excellent vehicle for judicial prejudices ... disguising the essentially class-based nature of the exercise being carried out').

[81] *Shoreham-by-Sea Urban District Council v Dolphin Canadian Proteins Ltd* (1972) 71 LGR 261 (QBD) 266 (May J). See similarly *Colls v Home and Colonial Stores Ltd* [1904] AC 179 (HL) 185 (Lord Halsbury LC).

[82] *Rushmer v Polsue & Alfieri Ltd* [1906] 1 Ch 234 (CA) (affirmed [1907] AC 121 (HL)).

to the **[473]** claim that private nuisance law is the judicial equivalent of zoning rules designed to prevent conflicts in land use. Rather:

> The character of the neighbourhood is invoked in the most general way as a recognition of the obvious fact that town, suburban and country life differ in the level of the sorts of noise and smells, and the proximity of commercial activity to one's residence, or other commercial activity to one's business, that one ought to expect.[83]

VI. TITLE TO SUE

The most controversial consequence of the fact that private nuisance is a property tort is the rule that the claimant in a nuisance action must have a proprietary interest in the land affected, a rule which was strongly reiterated by the House of Lords in *Hunter* following a period of uncertainty.[84] Lord Cooke, who dissented in *Hunter*, argued that the standing rule in nuisance was a question of 'policy';[85] however, if private nuisance is a tort protecting land rights, then there was no policy choice, and the majority's reasoning was self-evidently correct. Just as in other property torts, such as trespass to land and conversion – and indeed property damage claims in negligence[86] – it seems axiomatic that only someone with a right in the affected property should have standing to sue. In the words of Lord Hoffmann:

> Once it is understood that nuisances 'productive of sensible personal discomfort' do not constitute a separate tort of causing discomfort to people but are merely part of a single tort of causing injury to land, the rule that the plaintiff must have an interest in the land falls into place as logical and, indeed, inevitable.[87]

Furthermore, when we look at the detail of the standing rules in private nuisance, we can see that there is a clear equivalence with the rules governing who can sue in trespass to land, and also with the rules governing standing in wrongful interference with goods cases. As Lord Goff explained in *Hunter*, a claim in private nuisance is usually brought by the person in actual possession of the affected land, either as freeholder or tenant of the land, or exceptionally as a licensee with exclusive possession.[88] **[474]** In addition, a reversioner can bring an action where the nuisance threatens their reversionary interest.[89] Precisely the same rules determine standing to sue in trespass to land,[90] and the right to sue in

---

[83] JE Penner, 'Nuisance and the Character of the Neighbourhood' (1993) 5 *Journal of Environmental Law* 1, 11.

[84] The interest in land requirement was abandoned by the Court of Appeal in *Khorasandjian* (n 49), a decision followed by the same court in *Hunter* [1997] AC 655 (CA).

[85] *Hunter* (n 4) 717.

[86] *Leigh & Sillivan Ltd v Aliakmon Shipping Co Ltd (The Aliakmon)* [1986] AC 785 (HL).

[87] *Hunter* (n 4) 707.

[88] ibid 688. See also 724 (Lord Hope).

[89] See also the *Restatement, Second, Torts* (n 4) § 821E.

[90] See Oliphant (n 36) paras 10.13 ff.

conversion is also based on possession, with an action available to reversioners when their interests in goods are under threat.[91]

The extent of academic criticism of the standing rules of private nuisance,[92] and the watering down of those rules in at least one common law jurisdiction,[93] show that there is considerable resistance to a thoroughgoing property tort analysis of the cause of action. It seems to me, however, that the standing issue demonstrates the desirability of the property tort analysis, as becomes clear if we consider the implications of abandoning the requirement that the claimant have an interest in the affected land. First, the courts would have to fashion an entirely new standing rule, and it is difficult to see what it would be. *Some* link with the land would obviously be required, but the test formulated by the Court of Appeal in *Hunter* – that the claimant must have a 'substantial link' with the property[94] – was so vague as to be almost useless.[95] Secondly, since presumably even the critics of the interest in land requirement would retain it for cases of encroachment or physical damage to the land, abandoning the requirement in cases of interference with comfort and convenience would effectively split the tort down the middle, with two different versions of the cause of action emerging, each with its own standing rules. Quite apart from anything else, this would clearly complicate matters in cases straddling the divide.[96] Thirdly, it is difficult to see how the objective approach to the assessment of damages for private nuisance (which focuses on the impact of the interference on the utility of the land[97]) could survive a relaxation in the standing rules, and unclear what principles would emerge in its place. And finally, it is hard to see how the line could be held at private nuisance. A trespasser may well cause distress or inconvenience to licensees such as lodgers or children living in the family home, so there would be little logic in jettisoning the [475] interest in land requirement in private nuisance but maintaining it in the tort of trespass to land.

Tying the right to sue in private nuisance to 'a right to possession' or 'de facto occupation'[98] is nothing new – according to William Blackstone, for example, the action on the case for nuisance 'is maintainable by one that hath possession only'.[99] This reflects the fact that, as Lord Hoffmann said in the *Hunter* case, 'Exclusive possession de jure or de facto, now or in the future, is the bedrock of English land law',[100] and that more generally (as Stevens points out in his chapter

---

[91] See S Green and J Randall, *The Tort of Conversion* (Oxford, Hart Publishing, 2009) ch 4.

[92] See the citations by Lord Cooke in *Hunter* (n 4) 717.

[93] In Canada, family members living in the owner's house have successfully brought nuisance actions: see *Motherwell* (n 49); *Devon Lumber Co Ltd v MacNeill* (1987) 45 DLR (4th) 300 (New Brunswick CA).

[94] *Hunter v Canary Wharf Ltd* [1997] AC 655 (CA) 675 (Pill LJ).

[95] *Hunter* (n 4) 693 (Lord Goff).

[96] Such as *St Helen's Smelting* (n 78).

[97] See pt VIII below.

[98] *Hunter* (n 4) 703 (Lord Hoffmann).

[99] III Bl Comm 222.

[100] *Hunter* (n 4) 703.

in this book) 'property rights in relation to things arise from possession'.[101] The suggestion that the long-standing requirement of an interest in the land affected be abandoned therefore represents not only a threat to the coherence of the private nuisance action itself, but also to the very foundations of land law and property law more generally. This danger arises because critics of the standing rules have lost sight of the fact that property torts like trespass to land, private nuisance and conversion are not free-standing causes of action but are merely constituent elements of the wider law of property.[102] It follows that these torts are not free to establish their own standing rules, but that they presuppose 'some prior, independent method for defining and recognizing' the property rights which they protect.[103] Hence, the *Second Restatement of Torts* quite rightly defers to the *Restatement of Property* when it comes to the 'rules applicable in determining when a person's rights and privileges in respect to land constitute property rights and privileges' and so give title to sue in nuisance.[104] More than any other aspect of the cause of action, the rules on standing point ineluctably to the fundamental nature of private nuisance as a property tort.

VII. WHO CAN BE LIABLE

If private nuisance is a property tort, then since property rights are good against the whole world, it would follow that the creator of a nuisance should always be liable for it. This is indeed the case, and in particular there is no requirement that the defendant must be the owner or the occupier of the land from which the interference emanates, so that a trespasser[105] or licensee[106] on another's land can be sued if they create a **[476]** nuisance there, and a nuisance may originate on the public highway.[107] Limiting liability to the owner or occupier of the land which is the source of the interference would of course be highly illogical, as Henry LJ has observed:

> There would be no sense in a law which prevented you from playing your music at maximum volume in the middle of the night from your home but permitted you to walk around your neighbourhood with your 'ghetto-blaster' at full pitch.[108]

---

[101] R Stevens, 'Rights and Other Things' in Nolan and Robertson (n 46) 137.

[102] See pt XI below.

[103] Epstein (n 62) 52.

[104] *Restatement, Second, Torts* (n 4) § 821E, comment b.

[105] *Kraemers v A-G of Tasmania* [1966] Tas SR (Tas SC) 113.

[106] *Thompson v Gibson* (1841) 7 M & W 456, 151 ER 845; *Fennell v Robson Excavations Pty Ltd* [1977] 2 NSWLR 486 (NSWCA).

[107] *Halsey v Esso Petroleum Co Ltd* [1961] 1 WLR 683 (QBD); *Hubbard v Pitt* [1976] QB 142 (CA). See also *Hall v Beckenham Corp* [1949] 1 KB 716 (KBD), where it was assumed that persons flying model planes in a public park could be liable in nuisance.

[108] *Northampton Borough Council v Lovatt* (1997) 96 LGR 548 (CA) 556. See also *Southport Corp v Esso Petroleum Co Ltd* [1953] 2 All ER 1204 (Liverpool Assizes) 1207–1208 (Devlin J); *Lippiatt v South Gloucestershire Council* [2000] QB 51 (CA) 65 (Sir Christopher Staughton).

Surprisingly, however, the misconception that such a limitation exists is widespread,[109] and it was one of two reasons the Court of Appeal gave in *Hussain v Lancaster City Council*[110] for dismissing a private nuisance claim brought by shopkeepers on a council estate in respect of a campaign of harassment conducted by the defendant's tenants (the other, sound, reason being that a landlord's failure to evict a tenant he or she knows is creating a nuisance does not amount to an authorisation of that nuisance).

The origins of this misconception would seem to be threefold. First, it was true that the *assize* of nuisance lay only between freeholders,[111] although this was not true of the action on the case out of which the modern tort developed.[112] Secondly, the confusion may in part be attributable to loose definitions of private nuisance, which refer to 'neighbouring occupiers' and so forth.[113] And finally, the error may be connected to the necessity of distinguishing private nuisance from trespass. This was sometimes done by asking whether the act took place on or off the claimant's land, and since in the majority of cases, off the claimant's land meant on the defendant's land, the distinction was sometimes said to rest on whether the source of the interference was the claimant's or the defendant's land, a slip that may have contributed to the misapprehension in question.

[477] VIII. DAMAGES AND CONSEQUENTIAL LOSS

According to Stevens, when it comes to the assessment of damages for the commission of a tort, 'it is necessary to distinguish between damages awarded as a substitute for the right infringed and consequential damages as compensation for loss to the claimant ... consequent upon this infringement'.[114] The core 'substitutive' award is generally assessed objectively, so whether or not there is a loss to the claimant is irrelevant. Damages for consequential loss are subjective and require proof of loss having been suffered.[115] This analysis is broadly consistent with the approach of the courts to the assessment of damages in private nuisance cases, but there are a number of complications. As regards the core 'substitutive' award, it remains unclear precisely how this is to be calculated in cases where the nuisance has not diminished the capital value of the affected land. Furthermore, there is clearly some reluctance on the part of the courts to

---

[109] Fleming (n 19) 476 describes this misconception as the 'traditional view', but there is nothing 'traditional' about it.

[110] *Hussain v Lancaster City Council* [2000] QB 1 (CA).

[111] On the likely origins of this limitation, see D Ibbetson, *A Historical Introduction to the Law of Obligations* (Oxford, OUP, 1999) 99.

[112] AK Kiralfy, *The Action on the Case* (London, Sweet & Maxwell, 1951) 55–56.

[113] See, eg, *Sedleigh-Denfield v O'Callaghan* [1940] AC 880 (HL) 896–97 (Lord Atkin); *Miller* (n 65) 980 (Lord Denning MR); *Hunter* (n 4) 723 (Lord Hope); *Transco plc v Stockport Metropolitan Borough Council* [2003] UKHL 61, [2004] 2 AC 1 [9] (Lord Bingham). See also Weinrib (n 31) 191.

[114] Stevens, *Torts and Rights* (n 1) 60.

[115] ibid.

accept the full ramifications of the objective approach to the assessment of this award. As for damages for consequential loss, there is a lack of clarity about what types of consequential losses are recoverable, and why.

The House of Lords made clear in the *Hunter* case that the measure of the substitutive award is the reduction in the value of the affected land. In cases of physical damage to the land, this equates to the diminution in capital or resale value,[116] which is often (though not invariably) the same as the cost of reinstatement. In cases of interference with comfort and convenience, it equates to what the House of Lords in *Hunter* termed the diminution in the 'amenity value'[117] of the land during the period when the nuisance took place. This concept of amenity value encapsulates the fact that, as Lord Hoffmann pointed out with reference to a smell nuisance caused by a pig farm, 'the value of the right to occupy a house which smells of pigs must be less than the value of the occupation of an equivalent house which does not'.[118] But how is the diminution in amenity value to be assessed? According to the European Commission on Human Rights' interpretation of the reasoning in *Hunter*, the answer is by 'assessing a notional market rental value for [the] property without the presence of the environmental nuisance, assessing the reduction in such rental value caused by the presence of the nuisance and multiplying this reduction by the duration of the nuisance'.[119] This seems to be a sensible approach which should work in most cases, but it is unlikely that the reduction in [478] amenity value will always be captured by the market in this way,[120] and so it is desirable that a degree of flexibility should be maintained when it comes to the fixing of the substitutive award.

This focus on the impact of the nuisance on the land, as opposed to its occupiers, means that the objective approach taken to the assessment of the gravity of the interference is mirrored in the approach taken to the assessment of substitutive damages. Hence the quantum of damages is not affected by the number of people occupying the land in question – the 'reduction in amenity value is the same whether the land is occupied by the family man or the bachelor'[121] – but instead by the objective qualities of the land, such as its size, commodiousness and value.[122] It follows that if three identical flats are similarly affected by the

---

[116] *Hunter* (n 4) 695 (Lord Lloyd).

[117] ibid 696 (Lord Lloyd), 706 (Lord Hoffmann).

[118] ibid 706.

[119] *Khatun v United Kingdom* (1998) 26 EHRR CD 212 (ECommHR) 214. See also *Dobson v Thames Water Utilities Ltd* [2009] EWCA Civ 28, [2009] 3 All ER 319 [32] (Waller LJ), referring specifically to the opinion of Lord Hoffmann ('loss of (notional) rental value'); *Lawrence v Fen Tigers Ltd* [2011] EWHC 360 (QB) [314] (Judge Richard Seymour QC).

[120] This seems to have been the assumption of Lord Hope in *Hunter*, who spoke of the diminution in the 'capital or letting value' of the land as a 'relevant head of damages', but then referred to 'the measure of damages' in cases where the nuisance 'has resulted only in loss of amenity': *Hunter* (n 4) 724.

[121] ibid 696 (Lord Lloyd). See also at 706–707 (Lord Hoffmann) 724–25 (Lord Hope).

[122] ibid 706 (Lord Hoffmann).

same noise nuisance, the substitutive award made to the occupiers should be exactly the same, even if one lives in his flat with his family, one lives in her flat alone and is stone deaf, and one uses her flat as a *pied-à-terre* and stays there only once a fortnight.

Unfortunately, however, the Court of Appeal seemed to baulk at the full rigour of the objective approach to damages in its recent decision in *Dobson v Thames Water Utilities Ltd*.[123] In the course of a discussion of the impact (if any) of an award of private nuisance damages to someone with a legal interest in the affected land on a claim under the Human Rights Act 1998 in respect of the same interference by a person resident in the property, but lacking standing in nuisance,[124] Waller LJ suggested that 'a claimant must show that he has in truth suffered a loss of amenity before substantial damages can be awarded', with the result that where a house 'is unoccupied throughout the time of the (transitory) nuisance, has suffered no physical injury, loss of value or other pecuniary damage, and would not in any event have been rented out, we are unable to see how there can be any damages beyond perhaps the nominal'.[125] With respect, this statement appears to confuse the award of substitutive damages with recovery for consequential loss, and is difficult to square with the fact that (as Waller LJ himself acknowledged) following *Hunter* [479] nuisance damages 'are for injury to the property and not to the sensibilities of the occupier(s)'.[126] On the other hand, his Lordship's observation that when assessing damages for loss of amenity, account should be taken of 'the actual experience of the persons in occupation of the property during the relevant period'[127] is unproblematic, since although the subjective impact of the interference on the occupiers is not the measure of damages, it will usually be good evidence of the objective impact on the land. In any case, it is to be hoped that in future judges who are actually fixing damages awards in private nuisance cases will follow the clear guidance given by the House of Lords.

In *Hunter*, Lord Hoffmann said that the claimant in a private nuisance action may also be entitled to damages for losses consequential on the violation of his or her property rights:

> There may of course be cases in which, in addition to damages for injury to his land, the owner or occupier is able to recover damages for consequential loss. He will, for example, be entitled to loss of profits which are the result of inability to use the land

---

[123] *Dobson* (n 119).

[124] On this issue, and the relationship between the Human Rights Act 1998 and private nuisance more generally, see D Nolan, 'Nuisance and Human Rights' in D Hoffman (ed), *The Impact of the Human Rights Act on Private Law in England and Wales* (Cambridge, CUP, 2011).

[125] *Dobson* (n 119) [33]–[34].

[126] ibid [31]. '[I]t is a mistake to think that where no loss is suffered no claim for damages is available' (Stevens, *Torts and Rights* (n 1) 61).

[127] *Dobson* (n 119) [33].

for the purposes of his business. Or if the land is flooded, he may also be able to recover damages for chattels or livestock lost as a result.[128]

As this statement makes clear, foreseeable economic losses which flow from an unlawful interference with the claimant's land are therefore recoverable in a private nuisance action,[129] as where rental income is lost due to the flooding of the claimant's houses,[130] or expense incurred in investigating the extent of the damage done to the land.[131] Where the consequential economic loss exceeds the diminution in the capital or amenity value of the affected land, the claimant is entitled to the higher amount. In *Andreae v Selfridge & Co Ltd*,[132] for example, the owner of a hotel was compensated for a drop in takings attributable to the noise and dust from nearby building works, regardless of whether this exceeded the reduction in the notional rental value of the property attributable to the interference. (Conversely, it of course follows from the objective assessment of the substitutive award that if in this case the drop in takings had been *less* than the diminution in amenity value, the claimant could instead have asked for the latter.)

[480] Lord Hoffmann's statement also makes it clear that damages will be awarded for harm to the claimant's chattels which is consequential on an actionable interference with the claimant's land.[133] Such damages are not limited to cases in which the harm to the chattel results from physical damage to the claimant's land, as where stock was damaged when the claimant's shop was flooded,[134] but are also recoverable where they result from less tangible forms of interference, as where acid smuts from the defendant's oil refinery damaged washing hanging on the claimant's clothes line.[135] The principle in play here is that forms of injury which would not in themselves ground an action in private nuisance – such as economic loss and damage to personal property – may nevertheless be recoverable for when they result from the wrongful interference with the claimant's real property rights. (Another example of the operation of this principle is the rule that the damages awarded for a violation of the natural right to support of one's land may include compensation for damage to buildings affected by the loss of support, even where the right to have the buildings themselves supported

---

[128] *Hunter* (n 4) 706.

[129] Since such loss results from the injury to the claimant's land, it is misleading to describe it as 'pure economic loss', as does Fleming (n 19) 493.

[130] *Rust v Victoria Graving Dock Co* (1887) LR 36 Ch D 113 (CA) (loss too remote on the facts).

[131] *Jan de Nul (UK) Ltd v Axa Royale Belge SA* [2002] EWCA Civ 209, [2002] 1 Lloyd's Rep 583 [80] (Schiemann LJ).

[132] *Andreae v Selfridge & Co Ltd* [1938] Ch 1 (CA).

[133] See also *Hunter* (n 4) 719 (Lord Cooke). The same is perhaps implied by Blackstone in III Bl Comm 217: 'if one erects a smelting house for lead so near the land of another, that the vapor and smoke kills his corn and grass, *and damages his cattle therein*, this is held to be a nuisance' (emphasis added).

[134] *Howard Electric Ltd v A J Mooney Ltd* [1974] 2 NZLR 762 (NZSC).

[135] *Halsey* (n 107). £5 was awarded for the damaged linen. The claimant was also compensated for damage to his car caused by the acid smuts, but since his car was parked on the public highway the basis of this award was not private nuisance but public nuisance and the rule in *Rylands v Fletcher*.

has not yet been acquired.[136]) It is therefore surprising that in *Hunter* the House of Lords seemed to rule out recovery of damages for personal injury in private nuisance, even in cases where the injury is suffered by the right-holder and results from the nuisance.[137] After all, there would appear to be no logical distinction between consequential personal injury and consequential damage to personal property, and in the old case of *Malone v Laskey*[138] the Court of Appeal seem to have assumed that damages would be recoverable for the former if suffered by the owner or occupier.[139]

[481] IX. PRIVATE NUISANCE AND TRESPASS TO LAND

Commentators who are not persuaded by the property tort analysis of private nuisance typically distinguish it in this regard from the tort of trespass to land.[140] By contrast, I want to argue that in fact there is no fundamental distinction between the two torts, and indeed that certain issues in the law of private nuisance can be illuminated by considering trespass as an analogy. The inclusion of the word 'non-trespassory' in the definition of private nuisance makes it clear that the two torts are mutually exclusive, and the dividing line between them is the ancient distinction between a trespass action and an action on the case – whether the interference was direct or indirect.[141] Two principles determine that question: (1) if no person or physical object crosses the boundary of the claimant's land, then the interference is indirect;[142] and (2) where there is a projection of a physical object onto the claimant's land, the interference is direct if the act of the defendant was unlawful from the beginning, but indirect if the act of the defendant was initially lawful, but led afterwards to an invasion of the claimant's rights.[143] Hence a sign which when erected projects into

---

[136] See Gray and Gray (n 27) 21.

[137] *Hunter* (n 4) 676 (Lord Lloyd) 707 (Lord Hoffmann). *cf* 719 (Lord Cooke). See also *Corby* (n 5) [13] (Dyson LJ).

[138] *Malone v Laskey* [1907] 2 KB 141 (CA).

[139] See also Newark (n 7) 490 fn: 'It may well be that where an actionable nuisance is committed which in addition to interfering with the plaintiff's enjoyment of rights in land also damages his person or chattels, he can recover in respect of the damage to his person or chattels as consequential damages'.

[140] See, eg, Cane, 'What a Nuisance!' (n 11) 515 (trespass to land 'is unequivocally a property tort').

[141] *Southport Corp* (n 108) 1208 (Devlin J).

[142] McBride and Bagshaw (n 47) 367.

[143] *Reynolds v Clarke* (1725) 1 Str 634, 635; 93 ER 747, 748. *cf* McBride and Bagshaw (n 47) 368, arguing that what matters is the degree of control which the defendant has over the thing which causes the interference. In practice, this will usually (but not invariably) track the distinction drawn in the authorities between acts which are and are not initially lawful. Richard Wright (n 47) 510–11 distinguishes trespass to land and private nuisance by saying that while the former requires a physical invasion of the claimant's land by a tangible entity, a nuisance is always a physical invasion by an intangible entity. There are two errors here. The first is that Wright assumes that a nuisance must amount to a physical invasion, which we have seen is not the case (see pt IV above). The second is

the airspace over the claimant's shop is a trespass,[144] while a fence initially flush with the boundary line which subsequently comes to lean over adjoining land is a nuisance.[145]

Although it is also said (again reflecting the trespass/case distinction) that while trespass to land is actionable per se, private nuisance requires proof of damage, in practice this notional requirement of damage is synonymous with – and so adds nothing to – the requirement of substantial interference, which is where the real significance of the distinction between the two torts lies (there being no equivalent to this requirement in trespass). This distinction is, however, easily explained. As we have seen, in [482] private nuisance the substantial interference requirement is necessary to achieve an appropriate balance between the competing liberty and security interests in play; in cases of direct interference, by contrast, the threat posed to the claimant's security interests is usually greater, and the legitimate liberty interests of the defendant are less likely to be engaged, so a requirement of this kind is not appropriate (although where exceptionally an important liberty interest is engaged, a defence of necessity may be available[146]).

On a purely doctrinal level, therefore, it is difficult to see any fundamental distinction between the two principal causes of action protecting land rights. Two more theoretical distinctions are nevertheless sometimes drawn.[147] The first is that in the absence of a *vindicatio*-type action, trespass to land performs an important vindicatory function in common law systems, in the sense that it is used to *establish* as well as to *protect* rights in land. However, precisely the same is true of private nuisance. If I have a private right of way over your land, and you block the path, denying my right, then I must bring an action in private nuisance in order to establish that the right exists, and the same is true where you deny my acquired right to support, light and so on. Similarly, in cases concerning natural rights I must use private nuisance to establish my property right to be free, for example, from the intolerable stench of your pig farm, or the excessive noise of your factory. It follows that only on a reductionist view of land rights as limited to the core right to possession can a distinction be drawn in this respect between trespass and private nuisance.

The second, more theoretical, distinction which is sometimes drawn between the two torts is that while trespass lays down 'property rules', private nuisance

Wright's assumption that physical invasion by a tangible entity cannot be a nuisance, when in fact encroachment, as by tree roots or branches, is a well-established form of private nuisance involving a tangible entity: see further Oliphant (n 36) para 22.34.

[144] *Kelsen v Imperial Tobacco Co* [1957] 2 QB 334 (QBD).

[145] *Mann v Saulnier* (1959) 19 DLR (2d) 130 (New Brunswick CA).

[146] See, eg, *Rigby v Chief Constable of Northamptonshire* [1985] 1 WLR 1242 (QBD).

[147] For rejection of a third suggested distinction – that 'trespasses somehow involve misappropriations in a way that nuisances do not' – see C Rotherham, 'Gain-Based Relief in Tort after *Attorney General v Blake*' (2010) 126 LQR 102, 123–25.

lays down 'liability rules',[148] an argument which rests on the assumption that whereas injunctions are available as of right in trespass cases, generally in nuisance 'an injunction will not be granted … unless the costs of the damage exceed the costs of abating the damage'.[149] Now we should note that, even if this assumption were sound, it would establish only that nuisance law lays down a *combination* of property rules and liability rules, since injunctive relief is available – and so a property rule laid down – where this is the efficient outcome. But the real difficulty with this argument is that, whether or not a cost-benefit analysis of this kind determines the availability of specific relief in nuisance cases in the United [483] States,[150] it has certainly never done so in England, as is demonstrated by a host of authorities, ancient and modern.[151] The right-to-light cases are particularly instructive in this regard, since in some of these injunctions have been issued despite evidence that the economic cost to the defendant of compliance with the order would clearly exceed the economic benefit such compliance would bring to the claimant, in one case by a factor of up to 38 to one.[152] Nor is this refusal to take into account economic considerations at the remedy stage a peculiarity of English law: the Irish Supreme Court, for example, once issued an injunction in a nuisance case even though it was told that doing so would cause a critical shortage of cement throughout the whole country,[153] and in both Israel and Scotland the granting of damages in lieu of an injunction in such circumstances is regarded as an illegitimate expropriation of the claimant's rights.[154]

The conclusion must be, therefore, that there is in fact no fundamental distinction between trespass and private nuisance, and since it seems generally to be accepted that the former is a property tort, this is consistent with the property tort analysis of the latter. It also suggests that questions arising in private nuisance

---

[148] See, eg, WM Landes and RA Posner, *The Economic Structure of Tort Law* (Cambridge, Mass, Harvard UP, 1987) 42–48. On the distinction between these two types of rule, see G Calabresi and AD Melamed, 'Property Rules, Liability Rules and Inalienability: One View of the Cathedral' (1972) 85 *Harvard Law Review* 1089.

[149] Landes and Posner (n 148) 43.

[150] *Boomer v Atlantic Cement Co* 257 NE 2d 870 (NY 1970) is a famous example of an American court refusing an injunction for public interest reasons. See further Wright (n 47) 516–19.

[151] See, eg, *A-G v Birmingham Borough Council* (1858) 4 K & J 528, 70 ER 220; *Shelfer v City of London Electric Lighting Co* [1895] 1 Ch 287 (CA); *Kennaway* (n 65); *Watson v Croft Promosport Ltd* [2009] EWCA Civ 15, [2009] 3 All ER 249. *cf Miller v Jackson* (n 65); *Dennis* (n 65).

[152] *Regan v Paul Properties Ltd* [2006] EWCA Civ 1319, [2007] Ch 135 (reduction in value of claimant's land attributable to loss of light no more than £5500, but estimated cost to defendant of compliance with injunction up to £210 000). As Anthony Ogus and Genevra Richardson say in their study of the economics of private nuisance, the case law on injunctive relief 'manifestly demonstrates that … the judiciary have little regard for economic considerations': AI Ogus and GM Richardson, 'Economics and the Environment: A Study of Private Nuisance' [1977] *CLJ* 284, 309.

[153] *Bellew v Cement Ltd* [1948] IR 61 (Sup Ct Ire).

[154] See respectively *Ata Textile Co v Schwartz* (1976) 30(3) PD 785 (Sup Ct Isr) and *Ben Nevis Distillery (Fort William) Ltd v North British Aluminium Co Ltd* 1948 SC 592 (CSIH). Scottish courts

may be illuminated by considering trespass to land as an analogy. In addition to the rules on standing discussed above, there are at least two other issues where the analogy is instructive. The first is whether the fact that the claimant moved into his or her property knowing that it was subject to a nuisance should be a defence (the 'coming to the nuisance' idea).[155] The rule that it is not seems to me to be bolstered by the fact that it would surely be very odd to argue that if a person moved into a property knowing that someone else regularly trespassed on it, then for that reason he or she should be barred from [484] seeking an injunction to prevent further trespassing by that person, thereby short-circuiting (as would a coming to the nuisance defence) established principles governing the acquisition of land rights by prescription. And the second issue is the misguided notion that where the public benefit of the defendant's activity outweighs the harm it causes to the claimant, it should not be actionable in nuisance for that reason.[156] If the trespass analogy holds, then this is not altogether dissimilar to arguing that the owner of a factory should be able to extend it onto neighbouring land without the property owner's permission because doing so would create lots of new jobs, and the land in question is derelict and socially useless.[157]

X. THREE SOURCES OF CONFUSION

I hope to have shown thus far that private nuisance is a thoroughly coherent cause of action, once it is properly understood as a tort protecting rights in land. There are, however, a number of sources of confusion which have served to obscure the doctrinal clarity of the tort. In this part of the chapter I will advert briefly to what I perceive to be the most important of these.[158]

First and foremost is the much misunderstood relationship between the tort of private nuisance and the crime of public nuisance. The truth is that the origins of the two types of nuisance are entirely separate,[159] and although there are some overlaps between the operation of private nuisance and the action that lies where a public nuisance has caused the claimant particular damage – in particular, if its consequences are sufficiently widespread, an activity such as the generation of noxious fumes may be both a public nuisance and a private nuisance to

---

do not even have the power to refuse interdict and award damages in lieu: *The Laws of Scotland: Stair Memorial Encyclopaedia* (n 66) para 2150.

[155] As to which, see Oliphant (n 36) para 22.99.

[156] See pt V above.

[157] See also McBride and Bagshaw (n 47) 376–77.

[158] Other sources of confusion include the laboured (and it seems to me rather pointless) debates about the relationship between private nuisance and negligence, and the misconception that the rule in *Rylands v Fletcher* is an offshoot of private nuisance (a thesis criticised by J Murphy, 'The Merits of *Rylands v Fletcher*' (2004) 24 *OJLS* 643 and D Nolan, 'The Distinctiveness of *Rylands v Fletcher*' (2005) 120 *LQR* 421).

[159] See Kiralfy (n 112) 70; Ibbetson (n 111) 106 ('very different antecedents').

neighbouring properties – the two forms of nuisance have very little in common. In the words of Hayne J in a decision of the High Court of Australia:

> It is … important to recall that the crime of common or public nuisance and the tort of [private] nuisance were and are distinct. There can be no automatic transposition of the learning in one area to the other.[160]

Unfortunately, however, the terminological resemblance has caused considerable [485] confusion, which many who should have known better have compounded by failing adequately to differentiate the two.[161] A good recent example of this confusion was the deeply misguided argument of the defendant in *Corby Group Litigation Claimants v Corby Borough Council*[162] that because the House of Lords had said in the *Hunter* case that personal injury was not actionable in *private* nuisance it was not actionable in *public* nuisance either, despite a multiplicity of cases to the contrary, some going back 400 years.[163] Thankfully, the Court of Appeal was having none of it: the two causes of action were distinct and the rights protected by them were different.[164] One simple way of reducing the impact of this particular source of confusion would be for judges and commentators to be meticulous about referring to either 'private' or 'public' nuisance, rather than 'nuisance' in general.

A second terminological source of confusion is the use of the phrase 'unreasonable user' to describe the requirement of substantial interference.[165] So long as it is understood that it is the *interference* which must be unreasonable, and not the *defendant's conduct*, no harm is done, but inevitably this distinction is frequently lost, so that we end up with a reference to 'the centrality to the tort of nuisance of the fault-based concept of unreasonableness'[166] and the claim that no clear distinction can be drawn between negligence and nuisance, since in both 'the question is whether the defendant has acted reasonably'.[167] A recent example of the doctrinal chaos that can result is provided by the decision of the Court of Appeal in *Network Rail Infrastructure Ltd v Morris*, where Buxton LJ sought to abandon well-established principles of private nuisance law and to replace them with an 'analysis of the demands of reasonableness' in the particular case.[168] It is difficult to imagine a better recipe for uncertainty and incoherence.

---

[160] *Brodie v Singleton Shire Council* [2001] HCA 29, 206 CLR 512 [257].

[161] Newark (n 7) is a serial offender, who single-handedly caused great confusion in this regard. See also the *Restatement, Second, Torts* (n 4) ch 40 (where unhelpfully the two are dealt with in the same chapter); G Williams and BA Hepple, *Foundations of the Law of Tort* (London, Butterworths, 1976) 104–108; *Street on Torts* (n 75) 423 (failing to make clear that *Bolton v Stone* [1951] AC 850 (HL) was a public nuisance case).

[162] *Corby* (n 5).

[163] See, eg, *Fowler v Sanders* (1617) Cro Jac 446, 79 ER 382.

[164] *Corby* (n 5) [30] (Dyson LJ).

[165] See also Wright (n 47) 507–508 (arguing that the use of the word 'unreasonable' in this context is 'likely to mislead' and therefore best avoided).

[166] Cane, 'What a Nuisance!' (n 11) 520.

[167] Williams and Hepple (n 161) 107.

[168] *Network Rail Infrastructure Ltd v Morris* [2004] EWCA Civ 172, [2004] Env LR 41 [36].

Finally, confusion has arisen from the mistaken idea that 'a private nuisance always involves some degree of repetition or continuance',[169] a [486] claim which seems to have fed into the suggestion that cases of physical damage to land should be hived off into negligence, leaving private nuisance as a tort concerned only with amenity damage.[170] In fact, cases of physical damage caused by one-off floods, landslips and the like have long fallen within the scope of the cause of action. It would seem that the idea that some degree of continuity is required arises out of a failure to differentiate the action on the case for nuisance from the assize, a form of novel disseisin for which the primary remedy was specific relief, and which would not therefore have been appropriate once the nuisance had terminated.[171]

XI. PROPERTY AND OBLIGATIONS

Like the existence of other property torts such as trespass to land and conversion, acceptance of the property tort analysis of private nuisance calls into question the distinction commonly drawn between the 'law of property' on the one hand and the 'law of obligations' on the other. At the very least, it requires us to accept that the law of private nuisance is as much part of land law as the law of breach of contract is part of contract law (as Lord Hope said in the *Hunter* case, 'we are concerned here essentially with the law of property'[172]). It is noteworthy in this regard that the issues dealt with in common law systems by the tort of private nuisance are generally classified by civil law systems as falling within the law of property, not obligations.[173] Hence, for example, it is within the title of the Italian Civil Code dealing with property rights that we find Article 844, which refers to the obligation to tolerate 'emissions of smoke or heat, smells, noises, vibrations [and similar effects] where they do not exceed the customary measure of what is tolerable, with due consideration to the conditions prevailing within the locality'.[174] Similarly, in the German Civil Code, the provisions governing neighbour law are to be found in the sections on ownership, as elaborations of that right.[175] At the [487] same time, in civilian systems nuisance-type cases cannot straightforwardly be classified

---

[169] *A-G v PYA Quarries Ltd* [1957] 2 QB 169 (CA) 192 (Denning LJ). See also Newark (n 7) 489.
[170] Gearty (n 20).
[171] Kiralfy (n 112) 56. See also Ibbetson (n 111) 99.
[172] *Hunter* (n 4) 723.
[173] von Bar (n 60) 551: 'For the majority of European countries with civil codes, the law governing relationships between neighbours has traditionally been a part of property law'.
[174] Cited in ibid 559.
[175] §§ 906 ff BGB. See further A Their, 'Disturbances Between Neighbours in Germany 1850–2000' in Gordley (n 66) 87. In Scots law, the main role of nuisance has been described as 'a doctrine of *property law* or neighbourhood protecting interests in the use and enjoyment of land or public places from present and future interference': *The Laws of Scotland: Stair Memorial Encyclopaedia* (n 66) para 2017 (emphasis added).

as falling within the law of property because the availability of damages may give them a decidedly delictual flavour.[176] In both the common law and civilian legal traditions, therefore, 'the proper location of reparable wrongs against property ... is inherently ambivalent'.[177]

The taxonomic challenges posed by property torts like private nuisance are not without their practical implications. A good example is provided by the case of *Bradburn v Lindsay*,[178] where one of the issues was whether the owner of a semi-detached house could be liable for loss of support of a neighbouring house caused by his failure to keep his own house in good repair. The claim was in nuisance, for interference with an easement of support. Since an easement can be a right to do something, or a right not to have something done, but not a right to have something done, the authorities were clear: the easement of support does not impose a duty of positive action on the servient owner. His obligation is not to do anything to remove the support, and that is all.[179] However, Judge Blackett-Ord V-C held that the defendant *was* liable for his non-feasance. The learned judge pointed to private nuisance cases which imposed positive duties on occupiers, in particular *Leakey v National Trust*,[180] and distinguished the easement cases on the ground that they dealt with 'the nature of the right of support', while the claimants had put their case on the 'wider ground' of nuisance.[181] With respect, this purported distinction between the 'right of support' and 'nuisance' simply does not exist, for the two are mutually constitutive, in the sense that the rules of private nuisance law in part determine the content of the right of support, and vice versa. The same is true of the distinction drawn by another judge between the 'law of easements' and the 'modern law of nuisance'.[182] Only the failure to appreciate that private nuisance is part and parcel of the law of real property could have brought about such profound analytical errors.

[488] XII. CONCLUSION

There is a danger that rights analysis will be misinterpreted as a high-level unitary theory of private law along the lines of those put forward by corrective justice theorists. On the contrary, while acceptance of the rights model does have obvious implications for high-level theory of this type, and while the

---

[176] See Their (n 175) 103–104 (German law); AJ Verheij, 'Fault Liability Between Neighbours in the Netherlands 1850–2000' in Gordley (n 66) 110–15 (Dutch law); A Masferrer, 'Relations Between Neighbours in Spanish Law 1850–2000' in Gordley (n 66) 181–83 (Spanish law). On the taxonomical difficulties to which nuisance has given rise in Scots law, see Cameron (n 66) 156–61.

[177] Cameron (n 66) 159.

[178] *Bradburn v Lindsay* [1983] 2 All ER 408 (Ch D).

[179] *Sack v Jones* [1925] Ch 235 (Ch D) 240 (Astbury J); *Bond v Norman* [1940] 2 All ER 12 (CA) 18 (Sir Wilfred Greene MR).

[180] *Leakey v National Trust* [1980] QB 485 (CA).

[181] *Bradburn v Lindsay* [1983] 2 All ER 408 (Ch D) 413.

[182] *Abbahall Ltd v Smee* [2002] EWCA Civ 1831, [2003] 1 WLR 1472 [10] (Munby J).

connections between rights analysis and corrective justice theory are strong,[183] works like Stevens' *Torts and Rights*[184] are far more engaged with the detail of private law doctrine than the more abstract analysis which can be found in, for example, Ernest Weinrib's *The Idea of Private Law*[185] or Arthur Ripstein's *Equality, Responsibility, and the Law*.[186] This difference of emphasis reflects the fact that rights analysis is less concerned with identifying the philosophical foundations of private law at a general level than with understanding the internal structures and rules of private law in common law systems. It follows that to a large extent the merits of rights analysis stand to be assessed by its *analytical* force, in other words its ability to explain and rationalise not only 'the idea' of private law at a general level, but also particular private law doctrines, at a relatively high level of specificity. And in this chapter I hope to have shown that in the area of private nuisance law, at least, there is a marked degree of consistency between rights analysis and the principles and rules which emerge from the authorities.

Having said that, it would be a mistake to dismiss the rights analysis as a purely analytical exercise devoid of normative significance. As James Penner has pointed out in the context of private nuisance:

> When there is no judicial recognition of the distinction between rights and mere interests judges may decide that the law of nuisance turns on balancing interests. At this point the law of nuisance changes from one in which tortfeasors are restrained from violating the rights of land occupiers to one where the law is called upon to resolve conflicting land uses by sanctioning some interests over others: on the economic view the resolution is made by determining which interests have the higher social value.[187]

The normative power of rights analysis is well illustrated by the nineteenth-century nuisance case of *A-G v Birmingham Borough Council*,[188] where an injunction was issued to prevent the defendant local authority from discharging raw sewage into the River Tame, even though its counsel told the court that the effect of the injunction would be to turn the [489] city of Birmingham into 'one vast cesspool' and to bring about 'a plague, which will not be confined to the 250,000 inhabitants of Birmingham, but will spread over the entire valley and become a national calamity'.[189] Sir William Page Wood V-C was unimpressed:

> There are cases at law in which it has been held, that where the question arises between two portions of the community, the convenience of one may be counterbalanced by

---

[183] See D Nolan and A Robertson, 'Rights and Private Law' in Nolan and Robertson (n 46) pt IX.
[184] Stevens, *Torts and Rights* (n 1).
[185] Weinrib (n 31).
[186] Ripstein (n 52).
[187] Penner (n 83) 21.
[188] *Birmingham* (n 151).
[189] ibid 536, 224.

the inconvenience to the other, where the latter are far more numerous. But in the case of an individual claiming certain private rights, and seeking to have those rights protected against an infraction of the law, the question is simply whether he has those rights, and, if so, whether the Court, looking to the precedents by which it must be governed in the exercise of its judicial discretion, can interfere to protect them.[190]

Statements like this are apt to produce two slightly different varieties of negative response. The first such response is that they are symptomatic of an individualistic common law ethos which puts private property rights above the interests of the masses – in the *Birmingham* case, the riparian rights of an aristocratic landowner above the health of those living in one of England's biggest cities.[191] And the other response is that such statements reflect a failure on the part of some common law judges to recognise that private law rules exist not to protect private rights but to maximise overall social welfare.[192]

Although those who respond in these two different ways may not always share the same political outlook, they are guilty of the same two mistakes. The first mistake is the failure to appreciate that the appropriate forum for arguments regarding social welfare is not the private law court but the legislature. Only the most diehard libertarian would deny that sometimes private rights must give way to the public interest, but one of the strengths of the rights analysis of private law is that it reserves the power to make such decisions to legislators who are democratically accountable for their actions. The second mistake is the erroneous assumption that the judiciary are in a position to assess where the interests of the masses lie, or which outcome will maximise overall welfare. Indeed, the critics are wrong to assume that *they themselves* know the answers to these questions, as recent research on the aftermath of the *Birmingham* litigation demonstrates. For an illuminating article by Ben Pontin reveals that, far from bringing about the calamity predicted by counsel for the defendant, the decision in *Birmingham* to award an injunction [490] triggered a spate of similar actions against other local authorities, which had the effect of bringing about desperately needed municipal investment in modern systems of sewage purification.[193] Although the normative appeal of rights analysis would in no way be diluted if the practical effects of the injunction had been less positive, there is nevertheless a rich irony in the fact that a ruling founded on the force of private rights which was long lambasted as 'inefficient' and 'regressive' turns out to have had such beneficial long-term consequences.

---

[190] ibid 539, 225.

[191] This is the clear implication of WR Cornish and G de N Clark, *Law and Society in England 1750–1950* (London, Sweet & Maxwell, 1989) 157.

[192] L Rosenthal, 'Economic Efficiency, Nuisance and Sewage: New Lessons from *Attorney General v Council of the Borough of Birmingham*' (2007) 36 *Journal of Legal Studies* 27.

[193] B Pontin, 'The Secret Achievements of Nineteenth Century Nuisance Law: *Attorney General v Birmingham Corporation* (1858–95) in Context' (2007) 19 *Environmental Law and Management* 271.

10

The Essence of Private Nuisance

B McFarlane and S Agnew (eds), *Modern Studies in Property Law*,
Volume 10 (Oxford, Hart Publishing, 2019) 71–88

[71] I. INTRODUCTION

WHEN WE REFER to the 'essence' of something, we might mean a number of different things. One established usage of the word essence is 'a perfume or scent', for example. What, we might then ask, is the 'essence' of private nuisance in this sense? The stench of sewage?[1] The unmistakeable odour of a pig farm?[2] The pong of a waste disposal facility?[3] Or perhaps the 'pungent and nauseating' smell of oil from an oil depot?[4]

Happily, here I want to focus on a different meaning of the word 'essence'; what my dictionary refers to as 'the indispensable quality or element identifying a thing or determining its character',[5] or in other words the feature or set of features that *defines* a thing. And my claim is that the essence of private nuisance in this sense is interference with (or impairment of) the *usability* of the claimant's land. Although I would accept that a full definition of the tort of private nuisance requires the addition of certain qualifications (for example, that the interference must be non-trespassory), I maintain that this idea of interference with the usability of land is the central defining feature of the cause of action, in the sense that (subject to those qualifications) anything that interferes with the usability of land can in principle amount to a private nuisance, and anything that does not, cannot.

Since my claim is best understood as a clarification of the orthodox view that the central defining feature of a private nuisance is an interference with the use and enjoyment of land, you might be asking yourself why I feel it necessary to make it. There are three reasons for doing so. The first is that the clarification turns out to be an important one. The second is that, although this central defining feature of private nuisance is well-established, it has been the subject

---

[1] *Dobson v Thames Water Utilities Ltd* [2011] EWHC 3523 (TCC), 140 Con LR 135.
[2] *Bone v Seale* [1975] 1 WLR 797 (CA); *Wheeler v JJ Saunders Ltd* [1996] Ch 19 (CA).
[3] *Barr v Biffa Waste Services Ltd* [2012] EWCA Civ 312, [2013] QB 455.
[4] *Halsey v Esso Petroleum Co Ltd* [1961] 1 WLR 683 (QBD).
[5] *The Concise Oxford Dictionary*, 12th edn (Oxford, OUP, 2011).

of very little sustained analysis, and one of the aims of this chapter is to begin the task of plugging that gap.[6] And the final reason is that the orthodox conception of private nuisance has come under attack recently, and there is a danger that without a robust defence of it the coherence and utility of the tort will be compromised. In this chapter I seek to provide such a defence.

[72] The chapter is divided hereafter into three main sections. In section II, I show just how orthodox it is to define private nuisance by reference to interference with the use and enjoyment of land, seek to clarify this defining idea as concerned with the abstract usability of the land, and consider the implications of this analysis for the scope of the private nuisance action. In section III, I summarise and then critique a recent challenge to the orthodox conception of the tort, which I call the 'physical invasion' view. And in section IV, I briefly consider some of the implications for property theory of the orthodox conception of private nuisance, properly understood. It is important to emphasise that the scope of the chapter is limited to the question of identifying what is *capable* of amounting to a private nuisance, or (put differently) what is the key defining characteristic of all instances of private nuisance. I am not concerned with other questions, such as whether in a particular case an interference that is capable of being a private nuisance does actually amount to a nuisance on the facts (or for that matter with the question of *what determines* whether an interference capable of amounting to a nuisance is in fact one).[7]

II. THE ORTHODOX CONCEPTION OF PRIVATE NUISANCE

There are countless examples in the case law and the academic literature of definitions of private nuisance in terms of interference with the use and enjoyment of land. To give you a flavour of these, just consider the following examples, which come from a range of different jurisdictions:

> Private nuisance may be described as unlawful interference with a person's use or enjoyment of land, or some right over, or in connection with it.[8]

---

[6] It has been said, for example, that 'there is a relatively limited body of case law addressing the scope of what may possibly constitute the "interference" that is actionable in private nuisance' (*Shogunn Investments Pty Ltd v Public Transport Authority of Western Australia* [2016] WASC 42 [62] (Kenneth Martin J)).

[7] It seems that I am not alone in my view that the orthodox definition of private nuisance needs defending, and in preparing my defence I have had the advantage of reading C Essert, 'Nuisance and the Normative Boundaries of Ownership' (2016) 52 *Tulsa Law Review* 85, where the author trenchantly critiques the physical invasion view of the tort. I have few quibbles with Essert's analysis, and there are some significant overlaps between my criticisms and his. It is however important to emphasise that our agendas are different, in that Essert's concern in his article is to put forward what he calls a 'normatively attractive vision of nuisance law' as a whole, while my concern is the narrower one of identifying the appropriate definition or conception of the cause of action.

[8] WE Peel and J Goudkamp, *Winfield & Jolowicz on Tort*, 19th edn (London, Sweet & Maxwell, 2014) para 15-008.

A private nuisance is an unreasonable interference with the use and enjoyment of land.[9]

A private nuisance is a nontrespassory invasion of another's interest in the private use and enjoyment of land.[10]

[T]he main role [of nuisance in Scots law] is as a doctrine of property law or neighbourhood protecting interests in the use and enjoyment of land.[11]

Furthermore, this focus on the protection of interests in the use and enjoyment of land is not confined to the common law (and Scots law) of nuisance, but is also key to [73] understanding principles of neighbour law in civilian systems. According to § 906(1) of the German Civil Code (BGB), for instance:

The owner of a piece of land is not entitled to prohibit the intrusion of gases, vapours, smells, smoke, soot, heat, noises, shocks and similar interferences emanating from another piece of land to the extent that the interference does not or only immaterially prejudices the use of his piece of land.

Although the orthodox conception of private nuisance is well-established, it has been the subject of very little analysis, and in the remainder of this section of the chapter, I propose to clarify and to explore that conception, and to consider its implications for the scope of the cause of action.

The first thing to notice is that the word 'land' in the orthodox definition of private nuisance refers to the legal conception of land, which encompasses not only the physical land itself, but also the buildings and other things attached to it (trees, shrubs, crops etc), as well as acquired rights that run with the land.[12] Thus it is that private nuisance encompasses interferences with acquired rights or servitudes (easements and profits à prendre),[13] and that buildings and other fixtures fall under its protective cloak.

A second, crucially important, point to notice about the orthodox definition is that strictly speaking there is a flaw in it. This is because private nuisance is a 'tort against land'[14] – meaning (among other things) that the gist of the wrong

---

[9] K Barker et al, *The Law of Torts in Australia*, 5th edn (Melbourne, OUP Australia, 2012) 185. For an identical definition, see also AM Linden and B Feldthusen, *Canadian Tort Law*, 10th edn (Markham, Ont, LexisNexis Canada, 2015) 608.

[10] *Restatement, Second, Torts* (1977) § 821D.

[11] *The Laws of Scotland: Stair Memorial Encyclopaedia* (Edinburgh, Butterworths, 1988) vol 14, para 2017.

[12] See in particular the definition of 'land' in the Law of Property Act 1925, s 205(1)(ix). On the legal conception of land, see K Gray and SF Gray, *Elements of Land Law*, 5th edn (Oxford, OUP, 2009) ch 1.2.

[13] See K Oliphant (ed), *The Law of Tort*, 3rd edn (London, LexisNexis Butterworths, 2015) paras 22.25 ff. For the avoidance of doubt, it should be made clear that in the case of an easement, nuisance requires a substantial interference with the usability of the easement (right of way, etc), and not with the usability of the dominant tenement (though of course the former may entail the latter).

[14] See D Nolan, '"A Tort Against Land": Private Nuisance as a Property Tort' in D Nolan and A Robertson (eds), *Rights and Private Law* (Oxford, Hart Publishing, 2012). The definitive judicial statement of this understanding of the tort and its implications is to be found in Lord Hoffmann's judgment in *Hunter v Canary Wharf Ltd* [1997] AC 655 (HL).

is the diminished utility of the land itself, as opposed to the inconvenience and discomfort suffered by the occupiers. Hence, for example, '[a] sulphurous chimney in a residential area is not a nuisance because it makes house-holders cough and splutter but because it prevents them taking their ease in their gardens'.[15] And it follows from this that the wrong in nuisance is not interference with the use and enjoyment of the land per se, as the orthodox definition suggests, but rather interference with the *capacity* of the land in question to be used and enjoyed (its fitness 'for the ordinary purposes of life'[16]) – a more general notion of the 'usefulness'[17] or 'usability'[18] of the land that 'abstracts from the particularity of specific uses'.[19] This explains [74] why the test of substantial or unreasonable interference is an objective one, that takes no account of any abnormal sensitivity either of the claimant or of the use to which she puts her property,[20] and also why the damages in an amenity nuisance case are assessed objectively, in the sense that they compensate for the diminished utility of the land attributable to the wrongful interference, rather than the actual impact of the nuisance on the occupiers of the land.[21]

This turns out to be a critically important clarification. For a start, the clarification renders the orthodox conception of private nuisance compatible with rejection of a 'right to use' property – as opposed to a 'right to usability' of property – a right which property theorists have correctly identified as problematic.[22] It also explains, for instance, why it is that Roderick Bagshaw falls into error when he defines private nuisance in terms of 'some forms of interference with *a claimant's* use and enjoyment of his or her land', and then gives as an example of a form of such interference that falls outside the scope of the tort 'injuring or imprisoning the claimant'.[23] In fact, private nuisance is not concerned with whether the *claimant* can use or enjoy her land at all, but only with whether (and to what extent) her *land* is capable of being used and enjoyed. Furthermore, this clarification shows that on the orthodox conception of private nuisance one

---

[15] FH Newark, 'The Boundaries of Nuisance' (1949) 65 *LQR* 480, 489.

[16] See *Appleby v Erie Tobacco* (1910) 22 OLR 533 (Ont DC) 538 (Middleton J).

[17] See NJ McBride and R Bagshaw, *Tort Law*, 6th edn (Harlow, Pearson Education, 2019) 395.

[18] *Restatement, Second, Torts* (n 10) § 821D, comment b. The extent to which the concept of 'ordinary use' is built into this abstract notion of usability is a difficult question that I do not have the space to explore here. Clearly the ordinariness of the affected use is a consideration in nuisance cases, by virtue of the 'abnormal sensitivity' principle (as to which, see Oliphant (n 13) paras 22.44–22.45), but whether this goes to the defining notion of interference with the usability of the land or instead to the subsequent issue of 'substantial interference' is less obvious.

[19] EJ Weinrib, 'Ownership, Use, and Exclusivity: The Kantian Approach' (2018) 31 *Ratio Juris* 123, 130 (discussing Kant's theory of property).

[20] See *Network Rail Infrastructure Ltd v Williams* [2018] EWCA Civ 1514, [2019] QB 601 [43] (Sir Terence Etherton MR).

[21] See *Hunter* (n 14) 696 (Lord Lloyd), 706 (Lord Hoffmann).

[22] See, eg, JE Penner, *The Idea of Property in Law* (Oxford, OUP, 1997) 72–73 (though in concluding from this implausibility that 'the concept of exclusion, not use, dominates the legal analysis' Penner throws the 'usability' baby out with the 'use' bathwater).

[23] R Bagshaw, 'The Edges of Tort Law's Rights' in Nolan and Robertson (n 14) 417–18.

cannot plausibly explain the cause of action by reference to the resolution of competing uses of land,[24] since the law's concern is revealed as being with the *usability* of the claimant's land, not the *specific uses* to which the claimant puts it (and certainly not with the uses to which the defendant puts *his* land, not least because private nuisance liability can attach to conduct that does not amount to a use of the defendant's land at all[25]).

What more can we say about this definitional idea of interference with the capacity of the land in question to be used and enjoyed? The concept is certainly a broad one, which includes, for example, causing an alteration of the physical condition of land that reduces its utility[26] – hence the fact that physical damage to land falls within the scope of private nuisance.[27] On the other hand, the concept nevertheless excludes from the scope of private nuisance certain conduct which could be said to 'harm' the claimant's land, but without affecting its usability. Hence, for example, conduct that reduces the market value [75] of real property without impairing its utility is not wrongful,[28] so that a company which triggers a collapse in house prices in an area by closing down the main source of local employment does not thereby create a nuisance.[29]

Nor does the concept of interference with the usability of land extend to conduct that has a deleterious effect on a commercial enterprise operating on the claimant's land without diminishing the utility of the property more generally.[30] The classic illustration of this principle is *Victoria Park Racing and Recreation Grounds v Taylor*,[31] where the first defendant built a platform on his land which overlooked the plaintiff's racecourse and the second defendant stood on the platform and gave a live radio commentary on the races and announced the results, with the result that fewer people attended the races. According to

[24] *cf* R Coase, 'The Problem of Social Cost' (1960) 3 *Journal of Law & Economics* 1; G Calabresi and AD Melamed, 'Property Rules, Liability Rules, and Inalienability: One View of the Cathedral' (1972) 85 *Harvard Law Review* 1089. For an illuminating discussion highlighting this aspect of these economic approaches to nuisance, see HE Smith, 'Exclusion and Property Rules in the Law of Nuisance' (2004) 90 *Virginia Law Review* 965, 967–69.

[25] See Nolan (n 14) 475–76.

[26] See *Restatement, Second, Torts* (n 10) § 821D, comment b.

[27] Commentators sometimes question whether physical damage claims should be classified as nuisances (see, eg, C Gearty, 'The Place of Private Nuisance in a Modern Law of Tort' (1989) 48 *CLJ* 214), but while there is admittedly a case for separating such claims off from amenity nuisance claims and dealing with them in negligence – though also a case against doing this – the law's assumption that to physically damage land is substantially to interfere with its capacity for use and enjoyment seems a reasonable one. For a prominent example of judicial reasoning based on this assumption, see *Hunter* (n 14) 705–706 (Lord Hoffmann), and for a defence of this assumption, see M Lee, 'What is Private Nuisance?' (2003) 119 *LQR* 298, 308–10.

[28] For clear statements of this principle, see *Soltau v De Held* (1851) 2 Sim (NS) 133, 158; 61 ER 291, 301 (Sir RT Kindersley VC); *Harrison v Good* (1871) LR 11 Eq 338 (Ch D) 353 (Sir James Bacon VC); and *Network Rail Infrastructure* (n 20) [46]–[48] (Sir Terence Etherton MR).

[29] For discussion, see R Kidner, 'Nuisance and Rights of Property' [1998] *Conveyancer* 267, 276–79.

[30] See *Ricket v Metropolitan Railway Co* (1865) 5 B & S 156, 162–63; 122 ER 790, 795 (Exch Ch) (affirmed (1867) LR 2 HL 175 (HL)).

[31] *Victoria Park Racing and Recreation Grounds v Taylor* (1937) 58 CLR 479 (HCA).

the majority of the High Court of Australia, these actions of the defendants infringed no legal right of the plaintiff's, and in particular the mere fact that they had reduced the market value of the plaintiff's property and diverted custom away from its business did not make them a nuisance. According to Latham CJ, the defendants had 'not interfered in any way with the use and enjoyment of the plaintiff's land', since the racecourse remained 'as suitable as ever it was for use as a racecourse'.[32] Similarly, Dixon J said that 'the substance of the plaintiff's complaint' went to interference, not with 'its enjoyment of the land, but with the profitable conduct of its business'.[33]

The rejection of the private nuisance claim in *Victoria Park Racing* seems clearly to have been correct, and its key reasoning is reflected in more recent Australian case law rejecting nuisance claims for conduct that had affected the profitability of a business on the plaintiff's land, but was not considered to have interfered with the use and enjoyment of the land itself.[34] There are, however, also more borderline cases in the law reports. Three relatively recent decisions from across the common law world are instructive. The first is *Smith v Inco*,[35] where deposits from the defendant's factory led to an increase in the nickel content of the soil in the plaintiffs' neighbouring properties, which reduced their market value because of an (apparently false) community perception that these deposits might pose a health risk to occupiers. In this case, the Ontario Court of Appeal held that since the deposits had not objectively diminished the land's utility they were incapable of grounding a nuisance claim. On one level, this decision – which is consistent with the Court of Appeal's conclusion in *Birmingham Development v Tyler*[36] that a nuisance claim cannot lie in respect [76] of a false belief that the defendant's property may collapse onto the claimant's land – seems right.[37] We should be concerned in private nuisance with actual (not perceived) interferences with the capacity of the land to be used and enjoyed, just as a claimant in a battery case must establish that there was actually a touching, and not merely that she reasonably perceived that there was. On the other hand, the capacity of land to be used and enjoyed cannot be completely separated from the subjective perceptions of those occupying it; a noise or smell is more likely to be a nuisance if generally perceived as unpleasant, for example.[38]

---

[32] ibid 493. Note the way in which the usability of the land is here tied to its use 'as a racecourse'. The extent to which the usability idea that underlies nuisance is tied to the use of the affected land in a general sense (as, for example, a home, factory, shop, farm, racecourse etc) is a difficult one that lies beyond the scope of this chapter.

[33] ibid 508.

[34] See *Deepcliffe Pty Ltd v Council of the City of Gold Coast* [2001] QCA 342, 118 LGERA 117 (parking restrictions on street near restaurant); *Shogunn Investments* (n 6) (removal of turning lane in median strip near entrance to commercial car park).

[35] *Smith v Inco Ltd* [2011] ONCA 628, 107 OR (3d) 321.

[36] *Birmingham Development Co Ltd v Tyler* [2008] EWCA Civ 859, [2008] BLR 445.

[37] See also *Adkins v Thomas Solvent Co* 487 NW 2d 715 (Mich 1992); and *Adams v Star Enterprise* 51 F 3d 417 (4th Cir 1995).

[38] Commentators have been more sympathetic to claims based on unfounded fears than have the courts: see, eg, JPS McLaren, 'Nuisance in Canada' in AM Linden (ed), *Studies in Canadian Tort*

The second difficult decision is *D Pride & Partners (a firm) v Institute for Animal Health*,[39] where Tugendhat J rejected an argument that the defendants could be liable in private nuisance for causing an outbreak of foot-and-mouth disease that led to the introduction of government restrictions on the movement of the claimants' livestock. Intuitively, this seems right. After all, although the defendant's actions did (albeit indirectly) affect the ability of this particular land to be used for a particular purpose, namely raising cattle, they did not affect the usability of the land in a more general sense, and while blocking or substantially interfering with the access to the claimant's land can amount to a private nuisance, that seems a far cry from acting in such a way as to bring about a situation in which the claimant is prevented by the act of a third party from moving a particular class of chattels on or off her land.[40]

The third case, *Marsh v Baxter*,[41] raises similar questions. In this instance, occasional escapes of genetically modified canola from the defendant's property caused most of the plaintiffs' farmland to be stripped of its organic certification by an association with which it had a contractual relationship, even though none of the plaintiffs' crops or livestock could acquire any genetic traits from the canola. A nuisance argument was rejected by both the Supreme Court and the Court of Appeal of Western Australia, and again, this seems intuitively to be correct. At its highest, you could say only that the canola escapes interfered – also via a third party's intervention – with the use of the plaintiffs' land to 'farm organically', but in a case where in fact there was no risk of any transfer of genetic material this would seem to blur the important distinction drawn in the earlier cases between interfering with *the land* and 'interfering with' (or making less profitable) *a business* conducted on it. Having said that, it is noteworthy that both courts dismissed the claim on the grounds, not that there had been no interference with the use and enjoyment of the plaintiffs' land, but that any such interference had not been substantial, bearing in mind the abnormal sensitivity of the plaintiffs' use in the locality.

[77] Also tricky are the so-called 'affront' cases, of which the best known in England are *Laws v Florinplace*,[42] where it was held that there was a triable issue as to whether the mere presence of a sex shop in the locality of the claimants' properties could potentially amount to a nuisance, and the similar

Law (Toronto, Butterworths, 1968) 342–43; J Lowry and R Edmunds, 'Stigma Damages, Amenity and the Margins of Economic Loss: Quantifying Perceptions and Fears' in J Lowry and R Edmunds (eds), *Environmental Protection and the Common Law* (Oxford, Hart Publishing, 2000); Bagshaw (n 23) 420–21.

[39] *D Pride & Partners (a firm) v Institute for Animal Health* [2009] EWHC 685 (QB).

[40] cf *Exxon Corporation v Yarema* 516 A 2d 990 (Md 1986), where recovery was allowed in private nuisance after groundwater contamination caused by the defendants led to the imposition of severe controls on properties in the locality not otherwise affected by the contamination, including prohibitions on the use of groundwater, on the building of homes on the land, and on the sale of the land.

[41] *Marsh v Baxter* [2014] WASC 187, 46 WAR 377 (affirmed [2015] WASCA 169, 49 WAR 1).

[42] *Laws v Florinplace Ltd* [1981] 1 All ER 659 (Ch D).

earlier decision in *Thompson-Schwab v Costaki*,[43] where the Court of Appeal issued an interlocutory injunction to close down a brothel that had opened in the claimant's street. In retrospect these decisions certainly come close to countenancing liability for diminution in value per se.[44] In *Laws*, for example, Vinelott J quoted (as if relevant) the evidence of a home owner 'that the continuance of the defendants' business would severely injure the value of his property',[45] as well as the evidence of two estate agents who had expressed divergent opinions on the effect of the sex shop on local property prices.[46] Then again, a respectable argument can be made to the effect that – at least in extreme cases – the mere presence of a particular activity in the vicinity of a property could be so upsetting to an ordinary occupier as to amount to an interference with the capacity of the property to be used and enjoyed for normal purposes, and there are certainly some American cases to this effect.[47]

As these borderline cases suggest, it seems fair to say that the full implications of the orthodox conception of private nuisance have not yet been identified.[48] Could, for example, shutting off the supply of essential utilities such as water, gas and electricity to a property come within the orthodox conception of private nuisance, on the grounds that the absence of such amenities is capable of significantly diminishing the utility of the property?[49] In a first instance case, *Anglian Water Services Ltd v Crawshaw Robbins & Co Ltd*,[50] it was held that interrupting the supply of gas to a property could not be a nuisance, but the reasons given were unpersuasive. The first, that the right to the supply of gas was not a property right but a contractual right vis-à-vis the supplier, looks conclusory (after all, the right could be *both* contractual and proprietary). And the second, that the interference could be regarded as being with the use of gas appliances on the claimant's land, rather than with the use and enjoyment of the land itself, rests on a false dichotomy, since the fact that gas appliances cannot be used on my property may itself diminish the property's utility.[51] The decision is also hard to square with that of the Court of Appeal in *Guppys (Bridport) Ltd v Brookling*, where a landlord was held liable in nuisance for trying to force a

---

[43] *Thompson-Schwab v Costaki* [1956] 1 WLR 335 (CA).

[44] For telling criticism of the decisions, see Kidner (n 29) 277–78.

[45] *Laws* (n 42) 662. See similarly the mention of a plaintiff's concern about the effect of the defendants' activity on property values in *Thompson-Schwab* (n 43) 339.

[46] *Laws* (n 42) 663–64.

[47] See, eg, *Foley v Harris* 286 SE 2d 186 (Va 1982) (junk yard). See further, RR Coletta, 'The Case for Aesthetic Nuisance: Rethinking Traditional Judicial Attitudes' (1987) 48 *Ohio State Law Journal* 141.

[48] For an insightful exploration of these issues, see Bagshaw (n 23) 417–21.

[49] For an analogous case, see *Barratt Homes Ltd v DWR Cymru Cyfyngedig (Welsh Water) (No 2)* [2013] EWCA Civ 233, [2013] 1 WLR 3486, where Lloyd Jones LJ said (at [53]) that the claimant's ability to connect its properties to water and sewerage services was 'an essential adjunct' of its use of land, interference with which was arguably capable of amounting to a nuisance.

[50] *Anglian Water Services Ltd v Crawshaw Robbins & Co Ltd* [2001] BLR 173 (QBD).

[51] cf *Network Rail Infrastructure Ltd v CJ Morris* [2004] EWCA Civ 172, [2004] Env LR 41, where the nuisance claim failed, but it was not argued that the interference was incapable of being a nuisance because it interfered only with the use of certain devices on the claimant's property.

tenant out of the demised property by, inter alia, cutting off the supply of water and electricity.[52]

[78] One final point about the orthodox conception of private nuisance as an interference with the capacity of land to be used and enjoyed is a reminder that this is only the start of the nuisance enquiry. Even if the defendant's conduct falls within the scope of the nuisance cause of action in this sense, there are a host of other issues to consider, such as whether on the facts the interference was substantial, whether it was foreseeable, whether the claimant has standing to sue, whether any defences apply and so on. For the most part, the distinction between the definitional issue being explored in this paper and the other issues that may arise in a nuisance claim is reasonably clear, but there is at least one exception, where the blurring of the distinction has sometimes obscured analysis of the essential nature of the cause of action.

Although nuisance litigation is usually focused on whether on the facts of the case a *particular* interference with the use and enjoyment of land is a substantial one, another (often overlooked) question is whether the *type* of interference with the use and enjoyment of land in question is potentially actionable in private nuisance at all. This is because, as I have argued elsewhere,[53] the umbrella right instantiated by the tort of private nuisance – which we can loosely call 'the right to the usability of land' – is underlain by a complex substructure of more specific natural rights and acquired rights, and furthermore the tort does not protect against certain kinds of interference with the usability of land at all. Hence close inspection of private nuisance law reveals a threefold classification of *natural rights* (which attach automatically to the land), *acquired rights* (which the law recognises, but which must be acquired by grant or prescription) and *'no rights'* (which the law does not recognise at all), that operates as a preliminary filter in nuisance cases independent of, and anterior to, the question of whether on the facts the interference with the usability of the land is substantial.[54] For present purposes, the important thing to note about this substructure is that it is concerned with the classification of types of interference with the usability of land, and hence it is analytically *posterior* to the definitional question that is the subject-matter of this chapter. It follows that on the view of the tort taken here, it is a mistake to try to explain the 'no rights' cases at a definitional level, as falling outside the basic conception of the tort; rather, these cases should be understood as falling within that conception, but as nevertheless not actionable on the grounds that this particular type of interference is not considered to merit a legal response.

This observation can be illustrated by reference to perhaps the most prominent examples of these 'no rights' in English law, namely the rules that an occupier

---

[52] *Guppys (Bridport) Ltd v Brookling* (1984) 14 HLR 1 (CA).
[53] Nolan (n 14) 465–68.
[54] For the details, see Oliphant (n 13) paras 22.18–22.38.

has no right that others not obstruct the view from her land,[55] and no right to receive percolating water from a neighbour's property.[56] Now it seems fairly obvious that blocking a beautiful sea view from her house or causing her well to dry up are actions that interfere with the capacity of a neighbour's property to be used and enjoyed. Hence in theory such conduct could be held to amount to a private nuisance, even if English courts happen to have taken the view that such forms of interference are permissible.[57] What follows from this is that we cannot learn [79] anything about the essential nature of the private nuisance tort from the fact that such forms of interference are not actionable. Nevertheless, it seems clear that the failure to grasp this distinction between the basic scope or definition of the cause of action and its 'substructure' is one of the key drivers of the recent challenge to the orthodox conception of the tort.[58] That challenge is what I will call the 'physical invasion' view of private nuisance, and it is to that challenge that I now turn.

III. THE PHYSICAL INVASION VIEW

A. Summary of the Physical Invasion View

In broad terms the physical invasion view of private nuisance seeks to reformulate the cause of action as a sort of 'mini-trespass' tort, in which the focus is no longer on interference with the use and enjoyment of the claimant's land as such, but instead on the defendant being responsible for a physical invasion of the claimant's land that falls short of a trespass of the traditional kind.[59] In this section I seek to give an outline of this view, and to identify its most prominent proponents. The motivations that appear to lie behind this view are varied, and the proponents include scholars of libertarian, Kantian and utilitarian

---

[55] See *Aldred's Case* (1610) 9 Co Rep 57b, 58b; 77 ER 816, 821 (Wray CJ).

[56] *Chasemore v Richards* (1859) 7 HL Cas 349, 11 ER 140; *Bradford Corp v Pickles* [1895] AC 587 (HL).

[57] I emphasise 'English law' here because it is characteristic of the substructure of private nuisance that the classification of particular interference types is context-sensitive, so that different common law systems may classify the same kind of interference in different ways.

[58] See, eg, RA Epstein, 'Nuisance Law: Corrective Justice and Its Utilitarian Constraints' (1979) 8 *Journal of Legal Studies* 49, 60 ff; RW Wright, 'Private Nuisance Law: A Window on Substantive Justice' in Nolan and Robertson (n 14) 512–13; S Douglas, 'The Content of a Freehold: A "Right to Use" Land?' in N Hopkins (ed), *Modern Studies in Property Law*, vol 7 (Oxford, Hart Publishing, 2013) 374–75; S Douglas and B McFarlane, 'Defining Property Rights' in J Penner and HE Smith (eds), *Philosophical Foundations of Property Law* (Oxford, OUP, 2014) 231–32.

[59] There are weak echoes of the physical invasion view in dicta in a few English cases, of which the most prominent is the statement by Lord Goff that for an action to lie in private nuisance 'in respect of interference with the plaintiff's enjoyment of his land, it will generally arise from something emanating from the defendant's land' (*Hunter* (n 14) 685). In some subsequent cases Lord Goff's remark has in effect been taken as at least raising a presumption against a nuisance analysis where there is no such emanation: see, eg, *Anglian Water Services* (n 50) 197 (Burnton J).

persuasions. This reflects the broader point that (in the words of Larissa Katz), exclusion-based accounts of property 'emerge from a range of very different normative and methodological approaches'.[60] The question of what motivates this unlikely alliance of adherents to adopt forms of the physical invasion view is an interesting and important one, but unfortunately I do not have the space to explore that question here.[61] Instead, I seek simply to summarise the various forms of the physical invasion view that have been put forward, in order both to demonstrate the extent of its influence and to set the scene for my defence of the orthodox conception of private nuisance.

The first clear statement of the physical invasion view appears to be in a 1979 article by Richard Epstein.[62] Epstein there defined nuisances as 'invasions of the plaintiff's property that fall short of trespasses but which still interfere in the use and enjoyment of land'.[63] [80] Note that this version of the physical invasion view was not a full-scale assault on the orthodox conception of private nuisance, for two reasons: first, because (as his definition makes clear) Epstein still tied the physical invasion to the use and enjoyment of the claimant's land; and, second, because Epstein accepted that utilitarian considerations justified (in his words) 'making certain forms of noninvasive conduct actionable within the nuisance context',[64] giving as an example the removal of lateral support from the claimant's land.

Six years later, Thomas Merrill argued in the same journal that the law of nuisance was concerned with 'the right to exclude intrusions by others', and that the difference between trespass and nuisance was that while the former governed 'relatively gross invasions by tangible objects', nuisance applied to 'more indirect and intangible interferences'.[65] Merrill's thesis, which was based on what he called 'a simple economic model',[66] proved influential in property law circles, and other property scholars have since used economic analysis to explain private nuisance as a doctrine rooted (to a greater or lesser degree) in a property owner's core right to exclude. A good example is a sophisticated economic analysis of nuisance by Henry Smith,[67] who posited that '[i]nformation costs go a long way toward explaining why and how nuisance law rests on a foundation of exclusionary property rights',[68] while accepting that this was not the whole picture, and that more open-textured 'governance' rules also played a part in

---

[60] L Katz, 'Exclusion and Exclusivity in Property Law' (2008) 58 *University of Toronto Law Journal* 275, 279.

[61] For the beginnings of an explanation, see ibid 279–85; and H Dagan, *Property: Values and Institutions* (Oxford, OUP, 2011) ch 2.

[62] Epstein (n 58).

[63] ibid 53.

[64] ibid 94.

[65] TW Merrill, 'Trespass, Nuisance, and the Costs of Determining Property Rights' (1985) 14 *Journal of Legal Studies* 13, 13–14.

[66] ibid 14.

[67] Smith, 'Exclusion and Property Rules in the Law of Nuisance' (n 24).

[68] ibid 970.

the determination of nuisance cases. Smith's take on nuisance is summed up in a more recent paper in which he claims that '[m]uch of nuisance is "minitrespass", and otherwise it constitutes a fine-tuning of the exclusionary regime through governance'.[69]

The association of nuisance with a physical intrusion onto the claimant's land is not, however, limited to the work of property lawyers, for endorsement of the physical invasion view can also be found in the writings of tort lawyers of a Kantian persuasion, such as Richard Wright.[70] It is important to note, though, that not all Kantian private law scholars share this view of private nuisance, and that two of the most prominent such scholars, Ernest Weinrib and Arthur Ripstein, seem perfectly comfortable with the orthodox conception of the tort.[71] Indeed, in a recent article Weinrib characterises Kant's theory of property in terms of 'usability', an analysis that chimes with the central message of this chapter.[72]

That brings me to the most sustained and radical assault on the orthodox conception of private nuisance, which can be found in recent work by Simon Douglas and Ben McFarlane. Douglas and McFarlane's endorsement of the physical invasion view of private nuisance [81] law does not appear to rest on either an economic or a Kantian foundation, but instead arises in the course of a broader argument to the effect that private law *does* not (or at least *should* not) recognise a right to use and enjoy one's property, an argument summed up in the following statement:

> It thus seems that A, a freeholder of land, is owed no legal duty by B, C, D etc ... not to impair A's ability to use his land. Rather, A is merely owed a duty by B, C, D etc ... not to physically interfere with his land.[73]

Note that, although this broader argument appears to be completely at odds with the orthodox definition of private nuisance, the tension between the two is certainly reduced (and possibly even eliminated) by the clarification of that definition made earlier in this chapter, since in fact what private nuisance protects on the orthodox view is not the *use* but the *usability* of land. On the other hand, in an earlier sole-authored paper Douglas argued that it followed from the fact that there was or should be no claim-right in a freeholder to use her land that

---

[69] HE Smith, 'The Persistence of System in Property Law' (2015) 163 *University of Pennsylvania Law Review* 2055, 2079.

[70] See Wright (n 58) 512. See also the more nuanced argument in support of the claim that 'a person's right to land ... is exclusionary' in JW Neyers and J Diacur, 'What (is) a Nuisance?' (2011) 90 *Canadian Bar Review* 213, 219–20.

[71] See EJ Weinrib, *The Idea of Private Law*, revised edn (Oxford, OUP, 2012) 191; and A Ripstein, *Private Wrongs* (Cambridge, Mass, Harvard UP, 2016) 137.

[72] Weinrib, 'Ownership, Use, and Exclusivity' (n 19) 131 maintains that for Kant, ownership is 'the legal concept that pertains to the usability of things', and that '[u]sability lies at the heart of the Kantian account of ownership'.

[73] Douglas and McFarlane (n 58) 232.

'the gist of liability in nuisance is not the impairment of the utility of the free-holder's land, but the physical interference with it',[74] and this narrower claim is quite obviously inconsistent with the orthodox conception of the tort, even as clarified.

Three further observations should be made about the arguments of Douglas and McFarlane at this point. The first is that, whereas previous adherents of the physical invasion view (such as Epstein, Wright and Smith[75]) had maintained the connection with the claimant's use and enjoyment of land, Douglas and McFarlane break that link completely. The second point is that Douglas and McFarlane specifically connect their physical interference analysis with the idea of a boundary crossing, and endorse Merrill's distinction between trespass and nuisance as marking the difference between invasions by tangible and 'less tangible' things.[76] And the third point is that Douglas in particular acknowledges the difficulties that the traditional conception of private nuisance poses for his broader argument, and concedes that there are (in his words) a 'small number' of nuisance cases that are impossible to rationalise in terms of a physical interference with the claimant's land.[77]

B. Critique of the Physical Invasion View

In this subsection, I subject the physical invasion view of private nuisance to critical analysis and defend the orthodox conception of the tort. It is important to note that while some of my observations apply to all the various different forms of the physical invasion view that have been put forward, others are limited to one or more particular iterations of it.

The first and most obvious difficulty with the physical invasion view of nuisance is that it does not even come close to fitting the actual law. As Christopher Essert points out, '[t]he case books are rife with cases' in which liability does not rest on any kind of emanation [82] onto the claimant's land.[78] We might start with four types of case that Nicholas McBride and Roderick Bagshaw have aptly categorised as concerned with 'earth, water, air and light':[79]

> *Earth*: the rule that a removal of lateral support that causes your neighbour's land to collapse is actionable in nuisance.[80]

---

[74] Douglas, 'The Content of a Freehold' (n 58) 373.

[75] See Smith, 'Exclusion and Property Rules in the Law of Nuisance' (n 24) 992, 997.

[76] Douglas and McFarlane (n 58) 225–26. See also Douglas, 'The Content of a Freehold' (n 58) 369.

[77] Douglas, 'The Content of a Freehold' (n 58) 373.

[78] Essert (n 7) 96. See also Oliphant (n 13) para 22.12, and for judicial rejection of the suggestion that nuisance is so limited see, eg, *Victoria Park Racing* (n 31) 506–507 (Dixon J); *Thompson-Schwab* (n 43) 656 (Romer LJ); and *Barratt Homes* (n 49) [60] (Lloyd Jones LJ), [81] (Arden LJ).

[79] NJ McBride and R Bagshaw, *Tort Law*, 5th edn (Harlow, Pearson Education, 2015) 453–55.

[80] *Hunt v Peake* (1860) John 705, 70 ER 603; *Backhouse v Bonomi* (1861) 9 HL Cas 503, 11 ER 825.

Water: the rule that a person who diverts a natural stream or substantially alters its flow to the detriment of a downstream riparian owner is liable in private nuisance.[81]

Air: the rule that a person who obstructs the flow of air through a defined channel or aperture onto the claimant's land is liable in private nuisance if a right to the flow of air has been acquired by grant or prescription;[82] and

Light: the rule (in English and Commonwealth law, but not in American law[83]) that a person who substantially interferes with the light reaching the windows of a building on the claimant's property is liable in private nuisance if a right to light has been acquired by grant or prescription,[84] a rule explicitly understood in the case law as concerned with the effect of the diminution of the light on the 'comfort and convenience or *usefulness*' of the building in question.[85]

Two other examples of well-established types of nuisance that do not involve any physical invasion of the claimant's land are substantial interference with a private right of way, and impeding the access to the claimant's property from the highway.[86]

In addition to these well-established forms of private nuisance, there are several other examples of cases or types of case where nuisance liability has been imposed despite the absence of any kind of 'boundary crossing':

- The 'affront' cases, such as *Laws v Florinplace*, discussed earlier.[87]

- The suggestion in *Birmingham Development Co Ltd v Tyler*[88] that if the state of the defendant's property is such as to pose an actual danger of its collapsing onto the claimant's neighbouring land then this could amount to a nuisance.

- The unanimous view of the Court of Appeal in *Barratt Homes Ltd v Welsh Water (No 2)*,[89] that although in the light of the particular statutory context no action lay in nuisance for damage resulting from a refusal by a sewerage undertaker to allow a developer to [83] exercise its statutory right to connect newly built properties to a public sewer, the undertaker's conduct was capable of amounting to a nuisance.

---

[81] *Mason v Hill* (1833) 5 B & Ad 1, 110 ER 692; *Orr-Ewing v Colquhoun* (1877) 2 App Cas 839 (HL); *Fear v Vickers* (1911) 27 TLR 558 (CA). This rule forms part of a more complex set of principles that govern riparian rights: for further details, see J Getzler, *A History of Water Rights at Common Law* (Oxford, OUP, 2004).

[82] *Bass v Gregory* (1890) 25 QBD 481 (QBD).

[83] See, eg, *Fontainebleau Hotel Corp v Forty-Five Twenty-Five Inc* 114 So 2d 357 (Fla Dist Ct App 1959).

[84] *Bowry and Pope's Case* (1589) 1 Leon 168, 74 ER 155; III Bl Comm 216–17.

[85] See *Kine v Jolly* [1905] 1 Ch 480 (CA) 493 (Vaughan Williams LJ) (emphasis added). The seminal case on the nature of the right is *Colls v Home and Colonial Stores Ltd* [1904] AC 179 (HL).

[86] On the right of access, see Oliphant (n 13) para 22.85. This right is a private right appurtenant to the property, distinct from the public's right to pass along the highway: see, eg, *Toronto Transit Commission v Swansea (Village)* [1935] SCR 455 (SCC) 457 (Davis J).

[87] See text to nn 42 ff.

[88] *Birmingham* (n 36).

[89] *Barratt* (n 49).

- The decision in the Canadian case of *Nor-Video Services v Ontario Hydro*[90] that interference with television reception amounted to a private nuisance (a possibility also left open by the House of Lords in *Hunter v Canary Wharf*[91] unless the interference was caused by a building on the defendant's land).

Nor can the types of case I have described be dismissed as peripheral to some alleged paradigm of physical invasion, as Lord Goff suggested in the *Hunter* case.[92] On the contrary, if one looks, for example, at the chapter on nuisance in Baker and Milsom's *Sources of English Legal History*[93] (which covers English private law up to 1750), one finds that *all* of the cases in the first part of the chapter[94] concern rights of way, rights of common and diversion of water-courses, a clear indication that for much of its history the law of nuisance was dominated by cases that do not correspond with the physical invasion view of the tort. This ties into a broader weakness of the physical invasion view, namely that it fails to account for the operation of private nuisance in acquired rights cases (ie, those involving interference with easements and profits). Although these acquired rights cases are frequently under-emphasised in the modern literature on the tort of nuisance, they are in no way tangential, but are instead central to a proper understanding of both the historical and the contemporary operation of the cause of action.

   In addition to the many examples of nuisance case that do not involve a physical intrusion onto the claimant's land, there are a number of other problems with the physical invasion view (or versions of it). One, rather fundamental, such difficulty is that while the physical invasion view tells us that only things that cross the boundary can be nuisances, it then gives us little guidance as to which intangible boundary crossings are nuisances, and which are not (and why). (The problem with the physical invasion view, in other words, is not just that not all nuisances are boundary crossings, but that not all boundary crossings are nuisances – or trespasses.) In particular, if we follow Douglas and McFarlane in rejecting the idea that a nuisance is an interference with the use and enjoyment of the claimant's land, then we must obviously also reject the idea that nuisance liability turns on whether that interference is substantial or unreasonable. However, Douglas and McFarlane do not tell us what should replace that central stage of the nuisance enquiry, and yet *something* has to replace it, unless we are to believe that *every* sound wave, odour, ray of light, etc crossing the boundary of a person's property is wrongful, a proposition which

---

[90] *Nor-Video Services v Ontario Hydro* (1978) 84 DLR (3d) 221 (Ont HCJ).

[91] *Hunter* (n 14).

[92] ibid 685. See also the reference by Douglas (text to n 77) to 'a small number of claims successfully litigated in nuisance' where there was no physical emanation onto the claimant's land; and Douglas and McFarlane (n 58) 230 ('a small number of cases').

[93] J Baker, *Baker and Milsom's Sources of English Legal History: Private Law to 1750*, 2nd edn (Oxford, OUP, 2010).

[94] ibid 640–52.

is self-evidently nonsensical.[95] In his more moderate version of the physical invasion view, Epstein explains the focus on *substantial* interference (as encapsulated in the 'rule of give and take, live and let live',[96] the locality rule and so on) as a 'utilitarian constraint' on a pure form of [84] corrective justice focused on the boundary crossing *simpliciter*.[97] But, while this enables him formally to square his theory with the law, the suggestion that the conceptual apparatus that determines the vast majority of nuisance actions – and which lies 'at the heart of nuisance law'[98] – is a peripheral 'constraint' on the true nature of the cause of action rings hollow, and only goes to demonstrate 'the central failure of his account'.[99]

This first difficulty shades into a second one, which is that some versions of the physical invasion view fail plausibly to account for central doctrines of the law of private nuisance, most obviously the requirement that the interference with another's use and enjoyment must be substantial, or unreasonable.[100] Here the logic of the orthodox conception of the tort is clear: you begin by asking whether there is an interference with the capacity of land to be used and enjoyed at all, and then (if there is) you move on to consider how significant that interference is. By contrast, if you try to break the link with the land's utility, then the substantial interference question either makes no sense at all (substantial interference *with what*, on the Douglas/McFarlane approach?), or is pushed, rather implausibly, to the conceptual periphery (Epstein). Nor is this the only instance of a central aspect of private nuisance law which is clearly derivative of the conception of the tort as an interference with the usability of land. Another good example is the holding of the House of Lords in *Hunter v Canary Wharf* that the basic damages in a nuisance case are to be assessed by reference to the diminution in the value of the land attributable to the nuisance, and that in amenity nuisance cases (as opposed to physical damage cases) what this meant was the diminution in the *use or utility value* of the property.[101]

Sticking with the law itself, a further weakness of the physical invasion view is that the account its proponents give of the distinction between trespass and nuisance is unpersuasive. The alleged dichotomy between 'tangible' and 'intangible' things is clunky in the extreme;[102] makes little sense from a functional perspective (why should invasions of tangible and intangible things be subject to different legal regimes?); and is a poor match for the law, since there are many

---

[95] See also Essert (n 7) 97–98 (discussing light rays in particular).

[96] *Bamford v Turnley* (1862) 3 B & S 66, 84; 122 ER 27, 33 (Bramwell B).

[97] See Epstein (n 58) 82 ff.

[98] Essert (n 7) 104.

[99] ibid 104 fn. It is also worth noting that there is in fact nothing 'utilitarian' about these rules, but that is an argument for another day.

[100] For discussion of this requirement, see Oliphant (n 13) paras 22.39 ff.

[101] *Hunter* (n 14) 696 (Lord Lloyd), 706 (Lord Hoffmann).

[102] See Essert (n 7) 112, emphasising the arbitrary nature of the distinction. Unsurprisingly, the suggestion made to a US court that the two causes of action be distinguished in this way was roundly rejected: see *Martin v Reynolds Metals Co* 342 P 2d 790 (Or 1959).

examples of nuisances that *do* involve boundary crossings where the thing that crosses the boundary is eminently 'tangible' and not remotely 'ethereal',[103] such as stray golf balls[104] and cricket balls,[105] a collapsing fence or wall,[106] and encroaching tree branches and roots.[107] Although not free from difficulty, the traditional way of [85] drawing the distinction, which asks whether the interference is direct (trespass) or indirect (nuisance)[108] tracks the historical division between trespass and case, is easier to justify,[109] and is a much better fit with the cases.

Yet another difficulty with the physical invasion view is that the positive arguments that have been put forward for it are weak, and usually rely on what I hope to have shown is a misunderstanding of the orthodox conception of private nuisance (coupled, as argued earlier, with a failure to appreciate the role played by what I have called the 'substructure' of the tort[110]). Douglas, for example, says that what he terms a 'duty of non-impairment of use' owed to a freeholder of land could prove 'very onerous', since it could potentially entail 'a duty to refrain from doing *any act* that could prevent [the freeholder] from making a specific use of his land', and gives as an example buying up building materials that the freeholder needs in order to erect a building on his land.[111] As we have seen, however, what the tort of private nuisance protects is a relatively abstract notion of the *usability* of the claimant's *land*, rather than the ability of the *claimant* to actually *use* her land, whether generally or in specific ways. Once this is understood, the duty that Douglas thinks very onerous turns out to be entirely reasonable, and the building materials example is revealed as a red herring. Similarly, Douglas' other argument against a duty of non-impairment of use, that a freeholder will not usually be overly prejudiced by the loss of a specific liberty to use her land,[112] again misses the point that what private nuisance in fact protects is a more general interest in the usability of land, substantial interference with which is likely to be highly prejudicial to both freeholders and tenants alike.

---

[103] See Smith, 'Exclusion and Property Rules in the Law of Nuisance' (n 24) 998 ('nuisance is about invasions of a more ethereal sort').

[104] *Lester-Travers v City of Frankston* [1970] VR 2 (VSC); *Segal v Derrick Golf & Winter Club* (1977) 76 DLR (3d) 746 (Alta SC).

[105] *Miller v Jackson* [1977] QB 966 (CA).

[106] *St Anne's Well Brewery Co v Roberts* (1928) 140 LT 1 (CA) 6 (Scrutton LJ); *Mann v Saulnier* (1959) 19 DLR (2d) 130 (New Brunswick CA).

[107] For judicial confirmation that encroachment of tree branches or roots is a nuisance not a trespass, see, eg, *Lemmon v Webb* [1894] 3 Ch 1 (CA) 24 (Kay LJ); *Davey v Harrow Corpn* [1958] 1 QB 60 (CA) 70 (Lord Goddard CJ).

[108] *Southport Corp v Esso Petroleum Co* [1953] 2 All ER 1204 (QBD) 1208 (Devlin J).

[109] For such a justification, see Nolan (n 14) 481–82. See also the not dissimilar justification put forward by Essert (n 7) 112–24. Both justifications for the direct/indirect distinction centre on the fact that in nuisance it is necessary to show that the interference is substantial/unreasonable, but that no such limitation applies in trespass.

[110] See text following n 53.

[111] Douglas, 'The Content of a Freehold' (n 58) 376.

[112] ibid 376–77.

Finally, the physical invasion view, and in particular the rejection of a right to the usability of land, is counter-intuitive, and fairly obviously misses the point. After all, how plausible is an account of real property law according to which it is *not* an interference with your property rights to block all the access to your land, or to suck out all the air from your flat using a pump, or to make your house uninhabitable by cutting off all the utilities that service it?[113] And do we really believe that, as Douglas and McFarlane argue, an 'affront' case like *Thompson-Schwab*[114] is possibly explicable on the basis that the presence of the brothel or those frequenting it causes light rays to cross the boundary of the claimant's land[115] (which, we might note, is also true of the presence of every other person, building or thing visible from the claimant's property, including a cloud flitting past on the horizon or a star shining in the night sky)? [86]

IV. IMPLICATIONS FOR PROPERTY THEORY

Since it seems clear that at least some manifestations of the physical invasion view of private nuisance are rooted in attempts to square the tort with particular theories of property, it is now time to turn the tables, and to ask what implications the orthodox conception of the cause of action, properly understood, might have for property theory. After all, as Essert points out, '[u]nderstanding property requires understanding nuisance'.[116]

The most obvious such implication is that private nuisance demonstrates that it cannot be right to conceive of property rights solely in terms of a right to exclude others. While many private nuisance cases do in fact involve boundary crossings, many do not, and (more importantly) the essence of private nuisance does not lie in the idea of a physical invasion of the claimant's land, but rather in the impairment of the land's usability. A theory of property that cannot explain the essence of a cause of action so central to the lived reality of land law is not a persuasive one. Furthermore, the fact that the role nuisance plays in the protection of incorporeal hereditaments is such a problem for the physical invasion view of the tort serves as a useful reminder that theories of property need to be capable of explaining property rights of this kind, which clearly rest not on a right to exclude but on (something like) a right not to be excluded.

---

[113] Note that Douglas accepts that denying a person all access to his or her *chattel* can amount to a wrongful interference with it, actionable in conversion: S Douglas, *Liability for Wrongful Interferences with Chattels* (Oxford, Hart Publishing, 2011) 99.

[114] See n 43.

[115] Douglas and McFarlane (n 58) 232.

[116] Essert (n 7) 119–20. See also at 86, where he says that 'a complete theory of property would help explain what counts and what does not count as a nuisance', and that conversely 'a complete theory of nuisance would help explain the rights definitive of ownership of real property'.

Beyond the relatively simple claim that property rights cannot be conceived *solely* in terms of a right to exclude others, the implications of the orthodox conception of private nuisance for property theory become less clear-cut. After all, the claim that a plausible theory of property *must be capable of accommodating* a usability right is not necessarily inconsistent, for example, with the suggestion that the right to exclude is 'fundamental to the concept of property',[117] or indeed that exclusion or the right to exclude is the 'essence'[118] or 'core'[119] of property. On the other hand, the practical significance of private nuisance in common law systems of real property casts doubt even on these weaker claims, for, as Hanoch Dagan points out, doctrines such as nuisance 'are not marginal or peripheral to the life of property, but deal instead with some of our most commonplace human interactions'.[120]

Then again, my analysis of the essence of private nuisance is entirely consistent with some of the central arguments that have been made by commentators who have endorsed exclusion-based accounts of property, which suggests that, properly understood, private nuisance might not be as much of a problem for these theorists as it is for their theories. Take, for example, Douglas and McFarlane's 'core argument' that 'the distinctiveness of property rights is best understood, not by looking at the positive uses available to A, but rather at the negative duties owed to A by the rest of the world'.[121] Here the clarification of [87] the orthodox conception of private nuisance is significant, since it shows that what nuisance protects is not A's 'right to use' her land in particular ways, but a perfectly plausible 'right to usability' that corresponds to a duty not substantially to impair the usability of other people's land. Similarly, while the orthodox conception of private nuisance, properly understood, is incompatible with James Penner's argument that the interest we have in the use of property grounds *only* a formal right of exclusion,[122] it is perfectly consistent with what appears to be his more foundational claim that 'there is simply no basis in the legal institution of property rights to individuate or identify particular use-rights as legally recognised elements of the bundle [of rights]'.[123] And, again, by avoiding

---

[117] TW Merill, 'Property and the Right to Exclude' (1998) 77 *Nebraska Law Review* 730, 731.

[118] M Cohen, 'Property and Sovereignty' (1927) 13 *Cornell Law Quarterly* 8, 12–13. See also Penner, *The Idea of Property in Law* (n 22) 71 (describing exclusion as the 'formal essence' of the right to property).

[119] TW Merrill and HE Smith, *Property: Principles and Practice* (New York, Foundation Press, 2007) 22. For discussion of this idea, see Dagan (n 61) 38 ff.

[120] Dagan (n 61) 41.

[121] Douglas and McFarlane (n 58) 220.

[122] J Penner, 'Hohfeldian Use-Rights in Property' in JW Harris (ed), *Property Problems from Genes to Pension Funds* (London, Kluwer Law International, 1997) 168.

[123] ibid 172. Furthermore, it is also compatible with Penner's claim that 'the right to property does not *enable* use' (ibid 171), since we have seen that a proper understanding of the orthodox conception of nuisance shows it to be concerned with the usability of the land, not the ability of the claimant to use it.

the high information costs associated with the delineation of specific use rights, an abstract usability right would appear to be consistent with Smith's 'information-cost rationale for broad rights'.[124]

Tying these threads together, we can see that recognition of the underlying nature of private nuisance as a cause of action demonstrates that property rights need not (as many property theorists seem to assume[125]) be conceived of in strictly binary terms as *either* rights of exclusion *or* specific use rights: nuisance shows that there is a plausible third possibility, a right of usability that can profitably operate in tandem with an exclusion rule, as exemplified by its sister tort of trespass.

Finally, although my focus in this chapter is on the law of private nuisance, and so on property rights in *land*, we should also note the possibility that an exclusion/usability model may also underlie the protection of interests in chattels. As in the case of land, the implausibility of a 'right to use' personal property in particular ways[126] is not inconsistent with a more abstract right to the usability of chattels, and indeed there is some evidence of such a right in the law governing wrongful interference with personal property.[127] At the same time, it would be a mistake to ignore the important differences between land and chattels, and their implications for any usability analysis. In particular, the immovability or 'stuckness' of land means that it is more likely to be rendered unusable by the activities of others, whereas chattels are by definition movable and hence problems caused by their being rendered unusable in one location can generally be avoided by relocating them.[128] [88]

V. CONCLUSION

In this chapter, I have sought to defend and clarify the orthodox conception of private nuisance as a tort that responds to interference with the use and enjoyment of land. In doing so, I have argued for the rejection of an attenuated vision

---

[124] Smith, 'Exclusion and Property Rules in the Law of Nuisance' (n 24) 971. Similarly, a usability right would appear to satisfy Smith's test of a 'gatekeeper right that protects the owners' interests in a wide and indefinite class of uses without the need to delineate ... those uses at all' (ibid 973).

[125] See, eg, Merrill and Smith (n 119) 21. This assumption may reflect the influence of early law-and-economics scholarship, which characterised nuisance disputes as conflicts between particular land uses: see in particular the works by Coase and by Calabresi and Melamed, cited in n 24.

[126] As to which, see Douglas, 'The Content of a Freehold' (n 58) 376–77.

[127] See Douglas, *Liability for Wrongful Interferences with Chattels* (n 113) 66–68, 99, 117–18, 157. See also the discussion of a 'right to use' chattels in S Green, 'Rights and Wrongs: An Introduction to the Wrongful Interference Actions' in Nolan and Robertson (n 14).

[128] Though not always. If, for example, the defendant prevents the claimant from taking her car out of her garage he renders it immovable and hence unusable for its core purpose of transportation. See further, Bagshaw (n 23) 417. See also *England v Cowley* (1873) LR 8 Ex 126 (Exch) 128 (Pollock B). In the famous German 'Fleet case', it was held that trapping a ship in a canal for nine months amounted to a violation of ownership rights in the ship: BGH 21 December 1970, BGHZ 55, 153.

of real property which rests not only on a misguided 'isomorphism between the boundaries of the property right and the physical boundaries of the land',[129] but also (by ignoring incorporeal hereditaments) on a misconception of 'land' in its legal sense as a three-dimensional physical space, as opposed to a normative idea.[130] I hope thereby to have shown not only that private nuisance is a complex and sophisticated cause of action, but also that by looking through the lens of nuisance we can more clearly see the complexity and sophistication of the institution of property itself.[131]

---

[129] See RG Bone, 'Normative Theory and Legal Doctrine in American Nuisance Law: 1850 to 1920' (1986) *Southern California Law Review* 1101, 1157.

[130] See Essert (n 7) 107 fn. On the legal conception of land, see n 12.

[131] See Dagan (n 61) 37 (referring to property as 'a complex and heterogenous legal construct').

11

The Distinctiveness of Rylands v Fletcher

(2005) 121 *Law Quarterly Review* 421–451

EVER SINCE ITS inception, the rule in *Rylands v Fletcher* has been controversial. When the case came before the courts, the judiciary was divided between advocates of the fault principle and proponents of an older model of strict liability. The decision in *Rylands* was an important victory for the supporters of strict liability, but while they won this particular battle their opponents eventually won the war. By the turn of the twentieth century, therefore, the rule in *Rylands v Fletcher* already appeared incongruous, a throwback to earlier times. And yet the cause of action has proved surprisingly resilient. Although the contempt of the House of Lords was barely concealed in the post-war case of *Read v J Lyons & Co Ltd*,[1] their Lordships contented themselves with imposing severe constraints on the rule's operation, and refrained from abolishing it altogether. Little was heard of *Rylands v Fletcher* in the decades that followed, but more recently two decisions of the House of Lords, *Cambridge Water Co Ltd v Eastern Counties Leather plc*[2] and *Transco plc v Stockport Metropolitan Borough Council*,[3] have once again focused attention on the strict liability rule.

The waxing and waning of the rule's popularity has been accompanied by shifting perceptions as to the best explanation for the strict liability it imposes. Opinions differ as to the intentions of those who created it, and that difficult issue will be dealt with later. However, the subsequent triumph of the fault principle meant that a rationale was required for this outpost of strict liability, and the justification provided was that the defendant had been engaged in a peculiarly dangerous activity. The new understanding was epitomised by an article (published 20 years after *Rylands*) in which Pollock argued that while the general principle was no liability without fault, 'the law takes notice that certain things are a source of extraordinary risk, and a man who exposes his neighbour to such

---

[1] *Read v J Lyons & Co Ltd* [1947] AC 156 (HL).
[2] *Cambridge Water Co Ltd v Eastern Counties Leather plc* [1994] 2 AC 264 (HL).
[3] *Transco plc v Stockport Metropolitan Borough Council* [2003] UKHL 61, [2004] 2 AC 1.

risk is held ... to insure his neighbour against any consequent harm not due to some cause beyond human foresight and control'.[4] This was a perfectly sensible spin to put on the cause of action, particularly since the reinterpreted rule seemed an appropriate legal response to the more threatening innovations of the industrial age: hence the early deployment of *Rylands v Fletcher* against locomotives, traction-engines and electricity.[5] But this gradual transformation of the rule into a general principle of strict liability for ultra-hazardous activities was stopped in its tracks by *Read v Lyons*, where the House of [422] Lords denied the existence of any such principle,[6] and placed strict limits on the rule's operation. Once again, *Rylands v Fletcher* appeared anomalous. The most recent attempt at retrospective rationalisation came in *Cambridge Water*, where Lord Goff said that the rule was best regarded as an offshoot of the tort of private nuisance, an extension of that cause of action to isolated escapes. This 'offshoot theory' was endorsed by the House of Lords in *Transco*, and can now be described as the new orthodoxy.

The principal purpose of this article is to challenge the new orthodoxy. In particular, it will be argued that the offshoot theory is historically unsound, and that the consequences of its endorsement by the judiciary will be bad for *Rylands v Fletcher*, and bad for nuisance too. By way of contrast to the offshoot theory, the distinctiveness of the rule in *Rylands v Fletcher* will be asserted. Although the principal focus will be on the relationship between the rule and nuisance, that distinctiveness has also been threatened in another way. In *Burnie Port Authority v General Jones Pty Ltd*,[7] the High Court of Australia held, by a five-to-two majority, that the rule in *Rylands v Fletcher* should henceforth be treated as having been absorbed by the principles of ordinary negligence. The majority argued that over the years the gap between the rule and negligence liability had narrowed to almost nothing, and hence that assimilation of the two was now appropriate. This contention will be examined, and an attempt made to refute it. Finally, the future of a strict liability rule independent of nuisance will be considered. Would a renewed attempt to carve out a special regime for abnormally dangerous activities be a sensible way forward? And, if not, what should become of the rule in *Rylands v Fletcher*?[8]

---

[4] F Pollock, 'Duties of Insuring Safety: The Rule in Rylands v Fletcher' (1886) 2 *LQR* 52.

[5] See respectively *Jones v Festiniog Rly Co* (1868) LR 3 QB 733 (QBD); *Powell v Fall* (1880) 5 QBD 597 (CA); *National Telephone Co v Baker* [1893] 2 Ch 186 (Ch D) (defence of statutory authority on facts).

[6] *Read* (n 1) 172–73 (Lord Macmillan), 181–82 (Lord Simmonds), 186 (Lord Uthwatt). See also the thorough analysis of the American principle by Scott LJ in the Court of Appeal: [1945] KB 216 (CA) 108–11.

[7] *Burnie Port Authority v General Jones Pty Ltd* (1994) 179 CLR 520 (HCA). Mason CJ, Deane, Dawson, Toohey and Gaudron JJ gave a joint judgment; Brennan and McHugh JJ dissented.

[8] The subject-matter of this article overlaps with that of J Murphy, 'The Merits of *Rylands v Fletcher*' (2004) 24 *OJLS* 643, but not as much as I initially feared. Although Murphy also emphasises the distinctiveness of *Rylands v Fletcher*, many of his arguments are different from the ones on which I rely. Furthermore, while Murphy believes that the strict liability rule has an important role to play in the modern law of tort, I reach the opposite conclusion.

I. THE NEW ORTHODOXY

There is nothing particularly novel about the suggestion that the rule in *Rylands v Fletcher* is a sub-species of nuisance. Writing in the 1940s, Prosser posed the following question:[9]

> Let the reader now refer again to the doctrine of *Rylands v Fletcher* and ask himself whether there is any difference to be found, either in the nature of the harm done, the character of the defendant's conduct, [423] the type of hazard which arises, or the limitations upon liability in terms of 'natural' or 'reasonable' use, between that doctrine as it has developed in England and in the American courts which have accepted it by name, and the strict liability imposed under the guise of 'absolute' nuisance.

A number of others have shared Prosser's opinion, by far the most influential of them being Newark, who propounded the offshoot theory in his article 'The Boundaries of Nuisance'.[10] Newark argued that the main reason why difficulties surrounded the law of nuisance was that the boundaries of the tort had become blurred. And he claimed that one result of the blurring of the distinction between nuisance and other torts had been a 'misappreciation' of *Rylands v Fletcher*, namely that the case was a landmark in the law of tort. In fact, Newark maintained, the principle involved was a very simple one: that 'negligence is not an element in the tort of nuisance'.[11] The only novel aspect of the decision was that for the first time the law of nuisance had been applied to an isolated escape. Because by this time conceptions of the boundaries of nuisance were becoming fogged, this simple truth was not recognised, and the misguided perception took hold that the rule covered exceptional cases where liability was strict on account of the dangerous nature of the defendant's activity. This in turn led to the extension of the rule beyond the case of neighbouring property owners, and into the realm of personal injuries.

For the most part, this short passage of Newark's article consists merely of assertion. Although he points out that the judges who decided *Rylands v Fletcher* treated the case as a restatement of existing principles, this is far from proving Newark's point. The judiciary are understandably keen to make out that their decisions are in line with precedent, and in any case it will be argued that there is a more plausible explanation than the offshoot theory for the fact that those involved considered their reasoning to be consistent with earlier authority.[12] The only other evidence which Newark adduced in support of the offshoot theory was the fact that, in his judgment in *Rylands*, Blackburn J had cited the case

---

[9] WL Prosser, 'Nuisance Without Fault' (1942) 20 *Texas Law Review* 399, 420.

[10] FH Newark, 'The Boundaries of Nuisance' (1949) 65 *LQR* 480. For judicial support for the Prosser/Newark position, see, eg, *Read* (n 1) 183 (Lord Simonds); *Benning v Wong* (1969) 122 CLR 249 (HCA) 265 (Barwick CJ), 297 (Windeyer J).

[11] Newark (n 10) 487.

[12] See text to n 56.

of fumes escaping from an alkali works – a 'clear case of nuisance'[13] – as an instance of liability under the rule he was laying down. The significance of this will be addressed later: for now it is sufficient to note that the *locus classicus* of the new orthodoxy is more than a little flimsy.

Newark's analysis would have remained just another academic opinion had it not been for its enthusiastic adoption by Lord Goff in *Cambridge* [424] *Water*.[14] The defendants in this case were manufacturers of fine leather, who used a chemical solvent in their tanning process. Over the years, solvent that spilled on to the tannery floor seeped into the ground and contaminated the underground water that supplied a borehole used by the plaintiff water company. As a result, the plaintiffs were obliged to develop a new source of supply, and they sought recovery of the added expense from the defendants in negligence, private nuisance and under the rule in *Rylands v Fletcher*. At first instance, the judge dismissed the negligence and nuisance claims on the ground that the contamination of the borehole had not been reasonably foreseeable, and the *Rylands* action on the ground that the defendants' tannery was not a non-natural use of land. When the case reached the House of Lords, Lord Goff (who gave the only speech) held that the judge's finding on foreseeability was fatal to the *Rylands* claim, since 'foreseeability of damage of the relevant type should be regarded as a prerequisite of liability under the rule'.[15]

This conclusion was based on two considerations. The first was that the language Blackburn J employed in the *Rylands* case suggested that it had originally been envisaged that liability was limited to foreseeable harm.[16] However, it was the second consideration that proved the more significant, for Lord Goff went on to say that Newark had 'convincingly shown that the rule in *Rylands v Fletcher* was essentially concerned with an extension of the law of nuisance to cases of isolated escape',[17] and that since recovery of damages in private nuisance was conditional on foreseeability of the relevant type of damage it was therefore logical to extend that requirement to liability under the rule.[18] His Lordship added that it would lead to 'a more coherent body of common law principles if the rule were to be regarded essentially as an extension of the law of nuisance to cases of isolated escapes from land'.[19]

Two points can be made about Lord Goff's adoption of the offshoot theory in *Cambridge Water*. The first is that, although the analogy with nuisance influenced the outcome of the case, it was not necessary to the conclusion that

---

[13] Newark (n 10) 487.

[14] *Cambridge Water* (n 2).

[15] ibid 306.

[16] ibid 302. See *Fletcher v Rylands* (1866) LR 1 Exch 265 (Exch Ch), where Blackburn J refers (at 279) to 'anything likely to do mischief if it escapes', and (at 280) to liability for the 'natural and anticipated consequences' of the escape.

[17] *Cambridge Water* (n 2) 304.

[18] ibid.

[19] ibid 306.

reasonable foreseeability of the harm was required for *Rylands v Fletcher* liability. As his Lordship pointed out, this conclusion was consistent with the language used in the case itself, and it is also noteworthy that academic commentators had previously made the case for a foreseeability requirement without reference to the nuisance analogy.[20] [425] The other point is that in making the connection Lord Goff relied almost entirely on Newark's article. In addition to citing Newark, his Lordship merely drew attention to the fact that Blackburn J had not considered *Rylands* to be a revolutionary decision[21] – a point also made by Newark – and to what he considered to be the functional similarity between the doctrines of unreasonable user and non-natural use, the principal devices used to limit liability in nuisance and *Rylands v Fletcher* respectively.[22]

The speed with which Newark's thesis has been converted into orthodoxy since the *Cambridge Water* decision is remarkable. Two years after Lord Goff gave his speech, Judge Peter Bowsher QC said that, 'In view of the latest authority, it is difficult to separate off *Rylands v Fletcher* and nuisance',[23] and went on to remark that in *Cambridge Water* Lord Goff had treated nuisance and the strict liability rule as 'parts of the same cause of action'.[24] Similarly, at first instance in *Marcic v Thames Water Utilities Ltd* Judge Richard Havery QC commented that *Rylands v Fletcher* 'may be said to be a variety of nuisance'.[25] The alleged affinity with nuisance has also caused judges to call into question well-established principles of *Rylands v Fletcher* liability, such as the actionability of personal injuries and the absence of a *locus standi* rule requiring an interest in land affected by the escape.[26]

Any remaining doubts as to the impact of Lord Goff's reasoning were dispelled by the House of Lords in the *Transco* case.[27] *Transco* concerned an escape of water from the service pipe to a block of flats owned by the defendant council. The water that escaped caused the collapse of a nearby embankment, leaving the claimant's gas main exposed and unsupported, and the claimant sought to

---

[20] See, eg, RFV Heuston and RW Buckley, *Salmond & Heuston on the Law of Torts*, 20th edn (London, Sweet & Maxwell, 1992) 324–25.

[21] *Cambridge Water* (n 2) 299.

[22] ibid. It will be argued that in fact these devices share little in common: see text to n 93.

[23] *Ellison v Ministry of Defence* (1996) 81 BLR 101 (QBD) 117.

[24] ibid 120.

[25] *Marcic v Thames Water Utilities Ltd* [2001] 3 All ER 698 (QBD) 716.

[26] See *Ribee v Norrie* [2001] PIQR P8 (CA) [30], where Ward LJ said that Lord Goff's reasoning threw doubt on claims for personal injury under the rule; and *McKenna v British Aluminium Ltd* [2002] Env LR 30 (Ch D), where Neuberger J held that, in the light of the analysis in *Cambridge Water*, a claimant must have an interest in the land affected to bring an action under the rule. Only one judicial voice, that of Judge Anthony Thornton QC, has been raised against the new orthodoxy: see *Johnson v BJW Property Developments Ltd* [2002] EWHC 1131 (TCC), [2002] 3 All ER 574 [17] (the extent to which the causes of action in nuisance and *Rylands v Fletcher* have been assimilated remains unclear); and *Re-Source American International Ltd v Platt Service Ltd* [2003] EWHC 1142 (TCC), 90 Con LR 139 [171] ('a claimant relying on a *Rylands v Fletcher* type claim … need not himself have an interest in land').

[27] *Transco* (n 3).

recover the cost of the required repairs from the defendant under the rule in *Rylands v Fletcher.* The House of Lords declined an invitation from counsel for the defendant to abrogate the rule, but held that the escape did not attract strict liability because the supply of water to the flats was a natural user of the council's land.[28] Most **[426]** importantly, however, their Lordships confirmed that the rule was now to be regarded as, in Lord Bingham's words, a 'sub-species of nuisance'.[29] And since liability under *Rylands v Fletcher* was therefore 'a remedy for damage to land or interests in land',[30] it followed that personal injuries were not actionable under the rule,[31] and that only those with a proprietary interest in the land affected by an escape could sue.[32] The assimilation of the *Rylands* rule into the tort of private nuisance is now, therefore, complete. However, in the next section it will be argued that, far from making the common law more coherent, this realignment is both undesirable and historically unsound.

II. THE CASE AGAINST THE OFFSHOOT THEORY

A host of judges and academics have maintained that private nuisance and the rule in *Rylands v Fletcher* are distinct categories of liability. Lord Wright, for example, said that nuisance differed from the *Rylands* rule not only in its historical origin but also 'in its legal character and in many of its incidents and applications'.[33] And, in his article 'Nuisance as a Tort',[34] Winfield devoted a good deal of space to demolishing the view that *Rylands* was but a subset of nuisance. According to Winfield:[35]

> It would be incorrect ... to state baldly that the rule in *Rylands v Fletcher* is merely a species of nuisance. It is much nearer the truth to say that an accident of definition, or lack of definition, of nuisance, may bring the same set of facts within either kind of liability, but that they differ notably in details, and that it is only where none of these differences of detail is in question that it is immaterial whether the action is for nuisance or is on the rule in *Rylands v Fletcher.* Nuisance and that rule are related to one another as intersecting circles, not as the segment of a circle to the circle itself.

Moreover, two years earlier Stallybrass, though conceding that the strict liability rule was in some respects 'closely related' to nuisance, had cautioned that it

---

[28] Lord Scott felt that the appeal could also be dismissed on the ground that, since the water had remained on the defendant's land, there had been no 'escape': ibid [79].

[29] ibid [9]. Lord Walker took as read (at [94]) what Lord Goff had said in *Cambridge Water* about the inter-relationship of *Rylands v Fletcher* and nuisance.

[30] ibid [39] (Lord Hoffmann).

[31] ibid [9] (Lord Bingham), [35] (Lord Hoffmann), [52] (Lord Hobhouse).

[32] ibid [47] (Lord Hoffmann).

[33] *Northwestern Utilities Ltd v London Guarantee and Accident Co* [1936] AC 108 (PC) 119. See also his Lordship's speech in *Sedleigh-Denfield v O'Callaghan* [1940] AC 880 (HL) 903: 'There are ... well marked differences between the two juristic concepts'.

[34] Winfield, 'Nuisance as a Tort' (1931) 4 *CLJ* 189.

[35] ibid 195.

was not to be identified with it as it had sometimes been,[36] [427] while West later argued that the true distinction between nuisance and the rule in *Rylands v Fletcher* was that nuisance is a wrong caused *to* land, whereas *Rylands v Fletcher* is a wrong arising *from* land.[37] Here, four reasons will be put forward for rejecting the offshoot theory: (1) analysis of the *Rylands v Fletcher* case provides little support for the theory; (2) there are well-established distinctions between the rule in *Rylands v Fletcher* and private nuisance; (3) merger with the rule will be bad for nuisance; and (4) the version of the strict liability rule to which the offshoot theory has given rise is unappealing.

A. Analysis of the *Rylands v Fletcher* Case Provides Little Support for the Offshoot Theory

The defendants in *Rylands v Fletcher* had built a small reservoir to provide water for their mill. The design and construction of the reservoir were left in the hands of independent contractors. While excavating the bed of the reservoir the contractors had discovered some old shafts, filled in with soil. Neither the defendants nor the contractors knew that the shafts led to old workings under the reservoir site, which were in turn connected, by means of other underground workings, to the plaintiff's colliery. A few days after the reservoir was filled with water, one of the shafts burst downwards and the water passed through the old workings and flooded the plaintiff's mine. The action the plaintiff brought – which at the beginning looked like an ordinary negligence claim – was referred to an arbitrator, who found that the defendants had not been at fault, but that the contractors had been negligent in failing to block up the shafts. The arbitrator stated a special case, which came before the Court of Exchequer. By a majority, the court held that on these facts the plaintiff could not recover his losses from the defendants.[38]

It would appear that in the Court of Exchequer neither counsel referred to nuisance, nor indeed to any nuisance case. The focus was principally on trespass to land, though mention was also made of the action on the case. Henry

---

[36] WTS Stallybrass, 'Dangerous Things and the Non-Natural User of Land' (1929) 3 *CLJ* 376, 392. In the seventh edition of *Salmond on the Law of Torts*, Stallybrass made a point of taking the rule in *Rylands v Fletcher* from out of the middle of the chapter on nuisance, and giving it 'the dignity of a chapter to itself': WTS Stallybrass, *Salmond on the Law of Torts*, 7th edn (London, Sweet & Maxwell, 1928) ix. In the body of the text, he made clear (at 374) that, while Salmond believed the rule to be 'merely a branch of the law of nuisance', in his opinion the requirement of recurrent injury in nuisance cases differentiated the two causes of action.

[37] WA West, 'Nuisance or *Rylands v Fletcher*' (1966) 30 *Conveyancer* 95. Other writers who have emphasised the differences between the two causes of action are RJ Buxton, 'The Negligent Nuisance' (1966) 8 *Malaya Law Review* 1, 6–8; and RFV Heuston, *Salmond on the Law of Torts*, 11th edn (London, Sweet & Maxwell, 1953) 644–45 (though Heuston later changed his mind: see RFV Heuston, 'The Return of *Rylands v Fletcher*' (1994) 110 *LQR* 185).

[38] *Fletcher v Rylands* (1865) 3 H&C 774, 159 ER 737 (Exch).

Manisty QC, who appeared for the plaintiff, said that if a man collected water in a reservoir on his land and allowed it to escape on to the property of his neighbour, 'It is a trespass'.[39] He went on to draw an analogy with cattle trespass,[40] and cited *Tenant v Goldwin*[41] for the proposition that 'one who creates foul water in his own land must keep it [428] in that it may not trespass'.[42] For the defendants, George Mellish QC argued that the case was not one of trespass, and that an action on the case did not lie in the absence of fault.

Martin B, who gave the principal majority judgment, held that if the defendants had directly cast water on the plaintiff's land, then that would have been a trespass, but that since in this case the damage was 'mediate or consequential' no trespass action lay.[43] Although he referred to nuisance, Martin B dismissed it on the grounds that there had been nothing hurtful or injurious to the senses, and added that '[t]he making of a pond for holding water is a nuisance to no one'.[44] Furthermore, he took the view that in the absence of trespass or nuisance proof of negligence was required to recover for damage to real property, just as in cases of damage to personal property.[45] The dissenting judgment of Bramwell B is arguably of even greater significance, since the majority's reasoning was not followed in the higher courts. It is noteworthy, then, that – as Martin B pointed out – Bramwell B seemed to think that 'the act of the defendants was a trespass'.[46] The essence of Bramwell B's reasoning can be found in the following passage:[47]

> [The plaintiff] had a right to be free from what has been called 'foreign' water, that is, water artificially brought or sent to him directly, or indirectly by its being sent where it would flow to him. The defendants had no right to pour or send water on to the plaintiff's works. Had they done so knowingly it is admitted an action would lie; and that it would if they did it again ... the plaintiff's right then has been infringed; the defendants in causing water to flow to the plaintiff have done that which they had no right to do; what difference in point of law does it make that they have done it unwittingly? I think none, and consequently that the action is maintainable. The plaintiff's case is, you have violated my right, you have done what you had no right to do, and have done me damage.

There are three reasons why this passage suggests that Bramwell B had trespass in mind. First, he chose to conceptualise the issue in terms of the violation of a

---

[39] ibid 781.
[40] ibid.
[41] *Tenant v Goldwin* (1703) 2 Ld Raym 1089, 91 ER 314.
[42] *Fletcher* (n 38) 783. Note also that, when distinguishing another case, counsel commented (at 784) that the defendant was not 'as here, suffering a trespass to be committed on the plaintiff's land'.
[43] ibid 792.
[44] ibid.
[45] ibid 793.
[46] ibid 792.
[47] ibid 789.

specific right of the plaintiff. Secondly, the right he identified was envisaged as extending to cases of direct interference which would clearly amount to trespasses. And, finally, the language Bramwell B used to describe what took place – that the defendant 'poured' the water into the plaintiff's mine – is, though perhaps not entirely accurate, none the less [**429**] redolent of trespass.[48] For Bramwell B, the issue appears to have been whether, for liability in trespass to arise, the defendants must have been aware of what they were doing. His conclusion was that no such awareness was necessary: 'as a rule the knowledge or ignorance of the damage done is immaterial'.[49]

The Court of Exchequer Chamber unanimously reversed the decision of the Court of Exchequer, and found the defendants liable.[50] In reply to counsel for the defendants, counsel for the plaintiff once again made clear the basis on which he rested his case: '[H]ere the collecting of the water in such a manner as to invade the premises of the plaintiff was a trespass'.[51] Less obvious, though, is what Blackburn J, who delivered the judgment of the Exchequer Chamber, had in mind. He formulated the rule that made the case famous in the following terms:[52]

> We think that the true rule of law is, that the person who for his own purposes brings on his lands and collects and keeps there something likely to do mischief if it escapes, must keep it in at his peril, and, if he does not do so, is prima facie answerable for all the damage which is the natural consequence of its escape. He can excuse himself by shewing that the escape was owing to the plaintiff's default; or perhaps that the escape was the consequence of vis major, or the act of God; but as nothing of this sort exists here, it is unnecessary to inquire what excuse would be sufficient.

An investigation into the thinking behind this rule might usefully begin with Newark's point that the judges who sat in *Rylands v Fletcher* denied that they were laying down new law. Blackburn J later commented that he had wasted much time in the preparation of his judgment in the case if he did not succeed in showing that the law as he stated it had been law 'for at least 300 years',[53] and when the decision of the Exchequer Chamber was affirmed by the House of Lords, Lord Cairns LC remarked that the governing principles were 'extremely simple',[54] and Lord Cranworth came 'without hesitation' to the conclusion that the judgment of the court below was right.[55] It is by no means clear, however,

---

[48] See also *Nichols v Marsland* (1875) LR 10 Exch 255 (Exch) 260, where Bramwell B described *Rylands v Fletcher* as a case where 'the defendant poured the water into the plaintiff's mine. He did not know he was doing so; but he did it as much as though he had poured it into an open channel which led to the mine without his knowing it'.

[49] *Fletcher* (n 38) 789.

[50] *Fletcher* (n 16).

[51] ibid 277.

[52] ibid 279–80.

[53] *Ross v Fedden* (1872) 26 LT 966 (QBD) 968.

[54] *Rylands v Fletcher* (1868) LR 3 HL 330 (HL) 338.

[55] ibid.

that these remarks imply – as Newark went on to argue – that the judges involved regarded *Rylands* as a straightforward nuisance case, not least because no attempt was made to refute Martin B's cursory dismissal of a nuisance analysis in [430] the Court of Exchequer. A more plausible explanation for the self-assurance with which strict liability was imposed is that the judges were simply applying the ancient theory that a man acts at his peril. This was certainly the view of Holdsworth, according to whom 'the underlying principle [of *Rylands v Fletcher*] is the same as that which governed civil liability in general in the mediaeval common law'.[56]

It is entirely consistent with this analysis that the rule enunciated by Blackburn J should ground liability on causa rather than culpa.[57] While the act of building the reservoir was lawful, once the water escaped and did damage the plaintiff was entitled to recover without establishing negligence. The defendants' only hope would have been a causation argument: that the harm was caused not by them, but by an act of God, the claimant or a stranger. A similar causation-based analysis was evident in the House of Lords, where Lord Cranworth remarked that, in considering whether a defendant is liable for harm the plaintiff has sustained, 'the question in general is not whether the defendant has acted with due care and caution, but whether his acts have occasioned the damage'.[58] Now that statement was surely too sweeping: after all, by this time negligence had already become the touchstone of liability in road accident cases,[59] and was probably a prerequisite of recovery for personal injury more generally.[60] But *Rylands v Fletcher* indicated that the triumph of the fault principle was not yet complete: in the real property context, strict liability remained the norm. Moreover, it has been argued that this distinction between the two kinds of injury was not a new one: proof that the defendant had been 'utterly without fault' had long excused a defendant in trespass to the person cases, but not where the wrong was to land, as in cattle trespass and nuisance.[61]

This explains why Blackburn J cited an example from the law of nuisance: his point was that in this real property tort it was no defence for, say, the owner of an alkali works to prove that he had taken all reasonable steps to prevent the escape of chlorine fumes. But to extrapolate from this citation (as Newark did) that Blackburn J considered the *Rylands* rule to be simply an extension of nuisance is quite unwarranted. As we have seen, a close reading of the case suggests that trespass, rather than nuisance, was the established form of liability

---

[56] WS Holdsworth, *History of English Law*, 5th edn (London, Methuen, 1931) vol 8, 472. See also *Rickards v Lothian* [1913] AC 263 (PC) 275 (Lord Moulton); AKR Kiralfy, *Potter's Historical Introduction to English Law*, 4th edn (London, Sweet & Maxwell, 1958) 383.

[57] *Benning* (n 10) 298 (Windeyer J).

[58] *Rylands* (n 54) 341.

[59] See the remarks of Martin B in the Court of Exchequer: *Fletcher* (n 38) 793.

[60] GHL Fridman, 'The Rise and Fall of Rylands v Fletcher' (1956) 34 *Canadian Bar Review* 810, 812–13.

[61] ibid 814.

regarded as providing the closest analogy. And indeed the other two examples Blackburn J gave of the application of the strict liability rule were trespass-type cases. He stated that the most [431] common scenarios within the rule were instances of cattle trespass,[62] which (as its name suggests) was generally regarded as a form of trespass to land.[63] And the third example of strict liability cited by Blackburn J was *Tenant v Goldwin*,[64] where liability had been imposed for an escape of filth from the defendant's privy into his neighbour's cellar, and where, once again, the closest analogy was with trespass, rather than nuisance. According to Salkeld's report of this decision:[65]

> The reason he gave for his judgment was because it was the defendant's wall, and the defendant's filth, and he was bound of common right to keep his wall so as his filth might not damnify his neighbour, and that it was a trespass on his neighbour ....

Despite these strong connections with trespass to land, the judges who decided *Rylands v Fletcher* do not appear to have seen the case as a straightforward example of that cause of action, though Bramwell B perhaps came close to that position. This is understandable, for – as Francis Bohlen pointed out – if the shaft had given way as soon as the water was poured into the reservoir, then that would indeed have amounted to a trespass, but since in fact there was a 'rest in the course of events, a pause ... in the chain of causation', the harm was not a sufficiently direct consequence of the accumulation for trespass to lie.[66] Moreover, *Rylands v Fletcher* was framed as an action on the case.[67] At the same time, it would seem that in its conception the rule in *Rylands v Fletcher* was – as Newark argued – a tort against land, albeit not a form of nuisance but a *sui generis* cause of action. As we shall see, however, the later transformation of the

---

[62] ibid.

[63] In Blackstone's words (III Bl Comm 211): 'A man is answerable for not only his own trespass, but that of his cattle also: for if by his negligent keeping they stray upon the land of another ... and they there tread down his neighbour's herbage, and spoil his corn or his trees, this is a trespass for which the owner must answer in damages'.

See similarly *Read* (n 1) 166 (Viscount Simon); MJ Prichard, *Scott v Shepherd (1773) and the Emergence of the Tort of Negligence* (London, Selden Society, 1976) 9. As Williams points out (GL Williams, *Liability for Animals* (Cambridge, CUP, 1939) 127), the justification usually provided for this principle is a 'fanciful rule of early law', according to which trespass by one's cattle is equivalent to trespass by oneself: see, eg, F Pollock, *The Law of Torts*, 8th edn (London, Stevens & Sons, 1908) 497; *Read v J Lyons & Co Ltd* [1945] KB 216 (CA) 113 (Scott LJ). Williams concludes that this supposed principle was little better than a myth, and argues that cases involving escaping cattle ought logically to be classed under nuisance, but none the less the previously widespread acceptance of the vicarious trespass analysis suggests that Blackburn J would himself have associated cattle trespass with trespass to land rather than nuisance.

[64] *Tenant* (n 41).

[65] ibid 361.

[66] FH Bohlen, 'The Rule in Rylands v Fletcher: Part I' (1911) *University of Pennsylvania Law Review* 298, 311. See also *Read* (n 1) 166 (Viscount Simon).

[67] It is noteworthy, however, that in *Jones v Llanwrst Urban Council* [1911] 1 Ch 393 (Ch D) 402–403 Parker J seems to treat *Rylands* as a trespass case. See also WA Macfarlane and GW Wrangham, *Clerk and Lindsell on Torts*, 8th edn (London, Sweet & Maxwell, 1929) 392–93.

rule into a principle of liability for dangerous things severed the connection with real property, and opened the door to claims for personal injury.[68]

[432] In practical terms, the significance of *Rylands v Fletcher* was twofold:[69] first, Blackburn J took a liability rule previously applied to specifics, such as cattle and filth, and extended it to mischievous things generally;[70] and, secondly, the liability in question was imposed not only for the acts of oneself and one's servants but for the acts of anyone not classified as a stranger. (This explains why the defendants in *Rylands* were liable for the acts of their independent contractors a full ten years before such liability was imposed in nuisance.[71]) The broader significance of the case lay in the fact that it represented a victory for judicial opponents of the fault principle, but this is precisely why the rule so rapidly came to appear anomalous. Within a short time, the fault principle was ascendant, and only a few years later the facts of the case might well have been dealt with solely from the standpoint of negligence.

B. There Are Well-Established Distinctions Between the Rule in *Rylands v Fletcher* and Private Nuisance

There are a number of well-established distinctions between the rule in *Rylands v Fletcher* and private nuisance. Perhaps the two most obvious of these derive from the fact that while private nuisance is a tort against land the *Rylands* rule overcame its origins in the real property context and developed into a cause of action of more general application. As was made clear in *Hunter v Canary Wharf Ltd*,[72] if a wrong is characterised as one against land, then it follows that claims cannot be brought for personal injury, and that only those with an interest in the land affected have standing. Historically, neither restriction applied to actions brought under the rule. Before the *Cambridge Water* case, the only clear-cut judicial support for the analysis of *Rylands v Fletcher* as a tort limited to the protection of real property interests was to be found in *Read v Lyons*,[73] a case concerning a munitions inspector injured when an explosion took place in the factory where she was working. The House of Lords held that the inspector was not entitled to recover damages from the factory's owners under the strict liability rule because there had been no escape of a dangerous thing from their

---

[68] See text to n 82.

[69] Winfield (n 34).

[70] See also KS Abraham, '*Rylands v Fletcher*: Tort Law's Conscience' in RL Rabin and SD Sugarman (eds), *Torts Stories* (New York, Foundation Press, 2003) 215: 'The sense that something new was being decided in *Rylands* stems, I think, from the generality of the principle on which the opinions of Cairns and Blackburn are based'. Strangely, the general rule did not swallow up all its more specific antecedents, for cattle trespass remained distinct.

[71] *Bower v Peate* (1876) 1 QBD 321 (QBD).

[72] *Hunter v Canary Wharf Ltd* [1997] AC 655 (HL).

[73] *Read* (n 1).

premises, but Lord Macmillan added that the case also fell outside the ambit of the rule because *Rylands v Fletcher* [**433**] concerned 'the mutual duties of adjoining or neighbouring landowners', and had 'nothing to do with personal injuries',[74] recovery for which required proof of negligence.[75] Lord Uthwatt likewise said that the principle applied only to interference with land,[76] and, while Lords Porter and Simonds left open the question of recovery for personal injury, the latter inclined towards Lord Macmillan's position.[77]

Of course due weight must be accorded to these pronouncements, but it is important to remember that they were merely *dicta*, and that the House of Lords in *Read* was evidently concerned to limit as much as possible the scope of a principle they regarded with obvious disdain. In any case, there are numerous authorities to the contrary. As regards *locus standi*, the case law before *Cambridge Water* strongly suggested that the right to bring a claim was not dependent on possession of an interest in the property on to which the thing escaped. As Lawton J said in *British Celanese Ltd v AH Hunt (Capacitors) Ltd*: 'Once there has been an escape … those damnified may claim. They need not be the occupiers of adjoining land, or indeed of any land'.[78] Examples of this relaxed approach abound. One such is *Charing Cross Electricity Supply Co v Hydraulic Power Co*,[79] where water had escaped from the defendant's mains and damaged the plaintiff's electric cables, and where it was held that damages were recoverable under the strict liability rule, despite the fact that the plaintiff had no interest in the land where the cables were laid. *Rylands v Fletcher* has also been applied in cases where the damage occurred on a public highway,[80] and in a public park.[81] Some of the non-occupiers who successfully sued had suffered personal injury, but this was not seen as problematic either. In *Shiffman v Order of St John*,[82] for example, the plaintiff recovered damages under the *Rylands v Fletcher* rule after he was hurt by a falling flag pole in Hyde Park, and two years later, in *Hale v Jenning Bros*,[83] the Court of Appeal awarded the plaintiff damages under the rule after she was struck by a chair that became detached from a fairground chair-o-plane. Many [**434**]

---

[74] ibid 173.

[75] ibid 170–71.

[76] ibid 186.

[77] ibid 178 and 180, respectively.

[78] *British Celanese Ltd v AH Hunt (Capacitors) Ltd* [1969] 1 WLR 959 (QBD) 964. See also *Perry v Kendricks Transport Co Ltd* [1956] 1 WLR 85 (CA) 92, where Parker LJ said that (notwithstanding the *dicta* in *Read v Lyons*) it was not open to the Court of Appeal to hold that the rule applied only to damage to adjoining land or to a proprietary interest in land.

[79] *Charing Cross Electricity Supply Co v Hydraulic Power Co* [1914] 3 KB 772 (CA).

[80] *Miles v Forest Rock Granite Co* (1918) 34 TLR 500 (CA); *Halsey v Esso Petroleum Co Ltd* [1961] 1 WLR 683 (QBD). See also *Goodbody v Poplar Borough Council* (1914) 84 LJKB 122 (KBD), where the action failed on other grounds.

[81] *Shiffman v Order of St John* [1936] 1 All ER 557 (KBD).

[82] ibid.

[83] *Hale v Jenning Bros* [1938] 1 All ER 579 (CA). See also *Miles* (n 80) (plaintiff injured by defendant's blasting operations).

judges and commentators have noted these authorities, and concluded that the rule extends to cases of personal injury.[84]

The analysis of *Rylands v Fletcher* as a tort against land has not appealed to courts in other jurisdictions either,[85] while writers as distinguished as Winfield,[86] Stallybrass[87] and Fleming[88] have all rejected this narrow conception of the strict liability rule.[89] Moreover, there is evidence that Blackburn J did not subsequently consider that the rule he himself laid down was limited to the protection of real property interests. In *Cattle v Stockton Waterworks*,[90] water that leaked from the defendant's main made work the plaintiffs had contracted to do on a third party's land more onerous, and they sought recovery of the extra expense under the *Rylands v Fletcher* rule. The Divisional Court dismissed the claim on the ground that the harm (pure economic loss) was too remote. The importance of the case for present purposes lies in a passage in Blackburn J's judgment where – in making the point that economic loss was not recoverable – he said that, if it was, then in a case like *Rylands v Fletcher* the defendant would be liable,

> not only to an action by the owner of the drowned mine, *and by such of his workmen as had their tools or clothes destroyed*, but also to an action by every workman and person employed in the mine, who in consequence of its stoppage made less wages than he would otherwise have done.[91]

The words in italics suggest that at this time Blackburn J did not consider *Rylands v Fletcher* to be a real property tort.[92]

There are a number of other important distinctions between nuisance and *Rylands v Fletcher*. In *Cambridge Water*, Lord Goff pointed to what he called the 'similarity of function' between the nuisance principle of unreasonable user and the *Rylands* principle of non-natural use.[93] But whilst at a general level there is indeed a functional connection – each concept being the principal 'control mechanism' of the cause of action in question – closer scrutiny reveals marked differences between the two doctrines. The unreasonable user issue is ultimately

---

[84] See, eg, *Perry* (n 78) 92 (Parker LJ); *Hunter* (n 72) 719 (Lord Cooke); West (n 37) 96; JG Fleming, *The Law of Torts*, 9th edn (Sydney, Law Book Co, 1998) 384; Murphy (n 8) 652–54. A Canadian commentator has described the view that personal injuries are excluded as 'totally discredited': AM Linden, 'Whatever Happened to Rylands v Fletcher?' in L Klar (ed), *Studies in Canadian Tort Law* (Toronto, Butterworths, 1977) 335.

[85] See, eg, *Benning* (n 10) 275 (Barwick CJ), 277 (Menzies J), 319–20 (Windeyer J); and *Aldridge v Van Patter* [1952] 4 DLR 93 (Ont HC) (recovery under the rule by a spectator at a stock-car race).

[86] Winfield (n 34) 195.

[87] *Salmond on the Law of Torts*, 7th edn (n 36) 374.

[88] Fleming (n 84) 383–84.

[89] See also West (n 37) 101–102; JM Eekelaar, 'Nuisance and Strict Liability' (1973) 8 *Irish Jurist (NS)* 191, 205; Murphy (n 8) 646.

[90] *Cattle v Stockton Waterworks* (1875) LR 10 QB 453 (QBD).

[91] ibid 457 (emphasis added).

[92] Murphy (n 8) also draws attention (at 653) to these remarks, as well as pointing out that in *Jones v Festiniog Rly* (n 5) Blackburn J applied the strict liability rule to a haystack (ie, a chattel).

[93] *Cambridge Water* (n 2) 299.

concerned with [435] whether or not the interference with the claimant's land is tolerable, so the focus is not so much on the nature of the defendant's activity – though this is a factor to be considered – but on whether the resulting discomfort or inconvenience is something which the claimant can, in all the circumstances, be expected to put up with.[94] The non-natural use concept is quite different, for here the focus is not on the harm caused to the claimant, or even on a balancing of the two parties' interests, but simply on the nature of the defendant's activity.[95] At root, the question is whether the way the defendant is using his property is extraordinary or unusual, as opposed to humdrum or everyday.[96] Besides which, the doctrine of unreasonable user would be superfluous if applied to a *Rylands v Fletcher* case, since where there is physical damage to the claimant's land the requirement appears automatically to be satisfied.[97] Indeed, Cross points out that, unlike the non-natural use requirement in *Rylands v Fletcher*, the reasonable user principle has never been a general prerequisite of liability in nuisance: rather it is 'a test which has developed out of the need to establish, in a limited category of cases, whether the interference alleged surmounts the threshold of interference necessary to give rise to an action'.[98] The non-natural use requirement also shows up another important difference between the two torts, namely that while, by definition, things that arise naturally on the defendant's land fall outside the scope of the strict liability rule,[99] an occupier who fails to take reasonable steps to prevent such a thing causing damage to a neighbour's property can be sued in nuisance.[100]

A trickier issue is whether a distinction exists when it comes to the link required, if any, between the defendant and the land from which the interference emanates or the thing escapes. In nuisance, it is almost universally accepted that the creator is liable regardless,[101] but the defendant's occupation of the land in question has been said by some to be [436] a prerequisite of liability under

---

[94] See A Grubb (ed), *The Law of Tort* (London, Butterworths, 2002) para 22.38.

[95] M Lee, 'What is Private Nuisance?' (2003) 119 *LQR* 298, 313.

[96] See *Transco* (n 3) [11] (Lord Bingham); Prosser (n 9) 407–408.

[97] See Grubb (n 94) para 22.41. Roderick Bagshaw argues that it is hard to see how the nuisance principle of 'give and take, live and let live' can be a general solution to the 'non-natural user' conundrum 'because it is difficult to apply it to cases involving property damage caused by rare and isolated escapes' (R Bagshaw, '*Rylands* Confined' (2004) 120 *LQR* 388, 390).

[98] G Cross, 'Does Only the Careless Polluter Pay? – A Fresh Examination of the Nature of Private Nuisance' (1995) 111 *LQR* 445, 448. For other criticism of the conflation of the two concepts, see A Layard, 'Balancing Environmental Considerations' (1997) 113 *LQR* 254; MA Jones, *Textbook on Torts*, 8th edn (Oxford, OUP, 2002) 397–98; Lee (n 95) 313 ('non-natural use has generally not required a balancing of interests, but looks simply at what the defendant is doing'); and Murphy (n 8) 655–56 ('the supposedly related tests … serve quite different functions within their respective torts').

[99] *Bartlett v Tottenham* [1932] 1 Ch 114 (Ch D) 131 (Lawrence LJ); *Ellison* (n 23) 118 (Judge Peter Bowsher QC).

[100] *Leakey v National Trust* [1980] QB 485 (CA).

[101] See Grubb (n 94) para 22.11. For recent confirmation, see *Jones (Insurance Brokers) Ltd v Portsmouth City Council* [2002] EWCA Civ 1723, [2003] 1 WLR 427.

Rylands v Fletcher.[102] Indeed, it has been argued that the requirements of an accumulation on, and a non-natural use of, the defendant's land seem to force this conclusion,[103] and the same could be said of the escape requirement, since this has been defined in terms of an escape from a place which the defendant has occupation of, or control over, to a place outside his occupation or control.[104] There are, however, many authorities the other way.[105] That the rules governing liability for the acts of independent contractors differ as between the two causes of action is, on the other hand, not in doubt. In *Rylands v Fletcher*, the involvement of independent contractors makes no difference (as the leading case demonstrates), but in nuisance the general rule is that an occupier who employs a contractor to do work on his behalf is not liable if unlawful interference results,[106] though there are some exceptions, most notably where the task on which the contractor was engaged of its very nature involved a risk of damage to a third party.[107] When it comes to defences, we find that two (consent and statutory authority) are shared by both causes of action, but this is no surprise, since both are general defences to tort liability. The other three defences to actions under the rule in *Rylands v Fletcher* – act of God, act of a stranger, and default of the claimant – are causation based,[108] and no precise parallels exist in nuisance.

C. Merger with the Rule in *Rylands v Fletcher* Will Be Bad for Nuisance

The third objection to the merger of the rule in *Rylands v Fletcher* with private nuisance is that it will be bad for nuisance. There are three aspects to this objection. The first is that the assimilation of the two torts seems to be leading judges to apply principles developed in the *Rylands v Fletcher* context to ordinary nuisance cases, with unfortunate results. A good example is provided by *Dennis v Ministry of Defence*, where Buckley J held that because using an airfield to train Harrier jet pilots was an extraordinary use of land the noise

---

[102] See, eg, *Pett v Sims Paving and Road Construction Co Pty Ltd* [1928] VR 247 (VSC); Winfield (n 34) 196; West (n 37) 103–104. Such a requirement is also consistent with the language used in some of the English case law: see, eg, *Read* (n 1) 174 (Lord Macmillan) (neighbouring owners), 186 (Lord Uthwatt) (neighbouring occupiers); *Transco* (n 3) [11] (Lord Bingham), [57] (Lord Hobhouse) (referring to situations arising 'as between landowners').

[103] J Murphy, *Street on Torts*, 11th edn (London, Butterworths, 2003) 437.

[104] *Read* (n 1) 168 (Viscount Simon).

[105] See, eg, *Powell* (n 5); *Charing Cross* (n 79); *Shiffman* (n 81) 561 (Atkinson J); *Northwestern Utilities* (n 33) 118 (Lord Wright); *Rigby v Chief Constable of Northamptonshire* [1985] 1 WLR 1242 (QBD) 1255 (Taylor J); *Crown River Cruises Ltd v Kimbolton Fireworks Ltd* [1996] 2 Lloyd's Rep 533 (QBD) 547 (Potter J).

[106] *Matania v National Provincial Bank Ltd* [1936] 2 All ER 633 (CA) 645 (Slesser LJ); *Alcock v Wraith* (1991) 59 BLR 20 (CA) 26 (Neill LJ).

[107] See, eg, *Matania* (n 106). This principle is not limited to nuisance. The other three exceptions concern withdrawal of support, party-walls and fire: see Grubb (n 94) para 22.67.

[108] See text to n 164.

that resulted was a nuisance.[109] **[437]** Similarly, in *Crown River Cruises Ltd v Kimbolton Fireworks Ltd*, Potter J concluded that physical damage caused by a fireworks display on the River Thames was actionable in nuisance because such displays could 'hardly be said to be an ordinary and reasonable incident of river life'.[110] This sort of reasoning threatens to wreak havoc in the law of nuisance, since it follows that any interference with land caused by an extraordinary use will be actionable (no matter how trivial) and that any interference caused by an ordinary use will not be (no matter how intolerable). Indeed, the House of Lords has already taken a step towards the latter conclusion by holding that ordinary use of residential premises is never actionable in nuisance,[111] though that decision probably owed more to policy considerations than it did to the influence of *Rylands v Fletcher* reasoning.[112]

The second aspect of this objection is that extending private nuisance to isolated escapes undermines the essential nature of the cause of action. This becomes clear if we go back to the tort's origins in the assize of nuisance, for the object of the assize was abatement, a remedy which depended on the continuation of the interference down to the time of the action: hence Bohlen's definition of a nuisance as a 'condition capable of abatement after it is known to be injurious'.[113] Indeed, even in the modern law, the 'nuisance' is defined as the state of affairs that causes the interference, rather than the interference itself,[114] which presupposes an element of continuity. Moreover, because a nuisance is a wrongful state of affairs, it can be enjoined by a *quia timet* injunction before any harm has occurred.[115] *Rylands v Fletcher* liability is very different, since the initial accumulation is itself perfectly lawful: as Mellish LJ remarked in *Nichols v Marsland*, 'The wrongful act is not the making or keeping the reservoir, but the allowing or causing the water to escape'.[116] There is therefore no wrongful state of affairs which can properly be described as a nuisance,[117] and so a quia timet injunction will not lie. As Bagshaw has noted, this points to a fundamental distinction between the two causes of action:[118]

> One of the functions of private nuisance is to decide what activities people should be permitted to pursue in a particular locality, given the effects of those activities on

---

[109] *Dennis v Ministry of Defence* [2003] EWHC 793 (QB) [34].

[110] *Crown River Cruises* (n 105) 545. See also *Graham and Graham v ReChem International Ltd* [1996] Env LR 158 (QBD) [162] (Forbes J)(incineration of chemical waste potentially actionable in nuisance because it was not necessary for the common and ordinary use and occupation of the land); and *Arscott v The Coal Authority* [2004] EWCA Civ 892 [27] ff (Laws LJ).

[111] *Southwark London Borough Council v Tanner* [2001] 1 AC 1 (HL).

[112] See Grubb (n 94) para 22.40.

[113] Bohlen (n 66) 312.

[114] WA Seavey, 'Nuisance, Contributory Negligence and Other Mysteries' (1952) 65 *Harvard Law Review* 984, 985.

[115] Winfield (n 34) 196.

[116] *Nichols* (n 48) 5.

[117] Seavey (n 114) 986.

[118] Bagshaw (n 97) 389.

neighbours. But it is no part of the rule in *Rylands v Fletcher* to forbid particular activities. Rather ... it is a [438] rule which requires those who pursue particular activities to internalise the costs of escapes. It is a rule about who pays when things go wrong rather than about whether the defendant's activity is wrongful.

It might be objected that this second consideration loses some of its force because a body of nuisance cases involving one-off escapes already exists. However, most such authorities fall within the *Leakey v National Trust*[119] category – where liability is contingent on proof of carelessness – and these are best regarded as instances of negligence liability dressed up in nuisance clothing.[120] If we set aside the *Leakey*-type cases, there were only three examples of successful private nuisance actions based on one-off events prior to *Cambridge Water*, and none is persuasive. *Midwood & Co Ltd v Manchester Corporation*,[121] where an explosion was caused by the deficient insulation of the defendant's electric main, could surely have come under the *Rylands v Fletcher* rule, and was later treated as if it had.[122] The second such case is *British Celanese Ltd v AH Hunt (Capacitors) Ltd*,[123] where foil strips stored on the defendants' premises had blown on to the bus bars of a neighbouring electricity sub-station, and affected the electricity supply to the plaintiffs' factory. Since the plaintiffs suffered physical damage to their property as a result, recovery in negligence was straightforward. Rather strangely, however, Lawton J held that the defendants were also liable in nuisance, though it is difficult to see how the damage to the materials could be described as an interference with the plaintiffs' use and enjoyment of their land.[124] In the final case, *Spicer v Smee*,[125] defective electric wiring in the defendant's bungalow caused a fire that destroyed his neighbour's house. The decision of Atkinson J to award damages in nuisance was decidedly odd, for, as Winfield pointed out, 'during the course of the common law's development, liability for fire and liability for nuisance travelled in separate compartments'.[126] Besides, the legal gymnastics required to fit *Spicer v Smee* into nuisance included the conclusion that the 'nuisance' was the defective state of the wiring,[127] but if that were right then the plaintiff would have been entitled to an injunction requiring the defendant to put things right before the fire took place. In *Midwood*, Mathew LJ saw this problem coming and denied that [439]

---

[119] *Leakey* (n 100).
[120] C Gearty, 'The Place of Private Nuisance in a Modern Law of Torts' [1989] *CLJ* 214, 233–41. *Goldman v Hargrave* [1967] 1 AC 645 (PC), a leading authority in this category, reads like a negligence case as it is.
[121] *Midwood* [1905] 2 KB 597 (CA).
[122] *Charing Cross* (n 79).
[123] *British Celanese* (n 78).
[124] When a similar case reached the Court of Appeal three years later, the same judge made no mention of nuisance: *Spartan Steel & Alloys Ltd v Martin & Co (Contractors) Ltd* [1973] QB 27 (CA).
[125] *Spicer v Smee* [1946] 1 All ER 489 (KBD).
[126] Winfield (n 34) 203.
[127] *Spicer* (n 125) 493.

the defendants' system of electric lighting itself amounted to a nuisance, since this 'would seem to lead to the somewhat startling conclusion that, apart from actual mischief, it would be open to any one who might possibly be endangered by that system to indict the corporation for a nuisance in respect of it'.[128] And yet this concession to common sense amounts to an acceptance that in these cases there is no 'nuisance', in the sense of an injurious state of affairs, at all. Surely, then, the better view is that of Lord Denning:[129]

> I quite agree that a private nuisance always involves some degree of repetition or continuance. An isolated act which is over and done with, once and for all, may give rise to an action in negligence or an action under the rule in *Rylands v Fletcher*, but not an action for nuisance.

The final aspect of this objection is that fusion with the rule in *Rylands v Fletcher* will hinder rationalisation of private nuisance. Gearty has argued that if cases of physical damage to property were hived off into negligence, we would be left with a slimmed down, more coherent tort.[130] Assimilation of the two causes of action presents a significant obstacle to this apparently desirable development, since cases within the rule invariably concern physical harm.[131]

D. The Version of the Strict Liability Rule to Which the Offshoot Theory Has Given Rise Is Unappealing

The final objection to the offshoot theory is that it has given rise to a version of the strict liability rule which is unappealing. In the *Transco* case, Lord Bingham summed up the effect of the reformulated rule as follows:[132]

> An occupier of land who can show that another occupier of land has brought or kept on his land an exceptionally dangerous or mischievous thing in extraordinary or unusual circumstances is in my opinion entitled to recover compensation from that occupier for any damage caused to his property interest by the escape of that thing, subject to defences of act of God or of a stranger, without the need to prove negligence.

[440] This new version of the doctrine amounts, therefore, to a special category of liability for exceptionally hazardous activities that cause damage to land. An obvious objection is that greater protection is thereby given to proprietary

---

[128] *Midwood* (n 121) 610 (see also at 608 (Channell J), 609 (Romer LJ)). In *Sedleigh-Denfield* (n 33) – a leading case within the *Leakey* category – the House of Lords could not agree whether the nuisance was a blocked drainage pipe or the flooding it caused: see Gearty (n 120) 236–37.

[129] *Attorney-General v PYA Quarries Ltd* [1957] 2 QB 169 (CA) 192.

[130] Gearty (n 120).

[131] Lee, who opposes Gearty's proposed reform, points out that the assimilation of *Rylands v Fletcher* and nuisance serves to entrench the place of physical damage in the latter cause of action: (n 95) 305.

[132] *Transco* (n 3) [11].

interests than to personal interests, and that this would appear to be indefensible.[133] Indeed, it has been said that for the law to privilege real property interests in this way is suggestive of an 'alarming retrogressive tendency',[134] a throwback to a more primitive stage of the law's development. It is also worth pointing out that, while insurance against personal injury is relatively rare, insurance against property damage is relatively common. Although Lord Hoffmann's attempt in *Transco* to limit the *Rylands* rule to situations where the claimant could not reasonably have been expected to have insured himself[135] has been justly criticised,[136] nevertheless it seems odd that a strict liability rule often justified by reference to loss-spreading arguments should be deployed only where those arguments have the least bite.

Furthermore, in *Transco* their Lordships emphasised that the rule should henceforth be interpreted very narrowly. Lord Bingham did not think that the mischief or danger test would be at all easily satisfied: it must be shown that the defendant had done something which he recognised, or ought reasonably to have recognised, gave rise to an 'exceptionally high risk of danger or mischief' in the event of an escape.[137] And when it came to the question of non-natural use, it must be shown that the defendant had done something which he recognised, or ought to have recognised, was 'quite out of the ordinary' in the place and at the time when he did it.[138] Lord Hoffmann agreed that the criterion of exceptional risk must be taken seriously, and created a high threshold for the claimant to surmount.[139] It follows that in future there are likely to be even fewer cases where *Rylands v Fletcher* is pleaded successfully than there have been in the past, and it seems reasonable to conclude, therefore, that acceptance of the offshoot theory has resulted in a doctrine which is both arbitrary in its application and largely devoid of practical significance.

III. *RYLANDS v FLETCHER* AND NEGLIGENCE

Although in England the most serious challenge to the distinctiveness of *Rylands v Fletcher* has come from the offshoot theory, it has also been threatened in another way. The argument we are dealing with here is the [**441**] contention that the gap between *Rylands v Fletcher* liability and the tort of negligence has narrowed so much that the two causes of action are now

---

[133] See TH Tylor, 'The Restriction of Strict Liability' (1947) 10 *MLR* 396, 400; and Linden (n 84) 336: 'It is unthinkable that our courts could possibly value property interests over human safety.'
[134] FV Harper and F James, *The Law of Torts* (Boston, Little Brown, 1956) 806.
[135] *Transco* (n 3) [46].
[136] ibid [60] (Lord Hobhouse); Bagshaw (n 97) 390.
[137] *Transco* (n 3) [10].
[138] ibid [11].
[139] ibid [49].

virtually indistinguishable. Once again, there is nothing novel about this line of reasoning. As early as 1916, Thayer wrote that the difference between the two 'in the actual protection given by the law to the injured person is not very great',[140] and the following year Smith argued that *Rylands v Fletcher* could itself have been decided in negligence, since the contractors were careless, and the duty resting upon the defendants was non-delegable.[141] Since both Thayer and Smith were arch-proponents of the fault principle, their take on *Rylands v Fletcher* was unsurprising, but a similar analysis caused the High Court of Australia to hold, in *Burnie Port Authority v General Jones Pty Ltd*,[142] that the rule ought henceforth to be treated as having been absorbed by the principles of ordinary negligence. According to the Court, future cases should be dealt with under the usual negligence rules, with two provisos: the duty of care in situations falling within the scope of the *Rylands* rule would be non-delegable, and in the case of dangerous substances and activities the reasonably prudent person would exercise a particularly high degree of care.

Central to the reasoning of the majority (McHugh and Brennan JJ dissented) was the perception that, since its original formulation, the rule in *Rylands v Fletcher* 'has been progressively weakened and confined from within, and the area of its effective operation, in the sense of the area in which it applies to impose liability where it would not otherwise exist, has been progressively diminished by increasing assault from without'.[143] It was argued that the shrinkage of the space between negligence and *Rylands v Fletcher* was the result of a combination of the toughening and expansion of the former head of liability and the softening and constriction of the latter. Particularly noteworthy in this regard were – as regards negligence – the raising of the standard of care (especially in the context of dangerous activities), the doctrine of *res ipsa loquitur*, and the extension of liability for independent contractors; and – as regards *Rylands v Fletcher* – the development of exculpatory defences (such as act of God), the infusion of fault ideas into the concept of non-natural user, and the foreseeability requirement laid down in *Cambridge Water*. The end result was that, in terms of coverage, the difference between the two causes of action was negligible,[144] and hence the majority passed off the absorption [442] of the rule into negligence as, in Fleming's words, 'just a cleaning-up of the structural debris of outworn doctrine'.[145]

---

[140] E Thayer, 'Liability Without Fault' (1916) 29 *Harvard Law Review* 801, 808. For similar analyses, see V MacDonald, 'The Rule in Rylands v Fletcher and its Limitations' (1923) 1 *Canadian Bar Review* 140; Fridman (n 60); and MA Millner, *Negligence in Modern Law* (London, Butterworths, 1967) 190 ff.

[141] J Smith, 'Tort and Absolute Liability – Suggested Changes in Classification' (1917) 30 *Harvard Law Review* 409, 409–10.

[142] *Burnie Port Authority* (n 7).

[143] ibid 540.

[144] ibid 549, 555. For a similar conclusion, see *Transco* (n 3) [39] (Lord Hoffmann).

[145] JG Fleming, 'The Fall of a Crippled Giant' (1995) 3 *Tort Law Review* 56, 60.

Although it will be argued that this analysis is to some extent misguided, it is less invidious than the offshoot theory, for four reasons. First, it is not grounded on a misreading of the original case. Secondly, it is true that, while there are important theoretical differences between the two causes of action, in most cases application of the rule in *Rylands v Fletcher* and the tort of negligence will indeed lead to the same result. Thirdly, there is little danger that subsuming *Rylands v Fletcher* under negligence will distort the latter tort or reduce its coherence. And, finally, the outcome of the *Burnie* analysis, abrogation of the strict liability rule, is much more defensible than the state in which English law finds itself in the aftermath of *Transco*.[146]

Nevertheless, the way in which the majority sugared the pill of abolition was unconvincing, as McHugh J demonstrated in a strong dissenting judgment. His Honour pointed out that there were still important differences between the rule in *Rylands v Fletcher* and negligence, not least the fact that *Rylands v Fletcher* is a principle of strict liability, in the sense that the defendant may be held liable notwithstanding the fact that he exercised reasonable care. In particular, his Honour rejected the majority's argument that the presence of negligence has become a factor in determining whether the defendant's use of land is 'non-natural', claiming instead that the requirement of non-natural use was an important difference between the two causes of action.[147] This seems right. While it is certainly true that attempts have been made to infuse the doctrine of non-natural use with fault-based reasoning, the claim that reasonableness in negligence and non-natural user are essentially similar concepts[148] does not hold water.

There are two notions which have threatened to reduce the conceptual space between negligence and non-natural use, the first of which is that a use of benefit to the community is for that reason a natural one. This concern with social utility was not mentioned in the early case law, but surfaced in a couple of early twentieth century authorities, where it formed one element of a wider backlash against the strict liability rule.[149] However, although the idea was influential in the post-war years, the *Cambridge Water* decision signalled a return to orthodoxy, with Lord Goff remarking that if general benefit to the community were taken into account it was difficult to see how the natural user exception could be kept within [**443**] reasonable bounds.[150] His Lordship's scepticism was echoed by Lords Bingham and Walker in *Transco*, the latter denying that a court could

---

[146] Although since the majority's approach relies heavily on the difficult concept of non-delegable duty, and ties its application to the vagaries of 'dangerousness', it may be that the abrogation of the *Rylands* rule will give rise to as many problems as it solves. For a critique of the majority's reasoning on the non-delegable duty issue, see J Swanton, 'Another Conquest in the Imperial Expansion of the Law of Negligence' (1994) 2 *Torts Law Journal* 101, 109–15.

[147] *Burnie Port* (n 7) 588.

[148] See, eg, P Cane, 'Justice and Justifications for Tort Liability' (1982) 2 *OJLS* 30, 53–54.

[149] *Rickards* (n 56) 280 (Lord Moulton); *Read* (n 1) 169–70 (Viscount Simon).

[150] *Cambridge Water* (n 2) 308.

sensibly determine whether a use was ordinary or special 'by undertaking some utilitarian balancing of general good against individual risk'.[151]

The other threat to the distinction between the two doctrines has come from the notion that the manner as well as the nature of the use ought to be considered when determining whether it qualifies as non-natural.[152] In *Burnie Port* itself, for example, the Supreme Court of Tasmania held that the defendant's welding operations were a non-natural use because they were carried out in the vicinity of combustible material.[153] On appeal to the High Court of Australia, the majority agreed that when determining whether a use was non-natural regard could be had to its manner as well as to its nature.[154] There are also a handful of English cases where the courts have looked, not at the activity of the defendant *per se*, but at the way in which it has been carried out.[155] However, although this kind of reasoning obviously undermines the distinction between negligence and liability in *Rylands v Fletcher* (because the absence of reasonable care itself determines the applicability of the supposedly strict liability rule), it is surely an exaggeration to claim that this tendency has to all intents and purposes destroyed the latter cause of action as a separate entity.[156] Apart from these few cases, the authorities (including *Cambridge Water* and *Transco*) indicate that the issue of non-natural use should be determined not by reference to the manner of the defendant's operations but the character of his use of the land unit in question. The distinction with negligence is therefore maintained. In *Burnie Port*, McHugh J gave eloquent expression to the more orthodox approach:[157]

> Circumstances are relevant to the issue of non-natural use. But manner of performance is not. In determining whether a use is a natural use, regard must be had to what the occupier did. It is then necessary to determine whether that class of activity constitutes a [444] natural use having regard to the time, place and circumstances ... the exercise does not involve any close examination of the specifics.

---

[151] *Transco* (n 3) [105]. Lord Bingham commented (at [11]) that 'little help is gained (and unnecessary confusion perhaps caused) by considering whether the use is proper for the general benefit of the community'. Similar developments have occurred in the United States. According to the *Restatement, Second, Torts* (1977) § 520F, one factor which determines whether the strict liability rule for abnormally dangerous activities applies is the value to the community of the activity in question. However, in the draft of the third *Restatement*, the reference to the social utility of the activity has been dropped: *Restatement, Third, Torts: Liability for Physical Harm (Basic Principles)* (Tentative Draft No 1, 2001) § 20 and comment k.

[152] See DW Williams, 'Non-Natural Use of Land' [1973] *CLJ* 310, 311–17.

[153] *Burnie Port Authority v General Jones Pty Ltd* [1991] Tas R 203 (Tas SC).

[154] *Burnie Port* (n 7) 538–39.

[155] See, eg, *Balfour v Barty-King* [1956] 1 WLR 779 (QBD) (use of a blow-lamp in a loft, close to combustible material, a non-natural use) (affirmed on other grounds: [1957] 1 QB 496 (CA)); and *Mason v Levy Auto Parts of England Ltd* [1967] 2 QB 530 (Winchester Assizes) (method of storage of combustible material made it a non-natural use). For an example from Canada, see *Brady's Ltd v CNR* [1929] 2 DLR 549 (Alta SC) (cleaning a truck engine with gasoline without disconnecting the battery a non-natural use).

[156] Cane (n 148) 54.

[157] ibid 589–90.

Once it is understood that public benefit considerations have no place in the non-natural use inquiry, and that the non-natural use issue concerns only the general character of the defendant's activity, then the distinction between this concept and the requirement of unreasonable conduct in negligence becomes clear. As we have seen,[158] a use is non-natural because it is extraordinary or unusual: its reasonableness is neither here nor there.

Moving beyond the non-natural use requirement, there were two other developments in the law concerning *Rylands v Fletcher* actions which the majority in *Burnie Port* put forward as evidence of a gradual conflation with negligence. One was the decision in *Cambridge Water* to apply the principles governing remoteness of damage in negligence, so that foreseeability of damage of the relevant type became a prerequisite of liability under the rule. It is frequently alleged that this marked the end of strict liability in this context, but this is to ignore the fact that it is only the *consequences* of the escape, not the escape itself, that must be foreseeable,[159] and to make the mistake of confusing foreseeability with fault. Although there can be no fault without foreseeability, there can be foreseeability without fault: hence, if we assume that liability is strict where it is not conditional on proof of fault (or negligence), a foreseeability requirement is not inconsistent with a strict liability regime.[160] Furthermore, as Lord Goff pointed out in *Cambridge Water*, the language Blackburn J used in the *Rylands v Fletcher* case suggests that it was originally envisaged that liability under the rule would be limited to foreseeable harm.[161]

Finally, the majority in *Burnie Port* said that recognised defences to a *Rylands v Fletcher* claim, such as act of God, were more 'attuned to the notion of fault liability than that of strict liability'.[162] In saying this, their Honours were echoing academic commentators who have argued that the development of these defences has narrowed the gap between *Rylands v Fletcher* and negligence to almost nothing, and made it doubtful 'whether there is much left of the rationale of strict liability as originally contemplated in 1866'.[163] This reasoning is also flawed, however. Two of the five **[445]** established defences to an action under the rule, consent and statutory authority, are of general application in the law of tort. The other three – act of God, act of a stranger, and default of the claimant – all go to causation: the defendant is excused because there has

---

[158] See text to n 96.

[159] See further Grubb (n 94) para 23.29.

[160] See RFV Heuston and RW Buckley, *Salmond & Heuston on the Law of Torts*, 21st edn (London, Sweet & Maxwell, 1996) 314; T Weir, 'The Staggering March of Negligence' in P Cane and J Stapleton (eds), *The Law of Obligations: Essays in Celebration of John Fleming* (Oxford, OUP, 1998) 107. See also *Restatement, Third, Torts* (n 151) § 20, comment i (the principle of strict liability for abnormally dangerous activities is subject to a requirement of foreseeability).

[161] See text to n 16.

[162] *Burnie Port* (n 7) 545.

[163] Fleming (n 84) 385. See too AL Goodhart, 'The Third Man, or *Novus Actor Interveniens*' [1951] *CLP* 177.

been a novus actus interveniens, an interruption of the 'ordinary sequence of cause and consequence'.[164] Recognition of these defences is therefore entirely in keeping with the philosophy underpinning the strict liability rule, namely that responsibility rests on causa rather than culpa.[165] It comes as no surprise, therefore, to see that in his judgment in *Rylands v Fletcher* Blackburn J accepted that the defendant could excuse himself 'by shewing that the escape was owing to the plaintiff's default; or perhaps that the escape was the consequence of vis major, or the act of God'.[166] In any case, the line of argument in question exaggerates the significance of these exceptions to the strict liability rule – the scope of the act of God defence is so narrow, for example, that it appears to have been pleaded successfully on only two occasions.[167]

Why, then, is there such broad acceptance of the view that the strictness of the *Rylands* rule has been diluted? The explanation probably lies in anachronistic reasoning. Those who make this argument appear to be looking at a mid-nineteenth century case through contemporary spectacles, and ascribing to the judges who sat in it motivations that were almost certainly far from their minds. As we have seen,[168] the decision in the original case is most plausibly explained as a survival of the general principle of liability recognized by the medieval common law, namely that a man acts at his peril. This explains both the nature of the prima facie liability, and the character of the applicable defences.[169] The problem is that nowadays strict liability is generally justified by reference to internalisation of risk or insurance arguments, the logical conclusion of which is a liability model much tougher than that of the ancient common law: in essence, a regime of *absolute* liability.[170] Advocates of absolute liability are of course bound to consider the rule in *Rylands v Fletcher* something of a let-down, but they ought not to focus their disappointment on a [446] 'watering down' of the original rule which is largely the product of their own imaginations.

Of course, this analysis itself leads us to the conclusion that in practical terms the gap between the *Rylands* rule and fault-based liability was never

---

[164] *Benning* (n 10) 306 (Windeyer J). See also *Transco* (n 3) [59] (Lord Hobhouse). This analysis is borne out by the leading authorities on the three defences, which are suffused with causation reasoning: see *Nichols* (n 48) 6 (Mellish LJ) (act of God); *Carstairs v Taylor* (1871) LR 6 Exch 217 (Exch) 221 (Bramwell B); *Box v Jubb* (1879) 4 Ex D 76 (Exch D) 78–79 (Kelly CB); *Perry* (n 78) 90 (Jenkins LJ) (act of a stranger); and *Dunn v Birmingham Canal Co* (1872) LR 7 QB 244 (QBD) 260 (Cockburn CJ) (default of the claimant).

[165] See *Burnie Port* (n 7) 590 (McHugh J).

[166] *Fletcher* (n 38) 279–80.

[167] *Nichols* (n 48); *Carstairs* (n 164) (where there were also other grounds for dismissing the claim). The House of Lords took a particularly restrictive line in *Greenock Corporation v Caledonian Rly Co* [1917] AC 556 (HL).

[168] See text to n 56.

[169] Holdsworth (n 56) 472.

[170] It has been noted that the rule in *Rylands v Fletcher* is one of strict, rather than absolute, liability: *Benning* (n 10) 298–99 (Windeyer J); PH Winfield, *Text-book of the Law of Tort* (London, Sweet & Maxwell, 1937) 508.

that great. This should, however, come as no surprise, for, as Ibbetson has demonstrated, it is a mistake to exaggerate the contrast between the medieval regime of strict liability (subject to a range of exculpatory defences) and a regime of fault liability.[171] In particular, the operation of ideas of causation meant that 'strict liability was suffused through and through with ideas of fault'.[172] But Ibbetson also makes the point that 'fault' is not here a synonym for the modern notion of negligence, in the sense of an external standard according to which the wrongfulness of conduct could be assessed.[173] And of course it is impossible to make direct comparisons between an ancient system of strict liability heavily dependent on opaque jury verdicts and its modern manifestation as a series of rules applied by the courts. In any case, even if substantively the ancient and the modern approaches are not that dissimilar – since fault was usually present when 'strict' liability was imposed – the structure of the liability inquiry differs in one important respect. Under the old law – and, hence, under *Rylands v Fletcher* – the burden of proof as to 'fault' lay on the defendant, whereas in negligence it lies on the claimant.[174] In the end, therefore, it remains plausible to argue, not only that the rule in *Rylands v Fletcher* is quite distinct from negligence on a theoretical level, but also that application of the two causes of action will not infrequently lead to different outcomes.

IV. WHAT SHOULD BE DONE?

The final question to be answered is what, then, *should* be done with the rule in *Rylands v Fletcher*? Rejecting assimilation of the rule into private nuisance leaves three other options: a return to the status quo ante the *Cambridge Water* and *Transco* cases; transformation into a general principle of liability for abnormally dangerous activities; and abolition. The first of these options is unappealing, because even before the most recent developments the restrictions imposed on the rule's operation robbed it of any coherence, and fostered arbitrary distinctions: the escape requirement meant, for example, that the liability to two persons injured by an explosion while entering a factory could differ because one had paused [**447**] to let the other cross the threshold.[175] Since there was neither a clear picture of, nor any logical explanation for, the circumstances in which the usual

---

[171] D Ibbetson, *A Historical Introduction to the Law of Obligations* (Oxford, OUP, 1999) 58–63. See also PH Winfield, 'The Myth of Absolute Liability' (1926) 42 *LQR* 37.

[172] Ibbetson (n 171) 61.

[173] ibid.

[174] It is noteworthy that Pollock favoured abolition of the rule in *Rylands v Fletcher*, but reversal of the burden of proof as to fault in cases which would have come within the rule: see F Pollock, *The Law of Torts*, 10th edn (London, Stevens & Sons, 1916) 511, and clause 68 of his draft Civil Wrongs Bill for India (ibid 671–72). On the practical significance of the burden of proof point, see *Transco* (n 3) [110] (Lord Hobhouse).

[175] *Burnie Port* (n 7) 548.

negligence standard was displaced by the operation of strict liability, it is difficult to disagree with the Law Commission's condemnation of the rule as it stood in 1970 as 'complex, uncertain and inconsistent in principle'.[176]

The second option is closely associated with developments in the United States, where, despite some early opposition,[177] the rule in *Rylands v Fletcher* was eventually accepted in many states and served as the foundation of a principle of strict liability for abnormally dangerous activities.[178] Generality was achieved by doing away with the escape requirement and extending the principle to personal injuries. Furthermore, liability was imposed even where the immediate cause of the injury was the unforeseeable conduct of a third person – though perhaps not where this was intended to bring about the harm – or the unforeseeable operation of a force of nature.[179] As we have seen,[180] at one point English law appeared to be edging towards a similar doctrine based on the *Rylands v Fletcher* rule, but the transformation was nipped in the bud by the House of Lords in *Read v Lyons*,[181] and future development along these lines appears most unlikely. In *Cambridge Water*, Lord Goff made it clear that any such reform was now a matter for Parliament. This assessment – with which Lord Bingham agreed in *Transco*[182] – was based partly on the uncertainties and practical difficulties to which a general principle would give rise, and partly on the existence of a body of well-informed and carefully structured environmental protection legislation, which such a principle might overlap with or undermine.[183] And yet the chances of legislative intervention look slim. In the 1970s, the Pearson Commission recommended a statutory scheme which would have made the controller of any stipulated dangerous thing or activity strictly liable for personal injury or death the thing or activity occasioned.[184] At the time, this recommendation was ignored, and there is no reason to suppose that Parliament will be any more receptive to the idea in future: it is far more likely that the current legislative policy of [**448**] ad hoc imposition of strict liability on particular activities will prevail.[185]

---

[176] Law Commission, *Civil Liability for Dangerous Things* (Law Com No 32, 1970) para 20.

[177] Though the perception that the initial reception of the rule was generally frosty has been challenged: see JH Shugerman, 'The Floodgates of Strict Liability: Bursting Reservoirs and the Adoption of *Fletcher v Rylands* in the Gilded Age' (2000) 110 *Yale Law Journal* 333.

[178] See *Restatement, Second, Torts* (n 151) § 519(1): 'One who carries on an abnormally dangerous activity is subject to liability for harm to the person, land or chattels of another resulting from the activity, although he has exercised the utmost care to prevent the harm.'

[179] ibid § 522.

[180] See text to n 6.

[181] *Read v Lyons* (n 1).

[182] *Transco* (n 3) [7].

[183] *Cambridge Water* (n 2) 305.

[184] *Royal Commission on Civil Liability and Compensation for Personal Injury* (1978) Cmnd 7054, vol I, ch 31.

[185] See, eg, Gas Act 1965, s 14 (underground storage of gas); Nuclear Installations Act 1965, s 12 (nuclear matter); Water Resources Act 1991, s 209 (escape of water from a pipe vested in a water undertaker); Environmental Protection Act 1990, s 73(6) (unlawful deposit of waste).

In any case, the merits of a principle of strict liability for abnormally dangerous activities are doubtful. Far from being a panacea, it has been said that 'the doctrine plays a rather subsidiary role in modern American tort law', and may in some circumstances be even more conservative than the *Rylands* doctrine as developed in English law.[186] More generally, there is the problem of deciding which activities qualify as 'ultra-hazardous', a difficulty accentuated by the fact that 'in a progressive world, things which at one time were reckoned highly dangerous come to be regarded as reasonably safe'.[187] There is also the point that while at one stage tort law was fond of special rules for things 'dangerous in themselves' and so forth, such an approach now looks rather dated. The modern tendency is towards generalisation, perhaps because the concept of dangerousness has been overtaken by the complexity of contemporary industrial society;[188] perhaps because technological advances have in fact rendered many previously dangerous activities much safer, both in the eyes of the public and in fact;[189] or perhaps because the original appeal of 'dangerousness' lay in an outmoded perception of technology as alien and threatening. Finally, the rationale of a principle of this kind is far from clear. The justification usually given for the American doctrine is that the person who chooses to engage in an abnormally dangerous activity should bear the cost of any harm that results, because the risks his activity creates are not normal risks mutually created and borne by all.[190] Hence, according to Fletcher – who elevates this idea of non-reciprocal risks into a general justification for tort liability – the critical feature of *Rylands v Fletcher* was 'that the defendant created a risk of harm to the plaintiff that was of an order different from the risks that the plaintiff imposed on the defendant'.[191] Ripstein has articulated the rationale of strict liability in similar terms:[192] [449]

> If the standard of care is supposed to protect people equally from each other, it cannot leave one person free to choose any activity and then exercise care in relation to that activity. The choice of activities may itself expose others to undue risks, which the risk creator must bear.

---

[186] GT Schwartz, '*Rylands v Fletcher*, Negligence, and Strict Liability' in Cane and Stapleton (n 160) 238.

[187] *Read* (n 1) 172 (Lord Macmillan).

[188] W Friedmann, *Law in a Changing Society*, 2nd edn (London, Stevens & Sons, 1972) 164.

[189] Abraham (n 70) 224–25.

[190] *McLane v Northwest Natural Gas Co* 467 P 2d 635 (Or 1970) 638 (Holman J). See similarly *Restatement, Second, Torts* (n 151) § 522, comment a.

[191] G Fletcher, 'Fairness and Utility in Tort Theory' (1972) 85 *Harvard Law Review* 537, 546.

[192] A Ripstein, *Equality, Responsibility, and the Law* (Cambridge, CUP, 1999) 71. By contrast, Murphy's recent defence of the rule in *Rylands v Fletcher* (n 8) seems to be based on the fact that the defendant stands to profit from his risk-creating activity, rather than on the fact that the risks he creates are non-reciprocal. There are two problems with Murphy's position, however: one is that the rule is not limited to profit-making activities (indeed, it is not even clear whether the accumulation need have been for the defendant's benefit: see Grubb (n 94) para 23.27); the other is that his thesis does not explain why only risks created by unusual and 'dangerous' activities are caught by the rule.

There are two difficulties with this reasoning, however. The first is that its application across the board would transform the law of tort: it would require us, for example, to impose strict liability whenever a lorry collides with a pedestrian, since a clearer example of 'non-reciprocal risks' is hard to imagine. The second difficulty is that it makes no sense to characterise a given activity or thing as imposing a non-reciprocal risk in the abstract, for it all depends on the circumstances.[193] If I keep a lion in my back garden, and you keep an Alsatian in yours, which of us imposes the greater risk on the other depends on the precautions we take to keep our respective pets from escaping. Indeed, as Stanton points out, many of the most 'dangerous' activities – such as the transportation of nuclear waste – are carried on with such exceptional precautions that the level of risk they actually create is very low.[194] It is precisely because the risks an activity creates are bound up with the way in which it is conducted that there has been a tendency to consider the manner as well as the nature of the use when deciding whether an activity is non-natural for the purposes of the *Rylands v Fletcher* rule, but, as we have seen, this approach would eventually lead to the abandonment of strict liability, and its replacement by a negligence standard.

In the end, therefore, the best way forward appears to be abolition. The House of Lords refused to take this course in *Transco*, but the reasons their Lordships gave for this refusal were somewhat tenuous. One of the principal arguments – that the rule was too well-entrenched to be done away with by the courts[195] – is unconvincing, not least because the High Court of Australia did precisely that in the *Burnie Port* case. Nor were the other justifications provided for rejecting this option persuasive. Lord Hobhouse defended the rule (a 'useful and soundly based component of the law of tort'[196]) on the basis that where a landowner put his property to a dangerous use he ought to bear the resultant risk, but failed to explain why this principle extended only to interference with [450] property interests.[197] Lord Bingham felt that there was a category of case, however small, in which it seemed just to impose liability without fault, but provided no further elucidation. His Lordship also pointed out that in both French and

---

[193] As Millner puts it, 'danger is not a quality of a thing, but of a thing in relation to the attendant circumstances' (n 140) 195.

[194] KM Stanton, 'The Legacy of *Rylands v Fletcher*' in NJ Mullany and AM Linden (eds), *Torts Tomorrow: A Tribute to John Fleming* (Sydney, LBC Information Services, 1998) 92–93. Hence the so-called 'zero-infinity' problem in risk analysis: the idea that in the case of some activities the risk of an accident approaches zero, but the possible consequences of such an accident are almost infinite.

[195] *Transco* (n 3) [43] (Lord Hoffmann) ('too radical a step to take'), [82] (Lord Scott) (a 'rather drastic solution'). Lord Bingham commented (ibid [6]) that the fact that the House had refused to take this course in *Cambridge Water* was a reason not to take it in *Transco*, since 'stop-go' was 'in general as bad as an approach to legal development as to economic management'.

[196] ibid [52].

[197] His Lordship did say – presumably with negligence in mind – that liability for personal injuries was 'covered by other parts of the law of tort' (ibid), but negligence surely protects proprietary interests as assiduously as it does personal ones.

German law there is an element of strict liability protection in disputes between landowners – though not in Scotland, which has never adopted the *Rylands* principle. Finally, Lord Bingham was concerned that Parliament might have passed legislation on the assumption that *Rylands v Fletcher* liability would continue, though he had no way of knowing whether this was so. This would appear, however, to be an argument against any judicial development of the law at all, and in any case Parliament could easily deal with such a problem – if indeed it exists – by amending the relevant legislation.

V. CONCLUSION

Two conclusions of general significance can be drawn from the recent history of the rule in *Rylands v Fletcher*. The first is that it is unwise to base a sweeping reformulation of the law on a single article, particularly when it flies in the face of an abundance of authority to the contrary. The second is that, while there is a good deal of truth in Holmes's aphorism that 'it will be found that, when ancient rules maintain themselves ... new reasons more fitted to the time have been found for them, and that they gradually receive a new content, and at last a new form, from the grounds to which they have been transplanted',[198] sometimes it is better simply to extinguish the flickering flame that remains when legal developments leave past doctrines behind. In the case of *Rylands v Fletcher*, the reluctance to take this step may be down in part to legal sentimentalism. *Rylands* has always possessed a certain symbolic significance, despite – or perhaps because of – its relative practical irrelevance. It is no coincidence, for example, that *Rylands* is the only decision to feature in two books devoted to in-depth analysis of leading cases, Simpson's *Leading Cases in the Common Law*,[199] and a recent American collection entitled *Torts Stories*.[200] And in his essay in the latter work, Abraham argues that 'we study *Rylands* not only because of what it was and is, but also because of what it might have been and might still become'.[201] The case is 'one of tort law's greatest [451] hits'[202] because it is the emblem of a strict liability idea that serves as tort law's conscience: by reminding us that an alternative to the negligence paradigm exists, it forces us continually to assess whether the fault requirement accords with justice and public policy.

---

[198] Holmes, *The Common Law* (Boston, Little Brown, 1881) 36.

[199] AWB Simpson, *Leading Cases in the Common Law* (Oxford, OUP, 1995). Simpson's core thesis is that the decision in *Rylands v Fletcher* was influenced by a recent spate of dam-bursting disasters, though the evidence he marshals in support of this argument is (perhaps inevitably) circumstantial. He also seems to treat the decision as applying only to accumulations of water (see, eg, at 226, where he refers to the strict liability principle having 'acquired an assured status in the law in the special context of reservoir disasters'), but the rule Blackburn J formulated was not so limited.

[200] Rabin and Sugarman (n 70).

[201] Abraham (n 70) 227.

[202] ibid 226.

Be that as it may, the new orthodoxy has left the rule in *Rylands v Fletcher* a shadow of its former self, lacking either rationale or practical significance, and hedged about with arcane and indefensible restrictions. In *Transco*, their Lordships were at pains to point out that there have been very few cases in which actions under the rule have been successful, and Lord Hoffmann said that it was hard to escape the conclusion that the intellectual effort devoted to the rule by judges and writers over many years had 'brought forth a mouse'.[203] But if that is right – and his Lordship's conclusion appears inescapable – then would not putting this poor creature down have been more merciful than leaving it in the legal equivalent of a persistent vegetative state?

---

[203] *Transco* (n 3) [39]. See also Lord Bingham at [5]: it seems that over the past 60 years 'few if any claimants have succeeded in reliance on the rule in *Rylands v Fletcher* alone'.

Part III

Tort in General

12

Preventive Damages

(2016) 132 *Law Quarterly Review* 68–95

[68] 'Expenses incurred to prevent threatened damage amount to recoverable damage in so far as reasonably incurred.' *Principles of European Tort Law*, art 2.104

'A person who has reasonably incurred expenditure or sustained other loss in order to prevent that person from suffering an impending damage, or in order to limit the extent or severity of damage suffered, has a right to compensation from the person who would have been accountable for the causation of the damage.' *Principles of European Law on Non-Contractual Liability Arising out of Damage Caused to Another*, art 6.302

I. INTRODUCTION

IT SEEMS FAIR to say that for the most part common lawyers have not really woken up to the issue of 'preventive damages', the idea of which is neatly captured by the articles of the *Principles of European Tort Law* and *Principles of European Law on Non-Contractual Liability Arising out of Damage Caused to Another* reproduced above. If asked whether they thought that these articles represented the law in their jurisdiction, I suspect that most common lawyers would struggle to answer the question. They might intuitively feel that at least in some circumstances such preventive damages should be recoverable, and they might be able to identify some specific instances in which such damages have been awarded, but they would find it difficult to say with any confidence whether or not there is a general principle allowing their recovery, and what the precise parameters of any such principle are or should be.[1] As John Fleming put it in an essay which is an important exception to the general neglect of this topic, it is strange that 'our law is so neglectful of taking a stance on the cost of preventing threats to person or property'.[2]

---

[1] For a rare example of a textbook mentioning the issue, see C Sappideen and P Vines (eds), *Fleming's The Law of Torts*, 10th edn (Pyrmont, Thomson Reuters Professional (Australia), 2011) para 8.280.

[2] J Fleming, 'Preventive Damages' in N Mullany (ed), *Torts in the Nineties* (Sydney, Law Book Co, 1997) 65. The focus of Fleming's largely descriptive analysis was somewhat narrower than mine, since it was limited to three of the five scenarios I consider in Part III of this article (namely the

As the inclusion of such prominent provisions on the topic in the two sets of common European principles indicates, thinking on preventive damages is more advanced in continental legal systems. Hence, for example, article 249 of the German [69] Civil Code has been interpreted as allowing recovery of costs incurred to prevent or minimise a specific impending damage if compensation would have been recoverable for the damage had it occurred,[3] while article 419 of the Czech Civil Code states that a person who averts threatened damage shall be entitled to compensation 'of usefully spent costs and of damages suffered therein'. Furthermore, it seems that in France, Belgium and Spain, expenses incurred in preventing damage in cases of this kind themselves amount to legally recognised damage, and are therefore recoverable provided the general conditions of delictual liability are met.[4]

This article seeks to redress the balance somewhat by considering the issues raised by preventive damages claims from a common law perspective. Before I begin my exploration of the topic, however, four preliminary points should be made.

The first point is that the scope of my analysis is limited to the recovery of costs incurred before a wrong of a conventional kind has been committed, and not with the more routine case in which a claimant who has been the victim of a conventional wrong incurs costs in order to mitigate its consequences, as where a person who suffers personal injury at the hands of a negligent defendant pays for medical treatment to avert a possible complication. Cases of the latter kind appear relatively straightforward, and are dealt with fully in standard works on remedies (usually under the heading of mitigation of damage). They are therefore excluded from my analysis except insofar as they help to illuminate the more difficult issues raised by claims to recover costs incurred to avert a threatened wrong.

Secondly, my focus is on costs incurred in preventing wrongful interference with the person or property of the *claimant*. It does not therefore extend to costs incurred to protect the person or property of third parties, as where an occupier of premises with a dangerous defect attributable to the builder's negligence spends money to obviate a threat the danger poses to users of an adjacent highway.[5] Although cases of this kind raise some similar issues to cases where the threat is to the claimant, any recovery of preventive expenditure in the two types of case may well rest on different doctrinal foundations, and for this and other reasons they require separate analysis.

'collapsing crane', 'collapsing condominium' and 'medical monitoring' cases), and there was limited general discussion of the preventive damages question.

[3] C von Bar, *Principles of European Law on Non-Contractual Liability Arising out of Damage Caused to Another* (Oxford, OUP, 2009) art 6.302, note 5.

[4] ibid art 6.302, notes 1 and 2.

[5] *Murphy v Brentwood DC* [1991] 1 AC 398 (HL) 488–89 (Lord Oliver).

Thirdly, while the provisions reproduced above refer to expenditure incurred to prevent *damage*, in a common law context one can envisage a claim for the cost of averting a threatened wrong where that wrong would not have caused the claimant damage, as where the defendant threatened to enter the claimant's land or touch the claimant's body in a way that was harmless but nevertheless unlawful. It would in my view be wrong to dismiss such a claim out of hand, although the lack of threatened damage could be taken into account when applying the reasonableness test likely to govern preventive damages claims more generally.

And finally, I should make it clear at the outset that my analysis is a tentative one, with the emphasis on identifying the problems and possible solutions to them, rather than putting forward firmly held views as to how cases of this kind should be resolved. As we shall see, preventive damages claims give rise to some very [70] thorny problems, and – particularly in the light of the dearth of literature on the topic – for the most part it seems more sensible to pose questions rather than to answer them, at least in a way that purports to be definitive.

II. THE BROADER LEGAL CONTEXT

The issue of preventive damages as I have defined it for the purposes of this article cannot properly be understood without first considering the broader legal context surrounding claims of this kind. Three different aspects of the legal background will be highlighted, namely the rules governing contributory negligence and legal causation; mitigation of damage; and *quia timet* injunctions.

A. Contributory Negligence and Legal Causation

As regards contributory negligence, the important point to remember here is that the act or omission of the claimant which constitutes contributory negligence usually (or perhaps always) takes place before the wrong is committed, and may even occur before the faulty conduct of the defendant, as where the damages awarded to an injured car passenger are reduced because the passenger was not wearing a seatbelt at the time of an accident caused by the driver's negligence.[6] That a claimant's damages are reduced where he or she fails to take reasonable steps to avert a threatened injury and that failure is causally connected to some or all of a wrongful injury that then takes place is surely a good argument in favour of allowing a claimant who does take such steps to recover any costs incurred in doing so. Furthermore, we also need to recall that sometimes A's failure to take steps to avert the threat of injury to A posed by the prior negligent conduct of B may constitute a *novus actus interveniens*,

---

[6] See, eg, *Froom v Butcher* [1976] QB 286 (CA).

with the result that legal responsibility for the damage is deemed to lie entirely with A, who is then unable to bring a tort action against B in respect of it. If, for example, A uses a product in the knowledge that it is defective, this will break the chain of causation between any injury the defect causes A and any fault on the part of the manufacturer,[7] unless it was reasonable for A to run the risk, either because there was no practical alternative but to do so, or because A was unaware of the full extent of the danger.[8] The possibility that the failure to take preventive action will break the chain of causation in this way may have implications for the preventive damages analysis.

B. Mitigation of Damage

The wording of the provisions of the two sets of common European principles governing preventive damages seems broad enough to encompass expenses incurred to minimise the consequences of a past wrong, an issue dealt with in common law jurisdictions under the heading of 'mitigation of damage'. Since mitigation principles bite only after a wrong has been committed,[9] they do not themselves [71] offer a solution to the preventive damages problem, but they may nevertheless provide helpful analogies, and two particular rules relating to mitigation are noteworthy in this respect.

The first of these rules is the 'avoidable loss' rule, according to which a claimant cannot recover damages in respect of losses that the claimant could have avoided by the taking of reasonable steps.[10] And the second, connected, rule is that a claimant can recover the costs incurred in taking reasonable steps to mitigate the losses caused by a wrong.[11] A good example of the operation of this second rule is the case of *New Zealand Forest Products v O'Sullivan*,[12] where damages were awarded under the rule in *Rylands v Fletcher* for the costs the plaintiff incurred in trying to protect a pine forest on his property from a fire which had started on the defendant's land.[13] In reasoning highly pertinent to the issue under consideration, Mahon J said:

> If a claim may be sustained for damage to land and to chattels or fixtures on the land to which the fire had escaped, I can see no reason why the reasonable cost of

---

[7] See, eg, *Farr v Butters Bros & Co* [1932] 2 KB 606 (CA).

[8] See, eg, *Denny v Supplies and Transport Co* [1950] 2 KB 374 (CA).

[9] H McGregor, *McGregor on Damages*, 19th edn (London, Sweet & Maxwell, 2014) para 9-020. See also *Losinjska Plovidba v Transco Overseas (The Orjula)* [1995] 2 Lloyd's Rep 395 (QBD) 400, where Mance J assumes that the cause of action and the duty to mitigate arose at the same time.

[10] *British Westinghouse Electric and Manufacturing Co v Underground Electric Railways Company of London* [1912] AC 673 (HL) 689 (Viscount Haldane LC).

[11] *Restatement, Second, Torts* (1977) § 919(2).

[12] *New Zealand Forest Products v O'Sullivan* [1974] 2 NZLR 80 (NZHC).

[13] Note that the facts of this case would not now fall within the *Rylands* rule in English law, following the decision in *Gore v Stannard (t/a Wyvern Tyres)* [2012] EWCA Civ 1248, [2014] QB 1.

preserving such chattels or fixtures from damage should not be recoverable. The duty of a plaintiff to mitigate his loss is of general application in the law of damages and he may as a corollary recover from the defendant the expenses of mitigation.[14]

The same rule allows recovery of medical expenses reasonably incurred by a victim of wrongful personal injury[15] and of the costs of reasonable efforts to abate a nuisance affecting the claimant's land, so that where the encroaching roots of the defendant's tree had caused structural cracking in an apartment block, the owners were entitled to recover the cost of underpinning the building to prevent further damage.[16]

C. *Quia Timet* Injunctions

Finally, we should remember that a *quia timet* injunction may be granted where no wrong has yet occurred but there is the clear threat that one will be committed in the future. Of particular interest for present purposes is the possibility of a mandatory *quia timet* injunction, whereby a court orders the defendant to take positive steps to prevent their previous conduct from resulting in a future violation of the claimant's rights. Unless the defendant has acted 'wantonly and quite unreasonably in relation to his neighbour', account will be taken when deciding to issue a mandatory *quia timet* injunction of the cost to the defendant of doing the work required to prevent or reduce the likelihood of the future apprehended wrong, so that: [72]

> [T]he amount to be expended under a mandatory order ... must be balanced ... against the anticipated possible damage to the plaintiff and if, on balance, it seems unreasonable to inflict such expenditure on one who for this purpose is no more than a potential wrongdoer then the court must exercise its jurisdiction accordingly.[17]

Perhaps the most significant point to note here is that a court may award damages in lieu of a mandatory *quia timet* injunction, so that rather than the defendant being ordered to take the precautionary measures himself, the court orders him to compensate the claimant for the cost of her doing so instead. A good example of such a case is *Hooper v Rogers*,[18] where the defendant's excavation of a track on a steep slope threatened the stability of the claimant's farmhouse. The court found that there was a real probability that in time the defendant's actions would result in actual damage to the claimant's property, but instead of ordering the defendant to avert the danger by reinstating the track to

[14] *New Zealand Forest Products* (n 12) 83. See also *The Orjula* (n 9) 400.
[15] See, eg, *S v Distillers Co (Biochemicals)* [1970] 1 WLR 114 (QBD).
[16] *Delaware Mansions Ltd v Westminster CC* [2001] UKHL 55, [2002] 1 AC 321. For other examples, see K Oliphant (ed), *The Law of Tort*, 3rd edn (London, LexisNexis Butterworths, 2015) para 22.102.
[17] *Redland Bricks Ltd v Morris* [1970] AC 652 (HL) 666 (Lord Upjohn).
[18] *Hooper v Rogers* [1975] Ch 43 (CA).

its former condition, the court awarded the claimant the estimated cost of the work as damages in lieu of an injunction.[19] Of course, it will not always be realistic for the claimant to bring proceedings before incurring preventive expenses, and where the claimant incurs such expenses first and then brings an action to recover them afterwards, *Hooper v Rogers* would not provide a direct precedent for the claim, since any damages awarded could not be regarded as substituting for an injunction. Nevertheless, it is clearly arguable that the logic of the decision extends to at least some cases of preventive expenditure incurred prior to legal action being taken.

III. ILLUSTRATIVE CASES

In this section of the article I discuss a number of scenarios that squarely raise the question of whether preventive damages are and should be recoverable. The different examples are designed both to demonstrate the range of situations in which this issue can crop up, and to give a flavour of the difficulties to which it can give rise. They are not intended to represent a classification of preventive damages cases into distinct categories.

A. The Forest Fire Case

Suppose that B negligently allows a fire that B starts on B's own land to get out of control, with the result that it threatens to cross over into A's property, and destroy A's valuable pine forest. Alerted to the danger, A calls in a specialist squad of firefighters, who battle the blaze at the boundary of the two properties, and successfully prevent the fire from entering A's land and causing damage. Because the fire never enters A's land, B has not committed a wrong of a conventional kind, such as negligence or nuisance, and nor can B be held strictly liable for damage caused by the escape of a dangerous thing under the rule in *Rylands v* [73] *Fletcher*.[20] Assuming that A's expenses were reasonably incurred, are they recoverable from B?

The facts of this first scenario are based on the *New Zealand Forest Products* case[21] mentioned above, where a fire that began on the defendant's land spread onto the second plaintiff's land, threatening a forest on that land, and also a forest on adjoining land belonging to the first plaintiff. A contingent of firefighters provided by the two plaintiffs saved the trees, and they recovered the cost of the firefighting operation from the defendant under the rule in *Rylands v*

---

[19] See also *Barbagallo v J & F Catelan Pty Ltd* [1986] 1 Qd R 245 (QSC).

[20] Note that even if the fire crossed into A's land and caused damage, this now would not fall within the *Rylands* rule in English law, following the decision in *Gore* (n 13).

[21] *New Zealand Forest Products* (n 12).

Fletcher. Since the fire had spread to his land and caused some limited damage there, the recovery of these costs by the second plaintiff is explicable by reference to the second rule of mitigation discussed above, which allows the victim of a wrong to recover reasonable expenses incurred in attempting to minimise its consequences. However, since the fire never entered the first plaintiff's property, he was not the victim of a conventional wrong,[22] and hence his recovery of his expenses is a clear example of an award of preventive damages in the sense in which that term is being used in this article.

Other examples of the courts countenancing recovery of costs incurred to avert a direct threat of property damage can be given.[23] One is *The Port Victoria*, an admiralty case where it was held that:

> [I]f a vessel by negligence drags down towards another, and if it is a natural consequence that the other vessel is obliged to take a step which involves her in some expenditure, that is damage for which the first vessel is liable.[24]

And another example is the leading English decision on the *Rylands v Fletcher* rule, *Transco plc v Stockport MBC*,[25] where a large quantity of water had escaped from the service pipe to an apartment block owned by the defendant local authority. The escape of the water caused the collapse of a nearby embankment, and this in turn left a 27-metre section of the claimant's high-pressure gas main exposed and unsupported. There was an immediate and serious risk that the gas main would fracture, with potentially devastating consequences. The claimant acted to avert the danger by restoring support and covering the main, and then sought to recover the expense of doing so from the defendant under the rule in *Rylands v Fletcher*. Although the House of Lords dismissed the claim on the grounds that the supply of water to the tower block was not a sufficiently dangerous or extraordinary use of land to attract strict liability under that rule, it seems simply to have been taken as read that if the elements of a *Rylands v Fletcher* claim had been made out then the claimant would have been entitled to recover the cost of its preventive measures, even though in the event no property of the claimant was physically damaged, since its gas main was left unscathed (albeit vulnerable) and the embankment itself [74] belonged to the defendant.[26] The only member of the House who adverted to this question was Lord Hoffmann, who said that he was willing to assume that if damage to the

---

[22] ibid 84 (Mahon J).

[23] For an example of a statutory provision allowing such recovery, see the Merchant Shipping Act 1995, s 153(1)(b), which makes the owner of an oil tanker liable for the cost of reasonable measures taken to prevent or minimise damage caused by contamination resulting from a discharge or escape of oil from the tanker.

[24] *The Port Victoria* [1902] P 25 (PD) 27 (Sir FH Jeune P). On the facts, the plaintiffs recovered the value of an anchor and chain lost – and coals and stores consumed – when their vessel was forced to slip anchor and put to sea to avoid a collision.

[25] *Transco plc v Stockport MBC* [2003] UKHL 61, [2004] 2 AC 1. See also *Critelli Ltd v Lincoln Trust & Savings Co* (1978) 86 DLR (3d) 724 (Ont HC).

[26] *Transco* (n 25) [77].

pipe would have been actionable, then expense incurred in avoiding that damage would also have been recoverable.[27]

The apparently liberal attitude of the House of Lords towards preventive damages in *Transco* can be contrasted with the scepticism expressed about such claims in the private nuisance context in two lower court decisions, *Midland Bank plc v Bardgrove Property Services*[28] and *Yorkshire Water Services Ltd v Sun Alliance & London Insurance plc*.[29] In the *Midland Bank* case, the Court of Appeal refused a claim of this kind on facts similar to those of *Hooper v Rogers*,[30] the difference being that in this case the claimant had incurred expenditure shoring up land in its occupation *before* beginning proceedings against the defendant whose excavations threatened to cause a collapse. On the facts, this decision seems to have been justified, since before taking matters into its own hands the claimant should have given the defendant an opportunity to rectify the problem (or sought a mandatory *quia timet* injunction requiring it to do so),[31] but nevertheless the tenor of the judgments is unsympathetic to a claim that one of the judges said would expose the court and the parties to a 'wholly speculative enquiry' as to the likely future damage averted by the claimant's actions.[32] Similarly, in the *Yorkshire Water Services* case – where the claimant unsuccessfully sought recovery from its insurance company of sums it paid to a third party which had incurred preventive expenditure following an escape of sewage from the claimant's waste tip – Judge Humphrey Lloyd QC said that:

> The apprehension of damage, however well founded, does not entitle a party to recover damages in nuisance for the steps taken to anticipate such damage or its consequences whether by preventative measures or otherwise.[33]

Similar scepticism was apparent in the judgment of Dixon J of the Supreme Court of Victoria in *Gunnersen v Henwood*,[34] where the plaintiffs sought recovery of the cost of work on an escarpment adjacent to their home, which they alleged had been weakened by the defendant's conduct. On the facts, the failure of the claimants' action was again justified, this time on the grounds that the escarpment had been weakened by natural forces, rather than the defendant's conduct, but his Honour made it clear that he opposed awards of preventive damages in principle, citing 'the common law's well-established objection' to what he termed 'speculative damages', and describing such awards as an inappropriate move 'towards a concept of an attempted tort'.[35]

---

[27] ibid [47].
[28] *Midland Bank plc v Bardgrove Property Services* (1992) 65 P & CR 153 (CA).
[29] *Yorkshire Water Services Ltd v Sun Alliance & London Insurance plc* [1998] Env LR 204 (QBD).
[30] *Hooper* (n 18).
[31] See *Midland Bank* (n 28) 166 (Purchas LJ), 170 (Sir Christopher Slade).
[32] ibid 171 (Sir Christopher Slade).
[33] *Yorkshire Water Services* (n 29) 236.
[34] *Gunnersen v Henwood* [2011] VSC 440.
[35] ibid [350].

Finally, we should note with reference to this first scenario that while so far we have been concerned with averting the danger of an imminent threat of direct [75] physical damage to property, an analogous Norwegian case concerned an imminent threat of personal injury. The facts were that a train crash caused highly explosive propane gas to escape from two of the train's carriages, with the result that for several days the threat of a major explosion hung over the town where the accident took place. This in turn meant that local residents were forced to evacuate their homes and stay in hotels until the situation was brought under control. The Norwegian Supreme Court allowed the residents to recover the cost of the temporary accommodation from the railway company responsible for the accident.[36]

B. The Frozen Food Case

The second scenario differs from the first in that here the threat of physical damage to the claimant's property is arguably less direct, though equally real and equally imminent. This time the electricity supply to A's frozen food storage facility is interrupted when B's workers negligently cut through a cable belonging to the power company while doing road works in the street outside. As a result, A is forced to transfer the frozen food to another facility nearby, at considerable expense.[37] Let us assume for these purposes (a) that the full thawing out of the food in question would amount to physical damage, but that any thawing that takes place during the transfer of the food to the other facility does not; (b) that A is not at fault in not having an alternative source of electricity; and (c) that under the terms of A's contract with the electricity company, she has no redress against it in these circumstances. In these circumstances, can A recover her expenses from B in an action in tort?

It is of course a well-established rule in English law that a claimant cannot sue in negligence for a purely economic loss suffered as a result of physical damage to the property of a third party, as where a factory's operations are brought to a halt when the power supply is cut following negligently inflicted damage to a cable belonging to the electricity company.[38] On the other hand, provided the relevant elements of a negligence claim are made out, the factory owner would be entitled to recover in such a scenario if the cutting of the power caused

---

[36] Norges Høyesterett (Hr) 2 June 2006, Retstidende 2006, 691 (discussed in B Askeland, 'Norway' in H Koziol and B Steininger (eds), *European Tort Law 2006* (Vienna, Springer-Verlag, 2008) 361–63). For a similar scenario where a Canadian court held that no cause of action lay, having failed to advert to the preventive damages angle, see *Brooks v Canadian Pacific Railway Ltd* (2007) 283 DLR (4th) 540 (Sask Ct of QB).

[37] This scenario is based on examples used in J Smillie, 'Negligence and Economic Loss' (1982) 32 *University of Toronto Law Journal* 231, 250 fn; and P Benson, 'Economic Loss in Tort Law' in DG Owen (ed), *Philosophical Foundations of Tort Law* (Oxford, Clarendon Press, 1995) 438–39.

[38] *Spartan Steel & Alloys Ltd v Martin & Co (Contractors) Ltd* [1973] QB 27 (CA).

physical damage to the factory owner's property,[39] and so in our frozen food case, it seems clear that A would be able to bring an action if through no fault of A or A's employees the food had thawed out and been rendered worthless before the power cut had come to light.[40] It seems to follow that if preventive damages would be recoverable in the forest fire case, they ought also to be available here.

Although there do not appear to be any English or Commonwealth decisions that directly deal with this kind of scenario, there are analogous cases from the USA in which liability has been imposed. The best known of these is the decision of the US Court of Appeals for the Fifth Circuit in *Corpus Christi Oil & Gas Co v* [76] *Zapata Gulf Marine Corp*[41] As a result of the negligence of the defendant towboat operator, a barge under tow collided with a gas production platform owned by the plaintiff, damaging a gas riser connected to the platform, through which the gas flowed. The riser was owned by a third party. As a result, the plaintiff was unable to flow its gas through the riser, and in order to avoid the possibility of permanent damage to its gas wells, the plaintiff had to shut them in and flare gas for the two weeks it took to repair the riser. Although the court rejected a claim by the plaintiff for the revenues it had lost in that two-week period, it was permitted to recover from the defendant the value of the gas it had flared to save its wells, since those losses were 'directly attributable to its efforts to avoid the physical damages [to its wells] that would have rendered [the] defendant liable for much larger sums'.[42] Although strictly speaking the flaring of the gas amounted to physical damage to the plaintiff's property, the similarity of the facts of *Corpus Christi Oil* to those of the frozen food case is obvious, and the logic underlying the decision would seem to apply equally to the financial loss A suffers in that case.

C. The Collapsing Crane Case

The issue of preventive damages has most frequently come before the courts in common law jurisdictions in cases involving dangerously defective chattels and premises. It will be convenient to begin with an example involving a defective chattel, before going on to consider in the next scenario the additional complications to which defective premises give rise.

Suppose that A charters a log barge fitted with a crane designed and manufactured by B and takes it to a remote location in western Canada during the peak logging season to load logs. A subsequently discovers that a virtually identical crane also built by B has collapsed, killing its operator. A takes the barge back to Vancouver and on inspection finds serious structural defects in

---

[39] ibid.
[40] See, eg, *Seaway Hotels Ltd v Cragg (Canada) Ltd* (1959) 21 DLR (3d) 264 (Ont CA).
[41] *Corpus Christi Oil & Gas Co v Zapata Gulf Marine Corp* 71 F 3d 198 (5th Cir 1995).
[42] ibid 202.

the crane similar to those that caused the other crane to collapse. Assuming fault on B's part in the design and construction of the crane (and the absence of a contractual relationship between A and B), should A be able to recover the cost of making it safe from B?

In *Rivtow Marine Ltd v Washington Iron Works Ltd*,[43] a majority of the Supreme Court of Canada held that A could not sue B in tort in these circumstances, and that the cost of repairing the defective crane could be recovered from the manufacturer only under the terms of a contractual warranty of fitness. However, in a partially dissenting opinion, Laskin J argued that a manufacturer of a defective chattel which posed a threat of physical harm to persons or other property should be liable in tort to the chattel's owner for the cost of making the product safe to use. According to his Honour:

> The case is not one where a manufactured product proves to be merely defective (in short, where it has not met promised expectations), but rather one where by reason of the defect there is a foreseeable risk of physical harm from its use and where the alert avoidance of such harm gives rise to economic [77] loss. Prevention of threatened harm resulting directly in economic loss should not be treated differently from post-injury cure.[44]

Although the reasoning of Laskin J proved influential, it was eventually rejected by the House of Lords in *Murphy v Brentwood DC*[45] Lord Keith said in *Murphy* that he considered that the majority's decision in *Rivtow Marine* to reject the claim for the cost of repairing the crane had been correct, since that cost had been incurred in order that A could continue profitably to operate the crane. Once the danger was known about, it could have been averted by simply laying up the crane.[46] Lord Oliver agreed. The crane was dangerous only if A chose to go on using it for the purpose for which it was designed, and therefore the expenditure required to make it safe was incurred in order to enable A 'to reap such economic advantages as lay in [A's] continued ability to use it for that purpose'.[47]

These statements do not amount to rejection of the idea of preventive damages recovery. Rather, their Lordships were saying that in the case of a chattel known to be dangerous, the fact that any danger can usually be averted by abandoning or decommissioning the item means that the cost of repair is not generally necessary in order to prevent personal injury or property damage; rather, it is necessary in order to *continue to make use of the chattel*.[48] Properly understood, therefore, the cost of repair is not preventive expenditure at all.

---

[43] *Rivtow Marine Ltd v Washington Iron Works Ltd* [1974] SCR 1189 (SCC).

[44] ibid 1222. See similarly *Rutherford v Attorney-General* [1976] 1 NZLR 403 (NZHC), where Cooke J allowed a purchaser of an unsafe lorry to recover the cost of making it safe from the government body that had issued a certificate of fitness for the lorry before the sale.

[45] *Murphy* (n 5). See also the observations of Lord Bridge in *D & F Estates Ltd v Church Commissioners for England* [1989] AC 177 (HL) 206 (reiterated in *Murphy* at 475).

[46] *Murphy* (n 5) 470.

[47] ibid 489.

[48] See Benson, 'Economic Loss in Tort Law' (n 37) 436–37.

A possible objection to this reasoning is that the economic cost of abandoning the item is a cost incurred in order to obviate the danger (a 'preventive *cost*', as it were), and hence should be recoverable as preventive damages. However, the better view is that the preventive damages concept should be limited to *outlays* A makes in order to protect A's person or property, not least because recovery of 'preventive costs' of this kind would give rise to obvious anomalies.[49] Suppose, for example, that A buys a car that cannot be safely driven because it has defective brakes. Would it not be strange to allow A to recover the cost of repairing this defect, but to deny recovery if the reason A could not use the car was that it had a defective ignition, and so would not start?[50] Similarly, imagine another scenario, in which a consignment of plastic bottles ordered by a soft drinks producer have to be discarded because each bottle has a large hole in the base. The use of the bottles for their intended purpose would obviously result in the loss of other property of the drinks producer (the soft drink with which the bottles are filled), and yet it would seem very odd to allow recovery of the economic cost of discarding them as 'preventive damages', when no such claim would lie if they had to be [78] discarded because, for example, they were crushed flat during manufacture and so could not be filled in the first place.[51]

On the other hand, the concept of preventive damages *does* extend to expenditure A must incur in order to cease using the chattel, or to obviate a threat it poses even after it ceases to be used.[52] Suppose, for example, that B, a manufacturer of hydrochloric acid, packages the acid in unsuitable drums, and that a consignment of the drums begins to leak while on board A's ship. If the drums remain on the vessel, the leaking acid will damage the fabric of the vessel, and yet they cannot simply be abandoned at sea or on land. Instead, A is legally required as the custodian of the drums to put the vessel into a special decontamination dock and to pay for the drums to be removed and disposed of in compliance with environmental regulations. Since in this case A does not have the option of simply discarding the drums without further expense, a claim to recover from B the expenses A incurred in dealing with the danger is properly analysed as a claim for preventive damages. This conclusion is consistent with the reasoning of Mance J in the analogous case of *Losinjska Plovidba v*

---

[49] It follows that, for example, no claim for preventive damages would lie where (as in *Greenway v Johnson Mathey plc* [2014] EWHC 3957 (QB)) an employee negligently exposed to a substance by an employer becomes sensitised to it, with the result that in order to avoid an allergic reaction, the employee must forego future employment opportunities involving contact with the substance.

[50] This example is given by S Waddams, *Products Liability*, 5th edn (Toronto, Carswell, 2011) 41–42.

[51] See ibid 36. Another difficulty with granting recovery of the economic cost of abandoning a dangerous chattel in tort is that we then run into the problem that some uses of a product may be safe, and others dangerous – as where it is safe to sit *at* a table, but not to sit *on* the table – and yet the question of which uses the owner can legitimately expect to be safe may at least in part be a question of what Laskin J termed 'promised expectations', and so better governed by the law of contract.

[52] Benson, 'Economic Loss in Tort Law' (n 37) 440–41. See also S Perry, 'Protected Interests and Undertakings in the Law of Negligence' (1992) 42 *University of Toronto Law Journal* 247, 268–69.

Transco Overseas (The Orjula),[53] where he said that despite the statements in *D & F Estates* and *Murphy*, it was at least arguable that:

> [I]f property is put into circulation which remains positively dangerous unless preventive measures are taken to neutralize the danger, a person who is obliged to take such steps and does not have the option simply to abandon the property may have a claim in tort against a person who negligently put the article into circulation.[54]

D. The Collapsing Condominium Case

Further complexities arise where dangerously defective premises are involved. Suppose this time that A is the owner of an apartment in a condominium complex which turns out to have inadequate foundations because of the negligence of the builder B. Unless expensive remedial works are carried out, there is a real danger that the building will collapse, killing or injuring those inside. Can A recover their share of the cost of these works from B, despite the fact that A has no contractual relationship with B, having bought the apartment from a third party? This issue has dogged common law courts for the last four decades, and has met with a range of different judicial responses. One of those responses has been to hold that a remote purchaser of defective premises may be entitled to recover the diminution in value attributable to the negligent construction of the building from the builder (or another responsible party), regardless of whether the defect posed a threat of [79] personal injury or damage to other property.[55] Of more relevance to the present enquiry, however, have been two other responses to the defective premises problem.

The first of these responses gives no remedy in the case of non-dangerous but defective premises, but does allow a person who acquires premises that pose an imminent threat to the health or safety of those occupying them to recover the cost of making the building safe from a party responsible for the defect (usually the builder, but sometimes others, such as a local authority tasked with checking the construction work). This approach can be traced back to the decision of the Court of Appeal in *Dutton v Bognor Regis UDC*,[56] where Lord Denning MR rejected the argument of the defendant local authority that any duty of care it

---

[53] *The Orjula* (n 9).

[54] ibid 403.

[55] This is the position that has been taken by the courts in Australia and New Zealand. In Australia, whether a duty of care is in fact recognised depends on various considerations, including the vulnerability of the plaintiff: see *Bryan v Maloney* (1995) 182 CLR 609 (HCA); *Woolcock Street Investments Ltd v CDG Pty Ltd* [2004] HCA 16, 216 CLR 515; and *Brookfield Multiplex Ltd v Owners Corporation Strata Plan 61288* [2014] HCA 36, 254 CLR 185. For the current position in New Zealand law, see *North Shore CC v Body Corporate 188529* [2010] NZSC 158, [2011] 2 NZLR 289; and *Body Corporate No 207624 v North Shore CC* [2012] NZSC 83, [2013] 2 NZLR 297.

[56] *Dutton v Bognor Regis UDC* [1972] 1 QB 373 (CA).

might owe by virtue of its power to inspect buildings under construction did not extend to the purely economic costs of repairing a dangerous defect:

> If [that] were right, it would mean that, if the inspector negligently passes the house as properly built and it collapses and injures a person, the council are liable; but, if the owner discovers the defect in time to repair it – and he does repair it – the council are not liable. That is an impossible distinction. They are liable in either case.[57]

Dutton was later approved by the House of Lords in *Anns v Merton LBC*,[58] where it was held that in such cases damages were recoverable for the expenditure necessary to restore the dwelling to a condition in which it was no longer a danger to the health and safety of persons occupying it, as well as expenses arising out of any necessary displacement of the occupiers during the course of the repair work. And *Anns* was in turn followed by the Supreme Court of Canada in *Winnipeg Condominium Corp No 36 v Bird Construction Co*,[59] which allowed recovery of the reasonable cost of making safe a building that posed 'a substantial danger to the health and safety of the occupants' on facts similar to those of the scenario under discussion.[60] Both these decisions were influenced by the reasoning of Laskin J in the *Rivtow Marine* case, but in *Winnipeg Condominium* La Forest J also justified the award of preventive damages on the policy ground that it would incentivise claimants to mitigate potential losses and encourage economically efficient and socially responsible behaviour. Allowing recovery against negligent building contractors in tort for the cost of repairing dangerous defects therefore served 'an important preventative function'.[61]

The other response to the defective premises problem can be found in the decisions of the House of Lords in the *D & F Estates Ltd v Church Commissioners for England* and *Murphy v Brentwood DC* cases. In *D & F Estates*, Lord Bridge said that the argument that a chattel was no longer dangerous when a hidden defect [80] came to light might also apply in the case of defective premises,[62] and in *Murphy* the House overruled *Anns*, and held that in this type of case the cost of repair was no longer recoverable in tort. According to Lord Oliver:

> The injury which the plaintiff suffers in such a case is that his consciousness of the possible injury to his own health or safety or that of others puts him in a position in which, in order to enable him either to go on living in the property or to exploit its financial potentiality without that risk … he has to expend money in making good the defects which have now become patent.[63]

---

[57] ibid 396.
[58] *Anns v Merton LBC* [1978] AC 728 (HL).
[59] *Winnipeg Condominium Corp No 36 v Bird Construction Co* [1995] 1 SCR 85 (SCC).
[60] The court left open the question of whether damages were recoverable in the case of a non-dangerous defect: *Winnipeg Condominium* (n 59) 119–20.
[61] ibid 118.
[62] *D & F Estates* (n 45) 206.
[63] *Murphy* (n 5) 484.

For their Lordships, it was the distinction between dangerous defects that were known about and mere defects of quality which was an 'impossible' one, since in either case the loss was purely economic,[64] and in the former case no physical damage or personal injury would occur unless the claimant caused it to by courting a danger of which he was aware, so that the cost of repair was incurred 'not in preventing an otherwise inevitable injury but in order to enable him to continue to use the property'.[65]

One preliminary point that should be made about this issue is that, as with chattels, the preventive damages concept extends to costs – such as removal expenses – that A must incur in order to cease using dangerous premises. And although it is unlikely that these costs would exceed the cost of repairing the defect, where they would do so, the cost of repair should be recoverable as the minimum preventive expense.[66]

That takes us to a possible objection to the *Murphy* reasoning in defective premises cases, an objection that can be framed in one of two ways. The usual way of framing the objection is to say that, unlike in the case of a chattel, the owner of residential property realistically does not have the option of abandoning the property, but will in effect be forced to repair it in order to make it safe for continued occupation. As so framed, however, the objection lacks bite, since whether or not an occupier of dangerous residential premises can be expected to repair or abandon them is likely to depend on whether repair is worthwhile, and precisely the same is true of the occupier of dangerous commercial premises or the owner of a chattel. The other way of framing the objection packs more of a punch. This time the argument is that in residential premises cases the cost of making the premises safe ought properly to be recoverable as 'preventive damages', since the occupier has no choice but to run the risk of injury by staying put (abandonment not being a realistic option), and hence in this type of case – unlike in the chattel case – the expense involved in making the premises safe *is* necessary if the threat of personal injury is to be averted.

[81] While there is undoubtedly some force in this 'no choice' objection, on further scrutiny it becomes clear that it does not justify recovery of preventive

---

[64] ibid 465 (Lord Keith).

[65] ibid 488–89 (Lord Oliver).

[66] See J Neyers, '*Donoghue v Stevenson* and the Rescue Doctrine: A Public Justification of Recovery in Situations Involving the Negligent Supply of Dangerous Structures' (1999) 49 *University of Toronto Law Journal* 475, 505. Since my analysis is limited to expenditure necessary to obviate the threat of personal injury or property damage to the claimant, I am not concerned with cases where a dangerously defective building is a potential source of injury to persons or property on neighbouring land or an adjacent highway. In *Murphy* (n 5), Lord Bridge suggested (at 475) that in such a case the minimum cost of obviating the danger posed to third parties would be recoverable from a negligent builder, but subsequent case law is inconsistent on the point: compare *Morse v Barratt (Leeds) Ltd* (1992) 9 Constr LJ 158 (Ch D) (allowing such a claim) with *George Fischer Holding Ltd v Multi Design Consultants Ltd* (1998) 61 Con LR 85 (QBD) 110–11 (rejecting such a claim).

damages in cases of dangerously defective premises. An obvious difficulty with the argument is that it is simply not possible to draw a bright line in this regard between dwellings on the one hand and commercial premises and defective chattels on the other, since whether or not the owner of real or personal property can realistically abandon it will always depend on her individual circumstances. If subsidence affects adjacent properties in a Cotswolds village, for example, might it not be easier for the wealthy investment banker who uses one as a weekend getaway to abandon his property than it is for the owner of the small shop next door, who bought the premises with a large bank loan? And can a cleaner paid the minimum wage so easily 'discard' the dangerously defective car she needs to get to work?[67] Admittedly, this difficulty can be circumvented – at the cost of much uncertainty – by reframing the 'no choice' objection as an argument for recovery of preventive damages in all cases where the claimant will be unable to afford to abandon the premises or chattel in question. However, even as so reframed, the argument still fails to convince. This is because ultimately all that the 'no choice' objection does is to highlight the fact that, where it is expensive to replace or repair the dangerous property in question, the claimant's financial circumstances are likely to determine the amount of risk to which the claimant is prepared to be exposed in order to avoid incurring that cost. And while this seems right, it does not provide a convincing justification for awarding the cost of repair as preventive damages.

Consider two particular difficulties. First, where repair is not worthwhile, so that a wealthy owner would simply abandon the chattel or premises, what is the quantum of 'preventive damages' payable to the poorer claimant who would otherwise be forced to risk continued use? It makes little sense to award the claimant the cost of repair if this is greater than the cost of replacing the chattel or premises, and yet it would seem odd to award the cost of a replacement as 'preventive damages', and difficult to know how a court would decide what the minimum acceptable replacement would be. And secondly, where the risk associated with continued use of the property in question is very high (as where a house is likely to collapse within days), then no matter *how* straitened the claimant's circumstances are they will surely choose to abandon the property, so that paradoxically the argument for preventive damages – which is premised on the assumption that the claimant will run the risk of continued use – falls away. This most extreme of cases shows us that ultimately the 'no choice' objection fails because there always *is* a choice, even though it may not be a very palatable one. Tempting though it is to distinguish between collapsing cranes and collapsing condominiums in this context, therefore, it seems that there is not a good reason to do so.

---

[67] See *Messick v General Motors Corpn* 460 F 2d 485 (5th Cir 1972).

E. The Medical Monitoring Case

In the final scenario, toxic chemicals contaminate a town's water supply as a result of B's negligent operation of a landfill site. When the problem comes to light, a resident of the town, A, is advised by a doctor that A's consumption of the contaminated water has put A at increased risk of contracting a range of medical [82] conditions, including cancer. A is further advised that since early detection of these conditions may reduce the danger they pose, A should undergo a series of screening tests, which A will have to pay for. Can A recover the cost of this medical monitoring from B even though A cannot yet establish that the contaminated water has damaged A's health?

This scenario is based on the facts of *Ayers v Jackson Township*,[68] where the Supreme Court of New Jersey held that in such a scenario B should meet the cost of A's medical monitoring if in all the circumstances it could be shown to be reasonable and necessary. Similar claims have been allowed in a number of other jurisdictions in the USA.[69] In *Potter v Firestone Tire & Rubber Co*,[70] for example, the Supreme Court of California held that the costs of medical monitoring were recoverable provided medical testimony established that the need for such monitoring was a reasonably certain consequence of a wrongful toxic exposure and that the recommended monitoring was reasonable.[71]

An important point to note about these 'medical monitoring' claims is that they have only rarely resulted in payments of lump-sum damages to plaintiffs, with courts almost always requiring the establishment of a fund out of which disbursements can be made to plaintiffs as and when medical monitoring expenses are incurred.[72] This chimes with the argument made earlier that preventive damages claims ought to be limited to actual *outlays* A makes in order to protect A's person or property, from which it would follow that no such action lies for the *future need* to incur preventive expenses. It also provides a good illustration of the way in which preventive damages claims can blur the distinction between an award of damages for a past wrong and a more forward-looking grant of specific relief.

Allowing recovery of reasonable medical surveillance costs in cases such as these has been justified on various grounds, including the desirability of encouraging the early detection and treatment of the threatened health

---

[68] *Ayers v Jackson Township* 525 A 2d 287 (NJ 1987).

[69] Fleming, 'Preventive Damages' (n 2) 64–71.

[70] *Potter v Firestone Tire & Rubber Co* 863 P 2d 795 (Cal 1993).

[71] There, have, however also been many decisions rejecting such claims in the absence of an existing physical injury, and in recent years it seems that the tide has turned against actions of this kind: see V Schwartz and C Silverman, 'The Rise of "Empty Suit" Litigation: Where Should Tort Law Draw the Line?' (2015) 80 *Brooklyn Law Review* 599, 612–28.

[72] See, eg, *Metro-North Commuter RR Co v Buckley* 521 US 424 (1997), where the US Supreme Court rejected outright a claim for lump-sum damages for medical monitoring costs under the Federal Employers' Liability Act.

conditions,[73] which not only potentially benefits claimants by mitigating the severity of their illnesses, but also potentially benefits defendants, by reducing their future liabilities.[74] This explicitly preventive rationale is consistent with the judicial wariness of lump-sum awards, which could of course be put to other uses. On the other hand, the recovery of medical monitoring costs by asymptomatic plaintiffs has also attracted fierce criticism, with some commentators arguing that claims of this kind can open the floodgates of litigation and deplete the resources available to compensate those who have actually suffered physical injury as a result of the defendant's negligence.[75]

[83] Three further points should be made about the medical monitoring case. The first is that this scenario must be distinguished from claims for an increased risk of future injury, akin to a 'loss of a chance' claim. In the latter type of case, A seeks to recover an appropriate percentage of the quantum of the threatened future injury, whereas the claim in the medical monitoring case is limited to the expenses incurred by A in seeking to avoid the possibility of – or to mitigate the consequences of – that injury. The second point is that although negligent conduct that exposes others to an increased risk of future ill health may cause them to suffer other types of financial outlay (such as increased insurance premiums), these outlays are not incurred in order to reduce or eliminate the risk of personal injury, and so cannot ground a preventive damages claim.[76] And the final point is that two important distinctions can be drawn between the medical monitoring case and the more classic preventive damages scenario exemplified by the forest fire and frozen food cases. One is that, while in those cases it was highly likely (or inevitable) that physical damage would have occurred had the preventive expenses not been incurred, in the medical monitoring case the likelihood of the threatened health condition coming about may be much lower, which lends the claim a more speculative air. And the other is that, while in those cases the preventive expenditure is designed to prevent physical damage occurring at all, most medical monitoring is aimed at minimising the severity of an adverse health condition by expediting treatment, rather than preventing the condition arising in the first place. It follows from these distinctions that a rule permitting recovery of preventive damages in those more classic cases need not necessarily extend to the medical monitoring case.

---

[73] See, eg, *Ayers* (n 68) 311 (Stein J).

[74] See M Geistfeld, 'The Analytics of Duty: Medical Monitoring and Related Forms of Economic Loss' (2002) 88 *Virginia Law Review* 1921, 1947.

[75] See, eg, Schwartz and Silverman (n 71).

[76] E Voyiakis, 'The Great Illusion: Tort Law and Exposure to Danger of Physical Harm' (2009) 72 *MLR* 909 lumps the two together, and argues that both should be recoverable on the grounds that they are losses caused by a setback to the claimant's interest in 'keeping their physical health out of danger', but he fails to make good his claim that this interest is the subject of general protection by negligence law, and does not reconcile his analysis – which focuses on 'losses' – with the requirement of 'damage'. On the need to distinguish loss and damage in the negligence context, see D Nolan, 'Damage in the English Law of Negligence' (2013) 4 *Journal of European Tort Law* 259, 265–67.

IV. LIMITATIONS ON RECOVERY

On the assumption that preventive damages ought to be available in at least some of the scenarios discussed in the previous section, what limitations should be placed on the recovery of such damages? How clear must the danger be, must it be an 'imminent' one, what criteria will determine whether particular preventive action qualifies for compensation, and so on?

A number of general points can be made. First, when considering whether preventive damages should be recoverable, useful guidance may be given by the principles applicable to contributory negligence, self-defence and mitigation. Secondly, we shall see that there are a number of different possible rationales for the award of preventive damages, and the rationale that is favoured may have implications for the limits on recovery.[77] Thirdly, the general principles controlling relief in the tort in question must be borne in mind, so that if (for example) the cause of action is negligence, then A will have to show that the preventive [84] expenditure was reasonably foreseeable,[78] and causally connected to B's negligent conduct.[79] And finally, it seems inevitable that the central general limit on the recovery of preventive damages will be the *reasonableness* of the actions of the person seeking compensation of their preventive expenditure (hereafter 'A'), as is made clear in the provisions on preventive damages in the two sets of common European principles reproduced at the start of the article.[80] It will be helpful to take a closer look at this reasonableness criterion first, before going on to consider some further possible limits on recovery.

A. The General Criterion of Reasonableness

The general criterion of reasonableness should determine whether A can recover the particular expenditure incurred when seeking to avert the danger.[81] The same test of reasonableness applies to the recovery of expenses incurred in mitigation of a past wrong,[82] while the reasonableness of the measures demanded also determines the availability of *quia timet* injunctions.[83] Useful general

---

[77] This gives rise to a chicken-and-egg problem. It could be argued that, since the favoured rationale has implications for the limits on recovery, it would be better to consider the possible rationales before the limits issue. However, an assessment of the appropriate limits of recovery also informs the discussion of the various possible rationales, and in the end it seemed preferable to deal with the former first.

[78] See *Gunnersen* (n 34) [307].

[79] A requirement not satisfied on the facts of *Gunnersen* (n 34), where it was held that the risk mitigated by the preventive measures was a naturally occurring one.

[80] A reasonableness test has also been endorsed in the recent Australian case law on preventive damages: see *Dovuro Pty Ltd v Wilkins* [2000] FCA 1902, 105 FCR 476 [34] (Branson J) [127] (Finkelstein J); and *Gunnersen* (n 34) [268].

[81] See von Bar, *Principles of European Law on Non-Contractual Liability Arising out of Damage Caused to Another* (n 3) art 6:302, comment 3.

[82] McGregor (n 9) para 9-074.

[83] *Redland Bricks Ltd v Morris* [1970] AC 652 (HL) 666.

guidance on the operation of a reasonableness test in this context is provided by the *Restatement, Second, Torts*, which states that in determining whether the expenses incurred to avert harm were reasonable, 'the seriousness of the harm threatened, the degree of likelihood that it will occur, and the probable harm or expense to the threatened person are elements to be considered'.[84] As in contributory negligence,[85] where A is forced to respond quickly in an emergency situation created by B, the standard of reasonableness should not be pitched too high, but at the same time it must be borne in mind that, unlike in cases of contributory negligence and mitigation, here B may only be a *potential* wrongdoer.[86]

Four further points should be made on the reasonableness question. First, if some of the expenditure was reasonable and some unreasonable, A should be compensated for the former, as in the maritime doctrine of general average.[87] Secondly, it seems only right that the default position should be that the reasonableness of A's actions be assessed from the point of view of someone in A's position at the time the expenditure was incurred, in line with general tort principles.[88] Thirdly, it may sometimes be necessary to supplement the test of reasonableness with more specific requirements. In the medical monitoring case, for example, it might be thought appropriate to require A to show not only that B has exposed A to a toxin and that it would be reasonable for A to undergo medical [85] monitoring for health conditions associated with such exposure, but also that the exposure has significantly increased the risk of A contracting those conditions, since it might be perfectly 'reasonable' to incur the cost of such monitoring even if this were not the case. And finally, although it will not always be appropriate or practicable for A to give B notice of intended preventive expenditure, where B is in a position to avert the danger, it may be that it is unreasonable for A to incur costs without first giving B notice of the problem, and an opportunity to rectify matters at B's own expense. In the *Delaware Mansions* case,[89] for example, where the owners of an apartment block recovered the cost of underpinning the building from the local authority responsible for trees which had caused structural damage, the House of Lords made it clear that in such a case A must generally tell B of the problem and give B a reasonable opportunity

---

[84] *Restatement, Second, Torts* (1977) § 919, comment b.

[85] See, eg, *Jones v Boyce* (1816) 1 Stark 493, 171 ER 540.

[86] A point emphasised by Lord Upjohn in *Redland Bricks* (n 83) at 666 in the context of awards of *quia timet* injunctions. I say '*may* only be a potential wrongdoer' because of the possibility that the correct analysis of preventive damages cases is that they concern the violation of a right not to be threatened with impending damage, in which case the defendant in such cases is an actual wrongdoer: see further, text to n 119.

[87] FD Rose, *General Average: Law and Practice*, 2nd edn (London, LLP, 2005) para 2.68.

[88] See *Restatement, Second, Torts* (1977) § 919, comment b.

[89] *Delaware Mansions Ltd v Westminster CC* [2002] 1 AC 321 (HL). See also *Midland Bank* (n 28) 170 (Sir Christopher Slade). *cf Kirk v London Borough of Brent* [2005] EWCA Civ 1701, [2006] Env LR D7 [26] (Lloyd LJ), [37] (Pill LJ).

to deal with it before incurring remedial expenditure.[90] Furthermore, if in such a case B refuses to take the preventive measures in question, then it may be that A should seek a mandatory *quia timet* injunction requiring B to do so, before the incurring of expenditure by A.[91]

B. Further Possible Limits on Recovery

There are a number of further issues concerning the recovery of preventive damages that a test of reasonableness may not resolve. One such issue is the *specificity of the danger*. A may incur perfectly reasonable expenditure to avert a general danger that is not created by one particular potential wrongdoer, as where following an upsurge of burglaries in the neighbourhood, A installs expensive security locks in A's home. In a case of this kind, a claim by A to recover that expenditure as preventive damages from a subsequent individual wrongdoer – such as B, a burglar found breaking into A's house – runs into difficulties. After all, it is not clear why B should have to bear the total cost of expenditure incurred to avert a more general threat, and even if it were thought reasonable to shift a proportion of the cost onto B, it is hard to see how one would go about working out the proportion of the cost B should bear.[92]

The second such issue is the *necessity of the preventive measures*. A may reasonably believe that there is a threat of wrongful interference that justifies incurring preventive expenditure, but it may later turn out that the threat could never have materialised – in the forest fire case, for example, a sudden change of wind direction might have saved A's property in any case.[93] Here analogous areas of law provide less assistance. It is unclear, for example, whether a claim lies for general average if there is no peril, but the ship's master honestly and reasonably [86] believes that there is,[94] and in *Ashley v Chief Constable of Sussex Police*[95] the House of Lords left open the question of whether there would be a defence to a civil action for trespass to the person where the defendant had honestly and reasonably believed that it was necessary to defend himself but there was in fact

---

[90] An analogy can also be made with the case of the necessitous intervener: see FD Rose, 'Restitution for the Rescuer' (1989) 9 *OJLS* 167, 187.

[91] See the remarks of Dixon J in *Gunnersen* (n 34) at [349], although his Honour's apparent view that the possibility of *quia timet* intervention is a reason not to allow preventive damages claims *at all* fails to account for cases where there is not time to seek such intervention, or where for other reasons such intervention may not be appropriate.

[92] This explains why in a number of European jurisdictions a department store cannot recover part of the salary of a store detective it employs from a thief the detective apprehends: see U Magnus (ed), *Unification of Tort Law: Damages* (The Hague, Kluwer, 2001) 217.

[93] See *Dovuro* (n 80) 514.

[94] Rose (n 87) para 2.14. There are dicta to suggest not, but the author himself thinks there should be.

[95] *Ashley v Chief Constable of Sussex Police* [2008] UKHL 25, [2008] AC 962. For a note on *Ashley* taking a position on reasonable mistakes that tallies with the suggested approach here, see N McBride [2008] *CLJ* 461.

no actual or imminent attack.[96] Perhaps the best solution is to hold that if it turns out that there was in fact no danger, then to succeed in a preventive damages claim A must show not only that A honestly and reasonably believed that there was a danger, but also that B was at fault in bringing about that belief and should have foreseen that B's conduct might induce A to incur reasonable expenditure to avert the perceived threat. In the medical monitoring case, for example, this solution would pave the way for recovery in a case where it would be reasonable for A to undergo medical screening even though it is unclear whether A has in fact been exposed to the toxins B has negligently released into the environment.[97]

A third such issue is the *imminence of the danger*. Although it has been said that there must be proof of imminent danger for a *quia timet* injunction to be granted,[98] the better view is that what matters is the probability and likely gravity of damage.[99] In *Hooper v Rogers*, for example, damages were awarded in lieu of an injunction because there was a real probability of damage unless preventive measures were taken, even though the defendant's removal of support from the claimant's house might not have led to subsidence for many years.[100] Nor is the imminence of the danger a condition for the recovery of general average, since the law recognises the necessity of taking precautionary measures in good time.[101] There is therefore no particular magic in the imminence of the threat, not least because a threat of damage may be more difficult or more expensive to avert when it has become imminent than when it first becomes apparent, and a requirement of imminence gives potential claimants an incentive to delay preventive measures until they are urgently necessary.[102] Such a requirement would also

---

[96] *Ashley* (n 95). In *Cope v Sharpe (No 2)* [1912] 1 KB 496 (CA), it was held that a tenant of the sporting rights of another's land had a defence to a trespass action if the measures he took to fight a fire on the land were acts a reasonable man would have taken to meet the danger posed by the fire, even if it turned out that those measures had not in fact been necessary.

[97] This reasoning is consistent with the decision of the Federal Court of Australia in *Dovuro* (n 80) (reversed on other grounds: (2003) HCA 51, 215 CLR 317), where after a Western Australian farmer had planted a quantity of canola seed produced in New Zealand, the state authorities required him to take measures to eradicate three species of weed thought to be present in the seed. The farmer recovered the cost of those measures from the seed's producer, even though it was not established that the authorities' concerns had been warranted. According to Branson J, it was immaterial whether, if the preventive steps had not been taken, the weeds in question would have become established on his land: all that mattered was that 'the money spent to mitigate the risk was money reasonably spent' (at [34]). Meanwhile, Finkelstein J took the view (at [141]) that in preventive damages cases the plaintiff should be entitled to recover as long as the expenditure was foreseeable, and the plaintiff had reasonably suspected that there was a threat of damage.

[98] *Fletcher v Bealey* (1885) 28 Ch D 688 (Ch D) 698.

[99] See further, A Burrows, *Remedies for Torts and Breach of Contract*, 3rd edn (Oxford, OUP, 2004) 545.

[100] *Hooper* (n 18). See also *Barbagallo v J & F Catelan Pty Ltd* [1986] 1 Qd R 245 (QSC). This is also the approach favoured in J Murphy, 'Rethinking Injunctions in Tort Law' (2007) 27 *OJLS* 509.

[101] Rose, *General Average* (n 87) para 2.12.

[102] See Waddams (n 50) 37. The same point was made by critics of the holding in *Anns* that a claim for preventive damages arose only when the state of the defective premises posed a present or imminent danger to the health and safety of the occupiers: see, eg, *Murphy* (n 5) 480 (Lord Bridge), 497–98 (Lord Jauncey).

create [87] uncertainty.[103] It follows that in preventive damages cases the focus when applying the general test of reasonableness should generally be on the probability of the damage occurring and its likely gravity if it occurs, rather than the imminence of the danger, with the caveat that there may be instances in which the latter is also a relevant consideration.

Finally, it is suggested that provided the preventive expenditure is reasonably incurred, it should not be a condition of a claim for recompense that the *precautions taken were successful*. In the law of mitigation, the victim of a wrong who takes reasonable steps to minimise its consequences can recover the cost of those measures from the wrongdoer even if as it turns out the preventive action makes no difference – and indeed even if it actually make things worse[104] – and it is difficult to see why the rule should be different where measures are taken before a wrong has been committed. The right to compensation for the cost of preventive measures recognised in art 6.302 of the *Principles of European Law on Non-Contractual Liability Arising out of Damage Caused to Another* does not depend on the success of the measures taken,[105] and this is also the position taken in Austrian law,[106] and in the *Restatement, Second, Torts*.[107] Furthermore, if one of the primary reasons for awarding preventive damages is to encourage the taking of reasonable preventive measures, then that would seem to militate against making the success of those measures determinative, just as in the civilian doctrine of *negotiorum gestio*, where the goal of encouraging benevolent intervention in the affairs of others is generally thought to be furthered by allowing recovery in respect of reasonable interventions, regardless of success.[108]

V. JUSTIFYING RECOVERY

On an intuitive level, the case for allowing recovery of preventive damages in appropriate cases seems strong. In the words of Peter Cane:

> If the loss which is threatened would be compensatable if it occurred, there is surely good reason to allow damages to forestall it ... Both justice and economic good sense ('prevention is better than cure') seem to combine in favour of such a result.[109]

---

[103] How would a requirement of 'imminence' play out in the medical monitoring case, for example?.

[104] *New Zealand Forest Products* (n 12) 83; McGregor (n 9) para 9-097.

[105] von Bar, *Principles of European Law on Non-Contractual Liability Arising out of Damage Caused to Another* (n 3) art 6:302, comment 3.

[106] ibid art 6:302, note 6.

[107] *Restatement, Second, Torts* (1977) § 919, comment c.

[108] C von Bar, *Principles of European Law on Benevolent Intervention in Another's Affairs* (Oxford, OUP, 2006) art 3:101, comment 6. Compare the law of salvage, where success is required, but also rewarded.

[109] P Cane, *Tort Law and Economic Interests*, 2nd edn (Oxford, OUP, 1996) 469. See similarly, *New Zealand Forest Products* (n 12) 83; *Barnes v Mac Brown & Co Inc* 342 NE 2d 611 (Ind 1976) 621; *Dovuro* (n 80) 486 (Branson J) 514 (Finkelstein J); and A Mullis and K Oliphant, *Torts*, 4th edn (Basingstoke, Palgrave Macmillan, 2011) 55 ('intuitive appeal' of preventive damages recovery).

Furthermore, our intuitions are in this instance backed up by good arguments of both principle and policy for allowing such claims. An argument from *principle* for allowing recovery of preventive damages is that it is a logical corollary of the [88] law of contributory negligence and legal causation. After all, if a person who complains that they are the victim of a wrong can have their claim rejected or their damages reduced because they failed to take reasonable steps to avert the wrongful interference, then it seems only right that if they *do* in fact take such steps, they should be able to recover the cost of doing so from the person responsible for the danger.[110] This would appear to be the rationale of the rule permitting recovery of reasonable expenditure intended to mitigate the consequences of a wrong, which has been described as a corollary of the avoidable loss rule,[111] and it is hard to see why it should make a difference whether the measures are taken to avert a threatened wrong or to minimise the consequences of a wrong that has already taken place. We should however note that this argument is somewhat undermined by the fact that (unlike the mitigation doctrine) contributory negligence is a defence limited to certain torts – most notably negligence – and yet the intuitive appeal of preventive damages awards is more general, and a rule restricting their recovery to those torts would be hard to stomach.[112]

Turning from principle to policy, an obvious *policy* argument in favour of awarding preventive damages is that doing so serves to encourage those threatened with wrongful injury to take reasonable steps to reduce or eliminate the danger when best placed to do so – this being in the interests of everyone involved, not least the potential tortfeasor – whereas refusing such claims creates an incentive for them to sit back and wait for the injury to occur.[113] This looks to be a powerful argument, although it should be remembered that potential victims of wrongs are also incentivised to take reasonable care for their own safety by the instinct for self-preservation, and by the rules on contributory negligence and legal causation.[114]

---

[110] This connection is made in, eg, *Restatement, Second, Torts* (1977) § 919, comment a; and von Bar, *Principles of European Law on Non-Contractual Liability Arising out of Damage Caused to Another* (n 3) art 6:302, comment 1.

[111] *New Zealand Forest Products* (n 12) 83; McGregor (n 9) para 9-096.

[112] See, eg, *Restatement, Second, Torts* (1977) § 919, comment a.

[113] See, eg, *Winnipeg Condominium* (n 59) 120; *Dovuro* (n 80) 514. As we have seen (text to n 73), the need to encourage early detection of harmful health conditions caused by negligent conduct has been a key rationale for the award of medical monitoring damages by the US courts. It has also been argued that awards of preventive damages are justified by the need to deter dangerous conduct in the first place (see, eg, *Rivtow Marine* (n 43) 1221–22 (Laskin J); *Winnipeg Condominium* (n 59) 128 (La Forest J)), but this is an argument for negligence liability generally, not an argument for preventive damages in particular.

[114] This argument is also subject to a more general objection to deterrence-based arguments in the tort context, namely that they rest on the (usually false) assumption that the actors in question are conversant with the relevant legal principles.

A rule allowing recovery of preventive damages seems attractive, therefore, but can such recovery be reconciled with general tort principles? After all, does it not amount to an award of damages for a wrong that was threatened but never actually committed?[115] In this section of the article I identify and assess a number of possible ways in which awards of preventive damages might be reconciled with [89] general tort principles. Unfortunately, none of the potential solutions is straightforward.

A. Pure Economic Loss in Negligence

The first potential solution is to rationalise recovery of preventive damages as an exceptional instance of recovery of pure economic loss in negligence. After all, it would appear that recovery of preventive expenditure is seen as unproblematic in those continental legal systems, such as France and Spain, that take a liberal approach towards tort claims for pure economic loss.

However, it would be a mistake to think that a pure economic loss rationale offers a simple answer to the doctrinal challenge posed by claims for preventive damages. There are at least two difficulties. One is that recovery of preventive damages as pure economic loss may be difficult to square (either generally, or in a specific case) with the principles governing recovery of such loss in the negligence law of a particular jurisdiction: in English negligence law, for example, such loss is generally recoverable only where there has been a relevant assumption of responsibility by the defendant towards the claimant. This connects up with the fact that, for some tort scholars, recovery for pure economic loss in negligence is justifiable only where there has been a prior undertaking of the defendant,[116] so that for these scholars the extension of pure economic loss recovery to preventive damages claims would require some distinctive doctrinal rationale. And the other (perhaps intractable) difficulty with this rationalisation of preventive damages recovery is that a principle allowing such recovery ought ideally to be capable of extending to reasonable expenditure incurred in preventing any threatened wrong – including, for example, nuisance and trespass – and yet this rationalisation covers only cases where the threatened wrong would give rise to liability for negligence.

---

[115] A possible objection to this starting point is that in these cases B has wronged A by exposing her to an unreasonable risk of injury, and indeed Laskin J suggested in *Rivtow Marine* (n 43) 1220–21 that by putting a dangerously defective chattel into circulation the defendant had breached a duty of care owed to potential users of the chattel. However, this objection assumes that the wrong underlying negligence law is unreasonable risk creation, when in fact it is negligently causing injury (see D Nolan, 'Deconstructing the Duty of Care' (2013) 129 *LQR* 559, 561–63). For some other difficulties with this objection, see M Moran, 'Rethinking *Winnipeg Condominium*: Restitution, Economic Loss, and Anticipatory Repairs' (1997) 47 *University of Toronto Law Journal* 115, 130–33.

[116] See, eg, A Beever, *Rediscovering the Law of Negligence* (Oxford, Hart Publishing, 2007) ch 7; R Stevens, *Torts and Rights* (Oxford, OUP, 2007) ch 3.

B. 'Pre-emptive Right' or 'Extended Right'

A second possible response to the doctrinal challenge can be found in the writings of Peter Benson, who has sought to justify recovery of preventive damages (which he labels 'unavoidable economic loss') by arguing that despite the absence of actual physical injury to A's person or property, the cost of precautionary measures:

> [R]epresents a loss resulting from interference with [A's] person or property ... if, but *only* if, it is for a loss that arises unavoidably from the effort to prevent or mitigate the materialisation of a threatened injury to [A's] person or property.[117]

He continues:

> In these circumstances, the gravamen of the plaintiff's complaint is that his or her person or property be left alone by the defendant, in accordance with ordinary tort principles. The plaintiff claims no other right than that of [90] excluding the defendant from injuring his or her person or property without his or her consent. The fact that the plaintiff suffers loss, whether physical or purely financial, in the process of attempting to thwart or mitigate such interference does not change the fundamental legal character of the claim.[118]

There seem to be two different ways of conceptualising Benson's analysis. The first (which we might term the 'pre-emptive right' rationale) is to say that although in cases of this kind there has not actually been a wrongful interference with A's right to property or bodily integrity, that right nevertheless grounds an action to recover expenses unavoidably incurred in preventing such a wrongful interference, much as the right to use and enjoyment of land grounds the claim for an injunction against future interference in a private nuisance case. And the second (which we might call the 'extended right' rationale) is to say that at least some threats of damage to our property and person themselves constitute wrongful interferences with our rights to property and bodily integrity, so that reasonable expenses incurred in dealing with such threats are recoverable, in the usual way, as losses caused by a wrong.[119] (And if this second approach

---

[117] P Benson, 'The Basis and Limits of Tort Recovery for General Average Contribution Economic Loss' (2008) 16 *Torts Law Journal* 1, 18.

[118] ibid 19. See also Benson, 'Economic Loss in Tort Law' (n 37) 437–44. For a similar analysis, drawing on Benson's, see R Brown, 'Justifying the Impossibility of Recoverable Relational Economic Loss' (2005) 5 *Oxford University Commonwealth Law Journal* 155, 170–78.

[119] The two quotations from Benson reproduced above suggest an ambivalence as between these two possibilities, since while the former refers to 'a loss *resulting from interference*' with A's person or property, the latter refers to loss incurred 'in the process of *attempting to thwart or mitigate*' such interference. However, other statements in the same article appear consistent with the second analysis: see Benson, 'The Basis and Limits of Tort Recovery for General Average Contribution Economic Loss' (n 117) 9 ('fully actionable loss arising from wrongful interference with one's protected interests'), 12 ('a loss resulting from injury to [A's] exclusive proprietary right'), 18 (A 'must show that the payment represents a loss resulting from interference with his or her person or property').

seems counter-intuitive, recall that intentionally causing a person to fear imminent unlawful physical contact constitutes the tort of assault, even if no actual contact ensues, so that the right to bodily integrity seems to extend 'beyond one's body to protect one from the *apprehension* of unwanted physical contact'.[120])

As between these two alternative ways of rationalising Benson's argument for allowing recovery of preventive damages, there are good reasons for preferring the 'pre-emptive right' rationale to the 'extended right' rationale. One reason is that holding that all threats of damage to our person and property violate our rights *does* appear counter-intuitive (indeed downright implausible), and yet any attempt to distinguish those threats that do violate our rights from those that do not seems fraught with difficulty.[121] And another reason is that, if the correct analysis is that the threat of damage is sometimes itself wrongful, then that opens up various cans of worms, such as (1) whether in such cases a claim for nominal damages should lie, even if no preventive expenses are incurred; (2) whether all foreseeable losses caused by the threat should be recoverable, above and beyond reasonable preventive expenditure; (3) when precisely the 'wrong' occurs in a preventive damages action, which will have implications for the limitation analysis;[122] and (4) whether, where [91] there is both a wrongful threat and then subsequently a wrongful injury, there is one wrong, not two, so that if for example A recovers medical monitoring costs, a later claim for the onset of cancer would be barred by a defence of *res judicata*.[123]

Two final points should be made about Benson's analysis. One is that there is a difficulty with the 'pre-emptive right' rationale where A's failure to avert the threatened injury would have constituted a *novus actus interveniens*. In such a case, A's expenditure does not seem necessary to avert a *wrongful* interference with A's person or property, since had A not incurred the expenditure that inaction would have rendered the interference non-tortious. And the other point is that it has been argued that preventive damages ought to be recoverable in at least some cases where the claimant reasonably believed that there was a threat, but it turns out that there was no actual threat after all, and if that is right then recovery in this type of case would need to be reconciled with the 'pre-emptive right' or the 'extended right' rationale.

---

[120] Beever (n 116) 460.

[121] One basis on which such a distinction could be drawn would be the imminence of the threat. However, although this would mesh nicely with the tort of assault, it has been argued above that recovery of preventive damages should not be subject to a requirement of imminence, and so for present purposes it would be undesirable to use this as the determinative criterion.

[122] This is because it would seem to follow from the 'extended right' analysis that the wrong is committed (and hence the cause of action is complete) when the threat first arises, rather than when expenses are incurred in obviating it.

[123] For an argument to this effect in the medical monitoring context, see *Miranda v Shell Oil Co* 17 Cal App 4th 1651 (Cal Ct App 1993) 1658–59. cf *Ayers* (n 68) 311 (where it is argued that the problem does not arise because there are two separate causes of action). It might be possible for an English court to get round this problem by making a provisional damages award in the medical monitoring litigation: see Senior Courts Act 1981, s 32A.

C. *Negotiorum Gestio* or Unjust Enrichment

Another possibility is that the rationale for recovery of preventive damages lies outside the law of tort altogether, either in the civilian doctrine of *negotiorum gestio*, or in the law of unjust enrichment. However, neither explanation is convincing.

The *negotiorum gestio* rationale would be that by taking the preventive measures in question A has relieved B of a potential liability, and that as the beneficiary of this 'necessitous intervention' B ought to reimburse A for the expenditure incurred. There are three reasons why this explanation fails. First, the common law does not recognise any general right to recompense in cases of necessitous intervention.[124] Secondly, because the *negotiorum gestio* doctrine is generally considered to be based on a policy of encouraging beneficial intervention,[125] it is a condition of recovery under that doctrine that A act with the predominant intention of benefiting B,[126] and so it is inapplicable where (as here) A is motivated by self-preservation.[127] And finally, if A's failure to act would have amounted to a *novus actus interveniens*, then A's action is not capable of relieving B of any potential liability after all.

An unjust enrichment rationale for the recovery of preventive damages in the collapsing condominium case has been put forward by Mayo Moran[128] and endorsed by Robert Stevens, with the latter arguing that in this scenario A is 'compelled by [92] necessity' to incur the expenditure necessary to make the premises safe, and that B would otherwise have had to incur this expenditure 'in order to avoid the potentially much larger liability for personal injuries from accruing'.[129] Again, however, this suggestion runs into difficulties, particularly where (as is our present concern) the threat averted by the expenditure was to the claimant, as opposed to a third party.

First, there are problems with the claim that A's preventive expenditure enriches B. Moran claims that A's preventive action discharges a duty of B to make the building safe (thereby relieving B of a legally necessary expenditure),[130]

---

[124] See C Mitchell et al, *Goff & Jones on the Law of Unjust Enrichment*, 8th edn (London, Sweet & Maxwell, 2011) para 18-02; J Kortmann, *Altruism in Private Law: Liability for Nonfeasance and Negotiorum Gestio* (Oxford, OUP, 2005) 115; von Bar, *Principles of European Law on Benevolent Intervention in Another's Affairs* (n 108) 77.

[125] See Kortmann (n 124) ch 9.

[126] von Bar, *Principles of European Law on Benevolent Intervention in Another's Affairs* (n 108) art 1:101. See, eg, § 687(1) BGB (acts undertaken *for* another).

[127] von Bar, *Principles of European Law on Benevolent Intervention in Another's Affairs* (n 108) art 1:101, comment 19. For this reason, the Study Group on a European Civil Code specifically rejected this doctrine as the rationale for recovery of preventive damages: von Bar, *Principles of European Law on Non-Contractual Liability Arising out of Damage Caused to Another* (n 3) art 6:302, comment 2.

[128] Moran (n 115).

[129] Stevens (n 116) 31–32.

[130] Moran (n 115) 135.

but it is not clear why she believes that B is under a duty to repair in this case: if B is, then why does A not simply seek a mandatory injunction requiring B to carry out the repairs? At first blush, Moran's alternative argument that B is enriched by being relieved of a possible future liability to A for personal injury or property damage seems more promising. However, this enrichment is still highly specula-tive, since even if we are sure that the building will collapse – and we may well not be – we have no way of knowing whether A will suffer personal injury or property damage when it does, or whether the quantum of those claims would exceed the cost of repair. And while it is clear that a saved *inevitable* expense would count as an enrichment for these purposes,[131] extension of that concept to a saved *possible* expense (or even a saved *probable* expense) is controversial.[132] Finally, Moran fails to advert to the possibility that the continued occupation of the building by A would constitute a *novus actus interveniens* that would relieve B of that possible future liability in any case.[133]

Besides, even if we assume that B is enriched, it is unlikely that the enrichment would qualify as 'unjustified' on the English authorities. The argument seems to be that there is some kind of *compulsion* on A to incur the expenditure,[134] but this argument requires us to go well beyond the existing circumstances in which compulsion renders an enrichment unjust. The ground of unjust enrich-ment known as 'legal compulsion', for example, requires that A enrich B by discharging a liability of B to a third party under legal compulsion exercised or exercisable by that third party[135] but that is hardly the scenario here, where there is no third party and no existing (as opposed to future) liability of B discharged by A, and where in any case A is not legally compelled to act, being under no duty to do so.[136] Nor does the ground of unjust enrichment known variously as 'moral compulsion' or 'necessity' (and closely connected to the civilian *nego-tiorum gestio*) apply, because [93] A's expenditure is not incurred to preserve *another's* health or property, as this ground requires.[137]

---

[131] See, eg, A Burrows, *A Restatement of the English Law of Unjust Enrichment* (Oxford, OUP, 2012) s 7(3)(a).

[132] See D Stevens, '*The Regional Municipality of Peel v Canada*' (1994) 73 *Canadian Bar Review* 84, 97–98.

[133] It might be argued that the enrichment analysis is more convincing in the forest fire case, since there the probability of damage absent the preventive measures is very high, but even there it is doubtful whether it would often be possible to say that liability was otherwise *inevitable*, and the *novus actus* difficulty remains.

[134] See, eg, Moran (n 115) 139 ('wrongful compulsion'), 150 ('compelled by law'); Stevens (n 116) 31 ('compelled by necessity').

[135] See Burrows, *Restatement* (n 131) s 18.

[136] At one point, Moran claims that the plaintiffs in the *Winnipeg Condominium* and *Rivtow Marine* cases were 'charged with a duty to take steps to prevent the threatened harm' (Moran (n 115) 139), but any such duty must surely be predicated on a threat to third parties, rather than to the plaintiff's own interests.

[137] As to 'moral compulsion', see P Birks, *An Introduction to the Law of Restitution*, revised edn (Oxford, OUP, 1989) 193; as to 'necessity', see Burrows, *Restatement* (n 131) s 19.

And a final difficulty with the unjust enrichment rationale is that I have argued that preventive damages ought to be recoverable in cases where the danger is not real but is reasonably perceived, and where the preventive measures are reasonable but unsuccessful, and yet this would be particularly hard to square with unjust enrichment principles.

D. An Affirmative Duty to Rescue

Finally, we should note John Goldberg and Benjamin Zipursky's argument that B's obligation to meet A's expenses in the medical monitoring case is a manifestation of a principle that a person who has imperiled another comes under an affirmative primary duty to take reasonable steps to prevent the risk materialising and causing the other injury.[138] It follows that in these cases A is not seeking damages for a past wrong, but (in effect) an injunction requiring B to perform this primary duty by paying for A's medical monitoring, which seems consistent with the fact that US courts have generally ordered defendants to establish funds to meet plaintiffs' future monitoring costs, rather than awarding lump-sum damages.

The most important point to note about this argument for present purposes is that it is a rationale, not for the recovery of preventive damages per se, but for the grant of a particular type of injunctive relief in cases where A is threatened with harm by B's past conduct. And of course injunctive relief of this kind can offer a solution only where the preventive expenditure has not yet been incurred, as in the medical monitoring case, and possibly also in the collapsing crane and collapsing condominium cases. It is of no use to A if A must take the preventive measures before going to court because the danger is imminent, as in the forest fire and frozen food cases.

Even in cases where the preventive measures in question have not yet been taken, justifying recovery of the cost of those measures by reference to an 'affirmative duty of rescue' principle is by no means straightforward. For a start, the line of authority Goldberg and Zipursky draw upon does not provide a strong foundation for such recovery. Examples of the sort of cases that they have in mind are those where liability has been imposed on a manufacturer for injury caused by a negligent failure to alert past customers to a danger posed by goods that came to light only after they were marketed, or on an employer who failed to advise employees to undergo appropriate screening after discovering that they had been exposed to carcinogenic substances in the course of their employment, even though in neither case was the defendant to blame for the original danger.[139] However, the preventive

---

[138] J Goldberg and B Zipursky, 'Unrealized Torts' (2002) 88 *Virginia Law Review* 1625, 1701–15.
[139] *Hobbs (Farms) Ltd v The Baxenden Chemical Co Ltd* [1992] 1 Lloyd's Rep 54 (QBD); *Wright v Dunlop Rubber Co Ltd* (1972) 13 KIR 255 (CA).

measures expected of 'innocent' defendants such as these have been very limited ones – usually just to give warnings – and so it is quite a stretch from these cases to holding that a defendant at fault for creating a danger is subject to a much more onerous obligation to meet the cost of the measures required to [94] obviate that danger. Moreover, it is a feature of all these cases that the claimant was unable to protect themselves from the risk created by the defendant's conduct, whereas the whole point of the scenarios under discussion in this article is that A *is* able to do this, albeit at A's own expense. Another difficulty with Goldberg and Zipursky's explanation is that the dominant view among tort scholars seems to be that the primary duty underlying negligence law is a duty not negligently to injure, as opposed to a duty to take care,[140] an analysis which, as Nicholas McBride (a prominent critic of that view) has pointed out, is impossible to square with an affirmative primary duty of rescue enforceable by injunctive relief.[141] Finally, it seems unlikely that Goldberg and Zipursky's rationale for the recovery of preventive expenditure extends beyond instances of negligent risk-creation to threatened wrongs governed by a stricter liability regime.

VI. PREVENTIVE EXPENDITURE INCURRED BY A THIRD PARTY

A final point worth mentioning concerns cases where the preventive expenditure is incurred not by A but by a third party (X). Suppose for example that in the medical monitoring case, A's medical expenses are paid by a wealthy relative, or that in the forest fire case the fire is put out by the local fire service, at no cost to A. Since it has been argued that preventive damages actions should be grounded on actual preventive expenditure by A (and not on the *need* for such expenditure), it follows that A ought not to have a claim in this situation. The complication comes, however, when A is obliged to reimburse X for X's expenditure, for example by way of a contribution in general average. Since the cost of reimbursing X is not a cost A incurs in order to prevent damage to A's person or property, it seems that A ought not to be able to recover that sum from B as preventive damages. Note, however, that the 'extended right' rationale for recovery of preventive damages may entail a different conclusion here, since if the threatened interference is itself considered to amount to a violation of A's right to bodily integrity or property, then the expense A incurs in reimbursing X ought potentially to be recoverable as a loss flowing from that wrong.[142]

---

[140] See n 115. Indeed, Zipursky himself appears to subscribe to this view: see B Zipursky, 'Foreseeability in Breach, Duty, and Proximate Cause' (2009) 44 *Wake Forest Law Review* 1247, 1272.

[141] NJ McBride, 'Duties of Care: Do they Really Exist?' (2004) 24 *OJLS* 417, 428–29.

[142] This may explain why Benson argues that the rule that one who makes a general average contribution can recover it from a defendant who negligently created the peril that required the general average sacrifice or expenditure in the first place (*Morrison Steamship Co v Greystoke Castle (Cargo Owners) (The Greystoke Castle)* [1947] AC 265 (HL)) falls within his version of the preventive

VII. CONCLUSION

In this article I have considered the circumstances in which A can and should be permitted to recover from B expenses incurred in preventing B's conduct from resulting in a wrongful interference with A's person or property. I have identified and discussed a number of example cases that squarely raise this issue. In some [95] of these cases, the argument for recovery seems very strong. In others, it turns out that the claims are not properly analysed as claims for preventive damages, or other complications with the possibility of allowing recovery emerge. I have also discussed the test of reasonableness that is likely to act as a general limit on the recovery of preventive damages, and identified a number of issues that test may not resolve. Finally, I have highlighted the conceptual difficulties posed by claims for preventive damages and put forward some possible rationales for their recovery. I hope thereby to have shed some light on an issue of considerable practical and theoretical significance which has been the subject of surprisingly little analysis by common law scholars.

damages principle, though he muddies the waters a little with his (surely false) claim that in this scenario A suffers loss '*in the process of* attempting to thwart or mitigate' wrongful interference by B with A's property (Benson, 'The Basis and Limits of Tort Recovery for General Average Contribution Economic Loss' (n 117) 19 (emphasis added)). Smillie (n 37) also argues (at 248) that this rule falls within the preventive damages principle, but appears to conflate a general average *expense* (which he rightly describes as 'an extraordinary expense incurred to preserve ship and cargo from a situation of peril'), with a general average *contribution* (which surely does not fit this definition).

13

Rights, Damage and Loss

(2017) 37 *Oxford Journal of Legal Studies* 255–275

[255] A farmer had a horse, which ran away. Upon hearing the news, his neighbours sympathized, saying, 'This is such bad luck. Without a horse, your work will be much harder'. The famer replied, 'Maybe good, maybe bad. We shall see'.

The next day, the farmer's horse returned, bringing with it three wild horses. 'How lucky you are', his neighbours said, 'With four horses, the work on your farm will be much easier'. The farmer replied, 'Maybe good, maybe bad. We shall see'.

The next day, one of the wild horses kicked the farmer's only son, breaking his leg. His neighbours said, 'This is terrible. Now you will have to make do without your son's help until his leg recovers'. The farmer replied, 'Maybe good, maybe bad. We shall see.'

Shortly afterwards, a war broke out, and officials came to the farmer's village to draft all the young men into the army. Seeing that the farmer's son had a broken leg, they passed him by. The farmer's neighbours said to him, 'You are so fortunate! All the other young men will surely die.' The farmer replied, 'Maybe good, maybe bad. We shall see.'[1]

[256] I. INTRODUCTION

THIS ARTICLE IS an exploration of the relationship between the concepts of rights, damage and loss. The focus of the analysis is on the law of negligence, though some of the claims have wider ramifications. The article is divided into three main parts, with each part centred around a different relationship: first, the relationship between rights and damage; second, the relationship between rights and loss; and third, the relationship between damage and loss. In each of these three parts, a separate, but related, claim is made: (1) that a concept of damage is a necessary component of a plausible rights-based conception of negligence law; (2) that a right not to suffer loss is conceptually impossible; and (3) that damage and loss are fundamentally different

---

[1] This is an old Taoist story, also told by Zen Buddhists. The details of the story vary, but the message does not. See further H-G Moeller, *The Philosophy of the Daodejing* (New York, Columbia UP, 2006) esp ch 7.

concepts. Although these claims (or at least some of them) may appear to be radical ones, I hope to show that the truth of all of the claims is in fact rather obvious. Nevertheless, the claims are not unimportant, since a stronger grasp of the relationship between the concepts of rights, damage and loss will help to clarify our understanding, not only of negligence law, but of private law more generally.

Since a persistent theme of this article is the importance of terminology, I should begin by laying out working definitions of the three concepts at which I will be looking. When I refer to 'rights' in this article, then, I mean claim rights in the Hohfeldian sense of legal rights that correlate with legal duties,[2] such as a right not to be punched on the nose or to have the other party to a contract perform her contractual obligations. Clarifying the meaning of 'damage' is one of the central aims of the article, but suffice to say for now that when I refer to 'damage' I have in mind a certain kind of interference with a person's protected interests – paradigmatically either bodily or mental injury, or property damage – such as would ground a claim in negligence. Finally, by 'loss' I mean 'an abstract concept of being worse off', such that the suffering of a loss amounts to a 'detrimental difference' to the person who suffers it.[3]

[257] Staying with terminology for a moment, I should explain why I have chosen to focus my attention on damage and loss, as opposed to the not dissimilar concepts of 'harm' and 'injury'. The short answer is that I think it easier to ascribe meanings to the words 'damage' and 'loss' that correspond with the use of those terms in everyday language and that make for concepts that can play a useful role in explaining and understanding negligence law. By contrast, it seems to me that as generally understood the terms 'harm' and 'injury' lack the potential to make for useful concepts in this particular context.[4] This is not an

---

[2] WN Hohfeld, 'Some Fundamental Legal Conceptions as Applied in Judicial Reasoning' (1913) 23 *Yale Law Journal* 16, 32.

[3] Ironically, I have borrowed both these phrases from judicial definitions not of 'loss', but of 'damage': see respectively *Rothwell v Chemical & Insulating Co Ltd* [2007] UKHL 39, [2008] 1 AC 281 [7] (Lord Hoffmann) and *Tabet v Gett* [2010] HCA 12, 240 CLR 537 [66] (Hayne and Bell JJ). *cf* A Tettenborn, 'What is a Loss?' in J Neyers et al (eds), *Emerging Issues in Tort Law* (Oxford, Hart Publishing, 2007) 443 ('When we say someone has suffered a loss, we instinctively contemplate her being worse off in some factual, verifiable sense'); R Stevens, *Torts and Rights* (Oxford, OUP, 2007) 59, 78 (defining 'loss' in terms of being 'factually worse off'). As will become apparent, one of the central claims in this article is underpinned by the observation that whether a person has suffered loss in this sense cannot definitively be determined at any given moment in time (see text following n 32). This caused a referee to observe that I was defining loss as 'the condition of being worse off over one's whole life', and that this was not a definition of loss that it could sensibly be suggested the law should adopt. I agree with the characterisation of my definition of loss but am unclear as to why it is thought to be problematic. Of course, if the legal process reaches the conclusion that a person has suffered loss as I have defined it, this means only that at the relevant time (such as the time of trial) it *looks as if* the person is going to be worse off in this global sense, so that here 'loss' really means 'apparent loss', as judged at that time. But there is nothing particularly surprising or troubling about this, for *any* conclusion reached by the legal process is inevitably based on the circumstances as they appear at the relevant time.

[4] Of course, it does not follow that they cannot make for perfectly useful concepts in *other* contexts, as where it is said that a football player is 'recovering from injury', or when reference is made to the 'harm principle' in discussion of the appropriate limits of the criminal law.

easy claim to substantiate, but I would maintain that the central difficulty with using 'harm' and 'injury' when discussing negligence law is that as generally understood these terms produce concepts too broad to be used to draw helpful distinctions in this context. To take a simple example, it seems to me implausible to say that a sleeping person lightly kissed by a stranger has suffered either 'damage' or 'loss', but perfectly plausible to say that the kiss amounts to 'harm' or 'injury', since the word 'harm' can be said to encompass any significant interference with an important human interest[5] (including dignitary interests), while one well-known meaning of the word 'injury' when used legally is 'the violation of another's legal right'.[6] Put simply, then, my claim is that for a negligence lawyer the terminology of 'damage' and 'loss' is simply more useful – because more discriminating – than the terminology of 'harm' and 'injury'.

II. RIGHTS AND DAMAGE

The argument of this part of the article is that a concept of damage is a necessary component of a plausible rights-based analysis of negligence law. There are two reasons why this claim needs to be made. The first is that some rights theorists have sought to relegate the damage requirement in negligence cases from an element of the wrong itself to a condition of the wrong's actionability. And the second reason is that even rights theorists who have not explicitly adopted this approach have nevertheless either expressed scepticism about the damage requirement, or simply ignored it altogether.

The first of these two responses appears to represent a minority view, but the view seems to have some traction, and has forcefully been expressed by Nicholas McBride and Roderick Bagshaw.[7] At root, the issue is whether the wrong in negligence consists of exposing others to unreasonable risks of certain [258] kinds of interference with their bodily integrity, property and so forth, or whether it consists of negligently causing such interference to occur. On the latter view, where the interference is constitutive of the wrong itself, the question of precisely what interference is required (the essence of the 'damage' requirement) is central to the analysis; on the former view, by contrast, that question is less important, since at most it goes only to the *actionability* of a wrong the existence of which is independently determined. I have previously argued that for various reasons the former view, which equates to saying that we all have rights good against everyone else not to be exposed to certain kinds of risks,

---

[5] For a definition along these lines, see S Perry, 'Torts, Rights and Risk' in J Oberdiek (ed), *Philosophical Foundations of the Law of Torts* (Oxford, OUP, 2014) 54. Revealingly, Perry describes 'harm' as a 'relatively specific *moral* concept' (ibid, emphasis added).

[6] See, eg, BA Garner (ed), *Black's Law Dictionary*, 10th edn (St Paul, Minn, Thomson West, 2014) 905.

[7] NJ McBride and R Bagshaw, *Tort Law*, 5th edn (Harlow, Pearson Education, 2015) esp ch 5.

is impossible to accept,[8] and there is nothing to be gained by repeating those arguments here. Note, however, that even on the former view a damage concept is required, certainly for one reason, and possibly for two. The incontrovertible reason a damage concept is required is that the existence of the duty to act with reasonable care that (on this view) underpins negligence law depends on showing that it was reasonably foreseeable that the defendant's actions would result in the claimant suffering (as appropriate) physical injury or psychiatric illness, or damage to property in which the claimant had a sufficient interest at the time it was damaged.[9] And the other reason why damage may still be relevant on this view is that it may determine the actionability of the wrong constituted by the defendant's unreasonable conduct, though whether this is in fact the case depends on what McBride and Bagshaw mean when they refer to actionable 'loss' or actionable 'harm'.[10]

The more prevalent view among rights theorists is that the wrong in a negligence case is negligently injuring another person, and on this view the occurrence of 'injury' or 'damage' is therefore central to the defendant's wrongdoing – and hence also to the characterisation of the right violated by that wrongdoing. Nevertheless, there is little or no acknowledgement of the damage concept in the writings of these scholars, and there is a marked tendency to use the word 'injury' instead of 'damage', but then to confuse matters by also using the same word as a synonym for 'wrong'. For the sake of brevity, the discussion of this view will be limited to the work of two of the most prominent rights theorists who have subjected the law of negligence to sustained analysis, namely Allan Beever and Robert Stevens.

Beginning with Stevens, we find that he does acknowledge the damage concept as here understood, but then expresses scepticism, not about the concept itself, but about the language of 'damage' as employed in this context. His position is encapsulated in the following passage: [**259**]

> [F]or those who conceive of property damage and injury to person as species of loss ... the requirement of showing damage is not a requirement of showing injury but one of showing harm, so that the right disappears from the story. The slippery language of 'damage' elides the distinction between injury and consequential harm.[11]

Stevens then elaborates his claim that the language of damage is 'slippery' by citing a judicial definition of damage as 'an abstract concept of being worse off, physically or economically',[12] a definition that I have used as a definition

---

[8] D Nolan, 'Deconstructing the Duty of Care' (2013) 129 *LQR* 559, 561–64.

[9] See McBride and Bagshaw (n 7) ch 6. Hence McBride and Bagshaw do in fact discuss what counts as 'harm' to property, but only for the purposes of the *duty* analysis in property damage cases (ibid 165–75).

[10] For their discussion of actionability, see ibid ch 10.

[11] R Stevens, 'Rights and Other Things' in D Nolan and A Robertson (eds), *Rights and Private Law* (Oxford, Hart Publishing, 2012) 121.

[12] ibid, citing Lord Hofmann's definition in *Rothwell* (n 3).

of 'loss'. Unpicking this passage, we can see that Stevens equates 'harm' with (in my terminology) 'loss', and that he equates the word 'injury' with (in some sense) 'wrongfulness', such that disposing of the requirement of 'injury' entails abandoning a rights-based analysis. Finally, the language of 'damage' is seen as hovering uncertainly between 'injury' and 'loss'. Setting aside the appropriateness of equating 'harm' with 'loss', we are apparently left with an acceptance of the importance of a concept of 'injury' or 'damage' encapsulated in the opening reference to 'property damage and injury to person', but also with a clear preference for the word 'injury' over the word 'damage' as a way of capturing this concept.

Since my claim here is that a concept of 'damage' is an essential component of any plausible rights-based analysis of negligence law, it appears that my only disagreement with Stevens' position is semantic, since he seems to accept the claim, but simply prefers the language of 'injury' to that of 'damage'. Nevertheless, the need for clear and precise language is a central theme of this article, and so the semantics matter. So, which word better captures the concept in play, 'injury' or 'damage'? To my mind, the answer is the latter, since for me 'injury' is the slippery word here, not 'damage'. Recall that in its legal senses the word 'injury' has two possible meanings: the 'violation of another's legal right' (ie, a wrong) or 'harm or damage'.[13] It follows that in the negligence context it is actually the word 'injury' that is hovering uncertainly between two meanings, namely 'wrong' and 'damage'. Nor can Stevens respond to this slipperiness by saying that at least *for him* 'injury' has a specific meaning, because in his own use of the word he flits between these two alternative meanings.[14] In the passage reproduced above, for example, the two later uses of the word 'injury' seem to connote a wrong, while elsewhere in the same essay Stevens says that the duty in negligence is 'a duty not to injure, and not a duty not to expose to the risk of injury',[15] a claim that would be very odd if the word 'injury' meant 'wrong', but which makes perfect sense if it means [260] something like 'damage'. By contrast, although I would readily accept that the word 'damage' is sometimes treated in this context as synonymous with 'loss', this is attributable not to an inherent ambiguity in the general understanding of the word 'damage', but rather to a sloppiness of expression reflective of a broader failure to recognise the distinction between the concepts of loss and damage. Provided that distinction is acknowledged, and the appropriate language used accordingly, any ambiguity in the word 'damage' can easily be resolved.

Similar difficulties bedevil Beever's work. He seems to be trying studiously to avoid using the word 'damage' in his analysis of negligence law,[16] preferring (once again) to talk of 'injury'. However, like Stevens, Beever flits between the

---

[13] See *Black's Law Dictionary* (n 6) 905.

[14] I am not the first to point this out: see also NJ McBride, 'Rights and the Basis of Tort Law' in Nolan and Robertson (n 11) 363 fn.

[15] Stevens, 'Rights and Other Things' (n 11) 118.

[16] There is, however, at least one exception: see A Beever, *Rediscovering the Law of Negligence* (Oxford, Hart Publishing, 2007) 485 (where there is a passing reference to 'actionable damage').

two meanings of the word injury. In a central passage,[17] he argues that the true legal conception of injury is 'the violation of a legal right' (in other words, a wrong). But elsewhere in the same work Beever seems to use the word 'injury' in the more limited sense of damage or harm, as where he talks of whether the defendant caused 'the claimant's injury',[18] or when he says that, according to corrective justice, 'the issue is whether the appropriate normative connection exists between the defendant's negligence and the claimant's injury'.[19] As with Stevens, therefore, the semantic preference for 'injury' over 'damage' leads to confusion and ambiguity, and yet again the – this time implicit – rejection of the language of 'damage' seems not to reflect a rejection of an underlying concept of damage along the lines that I have outlined. (Beever readily acknowledges, for example, that to establish that the defendant committed a wrong, the claimant must show that the defendant '*damaged* something over which she had a right'.[20])

Two final points should be made about the relationship between rights and damage. The first is that one occasionally comes across instances where the word 'damage' is in effect being used (like 'injury') as a synonym for a rights violation, in other words a wrong.[21] Again, this kind of usage is to be deprecated, as when 'damage' is collapsed into 'wrong', the utility of the damage concept as a distinct element of the cause of action for negligence is lost.[22] And the second point is that intrinsic to the notion of damage in negligence is the idea that the damage is suffered *by someone* (so that we routinely refer to *the claimant's* damage). Now, this connection between the damage and the claimant clearly presents no difficulty when personal injury is involved: in such cases, *the claimant* suffers damage because it is her bodily integrity or mental [261] health that is impaired by the defendant's negligent conduct. However, in the case of property damage, the need to establish this connection between claimant and damage requires us to show not only that a particular item of property has suffered 'damage', in the sense of an impairment of its utility or value, but also that the claimant has a sufficient interest in the property in question.[23] While the issue of exactly *what* interest is required need not detain us here,[24] the fact that more than one person may have a sufficient interest to bring a claim in respect of damaged property – bailor *and* bailee, legal *and* equitable owner – shows us that 'damage' in this context is

---

[17] ibid 211.

[18] ibid 414.

[19] ibid 138.

[20] ibid 218 (emphasis added).

[21] The most famous example of this phenomenon is in *Ashby v White* (1703) 2 Ld Raym 938, 955; 92 ER 126, 137, where Holt CJ said that 'an injury imports a damage, when a man is thereby hindred [sic] of his right'.

[22] See similarly E Descheemaeker, *The Division of Wrongs: A Historical Comparative Study* (Oxford, OUP, 2009) 22 fn.

[23] See McBride and Bagshaw (n 7) 166–68.

[24] For a summary of the position, see WE Peel and J Goudkamp, *Winfield & Jolowicz on Tort*, 19th edn (London, Sweet & Maxwell, 2014) para 5-61.

a normative concept associated with a person, not a factual concept associated with a particular physical entity. In everyday parlance, we can certainly say that the claimant's body or car has been 'damaged', but the damage that grounds a negligence claim is the more intangible notion of a certain kind of interference with a person's protected interests.[25]

III. RIGHTS AND LOSS

In his book *Torts and Rights*, Robert Stevens stated that a right not to be caused economic loss could in theory be recognised and enforced by a legal system, while also making it clear that in his view such a right could not rightly be recognised by the courts, since doing so would inevitably require judges to answer policy questions that would take them beyond the 'political and technical limits placed upon judicial decision making'.[26] In a subsequent essay, however, Stevens took a different line, arguing that a right not to suffer loss was in fact a conceptual impossibility. His reasoning was as follows:

> A wrong, or injury, occurs in a moment of time, although some wrongs can be repeated, such as libel, or can be ongoing such as a trespass to land. D commits a civil wrong in relation to C whenever he breaches a duty to C not to do *x*. It is consequently meaningless to talk of a right not to be caused loss. If loss is suffered, it is a consequence of a breach of a duty; it cannot go to the definition of what D is under a duty to do or not to do.[27]

[262] Stevens' change of heart did not convince everyone. According to Nicholas McBride, his argument in the passage above does not work, as it does not follow from the fact that a wrong occurs in a moment of time that it is meaningless to talk of a right not to be caused loss. 'If A had a duty not to cause B loss', McBride argues, 'that duty would be breached exactly at the moment in time when A's actions first made B worse off'.[28] Furthermore, according to McBride,

---

[25] There is a parallel here with the French distinction between 'damage' as a factual concept and 'prejudice' as a legal concept, namely 'the consequence, in the juridical sphere, of damage' (C Quézel-Ambrunaz, 'Fault, Damage and the Equivalence Principle in French Law' (2012) 3 *Journal of European Tort Law* 21, 31). My argument is that the common law notion of damage is analogous to the French notion of 'prejudice'.

[26] Stevens, *Torts and Rights* (n 3) 337–38.

[27] Stevens, 'Rights and Other Things' (n 11) 119. Stevens may not have been the first person to make this claim, although (as far as I know) he was the first to make it explicitly. The impossibility of a right not to suffer loss may, for example, be thought to be implicit in some of the earlier work of Ernest Weinrib: see, eg, EJ Weinrib, *The Idea of Private Law* (Cambridge, Mass, Harvard UP, 1995) 132 ('As a matter of legal analysis, the fact that one person's action has made another worse off can never in itself be a basis for restoring the status quo ante'); and EJ Weinrib, 'The Disintegration of Duty' in MS Madden (ed), *Exploring Tort Law* (Cambridge, CUP, 2005) 159 ('harm [here apparently meaning 'loss'] considered in itself is not a notion from which one can, within the correlative structure of negligence law, impute a wrong').

[28] McBride (n 14) 363.

Stevens' argument is hard to reconcile with his insistence that the duty imposed by negligence law is a duty not to injure, and not to expose to the risk of injury, as (says McBride) 'a duty not to cause someone injury and a duty not to cause someone loss have exactly the same structure', and hence it is difficult to see why Stevens is prepared to accept that the first kind of duty can exist, but the second kind of duty cannot.[29] Similarly, in a review of the edited collection in which Stevens' essay was published, Sandy Steel said that he found the claim that a right not to suffer loss was conceptually impossible 'surprising', and that he suspected that 'many ... will be unconvinced by the idea that the concept of "loss" cannot – as a matter of conceptual fiat – enter into the specification of a person's primary legal rights or duties'.[30]

In this part of the article, I hope to demonstrate the truth of Stevens' claim that a right not to suffer loss is conceptually impossible, and to tease out some of the implications this has for the law of negligence, and indeed for private law more generally. The structure of my argument could not be simpler. It rests on two independent claims, from the truth of which the conclusion follows as a matter of logic. The claims are: (1) that a wrong (in other words, the violation of a right) occurs in a moment of time; and (2) that whether or not a person has suffered loss as a result of another's conduct cannot be determined at any given moment in time. It follows that the causing of loss cannot be a wrong, and hence that a right not to suffer loss is impossible.

The first of the two claims, that a wrong occurs in a moment of time, appears uncontroversial, and McBride does not challenge this claim in his critique of Stevens' argument. After all, it is surely right to conceive of a wrong as (in the words of Peter Birks) 'an event which happens in the world',[31] and an event which happens in the world obviously happens – or at least *starts* to happen – at a particular moment in time. Furthermore, we can point to legal doctrines that rest on the assumption that a wrong happens at a particular [263] moment in time, such as the principle in property torts that general damages are assessed by reference to the diminution in the value of the property at the time that the wrong occurred.[32]

Assuming, then, that the proposition that a wrong happens in a moment of time is accepted, we must turn to the second proposition, that whether or not a person has suffered loss as a result of another's conduct cannot be determined at any given moment in time. Recall that the working definition of loss that we are using is 'an abstract concept of being worse off', such that the suffering of a loss

---

[29] ibid 363–64.

[30] S Steel, 'Book Review' [2014] *CLJ* 466, 468. For an example of a commentator assuming the possibility of a right not to suffer loss in work predating Stevens' claim to the contrary, see D Priel, 'A Public Role for the Intentional Torts' (2011) 22 *King's Law Journal* 183, 198.

[31] P Birks, 'Rights, Wrongs and Remedies' (2000) 20 *OJLS* 1, 5. For a similar – though not identical – claim, see E Descheemaeker, 'Mapping Defamation Defences' (2015) 78 *MLR* 641, 646 ('any cause of action in tort is concerned with specific events happening in the real world').

[32] See, eg, *Coles v Hetherton* [2013] EWCA Civ 1704, [2015] 1 WLR 160 [27]–[29] (Aikens LJ).

amounts to a 'detrimental difference' to the person who suffers it. So the question we need to ask is whether it can be determined at any given moment in time that A's conduct has made B 'worse off'. Intuitively, we may feel that it is. Suppose, for example, that A's negligent driving causes an accident in which B's leg is broken. Can we not then say with some confidence at the time of the accident that A's conduct has left B worse off? In short, the answer is no: setting aside cases where A causes B's death (which raise difficulties that we need not engage with here[33]) it is never possible to say at any particular moment in time that A's conduct has left B worse off, because we can never know whether later events will affect the impact that A's conduct had on B's welfare. In the car accident case, for example, what if at the time of the accident B was driving to the airport to catch a plane that crashed on take-off, killing all those on board, so that B would almost certainly have been killed if A had not driven negligently? In this scenario, we might *think* in the immediate aftermath of the accident that A's conduct had made B worse off, but a later event (the plane crash) would falsify that belief.[34]

The impossibility of telling at any given moment whether A's conduct has left B worse off is nicely illustrated by the difficulties the courts have run into when trying to identify the time at which a claimant has suffered so-called 'damage' in negligence cases involving pure economic loss. In cases of this kind, the action is founded on the claim that A's negligence has left B financially worse off, where this financial loss is not the result of a separate wrong, such as negligently inflicted personal injury or property damage. No distinction can be drawn in such a case between damage and loss, so that if the concept of 'damage' is employed, it simply collapses into loss.[35] And since the **[264]** courts insist in these cases that, as elsewhere in negligence, the cause of action arises only when the claimant suffers 'damage', this means that for limitation purposes they must pinpoint the precise moment at which B became financially worse off as a result of A's conduct. However, for the reasons we have already identified, this is an impossible task, as there quite simply is no such moment. The result (unsurprisingly) has been a mass of confused and confusing case law on the limitation issue in economic loss cases, from which no clear principles have emerged.[36]

---

[33] One obvious difficulty is whether by killing someone you make that person 'worse off', since 'worse off' implies a comparison between two differing states of existence.

[34] For the example (and the point it so vividly makes), see EJ Weinrib, 'Right and Advantage in Private Law' (1989) 10 *Cardozo Law Review* 1283, 1283–84. There is one caveat that we need to add to the second proposition, which is that *at the moment of B's death* it may be possible to say that B has suffered loss as a result of A's conduct, since at that time it is no longer possible for any future events to alter the impact that A's conduct had on B's welfare. However, this caveat does not undermine the conclusion that a right not to suffer loss is conceptually impossible, since (as a matter of legal analysis, at any rate) it is not possible for A to wrong B if B no longer exists. I am grateful to John Mee for putting this point to me.

[35] For good examples of how damage collapses into loss in this type of case, see *DW Moore & Co Ltd v Ferrier* [1988] 1 WLR 267 (CA) 280 (Bingham LJ); and *Nykredit Mortgage Bank plc v Edward Erdman Group Ltd (No 2)* [1997] 1 WLR 1627 (HL) 1638–39 (Lord Hoffmann).

[36] See further on this case law, J O'Sullivan, 'The Meaning of "Damage" in Pure Financial Loss Cases: Contract and Tort Collide' (2012) 28 *Professional Negligence* 248; and R Walker, 'Pure

An example illustrates the problem. Suppose that A is a financial adviser who negligently advises B to invest his life savings in a high-risk investment fund, instead of advising him to build up a more diverse portfolio, with a mixture of high-risk and low-risk investments. In such a case, it is surely impossible to pinpoint any moment in time at which it becomes clear that B is worse off as a result. A month after he makes the investment, it might *seem as if* he is worse off, because his investment has fallen in value, but what if the fund then rebounds, so that after two months he stands to make a tidy profit?[37] And note that my claim is not merely that in *some* 'pure economic loss' cases it may be impossible to say at any given moment whether A's negligent conduct has made B financially worse off, but that it is *always* impossible to say this at any given moment. One scenario in which it might be thought clear that A's negligence has left B financially worse off is a disappointed beneficiary case, such as *White v Jones*,[38] where B, an intended beneficiary under a will, loses the intended legacy because solicitor A's negligence means that the testator's intentions are not carried into effect before the testator dies. However, even here it is possible to imagine circumstances in which A's negligence does not ultimately leave B worse off, as where the actual beneficiary under the will feels uncomfortable about receiving a legacy the testator intended for someone else, and so makes a gift of the relevant sum to B.

There are two objections that could be made to the proposition that whether or not B has suffered loss as a result of A's conduct cannot be determined at any given moment of time, but neither is persuasive. The first objection would be to say that in these cases we need to narrow down the 'loss' suffered by B in some way, so that in the car accident case, for example, we define the loss as the broken leg and the damaged car. Since nothing that happens after the accident can change the fact that B suffered a broken leg as a result of A's negligence, can we not now say at a particular moment in time that B has suffered loss as a result of A's negligence? Well of course we can indeed now [265] say that, but only because we are playing with words. The claim being made here is that *if* by 'suffering loss' we mean 'becoming worse off', *then* a right not to suffer loss is conceptually impossible, and that claim cannot be refuted by changing the meaning of 'suffering loss' to (in my terminology) 'sustaining damage'.

The second objection runs as follows. In both the car accident and the intended beneficiary cases, there may not be a given moment in time when we can say for sure that A's negligence has made B worse off, but surely there is a moment in time at which we can at least say that it is *highly likely* that it has.

Economic Loss: The Problem of Timing' (2012) 20 *Torts Law Journal* 77. And for judicial acknowledgement of the difficulties, see, eg, *Law Society v Sephton* [2006] UKHL 22, [2006] 2 AC 543 [10] (Lord Hoffmann).

[37] For an example along these lines from the case law on limitation of actions, see *Shore v Sedgwick Financial Services Ltd* [2008] EWCA Civ 863, esp [51]–[53] (Dyson LJ).

[38] *White v Jones* [1995] 2 AC 207 (HL).

And since civil law operates on a balance of probabilities standard of proof, why can we not just treat B as having suffered a loss at that moment, just as we would treat B as having suffered damage as a result of A's negligence even if it were not certain (but it *was* more likely than not) that he did? To see why this objection fails, we need to distinguish between what happens in the world and what we know about what happens in the world. Now, A's negligence either did or did not cause B's broken leg, but we may not *know* whether it did or not. In this case, it is perfectly proper to resolve the epistemic uncertainty with the use of a test such as the balance of probabilities standard. But the claim that is being made here is that a right not to suffer loss is impossible, because a rights violation (or wrong) happens in a moment of time, and at any given moment of time it can never be certain that A's conduct has *in fact* left B worse off. And whether *in fact* something happened in the world – as opposed to whether we are going to *treat* something as having happened in the world – is not a question that can be resolved on the balance of probabilities. Either it happened or it did not.

Furthermore, it is now clear that there is no bite in McBride's objections to Stevens' argument that a right not to suffer loss is impossible. Recall that his first objection was that it does not follow from the fact that a wrong occurs in a moment of time that it is meaningless to talk of a right not to be caused loss, as a duty not to cause B loss would be breached 'at the moment in time when A's actions first made B worse off'.[39] As we have seen, however, there quite simply is no such moment. Nor is there any force in McBride's other objection, which is that Stevens argues that the duty imposed by negligence law is a duty not to injure, and yet a duty not to cause injury and a duty not to cause loss 'have exactly the same structure', and so it is hard to see why one kind of duty can exist and the other kind of duty cannot.[40] We might first note that it is unclear why McBride thinks that it follows from the fact that two particular kinds of (purported) duty have the same *structure* that acceptance of the possibility of one entails acceptance of the possibility of the other. In any case, once it is appreciated that injury (in the sense of 'damage') and loss are very different [266] concepts, it becomes clear that there is no inconsistency in Stevens' position at all.

What, then, are the implications of the fact that a right not to suffer loss is a conceptual impossibility? A good place to start our consideration of this question might be to highlight three important limits to the claim being made. The first is that the claim concerns only what is capable of *being* a wrong (and, therefore, what is capable of *being* a right), and so there is nothing to stop the law from making the *actionability* of a wrong depend on whether at a given moment it looks as if the wrong has caused the claimant loss.[41] And indeed there are

---

[39] McBride (n 14) 363.
[40] ibid 363–64.
[41] See Stevens, 'Rights and Other Things' (n 11) 119 ('Loss is sometimes a necessary element of actionability, but it does not go to wrongfulness').

familiar examples of the law limiting the actionability of a wrong in this way, such as the rule that to sue in deceit you must show that the deceit has caused you loss, and the rule that slander is generally actionable only if the claimant has suffered 'special damage' (meaning financial loss, or loss capable of being estimated in money terms). As the actual wrong here happens in a moment of time – when the lie or slander is relevantly communicated – this technique is compatible with the claim that is being made, although in these cases the contingency inherent in the very concept of 'loss' may still give rise to difficulties, such as fixing the precise time at which the cause of action arises.

The second point that should be made about the limits of my claim is that the only type of right ruled out by the claim is a right not to suffer loss, where loss is defined as being 'worse off' in some way.[42] The claim therefore has no implications for the conceptual possibility of any other kind of right, and I am not seeking to place any other limits on the range of rights that might be recognised by the law. Hence a right that, for example, A not negligently cut off the power supply to B's factory[43] is not ruled out by the claim because in this case the occurrence of loss is not a defining feature of the wrong which is done if the right is violated, and so it is possible to pinpoint a precise moment at which that wrong occurs.[44] (Of course, this is not to say that such a right is desirable or even defensible: merely that it is *possible*.)

Finally, note that the claim I am making concerns only the range of *rights* that the law is capable of recognising, and not the range of *liabilities*.[45] There is nothing to stop the courts or Parliament laying down a liability rule under which the existence of a liability is contingent on B having suffered loss,[46] [**267**] because such a rule does not depend on the assumption that at any given moment of time B can be said to be worse off (in some definitive sense) as a result of A's conduct.[47]

Once these caveats are borne in mind, the implications of the claim that a right not to suffer loss is conceptually impossible become clearer. The most obvious implication is that there cannot be a right not to suffer so-called 'pure

---

[42] Though note that it also follows from my claim that a general right to be made *better* off is impossible: see n 48.

[43] See McBride (n 14) 338. *cf Anglian Water Services Ltd v Crawshaw Robbins & Co Ltd* [2001] BLR 173 (QBD) (interrupting the gas supply to a property is not actionable in private nuisance).

[44] For other examples of rights that would allow recovery in negligence for economic loss not consequential on personal injury or property damage, but which would not be ruled out by my claim, see R Bagshaw, 'The Edges of Tort Law's Rights' in Nolan and Robertson (n 11) 414–15.

[45] On the distinction between rights and liabilities, see D Nolan and A Robertson, 'Rights and Private Law' in Nolan and Robertson (n 11) 15–18.

[46] See, eg, Financial Services and Markets Act 2000, s 150 (making a breach of the rules regulating the financial services industry actionable at the suit of a private person who suffers loss as a result of the breach); Competition Act 1998, s 47A (allowing claims to recover financial losses caused by a breach of EU or domestic competition law).

[47] Hence the fact that there is no conceptual obstacle to pure economic loss recovery under article 1382 of the French *Code Civil*, which seems generally to be understood as establishing a liability rule.

economic loss' as a result of another's conduct.[48] For those who believe that the law of negligence is rights-based, this provides a straightforward explanation for the general no-recovery rule in respect of such loss in English negligence law. Again, however (to reiterate), it does not follow that there cannot be a right – such as a right not to have the power supply to one's factory cut off – that could ground recovery of financial loss in cases that have hitherto been seen as falling within the scope of the no-recovery rule,[49] and nor does it follow that the law cannot lay down a liability rule permitting recovery of pure economic loss in a given circumstance.

A connected implication of the claim being made is that the main exception to the no-recovery rule for pure economic loss – which is where A has assumed a relevant responsibility towards B – can only be reconciled with a rights analysis of negligence law if in such cases the suffering of financial loss by B goes not to the wrongfulness question itself, but only to the actionability of a wrong committed at an earlier time (presumably the moment at which A acted negligently and hence breached an undertaking to act with reasonable care). Since the wrong of breach of contract is not dependent on proof of damage or loss, this analysis is consistent with the origins of the assumption of responsibility idea in the old doctrine of assumpsit[50] (which also influenced the modern law of contract), and resonates with the familiar argument that [268] negligence cases in which liability arises out of an assumption of responsibility have at least as much in common with contract as they have with the rest of negligence law.[51]

---

[48] I originally thought that the claim might also have implications for omissions cases, where the gist of B's complaint is that A has failed to confer a benefit on her, since if it is impossible to say at any given moment of time whether A's conduct has made things *worse* for B, it must also be impossible to say at any given moment of time whether positive conduct by A would have made things *better* for B. However, while this does mean that a general right that A make things better for B is conceptually impossible, recognition of such a right need not underlie omissions liability, which can instead be based on a more specific right that A take reasonable steps to prevent B from suffering a recognised form of damage (usually personal injury), a right violated if and when B sustains the damage in question.

[49] Or indeed in cases of financial loss where recovery *has* been allowed in negligence, but which are not explicable on the basis of a prior assumption of responsibility by the defendant towards the claimant. The only clear-cut example of such a case in contemporary English law is *White* (n 38), where the violated right would have to be something along the lines of a right not negligently to be deprived of an intended legacy. Such a right would be violated when the testator dies, which is indeed when the cause of action in such a case has been held to arise (*Bacon v Howard Kennedy (a firm)* (1999) PNLR 1 (Ch D)). (Note that I am not commending the existence of such a right, but merely pointing out that this is the only sort of right on which recovery in this type of case could be grounded.)

[50] As to which, see P Mitchell, '*Hedley Byrne & Co Ltd v Heller & Partners Ltd* (1963)' in C Mitchell and P Mitchell (eds), *Landmark Cases in the Law of Tort* (Oxford, Hart Publishing, 2010).

[51] See, eg, Beever (n 16) esp ch 8. On the other hand, the fact that here the actionability of the wrong depends on the suffering of consequential loss also points to an important distinction between this category of case and cases where the defendant's undertaking is accompanied by the 'badges of enforceability' required by contract law, such as consideration: see Stevens, *Torts and Rights* (n 3) 11.

I am not the first scholar to argue that there is no 'right' of the claimant in play in cases of pure economic loss,[52] but it has been pointed out that earlier arguments to this effect are circular, or that (at most) they have established only the narrower proposition that there is no *property* right of the claimant in play in such cases.[53] There seem to be two difficulties here (difficulties that may well be connected). One is that the scholars who have made this argument seem to conceive of the rights *constituted by* the law of negligence – the rights which the law of negligence itself recognises – as somehow existing independently of negligence law, a conception nicely encapsulated in Beever's talk of the 'rights base' of the law of negligence[54] (as if this 'rights base' and the law of negligence are somehow distinguishable). If by 'rights' these scholars mean (as I do[55]) Hohfeldian claim rights, then this separation of negligence law and its underlying rights makes no sense, as a claim right – an assertion as to the import of the law from the standpoint of the beneficiary of a norm – is inseparable from the norm itself, and hence also from the area of law of which the norm is a part.[56] And the other difficulty is that at least some of these scholars seem to be presenting as a descriptive or logically undeniable claim an argument in fact premised on a particular philosophical conception of negligence law (essentially one founded on Kantian right). By contrast, the [269] claim being made here is in no way question-begging, and nor is it premised on any particular philosophical conception of negligence law. It is simply a conclusion that I have argued necessarily follows from two postulates. If the two postulates are both true, and the conclusion *does* necessarily follow from them, then the claim must itself be true. It is as simple as that.

[52] See, eg, P Benson, 'Economic Loss in Tort Law' in DG Owen (ed), *Philosophical Foundations of Tort Law* (Oxford, Clarendon Press, 1995) and P Benson, 'The Problem with Pure Economic Loss' (2009) 60 *South Carolina Law Review* 823; Beever (n 16) ch 7; JW Neyers, '*Tate & Lyle Food & Distribution Ltd v Greater London Council* (1983)' in Mitchell and Mitchell (n 50) 246; Stevens, 'Rights and Other Things' (n 11) 120.

[53] For such critiques, see, eg, McBride (n 14) 336–39, 349–50; K Barker, 'Relational Economic Loss and Indeterminacy: The Search for Rational Limits' in S Degeling at al (eds), *Torts in Commercial Law* (Pyrmont, Thomas Reuters (Professional) Australia, 2011) 171–73; and J Griffin, 'Pure Economic Loss: Out of Negligence and Into the Unknown' (2014) 3 *Oxford University Undergraduate Law Journal* 44, 48–49. For an example of the kind of reasoning these commentators deprecate, see Benson, 'Economic Loss in Tort Law' (n 52) 435–36, where it is argued that in a relational economic loss case the claimant 'seeks protection of an interest in the use of something from which he has no right to exclude the defendant', and that it follows from this that the claimant 'lacks a right on which to rest the interest that forms the very basis of his claim'. But why does the fact that the claimant lacks *one* kind of right – a property right in the damaged property – preclude recognition of *another* kind of right, such as a right not to suffer economic loss as a result of damage to someone else's property?

[54] Beever (n 16) 61–70.

[55] See text to n 2.

[56] The closest Beever comes to a definition of the 'rights' in what he calls the 'rights base' of negligence is when he refers to a primary right as 'a right recognised by the substantive law', such as a 'right to the performance of a contract, to property, to bodily integrity and to reputation': Beever (n 16) 212. The first example is a Hohfeldian claim right, and this seems consistent with the definition. However the remaining examples are not claim rights, but general 'rights' that are best

Although it is not my intention to spell out all the possible implications for private law of the claim that a right not to suffer loss is conceptually impossible, it is worth noting that the ramifications of the claim are not limited to the law of negligence. Consider for example the suggestion that there can be a right not to suffer a detriment as a result of reasonably relying on another's promise, a right that it has been argued might underlie the doctrine of promissory (or 'equitable') estoppel.[57] Since it can never be determined at any given moment of time that a person's reliance on another has been detrimental, no such right is capable of existing.[58] It does not follow that a doctrine of promissory estoppel cannot be rights-based: it might be, for example, that the giving of the promise creates a right in the promisee that the promise will be kept, but that (in the absence of consideration and so forth) the wrong of failing to keep the promise becomes actionable only when the promisee acts in reliance on the promise, or when such reliance appears to be detrimental.[59] And even if a rights-based analysis along these lines is thought unconvincing, another possible explanation

understood as references to constellations of legal norms – including claim rights – protective of a particular interest. Since these general rights are merely a way of expressing what the law *is*, it is difficult to see how they can form a 'rights base' of negligence law separate from negligence law itself. For further discussion of these kinds of rights, see Nolan and Robertson (n 45) at 9 and the literature there cited.

[57] See, eg, WA Seavey, 'Reliance upon Gratuitous Promises or Other Conduct' (1951) 64 *Harvard Law Rev* 913, 926 (the wrong in estoppel is 'in causing the plaintiff to change position to his detriment'). The argument in A Robertson, 'Estoppels and Rights-Creating Events: Beyond Wrongs and Promises' in J W Neyers et al (eds), *Exploring Contract Law* (Oxford, Hart Publishing, 2009) is more subtle, but still problematic. Robertson's claim that detrimental reliance on an assumption induced by another gives rise to a right at first looks unobjectionable (my claim, after all, is that a *wrong* occurs in a moment of time, not that the *existence of rights* cannot fluctuate over time, which of course they can and do). However, his claim that this is a 'right-creating *event*' must be rejected, since an event happens or starts happening in a moment of time, and we have seen that whether B's action on an assumption induced by A would cause B to suffer detriment if A did not adhere to it (ibid 210) cannot be determined at any particular moment. Furthermore, if we accept Peter Birks' plausible claim that all rights arise out of events (P Birks, 'The Concept of a Civil Wrong' in Owen (n 52) 31), then the right that Robertson posits cannot exist. Finally, the content of the purported right is not to be caused 'harm' by conduct inconsistent with the induced assumption (Robertson, 224), and since by 'harm' Robertson apparently means 'loss', a right of this kind is conceptually impossible for the reasons stated in this article.

[58] For the same reason, we must reject Peter Benson's suggestion that a right to recover economic loss in negligence can be grounded on justified detrimental reliance on an express or implied inducement by the defendant (see Benson, 'Economic Loss in Tort Law' (n 52) 450–54; and note in particular Benson's formulation of the defendant's duty as being to 'act in such a way that the plaintiff is not wrongfully *made worse off* than he would have been had he not abandoned or forgone the advantage' (ibid 455 fn, emphasis added)).

[59] This would explain why, despite the best efforts of scholars (including myself: see D Nolan, 'Following in their Footsteps: Equitable Estoppel in Australia and the United States' (2000) 11 *King's College Law Journal* 202) to argue that in such cases the courts should limit the remedy to the compensation of the promisee's detrimental reliance – which would tally with a 'right' not to suffer detriment in reliance on the promise – the clear tendency in practice is for the courts to award an expectation-based remedy – which would tally with a right that the promise be kept. See further, E Cooke, *The Modern Law of Estoppel* (Oxford, OUP, 2000) 150 ff (and for acceptance of this tendency by a leading proponent of a reliance-based remedy in promissory estoppel cases, see A Robertson, 'Reliance and Expectation in Estoppel Remedies' (1998) 18 *Legal Studies* 360, 360–61).

for the promissory estoppel [270] doctrine – or some part of it, at least[60] – would be a liability rule to the effect that if B reasonably relies to her detriment on A's promise, then A becomes liable to ensure that B suffers no such detriment, which seems to be the gist of the promise-detriment principle that Ben McFarlane has argued underlies some cases of both promissory and proprietary estoppel.[61] Again, a liability rule of this kind is perfectly compatible with the argument being put forward here, since (as McFarlane makes clear[62]) on this analysis there is no duty on the promisor – and hence no right in the promise – until the court order is made, so that the principle does not depend on the conceptual possibility of a right not to suffer loss.

IV. DAMAGE AND LOSS

It will be readily apparent from the above that I believe that damage (as an element of the cause of action for negligence) and loss are fundamentally different concepts, and in this part of the article I want to develop that claim, along with the related claim that the existence of damage cannot depend on the existence of loss. We should note first that the claim that damage and loss are fundamentally different concepts would appear to be controversial, as prominent judicial definitions of damage equate it to loss, in the sense of being 'worse off' (or having suffered some kind of 'detriment') as a result of the defendant's negligent conduct.[63] Furthermore, the fact that judges and academics frequently use the words 'damage' and 'loss' interchangeably in this context suggests that they see no fundamental difference between the two concepts, or perhaps more accurately that they do not believe that there are two separate concepts in play in the first place.[64] This reluctance to differentiate between damage and loss is surprising when one recalls that in everyday language the two words have quite distinct meanings, which seem to have obvious echoes in the different meanings I believe they have (or should have) in private law. Consider for example the film *Damage*, starring Juliette Binoche, Jeremy Irons and Miranda Richardson, in which a politician's affair with his son's girlfriend leads to his family being torn

---

[60] For the view that the doctrine is best understood as resting on at least three different principles, see B McFarlane, 'Promissory Estoppel and Debts' in A Burrows and E Peel (eds), *Contract Formation and Parties* (Oxford, OUP, 2010).

[61] B McFarlane, 'Understanding Equitable Estoppel: From Metaphors to Better Laws' (2013) 66 *CLP* 267.

[62] ibid 294 fn.

[63] See n 3. See also J Stapleton, 'Cause-in-Fact and the Scope of Liability for Consequences' (2003) 119 *LQR* 388, 413; O'Sullivan (n 36) 260; and J Varuhas, 'The Concept of "Vindication" in the Law of Torts: Rights, Interests and Damages' (2014) 34 *OJLS* 253, 260.

[64] See, eg, *Nykredit* (n 35) 1630–31 (Lord Nicholls); *Sephton* (n 36) [60] (Lord Mance); Descheemaeker (n 22) 22–23.

apart and his career destroyed.[65] Would not giving this film the title *Loss* have had a rather different, and less appropriate, connotation?

[271] Be that as it may, my claim that damage and loss are fundamentally different concepts is a legal one, and so I must turn to the law to make good the claim. And on closer inspection of the law, the truth of the claim seems rather obvious. After all, the example of the plane crash shows us that B can suffer damage for the purposes of negligence law without being worse off as a result of A's conduct, and numerous other examples can be used to illustrate the same point: a corporate claimant can for instance sue for negligently caused damage to its fully insured property,[66] and a bailee can sue for damage to the bailed property, regardless of whether he thereby comes under a liability to the bailor.[67] Conversely, B can be (apparently) worse off as a result of A's conduct, and yet not be considered to have suffered damage that grounds a negligence claim, as where A has negligently killed B's partner, or subjected B to a very unpleasant experience that does not result in any lasting psychological effects.[68]

The fundamental difference between damage and loss is most clearly demonstrated by property damage cases in which the person who is considered to have suffered damage (and so to have a claim) has suffered no loss, and the person who has suffered loss is considered not to have suffered damage (and so not to have a claim).[69] Suppose, for example, that a house is damaged by vibrations attributable to A's negligence while B is the owner, but that the damage only comes to light (thereby reducing the property's value) after B has sold the house to C. In that case, B is considered to have suffered 'damage' and so has a claim against A, while C – the person who is likely to end up worse off – is not considered to have suffered damage, and cannot sue. Similarly, a seller of goods can sue in tort for damage done to the goods before the property in them passed to the buyer, even if the risk had passed to the buyer at the relevant time,[70] whereas the buyer (the one who actually loses out) has no claim.[71]

---

[65] *Damage* (Studio Canal 1992). The film was based on a novel of the same name: J Hart, *Damage* (London, Chatto & Windus, 1991).

[66] I say 'corporate claimant' because a natural person may have an attachment to an item of property that renders it of more than merely financial value to her.

[67] *The Winkfield* [1902] P 42 (CA). For other examples, see Tettenborn (n 3) 450; C von Bar, 'The Notion of Damage' in AS Hartkamp and MW Hesselink (eds), *Towards a European Civil Code*, 4th revised edn (Alphen aan den Rijn, Wolters Kluwer, 2011) 394 (dilapidated building); D Nolan, 'Damage in the English Law of Negligence' (2013) 4 *Journal of European Tort Law* 259, 265–66 (unwanted clothes). As Stevens says ('Rights and Other Things' (n 11) 120), '[n]egligently injuring someone's person or property no more necessarily results in their being factually worse off as things turn out than does slandering their character or trespassing on their land'.

[68] See, eg, *Reilly v Merseyside Regional Health Authority* (1995) 6 Med LR 246 (CA) (elderly couple trapped in overcrowded lift for 80 minutes).

[69] This shows that, as Sarah Green has observed, '[t]he gist of negligent interference with assets is not that which the claimant has lost but that to which he or she is entitled' (S Green, 'Rights and Wrongs: An Introduction to the Wrongful Interference Actions' in Nolan and Robertson (n 11) 534).

[70] *The Charlotte* [1908] P 206 (CA); *The Sanix Ace* [1987] 1 Lloyd's Rep 465 (QBD).

[71] See, eg, *Leigh & Sillivan v Aliakmon Shipping Co (The Aliakmon)* [1986] AC 785 (HL).

One could point to these examples and argue that grounding negligence liability on damage rather than loss can produce unsatisfactory outcomes. But we should remember that there are second-order principles that may smooth things over. A straightforward example is an insurer's right to be subrogated to a property owner's claim for damage to insured property; another is the rule [272] that a bailee who successfully sues for damage to the bailed property holds the damages for the bailor.[72] Principles like this are perfectly compatible with the claims made in this article. Furthermore, I am not arguing that negligence liability cannot (or even should not) be grounded on loss rather than damage, but merely that grounding it on loss entails a liability rule analysis rather than a right/duty one. On the other hand, it does seem to me that in general terms a choice needs to be made between the two approaches, because while in theory they are capable of operating side-by-side – so that recovery could be grounded on *either* damage *or* loss – in practice this would surely lead to unacceptable results: it would, for example, expose a defendant to double liability in the cases discussed in the previous paragraph. Legislatures and courts in common law countries should bear this in mind when they decide to allow claims in negligence on the basis of loss rather than damage.[73]

That brings me to my related claim that if the damage concept is to be compatible with a rights-based analysis of negligence law then the existence of damage can never depend on the existence of loss. This claim follows inexorably from the others I have made. If a right not to suffer loss is conceptually impossible, then a right not to suffer damage cannot entail a right not to suffer loss, which of course it would if the existence of damage were contingent on the existence of loss. The broader point here is that if a violation of a right happens in a moment of time, then whether or not a person has suffered damage must be determinable at a particular moment in time if a requirement of damage is to be integral to a rights-based analysis of negligence law.

Setting aside the difficulties that arise when the language of 'damage' is invoked in cases of pure economic loss, the concept of damage as currently employed by the courts appears broadly consistent with these precepts. Of course at a practical level it may be difficult to pinpoint the moment at which the claimant has suffered damage, but the cases on limitation periods in the personal injury and property damage contexts obviously assume that such a moment exists, and there is no equivalent in this case law of the problems that have arisen from the attempts to pinpoint such a moment in the economic loss context. The time-specific nature of damage in negligence is demonstrated by the analysis in *The Starsin*,[74] where negligent stowage caused the condition of

---

[72] See *Hepburn v A Tomlinson (Hauliers) Ltd* [1966] AC 451 (HL) 468 (Lord Reid); WS Holdsworth, *History of English Law*, 2nd edn (London, Methuen, 1937) vol 7, 463.

[73] See, eg, Latent Damage Act 1986, s 3(1); *McMullin v ICI Australia Operations Pty Ltd* (1997) 72 FCR 1 (FCA) 74 (Wilcox J).

[74] *Homburg Houtimport BV v Agrosin Private Ltd (The Starsin)* [2003] UKHL 12, [2004] 1 AC 715.

various cargoes progressively to deteriorate during a sea voyage. The House of Lords held that in these circumstances causes of action in negligence arose once and for all when a cargo first suffered more than insignificant damage, and that only those with title to the cargo at that particular moment (and not [273] those who acquired title at a later point in the voyage) had the right to sue in tort. The same 'once and for all' principle applies in personal injury cases.[75]

Nevertheless, in property damage cases there is one potentially significant implication of the claim that on a rights-based analysis the existence of damage can never depend on the existence of loss, since it would then follow that whether A's negligent conduct has affected the market value of B's property cannot determine whether B has suffered damage for the purposes of a negligence claim. This is because a diminution in market value is a form of loss (being 'worse off'), and it shares with other forms of loss the characteristic of being contingent, as the market value of an asset is obviously capable of fluctuating over time.[76] Suppose for example that A (a graffiti artist) 'tags' a nineteenth-century landscape painting in B's collection without B's consent, significantly reducing its market value. But suppose further that A subsequently becomes so famous that a few years later the value of the painting has rebounded, and it is now worth far more than it would have been without the 'tag'.[77] If the existence of damage here depends on A's action having reduced the value of the painting in some general or definitive sense, then there would not be a single moment of time when it would be possible to say that the painting has been damaged, and indeed this will generally[78] be the case where the effect of A's conduct on the market value of B's property is determinative of the damage question.

The result is that we must tread carefully when we define 'property damage' in the negligence context. For example, an influential judicial definition of property damage as a 'physical change which renders the article less useful or less valuable'[79] is problematic, because on this test the actual impact of the physical change on the asset's market value may be determinative. Though the difference is subtle, an acceptable alternative definition (which has been used in the criminal damage context[80]) might be a 'physical change that *impairs* the value or

---

[75] See *Cartledge v E Jopling & Sons Ltd* [1963] AC 758 (HL) 771–72 (Lord Reid).

[76] Furthermore, it may be difficult to pinpoint when changes in market value occur: for an illustrative discussion in the defective premises context, see *Bank of East Asia Ltd v Tsien Wui Marble Factory Ltd* (1999) 2 HKCFAR 349, [2000] 1 HKLRD 268, 326–27 (Ching PJ).

[77] This is not a fanciful example. A mural spray-painted on the wall of an amusement arcade in Folkestone by the street artist Banksy was said to be worth up to £470,000, and the ownership of the relevant section of wall was subsequently contested in the courts: see *The Creative Foundation v Dreamland Leisure Ltd* [2015] EWHC 2556 (Ch).

[78] I say 'generally' because the position would be otherwise where the property in question is totally destroyed, and so no longer exists.

[79] *Hunter v Canary Wharf Ltd* [1997] AC 655 (CA) 676 (Pill LJ).

[80] See, eg, *R v Whiteley* (1991) 93 Cr App R 25 (CA) 28–29 (Lord Lane CJ).

utility' of the property,[81] provided this is understood to mean a physical change of a kind that tends to have a negative impact on the value or [274] utility of items of property like this one. Because this alternative shifts the focus from the *actual* impact of this particular change on the value of this particular item of property, it allows us to say definitively that at the moment that the change occurs the property has suffered damage. Hence in the example of the painting, while we cannot definitively say that the daubing of *this* tag on *this* painting will reduce its value, we can say that daubing tags on nineteenth-century landscape paintings tends to have this effect. An alternative solution would be simply to dispense with the reference to value altogether, and to focus instead on 'impairment' as a standalone concept, meaning that the thing in question is simply a *less good* thing as a result of the negligent conduct.[82] In the case of the painting, for example, the painting is impaired as soon as the tag is added, since it is simply a less good landscape painting than it was before, just as breaking someone's leg makes it a less good leg, or denting someone's car makes it a less good car.

V. CONCLUSION

I would like to make five points by way of a conclusion. The first is that my argument is not that loss is not a useful concept. On the contrary, it seems to me that the concept of loss may be valuable when it comes to the assessment of damages, and we have also seen that it is sometimes employed to determine the actionability of a wrong the existence of which is determined independently of it. In these contexts, the concept of 'loss' is certainly capable of playing an important role, and the precise parameters of the concept have usefully been investigated in scholarly analysis.[83]

The second point is that I should not be taken to be in any way implying that 'loss' is somehow less important or fundamental than 'damage' at a human

---

[81] For the use of a definition of property damage along these lines, see *Ranicar v Frigmobile Pty Ltd* [1983] Tas R 113 (Tas SC) 116 (Green CJ); and S Douglas, 'Actionable Interferences: A New Perspective on the Chattel Torts' in Degeling et al (n 53) 90. See also *Losinjska Plovidba v Transco Overseas (The Orjula)* [1995] 2 Lloyd's Rep 395 (QBD) 399 (Mance J) (describing the criminal law test as relevant guidance in a tort context). One of the definitions of 'damage' in the *Oxford English Dictionary* is 'injury, harm; *esp.* physical injury to a thing, such as impairs its value or usefulness'.

[82] I have argued elsewhere that some notion of 'impairment' is central to the law's conception of both personal injury and property damage in the negligence context: see Nolan (n 67). See also C Witting, 'Physical Damage in Negligence' [2002] *CLJ* 189, 190 fn ('The orthodox understanding of damage in negligence, whether personal or property damage, is predicated upon the damage being deleterious in the sense that it is an "impairment"'). This approach also tallies with that taken by the Ontario Court of Appeal in the interesting private nuisance case of *Smith v Inco Ltd* [2011] ONCA 628, 107 OR (3d) 321, where it was held that the deposit of nickel particles in the soil of the plaintiffs' properties did not constitute physical damage because even though public concern about the potential health consequences of the deposits had reduced the market value of the properties, the concern was baseless, and so objectively the deposits had had no detrimental effect on the land.

[83] See in particular Tettenborn (n 3).

level. On the contrary, in the grand scheme of things one's overall welfare is surely *more* significant than a broken window or for that matter a broken arm. The point is simply that the nature of loss is such that the concept cannot itself be constitutive of the rights and duties that we owe one another.

The third point is that although historical insights can significantly enhance our understanding of the current law, as scholars, practitioners and students of the law we ought not to be prisoners of history, but instead should strive to progress our discipline, so that the law of the future is better than the law of [275] the past. It follows that we must be prepared either to refine or to discard doctrines that are no longer fit for purpose, a good example of which in the present context is the old distinction between wrongs actionable per se and wrongs actionable only on proof of damage.[84] For here the word 'damage' really is slippery, since sometimes it means 'damage' in the sense in which I have used that word (so that damage is an element of the wrong); sometimes it means 'loss' in the sense in which I have used that word (so that the suffering of loss is a condition of the actionability of a wrong); and sometimes it really means nothing at all, as in the tort of private nuisance, where the concept of damage is synonymous with (and so adds nothing to) the central idea of a substantial interference with the use and enjoyment of land.[85]

The fourth point is the importance of using legal terminology thoughtfully and consistently. Needless to say, I do not expect everyone simply to accept the definitions of damage and loss that I have used in this article. However, I do think that it is reasonable to expect that legislators, judges and scholars will be consistent in their use of legal language, and will at least consider whether, for example, it is appropriate to use terms like 'damage', 'loss', 'injury' and 'harm' interchangeably, or whether it might not be more helpful to ascribe discrete meanings to these terms, in the hope that this might clarify the rule, principle or argument in question. Loose terminology both reflects and generates loose thinking.

And the final point is that my aim in this article has been the rather modest one of clarifying the nature and limits of some of the concepts that private lawyers use to make sense of their subject (or, perhaps, at times, and a little more ambitiously, of identifying and exploring some concepts that private lawyers could so use). Nevertheless, it would be a mistake to dismiss the importance of the kind of conceptual fine-tuning I have attempted in this article. On the contrary, I hope to have shown that carefully delineating the boundaries of the concepts that we use can significantly enhance both the theory and the practice of private law.

---

[84] For a similar judicial sentiment, see *Watkins v Secretary of State for the Home Department* [2006] UKHL 17, [2006] 2 AC 395 [74] (Lord Walker).

[85] See D Nolan, '"A Tort Against Land": Private Nuisance as a Property Tort' in Nolan and Robertson (n 11) 481.

14

Against Strict Product Liability

I. INTRODUCTION

SOME 10 YEARS ago I attended an international conference of tort scholars focused on product liability.[1] After two days of debate and discussion from a broad range of jurisdictional perspectives, and despite the best efforts of the participants to put forward plausible justifications for strict tortious liability for damage caused by defective products, I emerged with the distinct impression that no such justification existed. Having since looked more closely at the extensive literature which purports to provide such a justification that impression has hardened into a belief. In this chapter I explain why in my view the case for strict product liability in tort is weak, and why a negligence standard is to be preferred.

Had the chapter been written at the time of the conference in question, it would have been a purely hypothetical exercise as far as the law of the United Kingdom was concerned. That is because the statute that introduced strict product liability into UK law, the Consumer Protection Act 1987 ('the 1987 Act'), was passed to implement a European Directive ('the 1985 Directive'),[2] and so could not be repealed without a change of heart at the European level. However, following the UK's withdrawal from the European Union, Parliament is now free to repeal the 1987 Act, and I shall argue in this chapter that Parliament should indeed take that step. An alternative title for the chapter would therefore be: 'Why Part I of the Consumer Protection Act 1987 should be repealed'.

If the claim that the 1987 Act should be repealed appears to be a radical one, it is worth remembering that there are many common law countries in which product liability continues to be the exclusive preserve of the law of contract and the tort of negligence. Examples are Canada,[3] India and Singapore.[4] There seems to be no great clamour in these jurisdictions to move towards strict tort

---

[1] The conference was a meeting of the World Tort Law Society held in Harbin, China, in 2013. It resulted in the publication of H Koziol et al (eds), *Product Liability: Fundamental Questions in a Comparative Perspective* (Berlin, De Gruyter, 2017).

[2] Council Directive 85/374/EEC on Liability for Defective Products.

[3] See generally SM Waddams, *Products Liability*, 5th edn (Toronto, Carswell, 2011).

[4] Hence the absence of any extended discussion of product liability in G Chan and PW Lee, *The Law of Torts in Singapore*, 2nd edn (Singapore, Academy Publishing, 2016).

liability, and nor is it obvious that there are legal, economic or social factors that would explain why the UK requires strict liability and these countries do not. Of course, it does not follow that these countries have been right to stick to fault-based tort liability in this context. But it is important to bear in mind that repealing the 1987 Act would not leave the UK on its own as far as its product liability regime was concerned. It would be in some very respectable company in legal terms.

The argument I make in this chapter for repeal of the 1987 Act is primarily grounded on the conclusion that the justifications that have been put forward for imposing strict tort liability for damage caused by defective products do not hold up to scrutiny.[5] There is, however, a second string to the argument, which is that the imposition of strict product liability in a tort system primarily based on fault requires lines to be drawn that were always hard to justify and which technological change is making unsustainable. That technological change is undermining the distinctions which lie at the heart of modern product liability law has been widely acknowledged,[6] and this has now resulted in a proposal by the European Commission for a complete overhaul of the EU product liability regime, which would involve repealing the 1985 Directive and replacing it with a new Directive.[7] The Commission deserves credit for acknowledging and seeking to resolve the tensions generated by technological change in this field. However, it will be argued in this chapter that the only plausible way in which those tensions can be resolved is to abandon strict liability and revert to a fault standard.

It remains to be seen whether the Commission's proposal (or some modified version of it) will be adopted by the EU. However, if that were to happen, it would only strengthen the case for repeal of the 1987 Act, since it would pull the rug out from under any argument that it might be beneficial for the UK to share a common product liability law with the EU member states. On the contrary,

---

[5] It was suggested to me that it does not follow from the fact that the case for strict liability is weak that fault liability is to be preferred. However, it seems reasonable to assume that some special justification is needed for strict liability to be imposed, not least because in our legal system fault liability is clearly the default rule. This assumption also pervades the literature.

[6] See, eg, Law Commission and Scottish Law Commission, *Automated Vehicles: Joint Report* (Law Com No 404, 2022) para 13.32 ('We urge the UK Government to review the way that product liability law applies to new technologies'). For a helpful overview of the issues, see European Commission, 'Report on the Safety and Liability Implications of Artificial Intelligence, the Internet of Things and Robotics' COM(2020) 64 final.

[7] European Commission, 'Proposal for a Directive of the European Parliament and of the Council on Liability for Defective Products' COM(2022) 495 final. The proposed new Directive, inter alia, extends the scope of the EU product liability regime to encompass software and digital manufacturing files, loss or corruption of data, and some defects that arise after the product leaves the producer's hands; expands the categories of persons who are liable under the regime to include, inter alia, software producers, digital service providers and online platforms; and assists the claimant to establish liability by giving them rights of access to information in the defendant's hands and by reversing the burden of proof as to defectiveness and causation in certain circumstances. For a comprehensive evaluation of the proposal, see G Wagner, 'Liability Rules for the Digital Age: Aiming for the Brussels Effect' (2022) 13 *Journal of European Tort Law* 191, 199–220.

unless the UK were to follow suit and implement the new Directive – despite having had no say in its development – we would be left on our own, with a strict product liability regime established by an institution that had since discarded it as unsuited to modern conditions.

One final point which should be made at this stage is that, in moving away from strict product liability and returning to a fault standard, the UK would to some extent be tracking developments in the United States, where the third *Restatement of Torts* essentially reverted to a negligence standard for design and marketing defects, and retained true strict liability only for manufacturing defects.[8] Since strict tort liability for damage caused by defective products originated in the US, the importance of this development cannot be overstated.

The discussion in the remainder of the chapter unfolds as follows. I first investigate the differences between negligence liability and the strict liability regime established by the 1987 Act. Having clarified what is at stake, I proceed to consider the difficulties to which strict product liability has given rise. I then go on to identify the principal arguments that have been made for strict product liability in tort and subject them to critical examination. My conclusion is that none stand up to scrutiny. Finally, I consider various mitigating measures that could be taken if it were thought necessary to soften the blow of repealing the 1987 Act.

II. WHY IT MATTERS

It is difficult to evaluate the case for or against strict product liability without an appreciation of what is at stake. In this part of the chapter I therefore provide an overview of the differences between strict liability based on a defectiveness standard and fault liability based on a negligence standard in this context.[9] Although it might be thought to strengthen the case against strict liability to downplay those differences, in fact I will argue that the distinctions between the two standards are more significant than they are sometimes claimed to be.[10] Nevertheless, there is no doubt that in most product liability cases the outcome will be the same whichever standard is employed, and it is important to bear this

---

[8] See *Restatement, Third, Torts: Products Liability* (1998).

[9] The discussion draws on a more detailed analysis of these questions in my chapter on product liability in K Oliphant (ed), *The Law of Tort*, 3rd edn (London, LexisNexis, 2015).

[10] For examples of the downplaying of the differences, see J Stapleton, 'The Conceptual Imprecision of "Strict" Product Liability' (1998) 6 *Torts Law Journal* 1; G Wagner, 'Development of Product Liability in Germany' in S Whittaker (ed), *The Development of Product Liability* (Cambridge, CUP, 2010) 151; and P Cane and J Goudkamp, *Atiyah's Accidents, Compensation and the Law*, 9th edn (Cambridge, CUP, 2018) 90–91. Cane and Goudkamp claim, for instance, that the 'development risk' defence in s 4(1)(e) of the Consumer Protection Act 1987 is 'simply a plea of "no-negligence" in the designing, development and testing of the product'. This is not correct. It is possible for a defendant to be held liable for a design defect under the 1987 Act despite not having been negligent: see, eg, *Abouzaid v Mothercare (UK) Ltd*, *The Times* (CA, 20 February 2001).

in mind when considering some of the issues addressed later in the chapter, such as the difficulties to which strict liability gives rise.

The differences between strict liability and fault liability cannot be evaluated in a meaningful way without distinguishing three types of product defect, namely 'manufacturing defects' (resulting in a defective 'non-standard' product); 'design defects' (resulting in a defective 'standard' product); and 'marketing defects' (resulting in a product that is defective because of inadequate or misleading accompanying information, such as warnings and instructions). And since it seems generally to be accepted that under the UK's strict product liability regime there is little, if any, difference between strict liability and fault liability in marketing defect cases,[11] the discussion that follows will be limited to manufacturing defects and design defects.

A manufacturing defect can be defined as a dangerous departure from the product's intended design. It seems clear that a product which fails to offer the level of safety intended because it deviates from the manufacturer's design specifications is less safe than 'persons generally are entitled to expect' and hence has a defect applying the test set out in section 3(1) of the 1987 Act. Recovery should therefore be straightforward in this type of case under the Act, although matters are complicated somewhat by certain unfortunate dicta of Burton J in *A v National Blood Authority*.[12] In theory, there is a clear distinction between strict liability and negligence here, since in a negligence claim the claimant must prove that the flaw in the product is the defendant's fault. However, as has frequently been pointed out,[13] in fact the difference tends not to be significant, since once the claimant has established on the balance of probabilities that the product had a defect, and that this was present when it left the producer's hands, the burden will in practice shift to the producer to show that neither they nor any of their employees were to blame, a burden which will usually be very difficult to discharge.[14] It follows that in the manufacturing defect context the imposition of strict liability will make a difference only in the unusual case

---

[11] See, eg, C Newdick, 'The Future of Negligence in Product Liability' (1987) 103 *LQR* 288, 307–309; J Stapleton, 'Products Liability in the United Kingdom: The Myths of Reform' (1999) 34 *Texas International Law Journal* 45, 53. In *Worsley v Tambrands Ltd* [2000] PIQR P95 (QBD), where a warning was held to be adequate for the purposes of the 1987 Act, the analysis was essentially negligence-based. For a thorough analysis drawing on UK and US sources, see D Fairgrieve and R Goldberg, *Product Liability*, 3rd edn (Oxford, OUP, 2020) paras 12.08–12.12.

[12] *A v National Blood Authority* [2001] 3 All ER 289 (QBD). On these dicta, and their implications, see *The Law of Tort* (n 9) para 19.55.

[13] See, eg, Stapleton, 'The Conceptual Imprecision of "Strict" Product Liability' (n 10) 2; Cane and Goudkamp (n 10) 90.

[14] See *The Law of Tort* (n 9) para 19.20. The classic illustration of the difficulties faced by a manufacturer in such a case is *Grant v Australian Knitting Mills Ltd* [1936] AC 85 (PC). In the 1970s it was observed that there were very few reported cases in the previous four decades in which a claimant had established the existence of a manufacturing defect but failed to prove negligence: Law Commission and Scottish Law Commission, *Liability for Defective Products* (Law Com WP No 64, 1975) para 38(c).

where the producer can identify a cause of the defect for which they are neither personally nor vicariously responsible – such as that the problem lay with a component supplied by a third party, which they could not reasonably have guarded against.[15]

Matters are more complex when it comes to design defects, which are the mainstay of modern product liability litigation. A product is defective in design if it is unreasonably dangerous when manufactured as intended. And according to the UK case law on design defects under the 1987 Act, a product is unreasonably dangerous in this sense if the risks it creates outweigh its utility, with the easiest way of establishing this being to show that an alternative, safer, design was available at little or no extra cost.[16] As has again often been observed,[17] the use of a risk/utility analysis to determine design defectiveness under strict product liability leaves only a narrow gap between strict liability and fault liability in design defect cases, especially where (as in the 1987 Act[18]) the strict liability regime allows the producer to rely on a 'development risk' defence.

Although there is a tendency to overstate the degree of convergence between the 1987 Act and negligence in the design defect context,[19] there is still a gap between the two.[20] First, whereas in negligence the claimant bears the burden of establishing that the producer was at fault, under the Act the producer bears the burden of establishing that a product risk was not discoverable when the product was marketed for the purposes of the development risk defence. Second, the test of discoverability under that defence – whether the knowledge in question was 'accessible' – can apparently be satisfied even though a reasonable producer would not have discovered the risk (in which case there would of course be no liability in negligence).[21] Third, it may be that a reasonable producer would not

---

[15] See also *A v National Blood Authority* (n 12), where blood and blood products contaminated with the Hepatitis C virus were held to be defective under the 1987 Act but the producer had not been negligent because at the time of supply there was no way of screening blood for the presence of the virus.

[16] The leading case is *Wilkes v DePuy International Ltd* [2016] EWHC 3096 (QB), [2018] QB 627.

[17] See, eg, Cane and Goudkamp (n 10) 90.

[18] Consumer Protection Act 1987, s 4(1)(e).

[19] See, eg, Stapleton, 'The Conceptual Imprecision of "Strict" Product Liability' (n 10) 2, asserting that in relation to in-house design defects the liability imposed on producers under the 1987 Act is not strict, a claim contradicted by, for example, the *Abouzaid* case discussed in n 22 below. Similarly, Stapleton's claim (ibid 9) that as regards in-house design an assessment of the costs and benefits of the product 'is equivalent to judging the behaviour [of the producer] in making and supplying the product' is incorrect. Part of the problem is that Stapleton assumes (ibid 9–10) that under the 1987 Act the benefits of a product are to be assessed at the time of its supply, whereas in fact the cases show that both the costs and the benefits of the product are to be assessed with hindsight (in other words at the time of the trial): see, eg, *Gee v DePuy International Ltd* [2018] EWHC 1208 (QB), [2018] Med LR 347 [84]. She also claims that the development risk defence in s 4(1)(e) of the 1987 Act is 'based on reasonableness' (ibid 12), but again the case law contradicts this view: see n 21 below.

[20] See also K Oliphant, 'Statement from a European Common Law Perspective' in Koziol et al (n 1) 565–66.

[21] See Case C-300/95 *Commission v United Kingdom* [1997] ECR I-2649, para 28.

have identified the risk, not because it was undiscoverable in the light of the state of scientific and technical knowledge, but simply because it would not have crossed their mind. In such a scenario, there would be no liability in negligence, but there could be liability under the Act as the product is defective and the development risk defence is not available.[22] And finally, where the defect was the result of the work of a component manufacturer or an out-of-house designer, the producer can still be liable under the Act, but will not be liable in negligence unless they were at fault in either selecting that person or checking their work.[23] Nevertheless, even taking account of these differences, the distinction between the two regimes in design defect cases is not great and for the most part the same result will be reached whichever analysis is used.

A comparison of strict liability with common law negligence would not be complete without mentioning the types of defendants who can be held liable under the 1987 Act but who are unlikely to be at fault, and hence potentially liable in negligence. There are three such categories of defendant, namely apparent producers (such as supermarket 'own-branders'), importers of the product into the UK[24] and suppliers (such as sellers).[25] Although there is little evidence that claims against persons or entities in these three categories have been significant – all the reported cases seem to concern producers – the liability to which they are subject is potentially useful to a claimant where the producer cannot be identified, is insolvent or is based in another jurisdiction. Any repeal of the 1987 Act would deprive claimants of these advantages, although where the claimant is the purchaser of the product the availability of a contractual claim against the immediate supplier will to some extent mitigate the effect of this change, as will the possibility of a negligence claim against anyone in the supply chain who ought to have realised that the product had a defect.

The upshot of this brief comparison of the 1987 Act with negligence is that although there are important differences between the two product liability regimes, in practice the gulf between strict liability and fault liability in this context is not especially wide. It follows that while the repeal of the 1987 Act would have some concrete consequences for those involved in product liability litigation, in most cases the outcome of the litigation will be the same. This conclusion has significant implications for the discussion that follows. First, even if we believe that the advantages that a strict liability regime offers to claimants are welcome ones, it is questionable whether they justify the considerable complexity to which the existence of strict product liability in tort gives rise.

---

[22] See, eg, *Abouzaid* (n 10), where the producer of a pushchair accessory was held liable under the 1987 Act after a hook on its elastic strap caused an eye injury, even though it was held that the risk of this happening would not have been identified by a reasonable manufacturer before the accident occurred.

[23] See Stapleton, 'The Conceptual Imprecision of "Strict" Product Liability' (n 10) 6–7.

[24] Consumer Protection Act 1987, s 2(2)(b) and (c).

[25] ibid s 2(3).

Second, the very limited nature of the changes wrought by the 1987 Act should be borne in mind when considering some of the more grandiose justifications that have been put forward for strict product liability. And finally, it may be that many of the advantages that strict tort liability offers to claimants could also be achieved by making relatively straightforward changes to the liability rules in negligence and contract.

III. PROBLEMS WITH STRICT PRODUCT LIABILITY

One of the two foundations on which my case against strict product liability in tort rests is the difficulties to which such liability gives rise. Debates as to the merits of strict liability and fault liability tend to focus on the moral case for these forms of liability, or on consequentialist arguments which are said to favour one or other liability rule in a given context. However, in this part of the chapter I focus on a different kind of argument against strict liability. The argument is that creating a special strict liability regime for products within a tort system primarily based on fault inevitably results in the drawing of irrational distinctions, as well as high levels of complexity. The two problems are connected, as the distinctions that are drawn tend to generate complexity. Furthermore, both problems are now being exacerbated by technological change.

A. Products and Services

The key boundary between cases covered by a strict product liability regime and those that are not is the distinction between products and services. In the 1987 Act that boundary is set by the requirement that the damage be caused by a defect in a 'product', with a product being defined for these purposes as 'any goods or electricity'.[26] However, the distinction between products and services has always been hard to draw, and the fact that 'products and the provision of services are increasingly intertwined',[27] means that the problem is getting worse – so much so that the European Commission has said that in future the distinction may 'no longer be pertinent'.[28]

---

[26] ibid s 1(2). The reference to 'goods' reminds us of another dividing line drawn by the legislation, that between personal property and real property. Just as the strict product liability regime does not extend to services, it also does not extend to damage caused by buildings. Whether there is a justifiable distinction between real and personal property in this respect is an interesting question, but since this distinction does not seem to have given rise to much difficulty in practice, it is not the subject of further discussion here.

[27] European Commission, 'Report on the Safety and Liability Implications of Artificial Intelligence, the Internet of Things and Robotics' (n 6) 13.

[28] European Commission, 'Evaluation of Directive 85/374 on Liability for Defective Products' SWD(2018) 157 final, 52.

The difficulty of distinguishing between products and services is a notorious one. The problem is most obvious in the case of so-called 'information products', such as maps and cookbooks.[29] Should strict product liability extend to damage caused by defective information conveyed by such a product? If the answer is yes, then a troublesome distinction arises between misleadingly dangerous information conveyed in this way, which attracts strict liability, and the same information conveyed by another medium – the internet, for example, or television – which does not. Conversely, however, if damage caused by misleading information is excluded from the ambit of strict product liability, then it would seem to follow that strict liability would not attach to entire categories of product, such as traffic lights and smoke alarms, where any danger the product poses is likely to be result of the misleading information it implicitly conveys (such as 'It is safe to proceed/cross the road' or 'There is not excessive smoke in the house'). Furthermore, it would also call into question the extension of strict liability to marketing defects, since in all such cases the alleged defect arises out of the information (warnings, instructions, etc) that accompany the product.[30] The fact that both solutions produce indefensible anomalies suggests that there is simply no rational answer to the information product problem. As Jane Stapleton says, 'attempts to draw an explicit, coherent line between such cases are doomed to failure'.[31]

Similar problems arise when it comes to defective software. Where the software is downloaded online (as is now the norm) there is no physical product to which strict liability can attach, and so the situation seems to fall outside the ambit of the 1987 Act.[32] But should the position really be any different just because the software is installed from a tangible 'product', such as a CD? The difficulty is accentuated when physical products such as cars rely on software that is installed in the vehicle on manufacture, and which is then updated when the car is serviced. If a flaw in the software causes the vehicle to crash, injuring the driver, then there could be a strict liability claim under the 1987 Act if the flaw was present when the car was supplied by the producer (as it would constitute a 'defect' in the car). However, if the flaw had been introduced by a later software update, then the producer could rely on the defence in section 4(1)(d) of the Act that there was no defect in the car when they first supplied it,[33]

---

[29] See *The Law of Tort* (n 9) para 19.43. And for a recent CJEU decision on the issue, see Case C-65/20, *VI v KRONE–Verlag Gesellschaft mbH & Co KG* EU:C:2021:471.

[30] See Jane Stapleton's salt advice example: J Stapleton, 'Software, Information and the Concept of Product' (1989) 9 *Tel Aviv University Studies in Law* 147, 149. On the other hand, it may be possible to draw a meaningful distinction between a product (such as an aviation chart) which is dangerous solely by virtue of the misleading information it conveys and a product (such as a chainsaw) which is dangerous by virtue of a physical characteristic accentuated by inadequate or misleading accompanying information. The latter is the classic 'marketing defect' case.

[31] J Stapleton, *Product Liability* (London, Butterworths, 1994) 329.

[32] Stapleton, 'Software, Information and the Concept of Product' (n 30) 152.

[33] Consumer Protection Act 1987, s 4(1)(d).

and so would be liable only if at fault. Again, it is hard to see the logic of this distinction.[34]

Two further problems with the product/services distinction should be mentioned. The first relates to public utilities such as gas, water and electricity.[35] There is no obvious answer to the question of whether these are defective products or defective services, and this would seem to explain why the definition of 'product' in the 1987 Act expressly mentions electricity, the classification of which has apparently given rise to difficulties in the American case law on strict product liability.[36] And the other problem is the rise of artificial intelligence and automated systems, such as robots. To the extent that these end up undertaking tasks that were previously carried out by humans, the dividing line between products and services again comes under pressure.[37] For following automation it may be possible to characterise harm that would now straightforwardly be regarded as the result of provision of a service – such as a routine medical procedure, or the checking of a CT scan for abnormalities – as the result of a defect in a 'product', in the form of the artificially intelligent system or robot undertaking the task. This would then mean that liability for such harm would rest on fault where the task was performed by a human (such as a doctor) but would be strict where it was performed by an automated system.

For all these reasons it is difficult to escape the conclusion that the line between products and services cannot be held, and that this imposes 'considerable and perhaps intolerable expansionary pressure on the concept of "product"',[38] pressure which the European Commission's proposed new Directive shows it may no longer be possible for the architecture of strict product liability to resist.

B. Other Troublesome Distinctions

Strict product liability as encapsulated in the 1987 Act gives rise to several other troublesome distinctions, in addition to those generated by the product/services divide. It is difficult to catalogue all of these, so I will just flag some of the most obvious (or most obviously problematic).

One is between defects in the product when first supplied by the producer, to which strict liability applies, and defects introduced into the product later,

---

[34] The European Commission's proposed new Directive deals with this issue by classifying software as a 'product' whether stored on a device or not, and then classifying the 'developer or producer' of the software as a producer (European Commission, 'Proposal for a Directive' (n 7) recital 12). However, source code of software is not to count as a product since it is 'pure information' (ibid). One wonders why that description does not also apply to the software itself.

[35] See Stapleton, *Product Liability* (n 31) 330.

[36] ibid. The European Commission's proposed new Directive also clarifies 'for the avoidance of doubt' that electricity is a product (European Commission, 'Proposal for a Directive' (n 7) recital 14).

[37] See P Machnikowski, 'Conclusions' in P Machnikowski (ed), *European Product Liability* (Cambridge, Intersentia, 2016) 698.

[38] Stapleton, *Product Liability* (n 31) 324.

where section 4(1)(d) provides the producer with a defence to strict liability. This distinction makes sense when the product is supplied as a one-off thing, and the producer's involvement ceases once it leaves their hands. However, technological developments, such as the updating of product software after marketing, are increasingly putting the distinction under strain.[39] No such distinction is drawn in the law of negligence, where the producer's duty of care can simply be extended to reflect their continued involvement with the product after its initial supply.[40]

Another problematic distinction drawn by the 1987 Act is between damage caused before and after the defective product was put into circulation. In the former case, the producer again has a defence to strict liability, this time under section 4(1)(b),[41] and so liability is contingent on fault. However, it is not entirely clear why a person injured when a defective car crashes while being driven on the manufacturer's test circuit should have to prove fault, but a person injured when the same vehicle leaves the road while being driven home from a dealership by its first purchaser need not.[42]

Turning to the question of who can be liable for damage caused by a defective product under the 1987 Act, it will be helpful first to summarise the equivalent rules in contract and negligence. In contract, liability can be imposed only on a party who was in a contractual relationship with the person who suffered the injury or damage, unless the case falls within an exception to the privity doctrine, such as those created by the Contracts (Rights of Third Parties) Act 1999. And in negligence, anybody who takes on obligations regarding the production, supply, installation or repair of the product can be liable, so long as they were at fault, and the other basic requirements of negligence liability – such as foreseeability of injury – are met. Not only are these principles simple, they also have an internal logic that gives them coherence. A contractual counterparty is liable because they entered into a transaction which required them to sell (etc) a product of satisfactory quality. And a negligent defendant is liable because they were at fault.

By contrast, the rules on who can be liable under the 1987 Act do not always map very well onto possible justifications for imposing strict product liability in the first place. To the extent that such liability is based on deterrence concerns, for example, it should be 'directed to the person to whose conduct the injury is principally attributable',[43] but this is frequently not the case. Hence, where the

---

[39] See Wagner, *Liability Rules for the Digital Age* (n 7) 18–20.

[40] The post-sale duties of manufacturers in negligence are well recognised, although hitherto they have chiefly related to warnings and recalls in cases where a danger has come to light after the marketing of the product: see *The Law of Tort* (n 9) para 19.26.

[41] According to this provision it is a defence that the defendant 'did not at any time supply the product to another'.

[42] The anomalies created by this defence are emphasised by J Stapleton, 'Products Liability Reform: Real or Illusory?' (1986) 6 *OJLS* 392, 419–20, who argues that the distinction it draws is incompatible with the enterprise risk, loss distribution and deterrence arguments for strict liability.

[43] J Stapleton, 'Three Problems with the New Product Liability' in P Cane and J Stapleton (eds), *Essays for Patrick Atiyah* (Oxford, Clarendon Press, 1991) 264.

defect in the product is the result of the work of an out-of-house designer, the producer will be liable even though they took all reasonable steps in selecting the designer, and in checking their work, whereas the designer themselves bears no liability under the Act.[44] Similarly, were liability to be imposed under the Act for dangerously misleading information conveyed by a product,[45] the liability would fall on the producer of the physical product, rather than the person responsible for the misleading information. It follows that in the case of, say, an inaccurate guide to edible mushrooms, it would be the printer or publisher of the book (one of whom must presumably be its producer[46]) who would be liable under the Act, and not its author. This contrasts unfavourably with the position in negligence, where liability is placed on the person who is principally responsible for the damage, such as the out-of-house designer in the first example, and the author in the second.[47]

The problem of 'inappropriate parties'[48] being made responsible for product-related harm under a strict product liability regime is again made worse by technological change, while possible solutions to the problem threaten to make the issue of who is liable under such a regime yet more complex. These difficulties are not new. Over three decades ago, Stapleton pointed out that in the case of a computerised dialysis machine with defective software, the 1987 Act would place liability on the producer and supplier of the machine as a physical thing, but not on the 'producer' of the software (if different), and asked whether it was sensible for the software producer's liability to rest on the circumstances surrounding 'the origin of the physical conduit through which the defective [software] caused the injury'.[49] The difficulty is, however, exacerbated by increasing technological complexity, such as the advent of the 'Internet of Things', whereby more and more everyday products (from cars to fridges) are dependent on regular software updates which often occur automatically. Unless the update itself is treated as a 'product', no strict liability will arise for damage caused by a defect in the updating software, since the producer of the product will have a defence under section 4(1)(d) of the 1987 Act.[50] And although this apparent anomaly could in theory be solved by extending strict liability to 'the entity updating the digital content of a product previously put into circulation',[51] that would come at the price of additional complexity, and might well generate a different set of

---

[44] See ibid 264–65.

[45] See text following n 28.

[46] One would have thought that the printer would be the producer as the 'manufacturer' of the book (see the definition of a producer in the Consumer Protection Act 1987, s 1(2)(a)).

[47] To some extent these problems can be obviated in practice by building suitable indemnities into the relevant contracts (ie, those between the producer and the out-of-house designer, or the printer/publisher/author) but the point remains that the pattern of liability generated by the 1987 Act itself is hard to justify.

[48] Stapleton, 'Three Problems with the New Product Liability' (n 43) 265.

[49] Stapleton, 'Software, Information and the Concept of "Product"' (n 30) 152–53.

[50] That the defect did not exist in the product when supplied by the producer.

[51] As suggested by Machnikowski (n 37) 702.

anomalies. More generally, the European Commission rightly cautions that 'as products are more easily altered, adapted and combined with services, the definition of producer may become less clear', with the result that the definition 'may no longer be fully relevant in its current form'.[52]

The troublesome distinctions to which strict product liability gives rise are no accident. They flow inexorably from the absence of a convincing rationale for imposing strict liability in the first place (the theme of the next part of the chapter) and in particular for separating out damage caused by products – as opposed to, say, buildings or services – for special treatment in this regard. With reference to the product/services borderline, for example, it has been observed that '[w]ithout a clear understanding of *why* products cases are distinct, it has been difficult to ascertain *what* constitutes a products case in borderline situations presented by hybrid product-service transactions'.[53] In the absence of such an understanding, a strict product liability regime operating as an exception to a general system of fault-based liability is bound to give rise to anomalies and incoherence, and to 'inhibit the development of civil liability along broad rational principles'.[54] Indeed, we can go further. Not only are the troublesome distinctions generated by strict product liability a standalone reason to revert to fault liability in this context. The very existence of seemingly intractable boundary problems is powerful evidence that damage caused by defective products is not deserving of special treatment within the law of tort, and hence that there was never a good reason to move away from fault in the first place.

C. Complexity

An additional problem with strict product liability in tort is the complexity that it generates. All things being equal, the simpler the law is, the better it is. Simple laws help prevent litigation and make the resolution of the litigation that does occur easier, faster and cheaper. However, a strict liability tort regime exponentially complicates the law of product liability, when compared to the background rules of contract and negligence. After all, the basic principles governing strict liability for product defects in contract are well settled and reasonably straightforward.[55] Nor is liability for harm caused by defective products in negligence especially complex. The position is largely governed by general negligence principles, and although in the past there were distinct

---

[52] European Commission, 'Evaluation of Directive 85/374 on Liability for Defective Products' (n 28) 61.

[53] WC Powers Jr, 'Distinguishing between Products and Services in Strict Liability' (1984) 62 *North Carolina Law Review* 415, 418 (emphasis in original).

[54] Stapleton, *Product Liability* (n 31) 358.

[55] For a detailed account, see Fairgrieve and Goldberg (n 11) pt I.

rules pertaining to product liability in negligence, most of these have now been merged into those general principles, thereby simplifying the law.[56]

Again, the contrast with strict tort liability is stark. In principle, the liability regime established by the 1985 Directive is a simple one, and indeed the Directive itself is short and elegant, unlike the 1987 Act, which is badly drafted and over-complex. But although the basic conceptual structure of the European strict liability regime is straightforward enough – liability for damage caused by a defect in a product, with some defences, and a range of possible defendants – the basic building blocks of that regime (such as 'product', 'producer' and 'defect') have become encrusted with layer upon layer of interpretation and analysis, generated by decades of court judgments and academic commentary. And while of course it can be argued that some of this complexity was avoidable, the truth is that strict liability tort regimes tend to generate complexity, because of the reliance that they necessarily place on novel concepts not found elsewhere in the law of tort – such as 'defect' and 'product' – and, at least in some cases, because of the difficulty of separating out the situations governed by strict liability from those that are not. Only where there is a direct importation of general tort principles into the strict liability regime – as is the case in this context with the rules of causation[57] – can this additional complexity be avoided.

The concept of a 'defect' is instructive in this regard. Admittedly, when it comes to manufacturing defects, the defectiveness enquiry should be relatively straightforward, although even here the English courts have managed to complicate matters by not holding that a dangerous departure from the condition of the product as intended by the producer is by definition a defect for these purposes,[58] and thereby given the lie to John Fleming's (entirely sensible) observation that '[m]anufacturing defects pose no problems of definition'.[59] However, modern product liability litigation is dominated by design defect cases, where (unlike in manufacturing defect cases) there is no simple benchmark against which to assess the product's safety. The difficulty in assessing whether a product is defective in design has spawned a vast and complex literature, which has so far failed to produce anything close to a consensus on the

---

[56] A good example is the 'no intermediate examination' requirement, which was laid down as a limitation on the scope of the duty of care owed by a manufacturer of a product to the ultimate consumer in *Donoghue v Stevenson* [1932] AC 562 (HL), but the significance of which is now much reduced, and easily explained by reference to general principles of breach of duty and legal causation: see *The Law of Tort* (n 9) para 19.32.

[57] Strict product liability seems not to have thrown up particular problems regarding causation because the causation rules have simply been imported from negligence law: see *The Law of Tort* (n 9) para 19.72.

[58] The key decision in this respect is *A v National Blood Authority* (n 12), where regrettably Burton J refused to lay down this simple rule, although he did say that in the case of a harmful characteristic of a non-standard product a finding of defectiveness was 'likely to be straightforward' (at [66]).

[59] JG Fleming, 'Of Dangerous and Defective Products' (1989) 9 *Tel Aviv University Studies in Law* 11, 14.

question.[60] And although similar problems can arise when applying a fault standard in a design defect case, the switch of focus in strict liability from the producer's conduct to the condition of the product itself makes things even more difficult.[61] These complications were not anticipated by the pioneers of strict product liability, who had in mind only manufacturing defects, and who therefore believed (perfectly reasonably) that strict liability would simplify the law and reduce litigation, rather than the reverse.[62] More generally, the problems with the 'defect' requirement can be traced to its origins in sales law. The transposition of this essentially contractual concept into the law of tort was always likely to generate complexity and confusion, for tort is pre-eminently concerned with human behaviour, and not with the 'physical properties of things'.[63]

Many other examples could be given of the complexity to which the 1987 Act gives rise. One will suffice, which is the somewhat convoluted case law that has developed around the 'development risk' defence in section 4(1)(e) of the Act. As Stapleton has demonstrated in her writings on this defence, the concepts that underlie the defence as interpreted, such as 'scientific and technical knowledge' which is 'accessible' to the producer, are inherently problematic and (again) give rise to apparently indefensible distinctions.[64] Once again the contrast with the straightforward requirement in negligence that the claimant establish that the producer's conduct fell below the standard of the reasonable producer is obvious.

Two final points should be made on the complexity issue. The first is that adapting strict liability to take account of the technological changes which have already been highlighted in this essay is bound to make the law more complex, not less. Anyone who doubts the truth of this claim should read the original 1985 Directive alongside the Commission's proposed replacement Directive and ask themselves which set of rules is the simpler one. Similarly, the suggestion that the increasing difficulty of distinguishing between products and services should be dealt with by extending strict liability to services raises a host of difficult and complex questions, such as what a requirement of 'defectiveness' would entail in a services case, and how strict tort liability for defective services would interact with the law of contract.[65] And the second point is that the very existence of parallel liability regimes in negligence and under the 1987 Act adds hugely to

---

[60] Some sense of the complexities involved can be gained by looking at the extended discussion of the 'defect' issue in Fairgrieve and Goldberg (n 11), which runs to some 150 pages (317–468). See also the Reporters' Note to *Restatement, Third, Torts: Product Liability* (1998) § 2, comment d, entitled 'Design defects: general considerations', which runs to a remarkable 66 pages.

[61] See Fleming (n 59) 17. See also Stapleton, 'Products Liability Reform' (n 42) 412 (rejecting the notion that the shift from fault to a defect-based liability rule will simplify the analysis).

[62] See text to nn 70–71.

[63] See Wagner, 'Development of Product Liability in Germany' (n 10) 126.

[64] For an early critique, see Stapleton, *Product Liability* (n 31) 236–42.

[65] See WH van Boom, 'Statement from a Continental Perspective' in Koziol et al (n 1) 585.

the complexity of the law in this area. As Stapleton has pointed out, this has concrete implications for potential claimants and their legal advisers, who must necessarily consider all possible avenues of redress and defence, and who dare not risk suing only under the 1987 Act in case for some (perhaps unanticipated) reason the negligence route turns out to be more advantageous.[66] In difficult cases, the result is that 'far from simplifying the plaintiff's claim', the 1987 Act 'will have added a costly new dimension to it'.[67] Seen in this light, the belief of the early proponents of strict product liability that it would provide 'prompt and adequate compensation to injury victims',[68] and reduce the costs of product-related litigation,[69] looks to have been a pipe dream.

IV. RESPONDING TO THE ARGUMENTS FOR STRICT PRODUCT LIABILITY

Having identified some of the difficulties to which strict product liability in tort has given rise, I now turn to possible justifications for it. I conclude that none of them is convincing. Much of the material that follows covers ground which is already well-trodden, but I make no apology for that. On the contrary, the fact that the flimsiness of many of the arguments for strict liability in this context has frequently been pointed out by others adds weight to my critique. What is surprising is that the powerful criticisms of the various theories that lie behind strict liability have not led more commentators to question whether it is appropriate to impose such liability in defective product cases.

I group the possible justifications into three categories, namely: (1) loss-spreading/enterprise risk/risk community; (2) deterrence/prevention; and (3) other arguments. When considering these potential justifications, it is important to bear in mind not only the plausibility of the justification in general terms, but also whether it provides a reason for imposing strict liability for damage caused by defective products in particular. If not, then even if it might provide a reason for moving towards strict liability across the board, the justification does not explain why strict liability is *particularly appropriate* in product liability cases.

It is worth remembering when considering these arguments that many of them were first put forward by the early American proponents of strict product liability, who were almost entirely concerned with manufacturing defects.[70] For them, the paradigm product liability case was an exploding

---

[66] Stapleton, *Product Liability* (n 31) 355.

[67] ibid.

[68] B Feldthusen et al, 'Product Liability in North America' in Koziol et al (n 1) 368.

[69] See Law Commission, *Liability for Defective Products* (n 14) para 36(g) (arguing that strict tort liability might reduce legal costs by short-circuiting the contract chain, and because the court would not have to spend time on the negligence issue).

[70] See GL Priest, 'The Modern Irony of Civil Law: A Memoir of Strict Products Liability in the United States' (1989) 9 *Tel Aviv University Studies in Law* 93. According to Priest (at 98), the proponents of section 402A of the *Restatement, Second, Torts* (1965) 'intended its strict liability standard,

glass bottle of carbonated drink.[71] In their view, it made little sense to set the plaintiff in a case of this kind the near impossible task of proving that the explosion of the bottle was the fault of the manufacturer. It would be much simpler and more straightforward just to impose liability on the basis that there was a defect in the bottle, and that this had caused the plaintiff's injury. Furthermore, to the extent that these early proponents of strict liability considered design defect cases at all, it was 'the unanimous view' that they should be governed by a negligence standard.[72]

A. Loss-Spreading/Enterprise Risk/Risk Community

The 'loss-spreading' argument for strict product liability can be traced back to the seminal judgment of Traynor J in *Escola v Coca-Cola Bottling Co of Fresno*, where he said that:

> Those who suffer injury from defective products are unprepared to meet its consequences. The cost of injury and the loss of time or health may be an overwhelming misfortune to the person injured and a needless one, for the risk of injury can be insured by the manufacturer and distributed among the public as a cost of doing business.[73]

The essence of this justification was later summed up by Friedrich Kessler as follows:

> The manufacturer can either control the risk of defective products or can equitably distribute losses among all potential victims. He is strategically located to act not only as risk gatherer but also as risk distributor. Strict liability, therefore, is a good deal fairer than letting fate select the victim at random and letting him bear the full loss by denying him compensation; the seller by raising his price, spreads the loss over the community of consumers. The price paid by each consumer contains a small premium for accident insurance.[74]

Variations on this argument have been relied on by proponents of strict product liability ever since *Escola*. A popular modern variant is the 'enterprise risk' rationale, which posits that the losses caused by the producer's profit-making enterprise should be internalised to the enterprise by the imposition of strict

---

with minor exceptions, to apply *only* to what we now call manufacturing defect cases' (emphasis in original). Fleming (n 59) 13–16 concurs with Priest's analysis. In the US mass product liability tort cases alleging design defects were filed only in the 1970s, some time after section 402A was adopted by the American Law Institute: see KS Abraham, *The Liability Century* (Cambridge, Mass, Harvard UP, 2008) 146–47.

[71] On the significance of exploding bottle cases to the early debates on strict product liability, see K Graham, 'Strict Products Liability at 50: Four Histories' (2014) *Marquette Law Review* 580, 601 ff.

[72] Priest, 'The Modern Irony of Civil Law' (n 70) 104.

[73] *Escola v Coca-Cola Bottling Co of Fresno* 150 P 2d 436 (Cal 1944) 440–41.

[74] F Kessler, 'Products Liability' (1967) 76 *Yale Law Journal* 887, 927.

liability. This rationale has rightly been described as 'rather unfocused',[75] but the central underlying idea is that the person or entity that benefits from a given activity should also bear the burden of the losses that it causes.[76] According to Stapleton's theory of 'moral enterprise liability', for example, where products are made and marketed in the pursuit of financial profit, the producer should be liable for the injuries that they cause, regardless of fault, as a price to be paid for operating in the market.[77] Enterprise risk or enterprise liability arguments are not limited to the product liability context, but have also been relied upon as justifications for imposing strict liability on employers for workplace injuries,[78] and vicarious liability on employers for wrongful injury caused by their employees in the course of employment.[79]

A second variant of the loss-spreading justification is the 'risk community' theory, according to which the producer and consumers of a product are treated as 'part of one economic system in which the purchase price charged by the former may be seen as incorporating a heightened degree of protection of the latter from risk'.[80] According to one version of this argument, the price of the product is kept acceptable to consumers by not employing the very highest standards of safety and quality control, and hence they should also bear the costs that this imposes on the unlucky consumers who are injured as a result.[81]

None of these arguments is persuasive as a justification for strict product liability. In the UK, at least, the basic loss-spreading justification has rightly fallen out of favour in the modern era and it smacks of a post-war compensation-focused approach to tort liability that is now largely discredited. The objections to it are obvious. For a start, it is both inefficient and unfair, as David Owen points out:

> Its inefficiency is reflected by the very high transaction costs involved in the processing of claims, represented by the high costs of litigation for both parties and the courts. It is unfair, among other reasons, because of the regressive manner in which consumers pay an equal 'premium', as a part of the product's price, yet receive payouts based on sometimes greatly differing levels of income.[82]

---

[75] WH van Boom et al, 'Product Liability in Europe' in Koziol et al (n 1) 317.

[76] See, eg, *Restatement, Third, Torts: Product Liability* (1998) § 2, comment a.

[77] Stapleton, *Product Liability* (n 31) ch 8.

[78] See GL Priest, 'The Invention of Enterprise Liability: A Critical History of the Intellectual Foundations of Modern Tort Law' (1985) 14 *Journal of Legal Studies* 461, 466.

[79] See S Deakin, '"Enterprise-Risk": The Juridical Nature of the Firm' (2003) 32 *Industrial Law Journal* 97.

[80] Oliphant (n 20) 568.

[81] H Koziol, 'Introductory Lecture' in Koziol et al (n 1) 23.

[82] DG Owen, 'Products Liability: Principles of Justice' (1991) 20 *Anglo-American Law Review* 238, 245. On the efficiency advantages of first-party insurance over 'tort insurance' in this context, see M Geistfeld, '*Escola v Coca Cola Bottling Co*: Strict Products Liability Unbound' in RL Rabin and SD Sugarman (eds), *Torts Stories* (New York, Foundation Press, 2003) 256–57.

Coupling private first-party insurance with a public welfare system for those without insurance is both more efficient and more fair.[83] It should also be noted that a loss-spreading rationale is hard to reconcile with central tenets of the strict product liability regime created by the 1987 Act, including the requirement of a 'defect' and the development risk defence.

The benefit/burden idea that underpins the enterprise risk rationale also falls short as a justification for strict product liability. As has frequently been observed, on this approach only profit-making defendants should be subject to strict liability, but the 1987 Act extends to all producers and suppliers acting in the course of business,[84] including charities and state entities such as the National Health Service.[85] The idea that public hospitals and blood banks should be subject to strict product liability on the ground that 'he who takes the benefit should bear the burden' is singularly unpersuasive. And even in the case of commercial enterprises the benefit/burden idea is extremely crude. Do not consumers of products like fridges and cars also benefit from their production and marketing? If not, then why do they buy them in the first place? The truth is that in most cases the relationship of producer and consumer is a mutually beneficial one. Furthermore, product manufacture clearly has wider social and economic benefits, such as creating employment, supporting supplier businesses and funding public services through business taxation.[86] As Anthony Gray says, it is therefore folly to make the 'simplistic argument that an organisation derives all of the benefit of [its own] economic activity' and should therefore bear all of its costs.[87] In any case, the logic of enterprise risk or liability points to prima facie liability for all damage caused by products. On this rationale, the 'defect' requirement makes no sense.[88]

Although more sophisticated, the 'risk community' rationale also suffers from fatal flaws. Most importantly, it only serves as a justification for conferring the benefit of strict liability on the product purchaser, and cannot explain the extension of such liability to third parties such as family members and

---

[83] Owen (n 82) 245. As Mark Geistfeld points out, the insurance justification put forward by Traynor J in *Escola* was a contingent one, which depended on the lack of private health insurance, public healthcare provision and social insurance in the US in the 1940s: Geistfeld (n 82) 255–56. On the inadequacies of tort liability as a compensation mechanism more generally, see SD Sugarman, 'Doing Away with Tort Law' (1985) 73 *California Law Review* 555; and PS Atiyah, *The Damages Lottery* (Oxford, Hart Publishing, 1997).

[84] Although the fact that the defendant did not supply the product in the course of a business may afford them a defence under s 4(1)(c) of the 1987 Act, here as elsewhere in English law acting 'in the course of business' is a broad concept that encompasses many non-profit activities.

[85] A contrast can be drawn here with the position in Australia and Israel, where only commercial entities are subject to strict product liability: see EB Bourie et al, 'Product Liability in the Rest of the World' in Koziol et al (n 1) 463.

[86] On the 'multiplier effect' of economic activity of this sort, see A Gray, *The Evolution from Strict Liability to Fault in the Law of Torts* (Oxford, Hart Publishing, 2021) 173.

[87] ibid.

[88] See Geistfeld (n 82) 252, 254.

bystanders, who are not members of the 'risk community' in the first place.[89] Nor does it explain the application of strict liability to products supplied for free, such as medical devices and blood products provided by public healthcare systems. It is also subject to one of the most powerful counter-arguments to the loss-spreading justification, namely its regressive effect. All the members of the 'risk community' pay the same price for the protection that their membership affords them – namely the price premium associated with strict liability – but the wealthier members stand to gain much more from the compensation payments made to those who suffer product-related injury. The result is that the low-income product purchasers end up subsidising the high-income ones.

One final point can be made about the arguments discussed in this section, which is that they do not explain why product-related injuries should be singled out for strict liability. To the extent that the loss-spreading, enterprise risk and 'risk community' justifications do have any persuasive power, they would also serve as arguments for imposing strict tort liability in other contexts still governed largely by a fault standard, such as sub-standard service provision, defective premises and (in the case of the first two justifications) road traffic accidents. These rationales therefore offer no justification for 'the selective use of strict liability' in relation to injuries caused by defective products.[90]

B. Deterrence/Prevention

In *Escola*, Traynor J said that 'public policy demands that responsibility be fixed wherever it will most effectively reduce the hazards to life and health inherent in defective products', and that this militated in favour of strict liability.[91] The suggestion seemed to be that strict liability would help to prevent product-related injury, though it was not explained why it was more effective in this regard than a fault standard. Since *Escola* the claim that strict liability is more efficient than fault liability in this context has frequently been made, especially in the United States, but there is very little reason to suppose that this is in fact the case. In the discussion that follows I look first at arguments from what I will term 'specific' deterrence and then at arguments from 'market' (or 'general') deterrence, and finish by considering some objections to deterrence arguments for strict liability more generally. It is important to remember when considering these arguments that in economic terms the goal is not safer products per se, but an optimal level of product safety, which is to say the most efficient balance between product utility and cost on the one hand, and the amount of product-related injury on the other.

---

[89] It follows that any justificatory power of the 'risk community' idea is limited to strict *contract* liability for defective products and does not extend to strict *tort* liability.

[90] JCP Goldberg, 'Twentieth-Century Tort Theory' (2003) 91 *Georgetown Law Journal* 513, 543.

[91] *Escola* (n 73) 440–41.

i. Specific Deterrence

The specific deterrence argument for strict product liability posits that strict liability gives producers better incentives than a negligence rule to take cost-efficient precautions which will serve to reduce the level of product-related injury. This is a surprising idea. After all, the negligence standard should incentivise producers 'to adopt any safety measure that costs less than the harm expected to result from not taking the precaution'.[92] And as any additional safety measures must by definition cost more than the harm expected to result from taking them, the producer will not take those precautions, since *ex hypothesi* it is cheaper just to compensate the harm when it occurs. The result is that, as far as the rational and all-knowing producer assumed by this kind of economic analysis is concerned, there is quite simply 'no difference between the deterrence signal sent by negligence and strict liability'.[93]

It follows that any specific deterrence argument for strict liability must rest on a disparity between this basic model and what happens in the real world. Two main possibilities have been suggested in this regard. The first is that the difficulties of proving producer fault mean that a negligence standard will under-deter.[94] This is pure speculation, however. It is simply impossible to know whether in fact placing the burden of proof on claimants to establish fault causes under-deterrence or not. Much depends on the extent to which the courts are willing to help claimants to discharge that burden, and (as we have seen[95]) there is plenty of evidence that they will bend over backwards to assist claimants in this respect. Furthermore, in design defect cases the burden of proving fault may not be appreciably more onerous than the burden of proving that the product has a defect, in which case any force that this argument has is probably limited to manufacturing defects. Finally, even if the argument were to be accepted, the obvious solution to the problem would be to reverse the burden of proof in negligence, not to impose strict liability.[96]

A second reason why it has been suggested that there may be a disparity between the basic specific deterrence model and reality is that in practice the negligence standard may be set too low. Hence it has been claimed that a

---

[92] Feldthusen et al (n 68) 364.

[93] ibid. See also R Posner, 'Strict Liability – A Comment' (1973) 2 *Journal of Legal Studies* 205, 209 (comparative safety levels not affected by choice between negligence and strict liability in the short or long run).

[94] See Feldthusen et al (n 68) 364.

[95] See text to nn 13–14.

[96] See H Koziol, 'Conclusions from a Comparative Perspective' in Koziol et al (n 1) 533. Geistfeld (n 82) 246 fn rejects this solution on the ground that the difficulties of proving a negative mean that the result would be strict liability in all but name, and that therefore a strict liability rule is to be preferred because of the higher litigation costs associated with the reasonable care inquiry. However, it may be perfectly possible for a producer to prove on the balance of probabilities that they exercised reasonable care, and in any case Geistfeld's assumption regarding litigation costs takes no account of the complexities to which strict liability gives rise.

negligence standard may not incentivise producers to invest adequately in research and development, with the result that they fail to identify efficient safety measures that they could be taking.[97] However, this is again pure speculation, and, besides, if it is true that the courts set the fault standard too low, then the obvious answer is to raise it to a more appropriate level – or, more accurately, to apply the standard of the reasonable producer in a more appropriate way. For (to reiterate) if the courts are in fact applying that standard appropriately, then any additional deterrent effect of strict liability would inevitably be incentivising producers to take *unreasonable* precautions, the likely costs of which outweigh their likely benefits. And although it has been suggested that strict liability may in fact have such 'over-deterrence' (or 'overkill') effects,[98] clearly that would – if true – be undesirable from an efficiency perspective.[99]

The assumptions that underlie the specific deterrence justification for strict liability are in any case contestable. There is little evidence that the liability rule that is selected has any real impact on producer decision-making,[100] and nor is it realistic to suppose that product manufacturers are the omniscient rational actors that economic arguments like this take them to be.[101] It is also worth noting that, by channelling liability to producers, regardless of their fault, strict product liability may disincentivise participants in the process of product design and manufacture (such as out-of-house designers) whose liability remains fault-based, and who are therefore unlikely to be the targets of litigation.[102]

ii. Market Deterrence

Market deterrence arguments are typically associated with strict liability, and so at first blush look more promising. On closer inspection, however, they provide no more convincing a justification for strict product liability than specific deterrence arguments. In the case of specific deterrence, the problem lies with the absence of a plausible reason to depart from the basic model (which itself points to a negligence standard). In the case of market deterrence, by contrast, the problem lies with the implausibility of the basic model itself.

---

[97] See, eg, Fleming (n 59) 16 ('the negligence doctrine does not sufficiently encourage the search for and development of [safety] improvements').

[98] See text to nn 118–19.

[99] The development risk defence in s 4(1)(e) of the 1987 Act also reduces any incentive that strict liability gives producers actively to seek out hitherto unknown risks associated with their products.

[100] See Sugarman (n 83) 566, 588 (citing a study that found that changes in the law were not even transmitted by companies to those making design decisions and that firms treated product liability litigation as random 'noise', generating no clear signals to guide design decisions).

[101] See D More, 'Re-Examining Strict Products Liability's Goals and Justifications' (1989) 9 *Tel Aviv University Studies in Law* 165, 187–88.

[102] See Stapleton, 'Three Problems with the New Product Liability' (n 43) 264–65. In the absence of 'an adequately tight contribution rule' under the 1987 Act (ibid), this problem can only be countered by adding an indemnity to the contract between the producer and the party at fault.

According to the market deterrence argument, strict product liability ensures that all the costs associated with injuries caused by defective products are borne by the producers, so that the full social cost of a product is reflected in its price. This then means that the operation of market forces will result in a 'marginal shift to cheaper (because safer) substitutes if such exist'.[103] By contrast, if liability is based on fault, those injured by a defect in a product for which the producer is not to blame in effect subsidise the producer, thereby enabling products whose costs outweigh their benefits to remain on the market and inefficient producers to stay in business.[104]

The objections to market deterrence as a justification for strict liability are numerous. First, since the argument requires that the full social cost of a product be reflected in its price, it points towards a rule whereby all losses attributable to a product are internalised to its producer – what Stapleton calls 'full strict liability'[105] – and not only losses caused by a defect in a product. Second, the argument rests on the doubtful assumption that the damages paid out to tort victims in fact reflect the full social cost of their injuries. It seems much more likely that the assessment of damages either under- or over-estimates those costs, in which case strict liability will not mean that producers bear the full social cost – and only the full social cost – of accidents caused by their products. Third, any market deterrent effect of strict liability will be diluted by the failure of many victims of product-related injury to bring legal proceedings, and to the extent that those who do sue settle for less than a court would award them, or fail in their claims for want of proof of causation and such like.[106] Fourth, the assumption that liability costs will be reflected in the price of the relevant product is very doubtful. Setting aside the effect of liability insurance – to which we will come shortly – a producer will probably spread liability costs across the entire range of their products, rather than tying it to the particular product that gave rise to the liability.[107] Furthermore, the long latency period of many product liability claims (especially the design defect claims that dominate the modern law) means that any compensation payments are likely to be made by the producer many years after the product is first marketed and quite possibly after it has been taken off the market altogether.[108] Fifth, even if there *is* an effect on price, it is likely to be so negligible as to make very little difference to consumer preferences. According to one US study from the late 1970s, in the industry in which the totality of liability costs was then highest (rubber and plastics), they

---

[103] Stapleton, 'Products Liability Reform' (n 42) 396.
[104] This theory was first developed in G Calabresi, *The Costs of Accidents* (New Haven, Yale UP, 1970) 68–75.
[105] Stapleton, 'Products Liability Reform' (n 42) 397.
[106] ibid 420.
[107] Fleming (n 59) 19.
[108] See Stapleton, *Product Liability* (n 31) 148–49.

still amounted to only 0.58 per cent of sales income.[109] Bearing in mind that only part of that figure was attributable to product liability in particular, and that the market deterrence theory rests on the disparities between liability costs of different producers operating in the same market – which we can presume are lower than the total such costs averaged across the industry – the supposed shift to safer products predicted by the market deterrence theory looks optimistic, to say the least. And finally, there are likely to be market imperfections and positive externalities which for all we know may balance out any subsidy that a fault liability regime gives to product manufacturers, in which case that balance will be upset by the internalisation of all accident costs associated with the use of the product.[110]

iii. Problems with Deterrence Arguments in General

If we step back from the details of specific and market deterrence, we can also observe a raft of more general problems with the idea that strict product liability can be justified on deterrence grounds.[111] One of the most obvious of these is that deterrence arguments are seriously undermined by third-party insurance, which significantly dilutes the impact on producers of the imposition of liability for product-related injury. And while it can be countered that insurers will increase the premiums of firms with bad liability records, it seems that this is only likely to be true to a significant degree in the case of very large companies, as it is not worthwhile for insurers to 'experience rate' smaller firms individually in this way.[112] Furthermore, even when insurers do engage in experience rating, for various reasons it is unlikely to serve as 'an important promoter of safety'.[113] In reality the level of insurance premiums is likely to be governed primarily by the perceived liability risks of the product type in question (as opposed to the particular product or producer), along with the state of the insurance market. A second problem with deterrence theories is that any deterrent effect of liability rules in this context is likely to be completely dwarfed by the deterrent effect of the stringent regulations governing product safety, and of the potential reputational damage likely to result from having marketed a product found to have been

---

[109] See Sugarman (n 83) 570–71.

[110] See ibid 615. The point is that we have no good reason to assume that the price of products is optimal in efficiency terms *but for* any externalisation of accident costs. And yet that is precisely the assumption that the market deterrence theory makes.

[111] For more comprehensive critiques of efficiency rationales for strict product liability, see More (n 101) and Stapleton, *Product Liability* (n 31) ch 6. More generally, there is little empirical evidence that tort liability affects either individual or corporate behaviour, as compared to other influences, such as regulation, codes of conduct, ethics and culture: C Hodges, *Law and Corporate Behaviour* (Oxford, Hart Publishing, 2015) 145–57.

[112] Sugarman (n 83) 576.

[113] See ibid 576–77. On the distorting effect insurance has on the safety incentives of product manufacturers, see Stapleton, *Product Liability* (n 31) 150–54.

unsafe.[114] Nor should it be forgotten that manufacturers may well be subject to strict liability via indemnity claims up the contractual chain regardless of the position in tort. Finally, like the loss-spreading argument, deterrence arguments do not explain why product-related injuries *in particular* should be subject to strict liability. Similar arguments could be made for imposing strict liability in other contexts, such as road accidents, work-related injury, and damage caused by defective buildings.

For all these reasons, arguments from deterrence and prevention do not 'enable us to rank one form of liability as superior in efficiency terms to another', and so provide no justification for preferring strict liability to fault liability in this context.[115] As William Prosser pointed out many years ago, such arguments 'would appear to have been concocted in the heads of professors', rather than being based on 'any realities of the situation'.[116] Nor does the empirical evidence demonstrate that strict liability has reduced the frequency or severity of product-related injury.[117] Indeed, it is just as likely that strict liability has a *negative* effect on overall safety levels, by discouraging producers from developing beneficial new products for fear of liability for latent defects. According to the economist Kip Viscusi, in the US 'product liability often serves as a barrier to innovations that would reduce accidents',[118] while it has been argued that the imposition of strict liability on UK drug manufacturers has helped to create a situation in which useful medicines are less readily available, and that the first thing that should be done to encourage the development of new drugs is to revert to a negligence standard for product liability.[119]

C. Other Arguments

A range of other arguments have been put forward for strict product liability in tort, and here I deal with the four most prominent of these. The first two can

---

[114] See AM Polinsky and S Shavell, 'The Uneasy Case for Product Liability' (2010) 123 *Harvard Law Review* 1437, 1491 ('market forces and regulation frequently reduce the need for product liability to encourage safety'). The deterrent effect of reputational harm in this context was flagged by Prosser in his classic article on strict product liability: see WL Prosser, 'The Assault Upon the Citadel (Strict Liability to the Consumer)' (1960) 69 *Yale Law Journal* 1099, 1119. See also Wagner, 'Development of Product Liability in Germany' (n 10) 144 (pointing out that for reputational reasons car manufacturers launch product recalls even when the defect in question does not affect the safety of the vehicle but only inconveniences the owner).

[115] Stapleton, *Product Liability* (n 31) 156.

[116] Prosser (n 114) 1119.

[117] See, in the American context, WK Viscusi, 'Does Product Liability Make Us Safer?' (2012) 35 *Regulation* 24. Two reviews of empirical studies into the effect of product liability on product safety both reached agnostic conclusions: see JCP Goldberg and BC Zipursky, 'The Easy Case for Products Liability Law: A Response to Professors Polinsky and Shavell' (2010) 123 *Harvard Law Review* 1919, 1931.

[118] Viscusi, 'Does Product Liability Make Us Safer?' (n 117) 25.

[119] PJ Lachmann, 'The Penumbra of Thalidomide, the Litigation Culture and the Licensing of Pharmaceuticals' (2012) 105 *Quarterly Journal of Medicine* 1179.

be dismissed quickly, as they have no force whatsoever. The other two are more significant, and indeed are the only remotely persuasive arguments for strict liability in this context. Nevertheless, it will be contended that the issues that they highlight can be resolved in other ways, and that they come nowhere near to outweighing the many powerful arguments against strict liability.

i. The Representation Argument

The first of these four further arguments is the claim that strict liability should be imposed because the manufacturer implicitly represents that the product is safe, and so should be held to their representation. However, while this may serve to justify the strict contractual liability of a product supplier, it cannot explain why a producer is strictly liable to a consumer with whom the producer may have had no direct contact, still less a third party who by definition has not relied on any such representation in the first place,[120] or indeed a patient to whom a defective drug is administered during medical treatment. Like some of the other arguments that have been put forward for strict liability, this supposed justification is in truth little more than mere assertion.[121]

ii. The Risks Inherent in Modern Production Methods Argument

The second argument is also basically assertion, namely the claim made in the preamble to the 1985 Directive that strict liability is the 'sole means of adequately solving the problem, peculiar to our age of increasing technicality, of a fair apportionment of the risks inherent in modern technological production'.[122] This argument was later echoed by Advocate General Tesauro of the Court of Justice of the European Union, when he said that:

> With the ever increasing complexity of manufacturing processes, the risks associated with product defects multiplied and became difficult to avoid and it became clear that the system of liability founded on the producer's negligence was inappropriate to secure adequate protection for the consumer.[123]

Notice how in this sentence two groundless claims (that greater complexity in manufacturing processes caused the risks associated with product defects to multiply and become difficult to avoid) precede a conclusion that is a mere assertion ('it became clear that ...'). In fact, the supposed 'risks inherent in modern technological production' are a myth. Modern mass production processes are

---

[120] See Stapleton, *Product Liability* (n 31) 220.
[121] See, eg, *Restatement, Second, Torts* (1965) § 402A, comment c ('[T]he justification for the strict liability has been said to be that the seller, by marketing his product for use and consumption, has undertaken and assumed a special responsibility toward any member of the consuming public who may be injured by it; ... that reputable sellers stand behind their goods', etc, etc).
[122] Directive 85/374/EEC (n 2) recital 2.
[123] *Commission v United Kingdom* (n 21), Opinion of AG Tesauro, para 16.

safe by historical standards, so much so that manufacturing defects are now said to be 'rare events'.[124] And besides, even if it *were* true that modern production processes resulted in large numbers of defective products entering the market, this would not justify strict liability for design defects, nor the application of the strict liability regime to handmade goods, human body products, agricultural produce and the like. The conclusion that this 'argument' has no justificatory force whatsoever seems inescapable.

iii. The Contract Anomaly Argument

The third argument rests on the existence of strict liability in contract. Before we turn to it, we should note a separate contract-based argument, which is that requiring the injured purchaser of a defective product to sue the seller in contract in order to obtain the benefit of strict liability is 'needlessly circuitous',[125] since the liability will then simply be passed up the contract chain to the manufacturer in any case. This argument was relied on by Prosser in a seminal early article on strict product liability. According to Prosser, it was 'already possible to enforce strict liability by resort to a series of actions' up the contractual chain, but this was 'an expensive, time-consuming, and wasteful process' which could be 'interrupted by insolvency, lack of jurisdiction, disclaimers, or the statute of limitations'.[126] It followed that what was needed instead was 'a blanket rule which makes any supplier in the chain liable directly to the ultimate user, and so short-circuits the whole unwieldy process'.[127] But this seems a rather flimsy basis on which to ground a complex regime of strict product liability in tort, and it can be objected that the result is to bypass the contractual allocations of risk agreed upon by the commercial entities in the chain. Furthermore, there are other contexts – such as negligence recovery for pure economic loss – in which the law insists that parties sue up the chain of contracts, and it is not clear why product liability cases should be singled out for this kind of 'short-circuiting'.[128] Finally, this argument does not explain why strict product liability extends to product donees (for example, of blood transfusions) and third parties such as bystanders.

The more significant contract-based argument is that it is unjust to privilege the purchaser of the defective product – to whom the supplier is strictly liable in contract – over a third party, such as a family member of the purchaser, who must instead establish negligence vis-à-vis the manufacturer. According to Prosser:

> The result [of the operation of the privity rule in this context] has been such utterly preposterous decisions as those holding that the wife who buys the [defective]

---

[124] AD Twerski, 'Chasing the Illusory Pot of Gold at the End of the Rainbow: Negligence and Strict Liability in Design Defect Litigation' (2006) 90 *Marquette Law Review* 7, 18.

[125] *Escola* (n 73) 442 (Traynor J).

[126] Prosser (n 114) 1123–24.

[127] ibid 1124.

[128] See, eg, *Muirhead v Industrial Tank Specialities Ltd* [1986] QB 507 (CA).

sausage, handles it, cooks it, eats it, and is poisoned by it, cannot recover because she was merely buying as an agent for her husband, who was to pay the bill and so is regarded as the contracting party.[129]

The issue that Prosser highlighted in this passage could also arise under English law before the 1987 Act, as is shown by *Daniels and Daniels v R White & Sons Ltd*,[130] where a couple suffered injury after drinking lemonade containing grains of carbolic acid. Although the husband recovered damages from the retailer from whom he had bought the drink, his wife could not recover damages either from the retailer in contract (because of the privity rule) or from the manufacturer in tort (because she could not establish negligence).

Although there is unquestionably some force in this 'contract anomaly' argument, there is not enough weight in it to justify strict tort liability for defective products (which, as we have seen, generates anomalies of its own[131]). The problem is likely to arise only relatively rarely, and mostly in contexts that are far removed from the design defect cases involving drugs, medical devices and the like that currently dominate product liability litigation in the UK. Furthermore, the obvious solution to the problem is to reform contract law so as to extend the benefits of the purchaser's contractual protection to family members and similarly situated third party users of the product.[132] Indeed, to some extent the current contract rules already do this. The Contract (Rights of Third Parties) Act 1999, for example, enables a third party expressly identified in a contract to rely on a term of the contract if the contract says that they may do so, or if the contract purports to confer a benefit on them and the parties intended the contract to be enforceable by them.[133] Furthermore, even before the 1999 Act, the courts were willing in some cases to hold that an apparent donee had a contract with the retailer after all. In *Lockett v A & M Charles Ltd*,[134] for instance, a woman poisoned by infected food in a hotel was awarded damages in contract against the proprietors even though her husband had paid for the meal. Finally, it is worth noting that the real anomaly here is that in common law systems the mere fact that a person has paid for a product opens the door not only to a modest award of damages for economic loss caused by a defect in the product (typically the cost of repair or replacement), but also to potentially huge damages for personal injury, recoverable without proof of fault.[135] In many

---

[129] Prosser (n 114) 1118.

[130] [1938] 4 All ER 258 (KBD).

[131] See text following n 28.

[132] Graham (n 71) points out (at 620–21) that the US jurisdictions that extended consumer warranties to third parties tended to lag behind in adopting strict product liability in tort.

[133] On the implications of the 1999 Act in the present context, see Fairgrieve and Goldberg (n 11) paras 2.20–2.22.

[134] [1938] 4 All ER 170 (KBD).

[135] See Fairgrieve and Goldberg (n 11) para 1.04 ('An entitlement to recover the purchase price when goods are not as promised does not necessarily carry an implication that there is a right to claim compensation for physical injury which results from their use').

civilian legal systems, such as German law, strict contractual liability is mostly limited to what Kessler called 'the disturbed equivalence between the price paid and the quality of the commodity',[136] and in Scandinavia damages for personal injury are generally not recoverable in contract at all.[137] While it is not being suggested that English law should necessarily follow suit, the peculiarities of the common law of contract in this regard are hardly an auspicious foundation on which to construct a system of strict product liability in tort.[138]

iv. The Difficulty of Proving Negligence Argument

The final argument for strict liability which I wish to address is the alleged difficulty of establishing negligence in product liability cases. Like the contract anomaly argument, this justification admittedly has some force. However, once again, to the extent that the argument counts in favour of strict product liability it is heavily outweighed by the difficulties to which such liability gives rise.

In *Escola*, Traynor J drew attention to the fact that a person who suffers injury because of a defect in a product will often be unable to identify the cause of the defect, since 'he can hardly be familiar with the manufacturing process as the manufacturer himself is'.[139] He also argued that in the era of mass production manufacturing processes were more opaque than in earlier times when things were made by hand, and on a smaller scale.[140] More generally, product liability cases present problems of proof because any negligence is likely to have occurred 'at a time and place remote from the accident', making it hard for a claimant 'to ascertain specific facts about the manufacturer's behaviour'.[141] Furthermore, the place where any negligence occurred will almost certainly have been under the defendant's exclusive control, while the time lag between production and accident, coupled with the fact that the product may have passed through many different hands on its way to the final consumer, can make it difficult to establish whether the defect was introduced during the production process or only later on.[142]

As William Powers has argued, problems of proof provide a more plausible explanation for strict product liability than arguments from loss-spreading,

---

[136] Kessler (n 74) 912. See also van Boom et al (n 75) 275 (in Germany, contract liability for damage caused by a defective product is fault-based).

[137] See van Boom et al (n 75) 312.

[138] See also Stapleton, *Product Liability* (n 31) 92–93, arguing that if the law were 'feeling its way towards a consistent approach to claims for physical injury' it is not self-evident that the contractual strict liability standard would be regarded as the appropriate one.

[139] *Escola* (n 73) 441.

[140] ibid 443.

[141] Powers (n 53) 422. See also Law Commission, *Liability for Defective Products* (n 14) para 36(c).

[142] See, eg, *Evans v Triplex Safety Glass Co Ltd* [1936] 1 All ER 283 (KBD) (negligence claim against manufacturer of windscreen failed as it was unclear why it shattered, and whether the cause was present when it left the defendant's hands).

since they better explain the strict liability rules themselves. For example, the fact that there is a defect in the product at least raises an inference of fault, while the development risk defence is consistent with the fact that the claimant's inability to establish fault in the case of an unknowable danger is not attributable to problems of proof.[143] Furthermore, he also argues that since it will generally be easier for a claimant to prove fault in other types of case (such as those involving services) where the defendant's alleged negligence is likely to be more accessible to the claimant, problems of proof may be a reason – indeed, in his view, the *only* possible reason – for limiting strict liability to cases of injury caused by defective products.[144]

Nevertheless, as a justification for strict product liability problems of proof fall short. To some extent, they have been mitigated since the time of the *Escola* decision by a combination of more extensive pre-trial disclosure and scientific advances that make it easier for claimants to establish the cause of an accident. Furthermore, as we have seen,[145] there are various ways in which the courts help claimants to establish negligence in difficult cases. The result is that, as far as manufacturing defects are concerned, it is usually enough for the claimant to show that the defect was present when the product left the producer's hands, at which point the burden in effect shifts to the producer to show that they were not at fault. But most importantly, to the extent that the location of the burden of proof is thought to result in 'false negatives' in negligence claims for product-related injury, the obvious solution is to reverse the burden, and put the onus on the manufacturer of establishing that they were not at fault. Overlaying negligence with a complex regime of strict liability just to enable claimants to surmount problems of proof is the legal equivalent of using a sledgehammer to crack a nut.

V. MITIGATING MEASURES?

Enough has I hope been said to convince the reader that the case for strict product liability in tort is weak. It is particularly striking that, with the exceptions of the contract anomaly argument and the argument from difficulties of proof, the justifications that have been put forward for it are not unique to product cases. Properly understood, therefore, they are not arguments for strict *product* liability in particular, but for strict liability in tort more generally.[146] Moreover, because strict product liability rests on such shaky theoretical foundations,

---

[143] Powers (n 53) 426.

[144] ibid 429, 432.

[145] See text to nn 13–14.

[146] Hence, for example, it has been said that the enterprise risk justification 'supports the application of strict liability well beyond liability for injuries caused by products' (Feldthusen et al (n 68) 373).

'courts and legislatures have been left to build their rules on little more than intuition, mirage, and rhetoric'.[147] One obvious consequence is that the detailed rules of the strict product liability regimes that have developed bear little relation to any of the supposed justifications for imposing strict liability in the first place. It has been said, for example, that the 1985 Directive 'was neither based on a well-thought out and recognised overall concept for producer-liability nor on any theory-based, understandable justification of the legislators'.[148]

The overall picture presented by the modern UK law of product liability is not, therefore, an edifying one. However, the problem is easily solved: Parliament just needs to repeal the 1987 Act. Nevertheless, it may be that some will consider that solution too radical, at least in the absence of some sort of mitigating measures. With that in mind, in this section of the chapter I briefly consider a few ways in which the impact of that change could be lessened, without losing many of the benefits which repeal would bring in terms of the simplification and rationalisation of the law. And although I am not myself convinced that any such mitigation is necessary, I do believe that a combination of repeal of the 1987 Act and the adoption of one or more of these measures would leave product liability law in a better place than it is today.

The first possible mitigating measure would be to limit strict liability to manufacturing defects. Much of the complexity to which strict product liability gives rise is attributable to design defect cases. In particular, the concept of defectiveness is much more straightforward in manufacturing defect (or 'non-standard product') cases, where the safety of the standard product serves as a useful benchmark against which to assess the safety of the non-standard *ausreisser* ('runaway'). Moreover, the complex and somewhat incoherent development risks defence is of virtually no significance when it comes to manufacturing defects,[149] and could therefore be dispensed with were strict liability to be limited to cases of this kind. It is also generally quite straightforward to distinguish manufacturing defects from design defects, so that marking out the boundary of this more limited strict liability regime should not give rise to too many problems.

A second possible mitigating measure would be to reverse the burden of proof as to negligence.[150] This could either be done in all product liability cases, or it could be limited to manufacturing defect cases, where problems of proof tend to be most acute. There are many jurisdictions in which this step has already been

---

[147] Owen, 'Products Liability: Principles of Justice' (n 82) 239.

[148] Koziol, 'Introductory Lecture' (n 81) 21. See also Stapleton, *Product Liability* (n 31) 91 ('European reformers gave us a plethora of rationales, some of which are internally inconsistent, and with no indication of the weight and priority to be given to each').

[149] See *The Law of Tort* (n 9) para 19.67.

[150] This was a possibility canvassed by the Law Commission and Scottish Law Commission when they consulted on reform of product liability in the 1970s: see Law Commission, *Liability for Defective Products* (n 14) paras 39–45.

taken. In Germany, for example, it was held in the famous 'Chicken Pest' case that once the claimant shows that they have suffered injury as a result of a manufacturing defect in a product which was present when it left the producer's sphere of control, the burden of proof shifts to the producer to establish that they were not at fault.[151] Similar principles apply in Italy,[152] and (at least to some extent) in the Netherlands.[153] An argument in favour of this solution is the increasing complexity of products themselves. This will make it harder for claimants in the future to establish what went wrong, and why.[154] Reversing the burden of proof gives producers a clear incentive to make their processes as transparent as possible, in the hope that, if things do wrong, they will stand some chance of establishing that it was not their fault. (Another option would be to use the threat of a reversal of the burden of proof to encourage producer compliance with safety and cyber-security regulations, which might even extend to the transparency of the processes controlling the product.[155])

An attraction of reversal of the burden of proof is that it maintains the intuitively appealing idea of fault liability, while at the same time going some way to meeting one of the stronger arguments for strict liability, namely the difficulty of establishing negligence in defective product cases.[156] Conversely, it is a disadvantage of this measure that the courts would still be required to distinguish between products and services, since the burden of proof would be reversed only where a product caused the damage. Furthermore, the preconditions that would need to be satisfied before the burden of proof would be reversed (such as the presence of a 'defect') would necessarily give rise to some additional complexity, though if the measure were limited to manufacturing defects this would be minimal.

A third possible mitigating measure would be to reform the law of consumer contracts so as to enable certain third parties, such as members of the buyer's

---

[151] BGH 26 November 1968, BGHZ 51, 91. Later decisions extend this principle to design and marketing defects: see Fairgrieve and Goldberg (n 11) para 7.13. It would be possible to go further, and also put the onus on the producer of showing that the defect did not exist when the product left their hands, rather than requiring the claimant to establish (as the German rules does) that it did. After all, it may be difficult for a claimant to prove when the defect arose: see, eg, *Evans v Triplex Safety Glass* (n 142).

[152] N Coggiola, 'The Development of Product Liability in Italy' in Whittaker (n 10) 219, 233.

[153] I Giesen, 'The Development of Product Liability in the Netherlands' in Whittaker (n 10) 163, 177.

[154] See Machnikowski (n 37) 699. See also European Commission, 'Evaluation of Directive 85/374 on Liability for Defective Products' (n 28) 61.

[155] European Commission, 'Report on the Safety and Liability Implications of Artificial Intelligence, the Internet of Things and Robotics' (n 6) 14. In the new Directive proposed by the European Commission, the burden of proof as to defectiveness would be reversed in cases involving an obvious malfunction, and where the defendant has not complied with legal requirements pertaining to the collection and disclosure of product information, while the burden of proof regarding both defectiveness and causation would be reversed where 'it would be excessively difficult for the claimant, in light of the technical or scientific complexity of the case' to prove these matters: European Commission, 'Proposal for a Directive' (n 7) recitals 33–34.

[156] Law Commission, *Liability for Defective Products* (n 14) para 44.

family and donees of the buyer, to rely on the strict contractual warranties of fitness and safety in the contract of sale. This has been done by legislation in a range of common law systems, including the United States,[157] Canada,[158] Australia[159] and New Zealand.[160] And although this measure would only extend the benefit of strict product liability to some third parties, there may be good reasons for excluding from the protection of such liability bystanders who have no relationship with the buyer of the product.[161]

A fourth potential mitigating measure would be to adopt a simpler strict liability regime for certain kinds of products, shorn of the complications to which general strict product liability gives rise, such as the defect concept and the development risks defence. This measure could be a suitable response to new technologies, both because it may help them to gain social acceptance and because in such cases it may be particularly difficult to establish which party is responsible for the damage, and whether that party is at fault. Under this approach, legislation could simply lay down that if damage were caused by a product of the type in question (such as a robot or a drone) then a stipulated person or entity would be liable, subject to a limited range of defences which would ideally be kept as simple and straightforward as possible. An example of such a liability regime is the one recently established for driverless cars. Under the Automated and Electric Vehicles Act 2018, the insurer (or in some cases the owner) of a driverless vehicle is strictly liable for any damage that results from an accident caused by the vehicle when it is driving itself, but may seek an indemnity from other persons who are also liable for the damage under existing tort law rules.[162]

Finally, another mitigating measure that could be adopted would be to establish no-fault compensation schemes for injury caused by particular classes of product, as was done by the Vaccine Damage Payments Act 1979 in the case of vaccines.[163] This might be an appropriate solution to the thorny problem

---

[157] See Uniform Commercial Code, § 2-318, Alternative A, which extends retailer warranties to persons in the family or household of the buyer and guests in their home injured by the goods sold, and which has been adopted in most US jurisdictions. Alternatives B and C go further still. See Fairgrieve and Goldberg (n 11) paras 2.16–2.18.

[158] See, eg, Consumer Protection and Business Practices Act 2013 (Sask) s 35 (similar to Uniform Commercial Code, § 2-318, Alternative B).

[159] See the Australian Consumer Law (Competition and Consumer Act 2010 (Cth) Sched 2), which extends the protection of consumer warranties to 'affected persons', including those who acquire goods from a consumer buyer.

[160] Consumer Guarantees Act 1993 (NZ) s 24 (extending contract rights to donees of buyers).

[161] See Koziol, 'Conclusions from a Comparative Perspective' (n 96) 549–51.

[162] For a recent evaluation of the 2018 Act, and a helpful overview of the issues involved, see Law Commission, *Automated Vehicles* (n 6). Note that I am not holding up the 2018 Act as an exemplar of simplicity, which it assuredly is not. My point is merely that it should be possible to devise specific strict liability regimes for particular product types that are much simpler than the general strict liability regime under the 1987 Act.

[163] See Cane and Goudkamp (n 10) 94–95.

of drug-related injury, where it would save those involved from incurring the high costs of litigation – whether on a strict liability or negligence basis – while providing reassurance to patients that if they take a prescription drug which is likely to be beneficial they will be compensated if it turns out to cause them harm.[164]

VI. CONCLUSION

The experiment with strict product liability in tort has been a failure. Its adoption has made the law of product liability far more complex, and reliant on irrational distinctions which violate the fundamental precept that like cases should be treated alike. Technological change is also undermining the concepts that mark out the scope of the strict liability regime. This in turn threatens to generate yet more complexity as pressure grows to adapt those concepts to new realities.

Strict product liability also lacks a solid theoretical grounding, based as it is on a melange of mostly instrumentalist justifications that are now largely discredited. To the extent that these arguments ever had any real justificatory force it was limited to cases involving manufacturing defects. But although these were the cases that were foremost in the minds of the American pioneers of strict product liability, they have now largely disappeared, having long since been eclipsed by the design defect cases that dominate product liability litigation in the modern era.

The EU product liability regime, on which the 1987 Act is based, was an adaptation of an American model which has since largely been abandoned in the US itself. Furthermore, the political compromises that were required to obtain member state approval for the 1985 Directive robbed the European regime of any coherence that it might otherwise have had. As Stapleton has said: 'What was left was the almost empty shell of the special rule [of strict product liability] which itself generated many more anomalies than the one its proponents attacked, and generated virtually no consumer gain.'[165]

I have argued in this chapter that the time has come to call time on this failed experiment, and to revert to the law as it was before the reforms of

---

[164] In Sweden, there is a no-fault pharmaceutical insurance scheme, funded by the pharmaceutical industry, while voluntary drug insurance schemes have been established in Finland and Norway. See further, Fairgrieve and Goldberg (n 11) paras 9.47–9.49; C Hodges, 'Nordic Compensation Schemes for Drug Injuries' (2006) 29 *Journal of Consumer Policy* 143. The Independent Medicines and Medical Devices Safety Review recently recommended that no-fault redress schemes be introduced in the UK for pharmaceuticals and medical devices (albeit while leaving the liability landscape untouched): see *First Do No Harm: The Report of the Independent Medicines and Medical Devices Safety Review* (2020) app 3.

[165] Stapleton, *Product Liability* (n 31) 358.

the 1980s. The UK's withdrawal from the EU means that that can now easily be achieved by simply repealing Part I of the Consumer Protection Act 1987. In my view, nothing else needs to be done, although I have highlighted some mitigating measures that could be taken to soften the blow were that deemed to be necessary. Repeal of the 1987 Act would also solve the problem of what the UK should do (if anything) in response to the overhaul of the EU product liability rules recently proposed by the European Commission – a process in which the UK will of course have no say.

Although I have criticised the tendency to downplay the significance of strict product liability at a theoretical level, in practice the differences between fault liability and strict liability in this context are not great. In Canada, for example, it seems generally to be thought that the outcomes of negligence claims in respect of defective products 'are not markedly different from what they might be under strict tort [liability]'.[166] Furthermore, it is worth remembering that product liability is a relatively insignificant corner of the law of tort in modern times. Compared to the mid-twentieth century, when strict liability was born, the safety of products is heavily regulated today, and for this and other reasons the level of product-related injury is now low.[167] It seems unlikely that many product liability cases are brought, and certainly very few reach the courts.[168] When contrasted with the types of case that dominate the contemporary litigation landscape – such as accidents on the roads and at work, and claims against occupiers and healthcare providers – cases involving defective products are quite simply not that important.

One of the lessons for tort lawyers from the failure of strict product liability is the enduring appeal of the fault principle. Although much lambasted by the twentieth-century instrumentalists, the advantages of fault-based liability have not only ensured its survival, but also given rise to something of a renaissance, as many of the outposts of strict liability in the law of tort have either fallen to the forces of fault or been so ground down by them as to be rendered virtually irrelevant.[169] In the meantime the ideological underpinnings of strict liability have themselves collapsed, as the theories of tort advanced by the instrumentalists have fallen out of favour.[170]

---

[166] Feldthusen et al (n 68) 367.

[167] It is now largely forgotten that in the mid-twentieth century products were often extremely unsafe. For examples from the US, which included not only the exploding bottles that were a staple of product liability litigation, but also flammable children's clothing and lethal fridges, see Graham (n 71) 587–88, 601–602.

[168] The dearth of recent case law is not specific to the UK. The position is the same in Australia (Bourie et al (n 85) 495–96) and in Germany (Wagner, 'Development of Product Liability in Germany' (n 10) 143). For possible explanations of the phenomenon, including high levels of product safety, see Machnikowski (n 37) 685–86.

[169] See generally Gray (n 86).

[170] See, eg, the critical assessment of Goldberg (n 90). On the extent to which academic scholarship influenced the move to strict product liability in the US, see Priest, 'The Invention of Enterprise Liability' (n 78).

A creature of its times, the time for strict product liability in tort (if there ever was one) has long since passed.[171] And by the straightforward expedient of repealing the 1987 Act Parliament has the power, not just to return simplicity and rationality to the law of product liability, but also to ensure its fitness for purpose well into the future.

---

[171] See DG Owen, 'The Intellectual Development of Modern Products Liability Law: A Comment on Priest's View of the Cathedral's Foundations' (1985) 14 *Journal of Legal Studies* 529, 533 (referring to the fit between strict product liability and the 'dominant political sentiments of the 1960s'). See also GT Schwartz, 'The Beginning and the Possible End of the Rise of Modern American Tort Law' (1992) 26 *Georgia Law Review* 601, 615 (linking the willingness of the American courts in the 1960s to impose strong liabilities on major corporations to public antipathy to such corporations and the rise of the consumer movement); and Geistfeld (n 82) 243 (Traynor J's *Escola* opinion was influenced by legal realism, the 'dominant jurisprudential approach at the leading American law schools' in the 1940s).

Index

Abraham, Kenneth S, 334
acquired rights, 46, 61, 155, 261–2, 276, 286, 292, 298
adoption, 54
advocates, 40n69, 135n54
ambulance service, 101, 105, 108, 115–17, 132, 159, 161
armed forces: immunities, 79
Aronson, Mark, 173
asbestos, 230–4, 239–40
assumption of responsibility:
  arguments for, 143–5
  bailment, 127, 131, 137, 148–9, 153, 156
  beach scenario, 127–9, 135, 140–1, 143
  contract law and, 134–6, 147–8
  debate, 127, 144–5, 146–9, 156
  duty of care, 61, 137
  educational negligence, 222
  general undertaking, 154–5
  Hedley Byrne, 125, 127–8, 135, 136, 144, 145, 147, 148, 149, 156, 222
  loss of chance and, 248
  meaning, 129–40
  omissions, 140–1
  place, 145–9
  professional negligence, 153
  public authorities, 11, 114–20
    timing, 117–19
    voluntary assumption, 119–20
  pure economic loss, 141–2
  red herrings, 149–54
  reliance, 10–11, 143, 152–4, 155–6
  special skill/knowledge, 149–50
  standard of care, 138–9
  timing, 117–19, 155
  use, 125–7
  voluntariness, 150–2
  White v Jones, 131–2, 142
  wrongful conception and, 207
Atiyah, Patrick, 28
Australia:
  duty of care, 56
  negligent false imprisonment, 202, 204
  private nuisance, 289, 290
  product liability, 423
  standard of care, 158, 171, 173, 174
Austria:
  gross negligence, 183
  preventive damages, 361

Bagshaw, Roderick, 51, 107, 108, 112, 287, 296, 319n97, 321–2, 373, 374, 374n9
bailment, 127, 131, 137, 148–9, 156, 178
Baker, John, 256n3, 298
Barker, Kit, 145n112, 147n121
barristers, 40n69, 135n54
Beale, Joseph, 148
Beever, Allan, 33, 34, 122–3, 145, 147, 227, 236, 247–8, 260, 365, 375–6, 384n56
Belgium: preventive damages, 340
Benson, Peter, 364–5, 369n141, 385n58
bills of exchange, 179
Binoche, Juliette, 386–7
Birks, Peter, 378
Blackstone, William, 154, 269
bodily integrity, 105, 199, 208–9, 264, 364–5
Bohlen, Francis, 315, 321
Bracton, Henry of, 178
Brexit, 392, 425
brothels, 260, 291, 301
Buckland, WW, 28–9, 30
Burnham, Ulele, 204, 205
Burrows, Andrew, 2

Cameron, GDL, 281
Campbell, David, 144
Canada:
  gross negligence, 182
  negligent false imprisonment, 202, 204
  product liability, 392, 423
  standard of care, 158–9
Cane, Peter, 257, 279n166, 361
Cardi, Jonathan, 38
causation:
  basis of negligence, 4, 5
  but-for test, 15
  compensation, deterrence and, 227–8, 232–3, 249–51

corrective justice and, 227, 235–40, 249
goals of tort law and, 14–15, 226–51
indeterminacy, 228–40
instrumentalism, 227, 249
loss of chance, 14, 228, 241–8
medical delay, 241–8
novus actus interveniens, 40–1
overview, 14–15
preventive damages, 341–2, 362
probabilistic causation, 250
'two hunters problem', 230–40
child abuse, 100, 101–2, 104, 108–9, 186, 187
civilian legal systems, 3, 20, 61, 182–3, 280–1, 286, 340, 361, 366, 367, 419
cladding, 21
climate change, 20
combat immunity, 79, 89
common, rights of, 298
common European principles of tort law, 47, 339, 340, 342, 361
company prospectuses, 53
compensation
    see also damages
    corrective justice and, 227, 228
    deterrence and, 227–8, 249–51
    goal of tort law, 227–8
Conaghan, Joanne, 211, 212, 225
contract:
    assumption of responsibility and, 134–6, 147–8
    comparative law, 419
    loss of chance, 244–5
    product liability, 401
    strict liability, 417–19
    third parties, 401, 418, 422–3
    unfair contract terms, 189
contributory negligence, 21, 174, 204–5, 341–2, 357, 358, 362
conversion: title to sue, 268, 270
corrective justice, 34, 227, 228, 235–40, 249, 250, 281–2, 299, 376
credit references, 132, 147
Cross, Gerry, 319
Czech Republic: preventive damages, 340

Dagan, Hanoch, 302
damage:
    academic neglect, 193–4
    basis of negligence, 4, 5, 30, 193–4
    Commonwealth case law, 13
    educational negligence, 12, 196, 216–22, 223
    loss and, 21–2, 371–2, 386–90

meaning, 372, 391
mitigation
    avoidable loss, 342–3
    preventive damages and, 342–3, 361, 362
negligent imprisonment, 12, 195, 196–205, 223
new forms, 12–13, 193–225
private nuisance, 18
rights and, 21–2, 371–2, 373–7
terminology, 372–3, 374, 375, 391
wrongful conception, 12, 195, 206–16
Damage (film), 386–7
damages:
    conventional sum awards, 213–16
    educational negligence, 221
    false imprisonment, 224
    human rights, 9
    preventive damages *see* preventive damages
    private nuisance, 271–5, 279, 287
    wrongful conception, 206, 213–16
deterrence:
    causation and, 232–3
    compensation and, 249–51
    goal of tort law, 227–8
    strict product liability, 410–15
        market deterrence, 412–14
        specific deterrence, 411–12
Dobbs, Dan B, 38, 103
Douglas, Simon, 295–6, 298, 299, 300, 301, 302
driverless cars, 423
duty of care:
    acquired rights, 61
    assumption of responsibility *see* assumption of responsibility
    basic tests, 81–4
    basis of negligence, 27–8
    burden of proof, 45
    Caparo test, 57, 64–5, 66, 66–7, 67–8, 69–71, 81, 83–4, 86–7, 88, 126
    control device, 35
    critics, 28–9
    dispensing with, 4–6, 27–8, 43–60
        coherence argument, 53–5
        consistency argument, 49–50
        doctrinal clarity, 48–9
        drawbacks, 58–61
        general tests and, 55–7
        law and fact, 51–3
        missed issues, 50–1
        rationale, 47–57
    Donoghue v Stevenson, 37, 54, 56, 82, 88–9, 132, 139, 146, 163

dual role, 33–6
fault analysis and, 36–7
foreseeability test, 57
general test search, 55–7, 66, 82–8
    failure, 84–8, 90
immunities, 40, 45
instrumentalism and, 35, 55
malleability, 53–5, 58, 59, 65
Michael v Chief Constable of South Wales
        Police, 66–8
modern approach, 82
nature of duty, 369
neighbour principle, 38, 82, 146
notional duty
    concept, 33–5
    operation, 37–43
proximity, 56, 57, 66, 146
public authorities *see* public authorities
public interest and, 65
public policy and, 7, 75–6
reasonableness, 57, 68
remoteness and, 35, 44, 52–3
rights analysis and, 32–3, 35, 46–7
Robinson see Robinson v Chief Constable
        of West Yorkshire Police
third party actions and, 169–70
dyslexia, 166, 217–22

easements, 259, 261, 281, 286, 298
education:
    negligent damage, 12, 196, 216–22,
        223
    rights, 224
    special needs, 165, 166, 217–22
    standard of care, 165, 166, 167
employment references, 133, 135
Epstein, Richard, 294, 296, 299
Essert, Christopher, 285n7, 296, 299, 301
estoppel, 385–6
European Convention on Human Rights, 185,
        186, 272
European Union:
    Brexit, 392, 425
    product liability, 22, 392, 393, 400n34, 403,
        404, 405, 416, 421, 424
ex turpi causa principle, 42, 47, 60, 61

Fairgrieve, Duncan, 93, 188, 221
false imprisonment, 201–5
fault:
    basis of negligence, 4
    duty of care analysis and, 36–7

foreseeability and, 328
graduation, 12
non-natural use of land, 325
product liability and, 23, 394–8
Rylands v Fletcher and, 314
strict liability and, 22, 305–6
Feldthusen, Bruce, 406, 411, 425
fiduciary duties, 46, 61, 144, 148
Field, Iain, 21–2
fire brigades, 54, 105, 107, 116–17, 132
Fleming, John, 2, 20, 35, 48, 55, 235, 250, 318,
        325, 339, 404
Fletcher, George, 332
foster care, 166, 167, 187
France:
    administrative responsibility, 191
    grave fault, 182, 184, 190, 191
    gross negligence, 182
    negligence, 3
    preventive damages, 340
    pure economic loss, 363
    strict liability, 333–4
Fredman, Sandra, 211
freedom of movement, 197–8, 199, 200–1, 205,
        223–4

Gearty, Conor, 258, 259n25, 323
Germany:
    contractual liability, 419
    gross negligence, 182–3
    preventive damages, 340
    private nuisance, 280, 286
    product liability, 422
    standard of care, 158
    strict liability, 334
    wrongfulness, 46
Gibson, R Dale, 28
Goldberg, John, 35, 368–9
good Samaritans, 158–9, 174, 189
Gorringe v Calderdale MBC:
    application, 102
    entrapment, 110–11
    facts and decision, 96–8
    failing to confer benefits
        evaluation, 120–3
        private law principles, 106–20
        statutory duties/powers and, 94–105
    impact, 93, 98–9
        limiting, 100–5
    previous cases, 94–6
    reasonable expectation, 110
    significance, 93

statutory duties/powers and
  failing to confer benefits, 94–105
  human rights, 104–5
  targets or public duties, 101–4
Goudkamp, James, 70
graffiti, 389
Gray, Anthony, 409
Green, Michael D, 38
Green, Sarah, 387n69
gross negligence:
  19th century, 178–80
  comparative law, 182–3, 191
  current use, 180–3
  defining, 183–4
  manslaughter, 181, 183
  recklessness and, 184
  standard, 177–84

Handley, Elizabeth, 190
Hart, HLA, 129
health and safety authorities, 54
Heffey, Peter G, 200
Hepple, Bob, 28, 127, 279
Heuston, RFV, 85
Hickman, Tom R, 224
highways, 95–9, 110–11
Hoffmann, Leonard, 251
Hohfeld, WN, 29, 46, 262, 372, 384
Holdsworth, WS, 314
Holmes, Oliver Wendell, 32, 334
Honoré, Tony, 121, 141n92, 144, 156, 177
Howarth, David, 28, 93
human rights: public authorities failing
    to confer benefits, 104–5
Hurd, Heidi M, 239n52, 239n54

Ibbetson, David, 37, 193, 330
illegality defence, 42, 47, 60, 61
immunities:
  barristers, 40n69, 135n54
  combat immunity, 79, 89
  Crown immunity, 72n39
  duty of care, 40, 45, 61
  police, 64, 65, 67–8, 74, 75, 77
  public authorities, 99, 191
imprisonment *see* negligent imprisonment
India: product liability, 392
inhuman treatment, 104
instrumentalism, 14, 35, 55, 227, 228, 249,
    250–1, 424, 425
insurance, 15, 54, 131, 132, 181, 324, 346,
    409, 414

interference principle, 107–8
Ireland: standard of care, 159
Irons, Jeremy, 386–7
Italy:
  private nuisance, 280
  product liability, 422

Kantianism, 295, 384
Katz, Larissa, 294
Keene, Alexander R, 93
Kessler, Friedrich, 407, 419
Kidner, Richard, 260
Koziol, Helmut, 411n99, 421

land: definition, 259, 286
Law Commission:
  administrative redress, 93, 158
  gross negligence, 183
  occupiers' liability and trespass, 164
  product liability, 406n67, 421n150
  public law standard of care, 172, 173
  Rylands v Fletcher and, 331
  trustee exemption clauses, 178
Linden, Allen, 226
loss:
  damage and, 21–2, 371–2, 386–90
  meaning, 372
  rights and, 371–2, 21–2, 377–86
  terminology, 372–3, 375, 391
  useful concept, 390–1
loss of chance:
  assessing argument, 244–8
  causation, 14, 228, 241–8
  contract law, 244–5
  deterrence and, 250
  Gregg, 241, 242–4, 245, 247–8, 251
  Hotson, 241–2, 243, 244, 246, 248

McBride, Nicholas, 5, 51, 107, 108, 296, 369,
    373, 377–8, 381
McFarlane, Ben, 295–6, 298, 299, 301, 302, 386
McKerron, RG, 34
malicious prosecution, 200
manslaughter: gross negligence, 181, 183
Merrill, Thomas, 294, 296
Michael v Chief Constable of South Wales
    Police:
  duty of care, 66–8
  methodology, 88
Millner, MA, 91, 333n193
Milsom, SFC, 298
Mitchell, Paul, 148, 149

Moran, Mayo, 366–7
Morgan, Jonathan, 20
Morison, WL, 32, 33
Mullis, Alastair, 207, 210, 258

natural rights, 260–1, 274, 276, 292
negligence
    see also gross negligence
    basis of action, 4, 27
    duty of care *see* duty of care
    overview, 3–15
    proof of, 419–20
    pure economic loss, 363
    Rylands v Fletcher and, 314, 324–30
    standard of care *see* standard of care
negligent imprisonment:
    damage, 12, 195, 196–205, 223
    damages, 224
    false imprisonment, 201–5
    liability, 198–201
    malicious prosecution, 200
    scenarios, 196–7
negligent misstatements, 138, 141, 146–7
negotiorum gestio, 366
Netherlands: product liability, 422
New Zealand:
    manslaughter, 181
    product liability, 423
Newark, FH, 256–7, 258, 287, 307–8, 309, 313,
        314, 315
Norway: preventive damages, 347
novus actus interveniens:
    causation and, 40–1, 48–9
    duty of care and, 49–50, 57–8
    preventive damages context, 341–2, 365
    proximity and, 56
nuisance *see* private nuisance

occupiers' liability:
    duty of care, 57
    omissions, 162–4
    private nuisance, 162–3
    standard of care, 162–4, 175, 187–8
    trespass, 162–4, 175
Oliphant, Ken, 193, 258, 408
Owen, David, 38, 408–9, 421

Palmer, Norman, 146, 149
Pearson Report (1978), 331
Peel, WE, 285
Penner, James, 17–18, 267–8, 282, 287n22, 302
Perry, Stephen, 247, 373n5

Plunkett, James, 8, 79, 126n11
police
    see also Michael; Robinson
    assumption of responsibility, 116–17,
        132
    duty of care, 66–8, 73–5
    immunities, 64, 65, 67–8, 75, 77
Pontin, Ben, 283
Powers, William C, 403, 419–20
pregnancy *see* wrongful conception
preventive damages:
    causation, 341–2, 362
    comparative law, 340, 361
    contributory negligence, 341–2, 357, 358,
        362
    imminence of danger, 360–1
    issues, 20–1, 339–70
    justification, 361–9
        duty to rescue, 368–9
        extended right, 364–5
        negotiorum gestio, 366
        pure economic loss, 363
        unjust enrichment, 366–8
    mitigation of damage, 342–3, 357, 361,
        362
    necessity, 359–60, 366
    quia timet injunctions, 343–4, 346, 357,
        359, 360
    reasonableness, 357–9, 361
    restrictions, 357–61
    scenarios, 344–56
        collapsing condominium, 351–4, 366
        collapsing crane, 348–51
        contaminated water, 355–6
        defective premises, 351–4, 358–9, 360,
            366
        forest fire, 344–7
        frozen food, 347–8
        medical monitoring, 355–6, 358,
            365n123, 368
    self-defence, 357
    specificity of danger, 359
    third party expenditure, 369
Principles of European Tort Law, 47, 339, 340,
        342, 361
private nuisance:
    abnormal sensitivity and, 266–7
    affront cases, 290–1, 297, 301
    amenity value, 272–3, 287, 299
    beneficial activities, 265
    comparative law, 280–1
    constructive dispossession, 17–18

damage, 18
damages, 271–5, 287
    consequential loss, 271–5
    personal injuries, 275, 279
definition, 258–60, 271
    economic analysis and, 294–5
    essence, 284–304
    implications, 301–3
    orthodox view, 284–93
    physical invasion view, 285, 293–301
earth, water, air and light, 296–7
essence, 16–18, 284–304
incoherence, 258
liberty interest, 265
locality principle, 267–8
market value and, 260, 272, 288, 291, 299
noises and smells, 266, 267–8, 272, 276
occupiers' liability, 162–3
orthodox view, 284–93
physical invasion view, 293–301
    critique, 296–301
    proponents, 293–6
possible defendants, 270–1
preventive damages, 346
property tort, 15–16, 255–83
    academic debate, 257–8
    obligations, 280–1
    property theory, 301–3
    Rylands v Fletcher, 314–15
    'tort against land', 256–8, 286–7
public benefit and, 278, 328
public nuisance and, 258, 278–9
repetition, 280, 323
rights and, 260–3, 281–3, 292–3
    acquired rights, 268, 286, 292, 298
Rylands v Fletcher and *see Rylands v
    Fletcher*
substantial interference, 262, 263–8, 298–9
title to sue, 268–70, 317
trespass and, 15–16, 175, 255, 275–8, 293,
    294–5, 296, 299–300
unreasonable conduct, 264, 279
product liability:
    comparative law, 392–3, 422, 423
    contract law and, 401
    driverless cars, 423
    EU law, 392, 393, 400n34, 403, 404, 405,
        416, 421, 424
    information products, 399
    insurance, 413, 414–15
    later defects, 400–1
    manufacturing defects, 395–6, 404–5, 421

repealing 1987 Act, 392–4, 425–6
    mitigating measures, 420–4
software, 399–400, 402
strict liability, 22–3, 392–426
    arguments for, 406–20
    burden of proof, 421–2
    complexity, 403–6
    contract anomaly argument, 417–19
    deterrence argument, 410–15
    development risk defence, 396, 405, 409,
        420, 421, 423
    enterprise risk and, 407–8
    fault liability and, 23, 394–8
    inherent risk argument, 416–17
    loss-spreading argument, 407, 419–20
    problems, 398–406
    products v services, 398–400, 403, 422
    proving negligence argument, 419–20
    representation argument, 416
    risk community argument, 408–10
    third parties, 401–2
    types of defendants, 397
    utilities, 400
    vaccines, 423–4
professional negligence:
    assumption of responsibility, 125, 135, 141,
        153
    Bolam test, 166, 167
    standard of care, 160
profits à prendre, 259, 286
prospectuses, 53
Prosser, William, 2, 258, 307, 415, 417–18
psychiatric injury:
    duty of care, 75
    foreseeability, 41–2
    forms, 195
    learning disabilities, 222
    legal protection from, 81
    negligent imprisonment, 199–200
    remoteness, 44
    secondary victims, 75, 81, 89
public authorities:
    acts v omissions, 80–1, 92
    assumption of responsibility, 11, 114–20
    duty of care: *Robinson v Chief Constable
        of West Yorkshire Police*, 71–3
    equal liability principle, 67, 71–3, 89, 91
    failing to confer benefits, 8–10, 92–124
        additional damage, 106–9, 112
        assumption of responsibility and, 114–20
        claimant reliance, 109–13
        inconsistencies, 100–1

pre-*Gorringe*, 94–6
  private law principles, 106–20
  reasonable expectations, 109–13
  statutory duties/powers, 94–105
highways, 96–9, 110–11
identification of obligations, 122–3
justiciability, 37, 59
margins of appreciation, 167
public law standards, 171–4, 188
public policy and, 7, 77–9
remedies from, 122
standard of care, 11–12, 157–8, 164–8, 188
  modifying, 190
  serious fault test, 158, 172, 173
statutory duties/powers, 45
  failing to confer benefits and, 94–105
  human rights, 104–5
  targets or public duties, 101–4
public benefit: nuisance and, 278, 328
public policy:
  duty of care and, 124
  negligent imprisonment and, 205
  preventive damages and, 362
  private nuisance standing, 268
  Robinson, 7, 65, 75–6, 91
  strict product liability, 410
  wrongful conception and, 206
pure economic loss:
  assumption of responsibility and, 50, 140,
    141–2, 238
  contract, 417
  damage concept, 388
  general rule, 81, 383
  negligence, 363
  negligent advice, 380
  preventive damages and, 347–8
  property damage and, 13
  recoverability, 31, 40, 46, 195, 222, 379,
    381
  rights and, 384
  wrongful conception, 43, 47–8, 225

quia timet injunctions, 343–4, 346, 357, 359,
  360

Rabin, Robert L, 48, 334
Raz, Joseph, 147, 151–2, 223n163
remedies: scholarship, 1–2
responsibility:
  assumption *see* assumption of responsibility
  legal responsibility, 129
  meaning, 129

Richardson, Miranda, 386–7
rights:
  acquired rights, 46, 61, 155, 261–2, 276, 286,
    292, 298
  corrective justice and, 282
  damage and, 21–2, 371–2, 373–7
  duty of care analysis and, 32–3, 35, 46–7
  educational negligence, 224
  loss and, 21–2, 371–2, 377–86
  meaning, 372
  natural rights, 260–1, 274, 276, 292
  negligence and, 224–5
  private nuisance and, 260–3, 281–3,
    292–3
  right to a view, 293
  right to life, 105
  tort law and, 255
  wrongful conception and, 214–15
rights of common, 298
rights of way, 261, 262, 276, 297, 298
rights to light, 261, 262, 263, 277, 297
Ripstein, Arthur, 282, 295, 332
Robertson, Andrew, 45, 146, 385n57
*Robinson v Chief Constable of West Yorkshire
    Police*:
  acts v omissions, 80–1, 91
  disposal on facts, 75–6
  duty of care and, 6–8, 63–91
    general requirements, 68–71
    police, 73–5
    psychiatric injury, 81
    public authorities, 71–3, 91
    traditional approach, 81–4, 90
  facts, 64–6
  lower courts, 64–8
  public policy reasoning, 7, 65, 77–80, 91
  subsequent cases, 88–90
Rogers, WVH, 207, 259
Roman law, 175, 178, 179n134
Rylands v Fletcher:
  anomaly, 306
  distinctiveness, 18–19, 305–35
  facts, 311
  fire and, 19
  law reform, 330–4
  natural use of land, 307, 308, 319–20, 324,
    328
  negligence and, 314, 324–30
  new orthodoxy, 306, 307–10, 335
  nuisance and, 19, 310–11, 312, 314,
    316–20
    merger, 320–3

offshoot theory, 306, 308–9
  case against, 310–24
  strict liability rule, 305, 323–4
overview, 15–20
preventive damages, 345
significance, 316, 334
tort against land, 15–16, 318

Salmond, John, 2, 311n36
Scots law:
  private nuisance, 286
  Rylands v Fletcher and, 334
  trustee exemption clauses, 182
  trustee standard of care, 176
Scottish Law Commission, 178, 421n150
servitudes, 259, 261, 286
sewage, 282–3, 297
sex discrimination, 211
sex shops, 260, 290–1
Simpson, AWB, 334
Singapore: product liability, 392
Smith, Henry, 294–5, 296, 303
Smith, Jeremiah, 325
Smith, JC, 28
South Africa: duty of care, 34
Spain:
  gross negligence, 183
  preventive damages, 340
  pure economic loss, 363
sport: standard of care, 161–2
Stallybrass, WTS, 310–11, 318
standard of care:
  assumption of responsibility, 138–9
  good Samaritans, 158–9, 174, 189
  gross negligence standard, 177–84
  occupiers' liability, 162–4, 187–8
  professional negligence, 160
  public authorities, 11–12, 157–8, 164–8,
      188
    abandoning, 171–4
    serious fault test, 158, 172, 173
  reasonableness, 157–8, 160, 173–4
  recklessness and, 174
  third party actions, 168–71, 188, 189
  unfair contract terms and, 189
  varying, 11–12, 157–92
    abandoning, 171–4
    advantages/disadvantages, 185–7
    alternatives, 171–84
    contexts, 189–91
    English practice, 159, 160–71, 187–9
    overkill argument, 190–1

reasons for, 184–91
  subjectivising, 175–7, 188
  vicarious liability, 189
  wilful misconduct and, 174
standing: private nuisance, 268–70, 317
Stanton, Keith M, 333
Stapleton, Jane, 60, 235, 245, 246, 396n19,
    399, 401–2, 405, 403, 406, 408, 413,
    419n138, 424
Steel, Sandy, 5, 14, 378
Stevens, Robert, 127, 153, 227, 248, 255,
    269–70, 271, 282, 366, 374–5, 376,
    377–8, 381
strict liability:
  defences, 328–9
  nuisance and, 310–11, 314–16
  product liability *see* product liability
  Rylands v Fletcher, 305, 323–4, 327
    law reform, 330–4
Sugarman, Stephen D, 334, 412n100
suicide risks, 39, 51, 141
surveyors, 133

television reception, 261, 262, 263, 298
Thayer, Ezra, 325
trespass:
  actionability, 215
  cattle, 312, 315
  occupiers' liability, 162–4
  private nuisance and, 15–16, 175, 255,
      275–8, 293, 294–5, 296, 299–300
  Rylands v Fletcher and, 312–13, 315
  title to sue, 268, 269, 270
trespass to the person, 201–2
Trindade, FA, 204–5
trustees
  see also fiduciary duties
  charities, 130
  exemption clauses, 177–8
  gross negligence, 177–8, 179, 181–2
  standard of care: Scots law, 176
Twerski, Aaron D, 417

unfair contract terms, 189
United States:
  causation, 230
  duty of care, 28, 38
  gross negligence, 182
  preventive damages, 348, 349, 358
  private nuisance, 264, 270, 277, 286, 297, 332
  product liability, 406–7, 410, 413–14, 415,
      423, 424

rights to light and, 263
Rylands v Fletcher and, 331n178
standard of care, 174
voluntary emergency assistance: standard of care, 158–9
unjust enrichment, 55n169, 366–8
utilitarianism, 293–4, 299, 327

vaccines, 423–4
vicarious liability, 189, 216, 217, 408
view, right to a, 293
Viscusi, Kip, 415
volenti non fit injuria, 39, 42, 44
von Bar, Christian: *Principles of European Law on Non-Contractual Liability*, 47, 135n54, 264, 339, 361, 366

Wagner, Gerhard, 405, 415n114
Wang, Julia, 146
watercourses, 298
Weinrib, Ernest, 34, 227, 282, 287, 295
Weir, Tony, 2n3, 23, 39, 127–8, 144, 182, 185, 214, 245, 251

wilful misconduct, 171, 174, 184
Williams, Glanville, 279, 315n63
wills, 131–2, 380
Winfield, Percy, 2, 28, 60, 61n198, 148–9, 310, 318, 322
Witting, Christian, 208–9, 211, 212
Wright, Richard, 176–7, 180, 275n141, 276n143, 295, 296
wrongful conception:
    conventional sum awards, 213–16
    damage, 12, 195, 206–16
    damages, 206, 213–16
    duty of care, 49
    mode of analysis, 47–8
    parents' rights, 214–15
    pregnancy as personal injury, 206–12, 223
    scope, 43

Young, David, 159

Zipursky, Benjamin, 30, 35, 368–9

www.ingramcontent.com/pod-product-compliance
Lightning Source LLC
Chambersburg PA
CBHW031625210326
41599CB00021B/3301